W9-CAG-776

EYEWITNESS TRAVEL GUIDES

PARIS

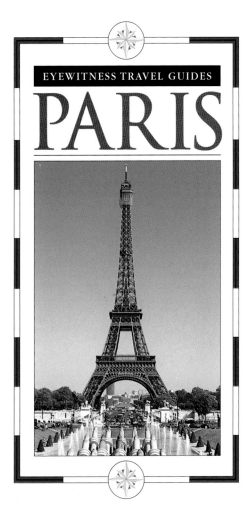

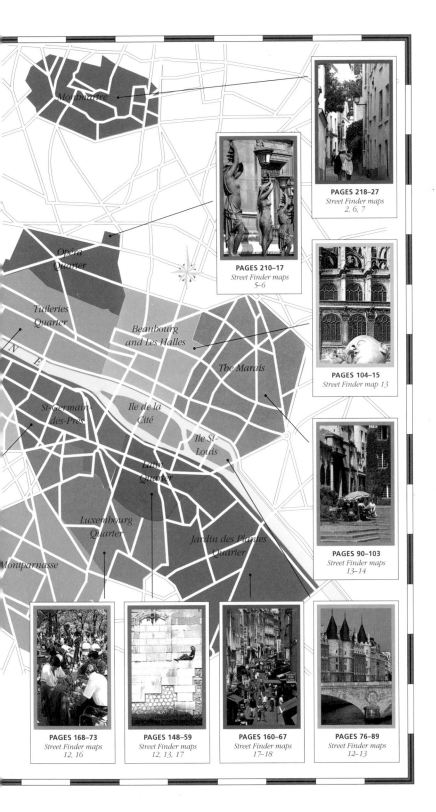

Montmartre

Opera
Quarter

Tuileries
Quarter

Beaubourg
and Les Halles

The Marais

St-Germain-
des-Prés

Ile de la
Cité

Ile St-
Louis

Latin
Quarter

Luxembourg
Quarter

Jardin des Plantes
Quarter

Montparnasse

N
E

PAGES 218–27
*Street Finder maps
2, 6, 7*

PAGES 210–17
*Street Finder maps
5–6*

PAGES 104–15
Street Finder map 13

PAGES 90–103
*Street Finder maps
13–14*

PAGES 168–73
*Street Finder maps
12, 16*

PAGES 148–59
*Street Finder maps
12, 13, 17*

PAGES 160–67
*Street Finder maps
17–18*

PAGES 76–89
*Street Finder maps
12–13*

EYEWITNESS TRAVEL GUIDES

PARIS

Main contributor: ALAN TILLIER

DK

LONDON, NEW YORK,
MELBOURNE, MUNICH AND DELHI
www.dk.com

PROJECT EDITOR Heather Jones
ART EDITOR Janis Utton
EDITOR Alex Gray
US EDITORS Mary Ann Lynch, Mary Sutherland
DESIGNER Vanessa Hamilton
DESIGN ASSISTANT Clare Sullivan

CONTRIBUTORS
Chris Boicos, Michael Gibson, Douglas Johnson

PHOTOGRAPHERS
Max Alexander, Neil Lukas, Robert O'Dea

ILLUSTRATORS
Stephen Conlin, Stephen Gyapay,
Maltings Partnership

This book was produced with the assistance of
Websters International Publishers.

Reproduced by Colourscan, Singapore
Printed and bound by South China Printing Co. Ltd., China

First American Edition, 1993
06 07 08 09 10 9 8 7 6 5 4 3 2

Reprinted with revisions 1997, 1999, 2000, 2001,
2002, 2003, 2004, 2005, 2006

Published in the United States by
DK Publishing, Inc., 375 Hudson Street,
New York, New York 10014

Copyright © 1993, 2006 Dorling Kindersley Limited, London

ALL RIGHTS RESERVED UNDER INTERNATIONAL AND PAN-AMERICAN
COPYRIGHT CONVENTIONS. NO PART OF THIS PUBLICATION MAY BE
REPRODUCED, STORED IN A RETRIEVAL SYSTEM, OR TRANSMITTED IN ANY
FORM OR BY ANY MEANS, ELECTRONIC, MECHANICAL, PHOTOCOPYING,
RECORDING, OR OTHERWISE, WITHOUT THE PRIOR WRITTEN
PERMISSION OF THE COPYRIGHT OWNER.
Published in Great Britain by Dorling Kindersley Limited.

ISSN 1542-1554
ISBN 0-7566-1547-X

THROUGHOUT THIS BOOK, FLOORS ARE REFERRED TO IN ACCORDANCE
WITH EUROPEAN USAGE, I.E. THE "FIRST FLOOR" IS ONE FLIGHT UP.

**The information in this
Eyewitness Travel Guide is checked annually.**
Every effort has been made to ensure that this book is as up-to-date
as possible at the time of going to press. Some details, however,
such as telephone numbers, opening hours, prices, gallery hanging
arrangements and travel information are liable to change. The
publishers cannot accept responsibility for any consequences arising
from the use of this book, nor for any material on third party
websites, and cannot guarantee that any website address in this
book will be a suitable source of travel information. We value the
views and suggestions of our readers very highly. Please write to:
Publisher, DK Eyewitness Travel Guides, Dorling Kindersley,
80 Strand, London WC2R 0RL, Great Britain.

CONTENTS

HOW TO USE THIS GUIDE 6

Henri II (1547–59)

INTRODUCING PARIS

Pont Alexandre III

Opéra de Paris Bastille

The Kiss by Rodin (1886)

Sacré-Coeur in Montmartre

An island in the Bois de Boulogne

Noisettes of lamb

The Panthéon

HOW TO USE THIS GUIDE

This Eyewitness Travel Guide helps you get the most from your stay in Paris with the minimum of practical difficulty. The opening section, *Introducing Paris*, locates the city geographically, sets modern Paris in its historical context and explains how Parisian life changes through the year. *Paris at a Glance* is an overview of the city's specialties. The main sightseeing section of the book is *Paris Area by*

Area. It describes all the main sights with maps, photographs and detailed illustrations. In addition, eight planned walks take you to parts of Paris you might otherwise miss.

Carefully researched tips for hotels, shops and markets, restaurants and bars, sports and entertainment are found in *Travelers' Needs*, and the *Survival Guide* has advice on everything from posting a letter to catching the metro.

PARIS AREA BY AREA

The city has been divided into 14 sightseeing areas. Each section opens with a portrait of the area, summing up its character and history, with a list of all the sights to be covered. These are clearly located by numbers on an *Area Map*. This is followed by a large-scale *Street-by-Street Map* focusing on the most interesting part of the area. Finding your way around the section is made simple by the numbering system used throughout for the sights. This refers to the order in which they are described on the pages that complete the section.

1 Area Map *For easy reference, the sights in each area are numbered and located on an area map. To help the visitor, the map also shows metro and mainline RER stations and parking lots.*

The **Conciergerie** ❽ is shown on this map as well.

Color-coding on each page makes the area easy to find in the book.

2 Street-by-Street Map *This gives a bird's-eye view of the heart of each sightseeing area. The most important buildings are picked out in stronger color, to help you spot them as you walk around.*

A locator map shows you where you are in relation to surrounding areas. The area of the *Street-by-Street Map* is shown in red.

Photographs of facades and distinctive details of buildings help you to locate the sights.

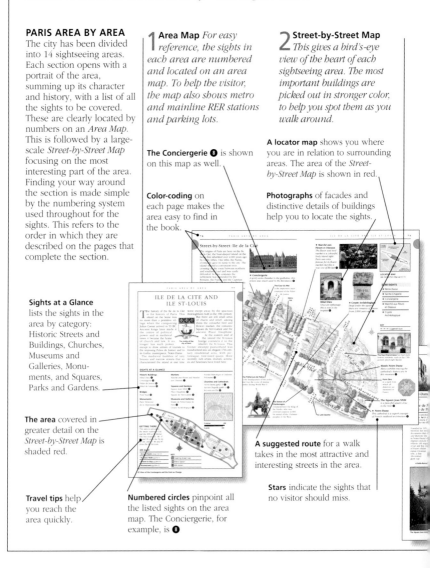

Sights at a Glance lists the sights in the area by category: Historic Streets and Buildings, Churches, Museums and Galleries, Monuments, and Squares, Parks and Gardens.

The area covered in greater detail on the *Street-by-Street Map* is shaded red.

Travel tips help you reach the area quickly.

Numbered circles pinpoint all the listed sights on the area map. The Conciergerie, for example, is ❽

A suggested route for a walk takes in the most attractive and interesting streets in the area.

Stars indicate the sights that no visitor should miss.

PARIS AT A GLANCE

Each map in this section concentrates on a specific theme: *Museums and Galleries, Churches, Squares, Parks and Gardens, Remarkable Parisians.* The top sights are shown on the map; other sights are described on the following two pages.

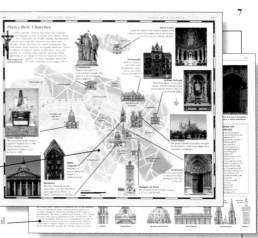

Each sightseeing area is color-coded.

The theme is explored in greater detail on the pages following the map.

3 Detailed information on each sight
All important sights in each area are described in depth in this section. They are listed in order, following the numbering on the Area Map. Practical information is also provided.

PRACTICAL INFORMATION
Each entry provides all the information needed to plan a visit to the sight. The key to the symbols used is on the inside back cover.

Nearest metro station

Sight number

Telephone number

Opening hours

Concièrgerie ❽

1 Quai de l'Horloge 75001.
Map 13 A3. **Tel** 01 53 73 78 50.
M Cité. ◯ Apr–Sep: 9.30am–6pm daily.

Map reference to *Street Finder* at back of book

Services and facilities available

Address

4 Paris's major sights *These are given two or more full pages in the sightseeing area in which they are found. Historic buildings are dissected to reveal their interiors; and museums and galleries have color-coded floor plans to help you find important exhibits.*

The Visitors' Checklist provides the practical information you will need to plan your visit.

The facade of each major sight is shown to help you spot it quickly.

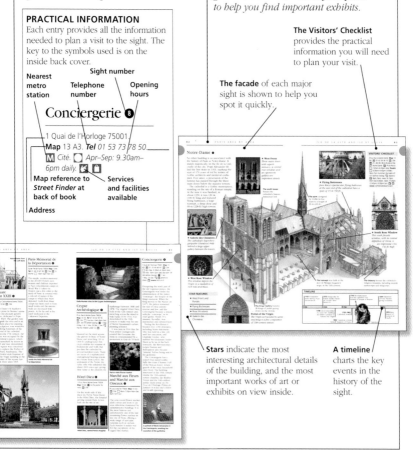

Stars indicate the most interesting architectural details of the building, and the most important works of art or exhibits on view inside.

A timeline charts the key events in the history of the sight.

INTRODUCING
PARIS

FOUR GREAT DAYS IN PARIS

Rodin's
Thinker

Paris is a city packed with wonderful things to see and do. There may be a temptation to spend the trip in a café letting the French way of life wash over you, but it would be a shame to miss its treasures. Here are the best of the city's must-dos. Energetic sightseers should manage everything on these itineraries, but this selection can also be dipped into for ideas. All are reachable by public transportation. Price guides are for two adults or for a family of two adults and two children, excluding meals.

Pyramide du Louvre, from across the fountain pools

ARTISTIC TREASURES

- Fabulous art at the Louvre
- Lunch at chic Café Marly
- A visit to the Rodin sculpture garden or take in the Musée Picasso
- Dine at Tokyo Eat

TWO ADULTS allow at least €60

Morning
Begin with the **Musée du Louvre** *(see pp122–9)*, one of the world's most impressive museums. The best way to start a tour of this huge collection is to beat the crowds by entering the little-known entrance at the Carrousel du Louvre. Save time by getting a floorplan and figuring out where you want to go and sticking to it.

Lunch
There are many cheap eateries nearby, but for a great lunch experience head to stylish **Café Marly** *(see p304)*. On warm days sit in the outside gallery or revel in the cozy red velvet and gilt splendor of the interior.

Afternoon
Choose from three museums for the afternoon. The fatigued should head to the sublime **Musée Rodin** *(see p187)* for a soothing stroll in the sculpture garden and a pensive moment next to *The Thinker*. Those seeking modern masterpieces should visit the **Musée Picasso** *(see pp100–1)*, which has works by Pablo Picasso, from early portraits and sketches to an amazing range of later paintings. To go even more modern, explore the crop of galleries that are known as "Scene Est" in the 13th arrondissement (district). "Scene Est" is three roads' full of cutting-edge galleries, with the **Rue Louise Weiss** *(Map 18 E4)* the most important and the Air de Paris gallery the most funky.

Evening
The **Palais de Tokyo** *(see p201)* is currently Paris's most fashionable exhibition space, with its multimedia displays open till midnight. After a quick tour around, stop at restaurant Tokyo Eat.

RETAIL THERAPY

- Buy foody treats at Le Bon Marché
- Lunch at a top department store restaurant
- Drinks and dinner at Kong

TWO ADULTS allow at least €22

Morning
One-stop shops for gourmets and gluttons include **Fauchon, Hediard** and **La Grande Epicerie** at **Le Bon Marché** *(see pp320–1)*. In fact, anything that is edible – as long as it's delicious – can be found here. Specialty shops include **Poilâne** for bread, **Richart** for chocolate, **Legrand** for wine and **Pierre Hermé** for cakes. Or head down the Rue Mouffetard, one of the city's best market streets.

Lunch
True shopaholics can eat in one of the main department stores. La Toupary at La Samaritaine (see p321) has a stunning rooftop view of the city, while the World Bar at

Interior of the elegant Café Marly, next to the Louvre

Au Printemps, designed by Paul Smith, is a super-cool eatery (see pp320–1).

Afternoon
Either shop till you drop in your chosen department store, or go esoteric and visit the **Musée de la Mode** at the Louvre *(see p121)*; a true temple to fashion, dedicated to beautiful clothes and accessories. Boutique lovers should go to **Claudie Pierlot, Agnes B, Isabelle Marant, Vanessa Bruno** *(see pp324–7)*.

Evening
Head for restorative drinks and dinner at **Kong** on top of Kenzo's flagship store and fashion shrine *(see pp317–8)*.

Reflections in La Géode, giant sphere at the Parc de la Villette

CHILD'S PLAY

- **Explore Parc de la Villette**
- **See animals at the zoo at Jardin des Plantes**
- **Stop for a café lunch**
- **Go up the Eiffel Tower**

FAMILY OF FOUR allow at least €128

Morning
Take receptive young minds to **Parc de la Villette**, which has an impressive children's program. **La Cité des Sciences et de l'Industrie** (Science City) is packed with interesting interactive exhibits for budding Einsteins *(see pp234–9)*. Family fun can be found at the **Ménagerie** *(see pp164)* in the Jardin des Plantes area where the zoo is

very popular. Even more exciting than the live animals for some are the skeletons and stuffed beasts in the **Muséum National d'Histoire Naturelle** *(see p167)*.

Lunch
There are lots of cafés in the Jardin des Plantes area or a more formal lunch can be had at **Mavromatis** *(see p307)*.

Afternoon
No child can resist a trip up the **Eiffel Tower**, so take them up in the afternoon for a great view of the city, or wait until nightfall and time your trip to coincide with the changing of the hour when thousands of lights twinkle for ten minutes *(see pp192–3)*. If there's time, take a tour of the waxworks at the **Grévin** museum *(see p216)*. Most of the models are of French celebrities, but big international names in art and sports can also be spotted.

THE GREAT OUTDOORS

- **Boat trip on the Seine**
- **Lunch on the Rue de Rivoli**
- **A walk to Luxembourg Garden**
- **Take a balloon ride**

TWO ADULTS allow at least €62

Morning
For today's trip the metro is banned, so instead take the hop-on-hop-off bateaubus up the Seine. The first "stop" is near the **Eiffel Tower** so a quick look around the

Modern water sculpture and greenhouse, Parc André Citroën

Champ-de-Mars underneath Gustave Eiffel's monument is recommended *(see p191)*. Continue on the bateaubus to the Louvre stop, jump off and wander around the **Jardin des Tuileries** *(see p130)*.

Lunch
The tea salon **Angélina** *(see p318)* is a cut above other cafés on Rue de Rivoli. Leave space for the famous Mont Blanc cake of chestnut purée and cream.

Afternoon
Reboard the boat and head up to **Notre-Dame** *(see pp82–5)*, then it's a good walk down the Boulevard St Michel to the **Jardin du Luxembourg** *(see p172)*. There's lots to see – chess tables, beehives and donkey rides – and the **Senate Art Gallery** hosts blockbuster shows. For a final blast of fresh air, cross the city to the **Parc André Citroën** and take a tethered balloon ride *(see p247)*.

A floral display in the Jardin des Plantes

Putting Paris on the Map

Paris, the capital of France, is a city of over two million
people covering 460 sq miles (1,200 sq km) of northern
France. It is on the Seine River at the center of the Ile-de-
France, the region which is home to ten million people,
around one-fifth of the French population. An important
European business and cultural center, it is the
focus of activity in the north of France.

WESTERN EUROPE

Western Europe

*Paris is in the heart of
industrial northern France,
with numerous road, rail
and air links to London,
Brussels, Amsterdam, and
the cities of western
Germany; by air, these take
under an hour to reach.*

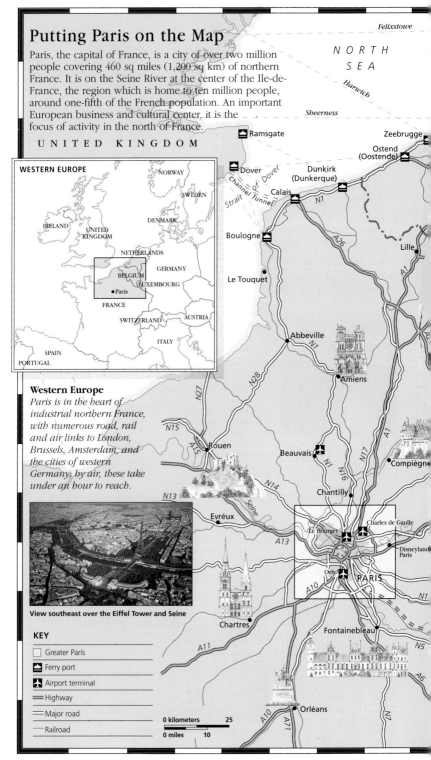

View southeast over the Eiffel Tower and Seine

KEY

☐ Greater Paris

⛴ Ferry port

✈ Airport terminal

═══ Highway

═══ Major road

─── Railroad

0 kilometers   25

0 miles   10

ILE-DE-FRANCE

N14
Cergy Pontoise
Oise
N1
N16
A1
N2

Seine
A13
Poissy

A15
St-Denis
Le Bourget
Charles de Gaulle
N3

Argenteuil
Aubervilliers
Lagny
Marne

Nanterre
Montreuil

St-Germain en-Laye
see next page
Vincennes
A4

N12
Versailles

N10
Sceaux
Créteil
N4

N118
Brie-Comte-Robert
N19

A10
Orly
N7
A6

N20
Corbeil-Essonnes

0 km   10

0 miles   5

Ile-de-France

*The Ile-de-France includes the conurbation of
Paris and many fascinating places such as
Chartres and Versailles. Central Paris is
bounded by the Périphérique beltway.
Important sights outside central Paris
are on pages 228–55.*

NETHERLANDS

Hook of Holland
(Hoek van Holland)

Rotterdam

N

Breda

Flushing
(Vlissingen)

Antwerp
(Antwerpen Anvers)

Gent
(Gand)

BELGIUM

Brussels
(Bruxelles Brussel)

Namur

Mons

GERMANY

St Quentin

Charleville-
Mézières

LUXEMBOURG

Trier

N2

Oise

N51

Luxembourg

Saarbrucken

N18

A31

Moselle

A32

Reims

N3

Verdun

Metz

A4

A4

Marne

Meuse

A4

Chalons

N44

N4

F R A N C E

Nancy

N4

A26

N4

Seine

Troyes

N19

Chaumont

A5

A31

Auxerre

Aerial view of central Paris

Central Paris

Napoleon's Arc de Triomphe

This book divides Paris into 14 areas, comprising central Paris and the nearby area of Montmartre. Most of the sights covered in the book lie within these areas, each one of which has its own chapter. Each area contains a range of sights that convey some of its history and distinctive character. The sights of Montmartre, for example, reveal its village charm and its colorful history as a thriving artistic enclave. In contrast, Champs-Elysées is renowned for its wide avenues, expensive fashion houses and opulent mansions. Most of the city's famous sights are within reach of the heart of the city and are easy to reach on foot or by public transportation.

Dôme Church
*The gilded Dôme Church
(see pp188–9) lies at the
heart of the Invalides.*

Eiffel Tower
*Named for the engineer
who designed and built it
in 1889, the Eiffel Tower is
the city's best known landmark (see pp192–3). It
towers more than 1,050 ft
(320 m) above Champ-de-
Mars park.*

Musée du Louvre
*Right in the heart of Paris, adjacent to the Seine River
and the Tuileries garden, lies the city's most impressive
museum, with an unrivaled collection of European
paintings from 1400 to 1850 (see pp122–9).*

KEY

	Star sights
Ⓜ	Metro station
🅡	SNCF (train) station
RER	RER station
⛴	Boat service boarding point
ℹ	Tourist information office

Sacré-Coeur
*Standing majestically above
Montmartre is the striking
basilica of Sacré-Coeur. Built
between 1875 and 1914, it is
dedicated to the sacred heart of
Jesus (see pp224–5).*

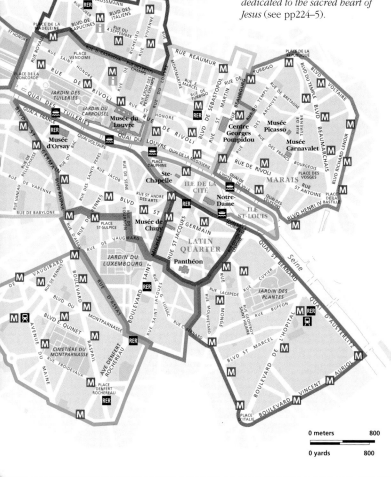

0 meters   800

0 yards   800

REPUBLIQUE FRANCAISE

LIBERTE EGALITE · FRATERNITE

THE HISTORY OF PARIS

The Paris conquered by the Romans in 55 BC was a small flood-prone fishing village on the Ile de la Cité, inhabited by the Parisii tribe. A Roman settlement soon flourished and spread onto the Left Bank of the Seine. The Franks succeeded the Romans, named the city Paris and made it the center of their kingdom.

Fleur-de-lys, the royal emblem

During the Middle Ages the city flourished as a religious center and architectural masterpieces such as Sainte-Chapelle were erected. It also thrived as a center of learning, enticing European scholars to its great university, the Sorbonne.

Paris emerged during the Renaissance and the Enlightenment as a great center of culture and ideas, and under the rule of Louis XIV it also became a city of immense wealth and power. But rule by the monarch gave way to rule by the people in the bloody Revolution of 1789. By the early years of the new century, revolutionary fervour had faded and the brilliant militarist Napoleon Bonaparte proclaimed himself Emperor of France and pursued his ambition to make Paris the center of the world.

Soon after the Revolution of 1848 a radical transformation of the city began. Baron Haussmann's grand urban scheme replaced Paris's medieval slums with elegant avenues and boulevards. By the end of the century, the city was the driving force of Western culture. This continued well into the 20th century, interrupted only by the German military occupation of 1940–44. Since the war, the city has revived and expanded dramatically, as it strives to be at the heart of a unified Europe.

The following pages illustrate Paris's history by providing snapshots of the significant periods in the city's evolution.

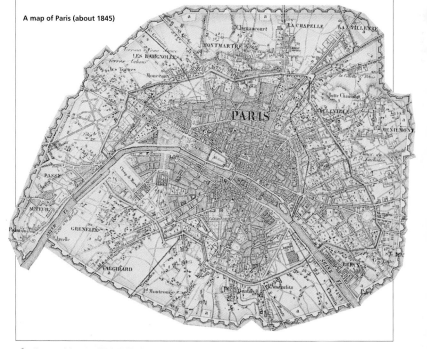

A map of Paris (about 1845)

◁ *Allegory of the Republic* (1848) by Dominique Louis Papety

Kings and Emperors in Paris

Paris became the power base for the kings of France at the beginning of the Capetian dynasty, when Hugh Capet ascended the throne. Successive kings and emperors have left their mark and many of the places mentioned in this book have royal associations: Philippe-Auguste's fortress, the Louvre Palace, is now one of the world's great museums; Henri IV's Pont Neuf bridge links the Ile de la Cité with the two banks of the Seine; and Napoleon conceived the Arc de Triomphe to celebrate his military victories. The end of the long line of kings came with the overthrow of the monarchy in 1848, during the reign of Louis-Philippe.

768–814 Charlemagne

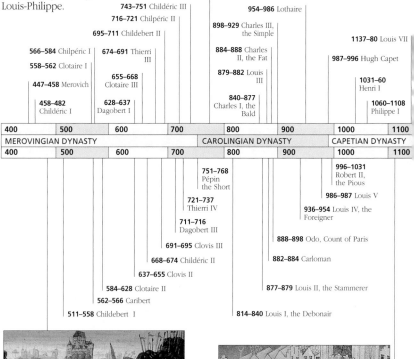

743–751 Childéric III
716–721 Chilpéric II
695–711 Childebert II
566–584 Chilpéric I
674–691 Thierri III
558–562 Clotaire I
447–458 Merovich
655–668 Clotaire III
458–482 Childéric I
628–637 Dagobert I

954–986 Lothaire
898–929 Charles III, the Simple
884–888 Charles II, the Fat
879–882 Louis III
840–877 Charles I, the Bald

1137–80 Louis VII
987–996 Hugh Capet
1031–60 Henri I
1060–1108 Philippe I

400	500	600	700	800	900	1000	1100
MEROVINGIAN DYNASTY				CAROLINGIAN DYNASTY		CAPETIAN DYNASTY	
400	500	600	700	800	900	1000	1100

751–768 Pépin the Short
721–737 Thierri IV
711–716 Dagobert III
691–695 Clovis III
668–674 Childéric II
637–655 Clovis II
584–628 Clotaire II
562–566 Caribert
511–558 Childebert I

996–1031 Robert II, the Pious
986–987 Louis V
936–954 Louis IV, the Foreigner
888–898 Odo, Count of Paris
882–884 Carloman
877–879 Louis II, the Stammerer
814–840 Louis I, the Debonair

482–511 Clovis I

1108–37 Louis VI, the Fat

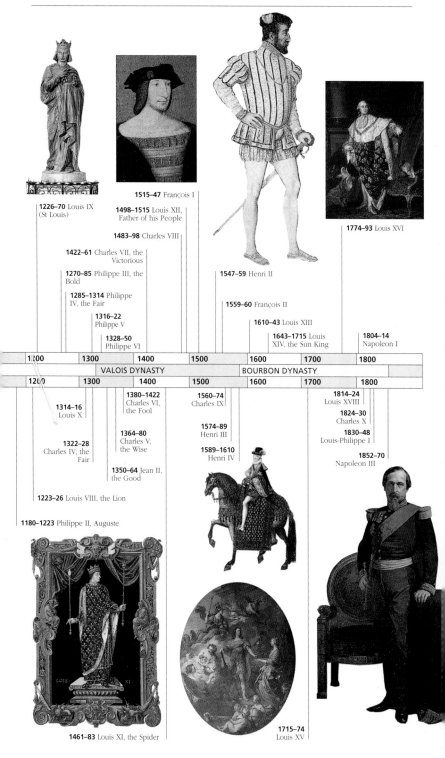

1226–70 Louis IX
(St Louis)

1515–47 François I

1498–1515 Louis XII,
Father of his People

1483–98 Charles VIII

1422–61 Charles VII, the
Victorious

1270–85 Philippe III, the
Bold

1547–59 Henri II

1285–1314 Philippe
IV, the Fair

1559–60 François II

1316–22
Philippe V

1610–43 Louis XIII

1328–50
Philippe VI

1643–1715 Louis
XIV, the Sun King

1774–93 Louis XVI

1804–14
Napoleon I

| 1200 | 1300 | 1400 | 1500 | 1600 | 1700 | 1800 |

VALOIS DYNASTY | BOURBON DYNASTY

| 1200 | 1300 | 1400 | 1500 | 1600 | 1700 | 1800 |

1314–16
Louis X

1380–1422
Charles VI,
the Fool

1560–74
Charles IX

1814–24
Louis XVIII

1824–30
Charles X

1322–28
Charles IV, the
Fair

1364–80
Charles V,
the Wise

1574–89
Henri III

1830–48
Louis-Philippe I

1350–64 Jean II,
the Good

1589–1610
Henri IV

1852–70
Napoleon III

1223–26 Louis VIII, the Lion

1180–1223 Philippe II, Auguste

1461–83 Louis XI, the Spider

1715–74
Louis XV

Gallo-Roman Paris

Paris would not have existed without the Seine. The river provided early peoples with the means to exploit the land, forests, marshes and islands. Recent excavations have unearthed canoes dating back to 4,500 BC, well before a Celtic tribe, known as the Parisii, settled there in the 3rd century BC, in an area known as Lutetia. From 59 BC, the Romans undertook

Roman enamel brooch

the conquest of Gaul (France). Seven years later Lutetia was sacked by the Romans. They fortified and rebuilt it, especially the main island (the Ile de la Cité) and the Left Bank of the Seine.

EXTENT OF THE CITY

▨ 200 BC	☐ Today

Bronze-Age Harness
Everyday objects like harnesses continued to be made of bronze well into the Iron Age, which began in Gaul around 900 BC.

Iron Daggers
From the 2nd century BC, short swords of iron replaced long swords and were sometimes decorated with human and animal shapes.

Baths

Theater

Forum

Present-day
Rue Soufflot

Glass Beads
Iron-Age glass beads and bracelets have been found on the Ile de la Cité.

Fired-Clay Vase
Pale ceramics with colored decoration were common in Gaul.

Present-day
Rue St-Jacques

TIMELINE

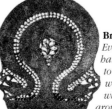

Helmet worn by Gaulish warriors

4500 BC Early boatmen operate from the banks of the Seine

52 BC Labienus, Caesar's lieutenant, defeats the Gauls under Camulogenes. The Parisii destroy their own city

4500	400		200	

Parisii gold coin minted on the Ile de la Cité

300 BC Parisii tribe settle on the Ile de la Cité

100 BC Romans rebuild the Ile de la Cité, and create a new town on the Left Bank

Roman Oil Lamp
The inhabitants of the densely populated Ile de la Cité derived comfort during the dark winter months from the warmth of central heating and the light from oil lamps.

Ile de la Cité

Gallo-Roman Goddess
Found in the arena, this head dates from the 2nd century AD.

Temple

WHERE TO SEE GALLO-ROMAN PARIS

Since the mid-19th century, excavations have yielded evidence of the boundaries of the Roman city which had as its central axes the present-day Rue St-Jacques and Rue Soufflot. In the Crypte Archéologique *(see p81)* under the square of Notre-Dame can be seen the remains of Gallo-Roman houses and Roman ramparts dating from the end of the 3rd century AD. Other Roman sites in Paris are the Arènes de Lutèce *(p165)* and the baths at the Musée de Cluny *(pp154 and 157)*.

The baths *(thermae)* at Cluny had three huge rooms of water with different temperatures.

Stage backdrop

Spectator seats

Arènes de Lutèce
This huge arena, built in the 2nd century AD, was used for circuses, theatrical performances and gladiatorial combat.

Ring Flask
From about 300 AD, this flask was found on the Ile de la Cité.

LUTETIA IN AD 200
Paris, or Lutetia, was laid out in a grid pattern with bridges linking the Ile de la Cité and the Left Bank.

Roman floor mosaic from the Cluny baths

200 Romans add arena, baths and villas

285 Barbarians advance, Lutetia swept by fire

360 Julien, prefect of Gaul, is proclaimed Emperor. Lutetia changes its name to Paris after the Parisii

| 0 | 200 | 400 |

250 Early Christian martyr, St Denis, beheaded in Montmartre

451 Sainte Geneviève galvanizes the Parisians to repulse Attila the Hun

485–508 Clovis, leader of the Franks, defeats the Romans. Paris becomes Christian

Medieval Paris

Manuscript illumination

Throughout the Middle Ages, strategically placed towns like Paris, positioned at a river crossing, became important centers of political power and learning. The Church played a crucial part in intellectual and spiritual life. It provided the impetus for education and for technological advances such as the drainage of land and the digging of canals. The population was still confined mainly to the Ile de la Cité and the Left Bank. When the marshes *(marais)* were drained in the 12th century, the city was able to expand.

EXTENT OF THE CITY

☐ 1300   ☐ Today

Sainte-Chapelle
The upper chapel of this medieval masterpiece (see pp88–9) was reserved for the royal family.

The Ile de la Cité, including the towers of the Conciergerie and Sainte-Chapelle, features in the pages for June.

Octagonal Table
Medieval manor houses had wooden furniture like this trestle table.

Drainage allowed more land to be cultivated.

Weavers' Window
Medieval craftsmen formed guilds and many church windows were dedicated to their crafts.

A rural life was led by most Parisians, who worked on the land. The actual city only occupied a tiny area.

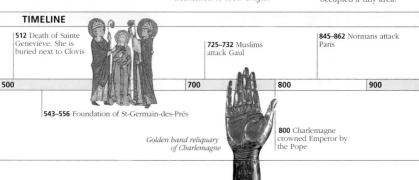

TIMELINE

512 Death of Sainte Geneviève. She is buried next to Clovis

725–732 Muslims attack Gaul

845–862 Normans attack Paris

500		700	800	900

543–556 Foundation of St-Germain-des-Prés

Golden hand reliquary of Charlemagne

800 Charlemagne crowned Emperor by the Pope

Notre-Dame
The great Gothic cathedrals took many years to build. Work continued on Notre-Dame from 1163 to 1334.

University Seal
The University of Paris was founded in 1215.

The Monasteries
Monks of many different orders lived in monasteries in Paris, especially on the Left Bank of the Seine.

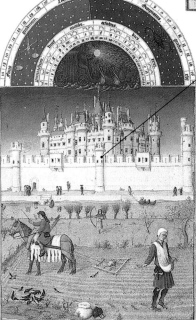

The Louvre of Charles V with its defensive wall is seen here from the Ile de la Cité.

The Nobility
From the mid-14th century, dress was considered to be a mark of class; noble ladies wore high, pointed hats.

THE MONTHS: JUNE AND OCTOBER
This illuminated prayer book and calendar, the Très Riches Heures (left and above), was made for the Duc de Berri in 1416. It shows many Paris buildings.

A MEDIEVAL ROMANCE
It was in the cloisters of Notre-Dame that the romance between the monk Pierre Abélard and the young Héloïse began. Abélard was the most original theologian of the 12th century and was hired as a tutor to the 17-year-old niece of a canon. A love affair soon developed between the teacher and his pupil. In his wrath, Héloïse's uncle had the scholar castrated; Héloïse took refuge in a convent for the rest of her life.

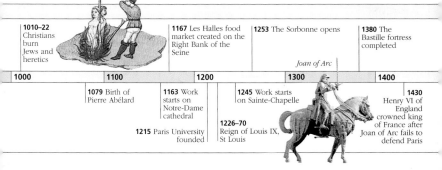

1010–22 Christians burn Jews and heretics

1167 Les Halles food market created on the Right Bank of the Seine

1253 The Sorbonne opens

1380 The Bastille fortress completed

Joan of Arc

1000 **1100** **1200** **1300** **1400**

1079 Birth of Pierre Abélard

1163 Work starts on Notre-Dame cathedral

1245 Work starts on Sainte-Chapelle

1430 Henry VI of England crowned king of France after Joan of Arc fails to defend Paris

1226–70 Reign of Louis IX, St Louis

1215 Paris University founded

Renaissance Paris

At the end of the Hundred Years' War with England, Paris was in a terrible state. By the time the occupying English army had left in 1453, the city lay in ruins, with many houses and woods burned. Louis XI brought back prosperity and a new interest in art, architecture, decoration and clothes. During the course of the 16th century, French kings came under the spell of the Italian Renaissance. Their architects made the first attempts at town planning, creating elegant, uniform buildings and open urban spaces like the magnificent Place Royale.

Couple in fine courtly dress

EXTENT OF THE CITY

☐ *1590*   ☐ *Today*

A Knight Preparing to Joust
The Place Royale was the setting for jousting displays well into the 17th century.

Printing Press (1470)
Religious tracts, mainly in Latin, were printed on the first press at the Sorbonne.

Jewel-Encrusted Pendant
A sign of the new prosperity, jewels became an important part of dress.

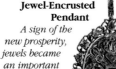

Pont Notre-Dame
This bridge with its row of houses was built at the start of the 15th century. The Pont Neuf (1589) was the first bridge without houses.

PLACE ROYALE
Built by Henri IV in 1609, with grand symmetrical houses around an open, central space, this was Paris's first square. Home to the aristocracy, it was re-named Place des Vosges in 1800 (see p94).

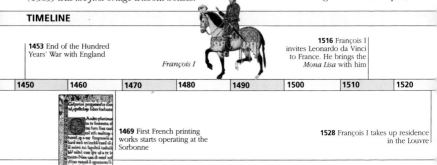

TIMELINE

1453 End of the Hundred Years' War with England

François I

1516 François I invites Leonardo da Vinci to France. He brings the *Mona Lisa* with him

1450	1460	1470	1480	1490	1500	1510	1520

1469 First French printing works starts operating at the Sorbonne

1528 François I takes up residence in the Louvre

16th-Century Knife and Fork Set
Ornate knife and fork sets were used in the dining rooms of the wealthy to carve roasts of meat. Diners used hands or spoons for eating.

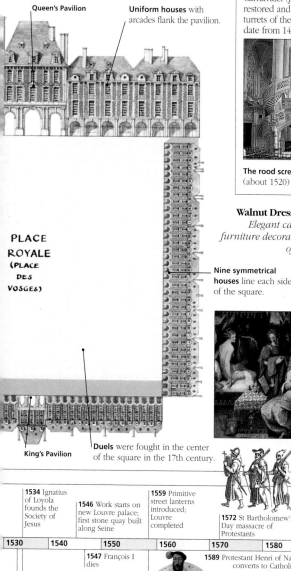

Queen's Pavilion

Uniform houses with arcades flank the pavilion.

PLACE ROYALE (PLACE DES VOSGES)

Nine symmetrical houses line each side of the square.

King's Pavilion

Duels were fought in the center of the square in the 17th century.

WHERE TO SEE RENAISSANCE PARIS TODAY
Besides the Place des Vosges with its fine buildings, there are many examples of the Renaissance in Paris today. Churches include the Tour St-Jacques (p115), St-Etienne-du-Mont (p153) and St-Eustache (p114). Mansions such as the Hôtel Carnavalet (pp96–7) have recently been restored and the staircases, courtyard and turrets of the Hôtel de Cluny (pp154–5) date from 1485–96.

The rood screen of St-Etienne-du-Mont (about 1520) is of outstanding delicacy.

Walnut Dresser (about 1545)
Elegant carved wooden furniture decorated the homes of the wealthy.

Hyante and Climente
Toussaint Dubreuil and other artists took up Renaissance mythological themes.

1534 Ignatius of Loyola founds the Society of Jesus

1546 Work starts on new Louvre palace; first stone quay built along Seine

1559 Primitive street lanterns introduced; Louvre completed

1572 St Bartholomew's Day massacre of Protestants

1589 Henri III assassinated at St-Cloud, near Paris

1609 Henri IV begins building Place des Vosges

1530	1540	1550	1560	1570	1580	1590	1600

1547 François I dies

1589 Protestant Henri of Navarre converts to Catholicism, crowned as Henri IV

1610 Henri IV is assassinated by Ravaillac, a religious fanatic

1534 Founding of the Collège de France

1589 Henri IV completes Pont-Neuf and improves capital's water supply

1533 Hôtel de Ville rebuilt

1559 Henri II killed in a Paris tournament

The assassin Ravaillac

The Sun King's Paris

Emblem of the Sun King

The 17th century in France, which became known as *Le Grand Siècle* (the great century), is epitomized by the glittering extravagance of Louis XIV (the Sun King) and his court at Versailles. In Paris, imposing buildings, squares, theaters and aristocratic *hôtels* (mansions) were built. Beneath this amazing surface lay the absolute power of the monarch. By the end of Louis' reign the cost of his extravagance and of waging almost continuous war with France's neighbors led to a decline in the monarchy.

EXTENT OF THE CITY

1657	Today

An open staircase rose from the internal courtyard.

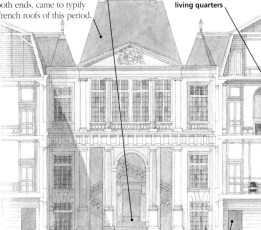

The mansard roof, with its slopes at both sides and both ends, came to typify French roofs of this period.

Cross section of the living quarters

The Gardens of Versailles
Louis XIV devoted a lot of time to the gardens, which were designed by André Le Nôtre.

Louis XIV as Jupiter
On ascending the throne in 1661, Louis, depicted here as Jupiter triumphant, ended the civil wars that had been raging since his childhood.

The ground floor contained the servants' quarters.

Chest of Drawers
This gilded piece was made by André-Charles Boulle for the Grand Trianon at Versailles.

TIMELINE

1610 Louis XIII's accession marks the start of *Le Grand Siècle*

Louis XIII

1624 Completion of Tuileries Palace

Cardinal Mazarin

1631 Launch of *La Gazette*, Paris's first newspaper

1643 Death of Louis XIII. Regency under control of Marie de Médicis and Cardinal Mazarin

1661 Louis XIV becomes absolute monarch. Enlargement of Château de Versailles begun

1610	1620	1630	1640	1650	1660

1622 Paris becomes an episcopal see

1629 Richelieu, Louis XIII's first minister, builds Palais Royal

1638 Birth of Louis XIV

1662 Colbert, Louis XIV's finance minister, founds Gobelins tapestry works

1614 Final meeting of the Estates Council (the main legislative assembly) before the Revolution

1627 Development of the Ile St-Louis

Weaving frame

Ceiling by Charles Le Brun
Court painter to Louis XIV, Le Brun decorated many ceilings like this one at the Hôtel Carnavalet (see p96).

Madame de Maintenon
When the queen died in 1683, Louis married Madame de Maintenon, shown here in a framed painting by Caspar Netscher.

Decorated Fan
For special court fêtes, Louis XIV often stipulated that women carry fans.

The Galerie d'Hercule with Le Brun ceiling

Formal Classical Garden

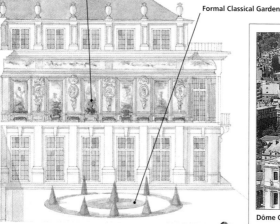

HOTEL LAMBERT (1640)
In the 17th century, the aristocracy built luxurious town houses with grand staircases, courtyards, formal gardens, coach houses and stables.

Neptune Cup
Made from lapis lazuli with a silver Neptune on top, this cup was part of Louis' vast collection of art objects.

Dôme Church (1706)

WHERE TO SEE THE SUN KING'S PARIS

Many 17th-century mansions such as the Hôtel Lambert still exist in Paris, but not all are open to the public. However, Hôtel des Invalides (p187), the Dôme Church (pp188–9), the Palais du Luxembourg (p172) and Versailles (pp248–53) give a magnificent impression of the period.

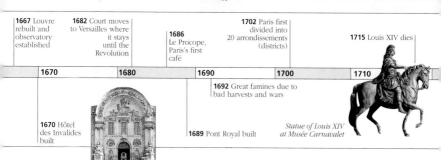

1667 Louvre rebuilt and observatory established

1682 Court moves to Versailles where it stays until the Revolution

1686 Le Procope, Paris's first café

1702 Paris first divided into 20 arrondissements (districts)

1715 Louis XIV dies

| 1670 | 1680 | 1690 | 1700 | 1710 |

1692 Great famines due to bad harvests and wars

1670 Hôtel des Invalides built

1689 Pont Royal built

Statue of Louis XIV at Musée Carnavalet

Paris in the Age of Enlightenment

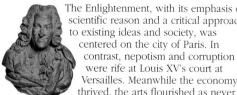

The Enlightenment, with its emphasis on scientific reason and a critical approach to existing ideas and society, was centered on the city of Paris. In contrast, nepotism and corruption were rife at Louis XV's court at Versailles. Meanwhile the economy thrived, the arts flourished as never before and intellectuals, such as Voltaire and Rousseau, were renowned throughout

Bust of François Marie Arouet, known as Voltaire

Europe. In Paris, the population rose to about 650,000: town planning was developed, and the first accurate street map of the city appeared in 1787.

EXTENT OF THE CITY

☐ *1720*   ☐ *Today*

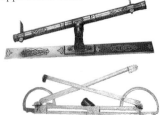

Nautical Instruments
As the science of navigation advanced, scientists developed telescopes and trigonometric instruments (used for measuring longitude and latitude).

18th-Century Wigs
These were not only a mark of fashion but also a way of indicating the wearer's class and importance.

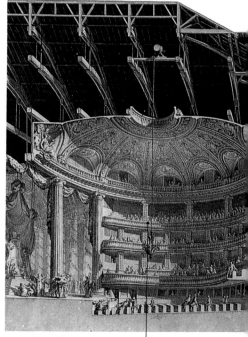

COMEDIE FRANÇAISE
The Age of Enlightenment saw a burst of dramatic activity and new theaters opened, such as the Comédie Française (see p120). Today the Théâtre Français company is based here.

The auditorium, with 1,913 seats, was the largest in Paris.

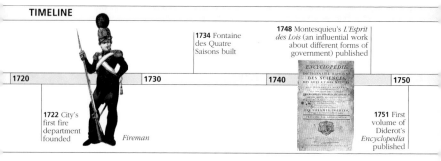

TIMELINE

1734 Fontaine des Quatre Saisons built

1748 Montesquieu's *L'Esprit des Lois* (an influential work about different forms of government) published

| 1720 | 1730 | 1740 | 1750 |

1722 City's first fire department founded

Fireman

1751 First volume of Diderot's *Encyclopedia* published

Madame de Pompadour
Although generally remembered as the mistress of Louis XV, she was renowned as a patron of the arts and had great political influence.

Chocolate Pot
By the 18th century, bourgeois families could afford tobacco, tea, chocolate and coffee from Asia and the New World.

Vestibule with painted ceiling

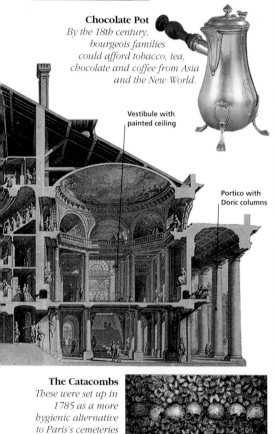

Portico with Doric columns

The Catacombs
These were set up in 1785 as a more hygienic alternative to Paris's cemeteries (see p179).

WHERE TO SEE ENLIGHTENMENT PARIS

The district around the Rue de Lille, the Rue de Varenne and the Rue de Grenelle *(p187)* has many luxurious town houses, or *hôtels*, which were built by the aristocracy during the first half of the 18th century. Memorabilia from the lives of the great intellectuals Voltaire and Jean-Jacques Rousseau are in the Musée Carnavalet *(pp96–7)*, along with 18th-century interior designs and paintings.

Churches were built throughout the Enlightenment. St-Sulpice *(p172)* was completed in 1776.

Le Procope *(p140)* is the oldest café in Paris. It was frequented by Voltaire and Rousseau.

1757 First oil street lamps

c.1760 Place de la Concorde, Panthéon and Ecole Militaire built

1760

1762 Rousseau's *Emile* and the *Social Contract*

1764 Madame de Pompadour dies

Rousseau, philosopher and writer, believed that humans were naturally good and had been corrupted by society.

1770

1774 Louis XV, great grandson of Louis XIV, dies

1778 France supports American independence

1780

1782 First sidewalks built, in the Place du Théâtre Français

1783 Montgolfier brothers make the first hot-air balloon ascent

1785 David paints the *Oath of the Horatii*

Paris During the Revolution

In 1789 most Parisians were still living in squalor and poverty, as they had since the Middle Ages. Rising inflation and opposition to Louis XVI culminated in the storming of the Bastille, the king's prison; the Republic was founded three years later. However, the Terror soon followed, when those suspected of betraying the Revolution were executed

A plate made in celebration of the Revolution

without trial: more than 60,000 people lost their lives. The bloody excesses of Robespierre, the zealous revolutionary, led to his overthrow and a new government, the Directory, was set up in 1795.

EXTENT OF THE CITY

☐ *1796*   ☐ *Today*

The prison turrets were set alight.

The French guards, who were on the side of the revolutionaries, arrived late in the afternoon with two cannons.

Declaration of the Rights of Man and the Citizen
The Enlightenment ideals of equality and human dignity were enshrined in the Declaration. This illustration is the preface to the 1791 Constitution.

Drawbridge

REPUBLICAN CALENDAR

The revolutionaries believed that the world was starting again, so they abolished the existing church calendar and took September 22, 1792, the day the Republic was declared, as the first day of the new era. The Republican calendar had 12 equal months, each subdivided into three ten-day periods, with the remaining five days of each year set aside for public holidays. All the months of the year were given poetic names which linked them to nature and the seasons, such as fog, snow, seed-time, flowers and harvest.

A colored engraving by Tresca showing *Ventôse*, the windy month (19 Feb–20 Mar) from the new Republican calendar

TIMELINE

Jul 14 Fall of the Bastille	**Aug 4** Abolition of feudalism
	Aug 26 Declaration of the Rights of Man and the Citizen
	Sep 17 Law of Suspects passed: the Terror begins

Aug 10 The storming of the Tuileries

1789	1790	1791	1792

Cartoon on the three Estates: the clergy, the nobility and the awakening populace

May 5 The Estates council meets

Lafayette, commander of the National Guard, takes his oath to the Constitution

Jul 14 Fête de la Fédération

Jul 17 Champ de Mars massacre

Apr 25 *La Marseillaise* composed

Paper Money
Bonds, called assignats, were used to fund the Revolution from 1790–93.

La Marseillaise
The revolutionaries' marching song is now the national anthem.

The Sans Culottes
By 1792, the wearing of trousers instead of breeches (culottes) was a political symbol of Paris's artisans and shopkeepers.

"Patriotic" Chair
The back of this wooden chair is topped by red bonnets, symbol of revolutionary politics.

Wallpaper
Commemorative wallpaper was produced to celebrate the Revolution.

The dead and wounded totaled 171 by the end of the day.

Coin tower

Great court

Well court

Guillotine
This was used for the first time in France in April 1792.

STORMING OF THE BASTILLE
The Bastille was overrun on July 14, 1789, and the seven prisoners held there released. The defenders (32 Swiss guards, 82 wounded soldiers and the governor) were massacred.

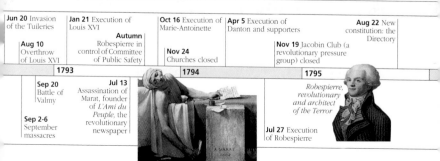

Jun 20 Invasion of the Tuileries

Aug 10 Overthrow of Louis XVI

Jan 21 Execution of Louis XVI

Autumn Robespierre in control of Committee of Public Safety

Oct 16 Execution of Marie-Antoinette

Nov 24 Churches closed

Apr 5 Execution of Danton and supporters

Nov 19 Jacobin Club (a revolutionary pressure group) closed

Aug 22 New constitution: the Directory

1793

1794

1795

Sep 20 Battle of Valmy

Sep 2-6 September massacres

Jul 13 Assassination of Marat, founder of *L'Ami du Peuple*, the revolutionary newspaper

Robespierre, revolutionary and architect of the Terror

Jul 27 Execution of Robespierre

Napoleonic Paris

Napoleon's imperial crown

Napoleon Bonaparte was the most brilliant general in the French army. The instability of the new government after the Revolution gave him the chance to seize power, and in November 1799 he installed himself in the Tuileries Palace as First Consul. He crowned himself Emperor in May 1804. Napoleon established a centralized administration and a code of laws, reformed France's educational system and set out to make Paris the most beautiful city in the world. The city was endowed with grand monuments and embellished with the spoils of conquest. His power was always fragile and dependent on incessant wars. In March 1814, Prussian, Austrian and Russian armies invaded Paris and Napoleon fled to Elba. He returned to Paris in 1815 but was defeated at Waterloo and died in exile in 1821.

EXTENT OF THE CITY

☐ *1810*   ☐ *Today*

Château de Malmaison
This was the favorite home of Josephine, Napoleon's first wife.

Ladies-in-Waiting hold Josephine's train.

Opaline-Glass Clock
The decoration on this clock echoed the fashion for draperies.

Elephant Project
This monument was planned for the center of the Place de la Bastille.

Eagle's Flight
Napoleon's flight to Elba in 1814 was satirized in this cartoon.

TIMELINE

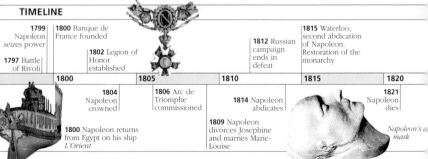

1799 Napoleon seizes power	**1800** Banque de France founded			**1815** Waterloo; second abdication of Napoleon. Restoration of the monarchy	
1797 Battle of Rivoli	**1802** Legion of Honor established		**1812** Russian campaign ends in defeat		
1800		**1805**	**1810**	**1815**	**1820**
	1804 Napoleon crowned	**1806** Arc de Triomphe commissioned	**1814** Napoleon abdicates		**1821** Napoleon dies
	1800 Napoleon returns from Egypt on his ship *L'Orient*		**1809** Napoleon divorces Josephine and marries Marie-Louise		*Napoleon's a mask*

Bronze Tabletop
Inlaid with Napoleon's portrait, this table marks the victory at Austerlitz.

Russian Cossacks in the Palais Royal
After Napoleon's defeat and flight in 1814, Paris suffered the humiliation of being occupied by foreign troops, including Austrians, Prussians and Russians.

Josephine kneels before Napoleon.

Napoleon holds the crown for his empress, Josephine.

The Pope makes the sign of the cross.

The Arc de Triomphe du Carrousel was erected in 1806 and crowned with the horses looted from St Mark's, Venice.

WHERE TO SEE NAPOLEONIC PARIS

Many of the grand monuments Napoleon planned for Paris were never built, but two triumphal arches, the Arc de Triomphe (pp208–9) and Arc de Triomphe du Carrousel (p122), were a major part of his legacy. La Madeleine church (p214) was also inaugurated in his reign and much of the Louvre was rebuilt (pp122–3). Examples of the Empire style can be seen at Malmaison (p255) and at the Carnavalet (pp96–7).

NAPOLEON'S CORONATION
Napoleon's rather dramatic crowning took place in 1804. In this recreation by J L David, the Pope, summoned to Notre-Dame, looks on as Napoleon crowns his empress just before crowning himself.

The Empress
Josephine was divorced by Napoleon in 1809.

1842 First railroad line between Paris and St-Germain-en-Laye opens

1825	1830	1835	1840	1845

1830 Revolution in Paris and advent of constitutional monarchy

1831 Victor Hugo's *Notre-Dame de Paris* published. Cholera epidemic hits Paris

1840 Reburial of Napoleon at Les Invalides

Napoleon's tomb

The Grand Transformation

In 1848 Paris saw a second revolution which brought down the recently restored monarchy. In the uncertainties that followed, Napoleon's nephew assumed power in the same way as his uncle before him – by a *coup d'état*. He proclaimed himself Napoleon III in 1851. Under his rule Paris was transformed into the most magnificent city in Europe. He entrusted the task of modernization to Baron Haussmann. Haussmann demolished the crowded, unsanitary streets of the medieval city and created a well-ordered capital within a geometrical grid of avenues and boulevards. Neighboring districts such as Auteuil were annexed, creating the suburbs.

EXTENT OF THE CITY

| | 1859 | | Today |

Lamppost outside the Opéra

Boulevard des Italiens
This tree-lined avenue, painted by Edmond Georges Grandjean (1889), was one of the most fashionable of the new boulevards.

Twelve avenues formed a star (*étoile*).

Arc de Triomphe

AVE DE FRIEDLAND

AVE HOCHE

AVE DE WAGRAM

AVE MAC-MAHON

PLACE

AVE CARNOT

Laying the Sewers
This engraving from 1861 shows the early work for laying the sewer system (see p190) from La Villette to Les Halles. Most was the work of the engineer Belgrand.

Circular Billboard
Distinctive billboards advertised opera and theater performances.

Grand mansions were built around the Arc de Triomphe between 1860 and 1868.

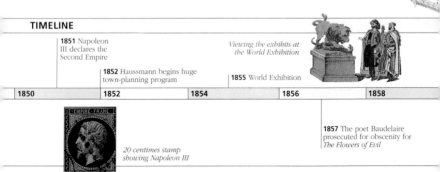

TIMELINE

1851 Napoleon III declares the Second Empire

1852 Haussmann begins huge town-planning program

Viewing the exhibits at the World Exhibition

1855 World Exhibition

| 1850 | 1852 | 1854 | 1856 | 1858 |

20 centimes stamp showing Napoleon III

1857 The poet Baudelaire prosecuted for obscenity for *The Flowers of Evil*

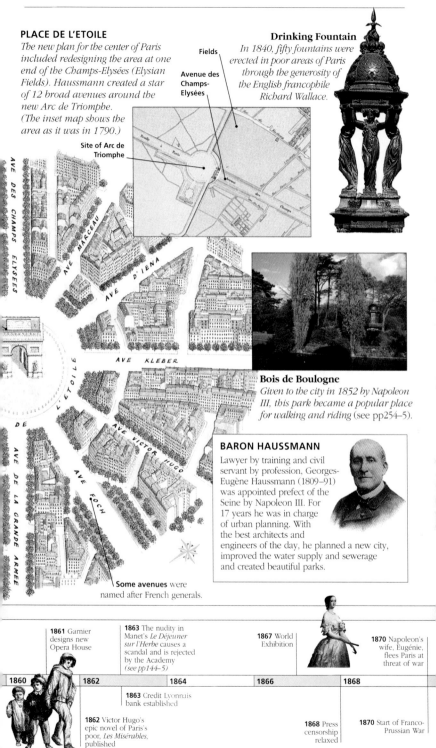

PLACE DE L'ETOILE

The new plan for the center of Paris included redesigning the area at one end of the Champs-Elysées (Elysian Fields). Haussmann created a star of 12 broad avenues around the new Arc de Triomphe. (The inset map shows the area as it was in 1790.)

Fields

Avenue des Champs-Elysées

Site of Arc de Triomphe

AVE DES CHAMPS ELYSEES

AVE MARCEAU

AVE D'IENA

L'ETOILE

DE

AVE KLEBER

AVE VICTOR HUGO

AVE FOCH

AVE DE LA GRANDE ARMEE

Some avenues were named after French generals.

Drinking Fountain

In 1840, fifty fountains were erected in poor areas of Paris through the generosity of the English francophile Richard Wallace.

Bois de Boulogne

Given to the city in 1852 by Napoleon III, this park became a popular place for walking and riding (see pp254–5).

BARON HAUSSMANN

Lawyer by training and civil servant by profession, Georges-Eugène Haussmann (1809–91) was appointed prefect of the Seine by Napoleon III. For 17 years he was in charge of urban planning. With the best architects and engineers of the day, he planned a new city, improved the water supply and sewerage and created beautiful parks.

1861 Garnier designs new Opera House

1863 The nudity in Manet's *Le Déjeuner sur l'Herbe* causes a scandal and is rejected by the Academy (*see pp144–5*)

1867 World Exhibition

1870 Napoleon's wife, Eugénie, flees Paris at threat of war

1860	1862	1864	1866	1868

1863 Credit Lyonnais bank established

1862 Victor Hugo's epic novel of Paris's poor, *Les Misérables*, published

1868 Press censorship relaxed

1870 Start of Franco-Prussian War

The Belle Epoque

The Franco-Prussian War culminated in the terrible Siege of Paris. When peace came in 1871, it fell to the new government, the Third Republic, to bring about economic recovery. From about 1890 life was transformed: the automobile, airplane, movies, telephone and gramophone all contributed to the enjoyment of life, and the *Belle Epoque* (beautiful age) was born. Paris became a glittering city where the new style, *Art Nouveau*, decorated buildings and objects. The paintings of the Impressionists, such as Renoir, reflected the *joie de vivre* of the times, while later those of Matisse, Braque and Picasso heralded the modern movement in art.

Art Nouveau pendant

EXTENT OF THE CITY

▨ 1895   ☐ Today

The interior was arranged as tiers of galleries around a central grand staircase.

Cabaret Poster
Toulouse-Lautrec's posters immortalized the singers and dancers of the cafés and cabaret clubs of Montmartre, where artists and writers congregated in the 1890s.

Electricity illuminated the window displays.

Windows facing onto the Boulevard Haussmann displayed the goods on offer.

Art Nouveau Cash Register
Even ordinary objects like this cash register were beautified by the new style.

Central Hall of the Grand Palais
The Grand Palais (pp206–7) was built to house two huge exhibitions of French painting and sculpture at the World Exhibition of 1889.

TIMELINE

1871 Third Republic established

1874 Monet paints first Impressionist picture: *Impression: Soleil levant*

Louis Pasteur

1889 Eiffel Tower built

| 1870 | 1875 | 1880 | 1885 | 1890 |

Zoo animals were shot to feed the hungry (see p224)

Entrance ticket to the exhibition

1891 First metro station opens

1870 Siege of Paris

1885 Louis Pasteur discovers rabies vaccine

1889 Great Exhibition

Citroën 5CV

France led the world in the early development of the automobile. By 1900 the Citroën began to be seen on the streets of Paris, and long-distance auto racing was popular.

WHERE TO SEE THE BELLE EPOQUE

Art Nouveau can be seen in monumental buildings like the Grand Palais and Petit Palais *(p206)*, while the Galeries Layfayette *(p321)* and the Pharamond restaurant *(p306)* have beautiful Belle Epoque interiors. The Musée d'Orsay *(pp144–7)* has many objects from this period.

The glass dome could be seen from all parts of the store.

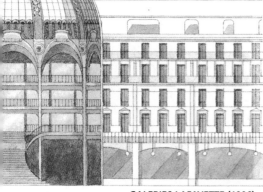

Moulin Rouge (1890)

The old, defunct windmills of Montmartre became nightclubs, like the world-famous Moulin Rouge (red windmill) (see p226).

The entrance to the metro at Porte Dauphine was the work of leading Art Nouveau designer Hector Guimard *(p226)*.

GALERIES LAFAYETTE (1906)

This beautiful department store , with its dome a riot of colored glass and wrought ironwork, was a sign of the new prosperity.

The Naughty Nineties

The Lumière brothers captured the daring negligée fashions of the 1890s in the first moving images of the cinematograph.

The doorway of No. 29 Avenue Rapp *(p191)*, in the Eiffel Tower quarter, is a fine example of Art Nouveau.

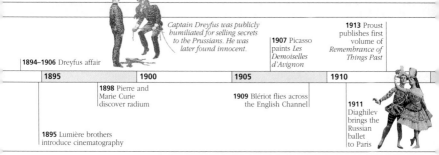

Captain Dreyfus was publicly humiliated for selling secrets to the Prussians. He was later found innocent.

1894–1906 Dreyfus affair

1907 Picasso paints *Les Demoiselles d'Avignon*

1913 Proust publishes first volume of *Remembrance of Things Past*

| 1895 | 1900 | 1905 | 1910 |

1898 Pierre and Marie Curie discover radium

1909 Blériot flies across the English Channel

1911 Diaghilev brings the Russian ballet to Paris

1895 Lumière brothers introduce cinematography

Avant-Garde Paris

Office chair by Le Corbusier

From the 1920s to the 1940s, Paris became a mecca for artists, musicians, writers and filmmakers. The city was alive with new movements such as Cubism and Surrealism represented by Cézanne, Picasso, Braque, Man Ray and Duchamp. Many new trends came from the USA, as writers and musicians including Ernest Hemingway, Gertrude Stein and Sidney Bechet took up residence in Paris. In architecture, the geometric shapes created by Le Corbusier changed the face of the modern building.

EXTENT OF THE CITY

☐ 1940   ☐ Today

Napoleon by Abel Gance
Paris has always been a city for filmmakers. In 1927 Abel Gance made an innovative movie about Napoleon, using triple screens and wide-angle lenses.

Occupied Paris
Paris was under occupation for most of World War II. The Eiffel Tower was a favorite spot for German soldiers.

Josephine Baker
Arriving in Paris in 1925, the outlandish dancer catapulted to fame in "La Revue Nègre" wearing nothing but feathers.

Sidney Bechet
In the 1930s and 1940s the jazz clubs of Paris resounded to the swing music of black musicians such as the saxophonist Sidney Bechet.

Stilts
supported the concrete shell.

Living space was made into a picture gallery.

LA ROCHE VILLA BY LE CORBUSIER
Made from concrete and steel, with straight lines, horizontal windows and a flat roof, this house (1923) epitomized the new style.

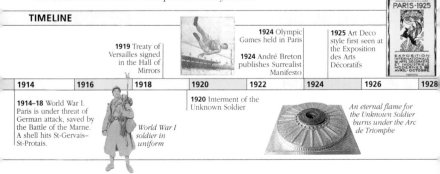

TIMELINE

1919 Treaty of Versailles signed in the Hall of Mirrors

1924 Olympic Games held in Paris

1924 André Breton publishes Surrealist Manifesto

1925 Art Deco style first seen at the Exposition des Arts Décoratifs

PARIS-1925

EXPOSITION INTERNATIONALE DES ARTS DECORATIFS ET INDUSTRIELS MODERNES AVRIL-OCTOBRE

| 1914 | 1916 | 1918 | 1920 | 1922 | 1924 | 1926 | 1928 |

1914–18 World War I. Paris is under threat of German attack, saved by the Battle of the Marne. A shell hits St-Gervais–St-Protais.

World War I soldier in uniform

1920 Interment of the Unknown Soldier

An eternal flame for the Unknown Soldier burns under the Arc de Triomphe

Fashion in the 1940s
After World War II, the classic look for men and women was reminiscent of military uniforms.

The roof was designed as a terrace.

Airmail Poster
Airmail routes developed during the 1930s, especially to French North Africa.

The bedroom was above the dining room.

The old Trocadéro was changed to the Palais de Chaillot *(see p198)* for the World Exhibition.

WHERE TO SEE AVANT-GARDE PARIS

La Roche Villa is now part of the Fondation Le Corbusier *(p254)* and can be visited in the Paris suburb of Auteuil. Hemingway's haunt, the bar-brasserie La Closerie des Lilas in Montparnasse *(p179)*, has retained much of its period decor. For fashion don't miss the Musée Galliera *(p201)*.

The kitchen was built at the back with a sloping glass roof.

The garage was built into the ground floor.

Claudine in Paris by Colette
The Claudine series of novels, written by Colette Willy, known simply as "Colette", were extremely popular in the 1930s.

Windows were arranged in a horizontal strip.

1930	1932	1934	1936	1938	1940	1942

1931 Colonial Exhibition

A visitor to the exhibition in colonial dress

1937 Picasso paints *Guernica* in protest at the Spanish Civil War

1940 World War II: Paris bombed and occupied by Nazis

1934 Riots and strikes in response to the Depression

1937 Palais de Chaillot built

Symbol of Free French super-imposed on the victory sign

Aug 1944 Liberation of Paris

The Modern City

In 1962, a program of renovation was started in Paris. Run-down districts like the Marais began to be restored. This work was continued by François Mitterrand's *Grand Travaux* (great works) program. Access was improved to historical monuments and art collections, such as the Grand Louvre *(see pp122–9)* and the Musée

Late President, François Mitterrand

d'Orsay *(pp144–7)*. The program was responsible for several monuments to the modern age, including the Opéra National de Paris Bastille *(p98)*, the Cité des Sciences *(pp236–9)* and the Bibliothèque Nationale in Tolbiac *(p246)*. With these, and the boldly modern Défense, Grande Arche and Stade de France, Paris prepared itself for the 21st century.

EXTENT OF THE CITY

▓ 1959	☐ Today

La Grande Arche
is taller and wider than Notre-Dame and runs in an axis linking the Arc de Triomphe and the Louvre Pyramid.

Christo's Pont Neuf
To create a work of art, the Bulgarian-born artist Christo wrapped Paris's oldest bridge, the Pont Neuf, in fabric in 1985.

Simone de Beauvoir
Influential philosopher and life-long companion of J-P Sartre, de Beauvoir fought for the liberation of women in the 1950s.

Shopping center

Citroën Goddess (1956)
With its ultramodern lines, this became Paris's most prestigious car.

TIMELINE

1945	1950	1955	1960	1965	1970	1975

1950 Construction of UNESCO, and the Musée de Radio-France

1962 André Malraux, Minister of Culture, begins renovation program for run-down districts and monuments

Ducting at the Pompidou Centre

1977 Pompidou Centre opens. Jacques Chirac is installed as first elected mayor of Paris since 1871

President de Gaulle

1958 Establishment of Fifth Republic with de Gaulle as president

1964 Reorganization of the Ile de France

1968 Student riots and workers strikes in the Latin Quarter

1969 Les Halles market transfers to Rungis

1973 Construction of Montparnasse Tower and the Périphérique (ring road)

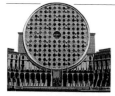

Marne La Vallée
Like a gigantic loudspeaker, this residential complex is in one of Paris's dormitory towns near Disneyland Resort Paris.

Chanel Designs
Paris is the center of the fashion world with important shows each year.

The Pompidou Centre
The nation's collection of modern art is housed here in this popular building (see pp110–13).

The Fiat Tower is one of Europe's tallest buildings.

Opéra National de Paris Bastille (1989)
It marks the bicentennial of the fall of the Bastille.

STUDENTS AT THE BARRICADES

In May 1968 Paris saw a revolution of a kind. The Latin Quarter was taken over by students and workers. What began as a protest against the war in Vietnam spread to other issues and became an expression of discontent with the government. President de Gaulle rode out the storm but his prestige was severely damaged.

Rioting students clash with police

The Défense Palace, housing the center for industry, is the oldest tower.

LA DEFENSE
This huge business center was started on the edge of Paris in 1958. Today 30,000 people commute here from Paris's surrounding areas.

1985 Christo wraps Pont Neuf

Participant of the bi-centennial wearing the French national colors

Victorious French soccer team holding aloft the World Cup trophy in Paris

1980	1985	1990	1995	2000	2005	2010

1980 Thousands greet Pope John-Paul on his official visit

1994 Eurostar inaugurated: Paris to London in 3 hrs

1989 Bicentennial celebrations to mark the French Revolution

2002 The euro replaces the franc as exclusive legal tender

1999 December hurricanes hit Paris: Versailles loses 10,000 trees

1998 France hosts – and wins – the 1998 soccer World Cup tournament

PARIS AT A GLANCE

There are nearly 300 places of interest described in the *Area by Area* section of this book. A broad range of sights is covered: from the ancient Conciergerie and its grisly associations with the guillotine *(see p81)*, to the modern opera house, the Opéra de la Bastille *(see p98)*; from No. 51 Rue de Montmorency *(see p114)*, the oldest house in Paris, to the elegant Musée Picasso *(see pp100–1)*. To help make the most of your stay, the following 20 pages are a time-saving guide to the best Paris has to offer. Museums and galleries, historic churches, spacious parks, gardens and squares all have a section. There are also guides to Paris's famous personalities. Each sight has a cross-reference to its own full entry. Below are the top tourist attractions to start you off.

PARIS'S TOP TOURIST ATTRACTIONS

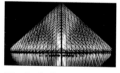

La Défense
See p255.

Sainte-Chapelle
See pp88–9.

Palace of Versailles
See pp248–53.

Pompidou Centre
See pp110–13.

Musée d'Orsay
See pp144–7.

Musée du Louvre
See pp122–9.

Jardin du Luxembourg
See p172.

Eiffel Tower
See pp192–3.

Bois de Boulogne
See pp254–5.

Notre-Dame
See pp82–5.

Arc de Triomphe
See pp208–9.

◁ The Dôme Church, adjoining the Hôtel des Invalides

Remarkable Parisians

By virtue of its strategic position on the Seine, Paris has always been the economic, political and artistic hub of France. Over the centuries, many prominent and influential figures from other parts of the country and abroad have come to the city to absorb its unique spirit. In return they have left their mark: artists have brought new movements, politicians new schools of thought, musicians and filmmakers new trends, and architects a new environment.

Actress Catherine Deneuve

ARTISTS

Sacré-Coeur by Utrillo (1934)

In the early 18th-century, Jean-Antoine Watteau (1684–1721) took the inspiration for his paintings from the Paris theater. Half a century later, Jean-Honoré Fragonard (1732–1806), popular painter of the Rococo, lived and died here, financially ruined by the Revolution. Later, Paris became the cradle of Impressionism. Its founders Claude Monet (1840–1926), Pierre-Auguste Renoir (1841–1919) and Alfred Sisley (1839–99) met in a Paris studio. In 1907, Pablo Picasso

(1881–1973) painted the seminal work *Les Demoiselles d'Avignon* at the Bateau-Lavoir, *(see p226)* where Georges Braque (1882–1963), Amedeo Modigliani (1884–1920) and Marc Chagall (1887–1985) also lived. Henri de Toulouse-Lautrec (1864–1901) drank and painted in Montmartre. So did Salvador Dalí (1904–89) who frequented the Café Cyrano, center of the Surrealists. The Paris School eventually moved to Montparnasse, home to sculptors Auguste Rodin (1840–1917), Constantin Brancusi (1876–1957) and Ossip Zadkine (1890–1967).

POLITICAL LEADERS

Hugh Capet, count of Paris, became king of France in 987. His palace was on the Ile de la Cité. Louis XIV, XV and XVI lived at Versailles *(see pp248–53)* but Napoleon *(see pp32–3)* preferred the Tuileries. Cardinal Richelieu (1585–1642), the power behind Louis XIII, created the Académie Française and the Palais-Royal *(see p120)*. Today the president lives in the Palais de l'Elysée *(p207)*.

Portrait of Cardinal Richelieu by Philippe de Champaigne (about 1635)

FILMS AND FILMMAKERS

Paris has always been at the heart of French film. The prewar and immediate post-war classics were usually made on the sets of the Boulogne and Joinville studios, where whole areas of the city were reconstructed, such as the Canal St-Martin for Marcel Carné's *Hôtel du Nord*. Jean-Luc Godard and other New Wave directors preferred to shoot outdoors. Godard's *A Bout de Souffle* (1960) with Jean-Paul Belmondo and Jean Seberg was filmed in and around the Champs-Elysées.

Simone Signoret (1921–1985) and Yves Montand (1921–1991), the most celebrated couple of French film, were long associated with the Ile de la Cité. Actresses such as Catherine Deneuve (b.1943) and Isabelle Adjani (b.1955) live in the city to be near their couturiers.

MUSICIANS

Jean-Philippe Rameau (1683–1764), organist and pioneer of harmony, is associated with St-Eustache *(see p114)*. Hector Berlioz (1803–69) had his *Te Deum* first performed there in 1855, and Franz Liszt (1811–86) his *Messe Solennelle* in 1866. A great dynasty of organists, the Couperins, gave recitals in St-Gervais–St-Protais *(see p99)*.

The stage of the Opéra *(see p215)* has seen many talents, but audiences have not always been appreciative. Richard Wagner (1813–83) had his *Tannhäuser* booed down. George Bizet's *Carmen*

(1838–75) was booed, as was *Peléas et Mélisande* by Claude Debussy (1862–1918).

Soprano Maria Callas (1923–77) gave triumphal performances here. The composer and conductor Pierre Boulez (b.1925) has devoted his talent to experimental music at IRCAM near the Pompidou Centre *(see p345)*, which he helped to found.

The diminutive *chanteuse* Edith Piaf (1915–63), known for her nostalgic love-songs, began singing in the streets of Paris and then went on to tour the world. There is now a museum devoted to her life and work *(see p232–3)*.

The Grand Trianon at Versailles, built by Louis Le Vau in 1668

Renée Jeanmaire as Carmen (1948)

ARCHITECTS

Gothic, Classical, Baroque and Modernist – all coexist in Paris. The most brilliant medieval architect was Pierre de Montreuil, who built Notre-Dame and Sainte-Chapelle. Louis Le Vau (1612–70) and Jules Hardouin-Mansart (1646–1708) designed Versailles *(see pp248–53)*. Jacques-Ange Gabriel (1698–1782) built the Petit Trianon *(see p249)* and Place de la Concorde *(see p131)*. Haussmann (1809–91) gave the city its boulevards *(see pp34–5)*. Gustave Eiffel (1832–1923) built his tower in 1889. A century later, I M Pei added the Louvre's glass pyramid *(see p129)*, Jean Nouvel created the Institut du Monde Arabe *(see p164)* and Dominique Perrault the new Bibliothèque Nationale de France *(see p246)*. The 21st century already has several new landmarks underway.

WRITERS

French has been dubbed "the language of Molière", after playwright Jean-Baptiste Poquelin, alias Molière, (1622–73), who helped create the Comédie-Française, now situated near his home in Rue Richelieu. On the Left Bank, the Odéon Théâtre de l'Europe was home to playwright Jean Racine (1639–99). It is near the statue of Denis Diderot (1713–84), who published his

L'Encyclopédie between 1751 and 1776. Marcel Proust (1871–1922), author of the 13-volume *Remembrance of Things Past*, lived on the Boulevard Haussmann. To the existentialists, the district of St-Germain was the only place to be *(see pp142–3)*. Here Sylvia Beach welcomed James Joyce (1882–1941) to her bookshop on the Rue de l'Odéon. Ernest Hemingway (1899–1961) and F Scott Fitzgerald (1896–1940) wrote novels in Montparnasse.

Proust by J-E Blanche (about 1910)

SCIENTISTS

Paris has a Quartier Pasteur, a Boulevard Pasteur, a Pasteur metro and the world-famous Institut Pasteur *(see p247)*, all in honor of Louis Pasteur (1822–95), the great French chemist and biologist. His apartment and laboratory are faithfully preserved. The Institut Pasteur is today home to Professor Luc Montagnier, who first isolated the AIDS virus in 1983. Discoverers of radium, Pierre (1859–1906) and Marie Curie (1867–1934), also worked in Paris. The Curies have been the subject of a long-running play in Paris, *Les Palmes de M. Schutz*.

EXILED IN PARIS

The Duke and Duchess of Windsor married in France after his abdication in 1936 as King Edward VIII. The city granted them a rent-free mansion in the Bois de Boulogne. Other famous exiles have included Chou En-Lai (1898–1976), Ho Chi Minh (1890–1969), Vladimir Ilyich Lenin (1870–1924), Oscar Wilde (1854–1900) and ballet dancer Rudolf Nureyev (1938–93).

The Duke and Duchess of Windsor

Paris's Best: Churches

The Catholic Church has been the bastion of Parisian society through time. Many of the city's churches are worth visiting. Architectural styles vary and the interiors are often spectacular. Most churches are open during the day and many have services at regular intervals. Paris's tradition of church music is still alive. You can spend an evening enjoying the interiors while listening to an organ recital or classical concert (*p345*). A more detailed overview of Paris churches is on pages 48–9.

Early crucifix in St-Gervais–St-Protais

La Madeleine
Built in the style of a Greco-Roman temple, this church is known for its fine sculptures.

Chaillot Quarter

Champs-Élysées

Tuileries Quarter

RIVER SEINE

Invalides and Eiffel Tower Quarter

St-Germain-des-Prés

Dôme Church
This memorial to the military engineer Vauban lies in the Dôme Church, where Napoleon's remains were buried in 1840.

Sainte-Chapelle
With its fine stained glass, this chapel is a medieval jewel.

Montparnasse

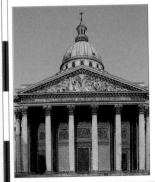

Panthéon
The Neoclassical Sainte-Geneviève, now the Panthéon, was inspired by Wren's St Paul's Cathedral in London.

0 kilometers

0 miles   0.5

Sacré-Coeur
Above the altar in this huge basilica, the chancel vault is decorated with a vast mosaic of Christ by Luc-Olivier Merson.

Montmartre

St-Eustache
With its mixture of Gothic and Renaissance styles, this is one of the finest churches in Paris.

Opéra Quarter

St-Paul–St-Louis
This Christ figure is one of the many rich furnishings in this Jesuit church, built in 1641 for Cardinal Richelieu.

Beaubourg and Les Halles

The Marais

Ile de la Cité

Ile St-Louis

Latin Quarter

Notre-Dame
The great cathedral was left to rot after the Revolution, until Victor Hugo led a restoration campaign.

Luxembourg Quarter

Jardin des Plantes Quarter

St-Séverin
The west door leads to one of the finest medieval churches in the city.

Mosquée de Paris
The minaret of this 1920s mosque is 100 ft (33 m) tall.

Exploring Paris's Churches

Some of Paris's finest architecture is reflected in the churches. The great era of church building was the medieval period, but examples survive from all ages. During the Revolution (see pp30–31) churches were used as grain or weapons stores but were later restored to their former glory. Many churches have superb interiors with fine paintings and sculptures.

Facade of Eglise de la Sorbonne

MEDIEVAL

Tower of St-Germain-des-Prés

Both the pointed arch and the rose window were born in a suburb north of Paris at the Basilica de St-Denis, where most of the French kings and queens are buried. This was the first Gothic building, and it was from here that the Gothic style spread. The finest Gothic church in Paris is the city cathedral, **Notre-Dame**, tallest and most impressive of the early French cathedrals. Begun in 1163 by Bishop Maurice de Sully, it was completed in the next century by architects Jean de Chelles and Pierre de

Montreuil, who added the transepts with their fine translucent rose windows. Montreuil's masterpiece is Louis IX's medieval palace chapel, **Sainte-Chapelle**, with its two-tier structure. It was built to house Christ's Crown of Thorns. Other surviving churches in Paris are **St-Germain-des-Prés**, the oldest surviving abbey church in Paris (1050); the tiny, rustic Romanesque **St-Julien-le-Pauvre**; and the Flamboyant Gothic **St-Séverin, St-Germain l'Auxerrois** and **St-Merry**.

RENAISSANCE

The effect of the Italian Renaissance swept through Paris in the 16th century. It led to a unique architectural style in which fine Classical detail and immense Gothic proportions resulted in an impure, but attractive, cocktail known as "French Renaissance". The best example in Paris is **St-Etienne-du-Mont**, whose interior has the feel of a wide and light basilica. Another is **St-Eustache**, the huge market church in Les Halles, and the nave of **St-Gervais–St-Protais** with its stained glass and carved choir stalls.

St-Gervais–St-Protais

BAROQUE AND CLASSICAL

Churches and convents flourished in Paris during the 17th century, as the city expanded under Louis XIII and his son Louis XIV. The Italian Baroque style was first seen on the majestic front of **St-Gervais–St-Protais**, built by Salomon de Brosse in 1616. The style was toned down to suit French tastes and the rational temperament of the Age of Enlightenment (see pp28–9). The result was a harmonious and monumental classicism in the form of columns and domes. One example is the **Eglise de la Sorbonne**, completed by Jacques Lemercier in 1642 for Cardinal Richelieu. Grander and more richly decorated, with a painted dome, is the church built by François Mansart to honor the birth of the Sun King at the **Val-de-Grâce** convent. The true gem of the period is Jules Hardouin-Mansart's **Dôme Church**, with its enormous gilded

TOWERS, DOMES AND SPIRES

The outlines of Paris's many churches have dominated its skyline since early Christian times. The Tour St-Jacques, in the Gothic style, reflects the medieval love of the defensive tower. St-Etienne-du-Mont, with its pointed gable and rounded pediment, shows the transition from Gothic to Renaissance. The dome, a much used feature of the French Baroque, was used to perfection in the Val-de-Grâce. By contrast, St-Sulpice with its severe arrangement of towers and portico is typical of the Neoclassical style. With its ornate spires, Sainte-Clotilde is a Gothic Revival church. Modern landmarks include the mosque with its minaret.

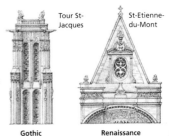

Tour St-Jacques

St-Etienne-du-Mont

Gothic

Renaissance

dome. Jesuit extravagance can be seen in **St-Paul–St-Louis** built in the style of Il Gesù in Rome. In contrast are Libéral Bruand's chapels, the **Salpêtrière** and **St-Louis-des-Invalides** with their severe geometry and unadorned simplicity. Other fine Classical churches are **St-Joseph-des-Carmes** and the 18th-century bankers' church, **St-Roch**, with its Baroque Marian chapel.

NEOCLASSICAL

Interior of the Panthéon

An obsession with all things Greek and Roman swept France in the mid-18th century and well into the 19th century. The excavations at Pompeii (1738) and the influence of the Italian architect Andrea Palladio produced a generation of architects fascinated by the column, geometry and engineering. The best example of such churches is Jacques-Germain Soufflot's Sainte-Geneviève, now the **Panthéon**. Begun in 1773, its colonnaded dome was also

inspired by Christopher Wren's St Paul's in London. The dome is supported by four pillars, built by Guillaume Rondelet, linking four great arches. The first colonnaded facade was Giovanni Niccolo Servandoni's **St-Sulpice**. Construction of this church began in 1733 and consisted of a two-story portico, topped by a triangular pediment. **La Madeleine**, Napoleon's grand temple to his victorious army, was constructed on the ground plan of a Greco-Roman temple.

SECOND EMPIRE AND MODERN

Franz Christian Gau's **Sainte-Clotilde** of the 1840s is the first and best example in Paris of the Gothic Revival or *style religieux*. Showy churches were built in the new districts created by Haussmann in the Second Empire *(pp34–5)*. One of the most lovely is Victor Baltard's St-Augustin, at the intersection of the Boulevard de Malesherbes and the Boulevard de la Madeleine. Here historic detail combines with modern iron columns and girders in a soaring interior space. The great basilica of the late 19th century **Sacré-Coeur** was built as a gesture of religious defiance. **St-Jean l'Evangéliste** by Anatole de Baudot is an interesting modern church combining the Art Nouveau style with Islamic arches. The modern gem of Islamic architecture, the **Mosquée de Paris**, is an attractive 1920s building in the Hispanic-Moorish style. It has a grand patio, inspired by the Alhambra, woodwork in cedar and eucalyptus, and a fountain.

The arches of St-Jean L'Evangéliste, reminiscent of Islamic architecture

FINDING THE CHURCHES

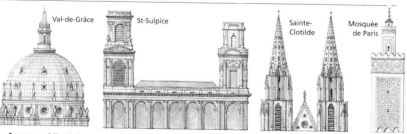

Val-de-Grâce   St-Sulpice   Sainte-Clotilde   Mosquée de Paris

Baroque and Classical   **Neoclassical**   **Second Empire**   **Modern**

Paris's Best: Gardens, Parks and Squares

Few cities can boast the infinite variety of styles found in Parisian gardens, parks and squares today. They date from many different periods and have been central to Parisian life for the past 300 years. The Bois de Boulogne and the Bois de Vincennes enclose the city with their lush, green open spaces, while elegant squares and landscaped gardens, such as the Jardin du Luxembourg, brighten the inner city and provide a retreat for those craving a few moments peace from the bustling city.

Parc Monceau
This English-style park features many follies, grottoes, magnificent trees and rare plants.

Champs-Elysées

Opéra Quarter

Chaillot Quarter

Tuileries Quarter

R I V E R   S E I N E

Invalides and Eiffel Tower Quarter

St-Germain-des-Prés

Luxembourg Quarter

Bois de Boulogne
The Bagatelle gardens, set in this wooded park, have an amazing array of flowers including the spectacular rose garden.

Montparnasse

Esplanade des Invalides
From this huge square, lined with lime trees, are some amazing views over the quays.

Jardin des Tuileries
These gardens are renowned for ornamental ponds, terraces and the collection of bronze figures by Aristide Maillol.

Parc des Buttes-Chaumont
Once a scraggy hilltop, this park was transformed to provide open spaces for the growing city. It is now beautifully landscaped with huge cliffs revealing caves.

0 kilometers 1

0 miles 0.5

Square du Vert-Galant
The square, named after Henri IV's nickname, forms the west point of the Ile de la Cité.

Place des Vosges
Considered one of the most beautiful squares in the world, it was finished in 1612 and is the oldest square in Paris.

Beaubourg
and
Les Halles

The Marais

Ile de la
Cité

Ile St-Louis

Jardin des Plantes
The botanical garden has a huge collection of plants and flowers from around the world.

Latin Quarter

Jardin des Plantes
Quarter

Jardin du Luxembourg
This park is a favorite with Parisians wanting to escape the bustle of the Latin Quarter.

Bois de Vincennes
The flower garden in this charming park is the perfect place to relax.

Exploring Gardens, Parks and Squares

Paris is dotted with many areas of parkland, intimate gardens and attractive tree-lined squares. Each is a reminder of the French capital's illustrious past. Many squares were formed during Napoleon III's transformation of the city, creating a pleasant environment for Parisians to live in (see pp34–5). This aim has been preserved right up to the present day. Paris's parks and gardens have their own character: some are ideal for a stroll, others for romance, while some provide space for pastimes such as a game of *boules*.

Royal built by Cardinal Richelieu in the 17th century. An elegant arcade encloses the garden. The 19th-century **Parc Monceau**, in the English picturesque style, has follies and grottoes. The flat **Jardins des Invalides** and the landscaped **Champ-de-Mars** were the grounds of the Hôtel des Invalides and the Ecole Militaire. They were the site of the Paris Universal Exhibition, whose reminder is the Eiffel Tower (pp192–3).

An attractive public garden is attached to the lovely Hôtel Biron, home of the **Musée Rodin**. The 17th-century botanical garden **Jardin des Plantes** is famous for its ancient trees, flowers, alpine garden, greenhouses and small zoo.

Engraving of the Jardin du Palais Royal (1645)

HISTORIC GARDENS

The oldest public gardens in Paris were created for the queens of France – the **Jardin des Tuileries** for Catherine de Médicis in the 16th century, and the **Jardin du Luxembourg** for Marie de Médicis in the 17th century. The Tuileries form the beginning of the axis running from the Arc du Triomphe du Carrousel through the Arc de Triomphe (pp208–9) to La Défense (p255). These gardens retain the formality devised by landscape architect André Le Nôtre, originally for the **Palace of Versailles**. Many of the Jardin des Tuileries's original sculptures survive, as well as modern pieces, notably the bronze nudes by Aristide Maillol (1861–1944).

The Jardin du Luxembourg also has the traditional formal plan – straight paths, clipped lawns, Classical sculpture and a superb 17th-century fountain. It is shadier and more intimate than the Tuileries, with lots of seats, pony rides and puppet shows to amuse the children.

The **Jardins des Champs-Elysées**, also by Le Nôtre, were reshaped in the English style during the 19th century. The gardens have Belle Epoque pavilions, three theaters (L'Espace Pierre Cardin, Théâtre Marigny and the Théâtre Barrault), chic restaurants – and the ghost of the novelist Marcel Proust, who once played here as a child.

A haven of peace in a busy district is the **Jardin du Palais**

19TH-CENTURY PARKS AND SQUARES

Aquatic Garden, Bois de Vincennes

The great 19th-century parks and squares owe much to Napoleon III's long exile in London before he came to power. The unregimented planting and rolling lawns of Hyde Park and the leafy squares of Mayfair inspired him to bring trees, fresh air

FOLLIES AND ROTUNDAS

Dramatic features of Paris's parks and gardens are the many follies and rotundas. Every age of garden design has produced these ornaments. The huge Gloriette de Buffon in the Jardin des Plantes was erected as a memorial to the great naturalist (p166). It is the oldest metal structure in Paris. The pyramid in the Parc Monceau, the oriental temple in the Bois de Boulogne and the recently restored 19th-century temple of love in the Bois de Vincennes reflect a more sentimental age. In contrast are the stark, painted-concrete follies that grace the Parc de la Villette.

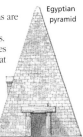
Egyptian pyramid

Parc Monceau

Relaxing in Jardin du Luxembourg

and park benches to what was then Europe's most congested and dirty capital. Under his direction, landscape gardener Adolphe Alphand turned two woods at opposite ends of the city, the **Bois de Boulogne** (known as the "Bois") and the **Bois de Vincennes**, into English-style parks with duck ponds, lakes and flower gardens. He also added a racecourse to the "Bois". Today it is traversed by traffic and by prostitutes at night. Its most attractive feature is the Bagatelle rose garden.

Far more pleasant are the two smaller Alphand parks, **Parc Montsouris** in the south and the **Parc des Buttes-Chaumont** in the northeast. The "Buttes" (hills), a favorite with the Surrealists, was a quarry transformed into two craggy mini-mountains with overhanging vegetation, suspended bridge, temple of love and a lake below.

Part of the town-planning programs for the old city included squares and avenues with fountains, sculptures, benches and greenery. One of the best is the **Square du Vert-Galant** on the Ile de la Cité. The Avenue de l'Observatoire in the **Jardin du Luxembourg** is rich in sculptures made by Jean-Baptiste Carpeaux.

Fountains and sculpture in the Jardins du Trocadéro

MODERN PARKS AND GARDENS

The shady **Jardins du Trocadéro** sloping down to the river from the Palais de Chaillot were planted after the 1937 Universal Exhibition. Here is the largest fountain in Paris and fine views of the river and the Eiffel Tower.

More recent Paris gardens eschew formality in favor of wilder planting, multiple levels, mazelike paths, children's gardens and modern sculpture. Typical are the gardens in front of the **Forum des Halles**, the **Parc André-Citroën**, the **Parc de la Villette** and the Jardins Atlantique above the Gare Montparnasse.

Pleasant strolls may be taken in Paris's waterside gardens: in the modern sculpture park behind Notre-Dame, at the Bassin de l'Arsenal at the Bastille, and along the quays of the Seine between the Louvre and the Place de la Concorde, or on the elegantly residential Ile St-Louis. The planted walkway above the **Viaduc des Arts** is a peaceful way to observe eastern Paris.

Parc Montsouris

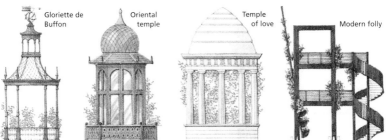

Gloriette de Buffon

Oriental temple

Temple of love

Modern folly

Jardin des Plantes   Bois de Boulogne   Bois de Vincennes   Parc de la Villette

Paris's Best: Museums and Galleries

Some of the oldest, the newest, and certainly some of the finest museums and galleries are found in Paris – many are superb works of art in their own right. They house some of the greatest and strangest collections in the world. Some of the buildings complement their themes, such as the Roman baths and Gothic mansion which form the Musée de Cluny, or the Pompidou Centre, a modern masterpiece. Elsewhere there is pleasing contrast, such as the Picassos in their gracious 17th-century museum, and the Musée d'Orsay housed in its grand old railroad station. Together they make an unrivaled feast for visitors.

Musée des Arts Décoratifs
Decorative and ornamental art like this Paris bathroom by Jeanne Lanvin is displayed here.

Champs-Elysées

Chaillot Quarter

R I V E R   S E I N E

Invalides
and
Eiffel Tower Quarter

Montparnasse

Petit Palais
A collection of works by the 19th-century sculptor Jean-Baptiste Carpeaux is housed here, including The Fisherman and Shell.

Musée Guimet
This 4th-century head of Buddha from India is part of a vast collection of Asian art and artifacts housed here.

Musée Rodin
The museum brings together works bequeathed to the nation by sculptor Auguste Rodin, like the magnificent Gates of Hell *doors.*

Musée d'Orsay
Carpeaux's Four Quarters of the World *(1867–72) can be found among this collection of 19th-century art.*

Musée du Louvre
The museum boasts one of the world's great collections of paintings and sculpture, from the ancient civilizations to the 19th century. This Babylonian monument, the Code of Hammurabi, *is the oldest set of laws in existence.*

Pompidou Centre
Paris's modern art collection from 1905 to the present day is housed here. The center also has art libraries and an industrial design center.

Opéra Quarter

Tuileries Quarter

Beaubourg and Les Halles

The Marais

St-Germain-des-Prés

Ile de la Cité

Ile St-Louis

Latin Quarter

Luxembourg Quarter

Jardin des Plantes Quarter

Musée Picasso
Sculptor and Model (1931) is one of many paintings on display in Picasso's private collection, "inherited" in lieu of tax by the French government after his death in 1973.

Musée Carnavalet
The museum is devoted to the history of Paris. Its historic buildings surround attractive garden courtyards.

Musée de Cluny
The remains of the old Gallo-Roman baths are part of this fine museum of ancient and medieval art.

0 kilometers		1
0 miles		0.5

Exploring Paris's Museums and Galleries

Paris holds great treasures in its museums and art galleries. The major national art collection is to be found at the **Musée du Louvre**, which began collecting 400 years ago and is still growing. Other important museums, such as the **Musée d'Orsay**, the **Musée Picasso** and the **Pompidou Centre**, have their own treasures, but there are scores of smaller, specialized museums, each with its own interest.

Dante and Virgil in the Underworld (1822) by Delacroix, Musée du Louvre

GREEK, ROMAN AND MEDIEVAL ART

Golden altar in the Musée de Cluny

Sculpture from Greek and Roman times is well represented in the **Musée du Louvre**, which also has fine medieval sculptures. The major medieval collection is at the **Musée de Cluny**, a superb 15th-century mansion. Among the highlights are the Unicorn Tapestries, the Kings' Heads from Notre-Dame and the golden altar from Basel Cathedral. Adjoining the Cluny are the 3rd-century Roman baths. Remains of houses from Roman and medieval Paris can be seen in the **Crypte Archéologique** near Notre-Dame cathedral.

OLD MASTERS

The Mona Lisa was one of the **Musée du Louvre's** first paintings, acquired 400 years ago. It also has other fine Leonardos. They are to be found along with superb Titians, Raphaels and other Italian masters. Other works include Rembrandt's *Pilgrims at Emmäus*, Watteau's *Gilles* and Fragonard's *The Bathers*. The **Musée Cognacq-Jay** has a small, but exquisite, collection of paintings and drawings by 18th-century French painters. The **Musée Jacquemart-André** has works by such masters as Mantegna, Uccello, Canaletto, Rembrandt and Chardin.

IMPRESSIONIST AND POST-IMPRESSIONIST ART

Installed in a converted 19th-century railroad station, the **Musée d'Orsay** boasts the world's largest collection of art from the period 1848–1904. Admired for its fine Impressionist and Post-Impressionist collections, it also devotes a lot of space to the earlier Realists and the formerly reviled 19th-century academic and "Salon" masters. There are superb selections of Degas, Manet, Courbet, Monet, Renoir, Millet, Cézanne, Bonnard and Vuillard, and some fine Gauguins, Van Goghs and Seurats, but these have to contend with poor lighting and an intrusive stone decor.

A great ensemble of late Monets is to be found at the **Musée Marmottan-Claude Monet** and another at the **Musée de l'Orangerie**, including Monet's last great waterlily murals (1920–5). Here also is a good collection of Cézannes and late Renoirs.

Three artists' studios and homes are now museums of their life and work. The **Musée Rodin**, in an attractive 18th-century mansion and garden, offers a complete survey of the master's sculptures, drawings and paintings. The **Musée Delacroix**, set in a garden near St-Germain-des-Prés, has sketches, prints and oils by the Romantic artist. The **Musée Gustave Moreau**, in an oppressive 19th-century town house, has an extraordinary collection of intricately painted canvases of legendary *femmes fatales* and dying youths. The **Petit Palais** has an interesting collection of 19th-century paintings with four major Courbets, including *The Sleep*.

Dead Poet in Musée Gustave Moreau

MODERN AND CONTEMPORARY ART

As the international center of the avant-garde from 1900 to 1940, Paris has a great concentration of modern painting and sculpture. The Pompidou Centre houses the **Musée National d'Art Moderne**, covering from 1905 to the present. It has a good selection of Fauvist and Cubist works, particularly by Matisse, Rouault, Braque, Delaunay, and Leger, as well as works by the 1960s' *Nouveaux Réalistes*.

The **Musée d'Art Moderne de la Ville de Paris**, in the elegant 1930s Palais de Tokyo also has an excellent collection, including Delaunays, Bonnards and Fauvist paintings. The highlight is Matisse's 1932 mural *The Dance*.

The **Musée Picasso**, in a lovely 17th-century mansion, has the world's largest Picasso collection. It also has his own personal collection of the work of his contemporaries. Picasso, Matisse, Modigliani, Utrillo and late Derains make up the collection of 1920s art dealer Paul Guillaume on display at the **Musée de l'Orangerie**. For modern sculpture, the small **Musée Zadkine** has Cubist work by a minor school whose leading light was Ossip Zadkine. The **Musée Antoine Bourdelle** and the **Musée Maillol** house work by these two sculptors, who were both influenced by Rodin, in very different ways.

Penelope by Bourdelle

FURNITURE, DECORATIVE ARTS AND OBJETS D'ART

The spotlight, after painting, must shine on furniture and the decorative arts, contained in a plethora of museums. Fine ensembles of French furnishings and decoration are in the **Louvre** (medieval to Napoleonic) and at the **Palace of Versailles** (17th–18th century). Furniture and *objets d'art* from the Middle Ages to the present century are arranged in period rooms at the **Musée des Arts Décoratifs**. The **Musée d'Orsay** has a large collection of 19th-century furniture, notably Art Nouveau. A superb example of Louis XV (1715–74) and Louis XVI (1774–93) furniture and decoration is in the **Musée Nissim de Camondo**, a mansion from 1910 facing the Parc Monceau. Other notable collections are the **Musée Cognacq-Jay**, the **Musée Carnavalet** (18th-century), the **Musée Jacquemart-André** (French furniture and earthenware), the **Musée Marmottan-Claude Monet** (Empire) and **Musée d'Art Moderne de la Ville de Paris** (Art Deco).

Jeweler's shop in the Carnavalet

SPECIALTY MUSEUMS

Devotees of antique hunting guns, muskets and hounds of the chase should head for the attractive Marais **Hôtel Guénégaud** (Musée de la Chasse et de la Nature). This museum also has some fine 18th-century animal paintings by Jean-Baptiste Oudry and Alexandre-François Desportes, as well as others by Rubens and Brueghel. The **Musée de la Contrefaçon** gives a fascinating insight into the world of counterfeit with examples from every luxury trade, including perfume, wines and spirits, and clothing. Numismatists will find an extensive coin and medallion collection housed in luxurious surroundings at

Candelabra in the Galerie Royale

the 18th-century Paris Mint at the **Musée de la Monnaie**. French coins are no longer minted here, but the old mint still makes medals which are on sale. Stamps are on show at the **Musée de la Poste**. The history of postal services is also covered, as are all aspects of philately old and new, with temporary shows on current philatelic design. Sumptuous silver dinner services and other antique glass- and silverware can be seen at the **Galerie Royale**. The items were made over a period of 150 years by the Paris firm whose founder was Charles Bouilhet-Christofle, silversmith to King Louis-Philippe and Napoleon III. Contemporary glass- and silverware is also for sale in nearby workshops.

FASHION AND COSTUME

The two rival fashion museums in Paris are the **Musée Galliera** at the Palais Galliera and the more recent national museum within the **Musée des Arts Décoratifs**. Neither displays a permanent collection, but both hold regular shows devoted to the great Paris couturiers, such as Saint Laurent and Givenchy. They also display fashion accessories and – more rarely but always fascinatingly – historical costumes.

PALAIS GALLIERA
10, avenue Pierre-I-de-Serbie, Paris XVI
du 24 octobre 1991 au 15 mars 1992

Poster for the Musée Galliera

ASIAN, AFRICAN AND OCEANIAN ART

The major collection of Asian art in France is housed at the **Musée National des Arts Asiatiques Guimet**, covering China, Tibet, Japan, Korea, Indochina, Indonesia, India and Central Asia. It includes Chinese bronzes and lacquerware and some of the best Khmer art outside Cambodia. The **Musée Cernuschi**, named after the banker, has a smaller but well-chosen Chinese collection, noted for its ancient bronzes and reliefs. France's premier showcase for African art and culture is the **Musée Dapper**, part of an important ethnographic research center, housed in an elegant 1910 *hôtel particulier* with an "African" garden. Its collection of tribal masks is particularly dazzling, with many examples of theatrical masks as well as masks worn during religious and ritualistic ceremonies.

Sri Lankan theatrical mask

HISTORY AND SOCIAL HISTORY

Café in Musée de Montmartre

Covering the entire history of the city of Paris, the **Musée Carnavalet** is housed in two historic Marais *hôtels*. It has period interiors, paintings of

the city and old shop signs, a fascinating section covering events and artifacts from the French Revolution, and even Marcel Proust's bedroom. Also in the Marais, the **Musée d'Art et d'Histoire du Judaisme** explores the culture of French Jewry. The **Musée de l'Armée**, in the Hôtel des Invalides, recounts French military history, and the Musée de l'Histoire de France, in the Rococo **Hôtel de Soubise**, has historical documents from the national archives on display. Famous *tableaux vivants* and characters, both current and historical, await the visitor at the **Grévin** wax museum. The intriguing

Musée de Montmartre, overlooking Paris's last surviving vineyard, holds exhibitions on the history of Montmartre.

ARCHITECTURE AND DESIGN

The Centre de la Création Industrielle holds modern and contemporary design and architecture exhibitions at the **Pompidou Centre**. Superb scale models of fortresses built for Louis XIV and later are on display at the **Musée des Plans-Reliefs**. The work of the celebrated Franco-Swiss architect forms the basis of the **Fondation Le Corbusier**. The showpiece is his 1920s villa for his friend, art collector Raoul La Roche. Some of his furniture is also on display.

THE FRENCH IMPRESSIONISTS

Impression: Sunrise by Monet

Impressionism, the great art revolution of the 19th century, began in Paris in the 1860s, when young painters, influenced in part by the new art of photography, started to break with the academic values of the past. They aimed to capture the "impression" of what the eye sees at a given moment and used brushwork designed to capture the fleeting effects of light falling on a scene. Their favorite subjects were landscapes and scenes from contemporary urban life.

The movement had no founder, though Edouard Manet (1832–83) and the radical Realist painter Gustave Courbet (1819–77) both inspired many of the

younger artists. Paintings of scenes of everyday life by Manet and Courbet often offended the academicians who legislated artistic taste. In 1863 Manet's *Le Déjeuner sur l'Herbe (see p144)* was exhibited at the Salon des Refusés, an exhibition set up for paintings rejected by the official Paris Salon of that year. The first time the term "Impressionist" was used to describe this new artistic movement was at another unofficial exhibition, in 1874. The name came from a painting by Claude Monet, *Impression: Sunrise*, a view of Le Havre in the mist from 1872. Monet was almost exclusively a landscape artist, influenced by the works of the English

Monet's sketchbooks

Harvesting (1876) by Pissarro

The living room of La Roche Villa by Le Corbusier (1923)

SCIENCE AND TECHNOLOGY

In the Jardin des Plantes the **Muséum National d'Histoire Naturelle** has sections on paleontology, minerology, entomology, anatomy and botany, plus a zoo and a botanical garden. In the Palais de Chaillot, the **Musée de l'Homme** is a major museum of anthropology, ethnology and prehistory with numerous African artifacts. Next door, the **Musée de la Marine** covers French naval history from the 17th century onward, with fine 18th-century models of ships and sculpted figure-heads. The **Musée des Arts et Métiers** displays the world of science and industry, of invention and manufacturing. The **Palais de la Découverte** covers the history of science and has a good planetarium, somewhat overshadowed by the spectacular one at the **Cité des Sciences** in the Parc de la Villette. This vast museum is on several levels, with a spher-ical movie screen, the Géode.

Gabrielle (1910) by Renoir

artists Constable and Turner. He always liked to paint out of doors and encouraged others to follow his example.

At the 1874 exhibition, a critic wrote that one should stand well back to see these "impressions" – the further back the better – and that members of the establishment should retreat altogether. Other exhibitors at the show were Pierre-Auguste Renoir, Edgar Degas, Camille Pissarro, Alfred Sisley and Paul Cézanne.

There were seven more Impressionist shows up to 1886. By then the power of the Salon had waned and the whole direction of art had changed. From then on, new movements were defined in terms of their relation to Impressionism. The leading Neo-Impressionist was Georges Seurat, who used thousands of minute dots of color to build up his paintings. It took later generations to fully appreciate the work of the Impressionists. Cézanne was rejected all his life, Degas sold only one painting to a museum and Sisley died unknown. Of the great artists whose genius is now universally recognized, only Renoir and Monet were ever acclaimed in their lifetimes.

Profile of a Model (1887) by Seurat

Artists in Paris

The city first attracted artists during the reign of Louis XIV (1643–1715), and Paris became the most sophisticated artistic center in Europe; the magnetism has persisted. During the 18th century, all major French artists lived and worked in Paris. In the latter half of the 19th century and early part of the 20th century, Paris was the European center of modern and progressive art, and movements such as Impressionism and Post-Impressionism were founded and blossomed in the city.

Monet's palette

ROCOCO ARTISTS
Boucher, François (1703–70)
Chardin, Jean-Baptiste-Siméon (1699–1779)
Falconet, Etienne-Maurice (1716–91)
Fragonard, Jean-Honoré (1732–1806)
Greuze, Jean-Baptiste (1725–1805)
Houdon, Jean-Antoine (1741–1828)
Oudry, Jean-Baptiste (1686–1755)
Pigalle, Jean-Baptiste (1714–85)
Watteau, Jean-Antoine (1684–1721)

BAROQUE ARTISTS
Champaigne, Philippe de (1602–74)
Coysevox, Antoine (1640–1720)
Girardon, François (1628–1715)
Le Brun, Charles (1619–90)
Le Sueur, Eustache (1616–55)
Poussin, Nicolas (1594–1665)
Rigaud, Hyacinthe (1659–1743)
Vignon, Claude (1593–1670)
Vouet, Simon (1590–1649)

Boucher's Diana Bathing *(1742), typical of the Rococo style (Louvre)*

1600	1650	1700	1750
BAROQUE		ROCOCO	NEOCLASSICISM
1600	1650	1700	1750

1627 Vouet returns from Italy and is made court painter by Louis XIII. Vouet revived a dismal period in the fortunes of French painting

1667 First Salon, France's official art exhibition; originally held annually, later every two years

1793 Louvre opens as first national public gallery

Philippe de Champaigne's Last Supper *(about 1652). His style slowly became more Classical in his later years (Louvre)*

1648 Foundation of the Académie Royale de Peinture et de Sculpture, which had a virtual monopoly on art teaching

Vouet's The Presentation in the Temple *(1641) with typically Baroque contrasts of light and shade (Louvre)*

David's The Oath of the Horatii *(1784), in the Neoclassical style (Louvre)*

NEOCLASSICAL ARTISTS
David, Jacques-Louis (1748–1825)
Gros, Antoine Jean (1771–1835)
Ingres, Jean-Auguste-Dominique (1780–1867)
Vigée-Lebrun, Elizabeth (1755–1842)

ROMANTIC AND REALIST ARTISTS

Courbet, Gustave (1819–77)
Daumier, Honoré (1808–79)
Delacroix, Eugène (1798–1863)
Géricault, Théodore (1791–1824)
Rude, Francois (1784–1855)

MODERN ARTISTS

Arp, Jean (1887–1966)
Balthus (1908–2001)
Brancusi, Constantin (1876–1957)
Braque, Georges (1882–1963)
Buffet, Bernard (1928–1999)
Chagall, Marc (1887–1985)
Delaunay, Robert (1885–1941)
Derain, André (1880–1954)
Dubuffet, Jean (1901–85)
Duchamp, Marcel (1887–1968)
Epstein, Jacob (1880–1959)
Ernst, Max (1891–1976)
Giacometti, Alberto (1901–66)
Gris, Juan (1887–1927)
Léger, Fernand (1881–1955)
Matisse, Henri (1869–1954)
Miró, Joan (1893–1983)
Modigliani, Amedeo (1884–1920)
Mondrian, Piet (1872–1944)
Picasso, Pablo (1881–1973)
Rouault, Georges (1871–1958)
Saint-Phalle, Niki de (1930–2002)
Soutine, Chaim (1893–1943)
Stael, Nicolas de (1914–55)
Tinguely, Jean (1925–91)
Utrillo, Maurice (1883–1955)
Zadkine, Ossip (1890–1967)

Giacometti's Standing Woman II *(1959), one of his many tall, thin bronze figures (see p112)*

Courbet's The Burial at Ornans *(1850), which showed Courbet to be the foremost exponent of Realism (Musée d'Orsay)*

Rude's Departure of the Volunteers in 1792 *(1836), a tribute to the French Revolution (see p209)*

1904 Picasso settles in Paris

1886 Van Gogh moves to Paris

1874 First Impressionist exhibition

1905 Birth of Fauvism, the first of the "isms" in modern art

1800	1850	1900	1950
ROMANTICISM/REALISM		IMPRESSIONISM	MODERNISM
1800	1850	1900	1950

1863 Manet's *Le Déjeuner sur l'Herbe* causes a scandalous sensation at the Salon des Refusés, both for "poor moral taste", and for its broad brushstrokes. The artist's *Olympia* was thought just as outrageous, but it was not exhibited until 1865 *(see p144)*

Monet's Impression: Sunrise *(1872), which led to the name Impressionism*

1938 International Surrealist exhibition in Paris

1977 Pompidou Centre opens

Delacroix's Liberty Leading the People *(1830) romantically celebrates victory in war (Louvre)*

1819 Géricault paints *The Raft of the Medusa*, one of the greatest works of French Romanticism *(see p124)*

IMPRESSIONIST AND POST-IMPRESSIONIST ARTISTS

Bonnard, Pierre (1867–1947)
Carpeaux, Jean-Baptiste (1827–75)
Cézanne, Paul (1839–1906)
Degas, Edgar (1834–1917)
Gauguin, Paul (1848–1903)
Manet, Edouard (1832–83)
Monet, Claude (1840–1926)
Pissarro, Camille (1830–1903)
Renoir, Pierre-Auguste (1841–1919)
Rodin, Auguste (1840–1917)
Rousseau, Henri (1844–1910)
Seurat, Georges (1859–91)
Sisley, Alfred (1839–99)
Toulouse-Lautrec, Henri de (1864–1901)
Van Gogh, Vincent (1853–90)
Vuillard, Edouard (1868–1940)
Whistler, James Abbott McNeill (1834–1903)

Tinguely and Saint-Phalle's Fontaine Igor Stravinsky *(1980), a modern kinetic sculpture (Pompidou Centre)*

PARIS THROUGH THE YEAR

Paris's attraction is strongest in spring – the season for chestnuts in blossom and tables under trees. From June Paris is slowly turned over to tourists; the city almost comes to a standstill for the French Tennis Open, and the major racetracks stage the big summer races. Next comes the July 14 Bastille Day parade down the Champs-Elysées; toward the end of the month the Tour de France ends here.

The end of July also sees the end of Paris's three-month Jazz Festival, after which most Parisians abandon the city to visitors until *la rentrée,* the return to school and work in September. Dates of events listed on the following pages may vary. For details consult the listings magazines, or contact Paris Infos Mairie *(see p357).* The Office du Tourisme *(see p367)* also produces an annual calendar of events.

SPRING

A good many of the city's 20-million annual visitors arrive in the spring. It is the season for fairs and concerts, when the marathon street race is held and the outdoor temperature is pleasant. Spring is also the time when hoteliers offer weekend packages, often with tickets for jazz concerts and with museum passes included.

French Tennis Open, Stade Roland Garros

MARCH

Foire du Trône *(late Mar–May),* Bois de Vincennes *(p233).* Large carnival.
Banlieues Bleues Festival *(Mar–early Apr),* Paris suburbs. Jazz, blues, soul & funk.
Jumping International de Paris *(3rd week),* Palais Omnisports de Paris-Bercy *(pp358–9).* International show jumping.
Salon International d'Agriculture *(1st week),* Paris-Expo, Porte de Versailles. Vast farming fair.
Spring flower shows at Parc Floral (Bois de Vincennes,

p233) and Bagatelle Gardens (Bois de Boulogne, *pp254–5).*
Chemin de la Croix *(Good Friday).* Beautiful Stations of the Cross procession from Montmartre to Sacré Coeur.

APRIL

Six Nations Trophy *(early Apr),* Stade de France *(p358).* International rugby.
Salon de la Musique à la Villette *(1st week).* International music extravaganza.
Shakespeare Garden Festival *(until Oct),* Bois de Boulogne *(pp254–5).* Classic plays performed outdoors.
Paris International Marathon *(April),* from Place de la Concorde to Avenue Foch.
Foire de Paris *(end-Apr–1st week May),* Paris Expo, Porte de Versailles. Food, wine, homes and gardens and tourism show.

MAY

Carré Rive Gauche *(one week, mid-month).* Exhibits

at antiques dealers near the Grand Louvre *(p135).*
Soccer Cup Final *(2nd week),* Stade de France.
Grands Eaux Musicales *(Apr–Oct: Sundays; Jul–Sep: Saturdays),* Versailles *(p248).* Open-air concerts.

Spring color, Jardin du Luxembourg

French Tennis Open *(last week May–1st week Jun),* Stade Roland Garros *(p358).* Parisian society meets sports!
Le Printemps des Rues *(3rd w/end).* Concerts and free street theater in Bastille/ République area.

Paris International Marathon

AVERAGE DAILY HOURS OF SUNSHINE

Hours

10
8
6
4
2
0

Jan Feb Mar Apr May Jun Jul Aug Sep Oct Nov Dec

Sunshine Hours
The northerly position of Paris gives it long and light summer evenings, but in winter the daylight recedes with few truly bright days.

SUMMER

Summer begins with the French Tennis Open, and there are many events and festivities until July. Thereafter the French begin thinking of their own annual vacation, but there are big celebrations on Bastille Day (July 14) with military displays for the president and his guests.

Jardin du Luxembourg in summer

JUNE

Festival St-Denis, Basilique St-Denis. Concerts with emphasis on large-scale choral works *(p346)*.
Fête du Cinéma, movies shown all over Paris for 1 nominal entry fee *(p354)*.

Final lap of the Champs-Elysées during the Tour de France

Fête de la Musique *(Jun 21)*, all over Paris. Nightlong summer solstice musical celebrations.
Flower show, Bois de Boulogne *(pp254–5)*. Rose season in the Bagatelle Gardens.
Gay Pride *(end Jun)*. Lively parade around the Bastille.
Paris Jazz Festival *(May–Jul)*, Parc Floral de Paris. Jazz musicians come to play in Paris *(pp349–50)*.
Paris Air and Space Technology Show *(mid-Jun)*, Le Bourget Airport.
Prix de Diane-Hermès *(2nd Sun)*, Chantilly. French equivalent of the British Ascot high society horse racing event.

JULY

Festival du cinéma en plein air *(mid-Jul–Aug)*, Parc de la Villette *(pp234–5)*.
Paris Quartier d'Eté *(mid-Jul–mid-Aug)*. Dance, music, theater, ballet.
Tour de France *(late Jul)*. The last stage of the world's greatest cycle race comes to a climax in the Champs-Elysées.
Fêtes de Nuit *(Jul–mid-Sep: Saturdays)*, Versailles. Son et lumière with music, dance and theater *(p249)*.
Paris-Plage *(mid-Jul–mid-Aug)*. Sand and palm trees are deposited on the Right Bank of the Seine to create a temporary beach.

Marching troops on Bastille Day (July 14)

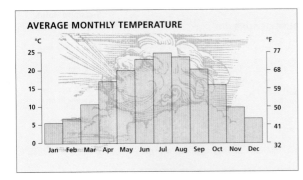

AVERAGE MONTHLY TEMPERATURE

Temperature
The chart shows the average minimum and maximum temperatures for each month. It is hottest in July and August and coolest between December and February, though Paris is rarely freezing cold. Temperatures are pleasant in the spring and the fall.

FALL

September sees the start of the social season, with gala performances of new movies, and parties in big houses on the Ile St-Louis. Paris is the world's largest convention center and there are a rush of shows in September, ranging from children's clothes and gifts to leisure and music. The pace barely slackens in October and November when Parisians begin to indulge their great love for the movies. French and Hollywood stars frequently make appearances at premiers staged on the Champs-Elysées.

SEPTEMBER

Festival d'Automne à Paris
(mid-Sep–end Dec), throughout Paris. Music, dance, theater *(pp346–7)*.
La Villette Jazz Festival *(mid-Sep)*. Jazz artists come blow their horns with gusto throughout the Cité de la Musique *(p234)*.

The Prix de l'Arc de Triomphe (October)

OCTOBER

Foire Internationale d'Art Contemporain (FIAC) *(last week)*, Paris-Expo, Porte de Versailles. Paris's biggest international modern and contemporary art fair.
Prix de l'Arc de Triomphe *(1st week)*, Longchamp. An international field competes for the richest prize in European horse-racing.
Salon de l'Automobile *(1st two weeks alternate years)*, Paris-Expo, Porte de Versailles. Commercial auto show, alternated annually with a motorcycle show.
Journées du Patrimoine *(usually 3rd week)*. Three hundred historic buildings, monuments, museums and ministries are open free to the public for two days, following an all-night party to kick off proceedings.

Jazz fusion guitarist Al di Meola playing in Paris

NOVEMBER

BNP Paribas Masters *(usually Nov)*, Palais Omnisports de Paris-Bercy *(pp358–9)*.
Festival d'Art Sacré *(Nov–Dec 24)*, at St-Sulpice, St-Eustache and St-Germain-des-Prés churches. Religious art festival.
Mois de la Photo *(Oct–Nov)*. Numerous photography shows.
Beaujolais Nouveau *(3rd Thursday Nov)*. Bars and cafés are crowded on this day, in a race to taste the new vintage.

Fall in the Bois de Vincennnes

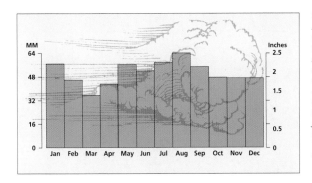

Rainfall

August is the wettest month in Paris as well as the hottest. In August and September you risk getting caught in storms. Sudden showers, sometimes with hail, can occur between January and April – notoriously in March. There is occasional snow in winter.

WINTER

Paris rarely sees snow; winter days tend to be invigorating rather than chilly. There are jazz and dance festivals, candlelit Christmas church services and much celebrating in the streets over the New Year. After New Year, the streets seem to become slightly less congested and on bright days the riverside quays are used as the rendezvous point of strollers and lovers.

Snow in the Tuileries, a rare occurrence

DECEMBER

Christmas illuminations *(until Jan)* in the Grands Boulevards, Opéra, Ave Montaigne, Champs-Elysées and the Rue du Faubourg St-Honoré.
Crèche *(early Dec–early Jan)*, under a canopy in Place de l'Hôtel de Ville, Marais *(p102)*. Lifesize Christmas nativity from a different country each year.

Horse & Pony Show *(1st two weeks)*, Paris-Expo, Porte de Versailles.
Paris International Boat Show *(1st two weeks)*, venue: as above.

JANUARY

Fête des Rois (Epiphany). *(Jan 6)*. The *boulangeries* are full of *galettes des rois*.
Prix d'Amérique *(mid-Jan)*. Europe's most famous trotting race, Hippodrome de Vincennes.
Fashion shows, summer collections. *(See* Haute Couture *p324)*

FEBRUARY

Carnaval *(2nd half month)*, Quartier de St-Fargeau.
Jeune Création *(mid-Feb)*, Parc de la Villette. Exhibition of works by young artists.
Floraisons *(all month)*, Parc Floral de Paris, Bois de Vincennes *(p233)* and Parc de Bagatelle, Bois de Boulogne *(pp254–5)*. Displays of crocuses and snowdrops.

PUBLIC HOLIDAYS

New Year's Day (Jan 1)
Easter Monday varies
Labour Day (May 1)
VE Day (May 8)
Ascension Day (6th Thu after Easter)
Bastille Day (Jul 14)
Assumption (Aug 15)
All Saints' Day (Nov 1)
Remembrance Day (Nov 11)
Christmas (Dec 25)

January fashion show

Eiffel Tower Christmas decorations

A RIVER VIEW
OF PARIS

Sculpture on the Pont Alexandre III

The remarkable French music-hall star Mistinguett described the Seine as a "pretty blonde with laughing eyes". The river most certainly has a beguiling quality, but the relationship that exists between it and the city of Paris is far more than one of flirtation.

No other European city defines itself by its river in the same way as Paris. The Seine is the essential point of reference to the city: distances are measured from it, street numbers determined by it, and it divides the capital into two distinct areas, with the Right Bank on the north side of the river and the Left Bank on the south side. These are as well defined as any of the supposedly official boundaries. The city is also divided historically, with the east more closely linked to the city's ancient roots and the west more closely linked to the 19th and 20th centuries.

Practically every building of note in Paris is either along the river or within a stone's throw. The quays are lined by fine bourgeois apartments, magnificent town houses, great museums and striking monuments.

Above all, the river is very much alive. For centuries fleets of small boats used it, but motorized land traffic stifled this once-bustling scene. Today, the river is busy with commercial barges and huge *bateaux mouches,* pleasure boats cruising sightseers up and down the river.

The octagonal lake in the Jardin de Luxembourg is a favorite spot for children to sail their toy boats. The Seine is host to larger craft, including many pleasure cruisers.

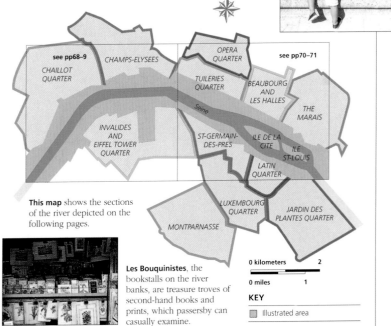

see pp68–9

CHAILLOT QUARTER

CHAMPS-ELYSEES

OPERA QUARTER

see pp70–71

TUILERIES QUARTER

BEAUBOURG AND LES HALLES

THE MARAIS

Seine

INVALIDES AND EIFFEL TOWER QUARTER

ST-GERMAIN-DES-PRES

ILE DE LA CITE

ILE ST-LOUIS

LATIN QUARTER

LUXEMBOURG QUARTER

JARDIN DES PLANTES QUARTER

MONTPARNASSE

This map shows the sections of the river depicted on the following pages.

Les Bouquinistes, the bookstalls on the river banks, are treasure troves of second-hand books and prints, which passersby can casually examine.

0 kilometers   2

0 miles   1

KEY

Illustrated area

◁ Pont Alexandre III, encrusted with exuberant statuary

From Pont de Grenelle to Pont de la Concorde

The soaring monuments and grand exhibition halls along this stretch of the river are remnants of the Napoleonic era and the Industrial Revolution with its great exhibitions. The exhilarating self-confidence of the Eiffel Tower, the Petit Palais and the Grand Palais is matched by more recent buildings, such as the Palais de Chaillot, the Maison de Radio-France and the skyscrapers of the Left Bank.

Palais de Chaillot
The curved wings and arching fountains make this a spectacular setting for three museums (p198).

Palais de Tokyo
Figures by Bourdelle adorn this museum (p201).

Bateaux Parisiens Tour Eiffel

Vedettes de Paris Ile de France

Passerelle

Trocadéro Ⓜ

The Statue of Liberty was given to the city in 1885. It faces west, toward the original Liberty in New York

Pont d'Iéna

Maison de Radio-France
Studios and a radio museum are housed in this imposing circular building (p200).

Ⓜ Passy

Pont de Bir-Hakeim

RER Champ de Mars

RER Prés. Kennedy Radio France

Eiffel Tower
The tower is the symbol of Paris (pp192–3).

The Pont Bir-Hakeim has a dynamic statue by Wederkinch rising at its north end.

Pont de Grenelle

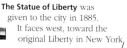

KEY

Ⓜ Metro station

RER RER station

Ⓞ Batobus stop

River trip boarding point

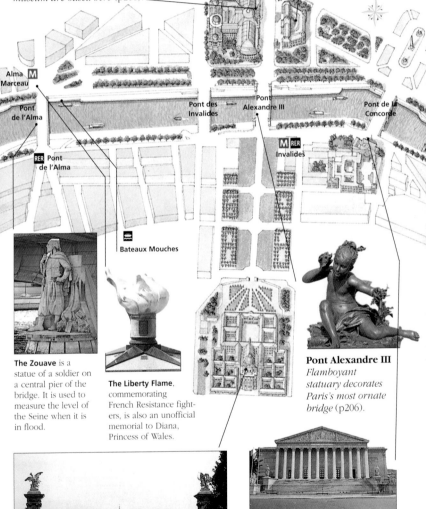

Grand Palais
Major exhibitions and a science museum are based here (p206).

Petit Palais
Now the Paris museum of fine arts, this was first designed as a companion to the Grand Palais (p206).

Champs-Elysées Clemenceau Ⓜ

Alma Marceau Ⓜ

Pont de l'Alma

RER Pont de l'Alma

Pont des Invalides

Pont Alexandre III

Pont de la Concorde

Ⓜ RER Invalides

Bateaux Mouches

The Zouave is a statue of a soldier on a central pier of the bridge. It is used to measure the level of the Seine when it is in flood.

The Liberty Flame, commemorating French Resistance fighters, is also an unofficial memorial to Diana, Princess of Wales.

Pont Alexandre III
Flamboyant statuary decorates Paris's most ornate bridge (p206).

Dôme Church
The majestic gilded dome (p188–9) is here seen from Pont Alexandre III.

Assemblée Nationale Palais-Bourbon
Louis XIV's daughter once owned this palace, which is now used by the Chambre des Députés as the national forum for political debate (p190).

From Pont de la Concorde to Pont de Sully

The historic heart of Paris lies on the banks and islands of the east river. At its center is the Ile de la Cité, a natural stepping stone across the Seine and the cultural core of medieval Paris. Today it is still vital to Parisian life.

Jardin des Tuileries
These are in the formal style (p130).

Musée du Louvre
Before becoming the world's greatest museum and home to the Mona Lisa, this was Europe's largest royal palace (pp122–9).

Pont de la Concorde

Assemblée Nationale
M

Passerelle Solférino

Quai d'Orsay RER

Pont Royal

Pont du Carrousel

Passerelle des Arts

Musée de l'Orangerie
An important collection of 19th-century paintings are on display here (p131).

The Passerelle des Arts
is a steel reconstruction of Paris's first cast-iron bridge (1804), and was inaugurated in 1984.

Bâteaux Vedettes du Pont Neuf

Musée d'Orsay
Paris's most important collection of Impressionist art is housed in this converted railroad station (pp144–7).

Hôtel des Monnaies
Built in 1768–85, this former mint has a fine coin collection in its old milling halls (p141).

Ile de la Cité
The medieval identity of this small island was almost completely erased in the 19th century by Baron Haussmann's grand scheme. Sainte-Chapelle and parts of the Conciergerie are the only buildings of the period that remain today (pp76–89).

Conciergerie
During the Revolution this building, with its distinctive towers, became notorious as a prison (p81).

The Tour de l'Horloge,
a 14th-century clock tower, features the first public clock in Paris. Germain Pilon's fine carvings continue to adorn the clock face.

Ile St-Louis
This has been a desirable address since the 17th century (p87).

St-Gervais–St-Protais
The oldest organ in Paris, dating from the early 17th century, is in this church (p99).

Pont Neuf
M

nt Neuf

M Châtelet

Hôtel de Ville

Pont au Change

M

Pont Notre Dame

Cité

M

Pont d'Arcole

RER M

St-Michel

Petit Pont

Pont au Double

Pont St Louis

Pont Louis Philippe

M Pont Marie

Pont Marie

Pont de Archevêché

Sully Morland

M

Pont de la Tournelle

Pont de Sully

Notre-Dame
This towering cathedral surveys the river (pp82–5).

Bâteaux Parisiens

How to Take a River or Canal Trip

Seine River cruises on *bateaux mouches vedettes* pleasure boats operate along the main sightseeing reaches of the river, taking in many of the city's famous monuments. The Batobus river service operates as a shuttle or bus service, allowing you to get on and off anywhere along the route. The main city canal trips operate along the old industrial canal at St-Martin in the city's east.

Pleasure-cruise boats passing under the Pont Alexandre III

Types of Boats
Bateaux mouches, *the largest of the pleasure-cruise boats, are a spectacular sight with their passenger areas enclosed in glass for excellent all-around viewing. At night floodlights are used to pick out river bank buildings. A more luxurious version of these is used on the Bateaux Parisien cruises. The vedettes are smaller and more intimate boats, with viewing through glass walls. The Canauxrama canal boats are flat-bottomed.*

SEINE CRUISES AND CANAL SHUTTLE SERVICES
The Seine cruises and shuttle services information below includes the location of boarding points, the nearest metro and RER stations, and the nearest bus routes. Lunch and dinner cruises must be reserved in advance, and passengers must board them 30 minutes before departure.

ILE de FRANCE

Vedettes de Paris Ile de France Seine Cruise
A fleet of nine boats carrying passengers in comfort and style on a cruise encompassing all major sights along the river. The boarding point is:

Port de Suffren
Map 10 D3. *Tel* 01 44 18 19 50. Ⓜ *Bir Hakeim.* 🚆 *Champ de Mars.* 🚌 *22, 30, 32, 44, 63, 69, 72, 82, 87.* **Departures** 10am–10pm (7pm winter) daily (every 30 mins). **Duration** 1 hr. **Dinner cruise** 8pm Sat. **Duration** 2 hr 30 min (phone to reserve). **www**.vedettesdeparis.com

CANAUXRAMA

Parc de la Villette Shuttle Service
This canal trip takes you from the Rotonde de Ledoux, in the Esplanade du Bassin de la Villette, to the Parc de la Villette *(see pp234–9)*. The boarding points are:

13 Quai de la Loire
Map 8 E1.
Tel 01 42 39 15 00.
Ⓜ *Jaurès.*
Parc de la Villette.
Ⓜ *Porte de Pantin.*
Departures
1:30pm–6:30pm daily (every 30 mins, if weather conditions are favorable). **Duration** 15 min.

Bateaux Parisiens

Bateaux Parisiens Notre-Dame Seine Cruise
This is the company that also organizes the Tour Eiffel trip. This trip, however, only operates during the summer months, following the same route but in the opposite direction. The boarding point is:

Quai de Montebello
Map 13 B4. *Tel* 01 44 11 33 44. Ⓜ *Maubert–Mutualite, St- Michel.* 🚆 *St-Michel.* 🚌 *24, 27, 47.* **Departures** Apr–Nov: 2:20–6:20pm daily (every hour).

Also 8:20pm & 9:20pm Fri, Sat. **Duration** 1 hr.

Bateaux Parisiens Tour Eiffel Seine Cruise
This company has a fleet of seven boats with a carrying capacity of 1,255 passengers. A commentary is provided in 12 languages. The boarding point is:

Port de la Bourdonnais
Map 10 D2. *Tel* 01 44 11 33 44 (cruise), 01 44 11 33 55 (dinner). Ⓜ *Trocadéro, Bir Hakeim.* 🚆 *Champs de Mars.* 🚌 *42, 82, 72.* **Departures** 10am–11pm (10pm winter) daily (every hour). **Duration** 1 hr. **Lunch cruise** 12:15pm daily. **Duration** 2 hr 15 min. **Dinner cruise** 7:45pm. **Duration** 3hrs. Unsuitable for children. Jacket & tie required. **www**.bateauxparisiens.com

Boarding Points

The boarding points for the river cruises and the Batobus services are easy to find along the river. Here you can buy tickets, and there are amenities such as snack bars. Major cruise companies also have foreign exchange booths. There is limited parking around the points, but none near the Pont Neuf.

River boarding point

Shuttle service. 1–2 day passes available. **Tel** 01 44 11 33 99. **Departures** May–Sep: 10am–9pm (7pm Mar, Apr, Oct; 4:30pm Nov–Feb) daily (every 15–25 min). Board at: **Eiffel Tower: Map** 10 D3. **M** Bir Hakeim. **Champs-Elysées: Map** 11 B1. **M** Champs-Elysées-Clemenceau. **Musée d'Orsay: Map** 12 D2. **M** Solferino. **Louvre: Map** 12 E2. **M** Louvre. **St-Germain-de-Prés: Map** 12 E3. **M** St-Germain-de-Prés. **Notre-Dame: Map** 13 B4. **M** Cité. **Hôtel de Ville: Map** 13 B4. **M** Hôtel de Ville. **www**.batobus.com

BATEAUX-MOUCHES

Bateaux Mouches Seine Cruise

This well-known pleasure boat company's fleet of 11 boats carries between 600 and 1,400 passengers at a time. The boarding point is:

Pont de l'Alma Map 10 F1. **Tel** 01 42 25 96 10. **M** Alma-Marceau. **RER** Pont de l'Alma. 28, 42, 49, 63, 72, 80, 83, 92. **Departures** Apr–Oct: 10am–8pm daily (every 30 min); Nov–Mar: 11am, 2:30pm, 4pm, 6pm, 9pm. **Duration** 1 hr 10 min. **Lunch cruise** 12:30pm daily. **Duration** 1 hr 45 min. Children under 12, half price. **Dinner cruise** 8:30pm Mon–Fri. **Duration** 2 hr 15 min. Jacket and tie required. **www**.bateaux-mouches.fr

Vedettes du Pont Neuf

Bateaux Vedettes Pont Neuf Seine Cruise

This company runs a fleet of six 80-passenger boats. The boats are of an older style, for a quainter cruise. The boarding point is:

Square du Vert-Galant (Pont Neuf). **Map** 12 F3. **Tel** 01 46 33 98 38. **M** Pont Neuf. **RER** Châtelet. 24, 27, 58, 67, 70, 72, 74, 75. **Departures** Mar–Oct: 10am, 11:15am, noon; 1:30–10:30pm daily (every 30 min); Nov–Feb: 10:30am, 11:15am, noon, 2–6:30pm (every 45 min), 8pm, 10:30pm Mon–Fri; 10:30am, 11:15am, noon, 2–6.30pm, 8pm, 9–10:30pm (every 30 min) Sat, Sun. **Duration** 1hr. Offer lunch/dinner cruises. **www**. vedettesdupontneuf.com

CANAL TRIPS

The Canauxrama company operates boat cruises along the city's Canal St-Martin and along the banks of the Marne River. The St-Martin journey passes along the tree-lined canal, which has nine locks, two swing bridges and eight romantic footbridges. The Bords de Marne cruise travels well into the suburbs, as far as Bry-sur-Marne. The **Paris Canal Company** (01 42 40 96 97; **www**. pariscanal.com) also has a St-Martin canal trip, from Parc de la Villette and extending beyond the canal, passing into the Seine River and as far as the Musée d'Orsay.

Canal St-Martin

The Canauxrama company offers many different trips along this canal, but it has two 125-passenger boats that operate regularly between the Bassin de la Villette and the Port de l'Arsenal. The boarding points are: **Bassin de la Villette. Map** 8 E1. **M** Jaurès. **Port de l'Arsenal. Map** 14 E4. **M** Bastille. **Tel** 01 42 39 15 00. **Departures** Apr–Nov, times may vary so phone to check and to make a reservation: Bassin de la Villette 9:45 am and 2pm; Port de l'Arsenal 9:45am and 2:30pm daily. On weekday mornings there are concessions for students, senior citizens and children under 12. Children under six travel free. Concert cruises are available on chartered trips on the Canal St-Martin and the Seine. **Duration** 2 hr 30 min.

Bords de Marne Croisière

This all-day cruise extends westward out of Paris down the Marne River. The trip includes a commentary, stories and dancing. The boarding point is: **Porte de l'Arsenal. Map** 14 E4. **M** Bastille. **Tel** 01 42 39 15 00. **Departures** 8.30am all-year-round. Reservations necessary. **Duration** 9 hr.

Canal-cruise boat in the Bassin de la Villette

PARIS AREA
BY AREA

ILE DE LA CITE AND ILE ST-LOUIS

T he history of the Ile de la Cité is the history of Paris. This island on the Seine was no more than a primitive village when the conquering Julius Caesar arrived in 53 BC. Ancient kings later made it the center of political power, and in medieval times it became the home of church and law. It no longer has such power, except to draw armies of tourists to the imposing Palais de Justice and to its Gothic masterpiece, Notre-Dame.

The medieval huddles of tiny houses and narrow streets that so characterized the island at one time

The motto of the city of Paris

were swept away by the spacious thoroughfares built in the 19th century. But there are still small areas of charm and relief, among them the colorful bird and flower market, the romantic Square du Vert-Galant and the ancient Place Dauphine.

At the eastern end of the island the St-Louis bridge connects it to the smaller Ile St-Louis. This former swampy pastureland was transformed into an elegant 17th-century residential area, with picturesque, tree-lined quays. More recently, rich artists, doctors, actresses and heiresses have lived here.

SIGHTS AT A GLANCE

Historic Buildings
Hôtel Dieu **6**
Conciergerie **8**
Palais de Justice **10**
Hôtel de Lauzun **16**

Bridges
Pont Neuf **12**

Monuments
Paris Mémorial de la Déportation **4**

Markets
Marché aux Fleurs and Marché aux Oiseaux **7**

Squares and Gardens
Square Jean XXIII **3**
Place Dauphine **11**
Square du Vert-Galant **13**

Museums and Galleries
Musée de Notre-Dame de Paris **2**
Crypte Archéologique **5**

Société Historique et Littéraire Polonaise **14**

Churches and Cathedrals
Notre-Dame pp82–5 **1**
Sainte-Chapelle pp88–9 **9**
St-Louis-en-l'Ile **15**

0 meters 400
0 yards 400

GETTING THERE
This area is served by the metro station at Cité and the RER at St-Michel. The bus routes 21, 38, 47, 85 and 96 cross the Ile de la Cité, and 67, 86 and 87 cross the Ile St-Louis.

SEE ALSO
• **Street Finder,** map 12–13
• **St-Louis Walk** pp262–3
• **Where to Stay** pp284–91
• **Restaurants** pp300–15

KEY
Street-by-Street map
M Metro station
RER RER station

◁ View of the Conciergerie and the Pont au Change

Street-by-Street: Ile de la Cité

The origins of Paris are here on the Ile de la Cité, the boat-shaped island on the Seine first inhabited over 2,000 years ago by Celtic tribes. One tribe, the Parisii, eventually gave its name to the city. The island offered a convenient river crossing on the route between northern and southern Gaul and was easily defended. In later centuries the settlement was expanded by the Romans, the Franks and the Capetian kings to form the nucleus of today's city.

There is no older place in Paris, and remains of the first buildings can still be seen today in the archaeological crypt under the square in front of Notre-Dame, the great medieval cathedral and place of pilgrimage for millions of visitors each year. At the other end of the island is another Gothic masterpiece, Sainte-Chapelle – a miracle of light.

★ Conciergerie
A grisly antechamber to the guillotine, this prison was much used in the Revolution ❽

The Cour du Mai
is the impressive main courtyard of the Palais de Justice.

Metro Cité

★ Sainte-Chapelle
A jewel of Gothic architecture and one of the most magical sights of Paris, Sainte-Chapelle is noted for the magnificence of its stained glass ❾

To Pont Neuf

The Quai des Orfèvres
owes its name to the goldsmiths (orfèvres) who frequented the area from medieval times onward.

Palais de Justice
With its ancient towers lining the quays, the old royal palace is today a huge complex of law courts. Its history extends back over 16 centuries ❿

The Préfecture de Police
is the headquarters of the police and was the scene of intense battles during World War II.

0 meters   100
0 yards   100

The Statue of Charlemagne
commemorates the king of the Franks, who was crowned emperor in 800. He united all the Christian peoples of the West.

★ Marché aux Fleurs et Oiseaux
The flower and bird market is a colorful, lively island sight. Paris was once famous for its flower markets but this is now one of the last **7**

LOCATOR MAP
See Central Paris Map pp14–15

STAR SIGHTS
- ★ Notre-Dame
- ★ Sainte-Chapelle
- ★ Conciergerie
- ★ Marché aux Fleurs et Oiseaux
- ★ Crypte Archéologique

Hôtel Dieu
Once an orphanage, this is now a city hospital **6**

★ Crypte Archéologique
Deep under the square, there are remains of houses from 2,000 years ago **5**

KEY
– – – Suggested route

The Rue Chanoinesse has had many famous residents, such as the 17th-century playwright Racine.

Musée Notre-Dame
Many exhibits tracing the cathedral's history are in this museum **2**

Point Zéro
is a mark from which all distances in France are measured.

The Square Jean XXIII
is a peaceful square close to the river **3**

★ Notre-Dame
This cathedral is a superb example of French medieval architecture **1**

To Latin Quarter

Notre-Dame from the Left Bank

Notre-Dame ❶

See pp82–5.

Musée de Notre-Dame de Paris ❷

10 Rue du Cloître-Notre-Dame 75004.
Map 13 B4. **Tel** *01 43 25 42 92.* Ⓜ
Cité. ℝℰℝ *St-Michel.* ◯ *2:30pm–6pm
Wed, Sat, Sun (last adm: 5:40pm).*

Founded in 1951, this
museum has exhibits and
documents that commemorate
and illustrate the great events
in Notre-Dame's history. The
displays include Gallo-Roman
objects, old engravings, works
of art and the city
of Paris's oldest
extant Christian
relic, a fine
4th-century
glass cup.

A Gallo-Roman coin

Square Jean XXIII ❸

Rue du Cloître-Notre-Dame 75004.
Map 13 B4. Ⓜ *Cité.*

Notre-Dame's St Stephen's
door (porte St-Etienne) opens
onto this pleasant garden
square dedicated to Pope
John XXIII. The garden runs
alongside the river and is an
excellent place for enjoying
the sculptures, rose windows
and flying buttresses of the
east end of the cathedral.
    From the 17th century, the
square was occupied by the
archbishop's palace, which
was ransacked by rioters in
1831 and later demolished.
A square was conceived
    to replace the Prefect of
        Paris, Rambuteau. The
        Gothic-style fountain of
    the Virgin standing in the
center of the square has
been there since 1845.

Paris Mémorial de la Déportation ❹

Sq de l'Ile de France 75004. **Map** 13 B4.
Tel *01 46 33 87 56.* Ⓜ *Cité.* ℝℰℝ *St-
Michel.* ◯ *10am–6pm Tue–Sun.*

The simple, modern memorial
to the 200,000 French men,
women and children deported
to Nazi concentration camps in
World War II (often via
Drancy, just a few miles to the
north of Paris) is covered with
a roll-call of names of the
camps to which they were
deported. Soil from these
camps has been used to form
small tombs, and the interior
walls are decorated with
poetry. At the far end is the
tomb dedicated to the
Unknown Deportee.

Inside the Paris Mémorial de
la Déportation

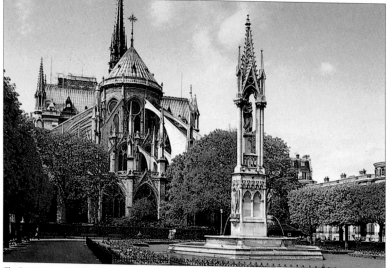

The Square Jean XXIII behind Notre-Dame

Gallo-Roman ruins in the Crypte Archéologique

Crypte Archéologique ❺

Pl du Parvis Notre-Dame 75004.
Map 13 A4. **Tel** 01 55 42 50 10.
Ⓜ Cité. ◑ Tue–Sun 10am–6pm (last adm: 30 min before closing). ● May 1, May 8, Nov 1 & 11, Dec 25, Jan 1. ✎ free for children under 12. ▣

Situated on the main square (the *parvis*) in front of Notre-Dame and stretching 393 ft (120 m) underground, this crypt exhibits the remains of foundations and walls that pre-date the cathedral by several hundred years. There are traces of a sophisticated underground heating system in a house from Lutèce, the settlement of the Parisii, the Celtic tribe who inhabited the island 2000 years ago, giving their name to the present city.

Hôtel Dieu ❻

1 Pl du Parvis Notre-Dame 75004.
Map 13 A4. ◑ to the public for visits. Ⓜ Cité.

On the north side of the place du Parvis Notre-Dame is the Hôtel Dieu, the hospital serving central Paris. It was built on the site of an

orphanage between 1866 and 1878. The original Hôtel Dieu, built in the 12th century and stretching across the island to both banks of the river, was demolished in the 19th century to make way for one of Baron Haussmann's urban-planning program.

It was here in 1944 that the Paris police courageously resisted the Germans; the battle is commemorated by a monument in Cour de 19-Août.

Paris's main flower market

Marché aux Fleurs and Marché aux Oiseaux ❼

Pl Louis-Lépine 75004. **Map** 13 A3.
Ⓜ Cité. ◑ 8am–7:30pm Mon–Sat; 8am–7pm Sun.

The year-round flower market adds color and scent to an area otherwise dominated by administrative buildings. It is the most famous and unfortunately one of the last remaining flower markets in the city of Paris, offering a wide range of specialized varieties such as orchids. Each Sunday it makes way for the cacophony of the caged bird market.

Conciergerie ❽

1 Quai de l'Horloge 75001. **Map** 13 A3. ⓘ 01 53 40 60 97. Ⓜ Cité. ◑ Apr–Sep: 9:30am–6:30pm daily; Oct–Mar: 9am–5pm daily (last adm: 30 min before closing). ● Jan 1, May 1, Dec 25. ✎ phone to check. ▣ www.monum.fr

Occupying the north part of the old Capetian palace, the Conciergerie was under the administration of the palace "concierge", the keeper of the king's mansion. When the king moved to the Marais (in 1417), the palace remained the seat of royal admini-stration and law; and the Conciergerie became a prison, with the "concierge" as its chief jailer. Henry IV's assassin, Ravaillac, was imprisoned and tortured here.

During the Revolution it housed over 4,000 prisoners, including Marie-Antoinette, who was held in a tiny cell until her execution, and Charlotte Corday, who stabbed Revolutionary leader Marat as he lay in his bath. Ironically, the Revolutionary judges Danton and Robespierre also became "tenants" before being sent to the guillotine.

The Conciergerie has a superb four-aisled Gothic Salle des Gens d'Armes (Hall of the Men-at-Arms), where guards of the royal household once lived. The building, renovated in the 19th century, retains the 11th-century torture chamber, the Bonbec Tower and the 14th-century public clock tower on the Tour de l'Horloge (Palais de Justice). It is the city's oldest and is still operating.

A portrait of Marie-Antoinette in the Conciergerie, awaiting her execution at the guillotine

Hôtel Dieu, central Paris's hospital

Notre-Dame ❶

No other building is so associated with the history of Paris as Notre-Dame. It stands majestically on the Ile de la Cité, cradle of the city. Pope Alexander III laid the first stone in 1163, marking the start of 170 years of toil by armies of Gothic architects and medieval craftsmen. Ever since, a procession of the famous has passed through the three main doors below the huge towers.

The cathedral is a Gothic masterpiece, standing on the site of a Roman temple. At the time it was finished, in about 1330, it was 430 ft (130 m) long and featured flying buttresses, a large transept, a deep choir and 228-ft (69-m) high towers.

★ West Front
Three main doors with superb statuary, a central rose window and an openwork gallery are important details.

The south tower houses the cathedral's famous Emmanuel bell.

★ Galerie des Chimères
The cathedral's legendary gargoyles (chimères) hide behind a large upper gallery between the towers.

★ West Rose Window
This window depicts the Virgin in a medallion of rich reds and blues.

STAR FEATURES

- ★ West Front and Portals
- ★ Flying Buttresses
- ★ Rose Windows
- ★ Galerie des Chimères

The Kings' Gallery features 28 Kings of Judah gazing down on the crowds.

Portal of the Virgin
The Virgin surrounded by saints and kings is a fine composition of 13th-century statues.

★ **Flying Buttresses**
Jean Ravy's spectacular flying buttresses at the east end of the cathedral have a span of 50 ft (15 m).

The spire, designed by Viollet-le-Duc, soars to a height of 295 ft (90 m).

VISITORS' CHECKLIST

Pl du Parvis-Notre-Dame. **Map** 13 B4. 🆔 01 42 34 56 10. Ⓜ️ Cité. 🚌 21, 38, 85, 96 to Ile de la Cité. 📷 Notre-Dame. 🅿️ Pl du Parvis. 🕐 7:45am–6:45pm daily. **Towers** 🕐 9:30am–4:45pm (winter), 9am–7pm (summer) (last adm 45 min before closing). 📷 (towers). ✝️ 8am, 9am, noon, 6:15pm Mon–Sat; 8:30am, 10am, 11:30am, 12:45pm, 6:30pm Sun. 📷 📷 **www**.cathedraledeparis.com

★ **South Rose Window**
This south facade window, with its central depiction of Christ, is an impressive 43 ft (13 m) high.

The transept was built at the start of Philippe-Auguste's reign, in the 13th century.

The treasury houses the cathedral's religious treasures, including ancient manuscripts and reliquaries.

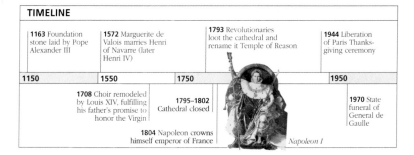

TIMELINE

1163 Foundation stone laid by Pope Alexander III	**1572** Marguerite de Valois marries Henri of Navarre (later Henri IV)	**1793** Revolutionaries loot the cathedral and rename it Temple of Reason	**1944** Liberation of Paris Thanksgiving ceremony
1150	**1550**	**1750**	**1950**
	1708 Choir remodeled by Louis XIV, fulfilling his father's promise to honor the Virgin	**1795–1802** Cathedral closed	**1970** State funeral of General de Gaulle
	1804 Napoleon crowns himself emperor of France	*Napoleon I*	

A Guided Tour of Notre-Dame

Notre-Dame's interior grandeur is instantly apparent on seeing the high-vaulted central nave. This is bisected by a huge transept, at either end of which are medieval rose windows, 43 ft (13 m) in diameter. Works by major sculptors adorn the cathedral. Among them are Jean Ravy's old choir screen carvings, Nicolas Coustou's *Pietà* and Antoine Coysevox's Louis XIV statue. In this majestic setting kings and emperors were crowned and royal crusaders were blessed. But Notre-Dame was also the scene of turmoil. Revolutionaries ransacked it, banished religion, changed it into a temple to the Cult of Reason, and then used it as a wine store. Napoleon restored religion in 1804 and architect Viollet-le-Duc later restored the buildings, replacing missing statues, as well as raising the spire and fixing the gargoyles.

A jeweled chalice of Notre-Dame

⑨ **North Rose Window**
This 13th-century stained-glass window depicts the Virgin encircled by figures from the Old Testament.

⑩ **View and Gargoyles**
The 387 steps up the north tower lead to sights of the famous gargoyles and magnificent views of Paris.

Stairs to the tower

Entrance

① **View of Interior**
From the main entrance, the view takes in the high-vaulted central nave looking down toward the huge transept, the choir and the high altar.

KEY

- - - Suggested route

② **Le Brun's "May" Paintings**
These religious paintings by Charles Le Brun hang in the side chapels. In the 17th and 18th centuries, the Paris guilds presented a painting to the cathedral on May Day each year.

⑧ **Carved Choir Stalls**
Noted for their early 18th-century carved woodwork, the choir stalls were commissioned by Louis XIV, whose statue stands behind the high altar. Among the details carved in bas-relief on the back of the high stalls are scenes from the life of the Virgin.

⑦ **Louis XIII Statue**
After many years of childless marriage, Louis XIII pledged to erect a high altar and to redecorate the east chancel to honor the Virgin if an heir was born to him. The future Louis XIV was born in 1638, but it took 60 years before the promises were made good. One of the surviving features from that time is the carved choir stalls.

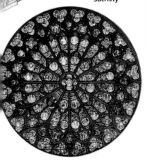

Entrance to Treasury

Entrance to Sacristy

⑥ **Pietà**
Behind the high altar is Nicolas Coustou's Pietà, standing on a gilded base sculptured by François Girardon.

⑤ **Chancel Screen**
A 14th-century high stone screen enclosed the chancel and provided canons at prayer with peace and solitude from noisy congregations. Some of it has survived to screen the first three north and south bays.

③ **South Rose Window**
Located at the south end of the transept, this window retains some of its original 13th-century stained glass. The window depicts Christ in the center, surrounded by virgins, saints and the 12 Apostles.

④ **Statue of the Virgin and Child**
Against the southeast pillar of the transept stands the 14th-century statue of the Virgin and Child. It was brought to the cathedral from the chapel of St Aignan, and is known as Notre-Dame de Paris (Our Lady of Paris).

The Pont Neuf, extending to the north and south of the Ile de la Cité

Sainte-Chapelle ❾

See pp88–9.

A Sainte-Chapelle decoration of angels with the Crown of Thorns

Palais de Justice ❿

4 Blvd du Palais (entrance by the Cour de Mai) 75001. **Map** 13 A3.
Tel *01 44 32 50 00.* **M** *Cité.*
⏺ *9am–6:30pm Mon–Fri.*
Ø 🖥 🍴

This huge block of buildings making up the law courts stretches the entire width of the Ile de la Cité. It is a splendid sight with its old towers lining the quays. The site has been occupied since Roman times and was the seat of royal power until Charles V moved the court to the Marais in the 14th century. In April 1793 the Revolutionary Tribunal began dispensing justice from the Première Chambre (gilded chamber). Today the site embodies Napoleon's great legacy – the French judicial system.

Place Dauphine ⓫

75001 (enter by Rue Henri-Robert).
Map 12 F3. **M** *Pont Neuf, Cité.*

East of Pont Neuf is this ancient square, laid out in 1607 by Henri IV and named after the Dauphin, the future Louis XIII. No. 14 is one of the few buildings to have avoided any subsequent restoration. This haven of 17th-century charm is popular with *pétanque* (boules) players and employees of the adjoining Palais de Justice.

Pont Neuf ⓬

75001. **Map** 12 F3. **M** *Pont Neuf, Cité.*

Despite its name (New Bridge), this bridge is the oldest in Paris and has been immortalized by major literary and artistic figures since it was built. The first stone was laid by Henri III in 1578, but it was Henri IV who inaugurated it and gave it its name in 1607. The bridge has 12 arches and spans 912 ft (275 m). The first stone bridge to be built without houses, it heralded a new era in the relationship between the Cité and the river and has been popular ever since. Fittingly, Henri IV's statue stands in the central section.

A sculptured relief on the Palais de Justice

Henri IV in Square du Vert-Galant

Square du Vert-Galant ⓭

75001. **Map** 12 F3. M *Pont Neuf, Cité.*

One of the magical spots of Paris, this square bears the nickname of Henri IV. This amorous and colorful monarch did much to beautify Paris in the early 17th century, and his popularity has lasted to this day. From here there are splendid views of the Louvre and the Right Bank of the river, where Henri was assassinated in 1610. This is also the point from which the Vedettes de Paris pleasure boats depart *(see pp72–3).*

Société Historique et Littéraire Polonaise ⓮

6 Quai d'Orléans 75004. **Map** 13 C4. **Tel** *01 55 42 83 83.* M *Pont Marie.* ◯ *2:15–5:45pm Thu.* 🎟 phone to reserve.

The Polish Romantic poet Adam Mickiewicz, who lived in Paris in the 19th century, was a major force in Polish cultural and political life, devoting his writing to helping his countrymen who were oppressed at home and abroad. His life is the focal point of the museum, which was founded in 1903 by the poet's son. Part of the famous

Polish library has moved to 74 rue Lauriston, but the archives remain. They form the finest Polish collection outside Poland: paintings, books, maps, emigration archive and Frédéric Chopin memorabilia, including his death mask.

St-Louis-en-l'Ile ⓯

19 bis Rue St-Louis-en-l'Ile 75004. **Map** 13 C4. **Tel** *01 46 34 11 60.* M *Pont Marie.* ◯ *9am–noon, 3pm–7pm Tue–Sun.* ● public hols. **Concerts.**

The construction of this church was begun in 1664 from plans by the royal architect Louis Le Vau, who lived on the island. It was completed and consecrated in 1726. Among its outstanding exterior features are the 1741 iron clock at the entrance and the pierced iron spire.

The interior, in the Baroque style, is richly decorated with gilding and marble. There is a statue of St Louis holding a crusader's sword. A plaque in the north aisle, given in 1926, bears the inscription "in grateful memory of St Louis in whose honor the City of St Louis, Missouri, USA is named". The church is also linked with Carthage cathedral in Tunisia, where St Louis is buried.

A bust of Adam Mickiewicz

The interior of St-Louis-en-l'Ile

Hôtel de Lauzun ⓰

17 Quai d'Anjou 75004. **Map** 13 C4. M *Pont Marie.* ● until 2006.

This splendid mansion was built by Louis Le Vau in the mid-1650s for Charles Gruyn des Bordes, an arms dealer. It was sold in 1682 to the French military commander Duc de Lauzun, who was a favorite of Louis XIV. It later became a focus for Paris's Bohemian literary and artistic life. It now belongs to the city of Paris and, for those lucky enough to see inside, offers an unsurpassed insight into wealthy lifestyles in the 17th century. Charles Le Brun worked on the decoration of its magnificent paneling and painted ceilings before moving on to Versailles.

The poet Charles Baudelaire (1821–67) lived on the third floor and wrote the major part of his controversial masterpiece *Les Fleurs du Mal* here in a room packed with antiques and bric-a-brac. The celebrated French Romantic poet, traveler and critic Théophile Gautier (1811–72), had apartments here in 1848. Meetings of the Club des Haschischines (the Hashish-Eaters' Club) took place on the premises.

Other famous residents were the Austrian poet Rainer Maria Rilke, the English artist Walter Sickert and the German composer Richard Wagner. Today it is used for public receptions by the mayor of Paris.

Sainte-Chapelle **9**

Ethereal and magical, Sainte-Chapelle has been hailed as one of the greatest architectural masterpieces of the Western world. In the Middle Ages the devout likened this church to "a gateway to heaven". Today no visitor can fail to be transported by the blaze of light created by the 15 magnificent stained-glass windows, separated by the narrowest of columns that soar 50 ft (15 m) to the star-studded, vaulted roof. The windows portray over 1,000 religious scenes in a kaleidoscope of red, gold, green, blue and mauve. The chapel was built in 1248 by Louis IX to house Christ's purported crown of thorns and other relics.

The spire rises 245 ft (75 m) into the air. It was erected in 1853 after three previous spires burned down.

The crown of thorns decorates the pinnacle as a symbol of the first relic bought by Louis IX.

★ Rose Window
Best seen at sunset, the religious story of the Apocalypse is told in 86 panels of stained glass. The window was a gift from Charles VIII in 1485.

STAR FEATURES

★ Rose Window

★ Window of Christ's Passion

★ Apostle Statues

★ Window of the Relics

Main Portal
The two-tier structure of the portal, the lower half of which is shown here, echoes that of the chapel.

ST LOUIS' RELICS

Louis IX was extremely devout, and was canonized in 1297, not long after his death. In 1239 he acquired the Crown of Thorns from the emperor of Constantinople and, in 1241, other relics, including a fragment of Christ's Cross. He built this beautiful chapel as a shrine to house them. Louis paid nearly three times more for the relics than he did for the whole of the construction of Sainte-Chapelle.

LOUIS IX.

VISITORS' CHECKLIST

4 Blvd du Palais. **Map** 13 A3.
01 53 40 60 80. Cité.
21, 38, 85, 96 to Ile de la Cité. St-Michel. Notre-Dame. Palais de Justice.
Mar–Oct: 9:30am–6:30pm daily; Nov–Feb: 9am–5pm daily. Last adm 30 mins before closing.
Jan 1, May 1, Nov 1, Nov 11, Dec 25.

The angel
once revolved so that its cross could be seen from anywhere in Paris.

UPPER CHAPEL WINDOWS

1 Genesis
2 Exodus
3 Numbers
4 Deuteronomy: Joshua
5 Judges
6 *left* Isaiah *right* Rod of Jesse
7 *left* St John the Evangelist *right* Childhood of Christ
8 Christ's Passion
9 *left* St John the Baptist *right* Story of Daniel
10 Ezekiel
11 *left* Jeremiah *right* Tobiah
12 Judith and Job
13 Esther
14 Book of Kings
15 Story of the Relics
16 Rose Window: The Apocalypse

Upper Chapel
The windows are a pictorial Bible, showing scenes from the Old and New testaments.

★ Window of Christ's Passion
The Last Supper is shown here in one of the most beautiful windows in the upper chapel.

★ Apostle Statues
These magnificent examples of medieval wood carving adorn the 12 pillars of the upper chapel.

Lower Chapel
Servants and commoners worshipped here, while the chapel above was reserved for the use of the king and the royal family.

★ Window of the Relics
This shows the journey of the true cross and the nails of the crucifixion to Sainte-Chapelle.

THE MARAIS

A place of royal residence in the 17th century, the Marais was all but abandoned during the Revolution, later descending into an architectural wasteland. Sensitive restoration brought the area to life again; some of Paris's most popular museums are now housed in its elegant mansions, while the main streets and narrow passageways bustle with chic boutiques, galleries and restaurants. Many merchants have been driven out by high prices, but enough artisans, bakers and small cafés survive, as does the ethnic mix of Jews, former Algerian settlers, Asians and others. Today, the Marais is also the center of the Parisian gay scene.

SIGHTS AT A GLANCE

Historic Buildings and Streets
Hôtel de Lamoignon ❷
Rue des Francs-Bourgeois ❸
Rue des Rosiers ❽
Hôtel de Ville ❿
Hôtel de Rohan ㉒

Churches
St-Paul–St-Louis ⓯
St-Gervais–St-Protais ⓲
Cloître des Billettes ⓴
Notre-Dame-des-Blancs-Manteaux ㉑

Museums and Galleries
Musée Carnavalet pp96–7 ❶
Musée Cognacq-Jay ❹
Maison de Victor Hugo ❻
Hôtel de Sully ❼
Hôtel de Coulanges ❾
Hôtel Libéral Bruand ❿
Musée Picasso pp100–1 ⓫
Hôtel de Sens ⓰
Hôtel de Soubise ㉓
Hôtel Guénégaud (Musée de la Chasse et de la Nature) ㉔
Musée des Arts et Métiers ㉕
Musée d'Art et d'Histoire du Judaïsme ㉗

Monuments and Statues
Colonne de Juillet ⓭
Mémorial du Martyr Juif Inconnu ⓱

Opera Houses
Opéra National de Paris Bastille ⓬

Squares
Place des Vosges ❺
Place de la Bastille ⓮
Square du Temple ㉖

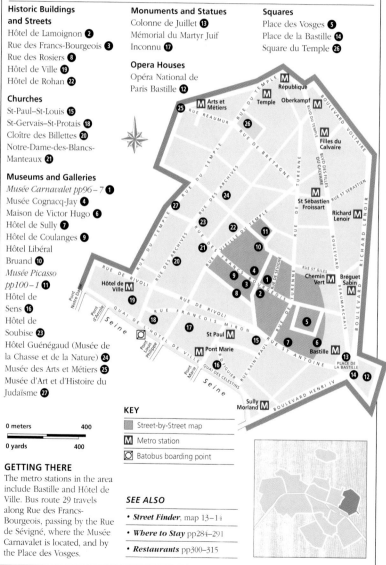

KEY
- Street-by-Street map
- **M** Metro station
- Batobus boarding point

0 meters 400
0 yards 400

GETTING THERE
The metro stations in the area include Bastille and Hôtel de Ville. Bus route 29 travels along Rue des Francs-Bourgeois, passing by the Rue de Sévigné, where the Musée Carnavalet is located, and by the Place des Vosges.

SEE ALSO
- *Street Finder*, map 13–14
- *Where to Stay* pp284–291
- *Restaurants* pp300–315

◁ **Lunchtime at a Marais park café**

Street by Street: The Marais

Once an area of marshland as its name suggests (*marais* means swamp), the Marais grew steadily in importance from the 14th century by virtue of its proximity to the Louvre, the preferred residence of Charles V. Its heyday was in the 17th century, when it became the fashionable area for the monied classes. They built many grand and sumptuous mansions (*hôtels*) that still dot the Marais today. Many of these *hôtels* have recently been restored and turned into museums. Once again fashionable with the monied classes, designer boutiques, trendy restaurants and cafés now line the streets.

To the Pompidou Centre

Rue des Francs-Bourgeois
This ancient street is lined with important museums ❸

Hôtel Libéral Bruand
Named after the architect who built it for his own use, this mansion is now used for temporary art exhibitions ❿

Rue des Rosiers
The smell of hot pastrami and borscht wafts from restaurants and shops in the heart of the Jewish area ❽

Musée Cognacq-Jay
An exquisite collection of 18th-century paintings and furniture is shown in perfect period setting ❹

STAR SIGHTS

★ Musée Picasso

★ Musée Carnavalet

★ Place des Vosges

KEY

– – – Suggested route

0 meters	100
0 yards	100

Hôtel de Lamoignon
Behind the ornate doorway of this fine mansion is Paris's historical library ❷

★ **Musée Picasso**
The palatial home of a 17th-century salt-tax collector is the setting for the largest collection of Picassos in the world, the result of a family bequest to the state **⑪**

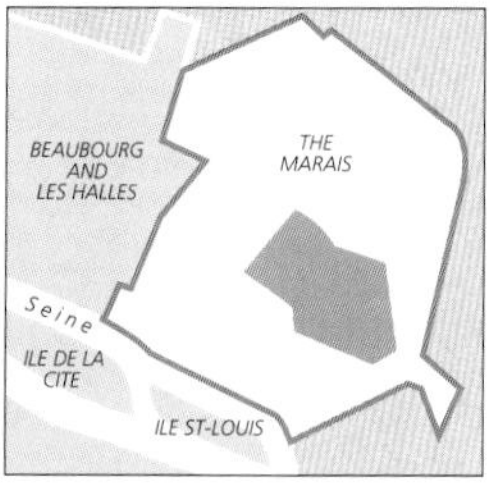

LOCATOR MAP
See Central Paris Map pp14–15

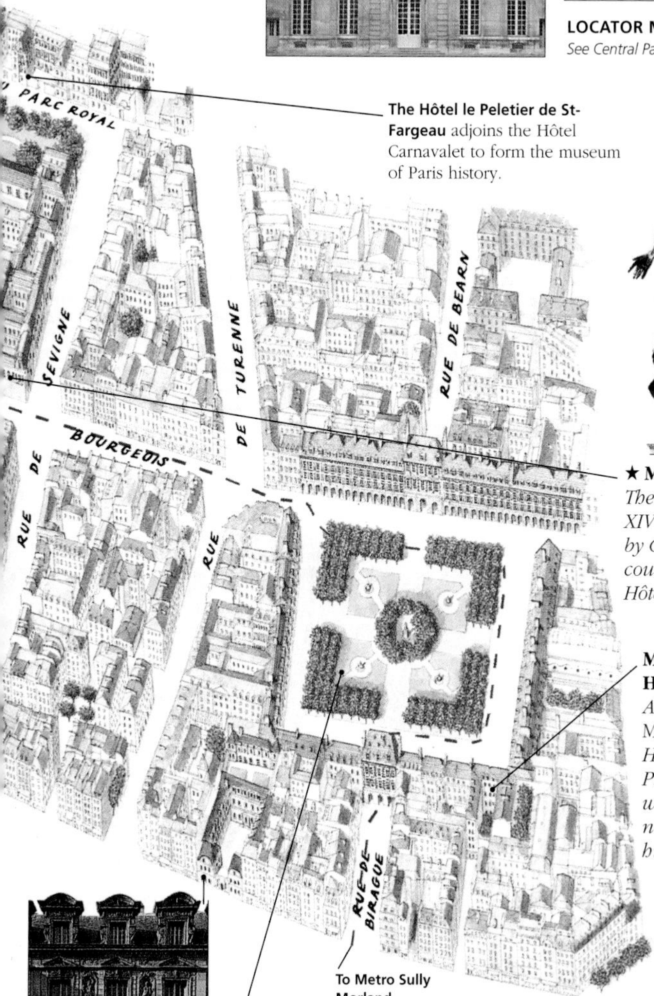

BEAUBOURG AND LES HALLES

THE MARAIS

Seine

ILE DE LA CITE

ILE ST-LOUIS

The Hôtel le Peletier de St-Fargeau adjoins the Hôtel Carnavalet to form the museum of Paris history.

PARC ROYAL

RUE DE SEVIGNE

DE TURENNE

RUE DE BEARN

RUE DE BOURGEOIS

RUE DE

RUE DE BIRAGUE

★ **Musée Carnavalet**
The statue of Louis XIV in Roman dress by Coysevox is in the courtyard of the Hôtel Carnavalet **❶**

Maison de Victor Hugo
Author of Les Misérables, *Victor Hugo lived at No. 6 Place des Vosges, where his house is now a museum of his life and work* **❻**

To Metro Sully Morland

★ **Place des Vosges**
Once the site of jousting and tournaments, the historic Place des Vosges, in the very heart of the Marais, is a square of perfect symmetry **❺**

Hôtel de Sully
This Renaissance hôtel was built for a notorious gambler **❼**

Musée Carnavalet ❶

See pp96–7.

Hôtel de Lamoignon ❷

24 Rue Pavée 75004. **Map** 14 D3.
Tel 01 44 59 29 40. M *St-Paul.*
◻ *1–6pm Mon–Sat.* ◻ *public hols & Aug 1–15.* ◻

The imposing Hôtel de Lamoignon is home to the historical library of the city of Paris. This mansion was built in 1585 for Diane de France, also known as the Duchesse d'Angoulême, daughter of Henri II. The building is noted for six high Corinthian pilasters topped by a triangular pediment and flourishes of dogs' heads, bows, arrows and quivers – recalling Diane's passion for hunting. The collection includes documents from the French Revolution and 80,000 prints covering the history of Paris.

Rue des Francs-Bourgeois ❸

75003, 75004. **Map** 14 D3.
M *Rambuteau, Chemin-Vert.*

This street is an important thoroughfare in the heart of the Marais, linking the Rue des Archives and the Place

Courtyard of the Musée Carnavalet

des Vosges, with the imposing Hôtel de Soubise at one end and the Musée Carnavalet at the other. The street got its name from the *francs* (free from taxes) – almshouses built for the poor in 1334 at Nos. 34 and 36. These were later closed because of illegal financial activities, although the state kept its pawnshop nearby, still there today.

Musée Cognacq-Jay ❹

Hôtel Donon, 8 Rue Elzévir 75004.
Map 14 D3. **Tel** 01 40 27 07 21.
M *St-Paul.* ◻ *10am–6pm Tue–Sun.*
◻ *public hols.* 🖼 🖼 *pre-book.* ◻
www.paris.fr/musees

This fine, small collection of French 18th-century works of art and furniture was formed by Ernest Cognacq and his wife, Louise Jay, founder of the Art Deco La Samaritaine, Paris's largest department store *(see p115)*. The private collection was bequeathed to the city and is now housed in the heart of the Marais at the Hôtel Donon – an elegant building dating from 1575 with an 18th-century extension and facade.

Place des Vosges ❺

75003, 75004. **Map** 14 D3.
M *Bastille, St-Paul.*

This square is considered among the most beautiful in the world by Parisians and visitors alike *(see pp24–5)*. Its impressive symmetry – 36 houses, nine on each side, of brick and stone, with deep slate roofs and dormer windows over arcades – is still intact after 400 years. It has been the scene of many historic events over the centuries. A three-day tournament was held here to celebrate the marriage of Louis XIII to Anne of Austria in 1615. The famous literary hostess, Madame de Sévigné, was born here in 1626; Cardinal Richelieu, pillar of the monarchy, stayed here in 1615; and Victor Hugo, the writer, lived here for 16 years.

A 19th-century engraving of the Place des Vosges

Maison de Victor Hugo ❻

6 Pl des Vosges 75004. **Map** 14 D3.
Tel 01 42 72 10 16. Ⓜ Bastille.
◯ 10am–5:40pm Tue–Sun.
● public hols. 🎫 📷 **Library**.
www.paris.fr/musees

The French poet, dramatist and novelist lived on the second floor of the former Hôtel Rohan-Guéménée, the largest house on the square, from 1832 to 1848. It was here that he wrote most of *Les Misérables* and completed many other famous works. On display are some reconstructions of the rooms in which he lived, pen-and-ink drawings, books and mementos from the crucially important periods in his life, from his childhood to his exile between 1852 and 1870.

Marble bust of Victor Hugo by Auguste Rodin

Hôtel de Sully ❼

62 Rue St-Antoine 75004. **Map** 14 D4. **Tel** 01 44 61 20 00. Ⓜ St-Paul. ◯ (courtyard only) 10am–6pm Tue–Sun. ● public hols. 🎫

This fine 17th-century mansion on one of Paris's oldest streets has been extensively restored, using old engravings and drawings as reference. It was built in 1624 for a notorious gambler, Petit Thomas, who lost his whole fortune in one night. The Duc de Sully, Henri IV's chief minister, purchased the house in 1634 and added some of the interior decoration as well as the Petit Sully orangery in the gardens. Today it is the head office of the Centre des Monuments Nationaux. The exterior of the *hôtel* has a late-Renaissance facade. Inside there is a courtyard with carved pediments, dormer windows and statues of the four seasons and sphinxes.

Late-Renaissance facade of the Hôtel de Sully

Rue des Rosiers ❽

75004. **Map** 13 C3. Ⓜ St-Paul.

The Jewish quarter in and around this street is one of the most colorful areas of Paris. The street's name refers to the rosebushes within the old city wall. Jews first settled here in the 13th century, with a second wave in the 19th century from Russia, Poland and central Europe. Sephardic Jews arrived from Algeria, Tunisia, Morocco and Egypt in the 1950s and 1960s. Some 165 students were rounded up and deported from the old Jewish Boys' school nearby at 10 rue de Hospitalières-St-Gervais. *N'Oubliez pas* (Lest we forget) is engraved on the wall. Today this area contains synagogues, bakeries and kosher restaurants, the most famous being Jo Goldenberg's *(see p333).*

Orthodox Jews in the Marais

Hôtel de Coulanges ❾

35 rue des Francs Bourgeois, 75004. **Map** 13 C3. **Tel** 01 44 61 85 85. Ⓜ St-Paul. ◯ 8:30am–6:30pm Mon–Fri. ● public hols. **www**.paris-europe.com

This hôtel is a magnificent example of the architecture of the early 18th century. The right wing of the building, separating the courtyard from the garden, dates from the early 17th century. The hôtel was given in 1640 to Phillipe II de Coulanges, the King's counselor. Renamed the "Petit hôtel Le Tellier" in 1662 by its new owner Le Tellier, this is where the children of Louis XIV and Madame de Montespan were raised in secrecy. It is home to the Maison de L'Europe, with exhibitions on themes relating to Europe.

Musée Carnavalet ❶

Carnavalet entrance

Devoted to the history of Paris, this huge museum occupies two adjoining mansions, with entire rooms decorated with paneling, furniture and *objets d'art*; many works of art such as paintings and sculptures of prominent personalities; and engravings showing Paris being built. The main building is the Hôtel Carnavalet, built as a town house in 1548 and transformed in the mid-17th century by François Mansart. The neighboring 17th-century mansion, Hôtel Le Peletier, features superb early 20th-century interiors, and the newly restored Orangery is devoted to prehistory and Gallo-Roman Paris.

Marie Antionette in Mourning *(1793) Alexandre Kucharski painted her at the Temple prison after the execution of Louis XVI.*

Memorabilia in this room is dedicated to 18th-century philosophers, in particular Jean-Jacques Rousseau and Voltaire.

★ Charles Le Brun Ceiling
Magnificent works by the 17th-century artist decorate the former study and great hall from the Hôtel de la Rivière.

★ Mme de Sévigné's Gallery
The gallery includes this portrait of Mme de Sévigné, the celebrated letter-writer, whose beloved home this was for the 20 years up to her death.

STAR EXHIBITS

- ★ Mme de Sévigné's Gallery
- ★ Charles Le Brun Ceiling
- ★ Hôtel d'Uzès Reception Room
- ★ Ballroom of the Hôtel de Wendel

★ Hotel d'Uzès Reception Room
The room was created in 1761 by Claude Nicolas Ledoux. The gold-and-white paneling is from a Rue Montmartre mansion.

Entran the mus

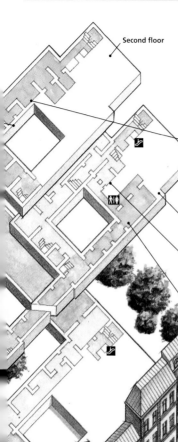

Second floor

First floor

Hôtel Le Peletier

Convention Room
Georges Danton's portrait is among the memorabilia of the Revolution.

VISITORS' CHECKLIST

23 Rue de Sévigné 75003.
Map 14 D3. *Tel* 01 44 59 58 58.
Ⓜ *St-Paul.* 🚌 *29, 69, 76, 96 to St-Paul, Pl des Vosges.* 🅿 *Hôtel de Ville, Rue St-Antoine.*
🕐 *10am–6pm Tue–Sun (rooms open in rotation; phone to check).*
🔵 *public hols.* ♿ *free Sun am.*
📷 🎥 *phone for times.* 🚻
www.carnavalet.paris.fr

Fouquet Jewelry Boutique *(1900)*
The Art Nouveau decor of this shop from Rue Royale is by A Moucha.

★ **Ballroom of the Hôtel de Wendel**
The early 20th-century ballroom interior has been reconstructed. This immense mural depicts the retinue of the Queen of Sheba and is by the Catalan designer and painter José María Sert y Badia.

Louis XV Room
This delightful room contains art from the Bouvier collection and paneling from the Hôtel de Broglie.

KEY TO FLOOR PLAN

- 🟦 Prehistory to Gallo-Roman
- ☐ Medieval Paris
- ☐ Renaissance Paris
- ☐ 17th-Century Paris
- ☐ Louis XV's Paris
- ☐ Louis XVI's Paris
- 🟦 Revolutionary Paris
- ☐ 19th Century
- ☐ 20th Century
- ☐ Temporary exhibitions
- ☐ Non-exhibition space

GALLERY GUIDE

The collection is mainly arranged chronologically. It covers the history of Paris up to 1789. The Renaissance is on the ground floor, and the exhibits covering the 17th century to the Revolution are on the first floor. In the Hôtel le Peletier the ground floor covers the First–Second Empires, with the new Prehistory–Gallo-Roman departments in the Orangery; from the Second Empire to the present day is on the first floor, and the second floor is devoted to the Revolution.

Hôtel Libéral Bruand ⑩

1 Rue de la Perle 75003. **Map** 14 D3.
Tel 01 42 77 79 62. **M** St-Paul,
Chemin-Vert. **Museum** ☐ for
temporary exhibitions; phone to
check. ● Aug & public hols. 📷

This small private house, built
by the architect Libéral
Bruand for himself in 1685,
is far removed, with its
elegant Italianate touches,
from his most famous work,
the gilded Hôtel des Invalides
(see p187).
    The building is usually
closed to the public but also
contains a museum, which
hosts temporary art exhibitions from time to time.

Musée Picasso ⑪

See pp100–1.

Opéra National de Paris Bastille ⑫

120 Rue de Lyon 75012. **Map** 14 E4.
Tel 01 40 01 17 89. 📠 08 92 89
90 90. **M** Bastille. ☐ phone for
details. ● certain public hols.
📷 ♿ 📷 compulsory.
Entertainment pp332–5.
www.opera-de-paris.fr

The controversial "people's
opera" was officially opened
on July 14, 1989, to coincide
with the bicentennial

The "genius of liberty" on top of
the Colonne de Juillet

celebrations of the fall of the
Bastille. Carlos Ott's imposing
building is a notable break
with 19th-century opera-
house design, epitomized by
Garnier's opulent Opéra in
the heart of the city (see
pp214–15). It is a huge,
modern, curved, glass
building. The main auditorium
seats an audience of 2,700;
its design is functional and
modern with black
upholstered seats contrasting
with the granite of the walls
and the impressive glass
ceiling. With its five movable
stages, this opera house is
certainly a masterpiece of
technological wizardry.

Colonne de Juillet ⑬

Pl de la Bastille 75004. **Map** 14 E4.
M Bastille. ● to the public.

Topped by the statue of the
"genius of liberty", this
column of hollow bronze
reaches 170 ft (51.5 m) into
the sky. It is a memorial to
those who died in the street
battles of July 1830 that led
to the overthrow of the
monarch (see pp32–33). The
crypt contains the remains of
504 victims of the violent
fighting and others who died
in the 1848 revolution.

Place de la Bastille ⑭

75004. **Map** 14 E4. **M** Bastille.

Nothing is now left of the
prison stormed by the
revolutionary mob on July 14,
1789 (see pp30–31) – an event
celebrated annually by the
French at home and abroad –
although the stones were used
for the Pont de la Concorde.
A line of paving stones from
Nos. 5 to 49 Blvd Henri IV
traces the former towers and
fortifications. Until recently,
the large, traffic-clogged square
which marks the site was the
border between central Paris
and the eastern working-class
areas (faubourgs). Gentrificat-
ion, however, is well underway, with a new marina, the
Port de Plaisance de l'Arsenal,
and attractive cafés and shops.

The glass facade of the
Bastille Opéra

St-Paul–St-Louis ⑮

99 Rue St-Antoine 75004. **Map** 14
D4. **Tel** 01 42 72 30 32. Ⓜ St-Paul.
◯ 8am–8pm daily. **Concerts**

A Jesuit church, St-Paul–St-Louis was an important symbol of the influence which the Jesuits held from 1627, when Louis XIII laid the first stone, to 1762 when they were expelled from France. The Gesù church in Rome served as the model for the nave, while the 180-ft high (60-m) dome was the forerunner of those of the Invalides and the Sorbonne. Most of the church's treasures were removed during periods of turmoil, but Delacroix's masterpiece, *Christ in the Garden of Olives,* can still be seen. The church stands on one of the main streets of the Marais, but can also be approached by the ancient Passage St-Paul.

Christ in the Garden of Olives by Delacroix in St-Paul–St-Louis

Hôtel de Sens ⑯

1 Rue du Figuier 75004. **Map** 13 C4.
Tel 01 42 78 14 60. Ⓜ Pont-Marie.
◯ 1.30pm–8.15pm Tue–Fri; 10am–8.15pm Sat. ● public hols. 🖼 for exhibitions. 🚫 🎥 by appointment only.

This is one of the few medieval buildings left in Paris. It now houses the Forney fine arts library. In the 16th century, at the time of the Catholic League, it was turned into a fortified mansion and occupied by the Bourbons, the Guises and Cardinal de Pellevé, whose religious fervor led him

to die of rage in 1594 on hearing that the Protestant Henri IV had entered Paris. Marguerite de Valois, lodged here by her ex-husband, Henri IV, led a life of breathtaking debauchery and scandal. This culminated in the beheading of an ex-lover, who had dared to assassinate her current favorite.

The memorial to the unknown Jewish martyr, dedicated in 1956

Mémorial du Martyr Juif Inconnu ⑰

17 Rue Geoffroy-l'Asnier 75004. 75004. **Map** 13 C4. **Tel** 01 42 77 44 72. Ⓜ Pont-Marie. ◯ 10am–6pm Sun–Fri (10am–10pm Thu). 🖼 ♿ 🅿 **www.**memorial-cdjc.org

The eternal flame burning in the crypt here is the simple memorial to the unknown Jewish martyr of the Holocaust. Its striking feature is a large cylinder that bears the names of the concentration camps where Jewish victims of the Holocaust died. In 2005 a stone wall, engraved with the names of 76,000 Jews – 11,000 of them children – who were deported from France to the Nazi death camps, was also erected here.

St-Gervais–St-Protais ⑱

Pl St-Gervais 75004. **Map** 13 B3.
Tel 01 48 87 32 02. Ⓜ Hôtel de Ville. ◯ 5:30am–10pm daily.

Named after Gervase and Protase, two Roman soldiers who were martyred by Nero, this remarkable church dates from the 6th century. It has the oldest Classical facade in Paris, which is formed of a three-tiered arrangement of columns: Doric, Ionic and Corinthian. Behind its facade lies a beautiful Gothic church renowned for its association with religious music. It was for the church's fine organ that François Couperin (1668–1733) composed his two masses. The church currently has a Roman Catholic monastic community whose liturgy attracts people from all over the world.

The facade of St-Gervais–St-Protais with its Classical columns

The Hôtel de Sens, now home to a fine arts library

Musée Picasso ⑪

On the death of the Spanish-born artist Pablo Picasso (1881–1973), who lived most of his life in France, the French state inherited many of his works in lieu of death duties. It used them to establish the Musée Picasso, which opened in 1985. The museum is housed in a large 17th-century mansion, the Hôtel Salé, in the Marais. The original character of the Hôtel, which was built in 1656 for Aubert de Fontenay, a salt-tax collector (*salé* means "salty"), has been preserved. The breadth of the collection reflects both the full extent of Picasso's artistic development, including his Blue, Pink and Cubist periods, and his use of so many different materials.

★ Self-Portrait
Poverty, loneliness and the onset of winter all made the end of 1901, when this picture was painted, a particularly difficult time for Picasso.

Violin and Sheet Music
This collage (1912) is from the artist's Synthetic Cubist period.

★ The Two Brothers
During the summer of 1906 Picasso returned to Catalonia in Spain, where he painted this picture.

★ The Kiss (1969)
Picasso married Jacqueline Roque in 1961, and at around the same time he returned to the familiar themes of the couple and of the artist and model.

GALLERY GUIDE

The collection is mainly presented in chronological order, starting on the first floor with the Blue and Pink periods, Cubist and Neo-classical works. Exhibitions change regularly – not all paintings are on show at any one time. On the ground floor there is a sculpture garden and works from the late 1920s to late 1930s, and from the mid-1950s to 1973.

Basement

KEY TO FLOORPLAN

☐ Paintings
☐ Illustrations
☐ Sculpture garden
☐ Ceramics
☐ Non-exhibition space

Woman with a Mantilla (1949)
Picasso extended his range when he began working in ceramics in 1948.

Painter with Palette and Easel (1928)
This Post-Cubist portrait in oils was painted at a time when Picasso's work was verging on Surrealism.

VISITORS' CHECKLIST

Hôtel Salé, 5 Rue de Thorigny.
Map 14 D2. 01 42 71 25 21.
St-Sébastien, St-Paul.
29, 96, 75, 86 to St-Paul,
Bastille, Pl des Vosges.
Châtelet-Les-Halles.
Rue St-Antoine, Bastille.
Apr–Sep: 9:30am–6pm Wed–
Mon; Oct–Mar: 9:30am–5:30pm
Wed–Mon. Dec 25, Jan 1.
groups by
appointment only.
www.musee-picasso.fr

First floor

★ **Two Women Running on the Beach** (1922)
In 1924 this was used for the stage curtain design for Diaghilev's ballet The Blue Train. It proved to be his last major design work for any theatre.

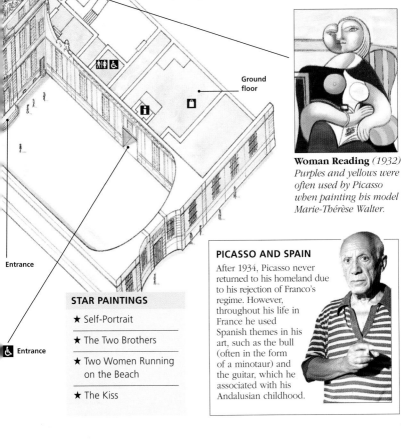

Ground floor

Woman Reading (1932)
Purples and yellows were often used by Picasso when painting his model Marie-Thérèse Walter.

Entrance

Entrance

STAR PAINTINGS

★ Self-Portrait

★ The Two Brothers

★ Two Women Running on the Beach

★ The Kiss

PICASSO AND SPAIN

After 1934, Picasso never returned to his homeland due to his rejection of Franco's regime. However, throughout his life in France he used Spanish themes in his art, such as the bull (often in the form of a minotaur) and the guitar, which he associated with his Andalusian childhood.

The town hall (Hôtel de Ville), overlooking a delightful square

Hôtel de Ville 🔟

Pl de l'Hôtel de Ville 75004. **Map** 13 B3. **Tel** 01 42 76 50 49. M Hôtel-de-Ville. ☐ groups: by arrangement. ● public hols, official functions. 🔣 🔲

Home of the city council, the town hall is a 19th-century reconstruction of the 17th-century town hall that was burned down in 1871. It is highly ornate, with elaborate stonework, turrets and statues overlooking a pedestrianized square which is a delight to stroll in, especially at night when the fountains are illuminated.

The square was once the main site for hangings, burnings and other executions. It was here that Ravaillac, Henri IV's assassin, was quartered alive, his body ripped to pieces by four strong horses.

Inside the Hôtel de Ville, a notable feature is the long Salles des Fêtes (ballroom), with adjoining salons devoted to science, literature and the arts. The impressive staircase, the decorated coffered ceilings with their chandeliers and the numerous statues and caryatids all add to the air of ceremony and pomp – a fitting power base for mayors of the city to hold elaborate banquets and receptions for foreign dignitaries in the building's grand halls. It is also the official residence of the mayor of Paris, though the current mayor, Bertrand Delanoë, lives elsewhere in the Marais.

Cloître des Billettes 🔟

26 Rue des Archives 75004. **Map** 13 B3. **Tel** 01 42 72 38 79. M Hôtel-de-Ville. ☐ **Cloister** noon–7pm daily; **church** 6:30–8pm Thu, 9:30am–4pm Sun.

This is the only remaining medieval cloister in Paris. It was built in 1427 for the Brothers of Charity, or *Billettes*, and three of its four original galleries are still standing. The adjoining church is a simple Classical building which replaced the monastic original in 1756.

The oldest cloister in Paris

Notre-Dame-des-Blancs-Manteaux 🔟

12 Rue des Blancs-Manteaux 75004. **Map** 13 C3. **Tel** 01 42 72 09 37. M Rambuteau. ☐ 10am–noon, 3pm–7pm daily. **Concerts**.

This church, built in 1685, takes its name from the white habits worn by the Augustinian friars who founded a convent on the site in 1258. It has a magnificent 18th-century Rococo Flemish pulpit, and its famous organ is best appreciated at one of its regular concerts of religious music.

Hôtel de Rohan 🔟

87 Rue Vieille-du-Temple 75003. **Map** 13 C2. **Tel** 01 40 27 60 09. M Rambuteau. ☐ for temporary exhibitions only.

Although not resembling it in appearance, the Hôtel de Rohan forms a pair with the Hôtel de Soubise. It was built by the same architect, Delamair, for Armand de Rohan-Soubise, a cardinal and bishop of Strasbourg. The *hôtel* has been home to a part of the national archives since 1927. In the courtyard over the doorway of the stables is the 18th-century sculpture *Horses of Apollo* by Robert Le Lorrain.

Horses of Apollo by Le Lorrain

Hôtel de Soubise ㉓

60 Rue des Francs-Bourgeois 75003.
Map 13 C2. **Tel** 01 40 27 60 96.
M Rambuteau. ☐ accessible
for research only; phone for
appointment.

The Hôtel de Soubise

This imposing mansion, built
from 1705 to 1709 for the
Princesse de Rohan, is one of
two main buildings housing
the national archives. (The
other is the Hôtel de Rohan.)
The Hôtel de Soubise displays
a majestic courtyard and a
magnificent interior decoration dating from 1735 to 1740
by some of the most gifted
painters of the day: Carl Van
Loo, Jean Restout, Natoire
and François Boucher.

Natoire's *rocaille* work on
the Princess's bedroom, the
Oval Salon, forms part of the
museum of French history –
which is unfortunately only
accessible to academics and
researchers. Other exhibits
include Napoleon's will, in
which he asks for his remains
to be returned to France.

Hôtel Guénégaud ㉔

60 Rue des Archives 75003.
Map 13 C2. **Tel** 01 53 01 92 40.
M Hôtel de Ville. ☐ 11am–6pm
Tue–Sun. ☐ public hols.
☒ ☐ ☐

The celebrated architect
François Mansart built this
superb mansion in the mid-
17th century for Henri de
Guénégaud des Brosses, who
was secretary of state and
Keeper of the Seals. One wing

now contains the Musée de la
Chasse et de la Nature
(Hunting Museum) inaugurated by André Malraux in
1967. The exhibits include a
fine collection of hunting
weapons from the 16th to the
19th centuries, many from
Germany and central Europe.
There are also animal trophies
from around the world, along
with drawings and paintings
by Oudry, Rubens, Rembrandt,
Monet and other artists.

Musée des Arts et Métiers ㉕

60 Rue Réaumur 75003. **Map** 13 B1-
C1. **Tel** 01 40 27 22 20. M Arts et
Métiers. ☐ 10am–6pm Tue–Sun
(9:30pm Thu). ☐ public hols. ☒ ☒
☒ ☐ ☐ **www.cnam.fr/museum**

Housed within the old
Abbey of Saint-Martin-des-
Champs, the arts and crafts
museum was founded in 1794
and closed down two
centuries later for interior
restructuring and renovation.
It reopened in 2000 as a high-
quality museum of science
and industry displaying 5,000
items. (It has 75,000 more items
in store available to academics
and researchers.) The theme
is man's ingenuity and the
world of invention and
manufacturing, covering such
topics as textiles, photography
and machines. Among the most
entertaining displays are ones
of musical clocks, mechanical
music instruments and
automata (mechanical figures),
one of which, the "Joueuse de
Tympanon", is said to
represent Marie-Antoinette.

Square du Temple ㉖

75003. **Map** 13 C1. M Temple.

A quiet and pleasant square
today, this was once a
fortified center of the medieval
Knights Templars. A state within a state, the area contained a
palace, a church and shops
behind high walls and a drawbridge, making it a haven for
those who were seeking to
escape from royal jurisdiction.
Louis XVI and Marie-Antoinette
were held here after their
arrest in 1792 (see pp30–31).
The king left from here for his
execution on the guillotine.

Musée d'Art et d'Histoire du Judaïsme ㉗

Hôtel de St-Aignan, 71 rue du Temple
75003. **Map** 13 B2. **Tel** 01 53 01 86
60. M Rambuteau. ☐ 11am–6pm
Mon–Fri, 10am–6pm Sun.
☐ Jewish hols. ☒ ☒ ☒ ☐ ☐
www.mah.org

Housed in an elegant Marais
mansion, the museum unites
collections formerly scattered
around the city, and commemorates the culture of French
Jewry from medieval times to
the present. There has been a
sizable Jewish community in
France since Roman times, and
some of the world's greatest
Jewish scholars were French.
Much exquisite craftsmanship
is displayed, with elaborate
silverware, Torah covers,
items of fine Judaica and religious objects. There are also
historical documents, photographs, paintings and cartoons.

"Being a Jew in Paris in 1939", a display in the Jewish museum

BEAUBOURG AND LES HALLES

This Right Bank area is dominated by the modernistic Forum des Halles and the Pompidou Centre. These two spectacular undertakings are thriving public areas of contact for shoppers, art lovers, students and tourists. Literally millions flow between the two squares. The Halles is for street fashion, with most of the shops underground, and the clientele strolling under the concrete and glass bubbles is young. The surrounding streets, colored by popular cheap shops and bars, are undergoing refurbishment

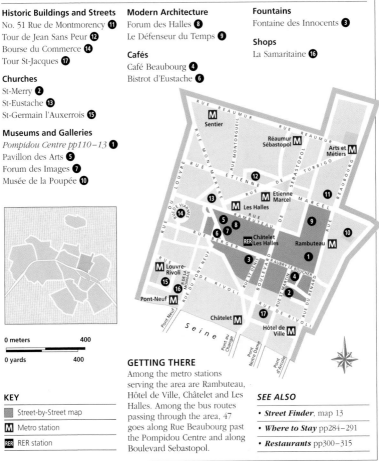

Fountain in the Place Igor Stravinsky

to combat their seedy image, and there are still enough specialty food shops, butchers and small markets to recall what Les Halles must have been like in its prime as the city's thriving market. All roads around Les Halles lead to the Beaubourg area and the Pompidou Centre, an avant-garde assembly of vast pipes, ducts and cables, renovated in the 1990s to cope with its 20,000 daily visitors. The adjoining streets, such as Rue St-Martin and Rue Beaubourg, house small contemporary art galleries in crooked, gabled buildings.

SIGHTS AT A GLANCE

Historic Buildings and Streets
No. 51 Rue de Montmorency ⑪
Tour de Jean Sans Peur ⑫
Bourse du Commerce ⑭
Tour St-Jacques ⑰

Churches
St-Merry ②
St-Eustache ⑬
St-Germain l'Auxerrois ⑮

Museums and Galleries
Pompidou Centre pp110–13 ①
Pavillon des Arts ⑤
Forum des Images ⑦
Musée de la Poupée ⑩

Modern Architecture
Forum des Halles ⑧
Le Défenseur du Temps ⑨

Cafés
Café Beaubourg ④
Bistrot d'Eustache ⑥

Fountains
Fontaine des Innocents ③

Shops
La Samaritaine ⑯

KEY

▢	Street-by-Street map
Ⓜ	Metro station
RER	RER station

GETTING THERE
Among the metro stations serving the area are Rambuteau, Hôtel de Ville, Châtelet and Les Halles. Among the bus routes passing through the area, 47 goes along Rue Beaubourg past the Pompidou Centre and along Boulevard Sebastopol.

SEE ALSO
• *Street Finder*, map 13
• *Where to Stay* pp284–291
• *Restaurants* pp300–315

◁ **St-Eustache and sculptured head,** *l'Ecoute,* **by Henri de Miller**

0 meters   400

0 yards   400

Street-by-Street: Beaubourg and Les Halles

When Emile Zola described Les Halles as the "belly of Paris" he was referring to the meat, vegetable and fruit market that had thrived here since 1183. Traffic congestion in the 1960s forced the market to move to the suburbs and Baltard's giant umbrella-like market pavilions were pulled down, despite howls of protest, and replaced by a shopping and leisure complex, the Forum. The conversion worked: today, Les Halles and the Pompidou Centre, which lies in the Beaubourg quarter and has been Paris's main tourist attraction ever since it opened in 1977, draw the most mixed crowds in Paris.

Pavillon des Arts
This is one of the mushroom-shaped pavilions overlooking the Forum. It houses changing exhibitions **5**

Bistrot d'Eustache
This lively café is a favorite venue for enthusiasts of both classic and modern jazz **6**

★ Forum des Halles
Beneath the shops, restaurants, theaters and swimming pool is the world's busiest subway station **8**

Forum des Images
Visitors watch videos in the Salle de Consultation **7**

To Metro Châtelet

Rue de la Ferronnerie
was where, in 1610, the religious fanatic Ravaillac assassinated Henri IV while his carriage was caught in traffic.

★ Fontaine des Innocents
This is the last Renaissance fountain left in Paris. It was designed by the sculptor and architect Jean Goujon **3**

IRCAM is an underground research center dedicated to pioneering new ways of making music.

STAR SIGHTS

* ★ Pompidou Centre
* ★ Le Défenseur du Temps
* ★ Fontaine des Innocents
* ★ Forum des Halles

KEY

— — — Suggested route

★ Le Défenseur du Temps
The passage of time is defended from attack by dragons on this mechanized clock **9**

The Rue Quincampoix is lined by 18th-century *hôtels* that have been beautifully restored and totally refurbished.

LOCATOR MAP
See Central Paris Map pp14–15

★ Pompidou Centre
Paris's museum of modern art is housed here, along with extensive art libraries and an industrial design center **1**

Metro Rambuteau

Place Igor Stravinsky is dominated by the first contemporary Parisian fountain, created by Niki de Saint Phalle and Jean Tinguely.

St-Merry
The pulpit of this beautiful church was designed by the Stodtz brothers in the mid-18th century and is supported by a pair of carved palm trees, one on each side **2**

0 meters   100
0 yards   100

Pompidou Centre ●

See pp110–13.

A nativity scene from the stained-glass windows in St-Merry

St-Merry ●

76 Rue de la Verrerie 75004. **Map 13 B3.** ***Tel*** *01 42 71 93 93.* Ⓜ *Hôtel-de-Ville.* ◯ *3–7pm daily.* ◩ *1st & 3rd Sun, pm.* **Concerts***.*

The site of this church dates back to the 7th century. St Médéric, the abbot of St-Martin d'Autun, was buried here at the beginning of the 8th century. The saint's name, which was eventually corrupted to Merry, was given to a chapel built nearby. The building of the church – in the Flamboyant Gothic style – was not completed until 1552. The west front is particularly rich in decoration, and the northwest turret contains the oldest bell in Paris, dating from 1331. It was the wealthy parish church of the Lombard moneylenders, who gave their name to the nearby Rue des Lombards.

Fontaine des Innocents ●

Sq des Innocents 75001. **Map 13 A2.** Ⓜ *Les Halles.* ⒭ *Châtelet-Les-Halles.*

This carefully restored Renaissance fountain stands in the Square des Innocents, the area's main crossroads.

Erected in 1549 on the Rue St-Denis, it was moved to its present location in the 18th century, when the square was constructed on the site of a former graveyard. Popular with the city's youth as a meeting place, the fountain is one of the landmarks of Les Halles.

Decoration on the Fontaine des Innocents

Café Beaubourg ●

100 Rue St-Martin, 75004. **Map 13 B2.** ***Tel*** *01 48 87 63 96.* Ⓜ *Les Halles.* ⒭ *Châtelet-Les-Halles.* ◯ *8am–1am Mon–Wed; 8am–2am Thu–Sat.*

Interior of the Café Beaubourg

Opened by Gilbert Costes in 1987, this stylish café was designed and decorated by one of France's star architects, Christian de Portzamparc, who created the impressive Cité de la Musique in the Parc de la Villette *(see p234).* Its vast terrace is lined with comfortable red and black wicker chairs. The spacious and coolly elegant interior is decorated with rows of books which soften its severely Art Deco ambience. The café is a favorite meeting point for art dealers from the surrounding galleries and Pompidou Centre staff. It serves light meals and brunch. If the crush gets too much around Les Halles, the Café Beaubourg is the ideal place to soothe the nerves.

Pavillon des Arts ●

101 Rue Rambuteau, Terrasse Lautréamont 75001. **Map 13 A2.** ***Tel*** *01 42 33 82 50.* Ⓜ *Les Halles.* ⒭ *Châtelet-Les-Halles.* ◯ *11:30am–6:30pm Tue–Sun.* ◉ *public hols.* ◪ ◪ ◪ *www.paris.fr/musees*

In creating this exhibition center in 1983, Paris opened up the newly revitalized quarter of Les Halles to the arts. Housed in the futuristic glass and steel of the Baltard Pavilion, its program of changing exhibitions often focuses on unusual or rarely seen subjects and works, drawn together from French and foreign museums. For example, past exhibitions have included Russian history as portrayed by Soviet photographers, Surrealists recalled through their collections of Indian dolls, or the Seine through the eyes of Turner.

Exterior of the Pavillon des Arts

Bistrot d'Eustache ❻

37 Rue Berger, 75001. **Map** 13 A2.
Tel *01 40 26 23 20.* Ⓜ *Les Halles.*
ℝℰℝ *Châtelet-Les-Halles.* ◯
noon–2am daily. **Live jazz, flamenco/
gypsy:** *phone for details.*

This compact café, decorated
with old wood paneling and
attractive mirrors, retains a
feeling of Paris as it was in
the 1930s and 1940s – a period
when jazz venues flourished
throughout the city. It is
always packed for live music
shows, when musicians
squeeze into a handkerchief-
sized space to play racy
guitar-led gypsy jazz. The
café serves a variety of traditional French food, at all
times throughout the day
and at very reasonable prices.

Terrace of the Bistrot d'Eustache

Forum des Images ❼

2 Grande Galerie, Forum des Halles
75001. **Map** 13 A2. **Tel** *01 44 76
62 00.* Ⓜ *Les Halles.* ℝℰℝ *Châtelet-
Les-Halles.* ◯ *1–9pm Tue–Sun.*
⬤ *public hols.* ♿ ⬛
www.forumdesimages.net

At the forum you can choose
from thousands of movies,
television and amateur films.
All feature the city of Paris.
There is footage on the
history of Paris since 1895
including a remarkable news-
reel of General de Gaulle
avoiding sniper fire during the
Liberation of Paris in 1944.
There are countless movies
such as Truffaut's *Baisers Volés*.
Admission includes two hours'
viewing of your chosen movie

in the Salle de Consultation
(see p106) and entry to two
auditoriums showing movies
linked by a theme.

François Truffaut's *Baisers Volés*

Forum des Halles ❽

75001. **Map** 13 A2. Ⓜ *Les Halles.*
ℝℰℝ *Châtelet-Les-Halles.*

The present Forum des
Halles, known simply as Les
Halles, was built in 1979,
amid much controversy, on
the site of the famous old
fruit and vegetable market.
The present complex occupies
7 ha (750,000 sq ft), above
and below ground. The
underground levels 2 and 3
are occupied by a varied array
of shops, from chic boutiques
to megastores. Above ground
there are well-tended gardens,
pergolas and mini-pavilions.
Also outside are the

Pygmalion by Julio
Silva in the
Forum des
Halles

palm-shaped buildings of
metal and glass which house
the Pavillon des Arts and the
Maison de la Poésie, cultural
centers for contemporary art
and poetry respectively. Sadly,
the area has recently become
rather seedy, and is not
recommended at night.

Le Défenseur du Temps ❾

Rue Bernard-de-Clairvaux 75003.
Map 13 B2. Ⓜ *Rambuteau.*

The modern Quartier de
l'Horloge (Clock Quarter) is
the location of Paris's newest
public clock, "The Defender
of Time" by Jacques
Monastier. An impressive
brass-and-steel mechanical
sculpture, it stands 13 ft (4 m)
high and weighs 1 ton. The
defender battles against the
elements: air, earth and water.
In the shape of savage beasts,
they attack him at the approach
of each hour, to the
accompanying sound of
earthquakes, hurricanes and
rough seas. At 2pm and 6pm
he overcomes
all three, as
watching
children cheer.

Pompidou Centre ❶

The Pompidou is like a building turned inside out: escalators, elevators, air and water ducts and even the huge steel struts that are the building's skeleton have all been placed on the outside. This allowed the architects, Richard Rogers, Renzo Piano and Gianfranco Franchini, to create an uncluttered and flexible space within it for the Musée National d'Art Moderne and for the Pompidou's other activities. Among the schools represented in the museum are Fauvism, Cubism and Surrealism. Outside in the piazza, large crowds gather to watch the street performers. The Pompidou has been completely renovated for the new millennium.

The escalator that rises step by step up the facade overlooking the piazza runs through a glass conduit. From the top there is a spectacular view over Paris that includes Montmartre, La Défense and the Eiffel Tower.

KEY

☐ Exhibition space

☐ Non-exhibition space

GALLERY GUIDE

The permanent collections are on Levels 5 & 4: works from 1905 to 1960 are on the former, with the latter reserved for contemporary art. Levels 1 & 6 are for major exhibitions, while Levels 1, 2 & 3 house an information library. The lower levels make up "The Forum", the focal public area, which include a performance center for dance, theater and music, a movie theater and children's workshop.

Portrait of the Journalist Sylvia von Harden (1926)
The surgical precision of Dix's style makes this a harsh caricature.

Le Cheval Majeur
This bronze horse (1914–16) by Duchamp-Villon is one of the finest examples of Cubist sculpture.

To Russia, the Asses and the Others (1911)
Throughout his life Chagall drew inspiration from the small Russian town of Vitebsk, where he was born.

VISITORS' CHECKLIST

Pl Georges Pompidou. **Map** 13
B2. **Tel** *01 44 78 12 33.*
Ⓜ *Rambuteau, Châtelet, Hôtel de Ville.* 🚌 *21, 29, 38, 47, 58, 69, 70, 72, 74, 75, 76, 81, 85, 96.*
RER *Châtelet-Les-Halles.*
◯ *MNAM & temp. exhibs: 11am–9pm Wed–Mon; Library: noon–10pm Wed– Mon; Atelier Brancusi: 2–6pm Wed–Mon.*
🚫 ♿ 📷 🎫 🍴 🛍 🚻
www.centrepompidou.fr

Sorrow of the King (1952)
Toward the end of his life, Matisse produced a number of collages using gouache-painted paper cutouts.

Basin and Sculpture Terrace

Le Duo (1937)
Georges Braque, like Picasso, developed the Cubist technique of representing different views of a subject in a single picture.

Basin and Sculpture Terrace

COLOR-CODING

The colored pipes that are the most striking feature at the back of the Pompidou, on the rue du Renard, moved one critic to compare the building to an oil refinery. Far from being merely decorative, the colors serve to distinguish the pipes' various functions: air-conditioning ducts are blue, water pipes green and electricity lines are painted yellow. The areas through which people move vertically (such as escalators) are red. The white funnels are ventilation shafts for the underground areas, and structural beams are clad in stainless steel. The architects' idea was to help the public understand the way the dynamics of a building function.

Exploring the Pompidou's Modern Art Collection

With a collection of over 50,000 works of art from more than 42,000 artists, the Pompidou encompasses all of the fine arts. Since its renovation, classic disciplines – painting, sculpture, drawing and photography – have been integrated with other media such as film, architecture, design, and visual and sound archives. The collections now represent a complete overview of modern and contemporary creation.

The Two Barges (1906) by André Derain

FROM 1905–60

The "historical" collections bring together the great artistic movements of the first half of the 20th century, from Fauvism to Abstract Expressionism to the changing currents of the 1950s. The rich collection of Cubist sculptures, of which the *Cheval Majeur* by Duchamp-Villon (1914–1916) is a fine example, is displayed, as well as examples of the great masters of the 20th century. Matisse, Picasso, Braque, Duchamp, Kandinsky, Léger, Miro, Giacometti and Dubuffet command large

areas at the heart of the collection. Toward the end of his life, Matisse made several collages from cut up large sheets of paper. Among others, the museum possesses *La Tristesse du Roi* (Sorrow of the King) which he created in 1952. With *Homme à la Guitare* (Man with a Guitar), Braque demonstrates his command of the Cubist technique which he pioneered along with Picasso. Considered as one of the first, if not

the first, Abstract painter, Kandinsky transformed works inspired by nature into constructions of color and form. The museum has a large collection of the Russian painter's works, of which the Impressions (*Impressions V, Parc*, 1911) mark the end of his Expressionist period before his plunge into Abstract art with *Improvisations XIV* or *Avec l'Arc Noir* (With the Black Arc) both dating from 1912 compositions.

The collection also shows the groups and the movements on which the history of modern art is based, or by which it has been affected, including Dada, Abstract Art and Informal. A pioneer of Informal art, Jean Fautrier is represented in the collections with *Otages* (Hostages), a commemoration of the suffering of the resistance fighters.

At the heart of this chronological progression, some newly opened spaces are a revelation. One set shows the Union des Artistes Modernes (Modern Artists Union) where architects, visual artists and designers met in the 1920s. Another room recreates the atmosphere of André Breton's workshop in which the works of his Surrealist friends are also shown. Silent pauses have also been allowed for: the room reserved for Miro's three huge *Bleus* (Blues) gives time and space for visitors to meditate on the explosion and revolutions of modern art.

With the Black Arc (1912)
by Vassily Kandinsky

BRANCUSI'S STUDIO

The Atelier Brancusi, on the rue Rambuteau side of the piazza, is a reconstruction of the workshop of the Romanian born artist Constantin Brancusi (1876-1957), who lived and worked in Paris from 1904. He bequeathed his entire collection of works to the French state on condition that his workshop be rebuilt as it was on the day he died. The collection includes sculptures and plinths, photographs and a selection of his tools. Also featured are some of his more personal items such as documents, pieces of furniture and his book collection.

Miss Pogany (1919–20) by Constantin Brancusi

The Good-bye Door (1980) by Joan Mitchell

ART SINCE 1960

The contemporary department opens with the 1960s and pays homage to Jean Tinguely. This sculptor/engineer was creator of the Stravinsky fountain situated near the center, along with Niki de Saint-Phalle. The display is organized around a central aisle from which the rooms holding the museum's collections lead off.

The 1960s saw the rise of Pop Art in America, which introduced advertising and mass-media images, along with objects from the consumer society, into art. Works by Jasper Johns, Andy Warhol and Claes Oldenburg are in the collection. In the Rauschenberg *Oracle*, for example, products become abstract shapes. Among other works of importance are *Ghost Drums Set* by Claes Oldenburg and *Electric Chair* by Andy Warhol.

In France, the New Realists, a heterogenous group including Yves Klein, César, Arman and others, were also interested in contemporary objects. They believed that by choosing mundane things from everyday life the artist could imbue them with artistic significance. Arman makes "accumulations",

Mobile on Two Planes (1955)
by Alexander Calder

Raymond Hains collects wall posters in order to make abstract canvases, while Jean Tinguely builds machines using materials collected.

The subtle eroticism of Balthus (Count Balthasar Klossowski de Rola) glows through *The Painter and His Model* (1980–81). In another area are ink drawings by poet-painter Henri Michaux.

Homogenous Infiltration (1966)
by Joseph Beuys

The work of Herbin, who founded the Abstraction-Création group, a loosely based association of non-figurative painters, is the focus for the work of the Geometric Abstractionists, while the Hard Edge Abstraction movement in America, which specializes in flat-colored, well-defined shapes, is represented by Ellsworth Kelly and Frank Stella, among others. Richard Serra's *Corner Prop No. 7 (For Natalie)* (1983) and Carl André's *144 Tin Square* (1975) are just two of the several Minimalist sculptures in the collection.

The museum has a selection of figurative art by Georg Baselitz, Gilbert and George, and Anselm Kiefer, as well as art from the abstract landscape painter Joan Mitchell.

Kinetic Art, Poor Art and Conceptual Art, and new trends in figurative and abstract painting, punctuate the route of the contemporary department's galleries.

Since the Pompidou's reopening, certain areas have been designated to bring together different disciplines around a theme and no longer around a school or movement. For example, the use of plastic materials in contemporary art is shown in the works of Jean Dubuffet, César or Claes Oldenburg and compared against the work of architects such as Richard Buckminster or Hans Hollein and designers such as Ettore Sottsass.

In its new arrangement the fourth floor offers areas allowing different aspects of the museum's collections to be discovered. They often reflect the museum's preference for the more ironic and conceptual forms. One display offered such works as Joseph Beuys's *Plight* (1985), which included a grand piano and wall and ceiling covered with about 7 tons of thick felt, and the video artist Nam June Paik's *Video Fish* (1979–85), in which video screens flashed manic sequences of images from behind aquaria populated by indifferent fish.

The museum gallery allows temporary exhibitions to be mounted from works held in reserve. A graphic arts exhibition room and a video area complete the arrangement. A screening room gives access to the museums' entire collection of videotapes and audio recordings of a wide range of modern artists.

Ben's Store (1973) by Ben (Vautier Benjamin)

Musée de la Poupée ❿

Impasse Berthaud 75003. **Map** 13 B2.
Tel 01 42 72 73 11. Ⓜ Rambuteau.
◯ 10am–6pm Tue–Sun. ⬛
for groups, by appt.
www.museedelapoupeeparis.com

An impressive collection of handmade dolls, from the mid-19th century to the present day, are on show in this charming museum. Thirty-six of the displays contain French dolls with porcelain heads ranging from 1850 to 1950. Another 24 display windows are devoted to themed exhibitions of dolls from around the world.

Father and son Guido and Samy Odin, who own the museum, are at your service if your doll needs medical care. The museum shop stocks everything you need to preserve and maintain these unique works of art. The Odins also offer comprehensive classes on doll-making for both adults and children.

A 19th-century French doll with porcelain head

No. 51 Rue de Montmorency ⓫

75003. **Map** 13 B1. Ⓜ Réaumur-Sébastopol. ◯ to the public.

This house is considered to be the oldest in Paris. No. 51 was built in 1407 by Nicolas Flamel, a book-keeper and alchemist. His house was always open to the poor, from whom he asked nothing more than that they should pray for those who were dead. Today, the house is a French restaurant.

The interior of St-Eustache in the 1830s

Tour de Jean Sans Peur ⓬

20 Rue Etienne-Marcel 75002.
Map 13 A1. **Tel** 01 40 26 20 28.
Ⓜ Etienne-Marcel. ◯ 1:30–6pm
Wed, Sat, Sun. ⬛

After the Duc d'Orléans had been assassinated on his orders in 1408, the Duc de Bourgogne feared reprisals. To protect himself, he had this 88-ft (27-m) tower built onto his home, the Hôtel de Bourgogne. He moved his bedroom up to the fourth floor of the tower (which was reached by climbing a flight of 140 steps) to sleep safe from the plots of his enemies.

No. 51 Rue de Montmorency, the oldest house in Paris

St-Eustache ⓭

Pl du Jour 75001. **Map** 13 A1. **Tel** 01 40 26 47 99. Ⓜ Les Halles. ⓡⓔⓡ Châtelet-Les-Halles. ◯ 9:30am–7pm daily. Ⓟ ⨍ 12:30pm Mon–Fri; 6pm Mon & Sat; 9:30am, 11am, 6pm Sun. **Organ recitals 5:30pm Sun.**

With its Gothic plan and Renaissance decoration, St-Eustache is one of the most beautiful churches in Paris. Its interior plan is modeled on Notre-Dame, with five naves and side and radial chapels. The 105 years (1532–1637) it took to complete the church saw the flowering of the Renaissance style, which is evident in the magnificent arches, pillars and columns. The stained-glass windows in the chancel are created from cartoons by Philippe de Champaigne.

The church has associations with many famous figures: Molière was buried here; the Marquise de Pompadour, official mistress of Louis XV, was baptized here, as was Cardinal Richelieu.

Entrance to the Bourse du
Commerce, the old grain exchange

Bourse du Commerce 🄌

2 Rue de Viarmes 75001. **Map** 12 F2.
Tel 01 55 65 55 65. Ⓜ Les Halles. ⓇⒺⓇ
Châtelet-Les-Halles. ◯ 9am–1pm, 2–
5pm Mon–Fri. 🄸 groups by appt. ♿

Compared by Victor Hugo to
a jockey's cap without a peak,
the old grain exchange building was constructed in the
18th century and remodeled
in 1889. Today its huge,
domed hall is filled with the
hustle and bustle of the com-
modities market for coffee
and sugar. It houses a World
Trade Center and the offices
of the Chambre de Commerce
et d'Industrie de Paris.

St-Germain l'Auxerrois 🄎

2 Pl du Louvre 75001.
Map 12 F2. **Tel** 01 42 60 13 96.
Ⓜ Louvre, Pont-Neuf.
◯ 8am–7pm daily. **Musical Hour**
4–5pm Sun.

After the Valois Court
decamped to the Louvre from
the Ile de la Cité in the 14th
century, this became the
favored church of kings, who
attended mass here.
   Its many historical associations include the horrific St
Bartholomew's Day Massacre
on August 24, 1572, the eve
of the royal wedding of Henri
of Navarre and Marguerite de
Valois. Thousands of
Huguenots who had been
lured to Paris for the wedding

were murdered as the church
bell tolled. Later, after the
Revolution, the church was
used as a barn. Despite many
restorations, it is a jewel of
Gothic architecture.

La Samaritaine 🄐

19 Rue de la Monnaie 75001.
Map 12 F2. **Tel** 01 40 41 20 20.
Ⓜ Pont-Neuf. ◯ 9:30am–7pm
Mon–Wed, Fri; 9:30am–9pm Thu;
9:30am–8pm Sat. 🄸 ▭ 🄿
See **Shopping** p313.

This fashionable department
store was founded in 1900 by
Ernest Cognacq. Built in 1926
with a framework of iron and
wide expanses of glass, La
Samaritaine is an outstanding
example of the Art Deco
style. The renovated interior
now has a fine Art Nouveau
ironwork staircase and
hanging galleries under
a large dome. The rooftop
restaurant, Le Toupary, has
some of the most spectacular
views of Paris. Cognacq was
also a collector of 18th-
century art, and his collection
is now on display in the
Musée Cognacq-Jay in the
Marais quarter (see p94).

The stylish Art Deco interior of
La Samaritaine

The Tour St-Jacques with its
ornate decoration

Tour St-Jacques 🄑

Square de la Tour St-Jacques 75004.
Map 13 A3. Ⓜ Châtelet. ◯ to the
public.

This imposing late Gothic
tower, dating from 1523, is
all that remains of an ancient
church that was a rendezvous
for pilgrims setting out on
long journeys. The church
was destroyed after the
Revolution. Earlier, Blaise
Pascal, the 17th-century
mathematician, physicist,
philosopher and writer, used
the tower for barometrical
experiments. There is a
memorial statue to him on the
ground floor of the tower.
Queen Victoria passed by on
her state visit in 1854, giving
her name to the nearby
Avenue Victoria.

The St Bartholomew's Day Massacre (c. 1572–84) by François Dubois

TUILERIES QUARTER

The Tuileries area is bounded by the vast expanse of the Concorde square at one end and the Grand Louvre at the other. This was a place for kings and palaces. The Sun King (Louis XIV) lives on in the Place des Victoires, which was designed solely to show off his statue. In Place Vendôme, royal glitter has been replaced by the precious stones of Cartier, Boucheron and Chaumet, and the fine cut of Arab, German and Japanese bankers, not to mention the chic ladies visiting the luxurious Ritz. The area is crossed by two of Paris's most magnificent shopping streets – the long Rue de Rivoli, with its arcades, expensive boutiques, bookshops and five-star hotels, and the Rue St-Honoré, another extensive street, bringing together the richest and humblest in people and commerce.

Ornate lamppost on
Place de la Concorde

SIGHTS AT A GLANCE

Historic Buildings
Palais Royal ❸
Banque de France ⑳

Museums and Galleries
Musée du Louvre pp122–9 ❶
Musée de la Mode et du Textile ❾
Musée de la Publicité ❿
Musée des Arts Décoratifs ⓫
Galerie Nationale du Jeu de Paume ⓯
Musée de l'Orangerie ⓰
Village Royal ⓲

Monuments and Fountains
Fontaine Molière ❻
Arc de Triomphe du Carrousel ⓬

Squares, Parks and Gardens
Jardin du Palais Royal ❺
Place des Pyramides ❽
Jardin des Tuileries ⓮
Place de la Concorde ⓱
Place Vendôme ⓳
Place des Victoires ㉑

Theaters
Comédie Française ❹

Shops
Louvre des Antiquaires ❷
Rue de Rivoli ⓭

Churches
St-Roch ❼

GETTING THERE
This area is well served by the metro system, with stations at Tuileries, Pyramides, Palais Royal and Louvre. There are frequent buses through the area. Routes 24 and 72 travel along the quayside passing the Jardin des Tuileries and the Musée du Louvre.

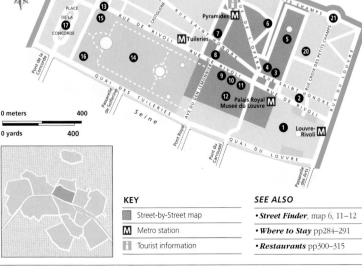

0 meters   400
0 yards   400

KEY
▨ Street-by-Street map
Ⓜ Metro station
ℹ Tourist information

SEE ALSO
• *Street Finder*, map 6, 11–12
• *Where to Stay* pp284–291
• *Restaurants* pp300–315

◁ **View of the Place de la Concorde and the Obelisk**

Street by Street: Tuileries Quarter

Elegant squares, formal gardens, street
arcades and courtyards give this part of
Paris its special character. Monuments to
monarchy and the arts coexist with
contemporary luxury: five-star hotels,
world-famous restaurants, fashion
emporiums and jewelers of international
renown. Sandblasting and washing have
given a new glow to the facades of the
Louvre and the Palais Royal square, where
Cardinal Richelieu's creation, the royal
palace, is now occupied by government
offices. From here the Ministry of Culture
surveys the cleaning and restoration of
the city's great
buildings. The other
former royal palace,
the Louvre, is now
one of the great
museums of the world.

The Normandy is an
elegant hotel in the Belle
Epoque style, a form of
graceful living that pre-
vailed in Paris at the turn
of the 20th century.

St-Roch
*The papal statue stands
in this remarkably long
17th-century church,
unusually set on a
north–south axis.
St-Roch is a
treasure house of
religious art* **7**

Metro Pyramides

**The Paris
Convention
and
Visitors'
Bureau**

★ **Jardin des Tuileries**
*Donkey rides are a popular
attraction in these formal
gardens, which were
designed by the royal
gardener André Le Nôtre
in the 17th
century* **14**

**Place des
Pyramides**
*Frémiet's gilded
statue of Joan of
Arc is the focus of
pilgrimage for
royalists* **8**

To the Quai
du Louvre

**Musée de la Mode
et du Textile**
The haute couture
*collections that are
kept in this museum
have given the
Louvre a new role* **9**

Musée des Arts Décoratifs
*A highlight of the museum's
displays of art and design is
the Art Nouveau collection* **11**

Fontaine Molière
Louis Visconti's fountain is of the famous playwright, who lived nearby **6**

★ Jardin du Palais Royal
The garden is a city haven, bordered by arcades with restaurants and art galleries alongside specialty shops **5**

LOCATOR MAP
See Central Paris Map pp14–15

Le Grand Véfour's 18th-century decor makes it one of the most beautiful restaurants in Paris. Napoleon Bonaparte and Victor Hugo were two of the many famous people who dined here. *(See p304.)*

★ Palais Royal
In the 18th century this former royal palace was a setting for fabulous gatherings, debauchery and gambling. Today modern sculptures grace the square **3**

Comédie Française
France's national theater is the setting for the works of great dramatists, such as Molière **4**

Metro Palais Royal

Louvre des Antiquaires
Three floors of a former department store house this chic art and antiques supermarket for the rich collector **2**

★ Musée du Louvre
Home to French kings for almost four centuries, the Louvre is now a museum with one of the world's great art collections **1**

STAR SIGHTS

★ Musée du Louvre

★ Palais Royal

★ Jardin du Palais Royal

★ Jardin des Tuileries

KEY

– – – Suggested route

0 meters   100

0 yards   100

The five-arched Pont Royal linking the Louvre with the Left Bank

Musée du Louvre ❶

See pp122–9.

Louvre des Antiquaires ❷

2 Pl du Palais Royal 75001. **Map** 12 E2. **Tel** *01 42 97 27 27.* ☐ *11am–7pm Tue–Sun (Jul & Aug: Tue–Sat).* ● *Jan 1, Dec 25.* 🍴 ☐ *See **Shopping** pp336–7.* **www**.louvre-antiquaires.com

One of the shops in the Louvre des Antiquaires market

A large department store – the Grands Magasins du Louvre – was converted at the end of the 1970s into this three-floor collection of art galleries and antique shops. Few bargains are found here, but the 250 shops of this chic market provide clues about what *nouveaux riches* collectors are seeking.

Palais Royal ❸

Pl du Palais Royal 75001. **Map** 12 E1. Ⓜ *Palais Royal.* **Buildings not open** to public.

This former royal palace has had a turbulent history. Starting out in the early 17th century as Richelieu's Palais Cardinale, it passed to the crown on his death and became the childhood home of Louis XIV. Under the control of the 18th-century royal dukes of Orléans it was the scene of fabulous gatherings, interspersed with periods of debauchery and gambling. The cardinal's theater, where Molière had performed, burned down in 1763, but was replaced by the Comédie Française. After the Revolution, the palace became a gambling house. It was reclaimed in 1815 by the future King Louis-Philippe, one of whose librarians was Alexandre Dumas. The building narrowly escaped the flames of the 1871 uprising.

After being restored again, between 1872 and 1876, the palace reverted to the state, and it now houses both the Council of State, the supreme legal body for administrative matters, and its more recent "partner", the Constitutional Council. Another wing of the palace is occupied by the Ministry of Culture.

Comédie Française ❹

1 Place Colette 75001. **Map** 12 E1. 🛈 *01 44 58 15 15.* Ⓜ *Palais Royal.* ☐ *for performances.* ☐ *9:30am, 10am, 10:30am Sat, Sun (01 44 58 13 16).* 📷 See ***Entertainment** pp342–4.*

A stone plaque to Pierre Corneille

Overlooking two charming, if traffic-choked, squares named after the writers Colette and André Malraux, sits France's national theater. The company has its roots partly in Molière's 17th-century players. In the foyer is the armchair in which Molière collapsed, dying, on stage in 1673 (ironically while he was performing *Le Malade Imaginaire – The Hypochondriac*). Since the company's founding in 1680 by Louis XIV, the theater has enjoyed state patronage as a center of national culture, and it has been based in the present building since 1799. The repertoire includes works of Corneille, Racine, Molière and Shakespeare, as well as those of modern playwrights.

Daniel Buren's stone columns (1980s) in the Palais Royal courtyard

Jardin du Palais Royal ❺

Pl du Palais Royal 75001. **Map** 12 F1.
Ⓜ *Palais Royal.*

The present garden is about a third smaller than the original one, laid out by the royal gardener for Cardinal Richelieu in the 1630s. This is due to the construction, between 1781 and 1784, of 60 uniform houses bordering three sides of the square. Today restaurants, art galleries and specialty shops line the square, which maintains a strong literary history – Jean Cocteau, Colette and Jean Marais are among its famous recent residents.

Statue in the Jardin du Palais Royal

Fontaine Molière ❻

Rue de Richelieu 75001. **Map** 12 F1.
Ⓜ *Palais Royal.*

France's most famous play-wright lived near here, in a house on the site of No. 40 Rue de Richelieu. The 19th-century fountain is by Louis Visconti, who also designed Napoleon's tomb at Les Invalides (*see pp188–9*).

St-Roch ❼

296 Rue St-Honoré 75001. **Map** 12 E1.
Tel 01 42 44 13 20. Ⓜ *Tuileries.*
◻ *8am–7pm daily.* ⛪ *non-religious public hols.* ✝ *Daily, times vary.*
Concerts. 📷

This huge church was designed by Lemercier, archi-tect of the Louvre, and its foundation stone was laid by

Vien's *St Denis Preaching to the Gauls* (1767) in St-Roch

Louis XIV in 1653. Jules Hardouin-Mansart added the large Lady Chapel with its richly decorated dome and ceiling in the 18th century and two further chapels extended the church to 413 ft (126 m), just short of Notre-Dame. It is a treasure house of religious art, much of it from now-vanished churches and monasteries. It also contains the tombs of the playwright Pierre Corneille, the royal gardener André Le Nôtre and the philosopher Denis Diderot. The facades reveal marks of Napoleon's attack, in 1795, on royalist troops who were defending the church steps.

Place des Pyramides ❽

75001. **Map** 12 E1. Ⓜ *Tuileries, Pyramides.*

Joan of Arc, wounded nearby fighting the English in 1429, is commemorated by a 19th-century equestrian statue by the sculptor Emmanuel Frémiet. The statue is a rallying point for royalists.

Musée de la Mode et du Textile ❾

107 Rue de Rivoli 75001. **Map** 12 E1.
Tel 01 44 55 57 50. Ⓜ *Palais Royal, Tuileries.* ◻ *11am–6pm Tue–Fri; 10am–6pm Sat, Sun.* 📷 🏠
www.ucad.fr

Set in the Louvre's Pavillon de Marsan, this museum promotes one of the city's oldest and most famous industries – fashion.

It houses an impressive collection of *haute couture* costumes and accessories and has become an important venue for temporary exhibitions of costumes.

Schiaparelli jacket in the museum

Musée du Louvre ❶

The Musée du Louvre, containing one of the most important art collections in the world, has a history extending back to medieval times. First constructed as a fortress in 1190 by King Philippe-Auguste to protect Paris against Viking raids, it lost its imposing keep in the reign of François I, who replaced it with a Renaissance-style building. Thereafter, four centuries of French kings and emperors improved and enlarged it. One of the more recent additions is a glass pyramid in the main courtyard from which all the galleries are reached.

The east facade, facing St-Germain l'Auxerrois

The Jardin du Carrousel, now part of the Jardin des Tuileries, was once the grand approach to the Tuileries Palace which was burned down in 1871 by the Communards.

Pavillon des Sessions

The Carrousel du Louvre underground visitors complex, with galleries, cloakrooms, shops, lavatories, parking and an information desk, lies beneath the Arc de Triomphe du Carrousel.

Denon Wing

The inverted glass pyramid brings light to the subterranean complex, echoing the museum's main entrance in the Cour Napoléon.

BUILDING THE LOUVRE

Over many centuries the Louvre was enlarged by a succession of French rulers, shown below with their dates.

MAJOR ALTERATIONS

- Reign of François I (1515–47)
- Catherine de' Médici (about 1560)
- Reign of Henri IV (1589–1610)
- Reign of Louis XIII (1610–43)
- Reign of Louis XIV (1643–1715)
- Reign of Napoleon I (1804–15)
- Reign of Napoleon III (1852–70)
- I M Pei (1989) (architect)

★ Arc de Triomphe du Carrousel
This triumphal arch was built to celebrate Napoleon's victories in 1805.

STAR FEATURES

- ★ Pyramid Entrance
- ★ Perrault Colonnade
- ★ Medieval Moats
- ★ Arc de Triomphe du Carrousel

Pavillon Richelieu
This imposing 19th-century pavilion is part of the Richelieu Wing, once home to the Ministry of Finance but now converted into magnificent galleries.

VISITORS' CHECKLIST

Map 12 E2. *Tel* 01 40 20 53 17; 01 40 20 55 00 (adv booking). ☎ 01 40 20 50 50. Ⓜ Palais Royal, Musée du Louvre. 🚌 21, 24, 27, 39, 48, 68, 69, 72, 81, 95. RER Châtelet-Les-Halles. Ⓞ Louvre. Ⓟ Carrousel du Louvre (entrance via Ave du General Lemonnier); Pl du Louvre, Rue St-Honoré. Ⓞ 9am–6pm Wed–Mon (not all departments are open daily – check schedule). Nocturnals Wed & Fri until 9:45pm (subject to change). ⬤ Jan 1, May 1, Dec 25. 🎫 (free 1st Sun of each month, for under 18, and for under 26 on Fri after 6pm). ♿ partial (01 40 20 59 90). ☎ phone 01 40 20 52 09. 🎧 **Lectures, films, concerts** (01 40 20 55 55). 🍴 ▯ www.louvre.fr

Cour Marly is the glass-roofed courtyard that now houses the Marly Horses *(see p125).*

★ Pyramid Entrance
The popular new main entrance, designed by the architect I M Pei, was opened in 1989.

Richelieu Wing

Cour Puget

Cour Khorsabad

Sully Wing

Cour Carrée

★ Perrault's Colonnade
The east façade with its majestic rows of columns was built by Claude Perrault, who worked on the Louvre with Louis Le Vau in the mid-17th century.

Cour Napoléon

The Salle des Caryatides
takes its name from the statues of women created by Jean Goujon in 1550 to support the upper gallery.

The Louvre of Charles V
In about 1360, Charles V transformed Philippe-Auguste's robust old fortress into a royal residence.

★ Medieval Moats
The base of the twin towers and the drawbridge support of Philippe-Auguste's fortress can be seen in the excavated area.

The Louvre's Collection

The Louvre's treasures can be traced back to the collection of François I (1515–47), who purchased many Italian paintings including the *Mona Lisa* (*La Gioconda*). In Louis XIV's reign (1643–1715) there were a mere 200 works, but donations and purchases augmented the collection. The Louvre was first opened to the public in 1793 after the Revolution, and has been continually enriched ever since.

The Lacemaker
In this exquisite picture from about 1665, Jan Vermeer gives us a glimpse into everyday domestic life in Holland. The painting came to the Louvre in 1870.

The Raft of the Medusa (*1819*)
Théodore Géricault derived his inspiration for this gigantic and moving work from the shipwreck of a French frigate in 1816. The painting shows the moment when the few survivors sight a sail on the horizon.

Cour Marly

Richelieu Wing

Main entrance

GALLERY GUIDE

The main entrance is beneath the glass pyramid. From here corridors radiate out to the museum's wings. The works are displayed on four floors: the painting and sculpture collections are arranged by country of origin. There are separate departments for Oriental, Egyptian, Greek, Etruscan and Roman anti-quities, objets d'art and prints and drawings. Arts from Africa, Asia, Oceania & the Americas are in the Pavillon des Sessions until 2006.

Underground visitors' complex

Pavillon des Sessions

Denon Wing

KEY TO FLOORPLAN

☐	Painting
☐	Objets d'art
☐	Sculpture
☐	Antiquities
☐	Non-exhibition space

★ **Venus de Milo**
Found in 1820 on the island of Milo in Greece, this ideal of feminine beauty was made in the Hellenistic Age at the end of the 2nd century BC.

★ Mona Lisa

Leonardo da Vinci painted this small portrait of a Florentine noblewoman, known as La Gioconda, *in about 1504. It was soon regarded as the prototype of the Renaissance portrait. The sitter's engaging smile has prompted endless commentary ever since. The painting has its own wall in the Salle des Etats (Denon wing).*

Second floor

★ Marly Horses

Since the 19th century, these wild horses by Guillaume Coustou have stood near the Place de la Concorde. Replicas have replaced them – the originals are now in a glass-covered courtyard in the Louvre.

First floor

Cour Puget

Cour Khorsabad

Cour Napoléon

Sully Wing

STAR EXHIBITS

- ★ Mona Lisa by Leonardo da Vinci
- ★ Venus de Milo
- ★ Marly Horses by Guillaume Coustou

The Dying Slave

Michelangelo sculpted this work between 1513 and 1520 as part of a group of statues for the base of the tomb of Pope Julius II in Rome.

Cour Carrée

Ground floor

Exploring the Louvre's Collections

It is important not to underestimate the size of these vast collections and useful to set a few viewing priorities before starting. The collection of European paintings (1400–1850) is comprehensive and 40 per cent of the works are by French artists, while the selection of sculptures is less complete. The museum's antiquities – Oriental, Egyptian, Greek, Etruscan and Roman – are of world renown and offer the visitor an unrivaled range of objects. The *objets d'art* on display are very varied and include furniture and jewelry.

The Fortune Teller (about 1594) by Caravaggio

EUROPEAN PAINTING: 1200 TO 1850

Painting from northern Europe (Flemish, Dutch, German and English) is well covered. One of the earliest Flemish works is Jan van Eyck's *Madonna of Chancellor Rolin* (about 1435) which shows the chancellor of Burgundy kneeling in prayer before the Virgin and Child.

Portrait of Erasmus (1523) by Hans Holbein

Hieronymus Bosch's *Ship of Fools* (1500) is a fine, satirical account of the futility of human existence. In the Dutch collection, Van Dyck's portrait *King Charles out Hunting* (1635) shows Charles I of England in all his refined elegance. Jacob Jordaens, best known for scenes of gluttony and lust, reveals unusual sensitivity in his *Four Evangelists*. The saucy smile of the *Gipsy Girl* (1628) displays Frans Hals' effortless virtuosity, in sharp contrast to Vermeer's highly finished *Lacemaker*. Rembrandt's *Self-portraits*, *Disciples at Emmaus* (1648) and *Bathsheba* (1654) are fine examples of his genius.

There is relatively little German painting, but the three major German painters of the 15th and 16th centuries are represented by important works. There is a *Self-portrait* by Albrecht Dürer as a young artist of 22 (1493), a *Venus* by Lucas Cranach (1529) and a portrait of the great humanist scholar Erasmus by Hans Holbein. Works by English artists include Thomas

Gainsborough's *Conversation in a Park* (about 1746), Sir Joshua Reynolds' *Master Hare* (1788) and several landscapes by J M W Turner.

Many of the master works in the Spanish collection depict the tragic side of life: El Greco's *Christ on the Cross Adored by Donors* (1576) and Francisco de Zurbarán's *Lying-in-State of St Bonaventura* (about 1629) with its dark-faced corpse are two of the Louvre's prize pieces. The subject of José de Ribera's *Club-Footed Boy* (1642) is a poor mute, who carries a scrap of paper requesting alms. In a lighter vein, there are several portraits by Goya from the 19th century.

The museum's collection of Italian paintings is large, covering the period 1200 to 1800. The father figures of the early Renaissance, Cimabue and Giotto, are here, as is Fra Angelico, with his *Coronation of the Virgin* (1435), and Pisanello, with his delightful *Portrait of Ginevra d'Este* (about 1435). There is also a fine portrait in profile of Sigismondo Malatesta by Piero della Francesca (about 1450) and an action-packed battle scene by Paolo Uccello. Several paintings by Leonardo da Vinci, for instance the *Virgin with the Infant Jesus and St Anne*, are as enchanting as his *Mona Lisa*.

The Louvre's fine collection of French painting ranges from the 14th century to 1848. Paintings after this date are housed in the Musée d'Orsay (see pp144–7). An outstanding

Gilles or Pierrot (about 1717) by Jean Antoine Watteau

LEONARDO DA VINCI IN FRANCE

Leonardo, artist, engineer and scientist, was born in 1452 and became a leading figure in the Italian Renaissance. François I met Leonardo in 1515 and invited him to live and work in France. The painter brought the *Mona Lisa* with him. Already in poor health, he died three years later in the arms of the king.

Self-portrait (early 16th century)

early work is Enguerrand Quarton's *Villeneuve-les-Avignon Pietà* (1455). Another early painting shows *Gabrielle d'Estrée*, mistress of Henri IV, in her bathtub. From the 16th and 17th centuries there are several splendid works by Georges de la Tour with the dramatic torch-light effect so typical of his work.

That great 18th-century painter of melancholy, Jean Watteau, is represented, as is J H Fragonard, master of the Rococo. His delightfully frivolous subjects are evident in *The Bathers* from 1770. In stark contrast is the classicism of Nicolas Poussin and the history painting of J L David. Most of J D Ingres' work is in the Musée d'Orsay, but the Louvre kept the erotic *Turkish Bath* of 1862.

EUROPEAN SCULPTURE: 1100 TO 1850

Early Flemish and German sculpture in the collection has many masterpieces such as Tilman Riemenschneider's *Virgin of the Annunciation* from the end of the 15th century and an unusual life-size nude figure of the penitent Mary Magdalen by Gregor Erhart (early 16th century). An ornate gilded-wood altarpiece of the same period exemplifies Flemish church art. Another important work of Flemish sculpture is Adrian de Vries's long-limbed *Mercury and Psyche* from 1593, which was originally made for the court of Rudolph II in Prague.

The French section opens with early Romanesque works, such as the figure of Christ by a 12th-century Burgundian sculptor and a head of St Peter. With its eight black-hooded mourners, the tomb of Philippe Pot (a high-ranking official in Burgundy) is one of the more unusual pieces. Diane de Poitiers, mistress of Henri II, had a large figure of her namesake Diana, goddess of the hunt, installed in the courtyard of her castle west of Paris. It is now in the Louvre. The works of Pierre Puget (1620–94), the great sculptor from Marseilles, have been assembled inside a glass-covered courtyard, Cour Puget. They include a figure of Milo of Crotona, the Greek athlete who got his hands caught in the cleft of a tree stump and was eaten by a lion. The wild horses of Marly now stand in the glass-roofed Cour Marly surrounded by other masterpieces of French sculpture, including Houdon's early 19th-century busts of Diderot and Voltaire, and two equestrian pieces by Coysevox.

The Italian sculpture collection includes pre-Renaissance work by Duccio and Donatello, and later masterpieces such as Michelangelo's *Slaves* and Cellini's Fontainebleau *Nymph*.

Tomb of Philippe Pot (late 15th century) by Antoine le Moiturier

ORIENTAL, EGYPTIAN, GREEK, ETRUSCAN AND ROMAN ANTIQUITIES

The range of antiquities in the Louvre is impressive. There are objects from the Neolithic period (about 6000 BC) to the fall of the Roman Empire. Important works of Mesopotamian art include the seated figure of Ebih-il, from 2400 BC, and several portraits of Gudea, Prince of Lagash, from about 2255 BC. A black basalt block bearing the code of the Babylonian King Hammurabi, from about 1700 BC, is one of the world's oldest legal documents.

The warlike Assyrians are represented by delicate carvings and a spectacular reconstruction of part of Sargon II's (722–705 BC) palace with its huge, winged bulls. A fine example of Persian art is the enameled brickwork depicting the king of Persia's personal guard of archers (5th century BC). It decorated his palace at Susa.

Most Egyptian art was made for the dead, who were provided with the things that they needed for the afterlife. It often included vivid images of daily life in ancient Egypt. One example is the tiny funeral chapel built for a high official in about 2500 BC. It is covered with exquisite carvings: men in sailing ships, catching fish, tending cattle and fowl.

It is also possible to gain insights into family life in ancient Egypt through a number of lifelike funeral portraits, like the squatting scribe, and several sculptures of married couples. The

Winged Victory of Samothrace (Greece, late 3rd–early 2nd century BC)

earliest sculpture dates from 2500 BC, the latest from 1400 BC.

From the New Kingdom (1555–1080 BC) a special crypt dedicated to the god Osiris contains some colossal sarcophagi, and a large number of mummified animals.

Some smaller objects of considerable charm include a 11-inch (29-cm) headless body of a woman, sensually outlined by the transparent veil of her dress and thought to be Queen Nefertiti (about 1365–1349 BC).

The department of Greek, Roman and Etruscan antiquities contains a vast array of fragments, among them some exceptional pieces. There is a large, geometric head from the Cyclades (2700 BC) and an elegant, swan-necked bowl, quite modern in its unadorned simplicity. It is hammered out of a single gold sheet and dates from about 2500 BC. The Archaic Greek period, from the 7th to the 5th century BC, is represented by the *Auxerre Goddess*, one of the earliest-known pieces of Greek sculpture, and the *Hera of Samos* from the Ionian Islands. From the height of the Classical Greek period (about the 5th century BC)

Winged Bull with Human Head from 8th century BC, found in Khorsabad, Assyria

there are several fine male torsos and heads such as the *Laborde Head*. This head has been identified as part of the sculpture that once decorated the west pediment of the Parthenon in Athens.

The two most famous Greek statues in the Louvre, the *Winged Victory of Samothrace* and the *Venus de Milo (see p 124)*, belong to the Hellenistic period (late 3rd to 2nd century BC) when more natural-looking human forms were beginning to be produced.

The undisputed star of the Etruscan collection is the terracotta *Sarcophagus of the Cenestian Couple*, who appear

Etruscan Sarcophagus (6th century BC)

as though they are attending an eternal banquet.

The sculptures in the Roman section demonstrate the great debt owed to the art of ancient Greece. There are many fine pieces: a bust of Agrippa, a basalt head of Livia, the wife of Augustus, and a splendid, powerful bronze head of Emperor Hadrian from the 2nd century AD. This has the look of a true portrait, unlike so many Imperial heads which are uninspired and impersonal.

Squatting Scribe (Egyptian, about 2500 BC)

OBJETS D'ART

The term *objets d'art* (art objects) covers a huge range of "decorative art" objects: jewelry, furniture, clocks, watches, sundials, tapestries, miniatures, silver and glassware, cutlery, small French and Italian bronzes, Byzantine and Parisian carved ivory, Limoges enamels, porcelain, French and Italian stoneware, rugs, snuffboxes, scientific instruments and armor. The Louvre has well over 8,000 items, from many ages and regions.

Many of these precious objects were in the Abbey of St-Denis, where the kings of France were crowned. Long before the Revolution, a regular flow of visitors had made it something of a museum. After the Revolution all the objects were removed and presented to the nation. Much was lost or stolen during the move but what remains is still outstanding.

The treasures include a serpentine stone plate from the 1st century AD with a 9th-century border of gold and precious stones. (The plate itself is inlaid with eight golden dolphins.) There is also a porphyry vase which Suger, Abbot of St-Denis, had mounted in gold in the shape of an eagle, and the golden scepter made for King Charles V in about 1380.

The French crown jewels include the coronation crowns of Louis XV and Napoleon, scepters, swords and other accessories of the coronation ceremonies. On view is also the Regent, one of the purest diamonds in the world. It was bought in 1717 and worn by Louis XV at his coronation in 1722.

One whole room is taken up with a series of tapestries called the *Hunts of Maximilian,* which were originally executed for Emperor Charles V

The Eagle of Suger (mid-12th century)

in 1530 after drawings by Bernard Van Orley.

The large collection of French furniture ranges from the 16th to the 19th centuries and is assembled by period, or in rooms devoted to donations by distinguished collectors such as Isaac de Camondo. On display are important pieces by exceptionally prominent furniture-makers such as André-Charles Boulle, cabinetmaker to Louis XIV, who worked at the Louvre in the late 17th to mid-18th centuries. He is noted for his technique of inlaying copper and tortoiseshell. From a later date, the curious inlaid steel and bronze writing desk, created by Adam Weisweiler for Queen Marie-Antoinette in 1784, is one of the more unusual pieces in the museum's collection.

THE GLASS PYRAMID

Plans for the modernization and expansion of the Louvre were first conceived in 1981. They included the transfer of the Ministry of Finance from the Richelieu wing of the Louvre to new offices elsewhere, and a new main entrance to the museum. A Chinese-American architect, I M Pei, was chosen to design the changes. He designed the pyramid as both the focal point and new entrance to the Louvre. Made out of glass, it enables the visitor to see the historic buildings that surround it while allowing light down into the underground visitors' reception area.

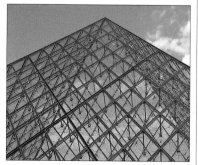

Musée de la Publicité ⓾

Palais du Louvre, 107 rue de Rivoli
75001. **Map** 12 E2.
Tel 01 44 55 57 50.
Ⓜ Palais Royal, Tuileries.
◯ 11am–6pm Tue–Fri; 10am–6pm
Sat–Sun. 🎫
www.ucad.fr

The Museum of Advertising
brings together over 40,000
historic posters dating from
the 18th century to 1949, plus
around 45,000 more recent
posters, and different varieties
of modern multimedia advertising. There is also a good
reference library.

Musée des Arts Décoratifs ⓫

Palais du Louvre, 107 Rue de Rivoli
75001. **Map** 12 E2. **Tel** 01 44 55 57
50. Ⓜ Palais Royal, Tuileries. ◯
11am– 6pm Tue, Thu, Fri; 11am–9pm
Wed; 10am– 6pm Sat & Sun. **Library**
🔲 publ hols. 🎫 🚻 **www**.ucad.fr

With five floors and over 100
rooms, this museum offers an
eclectic display of decorative
and ornamental art and
design from the Middle Ages
to the present. Among the
highlights are the Art
Nouveau and Art Deco rooms,
jewelry and Gallé glass. The
doll collection is remarkable.
   At the moment, however,
only the Galerie des Bijoux is
open, while the rest of the
museum undergoes extensive
renovation, until 2006. This
magnificent collection of over
1300 pieces, from medieval
brooches to contemporary
Cartier, still makes the museum
very much worth visiting.

Lemot's Restoration group of statues with the gilded figure of Victory

Arc de Triomphe du Carrousel ⓬

Pl du Carrousel 75001. **Map** 12 E2.
Ⓜ Palais Royal.

Built by Napoleon in 1806–
1808 as an entrance to the
former Palais des Tuileries, its
marble columns are topped by
soldiers of the Grande Armée.
They replaced the Horses of St
Mark's which he was forced to
return in 1815, after Waterloo.

Arcades along the Rue de Rivoli

Rue de Rivoli ⓭

75001. **Map** 11 C1 & 13 A2.
Ⓜ Louvre, Palais Royal, Tuileries,
Concorde.

The long arcades with their
shops, topped by Neoclassical
apartments, date back to the
early 18th century, though

they were only finished in the
1850s. Commissioned by
Napoleon after his victory at
Rivoli, in 1797, the street
completed the link between
the Louvre and the Champs-
Elysées, and became an
important artery as well as an
elegant center for commerce.
The Tuileries walls were
replaced by railings and the
whole area opened up.
   Today along the Rue de
Rivoli there are makers of
expensive men's shirts and
bookshops toward the Place
de la Concorde, and popular
department stores near the
Châtelet and Hôtel de Ville.
Angélina's, at No. 226, is
said to serve the best hot
chocolate in Paris (see p318).

Jardin des Tuileries ⓮

75001. **Map** 12 D1. **Tel** 01 40 20 90
43. Ⓜ Tuileries, Concorde.
◯ 7am–9pm Apr–Sep,
7:30am–7:30pm Oct–Mar.

These formal gardens were
once the gardens of the old
Palais des Tuileries. They are
an integral part of the
landscaped area running
parallel to the Seine from the
Louvre to the Champs-Elysées
and the Arc de Triomphe.
   The gardens were laid out
in the 17th century by André
Le Nôtre, royal gardener to
Louis XIV. Restoration has
created a new garden as well
as filling the entire area with
striking modern and
contemporary sculpture.

**A 17th-century engraving of the
Jardin des Tuileries by G Perelle**

Galerie Nationale du Jeu de Paume 15

Jardin des Tuileries, Pl de la Concorde 75008. **Map** 11 C1. **Tel** *01 47 03 12 50.* 🔊 *01 42 60 69 69.* Ⓜ *Concorde.* ⏰ *noon–9:30pm Tue, noon–7pm Wed–Fri, 10am–7pm Sat.* ⏰ *Jan 1, May 1, Dec 25.* 🎫 ⊘ ♿ 📷 ▢ 🎧 ▢

The Jeu de Paume – or *réal* tennis court – was built by Napoleon III in 1851. When *réal* (royal) tennis was replaced in popularity by lawn tennis, the court was used to exhibit art. Eventually an Impressionist museum was founded here. In 1986, the collection moved to the Musée d'Orsay (see pp144–7) across the river. The Jeu de Paume now houses the Centre National de la Photographie, and shows exhibitions of contemporary art.

Entrance to the Jeu de Paume

Musée de l'Orangerie 16

Jardin des Tuileries, Pl de la Concorde 75008. **Map** 11 C1. **Tel** *01 42 97 48 16.* Ⓜ *Concorde.* ⏰ *until early 2006.* 🎫 📷 ♿ 🎧 *by appointment.* ▢ **www.paris.fr/musees**

Claude Monet's crowning work, the water lily series, fills the oval ground floor rooms of this museum. Known as the *Nymphéas*, the series was painted in his garden at Giverny, near Paris, and presented to the public in 1927. This superb work is complemented well by the outstanding Walter-Guillaume collection of artists of the Ecole de Paris, from the late Impressionist era to the inter-war period. This is a remark-

Monet's water lilies, on display in the Musée de l'Orangerie

able concentration of masterpieces, including a room of dramatic works by Soutine and some 14 works by Cézanne – still lifes, portraits *(Madame Cézanne)* and landscapes, such as *Dans le Parc du Château Noir.*

Renoir is represented by 27 canvases, including *Les Fillettes au Piano (Young Girls at the Piano)*. There are early Picassos, works by Henri Rousseau – notably *Le Carriole du Père Junier (Old Junier's Cart)* – Matisse and a portrait of Paul Guillaume by Modigliani. All are bathed in the natural light which flows through the window.

Place de la Concorde 17

75008. **Map** 11 C1. Ⓜ *Concorde.*

This is one of Europe's most magnificent and historic squares, covering more than 20 acres (8 ha) in the middle of Paris. Starting out as Place Louis XV, for displaying a statue of the king, it was built in the mid-18th century by architect Jacques-Ange Gabriel, who chose to make it an open octagon with only the north side containing mansions.

The 3,200-year-old obelisk from Luxor

In the square's next incarnation, as the Place de la Révolution, the statue was replaced by the guillotine. The death toll in the square in two and a half years was 1,119, including Louis XVI, Marie-Antoinette (who died in view of the small, secret apartment she kept at No. 2 Rue Royale) and the revolutionary leaders Danton and Robespierre.

Renamed Concorde (originally by chastened Revolutionaries) in a spirit of reconciliation, the grandeur of the square was enhanced in the 19th century by the 3,200-year-old Luxor obelisk, two fountains and eight statues personifying French cities. It has become the culminating point of triumphal parades down the Champs-Elysées each July 14, most notably on the memorable Bastille Day of 1989 when the Revolution's bicentennial was celebrated by a million people and many world leaders.

Colonnaded entrance to the Village Royale

Village Royal ⓲

75008. **Map** 5 C5. **M** *Madeleine.*
Galerie Royale ◯ *10am–6pm Tue–Sat.* ● *public hols.*

This delightful enclave of 18th-century town houses sits discreetly between the Rue Royale and the Rue Boissy d'Anglas. The Galerie Royale is the former home of the Duchess d'Abrantès. It was converted in 1994 by architect Laurent Bourgois, who has combined classical and modern in superb style, reflecting both the antique glass- and silverware on display and the contemporary glassworkers and goldsmiths

who occupy the vaults. Beneath the original glass roof in the central courtyard, a statue of the goddess Pomona is lit by fiber-optics and colored with blue cabochons of Bohemian crystal. There is also a quiet, elegant Bernardaud Porcelain tearoom.

Place Vendôme ⓳

75001. **Map** 6 D5. **M** *Tuileries.*

Perhaps the best example of 18th-century elegance in the city, the architect Jules Hardouin-Mansart's royal square was begun in 1698. The original plan was to house academies and embassies behind the arcaded facades. However, bankers moved in and created opulent homes. Miraculously the square has remained virtually intact and is home to jewelers and bankers. Among the famous, Frederic Chopin died here in 1848 at No. 12 and César Ritz established his famous hotel at the turn of the 20th century at No. 15.

Banque de France ⓴

39 Rue Croix des Petits Champs 75001.
Map 12 F1. **M** *Palais Royal.* ◯ *for details phone 01 42 92 26 33.*

Founded by Napoleon in 1800, France's central bank is housed in a building intended for quite different purposes. The 17th-century architect François Mansart designed this mansion for Louis XIII's wealthy secretary of state,

Napoleon's statue in Place Vendôme

FORMAL GARDENS IN PARIS

The South Parterre at Versailles *(see pp248–9)*

For the past 300 years the main formal gardens in Paris have been open to the public and are a firm fixture in the city's life. Today the Jardin des Tuileries *(see p130)* has recently undergone extensive renovation and replanting; the Jardin du Luxembourg *(see p172)*, the private garden of the French Senate, is still beloved of Left Bankers; and the Jardin du Palais Royal *(see p121)* is enjoyed by those who seek peace and privacy.

French landscaping was raised to an art form in the 17th century, thanks to Louis XIV's talented landscaper André Le Nôtre, who created the gardens of Versailles *(see pp248–9)*. He achieved a brilliant marriage between the traditional Italian Renaissance garden and the French love of rational design.

The role of the French garden architect was not to tend nature but to transform it, pruning and planting to

The long Galerie Dorée in the Banque de France

Louis de la Vrillière, with the sumptuous 164-ft (50-m) long Galerie Dorée specially created for hanging his great collection of historical paintings. The house was later sold to the Comte de Toulouse, son of Louis XIV and Madame de Montespan. The building was extensively reconstructed in the 19th century after the ravages of the Revolution. The bank's most famous modern alumnus is Jacques Delors, president of the European Commission 1985–1994.

Place des Victoires ㉑

75002. **Map** 12 F1. Ⓜ *Palais Royal.*

This circle of elegant mansions was built in 1685 solely to offset the statue of Louis XIV by Desjardins, which was placed in the middle, with torches burning day and night. The proportions of the buildings and even the arrangement of the surrounding streets were all designed by the architect and courtier Jules Hardouin-Mansart to display the statue to its best advantage.

Unfortunately, the 1792 mobs were less sycophantic and tore down the statue. A replacement, of a different style, was erected in 1822 to the detriment of the whole system of proportions of buildings to statue. Yet the square retains much of the original design, and today it is the address of major names in the fashion business, most notably Thierry Mugler, Cacharel and Kenzo.

Louis XIV on Place des Victoires

A Bagatelle garden with floral color (see p255)

create leafy sculptures out of trees, bushes and hedges. Complicated geometrical designs that were created in beds and paths were interspersed with pebbles and carefully thought-out splashes of floral color. Symmetry and harmony were the landscaper's bywords, a sense of grandeur and magnificence his ultimate goal.

In the 17th century, as now, French formal gardens served two purposes: as a setting or backdrop for a château or palace, and for enjoyment. The best view of a formal garden was from the first floor of the château, from which the combination of boxwood hedges, flowers and gravel came together in an intricate, abstract pattern, a blossoming tapestry which complemented the château's interior. Paths of trees drew the eye into infinity, reminding the onlooker of how much land belonged to his host, and therefore establishing his undoubted wealth. So, early on the formal garden became a status symbol, and it still is. This is obvious in both private gardens and in grand public projects. Napoleon Bonaparte completed his vista from the Jardin des Tuileries with a triumphal arch. The late President Mitterrand applied the principle in building his Grand Arc de la Défense (*see pp40–41, 255*) along the same axis as the Tuileries and Arc de Triomphe.

But formal gardens were also made to be enjoyed. People in the 17th century believed that walking in the fresh air kept them in good health. What more perfect spot than a formal garden bedecked with statues and fountains for additional entertainment. The old and infirm could be pushed around in sedan chairs and people could meet one another around a boxwood hedge or on a stone bench under the marbly gaze of the goddess Diana.

ST-GERMAIN-DES-PRES

This Left Bank area is fuller and livelier, its streets and cafés more crowded than when it was at the forefront of the city's intellectual life in the 1950s. The leading figures of the time have now gone, and the rebellious disciples have retreated to their bourgeois backgrounds. But the new philosophers are there, the radical young thinkers who emerged from the 1960s upheavals, and the area still has its major publishing houses, whose executives entertain treasured writers and agents at the celebrated cafés. But they now share the area with the chic set, those who patronize Yves St-Laurent's opulent premises and the elegant Rue Jacob's top interior designers. On the south side of Boulevard St-Germain the streets are quiet and quaint, with lots of good restaurants, and at the Odéon end there are brassy cafés and a profusion of movie theaters.

Musée d'Orsay clock

SIGHTS AT A GLANCE

Historic Buildings and Streets

Palais Abbatial ❷
Boulevard St-Germain ❼

Rue du Dragon ❽
Rue de l'Odéon ❿
Cour de Rohan ⓬
Cour du Commerce St-André ⓭
Institut de France ⓯
Ecole Nationale Supérieure des Beaux-Arts ⓰
Ecole Nationale d'Administration ⓱
Quai Voltaire ⓲

Churches

St-Germain-des-Prés ❶

Museums and Galleries

Musée Eugène Delacroix ❸
Musée de la Monnaie de Paris ⓮
Musée d'Orsay pp144–7 ⓳
Musée Nationale de la Légion d'Honneur ⓴

Theaters

Odéon Théâtre de L'Europe ⓫

Cafés and Restaurants

Les Deux Magots ❹
Café de Flore ❺
Brasserie Lipp ❻
Le Procope ❾

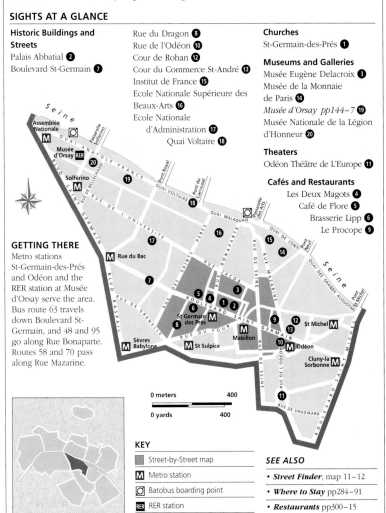

GETTING THERE

Metro stations St-Germain-des-Prés and Odéon and the RER station at Musée d'Orsay serve the area. Bus route 63 travels down Boulevard St-Germain, and 48 and 95 go along Rue Bonaparte. Routes 58 and 70 pass along Rue Mazarine.

0 meters 400
0 yards 400

KEY

▨ Street-by-Street map
Ⓜ Metro station
⬚ Batobus boarding point
RER RER station

SEE ALSO

• ***Street Finder***, map 11–12
• ***Where to Stay*** pp284–91
• ***Restaurants*** pp300–15

◁ **Les Deux Magots café beside the church of St-Germain-des-Prés**

Street-by-Street: St-Germain-des-Prés

After World War II, St-Germain-des-Prés became synonymous with intellectual life centered around bars and cafés. Philosophers, writers, actors and musicians mingled in the cellar nightspots and brasseries, where existentialist philosophy coexisted with American jazz. The area is now smarter than in the heyday of Jean-Paul Sartre and Simone de Beauvoir, the haunting singer Juliette Greco and the New Wave filmmakers. The writers are still around, enjoying the pleasures of sitting in Les Deux Magots, Café de Flore and other haunts. The 17th-century buildings have survived, but signs of change are evident in the plethora of affluent shops dealing in antiques, books and fashion.

Organ grinder in St-Germain

Les Deux Magots
The café is famous for the patronage of celebrities such as Hemingway ④

Café de Flore
In the 1950s, French intellectuals wrestled with new philosophical ideas in the Art Deco interior of the café ⑤

RUE DU DRAGON

RUE DU SABOT

RUE DE RENNES

RUE BONAPARTE

RUE DU FOUR

Metro St-Germain-des-Prés

Brasserie Lipp
Colorful ceramics decorate this famous brasserie frequented by politicians ⑥

★ **St-Germain-des-Prés**
Descartes and the king of Poland are among the notables buried here in Paris's oldest church ❶

★ **Boulevard St-Germain**
Café terraces, boutiques, cinemas, restaurants and bookshops characterize the central section of the Left Bank's main street ❼

Picasso's sculpture *Homage to Apollinaire is a tribute to the artist's friend, the poet Guillaume Apollinaire. It was erected in 1959, near the Café de Flore, where the poet held court.*

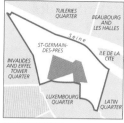

LOCATOR MAP
See Central Paris Map pp14–15

★ Musée Delacroix
Here, Delacroix created the splendid mural, Jacob Wrestling, for St-Sulpice (see p172) ❸

STAR SIGHTS

★ St-Germain-des-Prés

★ Boulevard
St-Germain

★ Musée Delacroix

Rue de Fürstenberg is a tiny square with old-fashioned street lamps and shady trees. It is often used as a movie setting.

KEY

--- --- Suggested route

0 metres   100

0 yards   100

Rue de Buci was for centuries an important Left Bank street and the site of some Real Tennis courts. It now holds a lively market every day.

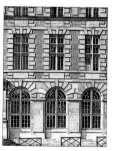

Palais Abbatial
This was the residence of abbots from 1586 till the 1789 Revolution ❷

Metro Odéon

Danton's statue *(1889), by Auguste Paris, is a tribute to the Revolutionary leader.*

Metro Mabillon

Marché St-Germain is an old covered food market which was opened in 1818, taking over the site of a former fairground. *(See p334.)*

St-Germain-des-Prés ❶

3 Pl St-Germain-des-Prés 75006. **Map**
12 E4. **Tel** 01 55 42 81 33. Ⓜ St-
Germain-des-Prés. ◯ 8am–7pm
daily. **Concerts** 8pm Tue, Thu. 🎨 📷

This is the oldest church in
Paris, originating in 542
when King Childebert built
a basilica to house holy relics.
It became an immensely
powerful Benedictine abbey,
which was suppressed during
the Revolution, when most of
the buildings were destroyed
by a fire in 1794. One of the
Revolution's most horrific
episodes took place in a
nearby monastery when 318
priests were hacked to death
by the mob on
September 3,
1792. The current
church dates from
about the 11th
century and was
heavily restored
in the 19th
century. One of
the three original
towers survives,
housing one of
the oldest belfries
in France. The
interior of the
church is an
interesting mix of
architectural styles,
with some 6th-
century marble
columns, Gothic
vaulting and
Romanesque

**Our Lady of
Consolation statue
in St-Germain-
des-Prés**

arches. Famous tombs include
those of the 17th-century
philosopher René Descartes,
the poet Nicolas Boileau and
John Casimir, king of Poland,
who later became abbot of St-
Germain-des-Prés in 1669.

Palais Abbatial ❷

1–5 Rue de l'Abbaye 75006.
Map 12 E4. Ⓜ St-Germain-des-Prés.
Not open to the public.

This brick and stone palace
was built in 1586 for Charles
of Bourbon who was
cardinal-abbot of St-Germain
and, very briefly, king of
France. Ten more abbots
lived there until the Revolution, when the building was

**An ironwork detail from the
facade of the Palais Abbatial**

sold. James Pradier, the 19th-
century sculptor who was
famous for his female figures,
established a studio here.
The palace is now noted
for its mixture of building
materials and its splendid
vertical windows.

Musée Eugène Delacroix ❸

6 Rue de Fürstenberg 75006.
Map 12 E4. **Tel** 01 44 41 86 50.
Ⓜ St-Germain-des-Prés. ◯ 9:30am–
4:30pm Wed–Mon (last adm: 4pm).
🎨 📷 **www**.musee-delacroix.fr

Eugène Delacroix

The leading nonconformist
Romantic painter, Eugène
Delacroix, known for his
passionate and highly
colored canvases, lived and
worked here from 1857 to his
death in 1863. Here he
painted *The Entombment
of Christ* and *The Way to
Calvary* (which now hang in
the museum). He also created
superb murals for the Chapel
of the Holy Angels in the
nearby St-Sulpice church,
which is part of the reason
why he moved to this area.

The first-floor apartment and
garden studio now form a
national museum, where
regular exhibitions of
Delacroix's work are held.
The apartment has a portrait
of George Sand, self-portraits,
studies for future works and
artistic memorabilia.
   The charm of Delacroix's
garden is reflected in the tiny
Fürstenberg square. With its
pair of rare catalpa trees and
old-fashioned street lamps,
the square is one of Paris's
most romantic corners.

Les Deux Magots ❹

6 Pl St-Germain-des-Prés 75006.
Map 12 E4. **Tel** 01 45 48 55 25.
Ⓜ St-Germain-des-Prés.
◯ 7:30am–1am daily.
⊗ for one week in Jan.
www.lesdeuxmagots.com

The café still trades on its
reputation as the meeting place
of the city's literary and
intellectual elite. This derives
from the patronage of
Surrealist artists and writers
including Ernest Hemingway
in the 1920s and 1930s, and
existentialist philosophers and
writers in the 1950s.
   The present clientele is
more likely to be publishers
or people-watchers than the
new Hemingway. The café's
name comes from the two
wooden statues of Chinese
commercial agents (*magots*)
that adorn one of the pillars.
This is a good place for
enjoying an old-fashioned hot
chocolate and watching the
world go by.

The interior of Les Deux Magots

Facade of the Café de Flore, former meeting place of existentialists

Café de Flore ❺

172 Blvd St-Germain 75006.
Map 12 D4. **Tel** 01 45 48 55 26.
Ⓜ St-Germain-des-Prés. ⬜
7:30am–1:30am daily. ♿ restricted.

The classic Art Deco interior of all-red seating, mahogany and mirrors has changed little since the war. Like its rival Les Deux Magots, it has hosted most of the French intellectuals during the post-war years. Jean-Paul Sartre and Simone de Beauvoir would meet "the Family" (their cronies) here and develop their philosophy of existentialism over a drink.

A waiter at the Brasserie Lipp

Brasserie Lipp ❻

151 Blvd St-Germain 75006. **Map** 12 E4. **Tel** 01 45 48 53 91. Ⓜ St-Germain-des-Prés. ⬜ 11:45am–12:45am daily. (See p305.)

Third of the famous cafés clustered around St-Germain-des-Prés, Brasserie Lipp combines Alsatian beer, sauerkraut and sausages (it was founded by a refugee from Alsace) with excellent coffee to produce a Left Bank fixture popular with French politicians and fashion gurus as well as visitors. Originally opened in the late 19th century, it is regarded by many as the quintessential Parisian brasserie, although the experience is more atmospheric than culinary these days. The interior is bright with ceramic tiles of parrots and cranes.

Boulevard St-Germain ❼

75006, 75007. **Map** 11 C2 & 13 C5. Ⓜ Solférino, Rue du Bac, St-Germain-des-Prés, Mabillon, Odéon.

The Left Bank's most celebrated thoroughfare, over 2 miles (3 km) long, curves across three districts from the Ile St-Louis to the Pont de la Concorde. The architecture is homogeneous because the boulevard was another of Baron Haussmann's bold strokes of 19th-century urban planning, but it encompasses a wide range of different lifestyles as well as a number of religious and cultural institutions. From the east (the low street numbers) the boulevard passes the late François Mitterrand's private town residence in the Rue de Bièvre, as well as the Maubert-Mutualité market square, the Musée de Cluny and the Sorbonne university, before crossing the lively Boulevard St-Michel.

It continues past the Ecole de Médecine and the Place de l'Odéon to St-Germain-des-Prés, with its historic church and café terraces. Fashion boutiques, theaters, restaurants and bookshops give this central portion its distinctive character. It is also here that one is most likely to see a celebrity. The area is active from midday to the early morning hours.

Continuing further, beyond this section the boulevard becomes more exclusively residential and then distinctly political with the Ministry of Defense and the National Assembly buildings.

Rue du Dragon ❽

75006. **Map** 12 D4.
Ⓜ St-Germain-des-Prés.

This short street, between the Boulevard St-Germain and the Carrefour de la Croix Rouge, dates back to the Middle Ages and still has houses from the 17th and 18th centuries. Notice their large doors, tall windows and ironwork balconies. A group of Flemish painters lived at No. 37 before the Revolution. The novelist Victor Hugo rented a garret at No. 30 when he was a 19-year-old bachelor.

A plaque at No. 30 Rue du Dragon commemorating Victor Hugo's house

Le Procope ❾

13 Rue de l'Ancienne-Comédie 75006.
Map12 F4. **Tel** 01 40 46 79 00.
Ⓜ *Odéon.* ◯ *noon–midnight daily.*
See **The History of Paris** pp26–7.

The rear facade of Le Procope restaurant

Founded in 1686 by the
Sicilian Francesco Procopio
dei Coltelli, this claims to be
the world's first coffee house.
It quickly became popular
with the city's political and
literary elite and with actors
from the Comédie-Française.

Its patrons have included
Benjamin Franklin and the
philosopher Voltaire – who
supposedly drank 40 cups of
his favorite mixture of coffee
and chocolate every day. The
young Napoleon would leave
his hat as security while he
went searching for the money
to pay the bill. Now a
restaurant, Le Procope was
revamped in 1989 in the style
of the 18th century.

**Odéon Théâtre de l'Europe, former
home of the Comédie-Française**

Rue de l'Odéon ❿

75006. **Map** 12 F5. Ⓜ *Odéon.*

Sylvia Beach's bookshop
Shakespeare & Company
(*see pp331–2*) stood at No. 12
from 1921 to 1940. She
befriended many struggling
American and British writers,
such as Ezra Pound, T S Eliot,
Scott Fitzgerald and Ernest
Hemingway. It was largely
due to her support – as
secretary, editor, agent and
banker – that James Joyce's
Ulysses was first published in
English. Adrianne Monnier's
French equivalent at No. 7
opposite, Les Amis des Livres,
was frequented by André
Gide and Paul Valéry.

Opened in 1779 to improve
access to the Odéon theater,
this was the first street in
Paris to have sidewalks with
gutters and it still has many
attractive houses and shops,
most of them dating from the
18th century.

Odéon Théâtre de l'Europe ⓫

1 Pl Paul-Claudel 75006. **Map** 12 F5.
Tel 01 44 41 36 00. Ⓜ *Odéon,
Luxembourg.* ◯ *for performances
only.* See **Entertainment** pp342–4.
www.theatre-odeon.fr

This Neoclassical theater
was built in 1779 by Marie-
Josephe Peyre and Charles
de Wailly on the grounds of
the former Hôtel de Condé.
The site had been purchased
by the king and given to the
city to house the Comédie
Française. The premiere of
The Marriage of Figaro, by
Beaumarchais, took place
here in 1784. With the arrival
of a new company in 1797
the name of the theater was
changed to Odéon. In 1807 the
theater was consumed by fire.
It was rebuilt later the same
year by the architect Jean-
François Chalgrin.

Following World War II, the
theater specialized in 20th-
century drama and was the
best attended in Paris. The
auditorium is particularly
impressive, not least for its
ceiling, painted by André
Masson in 1965.

A young Hemingway in the 1920s

Cour de Rohan ⓬

75006. **Map** 12 F4. Ⓜ *Odéon.*
Access from the Rue du Jardinet until
8pm; 8pm–8am access from the Blvd
St-Germain.

**The unusual middle courtyard in
the Cour de Rohan**

This picturesque series of
three courtyards was
originally part of the 15th-
century pied-à-terre of the
archbishops of Rouen
(corrupted to "Rohan"). The
middle courtyard is the most
unusual. Its three-legged
wrought-iron mounting block,
known as a *pas-de-mule*, was
used at one time by elderly
women and overweight
prelates to mount their mules.
It is probably the last
mounting block left in Paris.
Overlooking the yard is the
facade of a fine Renaissance
building, dating from the
beginning of the 17th century.
One of its important former
residents was Henri II's
mistress, Diane de Poitiers.

The third courtyard opens
on to the tiny Rue du
Jardinet, where the composer
Saint-Saëns was born in 1835.

Cour du Commerce St-André ⑬

75006. **Map** 12 F4. Ⓜ *Odéon.*

The grisly specter of the guillotine hangs over No. 9, since it was here that Dr Guillotin is supposed to have perfected his "philanthropic decapitating machine". In fact, although the idea was Guillotin's, it was Dr Louis, a Parisian surgeon, who was responsible for putting the "humane" plan into action. When the guillotine was first used for execution in 1792 it was known as a *Louisette*.

A print of a Revolutionary mob at a guillotine execution

Musée de la Monnaie de Paris ⑭

11 Quai de Conti 75006. **Map** 12 F3.
Tel *01 40 46 55 35.* Ⓜ *Pont-Neuf, Odéon.* ⬜ *11am–5:30pm Tue–Fri, noon–5:30pm Sat–Sun.* 🈳
🈳 🈳 ***Movies.***
www.monnaiedeparis.fr

When Louis XV decided to rehouse the mint in the late 18th century, he hit upon the idea of launching a design competition for the new

building. The present Hôtel des Monnaies is the result of this competition. It was completed in 1777, and the architect, Jacques Antoine, lived here until his death.

Coins were minted in the mansion until 1973, when the process was moved to Pessac in the Gironde. The minting and milling halls now contain the coin and medallion museum. The extensive collection is displayed in vertical glass stands so that both sides of the coins are visible, and everything is presented in the context of the history of the day. The final room of the museum shows a production cycle with late 19th-century and early 20th-century tools and machines on display.

Instead of minting coins, the building's workshops are now devoted to the creation of medallions, a selection of which are on sale in the museum shop.

Institut de France ⑮

23 Quai de Conti 75006.
Map 12 E3. ***Tel*** *01 44 41 44 41.*
Ⓜ *Pont-Neuf, St-Germain-des-Prés.* ⬜ *Sat & Sun by appointment only.*
🈳 🈳 **www**.institut-de-france.fr

Now home to the illustrious Académie Française, this Baroque building was built as a palace in 1688 and was given over to the Institut de France in 1805. Its distinctive cupola was designed by the palace's architect, Louis Le Vau, to harmonize with the Palais du Louvre.

The Académie Française is the most famous of the five academies within the institute. It was founded in 1635 by

A sign to the former Mint, which is now a museum

Cardinal Richelieu and charged with the compilation of an official dictionary of the French language. From the beginning, membership has been limited to 40, who are entrusted with working on the dictionary.

Ecole Nationale Supérieure des Beaux-Arts ⑯

13 Quai Malaquais 75006. **Map** 12 E3.
Tel *01 47 03 50 00.* Ⓜ *St-Germain-des-Prés.* ⬜ *groups by appt only (phone 01 47 03 52 15 to arrange).*
🈳 *Library.* **www**.ensba.fr

The main French school of fine arts occupies an enviable position at the corner of the Rue Bonaparte and the river-side Quai Malaquais. The school is housed in several buildings, the most imposing being the 19th-century Palais des Etudes.

A host of budding French and foreign painters and architects have crossed the large courtyard to study in the ateliers of the school. Young American architects, in particular, have studied there over the past century.

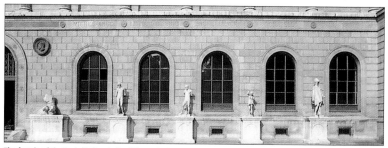
The facade of the Ecole Nationale Supérieure des Beaux-Arts

THE CELEBRATED CAFES OF PARIS

One of the most enduring images of Paris is the café scene. For the visitor it is the romantic vision of great artists, writers or eminent intellectuals consorting in one of the Left Bank's celebrated cafés. For the Parisian the café is one of life's constants, an everyday experience, providing people with a place to tryst, drink and meet friends, or to conclude business deals, or to simply watch the world go by.

The first café anywhere can be traced back to 1686, when the café Le Procope (*see p140*) was opened. In the following century cafés became a vital part of Paris's social life. And with the widening of the city's streets, particularly during the 19th century, and the building of Haussmann's Grands Boulevards, the cafés spread out on to the sidewalks, evoking Emile Zola's comment as to the "great silent crowds watching the street live".

The nature of a café was sometimes determined by the interests of its patrons. Some were the gathering places for those interested in playing chess, dominoes or billiards. Literary gents gathered in Le Procope during Molière's time in the 17th century. In the 19th century, First Empire imperial guards officers were drawn to the Café d'Orsay and Second Empire financiers gathered in the cafés along the Rue de la Chaussée d'Antin. The stylish set patronized the Café de Paris and Café Tortini, and theater-goers met at the cafés around the Opéra, including the Café de la Paix (*see p213*).

Newspaper reading is still a typical café pastime

Ecole Nationale d'Administration ⑰

13 Rue de l'Université 75007.
Map 12 D3. **Tel** *01 49 26 45 45.*
Ⓜ *Rue du Bac.* ⬤ *to the public.*

This fine 18th-century mansion was originally built as two houses in 1643 by Briçonnet. In 1713 they were replaced by a *hôtel*, built by Thomas Gobert for the widow of Denis Feydeau de Brou. It was passed on to her son, Paul-Espirit Feydeau de Brou, until his death in 1767. The *hôtel* then became the residence of the Venetian ambassador. It was occupied by Belzunce in 1787 and became a munitions depot during the Revolution until the restoration of the monarchy in 1815.

Until recently it housed the Ecole Nationale d'Administration (now in Strasbourg), where a high percentage of the elite in politics, economics and science were once students.

Plaque marking the house in Quai Voltaire where Voltaire died

Quai Voltaire ⑱

75006 and 75007. **Map** 12 D3.
Ⓜ *Rue du Bac.*

Formerly part of the Quai Malaquais, then later known as the Quai des Théatins, the Quai Voltaire is now home to some of the most important antiques dealers in Paris. It is also noted for its attractive 18th-century houses and for the famous people who lived in many of them, making it an especially interesting and pleasant street to walk along.

The 18th-century Swedish ambassador Count Tessin lived at No. 1, as did the sculptor James Pradier, famed for his statues and for his wife, who swam naked across the Seine. Louise de Kérouaille, spy for Louis XIV and created Duchess of Portsmouth by the infatuated Charles II of England, lived at Nos. 3–5.

Famous past residents of No. 19 included the composers Richard Wagner and Jean Sibelius, the novelist Charles Baudelaire and the exiled Irish writer and wit Oscar Wilde.

The French philosopher Voltaire died at No. 27, the Hôtel de la Villette. St-Sulpice, the local church, refused to accept his corpse (on the grounds of his atheism) and his body was rushed into the country to avoid a pauper's grave.

Entertainment in the Claude Alain café in the Rue de Seine during the 1950s

The most famous cafés are on the Left Bank, in St-Germain and Montparnasse, where the literati of old used to gather and where the glitterati of today love to be seen. Before World War I, Montparnasse was haunted by hordes of Russian revolutionaries, most eminently Lenin and Trotsky, who whiled away their days in the cafés, grappling with the problems of Russia and the world over a *petit café*. Cultural life flourished in the 1920s, when Surrealists like Salvador Dalí and Jean Cocteau dominated café life, and later when American writers led by Ernest Hemingway and Scott Fitzgerald talked, drank and worked in various cafés, among them La Coupole *(see p178)*, Le Sélect and La Closerie des Lilas *(see p179)*.

After the end of World War II, the cultural scene shifted northward to St-Germain. Existentialism had become the dominant creed and Jean-Paul Sartre its tiny charismatic leader. Sartre and his intellectual peers and followers, among them the writers Simone de Beauvoir and Albert Camus, the poet Boris Vian and the enigmatic singer Juliette Greco, gathered to work and discuss their ideas in Les Deux Magots *(see p138)* and the nearby rival Café de Flore *(see p139)*. The traditional habitué of these cafés is still to be seen, albeit mixing with the international jet-set and with self-publicizing intellectuals hunched over their notebooks.

Works by one of St-Germain's elite, Albert Camus (1913–60)

Musée d'Orsay ⑲

See pp144–7.

Musée Nationale de la Légion d'Honneur ⑳

2 Rue de Bellechasse (2 Rue de la Légion d'Honneur) 75007. **Map** 11 C2. **Tel** 01 40 62 84 25. Ⓜ Solférino. Ⓡ Musée d'Orsay. ⬭ (due to re-open in June 2006).

Next to the Musée d'Orsay is the enormous Hôtel de Salm. It was one of the last great mansions to be built in

The Musée d'Orsay, converted from a railroad station into a museum

the area (1782). The first owner was a German count, Prince de Salm-Kyrbourg, who was guillotined in 1794.

Today the building contains a museum where one can learn all about the Legion of Honor, a decoration launched by Napoleon I and so cherished by the French (and foreigners). Those

Napoleon III's Great Cross of the Legion of Honor

awarded the honor wear a small red rosette in their lapel. The impressive displays of medals and insignia are complemented by paintings. In one of the rooms, Napoleon's Legion of Honor is on display with his sword and breastplate.

The museum also covers decorations from most parts of the world, among them the British Victoria Cross and the American Purple Heart.

Musée d'Orsay ⑲

In 1986, 47 years after it had closed as a mainline railroad station, Victor Laloux's superb turn-of-the-century building was reopened as the Musée d'Orsay. Commissioned by the Orléans railroad company to be its Paris terminus, it avoided demolition in the 1970s following the outcry over the destruction of Baltard's pavilions at Les Halles food market. During the conversion much of the original architecture was retained. The museum, which is currently undergoing extensive renovation, was set up to present each of the arts of the period from 1848 to 1914 in the context of the contemporary society and all the forms of creative activity happening at the time.

The Museum, from the Right Bank
Victor Laloux designed the building for the Universal Exhibition in 1900.

Chair by Charles Rennie Mackintosh
The style developed by Mackintosh was an attempt to express ideas in a framework of vertical and horizontal forms, as in this tearoom chair (1900).

★ **The Gates of Hell** *(1880–1917)*
Rodin included figures that he had already created, such as The Thinker *and* The Kiss, *in this famous gateway.*

★ **Le Déjeuner sur l'Herbe** *(1863)*
Manet's painting, first exhibited in Napoleon III's Salon des Refusés, *is presently on display in the first area of the upper level.*

KEY TO FLOORPLAN

- ☐ Architecture & Decorative Arts
- ☐ Sculpture
- ☐ Painting before 1870
- ☐ Impressionism
- ☐ Neo-Impressionism
- ☐ Naturalism and Symbolism
- ☐ Art Nouveau
- ☐ Temporary exhibitions
- ☐ Non-exhibition space

GALLERY GUIDE

The collection occupies three levels. On the ground floor there are works from the mid to late 19th century. The middle level features Art Nouveau decorative art and a range of paintings and sculptures from the second half of the 19th century to the early 20th century. The upper level has an outstanding collection of Impressionist and Neo-Impressionist art.

The Dance *(1867–8)*
Carpeaux's sculpture caused a scandal when first exhibited.

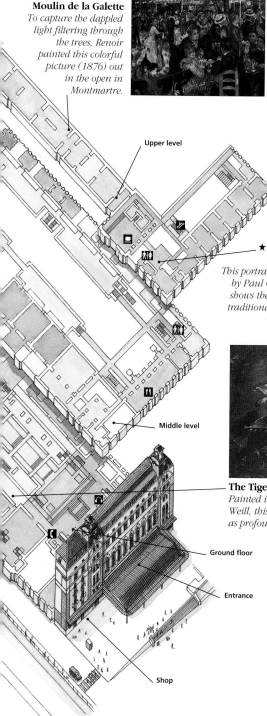

★ **Dancing at the Moulin de la Galette**
To capture the dappled light filtering through the trees, Renoir painted this colorful picture (1876) out in the open in Montmartre.

Upper level

Middle level

Ground floor

Entrance

Shop

VISITORS' CHECKLIST

Quai Anatole France. **Map** 12 D2.
Tel 01 40 49 49 78 (groups 01 53 63 04 50). Ⓜ *Solférino.* ﹏ *24, 68, 69, 84 to Quai A. France; 73 to Rue Solférino; 63, 83, 83, 94 to Blvd St-Germain.* RER *Musée d'Orsay.* Ⓟ *Musée d'Orsay.* Ⓟ *Rue du Bac, Blvd St-Germain.* Ⓞ *Jun–Sep: 9am–6pm Tue, Wed, Fri, Sat, Sun, 9am–9.45pm Thu; Oct–May: 10am– 6pm Tue, Wed, Fri, Sat, 10am–9.45pm Thu, 9am–6pm Sun.* Ⓞ *Jan 1, May 1, Dec 25.* Ⓞ Ⓞ Ⓞ Ⓞ
Concerts. Ⓞ Ⓞ Ⓞ
www.musee-orsay.fr

★ **La Belle Angèle**
This portrait (1889) by Paul Gauguin shows the sitter in traditional Breton costume.

The Tiger Hunt by Eugène Delacroix
Painted in 1854 for a dealer named Weill, this was described by Baudelaire as profound, sensual and terrible.

STAR EXHIBITS

★ The Gates of Hell by Rodin

─────────────

★ Le Déjeuner sur l'Herbe by Manet

─────────────

★ Dancing at the Moulin de la Galette by Renoir

─────────────

★ La Belle Angèle by Gauguin

Exploring the Orsay

Many of the exhibits now in the Musée d'Orsay originally came from the Louvre, and the superb collection of Impressionist art that was housed in the cramped Jeu de Paume until it closed in 1986 has been rehung here. In addition to the main exhibition, there are displays that explain the social, political and technological context in which the art was created, including exhibits on the history of cinematography.

Ceiling design (1911) by the artist and designer Maurice Denis

ART NOUVEAU

The Belgian architect and designer Victor Horta was among the first to give free rein to the sinuous line that gave Art Nouveau its French sobriquet of *Style Nouille* (noodle style). Taking its name from a gallery of modern design that opened in Paris in 1895, Art Nouveau flourished throughout Europe until World War I.

In Vienna, Otto Wagner, Koloman Moser and Josef Hoffmann combined high craft with the new design, while the School of Glasgow, under the impetus of Charles Rennie Mackintosh, developed a more rectilinear approach which anticipated the work of Frank Lloyd Wright in the United States.

René Lalique introduced the aesthetics of Art Nouveau into jewelry and glassware, while Hector Guimard, inspired by Horta, is most famous today for his once-ubiquitous Art Nouveau entrances to the Paris metro.

One exhibit not to be missed is the carved wooden bookcase by Rupert Carabin (1890), with its proliferation of allegorical seated female nudes, bronze palm fronds and severed bearded heads.

SCULPTURE

The museum's central aisle overflows with an oddly assorted selection of sculptures. These illustrate the eclectic mood around the middle of the 19th century when the classicism of Eugène Guillaume's *Cenotaph of the Gracchi* (1848–53) coexisted with the romanticism of François Rude. Rude created the relief on the Arc de Triomphe (1836), often referred to as *La Marseillaise (see p209)*.

There is a wonderful series of 36 busts of members of parliament (1832) – bloated, ugly, unscrupulous and self-important – by the satirist Honoré Daumier, and work by the vital but short-lived genius Jean-Baptiste Carpeaux, whose first major bronze, *Count Ugolino* (1862), was a character from Dante. In 1868 he produced his Dionysian delight, *The Dance*, which caused a storm of protest: it was "an insult to public morals". This contrasts with the derivative and mannered work of such sculptors as Alexandre Falguière and Hyppolyte Moulin.

Edgar Degas' famous *Young Dancer of Fourteen* (1881) was displayed during his lifetime, but the many bronzes on show were made from wax sculptures found in his

studio after his death. In contrast, the sculpture of Auguste Rodin was very much in the public eye, and his sensuous and forceful work makes him pre-eminent among 19th-century sculptors. The museum contains many of his works, including the original plaster of *Balzac* (1897). Rodin's talented companion, Camille Claudel, who spent much of her life in an asylum, is represented by a grim allegory of mortality, *Maturity* (1899–1903).

The turn of the 20th century is marked by the work of Emile-Antoine Bourdelle and Aristide Maillol.

PAINTING BEFORE 1870

The surprising diversity of styles in 19th-century painting is emphasized by the close juxtaposition on the ground floor of all paintings prior to 1870 – the crucial year in which Impressionism first made a name for itself. The raging color and almost Expressionistic vigor of Eugène Delacroix's *Lion Hunt* (1854) stands next to Jean-Dominiques Ingres' cool Classical *The Spring* (1820–56). As a reminder of the academic manner that dominated the century up to that point, the uninspired waxwork style of Thomas Couture's monumental *The Romans in the Age of Decadence* (1847) dominates the central aisle. In a class of their own are Edouard Manet's provocative *Olympia* and *Le Déjeuner sur l'Herbe* (1863), while works painted around the same time by his friends, Claude Monet, Pierre-Auguste Renoir, Frédéric Bazille and Alfred Sisley, give a glimpse of the Impressionists before the Impressionist movement began.

Young Dancer of Fourteen (1881) by Edgar Degas

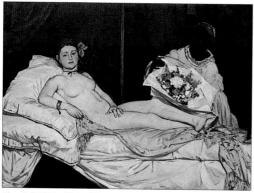

Olympia (1863) by Edouard Manet

IMPRESSIONISM

Rouen Cathedral caught at various moments of the day (1892–3) is one of the many works on show by Claude Monet, the leading figure of the Impressionist movement. Pierre-Auguste Renoir's plump nudes and his young people *Dancing at the Moulin de la Galette* (1876) were painted at the high point of his Impressionist period. Other artists on display include Camille Pissarro, Alfred Sisley and Mary Cassatt.

Edgar Degas, Paul Cézanne and Vincent Van Gogh are included here although their techniques differed from those of the Impressionists. Degas often favored crisp Realism, though he was quite capable of using the sketchy manner of the Impressionists, as, for instance, in *L'Absinthe* (1876). Cézanne was more concerned with substance than light, as can be seen in his *Apples and Oranges* (1895–1900). Van Gogh was momentarily influenced by the movement but then went his own way, illustrated here by works from the collection of Dr Gachet.

Breton Peasant Women (1894) by Paul Gauguin

NEO-IMPRESSIONISM

Although labeled Neo-Impressionism, the work of Georges Seurat (which includes *The Circus* from 1891) was quite unrelated to the older movement. He, along with Maximilien Luce and Paul Signac, painted by applying small dots of color that blended together when viewed from a distance. *Jane Avril Dancing* (1892) is just one of many pictures by Henri de Toulouse-Lautrec on display. The work Paul Gauguin did at Pont-Aven in Brittany is shown next to that of younger artists who knew him at the time, such as Emile Bernard and the Nabis group. There are also a number of paintings from his Tahitian period.

The Nabis (which included Pierre Bonnard) tended to treat the canvas as a flat surface out of which a sense of depth emerged as the viewer gazed upon it.

The dreamlike visions of Odilon Redon are in the Symbolist vein, while the naïve art of Henri (Douanier) Rousseau is represented by *War* (1894) and *The Snake Charmer* (1907).

NATURALISM AND SYMBOLISM

Three large rooms are devoted to paintings that filled the salons from 1880 to 1900. The work of the Naturalists was sanctioned by the Third Republic and widely reproduced at the time. Fernand Cormon's figure of *Cain* was highly acclaimed when it first appeared at the 1880 Salon. Jules Bastien-Lepage's interest lay in illustrating peasant life, and in 1877 he painted *Haymaking*, which established him as one of the leading Naturalists. His fairly free handling of paint was influenced by what he had learned from Manet and his friends. More somberly (and effectively) naturalistic is Lionel Walden's view of *The Docks of Cardiff* (1894).

Symbolism developed as a reaction against Realism and Impressionism and tended to be dominated by images of dreams and thoughts. This resulted in a wide variety of subjects and modes of expression. There is the over-sweet vision of levitating harpists, *Serenity* by Henri Martin (1899), Edward Burne-Jones' monumental work *Wheel of Fortune* (1883) and Jean Delville's *School of Plato* (1898). One of the most evocative paintings in this section is Winslow Homer's lyrical *Summer Night* (1890).

Blue Waterlilies (1919) by Claude Monet

LATIN QUARTER

15th-century stained glass in Musée de Cluny

Student bookshops, cafés, theaters and jazz clubs fill this ancient, riverside quarter between the Seine and the Luxembourg Gardens. Famous institutes of learning abound, among them the two most prestigious *lycées*, Henri IV and Louis le Grand, through which passes a large percentage of the future French elite.

As the leaders of the 1968 revolt *(see pp40–41)* disappeared into the mainstream of French life, so the Boulevard St-Michel, the area's spine, turned increasingly to commerce, not demonstrations. Today, there are cheap shops and fast-food outlets, and the maze of narrow, cobbled streets off the boulevard are full of inexpensive ethnic shops, quirky boutiques and avant-garde theaters and cinemas. But the area's 800 years of history are difficult to efface. The Sorbonne retains much of its old character and the eastern half of the area has streets dating back to the 13th century. And the Rue St-Jacques still remains, the long Roman road stretching out of the city, and the forerunner of all the city's streets.

A young musician playing music under the Pont St-Michel is part of the Latin Quarter's long tradition as a focus for the young from all walks of life.

SIGHTS AT A GLANCE

Historic Buildings and Streets
Boulevard St-Michel **2**
La Sorbonne **7**
Collège de France **8**

Museums and Galleries
Musée National du Moyen Age *pp154–7* **1**
Musée de la Préfecture de Police **6**

Churches and Temples
St-Séverin **3**
St-Julien-le-Pauvre **4**

Eglise de la Sorbonne **9**
St-Etienne-du-Mont **10**
Panthéon pp158–9 **11**

Squares
Place Maubert **5**

GETTING THERE
Metro stations in the area include those at St-Michel and Cluny La Sorbonne. The Balabus and routes 24 and 87 travel along Blvd St-Germain, and 38 travels along Blvd St-Michel, passing the Sorbonne and the Musée National du Moyen Age.

[Map of the Latin Quarter showing Seine, Metro stations, RER stations, and streets including Boulevard Saint Michel, Boulevard Saint Germain, Rue St Jacques, Quai de Montebello, Quai de la Tournelle, Rue Monge, Rue des Ecoles, Rue Soufflot, Place du Panthéon, Rue Clovis, with labels St Michel, Cluny-la-Sorbonne, Maubert Mutualité, Cardinal Lemoine, Luxembourg]

0 meters 400
0 yards 400

KEY

▢	Street-by-Street map
Ⓜ	Metro station
▣	Batobus boarding point
RER	RER station

SEE ALSO

◁ **A peaceful spot along a Latin Quarter quay**

Street-by-Street: Latin Quarter

Since the Middle Ages this riverside quarter has been dominated by the Sorbonne; it acquired its name from the early Latin-speaking students. It dates back to the Roman town across from the Ile de la Cité; at that time the Rue St-Jacques was one of the main roads out of Paris. The area is generally associated with artists, intellectuals and the bohemian way of life. It also has a history of political unrest. In 1871, the Place St-Michel became the center of the Paris Commune, and in May 1968 it was the site of the student uprisings. Today the eastern half has become sufficiently chic, however, to contain the homes of some of the Establishment.

Place St-Michel contains a fountain by Davioud. The bronze statue by Duret shows St Michael killing the dragon.

Metro St-Michel

Little Athens is a lively place in the evening, especially on the weekend, when the Greek restaurants situated in the picturesque streets around St-Séverin are at their busiest.

Metro Cluny La Sorbonne

★ **Boulevard St-Michel**
The northern end of the Boul'Mich, as it is affectionately known, is a lively mélange of cafés, book and clothes shops, with nightclubs and experimental movie theaters nearby ❷

★ **Musée National du Moyen Age**
One of the finest collections of medieval art in the world is kept here in a superb late 15th-century building ❶

No. 22 Rue St-Séverin is the narrowest house in Paris and used to be the residence of Abbé Prévost, author of *Manon Lescaut*.

★ St-Séverin
*Begun in the 13th century,
this beautiful church took
three centuries to build and
is a fine example of the
flamboyant Gothic style* ❸

Rue du Chat qui Pêche is a
narrow pedestrianized street
which has changed little in its
200-year history.

LOCATOR MAP
See Central Paris Map pp14–15

Shakespeare & Co *(see
pp331-2)* at No.37 Rue
de la Bûcherie is a
delightful, if chaotic,
bookshop. Any books
purchased here are
stamped with
*Shakespeare & Co
Kilomètre Zéro Paris.*

★ St-Julien-le-Pauvre
*Rebuilt in the 17th
century, this church was
used to store animal feed
during the Revolution* ❹

Rue de Fouarre
used to host
lectures in the
Middle Ages. The
students sat on straw
(fouarre) in the street.

STAR SIGHTS

★ Musée de Cluny

★ St-Séverin

★ St-Julien-le-Pauvre

★ Boulevard
St-Michel

Ⓜ
Metro
Maubert
Mutualité

Rue Galande was home
to the rich and chic
in the 17th century,
but subsequently
became notorious for
its taverns.

KEY

– – – Suggested route

0 meters — 100

0 yards — 100

Musée National du Moyen Age ❶

See pp154–7.

Boulevard St-Michel ❷

75005 & 75006. **Map** 12 F5 & 16 F2.
Ⓜ *St-Michel, Cluny-La Sorbonne.*
🚆 *Luxembourg.*

Cut through the area in 1869, the boulevard initially gained fame from its many literary cafés, but nowadays many have been replaced by clothes shops. Nos. 60–64 house the École Nationale Supérieure des Mines, one of France's leading engineering schools (*see p173*). In the Place St-Michel, marble plaques commemorate the many students who died here in 1944 fighting the Nazis.

Gargoyles adorning St-Séverin

St-Séverin ❸

1 Rue-des-Prêtres-St-Séverin 75005.
Map 13 A4. *Tel* 01 42 34 93 50.
Ⓜ *St-Michel.* ⬤ *11am–7:30pm daily.*
📷 *Concerts.*

One of the most beautiful churches in Paris, St-Séverin is a perfect example of the Flamboyant Gothic style. It is named after a 6th-century hermit who lived in the area and persuaded the future St Cloud, grandson of King Clovis, to take holy orders. Construction finished in the early 16th century and included a remarkable double ambulatory circling the chancel. In 1684 the Grande

Inside St-Julien-le-Pauvre

Mademoiselle, cousin to Louis XIV, adopted St-Séverin after breaking with her parish church of St-Sulpice and had the chancel modernized.

The burial ground here, which is now a garden, was the site of the first operation for gall stones in 1474. An archer who had been condemned to death was offered his freedom by Louis XI if he consented to the operation and lived. (It was a success, and the archer went free.) In the garden stands the church's medieval gable-roofed charnel house.

St-Julien-le-Pauvre ❹

1 Rue St-Julien-le-Pauvre 75005.
Map 13 A4. *Tel* 01 43 29 09 09.
Ⓜ *St-Michel.* 🚆 *St-Michel.*
⬤ *9:30am–1:30pm, 3pm–6pm daily.*
Concerts. See **Entertainment** *p336.*

At least three saints can claim to be patron of this church, but the most likely is St Julian the Hospitaller. The church, together with St-Germain-des-Prés, is one of the oldest in Paris, dating from between 1165 and 1220. The university held its official meetings in the church until 1524, when a student protest created so much damage that university meetings were barred from the church by parliament. Since 1889 it has belonged to the Melchite sect of the Greek Orthodox Church, and it is now the setting for chamber and religious music concerts.

Place Maubert ❺

75005. **Map** 13 A5.
Ⓜ *Maubert-Mutualité.*

From the 12th to the middle of the 13th century, "La Maub" was one of Paris's scholastic centers, with lectures given in the open air. After the scholars moved to the new colleges of the Montagne St-Geneviève, the square became a place of torture and execution, including that of the philosopher Etienne Dolet, who was burnt at the stake in 1546.

So many Protestants were burnt here in the 16th century that it became a place of pilgrimage for the followers of the new faith. Its dark reputation has been replaced by respectability and a notable street market.

Musée de la Préfecture de Police ❻

4 Rue de la Montagne Ste-Geneviève 75005. **Map** 13 A5.
Tel 01 44 41 52 50. Ⓜ *Maubert-Mutualité.* ⬤ *9am–5pm Mon–Fri; 10am–5pm Sat (last adm: 4:30pm).*
🚫 *public hols.*

Weapons in the police museum

A darker side to Paris's history is illustrated in this small museum. Created in 1909, the museum traces the development of the police in Paris from the Middle Ages to the 20th century. Curiosities on show here include arrest warrants for figures such as the famous revolutionary Danton, and a rather sobering display of weapons and tools used by famous criminals. There is also a section on the part the police played in the Resistance and subsequent liberation of Paris.

La Sorbonne ❼

47 Rue des Ecoles 75005.
Map 13 A5. **Tel** 01 40 46 22 11.
Ⓜ Cluny-La Sorbonne, Maubert-
Mutualité. ⃝ 9am–5pm Mon–Fri.
⬤ public hols. Ⓖ only, by appt:
write to Service des Visites.

The Sorbonne, seat of the
University of Paris, was
established in 1253 by Robert
de Sorbon, confessor to Louis
IX, for 16 poor students to
study theology. From these
modest beginnings the college soon became the center
of scholastic theology. In 1469
the rector had three printing
machines brought over from
Mainz, thereby founding the
first printing house in France.
The college's opposition to
liberal 18th-century philosophy led to its suppression
during the Revolution. It was
re-established by Napoleon in
1806. The buildings built by
Richelieu in the early 17th
century were replaced by the
ones seen today, with the
exception of the chapel.

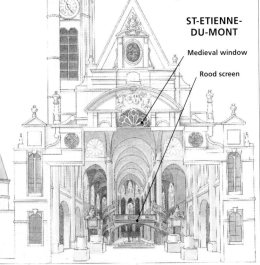

**16th-century
belfry tower**

**ST-ETIENNE-
DU-MONT**

Medieval window

Rood screen

Statues outside the college

Collège de France ❽

11 Pl Marcelin-Berthelot 75005.
Map 13 A5. **Tel** 01 44 27 12 11.
Ⓜ Maubert-Mutualité. ⃝ Oct– Jun:
9am–6pm Mon–Fri.

One of Paris's great institutes
of research and learning, the
college was established in
1530 by François I. Guided by
the great humanist Guillaume
Budé, the king aimed to
counteract the intolerance and
dogmatism of the Sorbonne.
A statue of Budé stands in the
west courtyard, and the
unbiased approach to
learning is reflected in the
inscription on the entrance to
the old college: *docet omnia*
(all are taught here).
Lectures are free and open
to the public.

Chapelle de la Sorbonne ❾

Pl de la Sorbonne 75005.
Map 13 A5. **Tel** 01 40 46 22 11.
Ⓜ Cluny-La Sorbonne,
Maubert-Mutualité. 🆁🅴🆁 Luxembourg.
⃝ for temporary exhibitions only.
♿

Designed by Lemercier and
built between 1635 and 1642,
this chapel is, in effect, a
monument to Richelieu, with
his coat of arms on the dome
supports and his white marble
tomb, carved by Girardon in
1694, in the chancel. The
chapel's attractive lateral
facade looks on to the main
courtyard of the Sorbonne.

Eglise de la Sorbonne clock

St-Etienne-
du-Mont ❿

Pl Ste-Geneviève 75005. **Map** 17 A1.
Tel 01 43 54 11 79. Ⓜ Cardinal
Lemoine. ⃝ 8:45am–7:30pm Tue–
Fri, noon–7:30pm Mon; w/e closed
midday. ⬤ Mon in Jul–Aug. 📷 Ⓘ

This remarkable church
houses not only the shrine of
Sainte Geneviève, patron saint
of Paris, but also the remains
of the great literary figures
Racine and Pascal. Some parts
are in the Gothic style and
others date from the
Renaissance, including a
magnificent rood screen. The
stained glass windows are
also of note.

Panthéon ⓫

See pp158–9.

Musée National du Moyen Age ❶

Medieval Mansion
The museum building, completed in 1500, was erected by Jacques d'Amboise, Abbot of Cluny.

Previously known as the Musée de Cluny, its original owner was Pierre de Chalus, Abbot of Cluny, who bought the ruins in 1330. Surrounded by imaginatively re-created medieval gardens, the museum is a unique combination of Gallo-Roman ruins, incorporated into a medieval mansion, and one of the world's finest collections of medieval art.

Head of St John the Baptist

Medieval chapel

★ Golden Rose of Basel *(1330)*
The goldsmith Minucchio da Siena made this rose for the Avignon Pope John XXII.

★ Lady with the Unicorn
This outstanding series of six tapestries is a fine example of the millefleurs *style, which was developed in the 15th and early 16th centuries. The style is noted for its graceful depiction of plants, animals and people.*

Gallo-Roman Baths
Built in AD 200, the baths lasted for about 100 years before being sacked by the barbarians.

Caldarium (hot bath room)

STAR EXHIBITS

- ★ Gallery of the Kings
- ★ Lady with the Unicorn
- ★ Golden Rose of Basel

Gallo-Roman Frigidarium
The arches of this cold bath room, dating from the late 2nd and early 3rd centuries, were once decorated with pairs of carved ship prows, the symbol of the association of Paris boatmen (nautes).

Books of Hours

The museum possesses two Books of Hours from the first half of the 15th century. The illuminated pages include scenes showing the Labors of the Months, accompanied by the relevant sign of the zodiac.

VISITORS' CHECKLIST

6 Pl Paul-Painlevé. **Map** 13 A5.
🛈 01 53 73 78 16. Ⓜ Cluny-La-Sorbonne, St-Michel, Odéon.
🚌 63, 86, 87, 21, 27, 85, 38 to Rue Soufflot, Rue des Ecoles.
ⓇⒺⓇ St-Michel, Cluny-La Sorbonne.
Ⓟ Blvd St-Germain, Pl Edmond Rostand. ⏲ 9:15am–5:45pm Wed–Mon. ⏲ Jan 1, May 1, Dec 25. 🎟 📷 🛍 🚻 *Concerts. Medieval poetry readings.*
www.musee-moyenage.fr

★ Gallery of the Kings

In 1977, 21 of the 28 stone heads of the Kings of Judah (carved around 1220 during the reign of Philippe Auguste) were unearthed during excavations in the Rue de la Chaussée-d'Antin behind the Opéra.

GALLERY GUIDE

The collection is spread throughout the two floors of the building. It is mainly medieval and covers a wide range of items, including illuminated manuscripts, tapestries, textiles, precious metals, alabaster, ceramics, sculpture and church furnishings. A number of Gallo-Roman artifacts are displayed around the sides of the frigidarium, *and the small circular room nearby contains some capitals.*

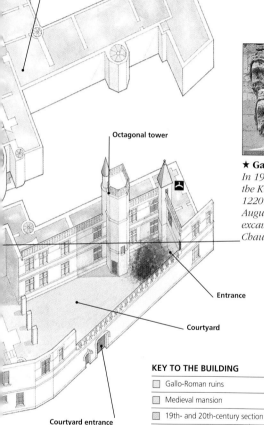

Octagonal tower

Entrance

Courtyard

Courtyard entrance

KEY TO THE BUILDING

- ☐ Gallo-Roman ruins
- ☐ Medieval mansion
- ☐ 19th- and 20th-century section

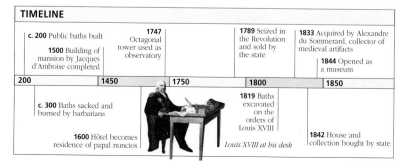

TIMELINE

c. 200 Public baths built		**1747** Octagonal tower used as observatory		**1789** Seized in the Revolution and sold by the state	**1833** Acquired by Alexandre du Sommerard, collector of medieval artifacts
	1500 Building of mansion by Jacques d'Amboise completed				**1844** Opened as a museum
200	**1450**		**1750**	**1800**	**1850**
c. 300 Baths sacked and burned by barbarians				**1819** Baths excavated on the orders of Louis XVIII	
	1600 Hôtel becomes residence of papal nuncios		*Louis XVIII at his desk*		**1842** House and collection bought by state

Exploring the Cluny's Collection

Alexandre du Sommerard took over the Hôtel de Cluny in 1833 and installed his art collection with great sensitivity to the surroundings and a strong sense of the dramatic. After his death the hôtel and its contents were sold to the state and turned into a museum.

The Grape Harvest tapestry

TAPESTRIES

The museum's tapestries are remarkable for their quality, age and state of preservation. The images present a surprising mixture of the naive with more complex notions. One of the earliest, *The Offering of the Heart* (early 15th century), shows a man who is literally proffering his heart to a seated medieval beauty. More everyday scenes are shown in the magnificent series *The Noble Life* (about 1500). Upstairs is the mysterious *Lady with the Unicorn* series.

CARVINGS

The diverse techniques of medieval European woodcarvers are well represented. From the Nottingham workshops in England, there are wood as well as alabaster works which were widely used as altarpieces all over Europe. Among the smaller works of this genre are *The School*, which is touchingly realistic and dates from the early 16th century.

Upstairs there are some fine Flemish and south German woodcarvings. The multicolored figure of St John is typical. Two notable altarpieces on display are the intricately carved and painted *Lamentation of Christ* (about 1485) from the Duchy of Clèves, and the Averbode altarpiece, which was made in 1523 in Antwerp, and depicts three scenes including the Last Supper. Not to be missed is a beautiful full-length figure of Mary Magdalene.

STAINED GLASS

Most of the Cluny's glass from the 12th and 13th centuries is French. The oldest examples were originally installed in the Basilique St-Denis in 1144. There are also three fragments from the Troyes Cathedral, destroyed by fire, two of which illustrate the life of St Nicholas while the third depicts that of Christ.

Numerous panels came to the Cluny from Sainte-Chapelle (*see pp88–9*), during its mid-19th-century restoration, and were never returned, including five scenes from the story of Samson dating from 1248.

The technique of contrasting colored glass with surrounding grisaille (gray-and-white panels) developed in the latter half of the 13th century. Four panels from the royal château at Rouen illustrate this.

Stained-glass scenes from Brittany (1400)

The School woodcarving (English, early 16th century)

Head of a queen from St-Denis
from before 1120

SCULPTURE

The highlight here is the Gallery of the Kings, a display of heads and decapitated figures from Notre-Dame. There is also a very graceful statue of Adam, sculped in the 1260s.

In the adjacent vaulted room are displays of fine Romanesque sculpture retrieved from French churches. Among the earliest are the 12 capitals from the nave of St-Germain-des-Prés, from the early 11th century. Retrieved from the portal of St-Denis is a boldly sculpted head of a queen (c.1140) which, though badly mutilated, is still compelling.

Other Romanesque and early Gothic capitals include six finely sculpted works from Catalonia and four of the museum's most famous statues, early 13th-century apostles made for Sainte-Chapelle.

EVERYDAY OBJECTS

Household goods show another side to medieval life, and this large collection is grouped in a sensitive way to illustrate their use – from wallhangings and caskets to kitchenware and clothing. Children's toys bring a very human aspect to the display, while travel cases and religious emblems evoke journeys of exploration and pilgrimage.

PRECIOUS METALWORK

The Cluny has a fine collection of jewelry, coins, metal and enamelwork from Gallic times to the Middle Ages. The showcase of Gallic jewelry includes gold torques, bracelets and rings, all of a simple design. In between these is one of the Cluny's most precious exhibits, the Golden Rose of Basel, a delicately wrought piece from 1330 and the oldest known of its kind.

The earliest enamelwork on display is the late Roman and Byzantine *cloisonné* pieces, culminating in the remarkable Limoges enamels, which flourished in the late 12th century. There are also two exceptional altarpieces, the Golden Altar of Basel and the Stavelot altarpiece.

Cross from
Italy (late
15th
century)

LADY WITH THE UNICORN TAPESTRIES

This series of six tapestries was woven in the late 15th century in the southern Netherlands. It is valued for its fresh harmonious colors and the poetic elegance of the central figure. Allegories of the senses are illustrated in the first five: sight (gazing into a mirror), hearing (playing a portable organ), taste (sampling candy), smell (sniffing carnations) and touch (the lady holding the unicorn's horn). The enigmatic sixth tapestry (showing jewels being placed in a box) includes the words "to my only desire" and is now thought to represent the principle of free choice.

The Pillar of the Nautes

GALLO-ROMAN RUINS

One of the main reasons for visiting the Musée de Cluny is to see the scale and layout of its earliest function, the Gallo-Roman baths. The vaulted *frigidarium* (cold bath room) was the largest of its kind in France. Here there is another of the Cluny's highlights, the recently restored Pillar of the Nautes (boatmen), unearthed during excavations beneath Notre-Dame in 1711. Composed of five carved stone blocks representing Gallic and Roman divinities, its crowning element is presumed to depict the Seine's boatmen. There are also the ruins of the *caldarium* and *tepidarium* (hot and tepid baths), and visitors can tour the underground vaults.

Unicorn on the sixth tapestry

Panthéon ⓫

When Louis XV recovered from desperate illness in 1744, he was so grateful to be alive that he conceived a magnificent church to honor Sainte Geneviève. The design was entrusted to the French architect Jacques-Germain Soufflot, who planned the church in Neoclassical style. Work began in 1764 and was completed in 1790, ten years after Soufflot's death, under the control of Guillaume Rondelet. But with the Revolution underway the church was soon turned into a pantheon – a location for the tombs of France's good and great. Napoleon returned it to the church in 1806, but it was secularized and then desecularized once more before finally being made a civic building in 1885.

The Facade
Inspired by the Rome Pantheon, the temple portico has 22 Corinthian columns.

The arches of the dome show a renewed interest in the lightness of Gothic architecture and were designed by Rondelet. They link four pillars supporting the dome, which weighs 10,000 tons and is 272 ft (83 m) high.

Pediment Relief
David d'Angers' pediment bas-relief depicts the mother country (France) granting laurels to its great men.

The Panthéon Interior
The interior has four aisles arranged in the shape of a Greek cross, from the center of which the great dome rises.

Entrance

STAR FEATURES

★ Iron-Framed Dome

★ Frescoes of Sainte Geneviève

★ Crypt

★ **Frescoes of Sainte Geneviève**
Murals along the south wall of the nave depict the life of Sainte Geneviève. They are by Pierre Puvis de Chavannes, the 19th-century fresco painter.

The dome lantern allows only a little light to filter into the church's center. Intense light was thought inappropriate for the place where France's heroes rested.

VISITORS' CHECKLIST

Pl du Panthéon. **Map** 17 A1.
Tel 01 44 32 18 00.
Ⓜ Jussieu, Cardinal-Lemoine.
🚌 84 to Panthéon; 21, 27, 38, 85 to Gare du Luxembourg.
RER St-Michel. Ⓟ Pl Edmond Rostand.
Crypt ◯ 10am– 7.15pm daily.
⬤ Jan 1, May 1, Nov 11, Dec 25. 🖩 📷 🅰

★ **Iron-Framed Dome**
The tall dome, with its stone cupolas and three layers of shells, was inspired by St Paul's in London and the Dôme Church (see pp188–9).

The dome galleries afford a magnificent panoramic view of France's capital.

Colonnade
The colonnade encircling the dome is both decorative and part of an ingenious supporting system.

Monument to Diderot
This is Alphonse Terroir's statue (1925) to the political writer Denis Diderot.

★ **Crypt**
Covering the entire area under the building, the crypt divides into galleries flanked by Doric columns. Many French notables rest here.

THE PANTHEON'S ENSHRINED

The first of France's great men to be entombed was the popular orator Honoré Mirabeau. (Later, under the revolutionary leadership of Maximilien Robespierre, he fell from grace and his body was removed.) Voltaire followed. A statue of Voltaire by Jean-Antoine Houdon stands in front of his tomb. In the 1970s the remains of the wartime Resistance leader Jean Moulin were reburied here. Pierre and Marie Curie's remains were transferred here in 1995, and Malraux's followed in 1996. Others here include Jean-Jacques Rousseau, Victor Hugo and Emile Zola.

JARDIN DES PLANTES QUARTER

This area, traditionally, has been one of the most tranquil corners of Paris. It takes its character from the 17th-century botanical gardens where the kings of the *ancien régime* grew medicinal herbs and where the National Natural History Institute stands today. The many hospitals in the area, notably Paris's largest, Pitié-Salpêtrière, add to the atmosphere. A colorful market takes over much of Rue Mouffetard every day, and the streets off Mouffetard are redolent of life in medieval times.

SIGHTS AT A GLANCE

Museums and Galleries
Musée de la Sculpture en Plein Air **2**
Collection des Minéraux de l'Université **4**
Muséum National d'Histoire Naturelle **10**
La Manufacture des Gobelins **13**

Modern Architecture
Institut du Monde Arabe **1**

Churches and Temples
St-Médard **8**
Mosquée de Paris **9**

Squares, Parks and Gardens
Ménagerie **3**
Place de la Contrescarpe **6**
Jardin des Plantes **11**

Historic Buildings and Streets
Arènes de Lutèce **5**
Rue Mouffetard **7**
Groupe Hospitalier Pitié-Salpêtrière **12**

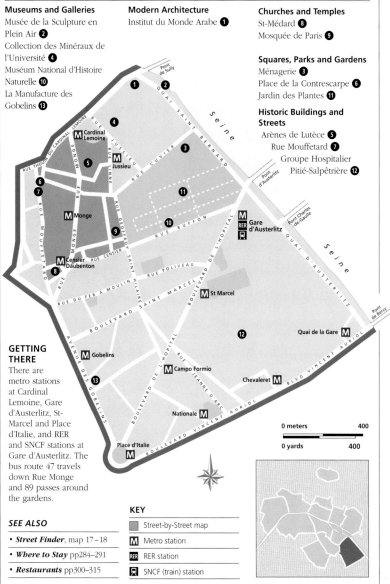

GETTING THERE
There are metro stations at Cardinal Lemoine, Gare d'Austerlitz, St-Marcel and Place d'Italie, and RER and SNCF stations at Gare d'Austerlitz. The bus route 47 travels down Rue Monge and 89 passes around the gardens.

SEE ALSO

KEY

▨	Street-by-Street map
M	Metro station
RER	RER station
🚆	SNCF (train) station

◁ **Market scene on the Rue Mouffetard**

Street-by-Street: Jardin des Plantes Quarter

Two physicians to Louis XIII, Jean
Hérouard and Guy de la Brosse,
obtained permission to establish the
royal medicinal herb garden in the
sparsely populated St-Victor suburb in
1626. The herb garden and gardens of
various religious houses gave the region
a rural character. In the 19th century the
population and thus the area expanded
and it became more built up, until it
gradually assumed the character it has
today: a well-to-do residential patchwork
of 19th- and early 20th-century buildings
interspersed with much older and some
more recent buildings.

Metro
Cardinal
Lemoine

Place de la Contrescarpe
*This village-like square
filled with restaurants
and cafés buzzes
with student life
after dusk* ❻

★ Rue Mouffetard
*Locals flock to the daily open-air market
here which is one of the oldest Paris street
markets. A hoard of* louis d'or *gold coins
from the 18th century were found at
No. 53 during its demolition in 1938* ❼

Pot de Fer fountain is one of 14 that
Marie de Médicis had built on the Left
Bank in 1624 as a source of water for her
palace in the Jardin du Luxembourg.
The fountain was rebuilt in 1671.

Metro
Monge

Passage des Postes is
an ancient alley which
was opened in 1830. Its
entrance is in the Rue
Mouffetard.

St-Médard
*This church was started
in the mid-15th century
and completed by 1655.
In 1784 the choir was
made Classical in style,
and the nave's 16th-
century windows were
replaced with contem-
porary stained glass* ❽

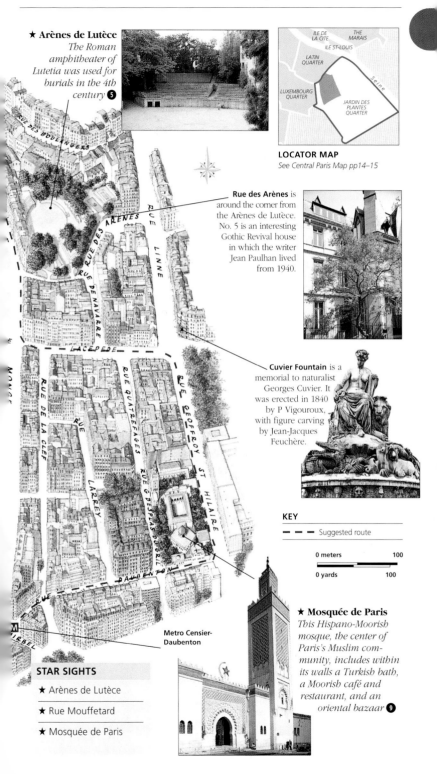

★ Arènes de Lutèce
The Roman amphitheater of Lutetia was used for burials in the 4th century ❺

LOCATOR MAP
See Central Paris Map pp14–15

Rue des Arènes is around the corner from the Arènes de Lutèce. No. 5 is an interesting Gothic Revival house in which the writer Jean Paulhan lived from 1940.

Cuvier Fountain is a memorial to naturalist Georges Cuvier. It was erected in 1840 by P Vigouroux, with figure carving by Jean-Jacques Feuchère.

KEY

— — — Suggested route

| 0 meters | 100 |
| 0 yards | 100 |

Metro Censier-Daubenton

STAR SIGHTS

★ Arènes de Lutèce

★ Rue Mouffetard

★ Mosquée de Paris

★ Mosquée de Paris
This Hispano-Moorish mosque, the center of Paris's Muslim community, includes within its walls a Turkish bath, a Moorish café and restaurant, and an oriental bazaar ❾

Institut du Monde Arabe ❶

1 Rue des Fossées St-Bernard 75005.
Map 13 C5. **Tel** 01 40 51 38 38.
Ⓜ Jussieu, Cardinal-Lemoine.
🔲 **Museum & temp exhibs:** 10am–
6pm Tue–Sun. **Library:** 1pm–8pm
Tue–Sat. 📷 🚶 🎬 **Lectures.**
🍴 🖥 www.imarabe.org

This cultural institute was
founded in 1980 by France
and 20 Arab countries with
the intention of fostering
cultural links between the
Islamic world and the West.
It is housed in a magnificent
modern building, designed by
the French architect Jean
Nouvel, that combines
modern materials with the
spirit of traditional Arab
architecture. The white marble
book tower, which can be
seen through the glass of the
west wall, spirals upward
bringing to mind the minaret
of a mosque. The emphasis

that is traditionally placed on
interior space in Arab architecture has been used here to
create an enclosed courtyard
reached by a narrow gap
splitting the building in two.
  From floors four to seven,
there is a fascinating display

of Islamic works of art from
the 9th to the 19th centuries,
including glassware, ceramics,
sculpture, carpets and a fine
collection of astrolabes, so
prized by ancient Arabic
astronomers. There is also a
library and media archive.

Musée de la Sculpture en Plein Air ❷

75004/ 75005. **Map** 13 C5.
Ⓜ Gare d'Austerlitz, Sully-Morland.

Butting up to the left-hand
corner of the Institut du
Monde Arabe, the Pont de
Sully links the Ile St Louis
with both banks of the Seine.
Opened in 1877 and built of
cast iron, the Pont de Sully is
not an especially beautiful
structure. Despite this, it is
well worth pausing for a
moment on the bridge for a
fabulous view of Notre-Dame
rising dramatically behind
the wonderfully graceful
Pont Marie.
  Running along the river
from the Pont de Sully as far
as the Pont d'Austerlitz is the
peaceful Quai St-Bernard.
Not always so sedate, Quai
St-Bernard was famous during
the 17th century as a spot
for nude bathing, until
scandalized public opinion
made it illegal. The grassy
slopes adjoining the quai
make a perfect spot to enjoy
a picnic. Opened in 1975,

they are known as the Jardin
Tino Rossi in honor of the
celebrated Corsican singer.
The garden has a display of
open-air sculpture known as
the Musée de la Sculpture en
Plein Air. Vandalism and other
problems have unfortunately
necessitated the removal of
some of the exhibits.

Ménagerie ❸

57 Rue Cuvier 75005. **Map** 17 C1.
Tel 01 40 79 37 94. Ⓜ Jussieu,
Austerlitz. 🔲 Oct–Mar: 9am–5pm
daily; Apr–Sep: 9am–6pm Mon–Sat.
📷 🍴 🖥

France's oldest public zoo is
situated in the lovely surroundings of the Jardin des
Plantes. It was set up during
the Revolution to house
survivors from the Royal
menagerie at Versailles – all
four of them. The state
then rounded up animals
from circuses and exotic
creatures were sent from
abroad. Unfortunately,
during the Prussian
siege of Paris
(1870–71), most of
them were
slaughtered to feed the
hungry citizens *(see p224)*.

Today the zoo specializes in
small mammals, insects, birds,
primates and reptiles, and it is
a great favorite with children
as it is possible for them to
get quite close to the animals.
The lion house contains an
impressive number of large
cats, including panthers from
China. Other attractions
include a large monkey house,
bear pits, a large waterfowl
aviary and wild sheep and goats.
  The displays in the vivarium
(enclosures of live animals in
natural habitat) are changed at
regular intervals and there is a
permanent exhibition of micro-
arthropods (also known as
creepy-crawlies!).

**Child playing
at the zoo**

Light Screens

The south elevation is made up of 1,600 high-tech metal screens which filter the light entering the building. Their design is based on moucharabiyahs (carved wooden screens found on the outsides of buildings from Morocco to Southeast Asia).

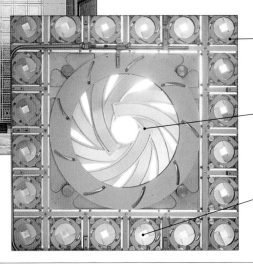

Each screen contains 21 irises which are controlled electronically, opening and closing in response to the amount of sunlight falling on photosensitive screens.

The central iris is made up of interlocking metal blades which move to adjust the size of the central opening.

The peripheral irises are linked to one another and to the central iris. They open and close in unison forming a delicate pattern of light and shade inside the institute.

Collection des Minéraux de l'Université ❹

Université Pierre et Marie Curie, 34 Rue Jussieu 75005. **Map** 13 C5. **Tel** 01 44 27 52 88. **M** Jussieu. ☐ 1pm–6pm Wed– Mon. ⚫ Jan 1, Easter, May 1, Jul 14, Nov 1, Dec 25. ✗ ☐ ☑ ☑ groups Tue pm.

This fascinating small museum is housed in the basement of the main university building, named after the distinguished scientists. The collection comprises cut and uncut gemstones and rock crystal from all over the world, shown to maximum advantage through the expert use of specialized lighting.

Topaz

Arènes de Lutèce ❺

Rue de Navarre 75005. **Map** 17 B1. **M** Jussieu. See p21.

The remains of this vast Roman arena (Lutetia was the Roman name for Paris) date from the late 2nd century. Its destruction began toward the end of the 3rd century at the hands of the barbarians, and later, parts of it were used to build the walls of the Ile de la Cité. The arena was then gradually buried and its exact location preserved only in old documents and the local name Clos des Arènes. It was rediscovered in 1869 during the construction of the Rue Monge and the allocation of building plots nearby.

Action toward its restoration began with the campaigning of Victor Hugo (among others) in the 19th century but work did not get really underway until 1918.

With a seating capacity of 15,000, arranged in 35 tiers, the original arena was used both for theatrical performances and as an amphitheater for the more gruesome spectacle of gladiator fights. This type of combined use was peculiar to Gaul (France), and the arena is similar to the other French ones in Nîmes and Arles.

The public park at the Arènes de Lutèce

BUFFON AND THE JARDIN DES PLANTES

At the age of 32 Georges Louis Leclerc, Comte de Buffon (1707–88), became the curator of the Jardin des Plantes at a time when the study of natural history was at the forefront of contemporary thought – Charles Darwin's *The Origin of Species* was to be published 120 years later. Buffon masterminded the reorganization of the Jardin, propelling it to a preeminent position within the scientific world. He was elected to the Académie Française in 1752 following the publication of his two main works, *Natural History* and *The Epoques of Nature*. He died in his house in the Jardin.

Illustration of a primate from Buffon's *Natural History*

Place de la Contrescarpe **6**

75005. **Map** 17 A1. *Place Monge.*

At one time this site lay outside the city walls. It gets its name from the backfilling of the moat that ran along Philippe-Auguste's wall. The present square was laid out in 1852. At No. 1 there is a memorial plaque to the old "pine-cone club" immortalized in the writings of Rabelais; here a group of writers known as *La Pléiade* (named after the constellation of The Pleiades) used to meet in the 16th century.

The area has always been used for meetings and festivals. Today it is extremely lively at weekends, and on Bastille Day (*see p65*) a delightful ball is held here.

Part of the medieval city wall

Cheese in the Mouffetard market

Rue Mouffetard **7**

75005. **Map** 17 B2. *Censier-Daubenton, Place Monge.*
Market *8am–1pm Tue–Sun.*
See **Shops and Markets** *p339.*

A major thoroughfare since Roman times, when it ran between Lutetia (Paris) and Rome, this street is one of the oldest in the city. In the 17th and 18th centuries it was known as the Grande Rue du Faubourg St-Marcel, and many of its buildings date from this period. Some of the small shops still have ancient painted signs, and some of the houses have mansard roofs. No. 125 has an attractive, restored Louis XIII facade, and the entire front of No. 134 has beautiful decoration of wild beasts, flowers and plants.

The whole area is well known for its open-air markets, especially those in Place Maubert, Place Monge, and Rue Daubenton, a side street where a lively African market takes place.

St-Médard **8**

141 Rue Mouffetard 75005.
Map 17 B2. **Tel** 01 44 08 87 00.
Censier-Daubenton.
8am–noon, 2:30–7:30pm Tue–Sun.

The origins of this charming church go back to the 9th century. St Médard, counselor to the Merovingian kings, was known for his custom of giving a wreath of white roses to young girls noted for their virtue. The churchyard, now a garden, became notorious in the 18th century as the center of the cult of the Convulsionnaires, whose hysterical fits were brought on by the contemplation of miracle cures. The interior has many fine paintings, including the 17th-century *St Joseph Walking with the Christ Child* by Francisco de Zurbarán.

Mosquée de Paris **9**

2 bis Pl du Puits de l'Ermite 75005.
Map 17 C2. **Tel** 01 45 35 97 33.
Place Monge. *9am–noon, 2pm–6pm Sat–Thu.* *Muslim hols.*
Library.
www.mosquee-de-paris.com

Built in the 1920s in the Hispano-Moorish style, this group of buildings is the spiritual center for Paris's Muslim community and the home of the Grand Imam. The complex comprises religious, educational and commercial sections; at its heart is a mosque. Each of

Decoration inside the mosque

the mosque's domes is decorated differently and the minaret stands nearly 100 ft (33 m) high. Inside is a grand patio inspired by the Alhambra in southern Spain, with mosaics on the walls and tracery on the arches.

Once used only by scholars, the mosque's place in Parisian life has grown over the years. The Turkish baths there can be enjoyed by both men and women but on alternate days.

Muséum National d'Histoire Naturelle ⑩

2 Rue Buffon 75005. **Map** 17 C2.
Tel *01 40 79 30 00.* Ⓜ *Jussieu, Austerlitz.* ◯ *10am–6pm Wed–Mon (10am–5pm winter).* ⬛ ♿ *restricted.*
⬛ ⬛ **Library.** www.mnhn.fr

Skull of the reptile dimetrodon

The highlight of the museum is the Grande Galerie de l'Evolution. There are also four other departments: paleontology, featuring skeletons, casts of various animals and an exhibition showing the evolution of the vertebrate skeleton; paleobotany, devoted to plant fossils; mineralogy, including gemstones; and entomology, with some of the oldest fossilized insects on earth. The bookshop is in the house that was occupied by the naturalist Buffon, from 1772 until his death in 1788.

Jardin des Plantes ⑪

57 Rue Cuvier 75005. **Map** 17 C1.
Ⓜ *Jussieu, Austerlitz.* ◯ *7am–8pm (5pm winter) daily.*

The botanical gardens were established in 1626 when Jean Hérouard and Guy de la Brosse, Louis XIII's physicians, obtained permission to found

a royal medicinal herb garden here and then a school of botany, natural history and pharmacy. The garden was opened to the public in 1640 and flourished under the inspired direction of Buffon. Now one of Paris's great parks, it includes a natural history museum, botanical school and zoo.

As well as beautiful vistas and walkways flanked by ancient trees and punctuated with statues, the park has a remarkable alpine garden with plants from Corsica, Morocco, the Alps and the Himalayas and an unrivaled display of herbaceous and wild plants. It also has the first Cedar of Lebanon to be planted in France, originally from Britain's Kew Gardens.

Groupe Hospitalier Pitié-Salpêtrière ⑫

47 Blvd de l'Hôpital 75013. **Map** 18
D3. Ⓜ *St-Marcel, Austerlitz.* Ⓡ *Gare d'Austerlitz.* ◯ *Chapel 8:30am–6:30pm daily.* ⬛ *3:30pm daily.* ⬛ ♿

The vast Salpêtrière Hospital stands on the site of an old gunpowder factory and derives its name from the saltpeter used in the making of explosives. It was founded by Louis XIV in 1656 to help sick or socially disadvantaged women and children and later became renowned for its pioneering humane treatment of the insane. It was here that Princess Diana died in 1997, following an automobile accident in a Paris underpass.

The Cedar of Lebanon in the Jardin

Outside the Hôpital Salpêtrière

La Manufacture des Gobelins ⑬

42 Ave des Gobelins 75013.
Map 17 B3. **Tel** *01 44 08 52 00.*
Ⓜ *Gobelins.* ◯ **guided tours only** *2pm, 2:45pm Tue–Thu (arrive 15 mins earlier). Groups by appt.*
⬛ ⬛ *public hols.*

Versailles tapestry by Le Brun

Originally a dyeing workshop set up in about 1440 by the Gobelin brothers, the building became a tapestry factory early in the 17th century. Louis XIV took it over in 1662 and gathered together the greatest craftsmen of the day – carpet weavers, cabinet makers and silversmiths – to furnish his new palace at Versailles (*see pp248–53*). Working under the direction of court painter Charles Le Brun, 250 Flemish weavers laid the foundations for the factory's international reputation. Today weavers continue to work in the traditional way but with modern designs, including those of Picasso and Matisse.

LUXEMBOURG QUARTER

Many a Parisian dreams of living in the vicinity of the Luxembourg Gardens, a quieter, greener and somehow more reflective place than its neighboring areas. Luxembourg is one of the most captivating places in the capital. Its charm is in its old gateways and streets, its bookshops, and in the sumptuous yet intimate gardens. Though writers of the eminence of Paul Verlaine and André Gide no longer stroll in its groves, the paths, lawns and avenues are still full of charm, drawing to them the numerous students from the nearby *grandes écoles* and *lycées*. And on

warm days old men meet under the chestnut trees to play chess or the traditional game of *boules*.

To the west the buildings are public and official, and on the east the houses are shaded by the tall chestnut trees of the Boulevard St-Michel.

Sailing boats are rented by children and adults to sail in the *grand bassin* (ornamental pond) in the Luxembourg Gardens.

SIGHTS AT A GLANCE

Museums
Musée du Service de Santé des Armées ❿
Ecole Nationale Supérieure des Mines ⓫

Historic Buildings
Palais du Luxembourg ❸
Institut Catholique de Paris ❻

Churches
St-Sulpice ❷
St-Joseph-des-Carmes ❼
Val-de-Grâce ❾

Squares and Gardens
Place St-Sulpice ❶
Jardin du Luxembourg ❺

Fountains
Fontaine de Médicis ❹
Fontaine de l'Observatoire ❽

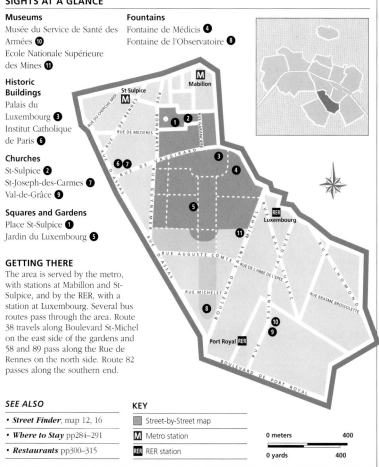

GETTING THERE

The area is served by the metro, with stations at Mabillon and St-Sulpice, and by the RER, with a station at Luxembourg. Several bus routes pass through the area. Route 38 travels along Boulevard St-Michel on the east side of the gardens and 58 and 89 pass along the Rue de Rennes on the north side. Route 82 passes along the southern end.

SEE ALSO

• **Street Finder**, map 12, 16

• **Where to Stay** pp284–291

• **Restaurants** pp300–315

KEY

▨	Street-by-Street map
Ⓜ	Metro station
🅁🅴🅁	RER station

0 meters 400
0 yards 400

◁ Playing chess in the Jardin du Luxembourg

Street-by-Street: Luxembourg Quarter

Situated only a few steps from the bustle of St-Germain-des-Prés, this graceful and historic area offers a peaceful haven in the heart of a modern city. The Jardin du Luxembourg and Palais du Luxembourg dominate the vicinity. The gardens became fully open to the public in the 19th century under the ownership of the Comte de Provence (later Louis XVIII), when for a small fee visitors could come in and feast on fruit from the orchard. Today the gardens, palace and old houses on the streets to the north remain unspoiled and attract many visitors.

★ St-Sulpice
This Classical church was built over 134 years to Daniel Gittard's plans. It has a facade by the Italian architect Giovanni Servandoni ❷

To St-Germain-des-Prés

Place St-Sulpice
The Fontaine des Quatre Points Cardinaux depicts four church leaders at the cardinal points of the compass. Point also means "never": the leaders were never made cardinals ❶

The Monument to Delacroix
(1890) by Jules Dalou is situated near the private gardens of the French Senate. Beneath the bust of the leading Romantic painter Eugène Delacroix are the allegorical figures of Art, Time and Glory.

RUE HENRI DE JOUVENEL
RUE FÉROU
RUE SERVANDONI
RUE GARANCIÈRE
RUE DE VAUGIRARD

STAR SIGHTS

★ St-Sulpice

★ Jardin du Luxembourg

★ Palais du Luxembourg

★ Fontaine de Médicis

★ Jardin du Luxembourg
Many fine statues were erected in the Luxembourg gardens in the 19th century during the reign of Louis-Philippe ❺

The Rue de Tournon is full of elegant architecture, boutiques and old bookshops. At No. 12 is the Grand Hôtel d'Entragues, reconstructed by Neveu in the 18th century during Louis XVI's reign.

LOCATOR MAP
See Central Paris Map pp14–15

KEY

– – – Suggested route

| 0 meters | 100 |
| 0 yards | 100 |

★ **Palais du Luxembourg**
In 1794, during the Revolution, the painter Jacques-Louis David was imprisoned here and made sketches for the Intervention of the Sabine Women ❸

★ **Fontaine de Médicis**
The 17th-century fountain is in the style of an Italian grotto and is thought to have been designed by Salomon de Brosse ❹

Sainte Geneviève, the patron saint of Paris, was a wealthy 5th-century Gallo-Roman land-owner. When Paris was invaded by the Huns in AD 451, she prayed with women friends that the city would be spared – their prayers were answered. This statue by Michel-Louis Victor (1845) pays homage to her.

The Octagonal Lake (Grand Bassin), attributed to Jean-François Chalgrin, is surrounded by formal terraces where visitors to the gardens often sunbathe.

RUE DE TOURNON

RUE DE MÉDICIS

Place St-Sulpice ❶

75006. **Map** 12 E4. Ⓜ *St-Sulpice.*

This large square, which is dominated on the east side by the enormous church from which it takes its name, was built in the last half of the 18th century.

Two main features of the square are the Fountain of the Four Bishops by Joachim Visconti (1844) and the pink-flowering chestnut trees. There is also the Café de la Mairie, a rendezvous of writers and students, which is often featured in French movies.

Stained-glass window of St-Sulpice

St-Sulpice ❷

Pl St-Sulpice 75006. **Map** 12 E5. **Tel** 01 46 33 21 78. Ⓜ *St-Sulpice.* ◯ 7:30am–7:30pm daily. ✝ frequent. ◙

It took more than a century, from 1646, for this huge and imposing church to be built. The result is a simple two-story west front with two tiers of elegant columns. The

overall harmony of the building is marred only by the towers, one at each end, which do not match.

Large arched windows fill the huge interior with light. By the front door are two enormous shells given to François I by the Venetian republic – they rest on rock-like bases sculpted by Jean-Baptiste Pigalle.

In the side chapel to the right of the main door are three magnificent murals by Eugène Delacroix: *Jacob Wrestling with the Angel (see p137), Heliodorus Driven from the Temple* and *St-Michael Killing the Dragon.* If you are lucky you can catch an organ recital.

Palais du Luxembourg ❸

15 Rue de Vaugirard 75006. **Map** 12 E5. **Tel** 01 42 34 20 00. Ⓜ *Odéon.* ℝℰℝ *Luxembourg.* ◪ Groups only: 1st Sun each mth, via CMN: **Tel** 01 44 61 21 66. ✉ www.senat.fr

Now the home of the French Senate, this palace was built to remind Marie de Médicis, widow of Henri IV, of her native Florence. It was de-signed by Salomon de Brosse and built in the style of the Pitti Palace in Florence. By the time it was finished (1631) she had been banished, but it remained a royal palace until the Revolution. Since then the palace has been used as a prison, and in World War II it was the head-quarters of the Luftwaffe, with air-raid shelters built underneath its famous gardens.

Figures on the Fontaine de Médicis

Fontaine de Médicis ❹

15 Rue de Vaugirard 75006. **Map** 12 F5. ℝℰℝ *Luxembourg.*

Built in 1624 for Marie de Médicis by an unknown architect, this vigorous Baroque fountain stands at the end of a long pond filled with goldfish and shaded by trees. The mythological figures were added much later by Auguste Ottin (1866).

Jardin du Luxembourg ❺

Blvd St-Michel 75006. **Map** 12 E5. **Tel** 01 42 34 20 00. ℝℰℝ *Luxembourg.* ◯ dawn–dusk daily. ▣

A green oasis covering 60 acres (25 ha) in the heart of the Left Bank, this is the most popular park in the whole of Paris. The layout of the gardens is centered around the Luxembourg Palace and is dominated by a great octagonal pool – usually full of toy sailing boats.

Apart from the aesthetic attraction of its formal terraces and broad avenues, statues of various queens of France are also dotted throughout the park, as well as an impressive figure of Saint Genevieve, the patron of Paris, and, by way of contrast, a Cyclops.

The park also includes an open-air café, a puppet theater, numerous tennis courts, a bandstand and a bee-keeping school.

Sculptures on Palais du Luxembourg

Institut Catholique de Paris ❻

21 Rue d'Assas 75006. **Map** 12 D5.
Ⓜ *St-Placide, Rennes.* **Musée Biblique** ⬤ *Sat: 4–6pm or by appt.* **Tel** *01 45 44 01 91.* **Musée Branly** ⬤ *by appt.* **Tel** *01 45 38 98 57.* **www.icp.fr**

Founded in 1875, this is one of the most distinguished teaching institutions in France. It also houses two small museums: the Musée Biblique which displays objects excavated in the Holy Land, and the Musée Branly, devoted to the physicist Edouard Branly, inventor of the radio conductor (which made the wireless possible).

Courtyard statue at the Institut Catholique

St-Joseph-des-Carmes ❼

70 Rue de Vaugirard 75006. **Map** 12 D5. **Tel** *01 44 39 52 00.* Ⓜ *St-Placide.* ⬤ *7am–7pm Mon–Sat; 9am–7pm Sun.* ⬤ *Easter Mon, Pentecost.* ♿ *restricted.* 📷 *3pm Sat.*

Completed in 1620, this church was built as the chapel for a Carmelite convent but was used as a prison during the Revolution. In 1792 more than a hundred priests met a grisly end in the church's courtyard as part of the September Massacres *(see pp30–31).* Their remains are now in the crypt.

Facade of St-Joseph-des-Carmes

Carpeaux's fountain sculpture

Fontaine de l'Observatoire ❽

Pl Ernest Denis, in Ave de l'Observatoire. **Map** 16 E2. 🚇 *Port Royal.*

Situated at the southern tip of the Jardin du Luxembourg, this is one of the liveliest fountains in Paris. Made of bronze, it has four women holding aloft a globe representing four continents – the fifth, Oceania, was left out for reasons of symmetry. There are some subsidiary figures, including dolphins, horses and a turtle. The sculpture was erected in 1873 by Jean-Baptiste Carpeaux.

Val-de-Grâce ❾

1 Pl Alphonse-Laveran 75005. **Map** 16 F2. **Tel** *01 40 51 51 92.* Ⓜ *Gobelins.* 🚇 *Port Royal.* ⬤ *noon–6pm Tue, Wed, Sat & Sun.* 📷 *(except for nave).* ⬆ *frequent, pm.* 📷 *appt.*

One of the most beautiful churches in France, it was built for Anne of Austria (wife of Louis XIII) in thanks for the birth of her son. Young Louis XIV himself laid the first stone in 1645. The design is in the style of the great architect François Mansart.

The church is noted for its beautiful imposing lead-and-gilt dome, which stands at an impressive 135 ft (41 m) and is 62 ft (19 m) in diameter. In the cupola is Pierre Mignard's enormous fresco, with over 200 triple-life-size figures.

The six huge, twisted marble columns that frame the altar are similar to those made by Bernini for St Peter's in Rome.

Henrietta of France (the wife of Charles I) is buried at this site, as well as 26 members of the French royal family.

Musée du Service de Santé des Armées ❿

1 Pl Alphonse-Laveran 75005. **Map** 16 F2. **Tel** *01 40 51 51 92.* 🚇 *Port Royal.* ⬤ *Tue, Wed, Sat & Sun 1–5pm.* 📷 📷 *phone to arrange.*

Founded during World War I and run by the army medical corps, this museum is also known as the Musée du Val-de-Grâce. It is in the west wing of the Val-de-Grâce church, where it became a military hospital in 1795.

The exhibits cover the history of medicine with some appropriately gruesome memorabilia such as artificial limbs and various surgical instruments. There are even reconstructions of military hospital trains that took wounded soldiers to hospital.

Ecole Nationale Supérieure des Mines ⓫

60 Blvd St-Michel. **Map** 16 F1. **Tel** *01 40 51 91 45.* 🚇 *Luxembourg.* ⬤ *1:30–6pm Tue–Sat.* 📷 📷 📷

Louis XIV set up the School of Mines in 1783 to train mining engineers. Today, it is one of the most prestigious *grandes écoles* – schools that provide the élite for the civil service and professions. It also houses the national collection of minerals – the Musée de Minéralogie.

MONTPARNASSE

I n the first three decades of the 20th century Montparnasse was a thriving artistic and literary center. So many modern painters and sculptors, new novelists and poets, the great and the young were drawn to this area. Its ateliers, conviviality and renowned Bohemian lifestyle made it a magnet for genius, some of it French, much of it foreign. The great epoch ended with World War II, and change continued with the destruction of many of the ateliers and the construction of the soaring Tour Montparnasse, Paris's tallest office tower, which heralded the more modern *quartier*. But the area has not lost its appeal. The great cafés remain very much in business and attract a lively international crowd. Small café-theaters have opened and the area springs to life on the weekends with theater crowds.

Monument to Charles Augustin Ste-Beauve in the Cimetière du Montparnasse

SIGHTS AT A GLANCE

Historic Buildings and Streets
Rue Campagne-Première ❸
Catacombes ❿
Observatoire de Paris ⓫

Cafés and Restaurants
La Coupole ❶
La Closerie des Lilas ⓬

Museums and Galleries
Musée Zadkine ❷
Musée Antoine Bourdelle ❻
Musée de la Poste ❼

Musée Montparnasse ❽
Fondation Cartier ❾

Modern Architecture
Tour Montparnasse ❺

Cemeteries
Cimetière du Montparnasse pp180–81 ❹

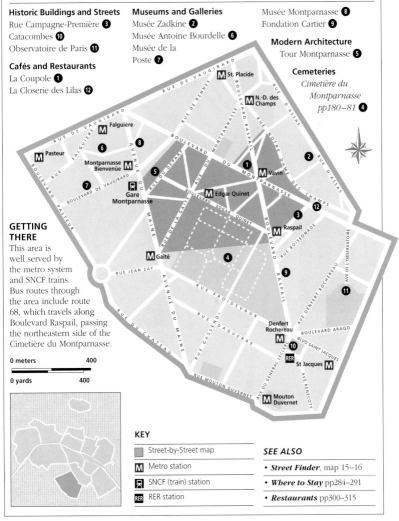

GETTING THERE

This area is well served by the metro system and SNCF trains. Bus routes through the area include route 68, which travels along Boulevard Raspail, passing the northeastern side of the Cimetière du Montparnasse.

| 0 meters | 400 |
| 0 yards | 400 |

KEY

▨	Street-by-Street map
Ⓜ	Metro station
🆁	SNCF (train) station
RER	RER station

SEE ALSO

• *Street Finder*, map 15–16
• *Where to Stay* pp284–291
• *Restaurants* pp300–315

◁ View of Tour Montparnasse from the Cimetière du Montparnasse

Street-by-Street: Montparnasse

Renowned for its mix of art and high
living, Montparnasse continues to live up
to its name: Mount Parnassus was the
mountain dedicated by the ancient
Greeks to Apollo, god of poetry, music
and beauty. That mix was especially
potent in the 1920s and 1930s, when
such artists and writers as Picasso,
Hemingway, Cocteau, Giacometti,
Matisse and Modigliani were to be seen
in the local bars, cafés and cabarets.

★ **La Coupole**
*This traditional
brasserie-style café,
with its large
enclosed terrace,
opened in 1927 and
became a famous
meeting place for
artists and
writers* ❶

★ **Tour Montparnasse**
*Europe's second-tallest tower
block rests on 56 piles that
extend 203 ft (62 m) below
the surface* ❺

Metro Edgar Quinet

★ **Cimetière du
Montparnasse**
This fine sculpture, The
Separation of a Couple
*by de Max, stands in
the smallest of the city's
major cemeteries* ❹

The Théâtre Montparnasse at
No. 31, with its fully restored
original 1880's decor.

RUE DU DEPART

RUE D'ODESSA

RUE DU MONTPARNASSE

BLVD

BLVD
EDGAR QUINET

RUE
DE LA GAITE

To Metro Gaîté

STAR SIGHTS

★ La Coupole

★ Tour Montparnasse

★ Rue Campagne-
  Première

★ Cimetière du
  Montparnasse

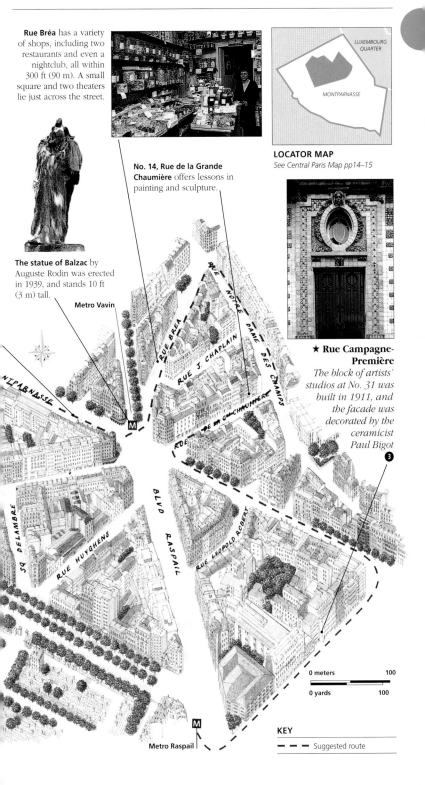

Rue Bréa has a variety of shops, including two restaurants and even a nightclub, all within 300 ft (90 m). A small square and two theaters lie just across the street.

No. 14, Rue de la Grande Chaumière offers lessons in painting and sculpture.

LOCATOR MAP
See Central Paris Map pp14–15

The statue of Balzac by Auguste Rodin was erected in 1939, and stands 10 ft (3 m) tall.

Metro Vavin

★ **Rue Campagne-Première**
The block of artists' studios at No. 31 was built in 1911, and the facade was decorated by the ceramicist Paul Bigot

❸

RUE BRÉA

RUE J. CHAPLAIN

RUE NOTRE DAME DES CHAMPS

RUE DE LA GRANDE CHAUMIÈRE

NIPARNASSE

SQ DELAMBRE

RUE HUYGHENS

BLVD RASPAIL

RUE LEOPOLD ROBERT

| 0 meters | 100 |
| 0 yards | 100 |

Metro Raspail

KEY

– – – Suggested route

The interior of La Coupole

La Coupole ●

102 Blvd du Montparnasse 75014.
Map 16 D2. **Tel** 01 43 20 14 20. Ⓜ
Vavin, Montparnasse. ◯ *8am–1am
Mon–Thu, 8:30am–1:30am Fri–Sun.*
See **Restaurants and Cafés** *p307.*

Established in 1927, this
historic café-restaurant and
dance hall underwent a face-
lift in the late 1980s. Its red
velvet seats and famous
columns, decorated by various
local artists, have survived.
Among its clientele have been
Jean-Paul Sartre, Josephine
Baker and Roman Polanski.

The museum's *Les Trois Belles*
(1950) by Ossip Zadkine

Musée Zadkine ●

100 bis Rue d'Assas 75116. **Map** 16
E1. **Tel** 01 55 42 77 20. Ⓜ *Notre-
Dame-Les Champs.* ◯ *10am–6pm
Tue–Sun.* ◐ *public hols.* 📷 🅿
by appt. ♿ *limited.*
www.paris.fr/musees/Zadkine

The Russian-born sculptor
Ossip Zadkine lived here

from 1928 until his death in
1967. The small house, studio
and daffodil-filled garden
contain his works. Here he
produced his great commemorative sculpture, *Ville Détruite*,
commissioned by Rotter-
dam after World War II,
and two monuments to
Vincent Van Gogh, one for
Holland and one for Auvers-
sur-Oise, where Van Gogh
died. The museum's works
span the development of
Zadkine's style, from his Cubist beginnings to Expressionism and Abstractionism.

Rue Campagne-Première ●

75014. **Map** 16 E2. Ⓜ *Raspail.*

This street has some interesting Art Deco buildings and a
long artistic tradition. Modigliani, ravaged by opium and
tuberculosis, lived at No. 3
during his last years. Between
the wars many artists resided
here, including Picasso, Joan
Miró and Kandinsky.

Cimetière du Montparnasse ●

See pp180–1.

Tour Montparnasse ●

Pl Raoul Dautry 75014. **Map** 15 C2.
Ⓜ *Montparnasse-Bienvenüe.* **Tel** 01
45 38 52 56. ◯ *Apr–Sep: 9:30am–
11:30 pm daily; Oct–Mar: 9:30am–
10:30pm daily.* 🎟 🍴 🅿 ♿

This was Europe's largest
office block when it was built
in 1973 as the focal point of a
new business sector intended
to revitalize a run-
down inner-city area.
It stands 690 ft (209
m) high, is made of
curved steel and
smoked glass, and
totally dominates the
quarter's skyline. The
bar, restaurant and
observatory on the
56th floor offer pano-
ramic views of the city
– up to 25 miles (40
km) on a clear day.

The Archer (1909) by Antoine
Bourdelle

Musée Antoine Bourdelle ●

18 Rue Antoine Bourdelle 75015.
Map 15 B1. **Tel** 01 49 54 73 73.
Ⓜ *Montparnasse-Bienvenüe.*
◯ *10am–6pm Tue–Sun*
◐ *public hols.* 📷 ♿ *limited.*
www.paris.fr/musees/Bourdelle

The prolific sculptor Antoine
Bourdelle lived and worked
in the studio here from 1884
until his death in 1929. The
house, studio and garden are
now a museum devoted to
his life and work. Among the
900 sculptures on display are
the original plaster casts of
his monumental works
planned for wide public
squares. They are housed in
the Great Hall in an extension
and include the group of
sculptures for the relief
decoration of the Théâtre des
Champs-Elysées.

Musée de la Poste ●

34 Blvd de Vaugirard 75015.
Map 15 B2. 📞 01 42 79 23 45.
Ⓜ *Montparnasse-Bienvenüe.*
◯ *10am–6pm Mon–
Sat.* ◐ *public hols.*
🅿 🎟 ♿ **Library.**
www.laposte.fr

Every conceivable
aspect of the history
of the French postal
service and methods
of transportation are
covered in this well
laid out collection.
There is even a
room devoted to

A view of the tower

mail delivery in times of war – carrier pigeons were used during the Franco-Prussian War with postmarks stamped on their wings. Postage stamp art is displayed in the gallery.

A Miró-designed postage stamp

Musée du Montparnasse ❽

21 Ave du Maine 75015. **Map** 15 C1. **Tel** 01 42 22 91 96. Ⓜ Montparnasse-Bienvenüe, Falguière. ⬤ 12:30–7pm Tue–Sun. 📷 **www**.museedemontparnasse.net

During World War I, this was a canteen for needy artists which, by its status as a private club, was not subject to curfew, and so the likes of Picasso, Braque, Modigliani and Léger could eat for 65 centimes and then party until late at night. This symbolic place is now a museum that recalls, through paintings and photos, how at the Vavin crossroads Western art turned some of the most beautiful pages of its modern history.

Fondation Cartier ❾

261 Blvd Raspail 75014. **Map** 16 E3. **Tel** 01 42 18 56 72. Ⓜ Raspail. ⬤ noon–8pm Tue–Sun. ⬤ Jan 1, Dec 25. 📷 ♿ 📷

This foundation for contemporary art is housed in a building designed by architect Jean Nouvel. He has created an air of transparency and light, as well as incorporating a cedar of Lebanon planted in 1823 by François-René de Chateaubriand. The structure complements the nature of the exhibitions of progressive art, which showcase personal, group or thematic displays, often including works by young unknowns.

Catacombes ❿

1 Pl Denfert-Rochereau 75014. **Map** 16 E3. **Tel** 01 43 22 47 63. Ⓜ Denfert-Rochereau. ⬤ 10am–5pm Tue–Sun (last admission 4pm). ⬤ public hols. 📷 📷 📷 **www**.catacombes.info

In 1786 a monumental project began here: the removal of the millions of skulls and bones from the unsanitary city cemetery in Les Halles to the ancient quarries formed by excavations at the base of the three "mountains": Montparnasse, Montrouge and Montsouris. It took 15 months to transport the bones and rotting corpses across the city in huge carts to their new resting place; the transportation was carried out at night.

Just before the Revolution, the Comte d'Artois (later Charles X) threw wild parties in the catacombs, and during World War II the French Resistance set up its headquarters here. Above the door outside are the words "Stop! This is the empire of death."

Observatoire de Paris ⓫

61 Ave de l'Observatoire 75014. **Map** 16 E3. **Tel** 01 40 51 22 21. Ⓜ Denfert-Rochereau. **Visits** (2 hrs) apply 2 mths ahead: 1st Sat of mth: 2:30pm; grps by appt. ⬤ Aug. 📷 📷 **www**.obspm.fr

In 1667 Louis XIV was persuaded by his scientists and astronomers that France needed a royal observatory. Building began on June 21,

the day of the summer solstice, and took five years to reach completion.

Astronomical research undertaken here included the calculation of the exact dimensions of the solar system in 1672, calculations of the dimensions of longitude, the mapping of the moon in 1679 and the discovery of the planet Neptune in 1846.

The facade of the Observatoire

La Closerie des Lilas ⓬

171 Blvd du Montparnasse 75014. **Map** 16 E2. **Tel** 01 40 51 34 50. Ⓜ Vavin. Ⓡ Port Royal. ⬤ Bar: 11–2am, brasserie: noon–1am daily.

Lenin, Trotsky, Hemingway and Scott Fitzgerald all frequented the numerous bars and cafés of Montparnasse, but the Closerie was their favorite. Much of Hemingway's novel *The Sun Also Rises* takes place here. Hemingway wrote it on the terrace in just six weeks. Today the terrace is ringed with trees and the whole place is more elegant in appearance, but much of the original decor remains (*see pp38–9*).

Skulls and bones stored in the catacombs

Cimetière du Montparnasse ❹

The Montparnasse Cemetery was planned by Napoleon outside the city walls to replace the numerous, congested small cemeteries within the old city, viewed as a health hazard at the turn of the 19th century. It was opened in 1824 and became the resting place of many illustrious Parisians, particularly Left Bank personalities. Like all French cemeteries it is divided into rigidly aligned paths forming blocks or divisions. The Rue Emile Richard cuts it into two parts, the Grand Cimetière and the Petit Cimetière.

★ **Charles Baudelaire Cenotaph**
This is a monument to the great poet and critic (1821–67), author of The Flowers of Evil.

Samuel Beckett, the great Irish playwright renowned for *Waiting for Godot*, spent most of his life in Paris. He died in 1989.

The Pétain tomb contains the family of the marshal who collaborated with the Germans during World War II. Pétain himself is buried on Ile d'Yeu, where he was imprisoned.

Guy de Maupassant was a 19th-century novelist.

Alfred Dreyfus was a Jewish army officer whose unjust trial for treason in 1894 provoked a political and social scandal.

Frédéric Auguste Bartholdi was the sculptor of the Statue of Liberty (1886) in New York.

André Citroën, an engineer and industrialist who died in 1935, founded the famous French car company.

AVE DU MIDI

AVE THIERRY

RUE EMILE RICHARD

AVE DE L'EST

FAMILLE CHARLES PIGEON

★ **Charles Pigeon Family Tomb**
This wonderfully pompous Belle Epoque tomb depicts the French industrialist and inventor in bed with his wife.

Charles-Augustin Sainte-Beuve was a critic of the French Romantic generation, and is generally described as the "father of modern criticism".

STAR FEATURES

★ Charles Baudelaire Cenotaph

★ Charles Pigeon Family Tomb

★ Jean-Paul Sartre and Simone de Beauvoir

★ Serge Gainsbourg

The Kiss by Brancusi
This is the famous Primitivo-Cubist sculpture (a response to Rodin's Kiss) by the great Romanian artist, who died in 1957 and is buried just off the Rue Emile Richard.

Camille Saint-Saëns, the pianist, organist and composer who died in 1921, was one of France's great post-Romantic musicians.

Serge Gainsbourg
The French singer, composer and pop on of the 1970s and 1980s is best known for his wistful and irreverent songs. He was married to the actress Jane Birkin.

VISITORS' CHECKLIST

3 Blvd Edgar Quinet. **Map** 16 D3.
Tel 01 44 10 86 50. Ⓜ *Edgar Quinet.* 🚌 *38, 83, 91 to Port Royal.* RER *Port Royal.* 🅿 *Rue Campagne-Première, Blvd St-Jacques.* ◻ Mid-Mar–Oct: 8am–6pm Mon–Fri, 8:30am–6pm Sat, 9am–6pm Sun; Nov–mid-Mar closes 5:30pm. **Adm free.** 📷 ♿

The Tower is all that remains of a 17th-century windmill. It was part of the old property of the Brothers of Charity on which the cemetery was built.

Génie du Sommeil Eternel
Horace Daillion's wistful bronze angel of Eternal Sleep (1902) is the cemetery's centerpiece.

Tristen Tzara, the Romanian writer, was leader of the literary and artistic Dada movement in Paris in the 1920s.

Henri Laurens
The French sculptor (1885–1954) was a leading figure in the Cubist movement.

Man Ray was an American photographer who immortalized the Montparnasse artistic and café scene in the 1920s and 1930s.

Charles Baudelaire, the 19th-century poet, is buried here in his detested step-father's family tomb, along with his beloved mother.

Chaïm Soutine, a poor Jewish Lithuanian, was a Montparnasse Bohemian painter of the 1920s. He was a friend of the Italian artist Modigliani.

Jean Seberg
The Hollywood actress, chosen by François Truffaut as the star for his film A bout de souffle, *was the epitome of American blonde beauty, youth and candor.*

JEAN PAUL SARTRE
1905 - 1980
SIMONE DE BEAUVOIR
1908 - 1986

★ Jean-Paul Sartre and Simone de Beauvoir
The famous existentialist couple, undisputed leaders of the post-war literary scene, lie here close to their Left Bank haunts.

INVALIDES AND EIFFEL TOWER QUARTER

Musée de l'Armée cannon

Everything in the area of Invalides is on a monumental scale. Starting from the sprawling 18th-century buildings of the Ecole Militaire on the corner of the Avenue de la Motte Piquet, the Parc du Champs de Mars stretches down to the Eiffel Tower and the Seine. The avenues around the tower are lined with lux-urious buildings, some in the Art Nouveau style, and numerous embassies. The area was already highly prized between the world wars when the noted actor Sacha Guitry lived there. Even earlier, in the 18th century, wealthy residents of the Marais moved to this part of the city, building the aristocratic town houses that line the Rue de Varenne and Rue de Grenelle.

SIGHTS AT A GLANCE

Historic Buildings and Streets
Hôtel des Invalides ⑥
Hôtel Matignon ⑧
Assemblée Nationale Palais-Bourbon ⑪
Rue Cler ⑫
Les Egouts ⑬
Champ-de-Mars ⑭
No. 29 Avenue Rapp ⑯
Ecole Militaire ⑱

Museums and Galleries
Musée de l'Ordre de la Libération ③
Musée de l'Armée ④

Musées des Plans-Reliefs ⑤
Musée Rodin ⑦
Musée Maillol ⑨

Churches and Temples
Dôme Church pp188–9 ①
St-Louis-des-Invalides ②
Sainte-Clotilde ⑩

Monuments and Fountains
Eiffel Tower pp192–3 ⑮

Modern Architecture
Village Suisse ⑰
UNESCO ⑲

GETTING THERE
The metro system serves this area well, with stations at Invalides, Solferino, Sèvres Babylone, Varenne, Latour Maubourg and Ecole Militaire. There are also several bus routes through the area. Route 69 passes along Rue St-Dominique heading east and along Rue de Grenelle on the way back. Route 87 travels along the Avenue de Suffren and 28 along Avenue de la Mottè Picquet.

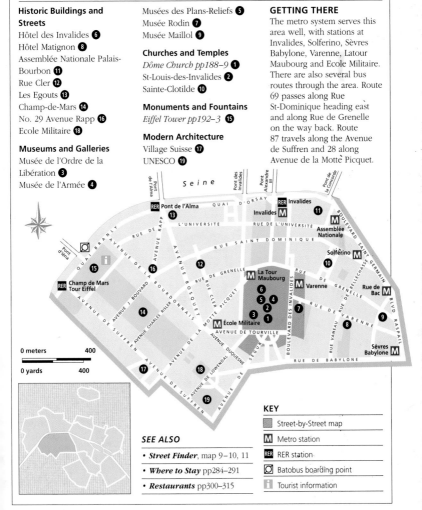

KEY

Street-by-Street map

M Metro station

RER RER station

◎ Batobus boarding point

ℹ Tourist information

SEE ALSO

- *Street Finder*, map 9–10, 11
- *Where to Stay* pp284–291
- *Restaurants* pp300–315

◁ **View of the Eiffel Tower**

Street-by-Street: Invalides

Mounted military policeman

The imposing Hôtel des Invalides, from which the area takes its name, was built from 1671 to 1676 by Louis XIV for his wounded and homeless veterans and as a monument to his own glory. At its center lies the glittering golden roof of the Sun King's Dôme Church, which marks the final resting place of Napoleon Bonaparte. The emperor's body was brought here from St Helena in 1840, 19 years after he died, and placed inside the majestic red sarcophagus, designed by Joachim Visconti, that lies at the center of the Dôme's circular glass-topped crypt. Just to the east of the Hôtel on the corner of the Boulevard des Invalides, the superb Musée Rodin offers artistic relief from the pomp and circumstance of the surrounding area.

The facade of the hôtel is 645 ft (196 m) long and is topped by dormer windows, each decorated in the shape of a different trophy. A head of Hercules sits above the central entrance.

Metro La Tour Maubourg

★ Musée de l'Armée
This museum covers military history from the Stone Age to World War II. It includes an exhibition on the development of the French flag, from the various standards of the ancien régime to the Tricolor ❹

STAR SIGHTS

- ★ Dôme Church and Napoleon's Tomb
- ★ St-Louis-des-Invalides
- ★ Musée de l'Armée
- ★ Musée Rodin

KEY

- – – Suggested route

| 0 meters | 100 |
| 0 yards | 100 |

Musée de l'Ordre de la Libération
The Order was set up to honor feats of heroism during World War II ❸

AVE DE TOURVILLE

Musées de Plans-Relief
This museum contains military models of forts and towns, as well as a display on model-making ❺

AVE DE SÉGUR

General de Gaulle's Liberation Order and compass

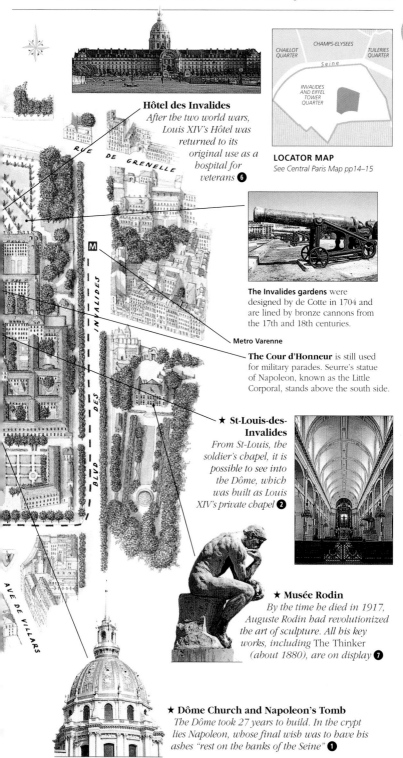

Hôtel des Invalides
After the two world wars, Louis XIV's Hôtel was returned to its original use as a hospital for veterans ❻

LOCATOR MAP
See Central Paris Map pp14–15

The Invalides gardens were designed by de Cotte in 1704 and are lined by bronze cannons from the 17th and 18th centuries.

Metro Varenne

The Cour d'Honneur is still used for military parades. Seurre's statue of Napoleon, known as the Little Corporal, stands above the south side.

★ St-Louis-des-Invalides
From St-Louis, the soldier's chapel, it is possible to see into the Dôme, which was built as Louis XIV's private chapel ❷

★ Musée Rodin
By the time he died in 1917, Auguste Rodin had revolutionized the art of sculpture. All his key works, including The Thinker *(about 1880), are on display* ❼

★ Dôme Church and Napoleon's Tomb
The Dôme took 27 years to build. In the crypt lies Napoleon, whose final wish was to have his ashes "rest on the banks of the Seine" ❶

Dôme Church ●

See pp188–9.

St-Louis-des-Invalides ●

Hôtel des Invalides 75007. **Map** 11
A3. **M** *Varenne, Latour-Maubourg.*
Tel *01 44 42 37 65.* ○ *Apr–Sep:*
10am–6pm daily; Oct–Mar:
10am–5pm daily.

Also known as the "soldiers' church", this is the chapel of the Hôtel des Invalides. It was built from 1679 to 1708 by Jules Hardouin-Mansart from the original designs by Libéral Bruand, architect of the Hôtel des Invalides. The imposing, but stark, interior is decorated with banners seized in battle.

The fine 17th-century organ was built by Alexandre Thierry. The first performance of Berlioz's *Requiem* was given on it in 1837, with an orchestra accompanied by a battery of outside artillery.

Musée de l'Ordre de la Libération ●

51 bis Blvd de Latour-Maubourg 75007.
Map 11 A4. **Tel** *01 47 05 04 10.* **M**
Latour-Maubourg. ○ *10am–5:45pm*
(4:45pm in winter) daily. ● *public*
hols. 🎫 📷 🎥 *apply 1 mth before.*

This museum is devoted to the wartime Free French and their leader, General Charles de Gaulle. The Order of

The facade of the Musée de l'Ordre de la Libération

Liberation was created by de Gaulle at Brazzaville in 1940. It is France's highest honor and was eventually bestowed on those who made an outstanding contribution to the final victory of the Allies in World War II. The *companions* who received the honor were French civilians and members of the armed forces, plus a handful of overseas leaders, including King George VI, Winston Churchill and General Dwight Eisenhower.

Cannons at the Musée de l'Armée

Musée de l'Armée ●

Hôtel des Invalides 75007.
Map 11 A3. **Tel** *01 44 42 37 72.*
M *Latour-Maubourg, Varenne.*
RER *Invalides.* ○ *10am–6pm (5pm*
winter) daily. ● *Jan 1, May 1, Nov 1,*
Dec 25. 🎫 📷 ♿ *grd floor only.*
🎥 📱 🎥 *Film.*
www.invalides.org

This is one of the most comprehensive museums of military history in the world, with exhibits ranging from the Stone Age to the final days of World War II. The museum is housed in galleries occupying two of the former four refectories on each side of the magnificent courtyard of the 17th-century Hôtel des Invalides, and in the "Priests' Wing" with the large World War II galleries.

In the Turenne gallery on the east side there is an impressive array of banners from 1619 to 1945, including Napoleon's flag of farewell flown at Fontainebleau in

1814, after his first abdication. The Restoration gallery on the second floor recalls the emperor's imprisonment on Elba, the Hundred Days War, Waterloo and his final exile on St Helena, with a reconstruction of the room where he died in 1821.

On the west side, the Oriental gallery has a rich display of arms and armour from China, Japan, India and Turkey; the Pauillac gallery has Renaissance swords and daggers; and the Arsenal has suits of armor, 1,000 helmets and hundreds of spears, swords and firearms.

Musées des Plans-Reliefs ●

Hôtel des Invalides 75007. **Map** 11
B3. **Tel** *01 45 51 95 05.* **M** *Latour-Maubourg, Varenne.* **RER** *Invalides.*
○ *10am–5:45pm (4:45pm in winter)*
daily. ● *Jan 1, May 1, Nov 1 & 11,*
Dec 25. 🎫 📷 📱

A map of Alessandria, Italy (1813)

The detailed models of French forts and fortified towns, some dating back to Louis XIV's reign, were considered top secret until the 1950s, when they were put on public display. The oldest model is that of Perpignan, dating to 1686. It shows the fortifications drawn up by the legendary 17th-century military architect Vauban, who built the defenses around several French towns, including Briançon.

The altar of St-Louis-des-Invalides

Hôtel des Invalides ❻

75007. **Map** 11 A3. **Tel** 01 44 42 37 72. Ⓜ Latour-Maubourg, Varenne. ⓞ 10am–6pm daily (5pm winter). ⓞ public hols. **www**.invalides.org

The Invalides main entrance

Founded by Louis XIV, this was the first military hospital and home for French war veterans and disabled soldiers who had hitherto been reduced to begging. The decree for building this vast complex was signed in 1670, and construction, following the designs of Libéral Bruand, was finished five years later.

Today the harmonious Classical facade is one of the most impressive sights in Paris, with its four storys, cannons in the forecourt, garden and tree-lined esplanade stretching to the Seine. The south side leads to St-Louis-des-Invalides, the soldiers' church, which backs on to the magnificent Dôme church of Jules Hardouin-Mansart. The dome was regilded in 1989 and now glitters anew.

Musée Rodin ❼

77 Rue de Varenne 75007. **Map** 11 B3. **Tel** 01 44 18 61 10. Ⓜ Varenne. ⓞ Apr–Sep: 9:30am–5:45pm Tue–Sun; Oct–Mar: 9:30am–4:45pm (gdn 1 hr later) Tue–Sun. ⓞ Jan 1, May 1, Dec 25. Ⓗ ⓞ ⓑ restricted. ⓞ ⓞ ⓞ occas. **www**.musee-rodin.fr

Auguste Rodin, widely regarded as the greatest 19th-century French sculptor, lived and worked in the Hôtel

Biron, an elegant 18th-century mansion, from 1908 until his death in 1917. In return for a state-owned apartment and studio, Rodin left his work to the nation, and it is now exhibited here. Some of his most celebrated sculptures are on display in the garden: *The Burghers of Calais, The Thinker, The Gates of Hell* and *Balzac*. The garden has a stunning array of 2,000 rose bushes.

The indoor exhibits are arranged in chronological order, spanning the whole of Rodin's career, with highlights such as *The Kiss* and *Eve*.

Hôtel Matignon ❽

57 Rue de Varenne 75007. **Map** 11 C4. Ⓜ Solférino, Rue du Bac. ⓞ to the public.

One of the most beautiful mansions in the Faubourg area, this was built by Jean Courtonne in 1721 and has been substantially remodeled since. Former owners include Talleyrand, the statesman and diplomat who held legendary parties and receptions here, and several members of the nobility. It has been the official residence of the French prime minister since 1958 and has the largest private garden in Paris.

Rodin's The Kiss (1886) at the Musée Rodin

Musée Maillol ❾

61 Rue de Grenelle 75007. **Map** 11 C4. **Tel** 01 42 22 59 58. Ⓜ Sèvres-Babylone, Rue du Bac. ⓞ 11am–6pm Wed–Mon. ⓞ public hols. ⓑ ⓞ ⓞ **www**.museemaillol.com

Once lived in by novelist Alfred de Musset, this museum was created by Dina Vierny, former model and muse to Aristide Maillol. All aspects of the artist's work are here: drawings, engravings, paintings, sculpture and decorative objects. Also displayed is Dina Vierny's private collection, in which naïve art sits alongside works by Matisse, Dufy, Picasso and Rodin.

Large allegorical figures of the city of Paris and the four seasons decorate Bouchardon's fountain in front of the house.

Sculptured figures at Ste-Clotilde

Sainte-Clotilde ❿

12 Rue de Martignac 75007. **Map** 11 B3. ⓕ 01 44 18 62 60. Ⓜ Solférino, Varenne, Invalides. ⓞ 9am–7pm daily. ⓞ non-religious public hols. ⓞ ⓞ

Designed by the German-born architect François-Christian Gau and the first of its kind to be built in Paris, this Neo-Gothic church was inspired by the mid-19th-century enthusiasm for the Middle Ages, made fashionable by such writers as Victor Hugo. The church is noted for its imposing twin towers, visible from across the Seine. The interior decoration includes sculpted stations of the cross by James Pradier and stained-glass windows with scenes relating to the patron saint of the church. The composer César Franck was the church organist here for 32 years.

Dôme Church ❶

Jules Hardouin-Mansart was asked in 1676 by the Sun King, Louis XIV, to build the Dôme Church among the existing buildings of the Invalides military refuge. A soldiers' church had already been built, but the Dôme was to be reserved for the exclusive use of the Sun King and for the location of royal tombs. The resulting masterpiece complements the surrounding buildings and is one of the greatest examples of 17th-century French architecture.

After Louis XIV's death, plans to bury the royal family in the church were abandoned, and it became a monument to Bourbon glory. In 1840 Louis-Philippe decided to install Napoleon's remains in the crypt, and the addition of the tombs of Vauban, Marshal Foch and other figures of military prominence have since turned this church into a French military memorial.

Gilded Dome
The cupola was first gilded in 1715.

① Tomb of Joseph Bonaparte
The sarcophagus of Napoleon's older brother, the king of Naples and later of Spain, is in the side chapel to the right as visitors enter.

Main entrance

② Memorial to Vauban
Commissioned by Napoleon I in 1808, this contains an urn with Sébastien le Prestre de Vauban's heart. He was Louis XIV's great military architect and engineer who died in 1707. His long military career culminated in his appointment as Marshal of France in 1703. He revolutionized siege warfare when he introduced his ricochet-batteries. His reclining figure by Antoine Etex lies on top of the memorial, mourned by Science and War.

⑥ **Glass Gallery**
Access to the glass-topped crypt containing Napoleon's tomb is by the curved stairs in front of the altar. The glass partition behind the altar separates the Dôme from the older Invalides chapel beyond.

VISITORS' CHECKLIST

Hôtel National des Invalides, 129 Rue de Grenelle. **Map** 11 A3.
Tel 01 44 42 37 72. M Latour-Maubourg, Varenne. ▦ 28, 49, 63, 69, 82, 83, 87, 92 to Les Invalides. ▦ Invalides. ◻ Tour Eiffel. ▣ Rue de Constantine.
◻ Oct– Mar: 10am–5pm; Apr–Sep: 10am–6pm daily. ◕ Jan 1, May 1, Jun 17, Nov 1, Dec 25.
▨ ◻ ▧ restricted. ◪ groups
Tel 01 44 42 37 72. ▣ ▣

KEY
▬ ▬ ▬ Tour route

⑤ **St Jérôme's Chapel**
Passing across the center of the church, the side chapel to the right of the main entrance contains the tomb of Napoleon's younger brother, Jérôme, king of Westphalia.

Stairs to crypt

④ **Dôme Ceiling**
Looking upward, Charles de la Fosse's circular painting (1692) on the ceiling shows the Glory of Paradise, *with Saint Louis presenting his sword to Christ.*

③ **Tomb of Marshal Foch**
Ferdinand Foch's imposing bronze tomb was built by Paul Landowski in 1937.

NAPOLEON'S RETURN
King Louis-Philippe decided to bring the Emperor Napoleon's body back from St Helena *(see pp32–3)* as a gesture of reconciliation to the Republican and Bonapartist parties contesting his regime. The Dôme Church, with its historical and military associations, was an obvious choice for Napoleon's final resting place. His body was encased in six coffins and finally placed in the crypt in 1861, in the culmination of a grand ceremony which was attended by Napoleon III.

Neoclassical facade of the Assemblée Nationale Palais-Bourbon

Assemblée Nationale Palais-Bourbon **⓫**

126 Rue de l'Université 75007.
Map 11 B2. **Tel** 01 40 63 60 00.
Ⓜ *Assemblée-Nationale.* 🆁🅴🆁 *Invalides.*
⏰ *2–5pm Mon, Fri, Sat. Enter at 33 Quai d'Orsay. ID necessary.* 🚻
✍ *for groups phone 01 40 63 64 08.*
www.assemblee-nat.fr

Built in 1722 for the Duchesse de Bourbon, daughter of Louis XIV, the Palais-Bourbon was confiscated during the Revolution. It has been home to the lower house of the French parliament since 1830.

During World War II, the palace became the Nazi administration's seat of government. The public can enter to watch parliament in action. The grand neo-Classical facade with its fine columns was added to the palace in 1806, partly to mirror the facade of La Madeleine church facing it across the Seine. The adjacent Hôtel de Lassay, built by the Prince de Condé, is now the residence of the president of the National Assembly.

Rue Cler **⓬**

75007. **Map** 10 F3.
Ⓜ *Ecole-Militaire, Latour-Maubourg.*
Market ⏰ *Tue–Sat. See **Shops and Markets** p338.*

This is the street market of the seventh arrondissement, the richest in Paris, for here live the bulk of senior civil servants, captains of industry and many diplomats. The market area occupies a pedestrian precinct stretching south from the Rue de Grenelle. It is colorful, but very much an exclusive market, with the best-dressed shoppers in town. As one would expect, the produce is excellent, the pâtisserie and cheese shops in particular.

Of architectural interest are the Art Nouveau buildings at No. 33 and No. 151.

Les Egouts **⓭**

93 Quai d'Orsay 75007. **Map** 10 F2.
📞 *01 53 68 27 81.*
Ⓜ *Alma-Marceau.* 🆁🅴🆁 *Pont de l'Alma.*
⏰ *11am–5pm (4pm in winter) Sat–Wed.* 🎟 *last 3 wks Jan.* 🚫 📷 ✍

One of Baron Haussmann's finest achievements, most of Paris's sewers (*égouts*) date from the Second Empire (*see pp32–3*). If laid end to end the 1,300 miles (2,100 km) of sewers would stretch from Paris to Istanbul. In the 20th century the sewers became a popular attraction with tourists. All tours have been limited to a small area around the Quai d'Orsay entrance and are now on foot. A sewer museum has now been established here where visitors can discover the mysteries of underground Paris. There are also displays of machinery used in the past and in the sewers of today.

The interior of a wine shop in the Rue Cler

Doorway at No. 29 Avenue Rapp

Champ-de-Mars ⓮

75007. **Map** 10 E3. Ⓜ Ecole-Militaire.
RER Champ-de-Mars–Tour-Eiffel.

The gardens stretching from the Eiffel Tower to the Ecole Militaire were originally a parade ground for the officer cadets of the Ecole Militaire. The area has since been used for horse-racing, balloon ascents and the mass celebrations for July 14, the anniversary of the Revolution. The first ceremony was held in 1790 in the presence of a glum, captive Louis XVI. Vast exhibitions were held here in the late 19th century, including the 1889 World's Fair for which the Eiffel Tower was erected. *Le Mur de la Paix*, Jean-Michel Wilmotte's monument to world peace, stands at one end.

A Paris balloon ascent

Eiffel Tower ⓯

See pp192–3.

No. 29 Avenue Rapp ⓰

75007. **Map** 10 E2. Ⓜ Pont-de-l'Alma.

A prime example of Art Nouveau architecture is No. 29, and it won its designer, Jules Lavirotte, first prize at the Concours des Facades de la Ville de Paris in 1901. Its ceramics and brickwork are decorated with animal and flower motifs intermingling with female figures. These are superimposed on a multi-colored sandstone base to produce a facade that is deliberately erotic, and was certainly subversive in its day. Also worth visiting is Lavirotte's building, complete with watchtower, which can be found in the Square Rapp.

Village Suisse ⓱

38-78 Ave de Suffren 75015.
Map 10 E4. Ⓜ Dupleix.
🕐 10:30am–7pm Thu–Mon.

The Swiss government built a mock-Alpine village for the 1900 Universal Exhibition held in the Champ-de-Mars nearby. It was later used as a center for dealing in secondhand goods. In the 1950s and 1960s antique dealers moved in, and everything became more fashionable and expensive. The village was renovated in the late 1960s.

Ecole Militaire ⓲

1 Pl Joffre 75007. **Map** 10 F4.
Ⓜ Ecole-Militaire. Visits by special permission only – contact the commandant in writing. 📷

The Royal Military Academy of Louis XV was founded in 1751 to educate 500 sons of impoverished officers. It was designed by architect Jacques-Ange Gabriel, and one of the features is the central pavilion. This is a magnificent example of the French Classical style, with eight Corinthian pillars and a quadrangular dome. The interior is decorated in Louis XVI style; of main interest are the chapel and a superb Gabriel-designed wrought-iron banister on the main staircase.

An early cadet at the academy was Napoleon, whose graduation report stated that "he could go far if the circumstances are right."

A 1751 engraving showing the planning of the Ecole Militaire

UNESCO ⓳

7 Pl de Fontenoy 75007. **Map** 10 F5.
Tel 01 45 68 10 00. 📠 01 45 68 10 60 (in English). Ⓜ Ségur, Cambronne.
🕐 9:30am–2:30pm Mon–Fri.
⬤ public hols & during conference sessions. 📷 ♿ 📷 🍴 📷
Exhibitions, films.
www.unesco.org

This is the headquarters of the United Nations Educational, Scientific and Cultural Organization (UNESCO). The organization's stated aim is to contribute to international peace and security through education, science and culture.

UNESCO is a trove of modern art, notably a huge mural by Picasso, ceramics by Joan Miró and sculptures by Henry Moore.

Moore's *Reclining Figure* at UNESCO (erected 1958)

Eiffel Tower ⑮

Eiffel Tower from
the Trocadéro

Originally built to impress visitors to the Universal Exhibition of 1889, the Eiffel Tower (Tour Eiffel) was meant to be a temporary addition to the Paris skyline. Designed by the engineer Gustave Eiffel, it was fiercely decried by 19th-century aesthetes. The author Guy de Maupassant lunched there to avoid seeing it. The world's tallest building until 1931, when New York's Empire State Building was completed, the tower is now the symbol of Paris. Since its recent renovation and installation of new lighting it has never looked better.

Ironwork Pattern

According to Eiffel, the complex pattern of pig-iron girders came from the need to stabilize the tower in strong winds. But Eiffel's design quickly won admirers for its pleasing symmetry.

Elevator Engine Room
Eiffel emphasized safety over speed in choosing the elevators for the tower.

STAR FEATURES

★ Eiffel Bust

★ Cinémax

★ Hydraulic Elevator Mechanism

★ Viewing Gallery

★ Cinémax
This small museum tells the history of the tower through a short movie. It includes footage of famous personalities who have visited the tower, including Charlie Chaplin, Josephine Baker and Adolf Hitler.

THE DARING AND THE DELUDED

The tower has inspired many crazy stunts. It has been climbed by mountaineers, cycled down by a journalist and used by trapeze artists and as a launch pad by sky divers. In 1912 a Parisian tailor, Reichelt, attempted to fly from the parapet with only a modified cape for wings. He plunged to his death in front of a large crowd. According to the autopsy, he died of a heart attack before even touching the ground.

Birdman Reichelt

★ Elevator Mechanism
Still in working order, this part of the original 1900 mechanism was automated in 1986.

The third level, 905 ft (276 m) above the ground, can hold 800 people at a time.

★ **Viewing Gallery**
On a clear day it is possible to see for 45 miles (72 km), including a distant view of Chartres Cathedral.

Double-Decker Elevators
During the tourist season, the limited capacity of the elevators means that it can take a couple of hours to reach the top. Lines for the elevators require patience and no fear of heights.

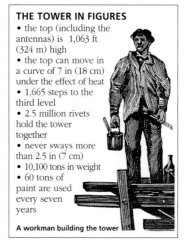

The second level is at 376 ft (115 m), separated from the first level by 359 steps, or a few minutes in the elevator.

Jules Verne Restaurant is one of the best restaurants in Paris, offering superb food and panoramic views (see p304).

The first level, at 187 ft (57 m), can be reached by elevator or by 360 steps. There is a post office here.

VISITORS' CHECKLIST

Champ de Mars. **Map** 10 D3.
Tel *01 44 11 23 23.* Ⓜ *Bir Hakeim.* 🚌 *42, 69, 72, 82, 87, 91 to Champ de Mars.* 🚇 *Champ de Mars.* 🅿️ *Tour Eiffel.* 🅿️ *on site.* ⏰ *Sep–mid-Jun: 9:30am–11pm daily (6:30pm for stairs); mid-Jun–Aug: 9am–midnight (last adm 1hr before).* 🎫 📷 ♿ *limited.* 🍴 🎬 *Films.* www.tour-eiffel.fr

THE TOWER IN FIGURES

- the top (including the antennas) is 1,063 ft (324 m) high
- the top can move in a curve of 7 in (18 cm) under the effect of heat
- 1,665 steps to the third level
- 2.5 million rivets hold the tower together
- never sways more than 2.5 in (7 cm)
- 10,100 tons in weight
- 60 tons of paint are used every seven years

A workman building the tower

★ **Eiffel Bust**
Eiffel's (1832–1923) achievement was crowned with the Légion d'Honneur in 1889. Another honor was the bust by Antoine Bourdelle, placed beneath the tower in 1929.

Gilded bronze statues by a number of sculptors decorating the central square of the Palais de Chaillot

Porte Dauphine M
Avenue Foch RER 10

BLVD FLANDRIN
RUE DE LA FAISANDER
RUE
AVE V

Avenue
Henri Martin
RER
AVE HENRI MARTIN
RUE DE

M La M
RUE DE

RER
Boulainvilliers-
La Muette
RUE DES
RUE DE BOULAINVILLIE

CHAILLOT QUARTER

The village of Chaillot was absorbed into Paris in the 19th century and transformed into an area rich in grand Second Empire avenues *(see pp34–5)* and opulent mansions. Some of the avenues converge on the Place du Trocadéro, renowned for its elegant cafés, which leads on to the Avenue du Président Wilson, with

Sculptures at the base of the Chaillot pool

a greater concentration of museums than any other street in Paris. Many of the area's private mansions are occupied by embassies, including the imposing Vatican embassy, and by major company headquarters. To the west is the territory of the *haute bourgeoisie*, one of Paris's most exclusive, if staid, residential neighborhoods.

SIGHTS AT A GLANCE

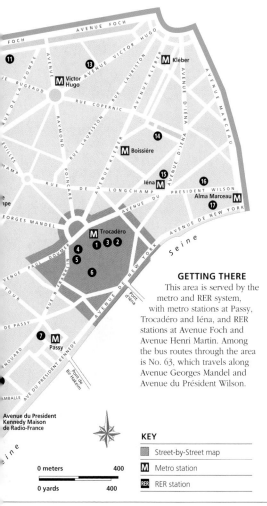

Museums and Galleries

Cinémathèque Française, Salle Chaillot ❷
Cité de l'Architecture et du Patrimoine ❸
Musée de l'Homme ❹
Musée de la Marine ❺
Musée du Vin ❼
Maison de Balzac ❽
Musée de Radio-France ❾
Musée de la Contrefaçon ❿
Musée National d'Ennery ⓫
Musée Arménien ⓬
Musée Dapper ⓭
Musée du Cristal de Baccarat ⓮
Musée National des Arts Asiatiques Guimet ⓯
Musée Galliera ⓰
Musée d'Art Moderne de la Ville de Paris ⓱

Gardens
Jardins du Trocadéro ❻

Modern Architecture
Palais de Chaillot ❶

GETTING THERE
This area is served by the metro and RER system, with metro stations at Passy, Trocadéro and Iéna, and RER stations at Avenue Foch and Avenue Henri Martin. Among the bus routes through the area is No. 63, which travels along Avenue Georges Mandel and Avenue du Président Wilson.

Avenue du President Kennedy Maison de Radio-France

KEY

▨	Street-by-Street map
Ⓜ	Metro station
RER	RER station

0 meters 400
0 yards 400

SEE ALSO

Street-by-Street: Chaillot

The Chaillot hill, with its superb position overlooking the Seine, was the site chosen by Napoleon for "the biggest and most extraordinary" palace that was to be built for his son – but by the time of his downfall only a few ramparts had been completed. Today, the monumental Palais de Chaillot, with its two huge curved wings, stands on the site. From the terrace in front of the Palais there is a magnificent view over the Trocadéro gardens and the Seine to the Eiffel Tower.

The statue of Marshal Ferdinand Foch, who led the Allies to victory in 1918, was unveiled on November 11, 1951. It was built by Robert Wlérick and Raymond Martin to commemorate the centennial of Foch's birth and the 33rd anniversary of the 1918 Armistice.

Metro Trocadéro

The Place du Trocadéro was created for the Universal Exhibition of 1878. Initially it was known as the Place du Roi-de-Rome, in honor of Napoleon's son.

★ **Musée de la Marine**
While concentrating on France's maritime history, this museum also has exhibits of navigational instruments **5**

Palais de Chaillot
This Neoclassical building was constructed for the World's Fair of 1937. It replaced the Palais du Trocadéro, which was built in 1878 **1**

★ **Musée de l'Homme**
This chair from Benin is just one of the many artifacts from Africa that the museum possesses **4**

Cité de l'Architecture et du Patrimoine
This huge complex houses an architecture museum, a school, library and archive, and various heritage organizations ❸

The Théâtre National de Chaillot,
beneath the terrace, includes a multi-purpose cultural center and a modern 1,200-seat theater. *(See pp342–4.)*

LOCATOR MAP
See Central Paris Map pp14–15

★ **Cinémathèque Française, Salle Chaillot**
Paris's film archive also screens old movies, such as the 1956 classic The Red Balloon, *directed by Albert Lamorisse* ❷

The Trocadéro fountains are operated in sequence, culminating in the huge water cannons in the center firing toward the Eiffel Tower. They are illuminated at night.

The Pont d'Iéna was built by Napoleon to celebrate his victory in 1806 over the Prussians at Jena (Iéna) in Prussia. It was widened in 1937 to complement the building of the Palais de Chaillot.

Jardins du Trocadéro
The present layout of the gardens was created by R Lardat after the World's Fair of 1937 ❻

KEY

– – – Suggested route

0 meters   100

0 yards   100

STAR SIGHTS

★ Cinémathèque

★ Musée de l'Homme

★ Musée de la Marine

Trocadéro fountains in front of the Palais de Chaillot

Palais de Chaillot ❶

17 Pl du Trocadéro 75016.
Map 9 C2. **Tel** *01 44 05 39 10.*
Ⓜ *Trocadéro.* ○ *9:45am–5:15pm
Wed–Mon.* 🚻 ▫ ▪

The palais, with its huge,
curved, colonnaded wings
each culminating in an
immense pavilion, houses
four museums, a theater and
the Cinémathèque. Designed
in Neoclassical style for the
1937 Paris Exhibition by Léon
Azéma, Louis-Hippolyte
Boileau and Jacques Carlu, it
is adorned with sculptures
and bas-reliefs. On the walls
of the pavilions there are gold
inscriptions by the poet and
essayist Paul Valéry.
The *parvis*, or square,
situated between the two
pavilions is decorated with
large bronze sculptures and
ornamental pools. On the
terrace in front of the *parvis*

stand two bronzes, *Apollo* by
Henri Bouchard and *Hercules*
by Albert Pommier. Stairways
lead from the terrace to the
Théâtre National de Chaillot
(see pp342–3), which, after
World War II, enjoyed huge
fame for its avant-garde
productions.

Cinémathèque Française, Salle Chaillot ❷

Palais de Chaillot, 7 Ave Albert de Mun
75016. **Map** 10 D2. 🎬 *01 56 26 01
01 for screenings.* Ⓜ *Trocadéro, Iéna.*
📷 *See* **Entertainment** *pp354–6.*

Devastated by fire in 1997,
this magnificent film library
has now been restored and
reopened. Its archive
contains a huge selection of
French film classics. Frequent retrospectives are still

held here, although the main
body of the Cinématique
Française has moved to Frank
Gehry's former American
Center *(see p246)*, alongside
the Musée du Cinéma and the
Maison du Cinéma.

Church model from Bagneux, Cité
de l'Architecture et du Patrimoine

Cité de l'Architecture et du Patrimoine ❸

Palais de Chaillot, Pl du Trocadéro
75016. **Map** 9 C2. **Tel** *01 44 05 39
10.* Ⓜ *Trocadéro.*
○ *9:30am–5:30pm Tue–Sun.*
📷 ▫ 🚻 ▪

Viollet-le-Duc's inspired
Musée des Monuments
Français (1789), which was
formerly housed here, is
now visible again as part of
this huge new architecture
complex, completed in 2003.
The complex includes an
enlarged architecture
museum, with extended
exhibition spaces, the
famous Ecole de Chaillot
"heritage" school, a
governmental architectural
agency, a library and archive
center and various heritage
organizations.

Sequence from the movie *Journey to the Moon* directed by Méliès in 1902

Musée de l'Homme ❹

Palais de Chaillot, 17 Pl du Trocadéro 75016. **Map** 9 C2. **Tel** 01 44 05 72 72. Ⓜ Trocadéro. ⬜ 9:45am–5:15pm Wed–Mon. ⬤ public hols. 📷 ✅ 2:30pm Sat. **Exhibitions, films.** 🍽 🖥 📖 www.mnhn.fr

Situated in the west wing of the Chaillot palace, this museum traces the process of human evolution through a series of anthropological, archaeological and ethnological displays. The anthropology section covers subjects as diverse as tattooing, mummification and head-shrinking.

Please note that the majority of the African collections are in the process of being gradually moved, for display in the Musée du Quai Branly (due to open in 2006). The Oceania and Americas collections will follow.

Gabon mask at Musée de l'Homme

Musée de la Marine ❺

Palais de Chaillot, 17 Pl du Trocadéro 75016. **Map** 9 C2. **Tel** 01 53 65 69 69. Ⓜ Trocadéro. ⬜ 10am–6pm Wed–Mon. ⬤ Jan 1, May 1, Dec 25. 📷 ✅ 📖 **Films, videos.** www.musee-marine.fr

French maritime history from the days of the royal wooden warships to today's aircraft carriers and nuclear submarines is told through wonderfully exact scale models (most of them two centuries old), mementoes of naval heroes, paintings and navigational instruments. The museum was set up by Charles X in

Relief outside the maritime museum

1827, and was then moved to the Chaillot palace in 1943. Exhibits include Napoleon's barge, models of the fleet he assembled at Boulogne-sur-Mer in 1805 for his planned invasion of Britain, and displays on underwater exploration and fishing vessels.

Jardins du Trocadéro ❻

75016. **Map** 10 D2. Ⓜ Trocadéro.

These lovely gardens cover 25 acres (10 ha). Their centerpiece is a long rectangular ornamental pool, bordered by stone and bronze-gilt statues, which look spectacular at night when the fountains are illuminated. The statues include *Man* by P Traverse and *Woman* by G Braque, *Bull* by P Jouve and *Horse* by G Guyot. On each side of the pool, the slopes of the Chaillot hill gently lead down to the Seine and the Pont d'Iéna. There is a freshwater aquarium in the northeast corner of the gardens, which are richly laid out with trees, walkways, small streams and bridges.

Musée du Vin ❼

Rue des Eaux, 5 Sq Charles Dickens 75016. **Map** 9 C3. **Tel** 01 45 25 63 26. Ⓜ Passy. ⬜ 10am–6pm. Tue–Sun. ⬤ Dec 24–Jan 1. 📷 🚫 ♿ ✅ groups only. 🍽 lunchtime only.

Waxwork figures and cardboard cutouts graphically illustrate the history of winemaking in these atmospheric vaulted medieval cellars, which were once used by the monks of Passy. The exhibits include a collection of old wine bottles, glasses and cork screws, as well as an array of scientific instruments that were used in the winemaking and bottling processes. There is also an excellent restaurant, wine for sale and tours which include a wine-tasting session.

Bridge in the Trocadéro gardens

Maison de Balzac ❽

47 Rue Raynouard 75016. **Map** 9 B3. **Tel** 01 55 74 41 80. Ⓜ Passy, La Muette. ⬜ 10am–6pm Tue–Sun (last adm: 5:30pm). ⬤ public hols. 📷 📷 ✅ 📖

The novelist Honoré de Balzac lived here from 1840 to 1847 under a false name, Monsieur de Brugnol, to avoid his numerous creditors. During this time he wrote many of his most famous novels, among them *La Cousine Bette* (1846).

The house now contains a reference library, with some of his original works, and a museum with memorabilia from his life. Many of the rooms have drawings and paintings portraying Balzac's family and close friends. The Madame Hanska room is devoted to the memory of the Russian woman who corresponded with Balzac for 18 years and was his wife for the five months before his death in 1850.

The house has a back entrance leading into the Rue Berton, which was used to evade unwelcome callers. Rue Berton, with its ivy-covered walls, has retained much of its old, country-like charm.

Plaque marking Balzac's house

Radio (1955) in radio museum

Musée de Radio-France ❾

116 Ave du Président-Kennedy
75016. **Map** 9 B4. **Tel** 01 56 40 15
16. Ⓜ Ranelagh. ◯ for tours only,
Mon–Sat. 🚻 public hols. 🏷 🚫 ♿
📷 10:30–11:30am, 2:30–4:30pm
Mon–Fri. **www**.radio-france.fr

Radio-France House is an impressive building designed by Henri Bernard in 1963 as the headquarters of the state-run Radio-France. The largest single structure in France, it is made up of three incomplete concentric circular constructions with a rectangular tower. The building covers an area of 5 acres (2 ha).

Here, in the 70-some studios and main public auditorium, French radio programs are produced. The museum traces the history of communications from the first Chappe telegraph, which took place in 1793, to the latest multimedia developments in radio-listening via the internet. It also gives a fascinating insight into how radio programs are made.

Musée de la Contrefaçon ❿

16 Rue de la Faisanderie 75016.
Map 3 A5. **Tel** 01 56 26 14 00.
Ⓜ Porte Dauphine. ◯ 2–5:30pm
Tue–Sun. 🚻 public hols. 🏷 📷
www.unifab.com

French cognac and perfume producers, and the luxury trade in general, have been plagued for years by counterfeiters operating around the world. This museum was set up by the manufacturers' union and illustrates the history of this type of fraud, which has been going on since Roman times. Among the impressive display of forgeries are copies of Louis Vuitton luggage, Cartier watches and fake wine from the Narbonne region. The museum also has a display on the fate that awaits anyone who may be tempted to imitate a product.

Musée National d'Ennery ⓫

59 Ave Foch 75016. **Map** 3 B5.
Tel 01 45 53 57 96. Ⓜ Porte
Dauphine. 🚻 for renovation until
early 2006. 📷

This mansion, which dates from the Second Empire period, houses two highly personal museums of precious *objets d'art*, the Musée d'Ennery and the Musée Arménien (see below), both currently closed for renovation. The former contains the huge collection of Chinese and Japanese items assembled by Adolphe d'Ennery, the 19th-century dramatist. Dating from the 17th to 19th centuries, the display includes human and animal figures, Japanese ceramic boxes, furniture and hundreds of *netsuke* – small, carved belt ornaments made of bone, wood or ivory.

Chinese vase (circa 18th century), Musée d'Ennery

Musée Arménien ⓬

59 Ave Foch 75016. **Map** 3 B5.
Tel 01 45 56 15 88. Ⓜ Porte
Dauphine. 🚻 for renovation until
further notice.

The ground floor of No. 59 Avenue Foch houses the Armenian museum, founded after World War II. Despite its small size the collection has many fascinating treasures, including church plates, exquisite miniatures, silverware, ceramics, carpets and contemporary paintings.

Khmer art in the Musée National des Arts Asiatiques Guimet

Musée Dapper ⓭

35 bis Rue Paul-Valéry, 75116.
Tel 01 45 00 01 50. Ⓜ Victor-Hugo.
◯ 11am-7pm Wed–Mon.

Not just a museum, but a world-class ethnographic research center called the Dapper Foundation, this is France's premier showcase of African art and culture. Located in an attractive building with an "African" garden, it is a treasure house of vibrant color and powerful, evocative work from the black nations. The emphasis is on precolonial folk arts, with sculpture, carvings, and tribal work, but there is later art too. The highlight is tribal masks, with a dazzling, extraordinary array of richly carved religious, ritual and funerary masks, as well as theatrical ones used for comic, magical or symbolic performances, some dating back to the 12th century. Anthropologists, locals and tourists mingle here for the themed exhibitions and events.

Armenian crown (19th century)

Musée du Cristal de Baccarat ⑭

11 Place des Etats Unis 75016. **Map** 4
D5. *Tel 01 40 22 11 00.*
Ⓜ *Boissière.* ○ *10am–7pm
Mon–Sat.* ◆ *public hols.* 🅿 📷 📹
🏠 www.baccarat.fr

The Musée du Cristal, also
known as the Musée
Baccarat, has on display over
1,200 articles made by the
Baccarat company, which
was founded in 1764 in
Lorraine. These include
services created for the royal
and imperial courts of Europe
and the finest pieces created
in the workshops.

Musée National des Arts Asiatiques Guimet ⑮

6 Pl d'Iéna 75116. **Map** 10 D1.
Tel 01 56 52 53 00. Ⓜ *Iéna.*
○ *10am–6pm Wed–Mon.* 🅿
🚫 ♿ 📹 🚻 📷 📹 *Panthéon
Bouddhique (additional galleries) at
19 Ave d'Iéna* **Tel** *01 40 73 88 11.*
www.museeguimet.fr

The Musée Guimet has the
finest collection of Khmer
(Cambodian) art in the West.
It was originally set up in Lyon
in 1879 by the industrialist
and orientalist Emile Guimet.
    Moved to Paris in 1884, it
meticulously represents every
artistic tradition from Afghani-

**Gabriel Forestier's sculpted doors,
Musée d'Art Moderne**

stan to India, to China and
Japan, to Korea and Vietnam
and the rest of southeast Asia.
With over 45,000 artworks,
the museum is acclaimed for
some especially unusual
collections, including the
Cambodian Angkor Wat
sculptures and 1600 displays
of Himalayan art. Other highlights include Chinese bronzes
and lacquerware, and many
statues of Buddha.

Musée Galliera ⑯

10 Ave Pierre 1er de Serbie 75116.
Map 10 E1. *Tel 01 56 52 86 00.*
Ⓜ *Iéna, Alma Marceau.* ○ *for
exhibitions only, 10am–6pm Tue–Sun.*
🅿 **Children's room.** www.paris.fr/
musees/musees_galliera

Devoted to the evolution of
fashion, this museum is
housed in the Renaissance-
style palace built for the
Duchesse Maria de Ferrari

Galliera in 1892. The collection
comprises more than 100,000
outfits, from the 18th century
to the present day. Some,
from more recent times, have
been donated by such fashionable women as Baronne
Hélène de Rothschild and
Princess Grace of Monaco.
Owing to the fragility of the
garments, they are displayed
in rotation twice per year.

Musée d'Art Moderne de la Ville de Paris ⑰

Palais de Tokyo, 13 Ave du Président-
Wilson 75016. **Map** 10 E1. *Tel 01 47
23 38 86.* Ⓜ *Iéna, Alma Marceau.*
○ *noon–midnight Tue–Sun.* 🅿
temp. exhibs.
♿ 📹 📷 🏠 *Films*
www.palaisdetokyo.com

This large, lively museum is
the municipality's own renowned collection of modern
art, covering all major 20th
century trends (the 21st
century included). The
museum occupies the vast east
wing of the Palais de Tokyo,
built for the 1937 World's Fair.
One of the highlights is Raoul
Dufy's gigantic mural *La Fée
Electricité*. Also notable are the
Cubists, Amadeo Modigliani,
Georges Rouault and the
Fauves, especially Henri
Matisse, whose *La Danse* is
here in both versions.

Garden and rear facade of the Musée Galliera

CHAMPS-ELYSEES

Two great streets dominate this area – the Avenue des Champs-Elysées and the Rue St-Honoré. The former is the capital's most famous thoroughfare. Its breadth is spectacular. The sidewalks are wide and their cafés, theaters and shops attract throngs of people, who come to eat and shop, but also to see and to be seen. Rond Point des Champs-Elysées is the pretty end, with shady chestnut trees and sidewalks colorfully bordered by flower beds. Luxury and political power are nearby. Five-star hotels, fine restaurants and upmarket shops line the nearby streets and avenues. And along Rue St-Honoré are the impressive, heavily guarded Palais de l'Elysée, the sumptuous town mansions of business chiefs, and the many embassies and consulates.

Ornate lamppost on Pont Alexandre III

SIGHTS AT A GLANCE

Historic Buildings and Streets
Palais de l'Elysée ❺
Avenue Montaigne ❻
Avenue des Champs-Elysées ❽
Place Charles de Gaulle (l'Etoile) ❾

Monuments
Arc de Triomphe pp208–9 ❿

Bridges
Pont Alexandre III ❶

Museums and Galleries
Grand Palais ❷
Palais de la Découverte ❸
Petit Palais ❹
Musée Jacquemart-André ❼

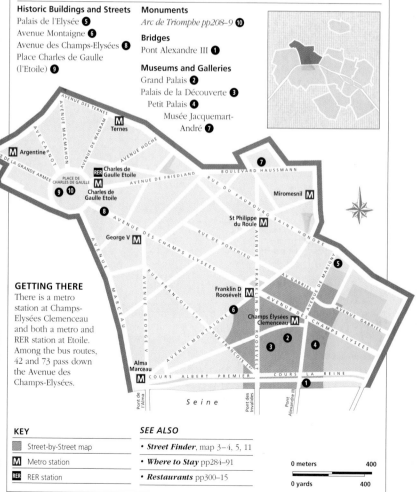

GETTING THERE
There is a metro station at Champs-Elysées Clemenceau and both a metro and RER station at Etoile. Among the bus routes, 42 and 73 pass down the Avenue des Champs-Elysées.

KEY

▨ Street-by-Street map

Ⓜ Metro station

ℝℰℝ RER station

SEE ALSO

• *Street Finder*, map 3–4, 5, 11
• *Where to Stay* pp284–91
• *Restaurants* pp300–15

0 meters   400
0 yards   400

◁ **View of the Arc de Triomphe at night**

Street-by-Street: Champs-Elysées

The formal gardens that line the Champs-Elysées from the Place de la Concorde to the Rond-Point have changed little since they were laid out by the architect Jacques Hittorff in 1838. They were used as the setting for the World's Fair of 1855, which included the Palais de l'Industrie, Paris's response to London's Crystal Palace. The Palais was later replaced by the Grand Palais and Petit Palais, which were created as a showpiece of the Third Republic for the Universal Exhibition of 1900. They sit on each side of an impressive vista that stretches from the Place Clémenceau across the elegant curve of the Pont Alexandre III to the Invalides.

The Théâtre du Rond-Point was the home of the Renaud-Barrault Company. There are plaques on the back door of the theater representing Napoleon's campaigns.

Metro Franklin D Roosevelt Ⓜ

Avenue Montaigne
Christian Dior and other haute couture *houses are based on this chic avenue* ❻

★ **Grand Palais**
Designed by Charles Girault, this grand 19th-century building is still used for major exhibitions ❷

The Lasserre restaurant is decorated in the style of a luxurious ocean liner from the 1930s.

LASSERRE

RUE JEAN GOUJON

RUE FRANÇOIS PREMIER

D ROOSEVELT

AVE G.¹ EISENHOWER

AVE FRANKLIN

PL DU CANADA

COURS L

PONT DES INVALIDES

STAR SIGHTS

★ Avenue des Champs-Elysées

★ Grand Palais

★ Petit Palais

★ Pont Alexandre III

Palais de la Découverte
Outside this museum of scientific discoveries is a pair of equestrian statues ❸

KEY

– – – Suggested route

0 meters	100
0 yards	100

★ Avenue des Champs-Elysées

This was the setting for the victory parades following the two world wars, and for the bicentennial parade in 1989 ⑧

LOCATOR MAP
See Central Paris Map pp14–15

CHAMPS-ELYSEES

CHAILLOT QUARTER

Seine

INVALIDES AND EIFFEL TOWER QUARTER

Metro Champs-Elysées-Clemenceau

The Jardins des Champs-Elysées, with their fountains, flower beds, paths and pleasure pavilions, became very popular toward the end of the 19th century. Fashionable Parisians, including Marcel Proust, often came here.

To the Place de la Concorde

★ Petit Palais

The art collections of the city of Paris are housed here. They contain a range of objects from antique sculptures to Impressionist paintings ④

To the Invalides

★ Pont Alexandre III

The bridge's four columns help to anchor the piers that absorb the immense forces generated by such a large single-span structure ①

Pont Alexandre III ❶

75008. **Map** 11 A1. Ⓜ *Champs-Elysées-Clemenceau.*

This is Paris's prettiest bridge with its exuberant Art Nouveau decoration of lamps, cherubs, nymphs and winged horses at each end. It was built between 1896 and 1900, in time for the Universal Exhibition, and it was named after Tsar Alexander III (father of Nicholas II) who laid the foundation stone in October 1896.

The style of the bridge reflects that of the Grand Palais, to which it leads on the Right Bank. The construction of the bridge is a marvel of 19th-century engineering, consisting of a 18-ft (6-m) high single-span steel arch across the Seine. The design was subject to strict controls that prevented the bridge from obscuring the view of the Champs-Elysées or the Invalides. So today you can still enjoy magnificent views from here.

Pont Alexandre III

Grand Palais ❷

Porte A, Ave Général Eisenhower 75008. **Map** 11 A1. **Tel** *01 44 97 78 04.* Ⓜ *Champs-Elysées-Clemenceau.* ◐ *for temporary exhibitions (usually 10am–8pm Thu–Mon,10am–10pm Wed, but phone to check).* ● *May 1, Dec 25.* 🖼 ∅ ♿ ⏰ *10am–1pm daily, Wed pm & Sat pm.* 🎧 🖥 ⓘ

Built at the same time as the Petit Palais and the Pont Alexandre III, the exterior of this huge palace combines an imposing Classical stone facade with a riot of Art

Nouveau ironwork. It has a splendid glass roof, and Récipon's colossal bronze statues of flying horses and chariots at its four corners. The building looks best at night, when the glass roof glows with the lights from inside and the statues are silhouetted against the sky. Sadly, this has not occurred since 1993, when the great hall closed for renovation. Temporary exhibitions are however still held in the Galeries Nationales du Grand Palais. The basement houses a major police station.

Palais de la Découverte

Palais de la Découverte ❸

Ave Franklin D Roosevelt 75008. **Map** 11 A1. Ⓖ *01 56 43 20 21.* Ⓜ *Franklin D Roosevelt.* ◐ *9:30am–6pm Tue–Sat; 10am–7pm Sun.* ● *Jan 1, May 1, Jul 14, Aug 15, Dec 25.* 🖼 🎧 *by permission.* ⓘ 🖥 www.palais-decouverte.fr

Opened in a wing of the Grand Palais for the World's Fair of 1937, this museum of scientific discoveries was an immediate success and has continued to be very popular ever since. The displays help to explain the basics of all the sciences.

Entrance to the Petit Palais

Petit Palais ❹

Ave Winston Churchill 75008. **Map** 11 B1. **Tel** *01 44 51 19 31.* Ⓜ *Champs-Elysées-Clemenceau.* ◐ *for renovation until 2006.* 🖼 📷 ⓘ *for exhibitions.*

Built for the Universal Exhibition in 1900, to stage a major display of French art, this jewel of a building now houses the Musée des Beaux-Arts de la Ville de Paris. Arranged around a pretty semicircular courtyard and garden, the palace is similar in style to the Grand Palais, and has Ionic columns, a grand porch and a dome which echoes that of the Invalides across the river.

The exhibits are divided into sections: the Dutuit Collection of medieval and Renaissance *objets d'art*, paintings and drawings; the Tuck Collection of 18th-century furniture and *objets d'art*; and the City of Paris collections of works by the French artists Jean Ingres, Eugène Delacroix and Gustave Courbet, as well as the landscape painters of the Barbizon School and the Impressionists.

Iron supports

Exhibition space

GRAND PALAIS

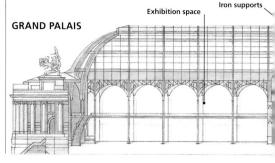

Palais de l'Elysée ❺

55 Rue du Faubourg-St-Honoré
75008. **Map** 5 B5. Ⓜ *St-Philippe-du-Roule.* **Not open** to the public.

Set amid splendid English-style gardens, the Elysée Palace was built in 1718 for the Comte d'Evreux and has been the official residence of the president of the republic since 1873. From 1805 to 1808 it was occupied by Napoleon's sister, Caroline, and her husband, Murat. Two charming rooms have been preserved from this period: the Salon Murat and the Salon d'Argent. General de Gaulle used to give press conferences in the Hall of Mirrors. Today, the president's modernized apartments are on the first floor across from the Rue de l'Elysée.

Elysée guard

Avenue Montaigne ❻

75008. **Map** 10 F1. Ⓜ *Franklin D Roosevelt.*

In the 19th century this avenue was famous for its dance halls and its Winter Garden, where Parisians went to hear Adolphe Sax play his newly invented saxophone. Today it is still one of Paris's most fashionable streets, bustling with restaurants, cafés, hotels and chic boutiques.

Glass cupola

Inside the Musée Jacquemart-André

Musée Jacquemart-André ❼

158 Blvd Haussmann 75008.
Map 5 A4. **Tel** *01 45 62 11 59.*
Ⓜ *Miromesnil, St-Philippe-du-Roule.*
◯ *10am–6pm daily.* 📷 🚫 🏠 🛍 🍴
www.musee-jacquemart-andre.com

This museum is known for its fine collection of Italian Renaissance and French 18th-century works of art, as well as its beautiful frescoes by Tiepolo. Highlights include works by Mantegna, Uccello's masterpiece *St George and the Dragon* (about 1435), paintings by Boucher and Fragonard and 18th-century tapestries and furniture.

Avenue des Champs-Elysées ❽

75008. **Map** 5 A5. Ⓜ *Franklin D Roosevelt, George V.*

Paris's most famous and popular thoroughfare had its beginnings in about 1667, when the landscape garden designer André Le Nôtre extended the royal view from the Tuileries by creating a tree-lined avenue which eventually became known as the Champs-Elysées (Elysian Fields). It has been the "triumphal way" (as the French call it) ever since the homecoming of Napoleon's body from St Helena in 1840. With the addition of cafés and restaurants in the second half of the 19th century, the Champs-Elysées became the place in which to be seen.

Place Charles de Gaulle (l'Etoile) ❾

75008. **Map** 4 D4. Ⓜ *Charles de Gaulle-Etoile.*

Known as the Place de l'Etoile until the death of Charles de Gaulle in 1969, the area is still referred to simply as l'Etoile, the star. The present *place* was laid out in accordance with Baron Haussmann's plans of 1854 *(see pp34–5)*. For drivers, it is the ultimate challenge.

Arc de Triomphe from the west

Arc de Triomphe ❿

See pp208–9.

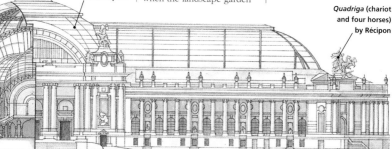

Quadriga (chariot and four horses) by Récipon

Arc de Triomphe ⑩

The east facade of the Arc de Triomphe

After his greatest victory, the Battle of Austerlitz in 1805, Napoleon promised his men, "You shall go home beneath triumphal arches." The first stone of what was to become the world's most famous triumphal arch was laid the following year. But disruptions to architect Jean Chalgrin's plans and the demise of Napoleonic power delayed the completion of this monumental building until 1836. Standing 164 ft (50 m) high, the Arc is now the customary starting point for victory celebrations and parades.

Thirty shields just below the Arc's roof each bear the name of a victorious Napoleonic battle fought in either Europe or Africa.

East facade

The frieze was executed by Rude, Brun, Jacquet, Laitié, Caillouette and Seurre the Elder. This east facade shows the departure of the French armies for new campaigns. The west side shows their return.

The Battle of Aboukir, a bas-relief by Seurre the Elder, depicts a scene of Napoleon's victory over the Turkish army in 1799.

Triumph of Napoleon
J P Cortot's high-relief celebrates the Treaty of Vienna peace agreement of 1810.

STAR FEATURES

★ Departure of the Volunteers in 1792

★ Tomb of the Unknown Soldier

★ **Tomb of the Unknown Soldier**
An unknown French soldier from World War I is buried here.

TIMELINE

1806 Napoleon commissions Chalgrin to build triumphal Arc	**1885** Victor Hugo's body lies in state under the Arc		**1944** Liberation of Paris. De Gaulle leads the crowd from the Arc
	1836 Louis-Philippe completes the Arc		

1800	1850	1900	1950

1840 Napoleon's cortège passes under the Arc

1815 Downfall of Napoleon. Work on Arc ceases

1919 Victory parade of Allied armies through the Arc

NAPOLEON'S NUPTIAL PARADE

Napoleon divorced Josephine in 1809 because she was unable to bear him children. A diplomatic marriage was arranged in 1810 with Marie-Louise, daughter of the Austrian emperor. Napoleon was determined to impress his bride by going through the Arc on their way to the wedding at the Louvre, but work had barely been started. So Chalgrin built a full-scale mock-up of the arch on the site for the couple to pass beneath.

VISITORS' CHECKLIST

Pl Charles de Gaulle. **Map** 4 D4.
Tel 01 55 37 73 77. **M** **RER** Charles
de Gaulle-Etoile. 22, 30, 31,
73, 92 to Pl C de Gaulle. **P** off Pl
C de Gaulle. **Museum** Apr–
Oct: 10am–11pm daily; Nov–Mar:
10am–10:30pm daily (last adm 30
mins earlier). Jan 1, May 1, Jul
14, Nov 11, Dec 25. www.monum.fr

The viewing platform affords one of the best views in Paris, overlooking the grand Champs-Elysées on one side. Beyond the other side is La Défense.

General Marceau's Funeral
Marceau defeated the Austrians in 1795, only to be killed the following year, still fighting them.

The Battle of Austerlitz by Gechter shows Napoleon's army breaking up the ice on the Satschan lake in Austria to drown thousands of enemy troops.

Officers of the Imperial Army are listed on the walls of the smaller arches.

Entrance to museum

★ **Departure of the Volunteers in 1792**
François Rude's work shows citizens leaving to defend the nation.

Place Charles de Gaulle
Twelve avenues radiate from the Arc at the center. Some bear the names of important French military leaders, such as Avenues Marceau and Foch.
(See pp34–5.)

OPERA QUARTER

The Opéra quarter bustles with bankers and stockbrokers, newspapermen and shoppers, theater-goers and sightseers. Much of its 19th-century grandeur survives in the Grands Boulevards of Baron Haussmann's urban design. These are still a favorite with thousands of Parisian and foreign promenaders, drawn by the profusion of shops and department stores, which range from the exclusively expensive to the popular.

Much more of the area's older character is found in the many *passages*, delightful narrow shopping arcades with steel and glass roofs. Fashion's bad boy, Jean-Paul Gaultier, has a shop in the toniest

Les Coulisses de l'Opéra (1889) by J Beraud

one, Galerie Vivienne. But more authentically old-style Parisian are the Passage des Panoramas and the Passage Jouffroy, the Passage Verdeau, with its old cameras and comics, and the tiny Passage des Princes. Two of Paris's finest food shops are in the area. Fauchon and Hédiard are noted for mouthwatering mustards, jams, pâtés and sauces. The area still has a reputation as a press center, although *Le Monde* has moved out, and a history of movies and theater – the Lumière brothers held the world's first public film show here in 1895, and the Opéra National de Paris Garnier staged grand theatrical events.

SIGHTS AT A GLANCE

Historic Buildings and Streets
Place de la Madeleine ❷
Les Grands Boulevards ❸
Palais de la Bourse ❾
Avenue de l'Opéra ⓬

Churches
La Madeleine ❶

Opera Houses
Opéra National de Paris Garnier ❹

Museums and Galleries
Musée de l'Opéra ❺
Grévin ❼
Cabinet des Médailles et des Antiques ❿
Bibliothèque Nationale ⓫

Shops
Drouot (Hôtel des Ventes) ❻
Les Passages ❽

GETTING THERE

This area is served by the metro and RER systems. Metro lines 3, 7 and 8 serve the station at the Opéra, line 14 stops at Madeleine and the RER Line A stops at Auber. Among the bus routes passing through the area, 42 and 52 travel along Boulevard Madeleine, and 21, 27 and 29 along Avenue de l'Opéra.

0 meters   400
0 yards   400

KEY

Street-by-Street map

Ⓜ Metro station

RER RER station

SEE ALSO

- *Street Finder*, map 5–6
- *Where to Stay* pp284–91
- *Restaurants* pp300–15

◁ Lamppost statues of the vestal virgins outside the Opéra National de Paris Garnier

Street-by-Street: Opéra Quarter

It has been said that if you sit for long enough at the Café de la Paix (across from the Opéra National de Paris Garnier) the whole world will pass by. During the day, the area is a mixture of commerce – France's top three banks are based here – and tourism. A profusion of shops, ranging from the chic, exclusive and expensive to the popular department stores, draw the crowds. In the evening, the theaters and movies attract a totally different crowd, and the cafés along the Boulevard des Capucines throb with life.

Statue by Gumery on the Opéra

Place de la Madeleine
On the north side of the square, the windows of the Fauchon shop are filled with food from around the world ❷

KEY

– – – Suggested route

0 meters   100

0 yards   100

RUE TRONCHET

RUE VIGNON

RUE GODOT DE MAUROY

RUE CAUMARTIN

PL DE LA MADELEINE

Metro Madeleine Ⓜ

BLVD DE LA MADELEINE

BLVD

STAR SIGHTS

★ La Madeleine

★ Boulevard des Capucines

★ Opéra National de Paris Garnier

★ **La Madeleine**
The final design of this church, which is dedicated to Mary Magdalene, differs from this original model, now in the Musée Carnavalet (see pp96–7) ❶

★ Opéra National de Paris Garnier
With a mixture of styles ranging from Classical to Baroque, this building from 1875 has come to symbolize the opulence of the Second Empire ❹

LOCATOR MAP
See Central Paris Map pp14–15

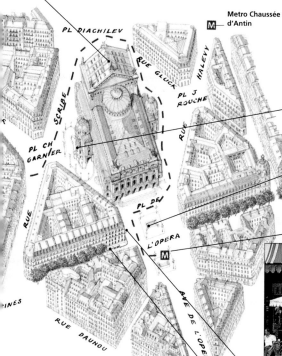

PL DIACHILEV

RUE GLUCK

RUE HALEVY

SCRIBE

PL J ROUCHE

PL CH GARNIER

RUE

Metro Chaussée d'Antin

PL DE

RUE

L'OPERA

Metro Opéra

RUE

AVE DE L'OPERA

RUE DAUNOU

INES

Musée de l'Opéra
Famous artists' work is often shown in temporary exhibition rooms ❺

The Place de l'Opéra
was designed by Baron Haussmann and is one of Paris's busiest intersections.

Metro Opéra

The Café de la Paix maintains its old-fashioned ways and still has its 19th-century decor, designed by Garnier. The café is now under renovation. *(See p319.)*

Harry's Bar was named after Harry MacElhone, a bartender who bought the bar in 1913. Past regulars have included F Scott Fitzgerald and Ernest Hemingway.

★ Boulevard des Capucines
At No. 14 a plaque tells of the world's first public screening of a movie, by the Lumière brothers in 1895; it took place in the Salon Indien, a room in the Grand Café ❸

Charles Marochetti's *Mary Magdalene Ascending to Heaven* (1837) behind the high altar of La Madeleine

La Madeleine ❶

Pl de la Madeleine 75008. **Map** 5 C5.
Tel *01 44 51 69 00*. **M** *Madeleine*.
⬜ *9am–7pm daily (9am Sat)*.
🚪 *frequent*. **Concerts**. 📷 🚹
See **Entertainment** pp346–7.

This church, which is dedicated to Mary Magdalene, is one of the best-known build-ings in Paris because of its prominent locat-ion and great size. It stands at one end of the curve of the Grands Boulevards and is the architectural counter-point of the Palais-Bourbon (home of the Assemblée Nationale, the French parliament) across the river. It was started in 1764 but not consecrated until 1845. There were proposals to convert it into a parliament, a stock exchange or a public library for the nation.

Napoleon decided to build a temple dedicated to military glory and he commissioned Pierre Vignon to design it, after the battle of Jena (Iéna) in 1806. A colonnade of 64-ft (20-m) high Corinthian columns encircles the building and supports a sculptured frieze. The bas-reliefs on the bronze doors are by Henri de Triqueti and show the Ten Commandments.

Fauchon tin

The inside is decorated with marble and gilt, and has some fine sculpture, notably François Rude's *Baptism of Christ*.

Place de la Madeleine ❷

75008. **Map** 5 C5.
M *Madeleine*. **Flower market** ⬜ *8am–7:30pm Tue–Sun*.

The place de la Madeleine was created at the same time as the Madeleine church. It is a food lover's paradise, with many shops special-izing in luxuries such as truffles, champagne, caviar and handmade chocolates. Fauchon, the millionaires' supermarket, is situated at No. 26 and stocks more than 20,000 items *(see pp333–5)*. The large house at No. 9 is where Marcel Proust spent his childhood. To the east of La Madeleine is a small flower market *(see p338)*.

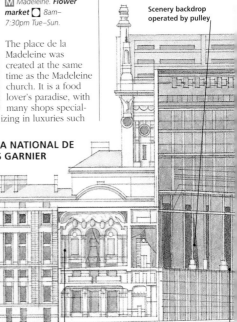

Scenery backdrop operated by pulley

OPERA NATIONAL DE PARIS GARNIER

Backstage area   **Stage**

Les Grands Boulevards ❸

75002 & 75009. **Map** 6 D5 –7C5.
M *Madeleine, Opéra, Richelieu-Drouot, Grands Boulevards.*

Eight broad boulevards – Madeleine, Capucines, Italiens, Montmartre, Poissonnière, Bonne Nouvelle, St-Denis and St-Martin – run from around La Madeleine to the Place de la République. They were constructed in the 17th century to turn obsolete city fortifications into fashionable promenades – *boulevard* came from the Middle Dutch *bulwerc*, which means bulwark or rampart. The boulevards became so famous in the 19th century that the name *boulevardier* was coined for one who cuts a figure on the boulevards.

Around the Madeleine church and the Opéra it is still possible to gain an impression of what the Grands Boulevards looked like in their heyday, lined with cafés and chic shops. Elsewhere, most of the cafés and restaurants have long since gone, and the old facades are now hidden by neon

advertising. However, the Grands Boulevards and the nearby department stores on the Boulevard Haussmann still attract large crowds.

Boulevard des Italiens

Opéra National de Paris Garnier ❹

Pl de l'Opéra 75009. **Map** 6 E4.
ℹ *01 40 01 22 63.* **M** *Opéra.*
⭕ *10am–4:30pm daily.* ● *public hols.* 🎫 🎟 *See* **Entertainment** *pp345–7.* **www**.operadeparis.fr

Sometimes compared to a giant wedding cake, this sumptuous building was designed by Charles Garnier for Napoleon III; construction started in 1862. Its unique appearance is due to a mixture of materials (including stone, marble and bronze) and styles, ranging from Classical to Baroque, with a multitude of columns, friezes and sculptures on the exterior. The building was not completed until 1875; work was interrupted by the Prussian War and 1871 uprising.

In 1858 Orsini had attempted to assassinate the emperor outside the old opera house. This prompted Garnier to include a pavilion on the east side of the new building, with a curved ramp leading up to it so that the sovereign could safely step out of his carriage into the suite of rooms adjoining the royal box.

The functions performed by each part of the building are reflected in the structure. Behind the flat-topped foyer, the cupola sits above the auditorium, while the triangular pediment that rises up behind the cupola marks the front of the stage. Underneath the building is a small lake, which provided inspiration for the phantom's hiding place in Paul Leroux's *Phantom of the Opera*.

Both the interior and the exterior have been recently refurbished. Don't miss the magnificent Grand Staircase, made of white marble with a balustrade of red and green marble, and the Grand Foyer, with its domed ceiling covered with mosaics. The five-tiered auditorium is a riot of red velvet, plaster cherubs and gold leaf, which contrast with the false ceiling painted by Marc Chagall in 1964.

Most operas are performed in the new Opéra Nationale de Paris Bastille (*see p98*), but the ballet remains here.

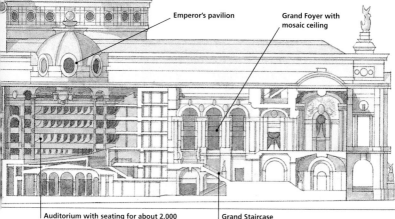

Statue by Millet

Copper-green roofed cupola

Emperor's pavilion

Grand Foyer with mosaic ceiling

Auditorium with seating for about 2,000

Grand Staircase

Sign outside the Grévin waxwork museum

Musée de l'Opéra ❺

Pl de l'Opéra 75009. **Map** 6 E5.
Tel 01 40 01 24 93. Ⓜ Opéra.
◻ 10am–6pm daily. ◉ Jan 1, May 1.
🖼 🎫 01 40 01 22 63. 🅱

The entrance to this small,
charming museum was ori-
ginally the emperor's private
entrance to the Opéra. The
museum relates the history of
opera through a large collection of musical scores, manuscripts, photographs and
artists' memorabilia, such as
the Russian dancer Waslaw
Nijinsky's ballet slippers and
tarot cards. Other exhibits
include models of stage sets
and busts of major composers.
The museum also houses a
superb library, containing
books and manuscripts on
theater, dance and music, as
well as more memorabilia.

Model of a set for *Les Huguenots* (1875) in the Musée de l'Opéra

Drouot (Hôtel des Ventes) ❻

9 Rue Drouot 75009. **Map** 6 F4. **Tel** 01
48 00 20 20. Ⓜ Richelieu Drouot.
◻ 11am–6pm Mon–Sat. 🚫 🎫 🅱
See **Shops and Markets** pp336–7.
www.gazette-drouot.com

This is the leading French
auction house (Hôtel des
Ventes) and it takes its name
from the Comte de Drouot
who was Napoleon's aide-de-
camp. There has been an
auction house on the site
since 1858, and in 1860
Napoleon III visited the hôtel
and purchased a couple of
earthenware pots. It has been
known as the Nouveau
Drouot ever since the 1970s,
when the existing building was
demolished and replaced with
today's rather dull structure.
    Although overshadowed
internationally by Christie's
and Sotheby's, auctions at the
Nouveau Drouot nevertheless
provide a lively spectacle and
involve a fascinating range of
rare objects. Its presence in
the area has attracted many
antique and stamp shops.

Grévin ❼

10 Blvd Montmartre 75009.
Map 6 F4. **Tel** 01 47 70 85 05.
Ⓜ Grands Boulevards
◻ 10am–6:30pm Mon–Fri, 10am–
7pm Sat & Sun. (last admission
1 hour before closing). 🖼 🅱
www.grevin.fr

This waxwork museum was
founded in 1882 and is now a
Paris landmark, on a par with
Madame Tussauds in London.

It contains tableaux of vivid
historical scenes (such as
Louis XIV at Versailles and
the arrest of Louis XVI),
distorting mirrors and the
Cabinet Fantastique, which
includes regular conjuring
shows given by a live
magician. Famous figures
from the worlds of art, sports
and politics are also on show,
with new celebrities replacing
faded and forgotten stars.

Galerie Vivienne

Les Passages ❽

75002. **Map** 6 F5. Ⓜ Bourse.

The early 19th-century
Parisian shopping arcades
(known as *passages* or
galeries) are located between
the Boulevard Montmartre
and the Rue St-Marc (the
extensive Passage des
Panoramas). Other arcades
are found between the Rue
du Quatre Septembre and the
Rue des Petits Champs.
    At the time of their
construction, the Passages
represented a new traffic-free
area for commerce, work-
shops and apartments. They
fell into disuse, but were
dramatically revamped in the
1970s and now house an
eclectic mixture of small
shops selling anything from
designer jewelry to rare
books. They have high,
vaulted roofs of iron and
glass. One of the most
charming is the Galerie
Vivienne (off the Rue
Vivienne or the Rue des Petits
Champs) with its mosaic floor
and excellent tearoom.

The colonnaded Neoclassical facade of the Palais de la Bourse

Palais de la Bourse ❾

(Bourse des Valeurs) 4 Pl de la Bourse 75002. **Map** 6 F5. **Tel** 01 49 27 55 54 (tours). Ⓜ Bourse. ☐ by appt only. 🗌 🗌 🗌 compulsory. **Films**.

This Neoclassical temple of commerce was commissioned by Napoleon and was home to the French Stock Exchange from 1826 to 1987. Today the French stock market, located at 29 rue Cambon (not open to visits), is fully computerized. The hectic floor trading of the Palais de la Bourse has been considerably reduced and is limited to the Matif (the futures market) and the Monep (the traded options market).

Sainte-Chapelle cameo in the Cabinet des Médailles

Cabinet des Médailles et des Antiques ❿

58 Rue de Richelieu 75002. **Map** 6 F5. **Tel** 01 47 03 83 30. Ⓜ Bourse. ☐ 1–6pm Mon–Sat (5pm Sat); noon–6pm Sun. ◼ public hols. 🗌 🗌 🗌 www.bnf.fr

This valuable collection of coins, medals, jewels and Classical objects is part of the Bibliothèque Nationale. Exhibits include the Berthouville Treasure (1st-century Gallo-Roman silverware) and the Grand Camée (cameo) from Sainte-Chapelle.

Bibliothèque Nationale ⓫

58 Rue de Richelieu 75002. **Map** 6 F5. **Tel** 01 53 79 81 26. Ⓜ Bourse. ☐ 9am–6pm Mon–Sat. www.bnf.fr

The Bibliothèque Nationale (National Library) originated with the manuscript collections of medieval kings, to which a copy of every French book printed since 1537, has, by law, been added. The collection, which includes two Gutenberg Bibles, is partially housed in this complex, created in the 17th century by Cardinal Mazarin. Despite the recent removal of the printed books, periodicals and CD-ROMs to the newly built Bibliothèque Nationale de France (see p246) at Tolbiac, the rue Richelieu buildings still contain a huge variety of items, including original manuscripts by Victor Hugo and Marcel Proust, among others. The library also has the richest collection of engravings and photographs in the world, and departments for maps and plans, theatrical arts, and musical scores. Sadly, the 19th-century reading room is not open to the public.

Bibliothèque Nationale

Avenue de l'Opéra ⓬

75001 & 75002. **Map** 6 E5. Ⓜ Opéra, Pyramides.

This broad avenue is a notable example of Baron Haussmann's dramatic modernization of Paris in the 1860s and 1870s (see pp34–5). Much of the medieval city (including a mound from which Joan of Arc began her crusade against the English) was cleared to make way for the wide thoroughfares of today. The Avenue de l'Opéra, running from the Louvre to the Opéra de Paris Garnier, was completed in 1876. The uniformity of the five-story buildings that line it contrast with those found in nearby streets, which date from the 17th and 18th centuries. Nearby, in the Place Gaillon, is the Café and Restaurant Drouant where the prestigious Goncourt Prize for literature is awarded. The avenue is dominated by travel and luxury shops. At No. 27 there is the National Center for the Visual Arts, which has a false entrance.

Avenue de l'Opéra

MONTMARTRE

Montmartre and art are inseparable. By the end of the 19th century the area was a mecca for artists, writers, poets and their disciples, who gathered to sample the bordellos, cabarets, revues and other exotica which made Montmartre's reputation as a place of depravity in the eyes of the city's more sober, upstanding citizens. Many of the artists and writers have long since left the area and the lively night life no longer has the same charm.

But the hill of Montmartre (the butte) still has its physical charms and the village atmosphere remains

Street theater
in Montmartre

remarkably intact. Mobs of eager tourists ascend the hill, most of them gathering in the most spacious parts, particularly where quick portrait artists and souvenir sellers thrive, as in the old village square, the Place du Tertre. Elsewhere there are tiny, exquisite squares, winding streets, small terraces, long stairways, plus the butte's famous vineyard where the few grapes are harvested in an atmosphere of revelry in early autumn. And there are spectacular views of the city from various points, most especially from the monumental Sacré-Coeur.

SIGHTS AT A GLANCE

Historic Buildings and Streets
Bateau-Lavoir ⑪
Moulin de la Galette ⑭
Avenue Junot ⑮

Churches
Sacré-Coeur pp224–5 ①
St-Pierre de Montmartre ②
Chapelle du Martyre ⑧
St-Jean l'Evangéliste de Montmartre ⑩

Museums and Galleries
Espace Dalí Montmartre ④
Musée de Montmartre ⑤
Musée d'Art Naïf Max Fourny ⑦

Squares
Place du Tertre ③
Place des Abbesses ⑨

Cemeteries
Cimetière de Montmartre ⑬

Theaters and Nightclubs
Au Lapin Agile ⑥
Moulin Rouge ⑫

GETTING THERE

This area is served by several metro stations, including Abbesses and Pigalle. The Montmartobus leaves Pigalle for the village area and bus route 80 passes Montmartre's cemetery. Route 85 passes along Rue de Clignancourt.

KEY

▨	Street-by-Street map
Ⓜ	Metro station

0 meters   400
0 yards   400

◁ **The narrow Rue St-Rustique winding up the hill to Sacré-Coeur**

Street-by-Street: Montmartre

The steep butte (hill) of Montmartre has been associated with artists for 200 years. Théodore Géricault and Camille Corot came here at the start of the 19th century, and in the 20th century Maurice Utrillo immortalized the streets in his works. Today street painters thrive on a lively tourist trade, as travelers flock to this picturesque district which in places still preserves the atmosphere of prewar Paris. The name of the area is ascribed to local martyrs tortured in Paris around AD 250, hence *mons martyrium.*

Streetside painter

Montmartre vineyard is the the last surviving vineyard in Paris. On the first Saturday in October the start of the grape harvest is celebrated.

Metro Lamarck Caulaincourt

RUE ST-

RUE DE L'ABREUVOIR

RUE DES SAULES

RUE &

RUE ST-R

RUE

NORVINS

RUE LEPIC

PL & B CLEMENT

RUE POULBOT

RUE DES MILA

RAVIGNAN

PL E GOUDEAU

RUE

RUE

RUE

RUE DES TROIS FRERES

★ **Au Lapin Agile**
Literary meetings have been held in this rustic nightclub ("The Agile Rabbit") since 1910 ❻

A La Mère Catherine was a favorite eating place of Russian Cossacks in 1814. They would bang on the table and shout *"Bistro!"* (Russian for "quick") – hence the bistro was named.

Espace Dalí Montmartre
The exhibition pays homage to the eclectic artist Dalí. Some of the works are on public display for the first time in France ❹

STAR SIGHTS

★ Sacré-Coeur
___
★ Place du Tertre
___
★ Musée de Montmartre
___
★ Au Lapin Agile

★ **Place du Tertre**
The square is the tourist center of Montmartre and is full of portraitists. No. 3 commemorates local children, as popularized in the artist Poulbot's drawings ❸

KEY

‒ ‒ ‒ Suggested route

0 meters   100

0 yards   100

★ **Musée de Montmartre**

The museum includes the work of artists who lived in the area: this Portrait of a Woman (1918) *is by the Italian painter and sculptor Amedeo Modigliani* ❺

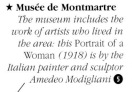

LOCATOR MAP
See Central Paris Map pp14–15

★ **Sacré-Coeur**

This Romano-Byzantine church, started in the 1870s and completed in 1914, has many treasures, such as this figure of Christ by Eugène Benet (1911) ❶

St-Pierre de Montmartre
This church became the Temple of Reason during the Revolution ❷

To metro Anvers

The funiculaire, or cable railroad, at the end of the Rue Foyatier takes you to the foot of the basilica of the Sacré-Coeur. Metro tickets are valid on it.

Square Willette lies below the forecourt of the Sacré-Coeur. It is laid out on the side of the hill in a series of descending terraces with lawns, shrubs, trees and flower beds.

Musée d'Art Naïf Max Fourny
The museum houses 580 examples of naive art. This oil painting, L'Opéra de Paris (1986), *is by L Milinkov* ❼

Montmartre streetside paintings

Sacré-Coeur ❶

See pp224–5.

St-Pierre de Montmartre ❷

2 Rue du Mont-Cenis 75018. **Map** 6 F1.
Tel *01 46 06 57 63.* Ⓜ *Abbesses.*
◯ *8am–7pm daily.* ✝ *frequent.* ◉
♿ **Concerts.**

Situated in the shadow of Sacré-Coeur, St-Pierre de Montmartre is one of the oldest churches in Paris. It is all that remains of the great Benedictine Abbey of Montmartre, founded in 1133 by Louis VI and his wife, Adelaide of Savoy, who, as its first abbess, is buried here.

Inside are four marble columns supposedly from a Roman temple which originally stood on the site. The vaulted choir dates from the 12th century, the nave was remodeled in the 15th century and the west front in the 18th. During the Revolution the abbess was guillotined, and the church fell into disuse. It was reconsecrated in 1908. Gothic-style stained-glass windows replace those destroyed by a stray bomb in World War II. The church also has a tiny cemetery, which is open to the public only on November 1.

Place du Tertre ❸

75018. **Map** 6 F1. Ⓜ *Abbesses.*

Tertre means "hillock", or mound, and this picturesque square is the highest point in Paris at some 430 ft (130 m). It was once the site of the abbey gallows but is associated with artists, who began exhibiting paintings here in the 19th century. It is lined with colorful restaurants – La Mère Catherine dates back to 1793. The house at No. 21 was formerly the home of the "Free Commune", founded in 1920 to perpetuate the Bohemian spirit of the area. It is now the site of the Old Montmartre information office.

The Spanish artist Salvador Dalí

Espace Dalí Montmartre ❹

Doors to St-Pierre church

11 Rue Poulbot 75018.
Map 6 F1. **Tel** *01 42 64 40 10.* Ⓜ *Abbesses.*
◯ *Sep–Jun: 10am–6:30pm daily; Jul & Aug: 10am–9pm daily.* 📷
📷 *groups by appt.*

A permanent exhibition of 330 works of the painter and sculptor Salvador Dalí is on display here at the heart of Montmartre. Inside, the vast, dark setting reflects the dramatic character of this 20th-century genius as moving lights grace first one, then another, of his Surrealist works. This in turn is counterpointed with the rhythm of Dalí's recorded voice. There is an art gallery as well as a library housed in this original museum.

Musée de Montmartre ❺

12 Rue Cortot 75018. **Map** 2 F5.
Tel *01 46 06 61 11.* Ⓜ *Lamarck-Caulaincourt.* ◯ *10am–6pm Tue–Sun.*
📷 📷 📷

During the 17th century this charming home belonged to the actor Roze de Rosimond (Claude de la Rose), a member of Molière's theater company who, like his mentor Molière, died during a performance of Molière's play *Le Malade Imaginaire*. From 1875 the big white house, undoubtedly the finest in Montmartre, provided living and studio space for numerous artists, including Maurice Utrillo and his mother, Suzanne Valadon, a former acrobat and model who became a talented painter, as well as Raoul Dufy and Pierre-Auguste Renoir.

The museum recounts the history of Montmartre from the days of the abbesses to the present, through artefacts, documents, drawings and photographs. It is particularly rich in memorabilia of Bohemian life, and even has a reconstruction of the Café de l'Abreuvoir, Utrillo's favorite watering hole.

Café de l'Abreuvoir reconstructed

The deceptively rustic exterior of Au Lapin Agile, one of the best-known nightspots in Paris

Au Lapin Agile ❻

22 Rue des Saules 75018.
Map 2 F5. **Tel** *01 46 06 85 87*.
Ⓜ *Lamarck-Caulaincourt.*
◯ *9pm–2am Tue–Sun.*
See **Entertainment** pp342–3.

The former Cabaret des
Assassins derived its current
name from a sign painted by
the humorist André Gill. His
picture of a rabbit escaping
from a pot *(Le Lapin à Gill)*
became known as the nimble
rabbit *(Lapin Agile).* The club
enjoyed popularity with
intellectuals and artists at the
turn of the 20th century. Here
in 1911 the novelist Roland
Dorgelès' hatred for modern
art, as practiced by Picasso
and the other painters at the
"Bateau-Lavoir" (No. 13 Place
Emile-Goudeau), led him to
play an illuminating practical
joke on one of the customers, Guillaume Apollinaire,
who was a poet, art critic
and champion of Cubism.
He tied a paintbrush to the
tail of the café-owner's
donkey, and the resulting
daub was shown at a Salon
des Indépendents exhibition
under the enlightening title
Sunset over the Adriatic.

In 1903 the premises were
bought by the cabaret
entrepreneur Aristide Bruand
(painted in a series of posters
by Toulouse-Lautrec). Today
it manages to retain much of
its original atmosphere.

Musée d'Art Naïf Max Fourny ❼

Halle St-Pierre, 2 Rue Ronsard 75018.
Map 7 A1. **Tel** *01 42 58 72 89.*
Ⓜ *Anvers.* ◯ *10am–6pm daily.*
🎨 ⍉ ♿ ▢ 🏢
www.hallesaintpierre.org

Naive art is usually characterized by simple themes,
bright, flat colors and a
disregard for perspective. Max
Fourny's publishing activities
brought him into contact with
many naive-style painters and
this unusual museum, located
in the Halle St-Pierre, contains
his collection of paintings and
sculptures from more than 30
countries, with exhibitions on

***The Wall* by F Tremblot (1944)**

selected themes. Many of the
paintings shown here are
rarely seen in museums.

The museum also organizes
temporary exhibitions of
outsider art, folk art and work
by self-taught artists, as well
as conducting children's
workshops. The building
itself is a 19th-century iron-
and-glass structure which was
once part of the St-Pierre
fabrics market.

Chapelle du Martyre ❽

9 Rue Yvonne-Le-Tac 75018.
Map 6 F1. Ⓜ *Pigalle.*
◯ *10am–noon, 3pm–5pm Fri–Wed.*

This 19th-century chapel
stands on the site of a
medieval convent's chapel,
which was said to mark the
place where the early Christian martyr and first bishop of
Paris, Saint Denis, was
beheaded by the Romans in
AD 250. It remained a major
pilgrimage site throughout the
Middle Ages. In the crypt of
the original chapel in 1534
Ignatius de Loyola, founder of
the Society of Jesus (the mighty
Jesuit order designed to save
the Catholic Church from the
onslaught of the Protestant
Reformation), took his Jesuit
vows with six companions.

Sacré-Coeur ❶

Southeast rose window (1960)

At the outbreak of the Franco Prussian War in 1870, two Catholic businessmen made a private religious vow. It was to build a church dedicated to the Sacred Heart of Christ, should France be spared the impending Prussian onslaught. The two men, Alexandre Legentil and Hubert Rohault de Fleury, lived to see Paris saved from invasion despite the war and a lengthy siege – and the start of what is the Sacré-Coeur basilica. The project was taken up by Archbishop Guibert of Paris. Work began in 1875 to Paul Abadie's designs. They were inspired by the Romano-Byzantine church of St-Front in Périgueux. The basilica was completed in 1914, but the German invasion forestalled its consecration until 1919, when France was victorious.

The Facade
The best view of the domed and turreted Sacré-Coeur is from the gardens below.

The belltower (1895) is 252 ft (83 m) high and contains one of the heaviest bells in the world. The bell itself weighs 18.5 tons and the clapper 1,900 lb (850 kg).

★ **Great Mosaic of Christ**
The colossal mosaic (1912–22) dominating the chancel vault was designed by Luc Olivier Merson and Marcel Magne.

Virgin Mary and Child *(1896) This Renaissance-style silver statue is one of two in the ambulatory by P Brunet.*

THE SIEGE OF PARIS

Prussia invaded France in 1870. During the four-month siege of Paris, instigated by the Prusso-German statesman Otto von Bismarck, Parisians became so hungry that they ate all the animals in the city.

★ **Crypt Vaults**
A chapel in the basilica's crypt contains Legentil's heart in a stone urn.

STAR FEATURES

★ Great Mosaic
of Christ

★ Bronze Doors

★ Ovoid Dome

★ Crypt Vaults

VISITORS' CHECKLIST

35 Rue adu Chevalier de la Barre
75018. **Map** 6 F1.
Tel *01 53 41 89 00.*
M *Abbesses (then take the
funiculaire to the steps of the
Sacré-Coeur), Anvers, Barbès-
Rochechouart, Château-Rouge,
Lamarck-Caulaincourt.*
30, 54, 80, 85.
P *Blvd de Clichy, Rue Custine.*
Basilica ◯ *6am–11pm daily.*
Dome and crypt ◯ *9am–7pm
daily (6pm winter).* **for crypt
and dome.** *11:15am,
6:30pm, 10pm Mon–Fri (& 3pm
Fri); 11:15am Sat; 11am, 6pm,
10pm Sun.* *restricted.*
www.sacre-coeur-
montmartre.com

★ Ovoid Dome
*This is the second-highest
point in Paris, after the
Eiffel Tower.*

Spiral staircase

The inner structure
supporting the
dome is made
from stone.

**The stained-
glass gallery**
affords a
view of
the whole
of the
interior.

Statue of Christ
*The basilica's most
important statue is
symbolically
placed above the
two bronze saints.*

Equestrian Statues
*The statue of Joan of Arc is
one of a pair by H Lefèbvre.
The other is of Saint Louis.*

★ Bronze Doors
*Relief sculptures on
the doors in the
portico entrance
illustrate scenes
from the life of
Christ, such as the
Last Supper.*

Main entrance

The famous silhouette of the Moulin Rouge nightclub

Place des Abbesses ❾

75018. **Map** 6 F1. **M** *Abbesses.*

This is one of Paris's most picturesque squares. It is sandwiched between the rather dubious attractions of the Place Pigalle with its strip clubs and the Place du Tertre which is mobbed with hundreds of tourists. Do not miss the Abbesses metro station with its unusual, green wrought-iron arches and amber lights. Designed by the architect Hector Guimard, it is one of the few original Art Nouveau stations.

St-Jean l'Evangéliste de Montmartre ❿

19 Rue des Abbesses 75018.
Map 6 F1. **Tel** *01 46 06 43 96.*
M *Abbesses.* ◯ *9am–noon, 3pm–7pm Mon–Sat; 2pm–7pm Sun.* ✝ *frequent.*
📷 🎞 *once a month.*

Designed by Anatole de Baudot and completed in 1904, this church was the first to be built from reinforced concrete. The flower motifs on the interior are typical of Art Nouveau, while its interlocking arches suggest Islamic architecture. The red-brick facing has earned it the nickname St-Jean-des-Briques.

Entrance to the Abbesses metro

Bateau-Lavoir ⓫

13 Pl Emile-Goudeau 75018.
Map 6 F1. **M** *Abbesses.*
🌑 *to public.*

This artistic and literary mecca was an old piano factory. Its name comes from its resemblance to the laundry boats that used to travel along the Seine River. Between 1890 and 1920 it was home to some of the most talented artists and poets of the day. They lived in squalid conditions with just one faucet for water and took turns to sleep in the beds. The artists Picasso, Van Dongen, Marie Laurencin, Juan Gris and Modigliani were just a few of the residents. It was here that Picasso painted *Les Demoiselles d'Avignon* in 1907, usually regarded as the painting that inspired Cubism. The shabby building burned down in 1970, but a concrete replica has been built – with studio space for up-and-coming artists.

Moulin Rouge ⓬

82 Blvd de Clichy 75018. **Map** 6 E1.
Tel *01 53 09 82 82.* **M** *Blanche.*
◯ *Dinner: 7pm; shows: 9pm and 11pm daily.* 🎫 *See Entertainment p343-4.* **www**.moulin-rouge.com

Built in 1885, the Moulin Rouge was turned into a dance hall as early as 1900. The cancan originated in Montparnasse, in the polka gardens of the Rue de la Grande-Chaumière, but it will always be associated with the Moulin Rouge where the wild and colorful dance shows were immortalized in the posters and drawings of Henri de Toulouse-Lautrec. The high-kicking routines of famous Dorriss dancers such as Yvette Guilbert and Jane Avril continue today in a glittering, Las Vegas-style revue that includes computerized lights and displays of magic.

Detail of St-Jean l'Evangéliste facade

Waslaw Nijinsky lies in Montmartre

Cimetière de Montmartre 🔞

20 Ave Rachel 75018. **Map** 2 D5. **Tel** *01 53 42 36 30.* Ⓜ *Place de Clichy, Blanche.* ◯ *8am–5:30pm daily (opens 8:30am Sat, 9am Sun; closes 6pm daily in summer).* ♿

This has been the resting place for many artistic luminaries since the beginning of the 19th century. The composers Hector Berlioz and Jacques Offenbach (who wrote the famous cancan tune), are buried here, alongside many other celebrities such as La Goulue (stage name of Louise Weber, the high-kicking danceuse who was the can-can's first star performer and Toulouse-Lautrec's model), the painter Edgar Degas, writer Alexandre Dumas *fils*, German poet Heinrich Heine, Russian dancer Waslaw Nijinsky, and film director François Truffaut. It's an evocative, atmospheric

place, conveying some of the heated energy and artistic creativity of Montmartre a century ago.

Nearby, close to Square Roland Dorgeles, there is another, smaller, often overlooked Montmartre cemetery – **Cimetière St-Vincent**. Here lie more of the great artistic names of the district, including the Swiss composer Arthur Honegger and the writer Marcel Aymé. Most notable of all at St-Vincent is the grave of the great French painter Maurice Utrillo, the quintessential Montmartre artist, many of whose works are now some of the most enduring images of the area.

Moulin de la Galette 🔞

T-junction at Rue Tholoze and Rue Lepic 75018. **Map** 2 E5. Ⓜ *Lamarck-Caulaincourt.*

More than 30 windmills once dotted the Montmartre skyline and were used for grinding wheat and pressing grapes. Now only two remain: the Moulin du Radet, which stands further along the Rue Lepic, and the rebuilt Moulin de la Galette, now converted into a restaurant. The latter was built in 1622 and is also known as the Blute-fin; one of its mill owners, Debray, was supposedly crucified on the windmill's sails during the 1814 Siege of Paris. He had been trying to repulse the invading Cossacks. At the turn of the 20th century the

mill became a famous dance hall and provided inspiration for many artists, notably Pierre-Auguste Renoir and Vincent Van Gogh.

The steep Rue Lepic is a busy shopping area with a good market *(see p339).* The Impressionist industrial and seascape painter Armand Guillaumin once lived on the first floor of No. 54, and Van Gogh inhabited its third floor.

Moulin de la Galette

Avenue Junot 🔞

75018. **Map** 2 E5. Ⓜ *Lamarck-Caulaincourt.*

Opened in 1910, this broad, peaceful street includes many painters' studios and family houses. No. 13 has mosaics designed by its former illustrator resident Francisque Poulbot, famous for his drawings of urchins. He is credited with having invented a bar billiards game. At No. 15 is Maison Tristan Tzara, named after its previous owner, the Romanian Dadaist poet. Its eccentric design by the Austrian architect Adolf Loos aimed to complement the poet's character. No. 23 bis is the Villa Léandre, a group of perfect Art Deco houses.

Just off the Avenue Junot up the steps of the Allée des Brouillards is an 18th-century architectural folly, the Château des Brouillards. In the 19th century it was the home of the French symbolist writer Gérard de Nerval, who committed suicide in 1855.

Sacré-Coeur, Montmartre, **by Maurice Utrillo**

FARTHER AFIELD

Many of the great châteaux outside Paris, originally built as country retreats for the aristocracy and post-revolutionary bourgeoisie, are now preserved as museums. Versailles is one of the finest, but if your tastes are Modernist, there's also Le Corbusier architecture to see. There are two theme parks – Disneyland Resort Paris and Parc de la Villette – to amuse adults and children alike, and excellent parks to relax in when the bustle of the city gets too much.

SIGHTS AT A GLANCE

Museums and Galleries
Musée Nissim de Camondo ❸
Musée Cernuschi ❹
Musée Gustave Moreau ❺
Musée Edith Piaf ⓬
Musée Marmottan-Claude
Monet ㉙
Musée des Années 30 ㉛
Palais de la Porte Dorée ⓰

Churches
St-Alexandre-Nevsky
Cathedral ❶
Basilique Saint-Denis ❼
Notre-Dame du Travail ㉓

Historic Buildings and Streets
Bercy ⓲
Bibliothèque Nationale de
France ⓳
13th Arrondissement ⓴
Cité Universitaire ㉒
Institut Pasteur ㉔
Versailles pp248–53 ㉖
Rue de la Fontaine ㉗
Fondation Le Corbusier ㉘
La Défense ㉜
Château de Malmaison ㉝

Markets
Marché aux Puces de St-Ouen ❻
Portes St-Denis et St-Martin ❽
Marché d'Aligre ⓯

Parks, Gardens and Canals
Parc Monceau ❷
Canal St-Martin ❾
Parc des Buttes-Chaumont ❿
Château et Bois de
Vincennes ⓱
Parc Montsouris ㉑
Parc André Citroën ㉕
Bois de Boulogne ㉚

Cemeteries
Cimetière du Père Lachaise
pp240–41 ⓭

Theme Parks
Parc de la Villette pp234–9 ⓫
Disneyland Resort Paris
pp242–5 ⓮

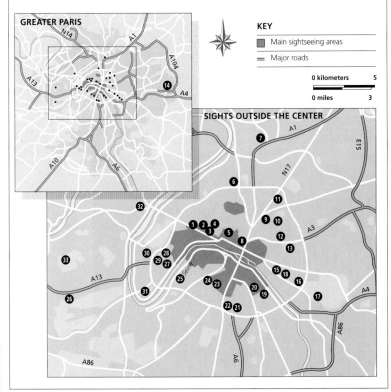

GREATER PARIS

KEY

◼ Main sightseeing areas

═ Major roads

0 kilometers   5

0 miles   3

SIGHTS OUTSIDE THE CENTER

◁ A landscaped island in the Bois de Boulogne

North of the City

St-Alexandre-Nevsky Cathedral

St-Alexandre-Nevsky Cathedral ❶

12 Rue Daru 75008. **Map** 4 F3.
Tel 01 42 27 37 34. M Courcelles.
◯ 3pm–5pm Tue, Fri, Sun.
✝ 6pm Sat, 10:30am Sun. ✐ 🖼

This imposing Russian
Orthodox cathedral with its
five golden-copper domes
signals the presence of a large
Russian community in Paris.
Designed by members of the
St Petersburg Fine Arts
Academy and financed jointly
by Tsar Alexander II and the
local Russian community, the
cathedral was completed in
1861. Inside, a wall of icons
divides the church in two. The
Greek-cross plan and the rich
interior mosaics and frescoes
are Neo-Byzantine in style,
while the exterior and gilt
domes are traditional Russian
Orthodox in design.

The Russian population in
the city increased dramatically
following the Bolshevik
Revolution of 1917, when
thousands of Russians fled to
Paris for safety. The Rue Daru,
in which the cathedral stands,
and the surrounding area form
"Little Russia", with its Russian
schools and many dance
academies, and delightful tea
shops and bookshops where
visitors can browse.

Parc Monceau ❷

Blvd de Courcelles 75017. **Map** 5 A3.
Tel 01 42 27 08 64. M Monceau.
◯ 7am–8pm daily (11pm summer).
See **Eight Guided Walks** pp258–9.

This green haven dates back
to 1778 when the Duc de
Chartres (later Duc d'Orléans)
commissioned the painter-
writer and amateur landscape
designer Louis Carmontelle to
create a magnificent garden.
Also a theater designer,
Carmontelle created a "garden
of dreams", an exotic landscape
full of architectural follies in
imitation of English and
German fashion of the time.
In 1783 the Scottish landscape
gardener Thomas Blaikie laid
out an area of the garden in
English style. The park was
the scene of the first recorded
parachute landing, made by
André-Jacques Garnerin on
October 22, 1797. Over the
years the park changed hands,
and in 1852 it was acquired
by the state and half the land
sold off for property development. The remaining 22 acres
(9 ha) were made into public
gardens. These were restored
and new buildings erected by
Adolphe Alphand, architect of
the Bois de Boulogne and the
Bois de Vincennes.

Today the park remains one
of the most chic in the capital
but has unfortunately lost
many of its early features. A
naumachia basin flanked by
Corinthian columns remains.
This is an ornamental version
of a Roman pool used for
simulating naval battles. There
are also a Renaissance arcade,
pyramids, a river and the
Pavillon de Chartres, a
charming rotunda designed
by Nicolas Ledoux which was
once used as a tollhouse. Just
south of here is a huge red
pagoda, which now houses a
gallery devoted to Asian art.

Musée Nissim de Camondo ❸

63 Rue de Monceau 75008.
Map 5 A3. 📷 01 53 89 06 40.
M Monceau, Villiers.
◯ 10am–5pm Wed–Sun
(last adm: 4:30pm). ● public hols.
🖼 🖼 (01 44 55 59 26). ◯

Comte Moïse de Camondo,
a leading Jewish financier,
commissioned this mansion in
1914 to be designed
in the style of the
Petit Trianon at
Versailles (see
pp248–9) to house
a collection of rare
18th-century
furniture, tapestries,
paintings and other
precious objects.
The museum has
been faithfully and
lovingly restored to
recreate an
aristocratic town
house of the Louis
XV and XVI eras.
In the museum
there are Savonnerie
carpets, Beauvais
tapestries, and the
Buffon service

Colonnade beside the *naumachia* basin in Parc Monceau

(Sèvres porcelain). The very latest gadgets, for the period, are now displayed in the restored kitchen and service quarters, equipped with the utmost efficiency, taste and forethought by their owner.

Musée Nissim de Camondo

Musée Cernuschi ❹

7 Ave Vélasquez 75008. **Map** 5 A3. **Tel** 01 45 63 50 75. Ⓜ Villiers, Monceau. ⬜ 10am–5:40pm Tue–Sun. ⬤ public hols. 🏛 ⌀ 🎫 ⏍ **www**.paris.fr/musees

This mansion near Parc Monceau contains an intriguing private collection of late East Asian art which was amassed by the Milanese-born politician and banker Enrico Cernuschi (1821–96). The original bequest of 5,000 lacquered, ceramic, bronze and ivory items has been augmented by donations and acquisitions over the years. The wide-ranging collection, now about ten thousand items, includes a 5th-century seated Bodhisattva (Buddhist divine being) from Yunkang; *La Tigresse* (a 12th-century BC bronze vase); and *Horses and Grooms*, an 8th-century T'ang painting on silk attributed to the era's greatest horse painter, court artist Han Kan.

Bodhisattva in the Musée Cernuschi

Musée Gustave Moreau ❺

14 Rue de la Rochefoucauld 75009. **Map** 6 E3. **Tel** 01 48 74 38 50. Ⓜ Trinité. ⬜ 10am–12:45pm, 2pm–5:15pm Wed–Mon. ⬤ Jan 1, May 1, Dec 25. 🏛 📷 ⏍ **www**.musee-moreau.fr

The symbolist painter Gustave Moreau (1825–98), known for his vivid, imaginative works depicting biblical and mythological fantasies, left to the French state a vast collection of more than 1,000 oils, watercolors and some 7,000 drawings in his town house. One of Moreau's best-known and most outstanding works, *Jupiter and Semele*, can be seen here. There is also a superb collection of his unfinished sketches.

Marché aux Puces du St-Ouen, a large antique market

Marché aux Puces de St-Ouen ❻

Rue des Rosiers, St-Ouen 75018. **Map** 2 F2. Ⓜ Porte-de-Clignan-court. ⬜ 9am–6pm Sat–Mon. See **Markets** p335. **www**.les-puces.com

This is the oldest and largest of the Paris flea markets, covering 15 acres (6 ha). In the 19th century, rag merchants and tramps would gather outside the city limits and offer their wares for sale. By the 1920s there was an actual market here, where masterpieces could sometimes be purchased cheaply from

Angel Traveler by Gustave Moreau, in the Musée Gustave Moreau

the then-unknowing sellers. Today it is divided into specialty markets. Known especially for its profusion of furniture and ornaments from the Second Empire (1852–70), few bargains are to be found these days, yet some 150,000 bargain-hunters, tourists and dealers still flock here to browse among more than 2,000 open or covered stalls.

Basilique Saint-Denis ❼

2 Rue de Strasbourg, 93200 St-Denis. **Tel** 01 48 09 83 54. Ⓜ St-Denis-Basilique. 🚄 St-Denis. ⬜ Apr–Sep: 10am–6:15pm Mon–Sat, noon–6:30pm Sun; Oct–Mar: 10am–5pm Mon–Sat, noon–5:15pm Sun (last adm: 15 minutes before closing). ⏏ 8:30am, 10am Sun. 🏛 📷 🎫 ⏍

Constructed between 1137 and 1281, the Basilica is on the site of the tomb of St Denis, the first bishop of Paris, who was beheaded in Montmartre in AD 250. The building was the original influence for Gothic art. From Merovingian times it was a burial place for rulers of France. During the Revolution many tombs were desecrated and scattered, but the best were stored and now represent a collection of funerary art. Memorials include those of Dagobert (died 638), Henri II (died 1559) and Catherine de'Medici (died 1589), and Louis XVI and Marie-Antoinette (died 1793).

Western arch of the Porte St-Denis, once the entrance to the city

Portes St-Denis et St-Martin **8**

Blvds St-Denis & St-Martin 75010.
Map 7 B5. **M** St-Martin, Strasbourg-St-Denis.

These gates offer access to the two ancient and important north–south thoroughfares whose names they bear. They once marked the entrance to the city. The Porte St-Denis is 76 ft (23 m) high and was built in 1672 by François Blondel. It is decorated with figures by Louis XIV's sculptor, François Girardon. They commemorate victories of the king's armies in Flanders and the Rhine that year. Porte St-Martin is 56 ft (17 m) tall and was built in 1674 by Pierre Bullet. It celebrates Besançon's capture and the defeat of the Triple Alliance of Spain, Holland and Germany.

Boats berthed at Port de l'Arsenal

East of the City

Canal St-Martin **9**

Map 8 E2. **M** Jaurès, J Bonsergent, Goncourt. See pp260–61.

The 3-mile (5-km) canal, opened in 1825, provides a shortcut for river traffic between loops of the Seine. It has long been loved by novelists, film directors and tourists alike. It is dotted with barges and pleasure boats that leave from the Port de l'Arsenal. At the north end of the canal is the Bassin de la Villette waterway and the elegant Neoclassical Rotonde de la Villette, spectacularly floodlit at night.

Parc des Buttes-Chaumont **10**

Rue Manin 75019 (main access from Rue Armand Carrel). **M** Botzaris, Buttes-Chaumont. ◻ Oct–Apr: 7am–9pm daily; May–Sep: 7am–10pm daily. **11** See pp268–9.

For many this is the most pleasant and unexpected park in Paris. The panoramic hilly site was converted in the 1860s by Baron Haussmann from a garbage dump and quarry with a gallows below. Haussmann worked with the

landscape architect/designer Adolphe Alphand, who organized a huge 1860s program to furnish the new sidewalk-lined avenues with benches and lampposts. Others involved in the creation of what was then a highly praised park were the engineer Darcel and the landscape gardener Barillet-Deschamps. They created a lake, made an island with real and artificial rocks, gave it a Roman-style temple and added a waterfall, streams, foot-bridges leading to the island, and beaches and firs. Today visitors will also find boating facilities and donkey rides.

Parc de la Villette **11**

See pp234–9.

Musée Edith Piaf **12**

5 Rue Crespin du Gast 75011.
Tel 01 43 55 52 72. **M** Ménilmontant. ◻ 1pm–6pm Mon–Thu (last adm: 5:30pm), by appointment only. ▣ public hols. ▨ ⊘ ▦ ▯

Edith Piaf – "the little sparrow" (1915–63)

Born Edith Gassion in the working-class east end of Paris in 1915, Edith Piaf took her stage name from her nickname meaning "the little sparrow". She started her career as a singer in local cafés and bars before becoming an international star in the late 1930s.

She never lived at the address of this museum, which was founded in 1967 by an association of fans, Les Amis d'Edith Piaf. Since then, they have collected a host of memorabilia and squeezed it into this small apartment. It contains many photographs and portraits, lithographs by Charles Kiffer, intimate letters, clothes and books – gifts from Piaf's parents-in-law or bequests from other singers. Records by the singer, who died in 1963 and lies in Père Lachaise cemetery (*see pp240–41*), are played in the museum on request. (Visits are by appointment only.)

Cimetière du Père Lachaise ⑬

See pp240–41.

Disneyland Paris ⑭

See pp242–5.

Marché d'Aligre ⑮

Place d'Aligre 75012. **Map** 14 F5.
Ⓜ *Ledru-Rollin.* ◯ *7:30am–12:30pm daily.*

On Sunday mornings this lively market offers one of the most colorful sights in Paris. French, Arab and African traders hawk fruit, vegetables, flowers and clothing on the streets, while the adjoining covered market, the Beauveau St-Antoine, offers meats, cheeses, pâtés and many intriguing international delicacies.

Aligre is where old and new Paris meet. Here the established community of this old artisan quarter coexists with a more

Exterior relief on Palais de la Porte Dorée

The imposing Château de Vincennes

recently established group of up-and-coming young people. They have been lured here to live and work by the recent transformation of the nearby Bastille area (*see p98*).

Palais de la Porte Dorée ⑯

293 Ave Daumesnil 75012. **Tel** 01 44 74 84 80. Ⓜ *Porte Dorée.* ◯ *10am–5:15pm Wed–Mon.* ✗ ♿ *restricted.* Ⓕ www.palais-portedoree.org

This museum and aquarium is housed in a beautiful Art Deco building which was designed especially for the 1931 Colonial Exhibition. The impressive facade has a huge frieze by A Janniot, depicting the contributions of France's overseas territories. The museum was, until early 2003, the Musée National des Arts d'Afrique et d'Océanie, with a remarkable display of primitive and tribal art covering West, Central and North Africa, as well as Oceania and Australasia. This entire collection is in storage, awaiting the opening of a museum of primitive art on Quai Branly in 2006.

The Palais de la Porte Dorée still has plenty to offer, with reconstructions of 1930s-style rooms, a remarkable African-Asian salon and a stunning Art Deco ballroom. In the basement there is a magnificent tropical aquarium filled with colorful fish, as well as terrariums containing tortoises and crocodiles.

Château et Bois de Vincennes ⑰

Ⓜ *Château de Vincennes.* ⒭ⒺⓇ *Vincennes.* **Château** Ave de Paris 94300 Vincennes. **Tel** 01 48 08 31 20. ◯ *10am–6pm (5pm winter) daily.* ● *public hols.* Ⓕ ✦ *compulsory in keep & chapel.* ✦
Bois de Vincennes ◯ *dawn to dusk daily.* **Zoological Park** 53 Ave de St-Maurice 75012. Ⓕ 01 44 75 20 10. ◯ *9am–5:30pm (5pm winter) daily (last adm 30 min before).* ♿ Ⓕ ✦ ✦ www.chateau-vincennes.fr

The Château de Vincennes, enclosed by a defensive wall and a moat, was once a royal residence. It was here that Henry V of England died painfully of dysentery in 1422. His body was boiled in the château's kitchen to prepare it for shipping back to England. Abandoned when Versailles was completed, the château was converted into an arsenal by Napoleon.

The 14th-century keep is a fine example of medieval military architecture and houses the château's museum. The Gothic chapel was finished around 1550, with beautiful stone rose windows and a magnificent single aisle. Two 17th-century pavilions house a museum of army insignia.

Once a royal hunting ground, the forest of Vincennes was given to the city of Paris by Napoleon III in 1860. Baron Haussman's landscape architect added ornamental lakes and cascades. Among its main attractions are the zoo and the largest carnival in France (from Palm Sunday to end of May).

Parc de la Villette ⑪

The old slaughterhouses and livestock market of Paris have been transformed into this huge urban park, designed by Bernard Tschumi. Its vast and ambitious facilities stretch across 88 acres (35 ha) of a previously run-down part of the city. The great plan is to revive the tradition of parks for meetings and activities and to stimulate interest in the arts and sciences. Work began in 1984 and the park has grown to include a huge science museum, a pop concert hall, an exhibition pavilion, a spherical theater and a music center. Linking them all is the park itself, with its follies, walkways, gardens and playgrounds.

The Follies
These red cubes punctuate the park and provide a variety of services, such as a daycare center, café and a children's workshop.

Children's Playground
A dragon slide, sand pits and colorful play equipment in a maze-like setting make the playground a paradise for young children.

★ **Grande Halle**
The old cattle hall has been transformed into a flexible exhibition space with mobile floors and auditorium.

Entrance

STAR BUILDINGS

★ Cité des Sciences et de l'Industrie

★ Grande Halle

★ Cité de la Musique

★ Zénith Theater

★ **Cité de la Musique**
This quirky but elegant all-white complex holds the music conservatory, a concert hall, library, studios and a museum.

Maison de la Villette is a history center with documents and displays on the history of the site and area.

Entrance

★ **Cité des Sciences et de l'Industrie**
This huge science museum boasts the latest in futurist equipment and has dazzling hands-on displays (see pp236–9).

La Géode
The theater's gigantic 180° movie screen combines visual and sound effects to create fantastic experiences, such as the sense of traveling in space.

★ **Zénith Theater**
This huge polyester tent was built as a venue for pop concerts and has capacity to seat more than 6,000 spectators.

L'Argonaute
The exhibit consists of a 1950s submarine and a nearby navigation museum.

Musicians from Guadeloupe performing outside the museum

LE MUSEE DE LA MUSIQUE

This museum brings together a collection of over 4,500 instruments, objects, tools and works of art covering the history of music since the Renaissance. The permanent collection of over 900 items is displayed chronologically and can be traced using infrared audio headphones.

La Villette: Cité des Sciences et de l'Industrie

This immense science and technology museum occupies the largest of the old Villette slaughterhouses. The building soars 133 ft (40 m) high and stretches over 7 acres (3 ha). Architect Adrien Fainsilber has created an imaginative interplay between the building and three natural themes: water surrounds the structure; vegetation penetrates through the greenhouse; and light flows in through the cupolas. The museum is on five levels. Its heart is the Explora exhibits on levels 1 and 2, where lively and entertaining displays of equipment and activities promote an

A young visitor at La Villette interest in science and technology. Visitors can actively engage in computerized games on space, computers and sound. On other levels there are theaters, a Children's Science City, a library, restaurants and shops.

Cupolas
The two glazed domes, 56 ft (17 m) in diameter, filter the flow of natural light into the main hall.

★ Planetarium
In this 260-seat auditorium, special effects projectors and the latest sound systems create exciting images of the stars and planets.

Main Hall
A soaring network of shafts, bridges escalators and balconies creates a cathedral-like atmosphere here.

STAR EXHIBITS

★ Planetarium

★ Ariane Rocket

★ La Géode

★ Ariane Rocket
The fascinating displays of rockets explain how astronauts are launched into outer space, and include an example of the European rocket Ariane.

The moat was designed by Fainsilber at 43 ft (13 m) below the level of the park, so that natural light could penetrate into the lower levels of the building. The sense of the building's enormous scale is enhanced by reflections in the water.

Mirage Aircraft
A full-scale model of the French-built jet fighter plane is just one of the exhibits illustrating dramatic advances in technology.

Children's Science City
In this lively, extensive area children can experiment and play with interactive machines that show them how scientific principles work.

The greenhouse
is a square structure, 105 ft (32 m) high and wide, linking the park to the building.

To the Géode

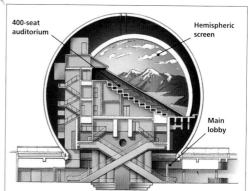

400-seat auditorium

Hemispheric screen

Main lobby

LA GÉODE
This giant entertainment sphere, 116 ft (36 m) in diameter, has a "skin" composed of 6,500 stainless-steel triangles, which reflect the surroundings and the sky. Inside, a huge hemispherical movie screen, 11,000 sq ft (1,000 sq m), shows films on nature, travel and space.

Walkways
The walkways cross the encircling moat to link the various floors of the museum to the Géode and the park.

Cité des Sciences et de l'Industrie: Explora

The Explora exhibits on levels 1 and 2 of the Cité are a fascinating guide to the worlds of science and technology. Our understanding of computers, space, ocean, earth, sound and film is heightened by bold, imaginative presentations of multimedia displays, interactive computer exhibits and informative models. Children and adults can learn while playing with light, space and sound. Young children can walk through the sound sponge, experience optical illusions, see how astronauts live in outer space, whisper to one another through the parabolic sound screen, and listen to talking walls. Older children can learn more about how man lives and works under water, how special effects are made in movies, listen to the story of a star, and see the birth of a mountain.

Sound Dishes
These parabolic sound screens transmit a conversation between people standing 54ft (17m) apart.

★ Star Display
Ten thousand stars are projected onto the dome of the Planetarium by the astronomic simulator. The visual and sound effects simulate breathtaking voyages through space.

Level 2

The Nautile
One of the country's most recent scientific exploration submarines, the Nautile is one of the most sophisticated machines in the world and a technological marvel.

Level 1

The self-service media library contains books, magazines and CD-ROMs on all fields of science and technology.

KEY TO FLOORPLAN

☐	Permanent exhibitions
▨	Temporary exhibitions
☐	Planetarium
☐	Future exhibition space
▨	Non-exhibition space

STAR EXHIBITS

★ Star Display

★ Man and His Genes

Light Games
This exhibition features interactive experiments with light, creating surprising optical illusions.

VISITORS' CHECKLIST

30 Ave Corentin-Cariou 75019.
01 40 05 80 00. Porte de la Villette. 75, 139, 150, 152, PC to Pte de la Villette.
10am– 6pm Tue–Sat (7pm Sun).
Concerts, films, videos. Conference center. Library.
www.cite-sciences.fr

Images Exhibition
Make the Mona Lisa talk by lending her your own voice; include yourself in a TV commercial and explore the world of images with a virtual camera.

The Flight Simulator
re-creates a hands-on experience of an aircraft flight with feed-in and feedback computer data.

★ Man and His Genes
Chromosomes are magnified in a bubble as part of a study of genes, the evolution of the species, reproduction and the bioethics debate.

Cimetière du Père Lachaise ⓭

Paris's most prestigious cemetery is set on a wooded hill overlooking the city. The land was once owned by Père de la Chaise, Louis XIV's confessor, but it was bought by order of Napoleon in 1803 to create a new cemetery. The cemetery became so popular with the Paris bourgeoisie that it was expanded six times during the century. Here were buried celebrities such as the writer Honoré de Balzac and the composer Frédéric Chopin, and more recently, the singer Jim Morrison and the actor Yves Montand. Famous graves and striking funerary sculpture make this a pleasant place for a leisurely, nostalgic stroll.

The Columbarium was built at the end of the 19th century. The American dancer Isadora Duncan is one of the many celebrities whose ashes are housed here.

Marcel Proust
Proust brilliantly chronicled the Belle Epoque in his novel Remembrance of Things Past.

★ Simone Signoret and Yves Montand
France's most famous post-war moviecouple were renowned for their left-wing views and long turbulent relationship.

Allan Kardec was the founder of a 19th-century spiritual cult, which still has a strong following. His tomb is forever covered in pilgrims' flowers.

Sarah Bernhardt
The great French tragedienne, who died in 1923 aged 78, was famous for her portrayal of Racine heroines.

Monument aux Morts
by Paul Albert Bartholmé is one of the best monumental sculptures in the cemetery. It dominates the central avenue.

Entrance

STAR FEATURES

★ Oscar Wilde

★ Jim Morrison

★ Edith Piaf

★ Simone Signoret and Yves Montand

Frédéric Chopin, the great Polish composer, belonged to the French Romantic generation.

Théodore Géricault
The French Romantic painter's masterpiece, The Raft of Medusa *(see p124), is depicted on his tomb.*

★ Oscar Wilde
The Irish dramatist, aesthete and great wit was cast away from virtuous Britain to die of drink and dissipation in Paris in 1900. Jacob Epstein sculpted the monument.

The remains of Molière, the great 17th-century actor and dramatist, were transferred here in 1817 to add historic glamour to the new cemetery.

VISITORS' CHECKLIST

16 Rue du Repos. **Tel** *01 55 25 82 10.* Ⓜ️ *Père Lachaise, Alexandre Dumas.* 🚌 *62, 69, 26 to Pl Gambetta.* 🅿️ *Pl Gambetta.* ⏺ *8am–5.30pm daily (8.30am Sat, 9am Sun).* 📷 ✔️ ℹ️

Mur des Fédérés is the wall against which the last Communard rebels were shot by government forces in 1871. It is now a place of pilgrimage for left-wing sympathizers.

★ Edith Piaf
Known as "the little sparrow" because of her size, Piaf was the 20th century's greatest French popular singer. In her tragic voice she sang of the sorrows and love woes of the Paris working class.

Victor Noir
The life-size statue of this 19th-century journalist shot by Pierre Bonaparte, a cousin of Napoleon III, is said to have fertility powers.

George Rodenbach, the 19th-century poet, is depicted as rising out of his tomb with a rose in the hand of his outstretched arm.

Elizabeth Demidoff, a Russian princess who died in 1818, is honored by a three-story Classical temple by Quaglia.

★ Jim Morrison
The death of The Doors' lead singer in Paris in 1971 is still a mystery.

François Raspail
The tomb of this much-imprisoned partisan of the 1830 and 1840 revolutions is in the form of a prison.

Disneyland Resort Paris ⑭

Disneyland Resort Paris is built on a massive scale – the 5,000-acre (2,000-ha) site encompasses two theme parks; seven hotels (several with swimming pools), a shopping, dining and entertainment village; a seasonal ice-skating rink; lakes; two convention centers; and a golf course. One stop down the line from their very own train station lies Val d'Europe, a huge new shopping mall with more than 180 shopping outlets, including 60 discount stores, and a Sea World center.

Unbeatable for complete escapism, combined with vibrant excitement and sheer energy, the parks offer extreme rides and gentle experiences, all accompanied by phenomenal visual effects.

The Queen of Hearts' Castle, in Alice's Curious Labyrinth

THE PARKS

Disneyland Resort Paris consists of Disneyland Park and Walt Disney Studios Park. Disneyland Park is based on the Magic Kingdom of California and has 42 rides or attractions. The newest park is the Walt Disney Studios Park, where interactive exhibits and live shows bring alive the artistic and technical wizardry that has made the movie and television industry so enthralling. Find out more at: www.disneylandparis.com

GETTING THERE

By Car
Disneyland Resort Paris lies 20 miles (32 km) to the east of Paris, and has its own link (exit 14) from the A4 westbound from Paris and eastbound A4 from Strasbourg. Simply follow the signs to Marne la Vallée (Val d'Europe) until you see the Disneyland signs. (The Davy Crockett Ranch is exit 13.)

By Air
Both Orly and Charles de Gaulle airports have a shuttle bus which runs every 30 minutes (45 in the low season). No reservation is required. The fare is about 12€ per person.

By Train
The Paris RER runs directly to the parks, as does the TGV which has connections throughout Europe.

PARKING

There is space for over 12,000 vehicles, and an efficient moving sidewalk conveys you to the exit. Parking costs 8€ per day for cars, and 10€ for campers and buses. Parking at Disneyland Resort Paris hotels is free to guests, and the Disneyland and New York hotels offer valet parking.

OPENING HOURS

Generally, the parks open at 9am in high season and 10am otherwise. Disneyland Park closes at 11pm in high season and 8pm in low season. The Walt Disney Studios Park closes at 8pm in high season and 6pm in low season. Special events, such as Halloween, can mean extended hours.

WHEN TO VISIT

The busiest times are Christmas and New Year, mid-February to early April and July to early September, and mid-October. Busiest days are Saturday–Monday; Tuesday and Wednesday are quietest.

LENGTH OF VISIT

To experience everything Disneyland Resort Paris has to offer you really need to spend three or four days at the resort. Although it is possible to tour the parks in one day each (just), to enjoy them at less than breakneck pace you need at least two days for Disneyland Park alone, and if you want to include Buffalo

---

EATING AND DRINKING

There's no need to leave the park to eat during the day. **Au Chalet de la Marionnette** (Fantasyland) is excellent for kids (and almost deserted at 3pm) as is the **Cowboy Cook-out Barbecue** (Frontierland), which tends to be rather more crowded. **Colonel Hathi's Pizza Outpost** (Adventureland) is worth a visit just to see the authentic colonial gear, while **Café Hyperion – Videopolis** (Discoveryland) offers good food plus excellent entertainment, but service is very slow.

You pay a premium for full-service restaurants but the experience of eating in **Blue Lagoon Restaurant** (Adventureland) is one you will remember. You dine on the "shore" of a Caribbean Pirate hideaway while the boats from Pirates of the Caribbean glide past. **Walt's**, on Main Street, USA, is also a good but pricey restaurant offering American fare. If you're lucky, they'll seat you so that you can watch the afternoon Main Street parade in comfort from an upstairs window.

In Disney Village **Annette's Diner** is staffed by roller-skating waitresses against a background of '50s records. **Planet Hollywood** is another good option, and the **Rainforest Cafe** provides an interestingly animated meal. The **Steakhouse** is excellent, although a little pricey, while a giant **McDonald's** serves the usual fare. The hotel restaurants are more expensive the nearer they are to the park.

Bill's Wild West show or visit some of the nightclubs in Disney Village, then you'll be pushed to manage it all in under four days. Locals turn up on a daily basis from Paris, which is only 35 minutes away on the RER, but most guests from further afield will stay in hotels. Disney offer several packages for those who wish to savor the delights of staying on site. These include passes for the parks, and accommodation with continental breakfast included. All inclusive packages are available.

TICKETS

If you buy a package, tickets will be included in the price. Tickets for both parks can be bought from any Disney Store before you leave home, or at the park upon arrival – though this means wasting good riding time waiting at a ticket booth. 1,2 or 3 day tickets are available, and prices vary according to season. The Hopper ticket allows entry to both parks on the same day.

GETTING AROUND

Disney provide an efficient transportation system between parks and the hotels (excluding Davy Crockett Ranch) with buses on the half hour. In summer, a fleet of little open-top buses drive slowly around Lake Disney, ferrying guests between the three lakeside hotels and Disney Village. If you're staying at any of the on-site hotels it's only a short walk (20 minutes at most) to the park gates.

Sleeping Beauty Castle, the centerpiece of the park

WHICH HOTEL?

There are six hotels on site, and one in woodland 3 miles (2 km) away. The best hotels are the closest to the parks.

Hotel Santa Fe: basic, small and reasonably inexpensive. The only hotel offering parking immediately outside your room.
Hotel Cheyenne: a Wild West theme hotel, about 17 minutes walk from the park. Small rooms (with bunks for the kids), a Native American village play area. Inexpensive and a great experience. Kids love this hotel.
Sequoia Lodge: a lakeside "hunter's lodge", moderately priced with more than 1,000 rooms. Ask for a room in the main building. Rooms at the front have great views.
Newport Bay Club: a huge, nautically themed hotel on the lakeside. Moderately priced, this massive hotel has a huge convention center, magnificent swimming pool and three floors offering extra services for a supplement.
Hotel New York: expensive and business-oriented; not a lot for the kids. This hotel also has a large convention center, and there's an ice-skating rink from October to March.
Disneyland Hotel: the jewel in the crown. Expensive, but right at the entrance to the Disneyland Park. Full of delightful touches, such as grandfather clocks and ever-present Disney characters. The Castle Club is a 50-room hotel-within-a-hotel. If you can afford it, a week of decadent fawning and unrestrained hedonism can be yours!
Davy Crockett Ranch: log cabins sleeping 4–6 are grouped around a woodland trail, as well as traditional camping facilities. Some excellent facilities: the pool ranks as one of the best in Disneyland Resort Paris.

MONEY

Credit cards are accepted everywhere within the resort. ATMs and commission-free foreign exchange are available immediately inside the park entrances and at reception in all the hotels.

DISABLED TRAVELERS

City hall (immediately within Disneyland Park) has a brochure outlining the facilities for the disabled, and a Disabled Guest Guide can be pre-ordered (free) from the Disneyland Resort Paris website. The complex is designed very much with the disabled in mind, but note that cast members are not allowed to assist with lifting people or moving wheelchairs.

STAYING IN A DISNEY HOTEL

The on-site hotels offer rooms at a wide range of prices, with the rule of thumb being that those closest to the parks are the most expensive. Advantages include virtually

The runaway mine-train track of Big Thunder Mountain

no traveling to reach the parks, and "early bird" entry to the parks on selected dates (usually at peak times).

If you stay at a Disney Hotel you will be given a hotel ID card. This unprepossessing little item is very important. As well as being used to charge anything you buy back to your hotel room (and have it delivered there), it also allows you entry to the Disneyland hotel grounds early in the morning while they're still shut to day trippers. (The grounds also act as an entrance to the park.)

For children (of any age), one of the most exciting bonuses of staying in an on-site hotel is the chance to dine with Disney characters.

Exploring Disneyland Resort Paris

The resort is comprised of two large entertainment areas, the Disneyland Park and the Walt Disney Studios Park. The former celebrates lands from a past strongly colored by Hollywood folklore, and the latter highlights the ingenuity of the production processes involved in movies, animation and television. The resort offers a plethora of attractions and themed parades chosen from the "Wonderful World Of Disney".

DISNEYLAND PARK

MAIN STREET, USA

Main Street represents a fantasy small-town America, right down to the traffic, which includes horse-drawn rail cars, a paddy wagon and other vintage transportation in a system that runs between Town Square and Central Plaza. The Victorian facades offer a wealth of detail, and hide several interesting stores. The Emporium is the place for gifts. Further along, you can snack at Casey's Corner or succumb to the aromas from Cookie Kitchen or the Cable Car Bake Shop. On each side of the shops are the Discovery and Liberty Arcades, offering a covered route to the Central Plaza and hosting displays and cute small stalls.

At night, thousands of lights set Main Street's paving a-glow. Disney's Fantillusion, a fantasy of music, live action and illuminated floats, begins at Town Square. From Main Street you can ride a 19th century "steam" engine. Do note that boarding elsewhere than Main Street is not always possible before noon.

FRONTIERLAND

This homage to America's Wild West hosts some of the park's most popular attractions. Big Thunder Mountain, a rollercoaster ride, is circled by two paddle steamers that take a musical cruise around America's finest natural monuments. Phantom Manor is a ghost ride, and at the outdoor Chaparral Theater you can see some amazing stage performances.

Pocahontas Indian Village and Critter Corral are both popular with younger children.

ADVENTURELAND

Enjoy the wild rides and Audio-Animatronics™ of Adventureland. Indiana Jones™ and the Temple of Peril hurtles you through a derelict mine. The ride has torches, steep drops and tight 360° loops.

Pirates of the Caribbean is a great boat ride through underground prisons and past 16th-century fighting galleons. *La Cabane des Robinson*, based on Jonathan Wyss's *Swiss Family Robinson*, starts with a shaky climb up a 88-ft (27-m) Banyan Tree. From here you explore the rest of the island, including the caves of Ben Gunn from *Treasure Island* and the awe-inspiring suspension bridge near Spyglass Hill. The children's playground, Pirates' Beach, is also well worth a visit.

FANTASYLAND

The buildings here are modeled on those in animated movies. Many attractions are for younger children, such as Snow White and the Seven Dwarfs, and Pinocchio's Fantastic Journey. The very young will love Dumbo the Flying Elephant. Peter Pan's Flight is a triumph of imagination and technology, flying you high over the streets of London. A popular diversion is Alice's Curious Labyrinth.

Hourly, there's a musical parade of clockwork figures at "It's a Small World". Aboard a boat, you meander through lands of animated models to the strains of the eponymous song. Le Pays des Contes des Fées (Storybook Land) is another boat ride. Next, hop aboard Casey Jr for a train ride circling the boats.

DISCOVERYLAND

Science fiction and the future are the themes here. The multi-loop ride Space Mountain draws crowds from the outset, but at the end of the day you can often walk straight on. Les Mystères du Nautilus takes you right into the submarine from *20,000 Leagues Under the Sea*. Autopia, where you can drive a real, gas-engined car, is a magnet for youngsters. Orbitron features spaceships and soon gets crowded, but is worth experiencing. Star Tours makes you a passenger in a star shuttle on a breathtaking journey of narrow escapes.

The best shows are in Videopolis, a cavernous café showing cartoons between shows. Honey, I Shrunk the Audience is a masterpiece of total sensory stimulation.

WALT DISNEY STUDIOS PARK

FRONT LOT

Inside the giant studio gates, the central feature of Front Lot is a fountain in the shape of Mickey Mouse as he appears in *The Sorceror's Apprentice*. It's also hard to miss 'Earful Tower', a massive studio icon based on the water tower at the Disney Studios in California. Disney Studio 1 houses a film set boulevard, complete with facades that front a street and represent stylized locations such as the 1930's-style Club Swankedero, the Liki Tiki tropical bar and the ultracool rat-packesque Hep Cat Club.

ANIMATION COURTYARD

Celebrating the key art that facilitated Disney's great success, the courtyard is made up of three areas. A huge *Sorcerer's Apprentice* hat marks the entrance to the Art of Disney Animation, an interactive attraction tracing the entire history of moving imagery. Animagique is a show that brings together some of the greatest moments from the Disney corpus. In Flying Carpets over Agrabah, the genie from *Aladdin* invites spectators to enjoy an astonishing magic carpet ride all around a magical set whose amazing centerpiece is a giant genie's bottle. Participants even get to be the stars of a movie directed by the magical man himself.

PRODUCTION COURTYARD

Here the emphasis is on the production process. At the Walt Disney Television Studios you can see behind the scenes of television production, while Ciné-Magique is a must for film buffs, as it covers the history of both American and European cinema. The Studio Tram Tour gives you a tour of the studio premises, including a visit to Catastrophe Canyon, where you can enjoy the fun of a spectacular film shoot.

BACKLOT

This area concentrates its focus on the topics of special effects, film music recording and crazy daredevil stunts. Armageddon Special Effects presents a tour of movie trickery, while Rock 'n' Roller Coaster is a high-speed attraction (in fact, it is the fastest ride in any Disney theme park) that combines a once-in-a-lifetime ride set against a pulsating musical soundtrack provided by rock legends Aerosmith.

RIDES AND ATTRACTIONS

This chart is designed to help you make the best use of your time at Disneyland Paris, decide on which rides and tours are best for you, and choose when to visit them.

	Queues	Height / Age Restriction	Best Time to Ride or Visit	Fastpass	Scary Rating	May Cause Motion Sickness	Rating Overall
Phantom Manor	◗		Any		❷		★
Rivers of the Far West	○		Any		❶		▼
Big Thunder Mountain	●	48in	FT	✔	❷		★
Pocohantas Indian Village	○		Any		❶		▼
Indiana Jones & the Temple of Peril	●	55in	LT	✔	❸	✔	★
Adventure Isle	○		Any		❶		▼
La Cabane des Robinson	○		Any		❶		▼
Pirates of the Caribbean	○		Any		❶		★
Peter Pan's Flight	●		FT	✔	❶		◆
Snow White & the Seven Dwarfs	●		►11		❶		◆
Pinocchio's Fantastic Journey	●		►11		❶		▼
Dumbo the Flying Elephant	●		FT		❶		▼
Mad Hatter's Teacups	◗		►12		❶		▼
Alice's Curious Labyrinth	○		Any		❶		▼
"It's a Small World"	○		Any		❶		◆
Casey Jr – Le Petit Train du Cirque	○		►11		❶		◆
Le Pays des Contes des Fees	○		Any		❶		◆
Star Tours	○	52in	Any	✔	❶		★
Space Mountain	●	55in	LT	✔	❸	✔	★
Honey, I Shrunk the Audience	○		Any		❶		★
Autopia	●		FT		❶		▼
Orbitron	●	48in	FT		❶		▼
Disney Studio 1	◗		Any		❶		◆
Art of Disney Animation	◗		Any		❶		▼
Animagique	●		Any		❶		◆
Flying Carpets Over Agrabah	●	48in	FT		❶	✔	◆
Walt Disney Television Studios	●		Any		❶		◆
CinéMagique	◗		Any		❶		◆
Studio Tram Tour	●		FT		❶		★
Armageddon Special Effects	●		Any		❶		▼
Rock 'n' Roller Coaster	●	48in	Any		❸	✔	★

Short - ○   Medium - ◗   Long - ●   Anytime - Any   Before 11 - ►11   First thing - FT   Last thing - LT
Not Scary - ❶   Slightly - ❷   Very - ❸   Quite good - ▼   Very good - ◆   Outstanding - ★

Bercy ⓲

75012. **Map** 18 F3. Ⓜ *Bercy, Cour St-Emilion.* *Port de Bercy (01 43 43 40 30).*

This former wine-trading quarter just east of the city center, with its once-grim warehouses, pavilions and slum housing, has been transformed into a modern district. An automatic metro line (Line 14) links it to the heart of the city.

The centerpiece of Bercy is the Palais Omnisports de Paris-Bercy, now the city center's principal venue. The vast pyramidal structure has become a contemporary landmark. Many sports events are held here, as well as classical operas and rock concerts (*see pp345 and 349*).

Other architecturally adventurous buildings dominate Bercy, notably Chemetov's building for the Ministry of Finance, and Frank Gehry's American Center (which houses the Maison du Cinema and the mighty Cinemathèque Française).

At the foot of these structures, the imaginatively designed 173-acre (70-ha) Parc de Bercy provides a welcome green space for this part of the city. The park's attractions for children include a traditional carousel.

Former wine stores and cellars along Cours St Emilion have been restored as bars, restaurants and shops, and one of the warehouses now contains the Musée des Arts Forains (Fairground Museum).

Bibliothèque Nationale de France

Nearby, the Viaduc des Arts houses artists' workshops, boutiques and restaurants.

The Marina de Bercy is the starting and finishing point for cruises along the Seine.

Bibliothèque Nationale de France ⓳

Quai François-Mauriac 75013. **Map** 18 F4. *01 53 79 59 59.* Ⓜ *Bibliothèque F Mitterrand, Quai de la Gare.* *10am–8pm Tue– Sat; noon–7pm Sun.* *public hols & 2 wks mid-Sep.* **www**.bnf.fr

Dominique Perrault's 1996 landmark national library is the most striking of all the *Grands Projets* with which President Mitterand revitalized this eastern part of the city. Four towers house 12,000,000 volumes, with reference and research libraries in the central podium. Resources include 50,000 digitized illustrations, sound archives and CD-ROMs.

Bercy's striking American Center, designed by Frank Gehry

South of the City

13th Arrondissement ⓴

Zac Paris Rive Gauche, 75013. Ⓜ *Bibliotheque F Mitterrand.* **Map** 18 F5

Following a ten-year project called the Zac Paris Rive Gauche, the 13th arrondissement has become an area of startling urban regeneration. The once disused area of land between Gare d'Austerlitz and Ivry-sur-Seine has now been revived for a new university that will house some 30,000 students. The area also boasts the MK2 Bibliothèque, a vast movie complex which, with its 14 screens, cafés and exhibition areas, is already attracting avid film-goers.

Connected to Bercy by a bridge due to open in 2005, the area also offers new housing, schools and business oportunities.

Parc Montsouris ㉑

Blvd Jourdan 75014. ***Tel*** *01 45 88 28 60.* Ⓜ *Porte d'Orléans.* RER *Cité Universitaire.* *summer: 7:30am– 7pm daily; winter: 7:30am–5:30pm daily.*

This English-style park was laid out by the landscape architect Adophe Alphand, between 1865 and 1878. It has a restaurant, lawns, slopes, elegant trees and a lake which is home to many species of birds. The park is the second largest in central Paris and is also home to the municipal meteorological weather station.

Cité Universitaire 22

19–21 Blvd Jourdan 75014.
🗻 *01 44 16 64 00.* RER *Cité Universitaire.* **www**.ciup.fr

This is an international city in miniature for more than 5,000 foreign students attending the University of Paris. Created in the 1920s, it now contains 37 houses and, fascinatingly, each is in an architectural style linked to different countries. The Swiss House and the Franco-Brazilian House were designed by the Modernist architect Le Corbusier. The International House, donated by John D Rockefeller in 1936, has a library, restaurant, swimming pool and theater. The student community makes this a lively and stimulating area of the city to visit.

Japan House at Cité Universitaire

Notre-Dame du Travail 23

59 Rue Vercingetorix 75014. **Map** 15 B3. **Tel** *01 44 10 72 92.* M *Pernety.* ⏱ *10am–noon, 2pm–5pm daily.* ✝ *9am, 7pm Mon–Fri, 6pm Sat, 9am, 11am Sun.*

This church dates from 1901 and is made of an unusual mix of materials: stone, rubble and bricks over a riveted steel and iron framework. It was the creation of Father Soulange-Boudin, a priest who organized cooperatives and sought to reconcile labor and capitalism. Local parishioners

The Sebastopol Bell in Notre-Dame du Travail

raised the money for its construction, but lack of funds meant that many features, such as the bell towers, were never built. On the façade hangs the Sebastopol Bell, a trophy from the Crimean War given to the people of the Plaisance district by Napoleon III. The Art Nouveau interior has been completely restored, and features paintings of patron saints.

Institut Pasteur 24

25–28 Rue du Docteur Roux 75015.
Map 15 A2. **Tel** *01 45 68 80 00.* M *Pasteur.* ⏱ *2pm–5:30pm Mon–Fri (last adm: 4:45pm).* ● *Aug, public hols.* 🎫 📷 *Films, videos.* 📷 *compulsory.* 📷 **www**.pasteur.fr

The Institut Pasteur is France's leading medical research center and was founded by the world-renowned scientist Louis Pasteur in 1888–9. He discovered the process of milk pasteurization as well as vaccines against rabies and anthrax. The center houses a museum which includes a reconstruction of Pasteur's apartment and laboratory. It was designed by his grandchildren (also scientists) and is faithful to the original down to the last detail. Pasteur's tomb is in a basement crypt built in the style of a small Byzantine chapel. The tomb of Dr Emile Roux, the inventor of the

Louis Pasteur

treatment of diphtheria by serum injection, lies in the garden. The institute has laboratories for pure and applied research, lecture theaters, a reference section, and a hospital founded to apply Pasteur's theories.

There is also a library – the institute's original building from 1888 – where research into AIDS is carried out, led by pioneering Professor Luc Montagnier who discovered the HIV virus in 1983.

Garden in the Parc André Citroën

Parc André Citroën 25

Rue Balard 75015. **Tel** *01 56 56 11 56.* M *Javel, Balard.* ⏱ *7:30am–dusk Mon–Fri (9am Sat, Sun & public hols).*

Opened in 1992, this park is the third large-scale vista on the Seine, along with Les Invalides and the Champ-de-Mars. Designed by both landscapers and architects, it is a fascinating blend of styles, ranging from wildflower meadow in the north to the sophisticated mono-chrome mineral and sculpture gardens of the southern section. Numerous modern water sculptures dot the park, and huge greenhouses nurture a range of environments from a Mediterranean garden and a southern hemisphere zone to an Orangery which is used for horticultural shows in summer.

Versailles 26

See pp248–53.

The Palace and Gardens of Versailles ㉖

Garden statue
of a flautist

Visitors passing through the rich interior of this colossal palace, or strolling in its vast gardens, will understand why it was the glory of the Sun King's reign. Starting in 1668 with his father's modest hunting lodge, Louis XIV built the largest palace in Europe, housing 20,000 people at a time. Architects Louis Le Vau and Jules Hardouin-Mansart designed the buildings, Charles Le Brun did the interiors, and André Le Nôtre, the great landscaper, redesigned the gardens. The gardens are formally styled into regular patterns of paths and groves, hedges and flower beds, pools of water and fountains.

★ **Formal Gardens**
Geometric paths and shrubs are features of the formal gardens.

The Orangery was built beneath the Parterre du Midi to house exotic plants in winter.

The South Parterre's shrubbery and ornate flower beds overlook the Swiss pond.

★ **The Château**
Louis XIV made the château into the center of political power in France (see pp250–53).

The Water Parterre's vast pools of water are decorated with superb bronze statues.

Fountain of Latona
Marble basins rise to Balthazar Marsy's statue of the goddess Latona.

Dragon Fountain
The fountain's centerpiece is a winged monster.

The King's Garden with Mirror Pool are a 19th-century English garden and pool created by Louis XVIII.

Colonnade
Mansart designed this circle of marble arches in 1685.

VISITORS' CHECKLIST

Versailles. **Tel** 01 30 83 78 00. 01 30 83 77 77. 171 to Versailles. Versailles Rive Gauche. **Château** Oct–Mar: 9am–5pm Tue–Sun; Apr–Sep: 9am–6pm Tue–Sun.

Grand Trianon & Petit Trianon
Apr–Oct: noon–6:30pm daily; Nov–Mar: noon–5:30 daily. *Les Grandes Eaux Musicales (Apr–Sep); Les Fêtes de Nuit (Aug–Sep); Les Grandes Eaux Nocturnes (Sat during summer).* www.chateauversailles.fr

The Grand Canal was the setting for Louis XIV's many boating parties.

Fountain of Neptune
Groups of sculptures spray spectacular jets of water in Le Nôtre and Mansart's 17th-century fountain.

Petit Trianon
Built in 1762 as a retreat for Louis XV, this small château became a favorite of Marie-Antoinette.

STAR SIGHTS

★ The Château

★ Formal Gardens

★ Grand Trianon

★ Grand Trianon
Louis XIV built this small palace of stone and pink marble in 1687 to escape the rigors of court life, and to enjoy the company of his mistress, Madame de Maintenon.

The Main Palace Buildings of Versailles

Gold crest from the Petit Trianon

The current palace grew as a series of envelopes enfolding the original hunting lodge, whose low brick front is still visible in the center. In the 1660s, Louis Le Vau built the first envelope, a series of wings which expanded into an enlarged courtyard. It was decorated with marble busts, antique trophies and gilded roofs. On the garden side, columns were added to the west facade and a great terrace was created on the first floor. Mansart took over in 1678 and added the two immense north and south wings and filled Le Vau's terrace to form the Hall of Mirrors. He designed the chapel, which was finished in 1710. The Opera House (*L'Opéra*) was added by Louis XV in 1770.

South Wing
The wing's original apartments for great nobles were replaced by Louis-Philippe's museum of French history.

The Royal Courtyard
was separated from the Ministers' Courtyard by elaborate grillwork during Louis XIV's reign. It was accessible only to royal carriages.

Louis XIV's statue, erected by Louis Philippe in 1837, stands where a gilded gateway once marked the beginning of the Royal Courtyard.

STAR SIGHTS

★ Marble Courtyard

★ L'Opéra

★ Chapelle Royale

Ministers' Courtyard

Main Gate
Mansart's original gateway grille, surmounted by the royal arms, is the entrance to the Ministers' Courtyard.

TIMELINE

1667 Grand Canal begun	*Louis XV*		**1793** Louis XVI and Marie-Antoinette executed	**1833** Louis-Philippe turns the château into a museum
1668 Construction of new château by Le Vau	**1722** 12-year-old Louis XV occupies Versailles			
1650	**1700**	**1750**	**1800**	**1850**
1671 Interior decoration by Le Brun begun	**1715** Death of Louis XIV. Versailles abandoned by court		**1789** King and queen forced to leave Versailles for Paris	
	1682 Louis XIV and Marie-Thérèse move to Versailles			**1919** Treaty of Versailles signed on June 28
1661 Louis XIV enlarges château			**1774** Louis XVI and Marie-Antoinette live at Versailles	

The Clock
Hercules and Mars flank the clock overlooking the Marble Courtyard.

★ **Marble Courtyard**
The courtyard is decorated with marble paving, urns, busts and a gilded balcony.

North Wing
The chapel, Opéra and picture galleries occupy this wing, which originally housed royal apartments.

★ **L'Opéra**
The Opéra was completed in 1770, in time for the marriage of the future Louis XVI and Marie-Antoinette.

★ **Chapelle Royale**
Mansart's last great work, this two-story Baroque chapel, was Louis XIV's last addition to Versailles.

Inside the Château of Versailles

The sumptuous main apartments are on the first floor of the vast château complex. Around the Marble Courtyard are the private apartments of the king and the queen. On the garden side are the state apartments where official court life took place. These were richly decorated by Charles Le Brun with colored marbles, stone and wood carvings, murals, velvet, silver and gilded furniture. Beginning with the Salon d'Hercule, each state room is dedicated to an Olympian deity. The climax is the Hall of Mirrors, where 17 great mirrors face tall arched windows.

STAR SIGHTS

★ Chapelle Royale

★ Salon de Venus

★ Hall of Mirrors

★ Queen's Bedroom

KEY

▨	South wing
▨	Coronation room
▨	Madame de Maintenon's apartments
▨	Queen's apartments and private suite
▨	State apartments
▨	King's apartments and private suite
▨	North wing
▨	Non-exhibition space

★ Queen's Bedroom
In this room the queens of France gave birth to the royal children in full public view.

Entrance

Louis XVI's library features Neoclassical paneling and the king's terrestrial globe.

The Salon du Sacre is adorned with huge paintings of Napoleon by Jacques-Louis David.

Entrance

★ Salon de Venus
A Louis XIV statue stands amid the rich marble decor of this room.

★ Chapelle Royale
The chapel's first floor was reserved for the royal family and the ground floor for the court. The interior is richly decorated in white marble, gilding and Baroque murals.

★ Hall of Mirrors
Great state occasions were held in this multi-mirrored room stretching 233 ft (70 m) along the west façade. Here in 1919 the Treaty of Versailles was ratified, ending World War I.

Oeil-de-Boeuf

The King's Bedroom is where Louis XIV died in 1715, aged 77.

Salon de la Guerre
The room's theme of war is dramatically reinforced by Antoine Coysevox's stuccoed relief of Louis XIV riding to victory.

The Cabinet du Conseil is where the king received his ministers and his family.

Salon d'Apollon
Designed by Le Brun and dedicated to the god Apollo, this was Louis XIV's throne room. A copy of Hyacinthe Rigaud's famous portrait of the king (1701) hangs here.

Salon d'Hercule

Stairs to ground floor reception area

PURSUIT OF THE QUEEN

On October 6, 1789, a Parisian mob invaded the palace seeking the despised Marie-Antoinette. The queen, roused in alarm from her bed, fled toward the king's rooms through the anteroom known as the Oeil-de-Boeuf. As the mob tried to break into the room, the queen beat on the door of the king's bedroom. Once admitted she was safe, at least until morning, when she and the king were removed to Paris by the cheering and triumphant mob.

West of the City

An Art Nouveau window in the Rue la Fontaine

Rue la Fontaine ⓲

75016. **Map** 9 A4. M *Jasmin, Michel-Ange Auteuil.*

The Rue la Fontaine and surrounding streets act as a showcase for some of the most exciting architecture of the early 20th century. At No. 14 stands the Castel Béranger, a stunning apartment block made from cheap building materials to keep costs low, yet featuring stained glass, convoluted ironwork, balconies and mosaics. It established the reputation of Art Nouveau architect Hector Guimard, who went on to design the entrances for the Paris metro. Several more examples of his work can be seen further along the street, such as the Hôtel Mezzara at No. 60.

Fondation Le Corbusier ⓲

8–10 Square du Docteur Blanche 75016. **Tel** *01 42 88 41 53.* M *Jasmin.* ⬤ *1:30pm–6pm Mon, 10am–12:30pm, 1:30pm–6pm (5pm Fri) Tue–Fri.* ⬤ *public hols, Aug, Dec 24–Jan 2.* 🈲 ⎙ *Films, videos.* 🇮 *See History of Paris pp38–9.* **www.**fondationlecorbusier.asso.fr

In a quiet corner of Auteuil stand the villas La Roche *(see p265)* and Jeanneret, the first two Parisian houses built by the brilliant 20th-century architect Charles-Edouard Jeanneret, known as Le Corbusier. Built in the 1920s, they show his revolutionary use of white concrete in Cubist forms. Rooms flow into each other allowing maximum light, and the houses stand on stilts with windows along their entire length.

Villa La Roche was owned by the art patron Raoul La Roche. Today both villas serve as a fascinating documentation center on Le Corbusier.

Musée Marmottan-Claude Monet ⓲

2 Rue Louis Boilly 75016. 🇮 *01 40 50 65 84.* M *Muette.* ⬤ *10am–6pm Tue–Sun (last adm: 5:30pm).* ⬤ *Jan 1, May 1, Dec 25.* 🈲 🇮 **www.**musee-marmottan.com

The museum was created in the 19th-century mansion of the art historian Paul Marmottan in 1932, when he

bequeathed his house and his Renaissance, Consular and First Empire collections of paintings and furniture to the Institut de France. The focus of the museum changed after the bequest by Michel Monet of 65 paintings by his father, the Impressionist Claude Monet. Some of his most famous paintings are here, including *Impression – Sunrise*, a beautiful painting of Rouen Cathedral and several *Water Lilies*.

Part of Monet's personal art collection also passed to the museum, including paintings by Camille Pissarro and the Impressionists Pierre Auguste Renoir and Alfred Sisley. The museum also displays medieval illuminated manuscripts.

***La Barque** (1887) by Claude Monet, in the Musée Marmottan*

Bois de Boulogne ⓲

75016. M *Porte Maillot, Porte Dauphine, Porte d'Auteuil, Sablons.* ⬤ *24 hrs daily.* 🈲 *to specialty gardens and museum.* 🇮 **Shakespeare garden** 🎭 *Open-air theater* **Tel** *01 40 19 95 33/01.* ⬤ *May–Sep.* **Bagatelle & Rose gardens. Tel** *01 40 67 97 00.* ⬤ *8:30am. Closing times vary from 4:30pm to 8pm according to season.* **Jardin d'Acclimatation Tel** *01 40 67 90 82.* ⬤ *10am–7pm daily (Oct–May: 6pm).* 🇮 🇮 **Musée en Herbe. Tel** *01 40 67 97 66.* ⬤ *10am–6pm Mon–Fri, 2pm–6pm Sat.* 🈲 🇮 **Musée des Arts et Traditions Populaires. Tel** *01 44 17 60 00.* ⬤ *9:30am–5:15pm Wed–Mon.* 🈲 🇮 🇮 *by appt.*

Between the western edges of Paris and the River Seine this 2,137-acre (865-ha) park offers greenery for strolling, boating, picnicking or

Villa La Roche, home of the Fondation Le Corbusier

Kiosque de l'Empereur, on an island in the Grand Lac, Bois de Boulogne

spending a day at the races. The Bois de Boulogne is all that remains of the vast Forêt du Rouvre. In the mid-19th century Napoleon III had it redesigned and landscaped by Haussmann along the lines of London's Hyde Park.

There are many beautiful areas within the Bois. The Pré Catelan is a self-contained park with the widest beech tree in Paris, and the charming Bagatelle gardens feature architectural follies and an 18th-century villa famous for its rose garden, where an international rose competition is held in June. The villa was built in 64 days as a bet between the Comte d'Artois and Marie-Antoinette. The Bois has a reputation as a seedy area after dark so is best avoided at night.

Musée des Années 30 ❸❶

28 Ave André Morizet, Boulogne-Billancourt 92100. *Tel 01 55 18 46 42.* 🅼 *Marcel Sembat.* ⬜ *noon–5:45pm Tue–Sun.* 🦽♿⬛🚪
www.boulognebillancourt.com

La Grande Arche in La Défense

Inaugurated in 1998, this museum of the 1930s forms part of an arts complex, the Espace Landowski, named after Paul Landowski, a sculptor who lived in Boulogne-Billancourt from 1905 until his death in 1961, and his musician brother, Marcel. Several of Paul's works are on show in the museum. The complex also includes a library, a gallery of video directors and a move theater, and will soon have a multimedia center with artists studios.

Through paintings, drawings, sculpture and artifacts, the museum gives a vivid impression of the aesthetic mood of the era. The museum also organizes temporary thematic exhibitions relating to the period. Themed tours of the architectural and industrial heritage of Boulogne-Billancourt are also run.

La Défense ❸❷

La Grande Arche. *Tel 01 49 07 27 57.* 🆁🆁🆁 *La Défense.* ⬜ *9am–6pm daily (last adm: 30 min before closing).* 🎫⬛ℹ️ *See **History of Paris** pp38–9.* **www**.grandearche.com

This skyscraper business city on the western edge of Paris is the largest new office development in Europe and covers 198 acres (80 ha). It was launched in the 1960s to create a new home for leading French and multi-national companies. Since then, a major artistic scheme has transformed many of the squares into fascinating open-air museums.

In 1989 La Grande Arche was added to the complex, an enormous hollow cube large enough to contain Notre-Dame cathedral. This was designed by Danish architect Otto von Spreckelsen as part of major construction works, or *Grands Travaux*, which were initiated by (and are now a memorial to) the late President François Mitterrand.

The arch now houses an exhibition gallery and a conference center, and commands a superb view over the city of Paris.

Château de Malmaison ❸❸

Ave du Château 92500 Rueil-Malmaison. *Tel 01 47 49 48 15.* 🆁🆁🆁 *La Défense then bus 258.* ⬜ *10am–5pm Wed–Mon; closing times vary; phone for details.* 🎫⬛ *See **History of Paris** pp32–3.* **www**.napoleon.org

This 17th-century château was bought in 1799 by Josephine de Beauharnais, wife of Napoleon I. A magnificent veranda, Classical statues and a small theater were added. After his campaigns, Napoleon and his entourage would come here to relax. The château became Josephine's main residence after their divorce. Today, it is an important Napoleonic museum, together with the nearby Château de Bois-Préau.

Furniture, portraits, artifacts and mementoes of the imperial family are displayed in rooms reconstructed in the style of the First Empire.

Part of the original grounds still exists, including Josephine's famous rose garden.

The Empress Josephine's bed in the Château de Malmaison

EIGHT GUIDED WALKS

Paris is a city for walking. It is more compact and easier to get around than many other great capitals. Most of its best sights are within walking distance of each other and they are close to the heart of the city, the Ile de la Cité.

There are 14 classic tourist areas described in the *Area by Area* section of this book, each with a short walk marked on its *Street-by-Street* map, taking you past many of the most interesting sights. Yet Paris

Parc Monceau statue

offers a wealth of lesser known but equally remarkable areas, whose special history, architecture and local customs reveal other facets of the city.

The eight walks around the following neighborhoods take in the main sights and also introduce visitors to their subtle details, such as street markets, quirky churches, canals, gardens, old village streets and bridges. And the literary, artistic and historical associations allow the past and present to blend into the changing and vibrant life of the modern city.

Auteuil is renowned for its luxurious modern residential architecture, Monceau for its sumptuous Second Empire mansions and St-Louis for its *ancien régime* town houses, narrow streets and literati residents. The old-fashioned charm of the iron footbridges survives along Canal St-Martin, and steep village streets that were once home to famous artists still enrich Montmartre. A tranquil village atmosphere also pervades two lesser-known hilltop districts – Buttes-Chaumont, with one of Paris's loveliest parks, and Butte-aux-Cailles, whose quaint, cobbled alleyways belie its association with the ill-fated Paris Commune of 1871, while the once working-class area of Faubourg St-Antoine has been given a new lease on life as a pleasure-boat harbor and artisans' quarter.

All the walk areas are accessible by public transportation and the nearest metro stations and bus routes are listed in the *Tips for Walkers* boxes. For each walk there are suggestions on convenient resting points, such as cafés and squares, along the route.

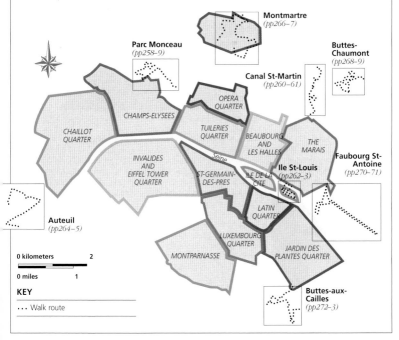

Montmartre
(pp266–7)

Parc Monceau
(pp258–9)

Buttes-Chaumont
(pp268–9)

Canal St-Martin
(pp260–61)

OPERA QUARTER

CHAMPS-ELYSEES

CHAILLOT QUARTER

TUILERIES QUARTER

BEAUBOURG AND LES HALLES

THE MARAIS

Faubourg St-Antoine
(pp270–71)

INVALIDES AND EIFFEL TOWER QUARTER

Seine

ST-GERMAIN-DES-PRES

ILE DE LA CITE

Ile St-Louis
(pp262–3)

Auteuil
(pp264–5)

LATIN QUARTER

LUXEMBOURG QUARTER

JARDIN DES PLANTES QUARTER

MONTPARNASSE

0 kilometers   2

0 miles   1

KEY

••• Walk route

Buttes-aux-Cailles
(pp272–3)

◁ **Bridge over the canal St-Martin**

A 90-Minute Walk around Parc Monceau

This leisurely walk passes through the exquisite late-18th-century Parc Monceau, the centerpiece of a chic Second Empire district. It then follows a route along surrounding streets, where groups of opulent mansions stunningly convey the magnificence in which some Parisians live, before ending at Place St-Augustin. For details on Monceau sights, see pages 230–31.

Ruysdaël gate

Parc Monceau to Avenue Velasquez

The walk starts at the Monceau metro station ① on the Boulevard de Courcelles. Enter the park where Nicolas Ledoux's 18th-century tollhouse ② stands. On

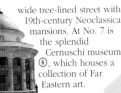

Parc Monceau's tollhouse ②

each side are sumptuously gilded 19th-century wrought-iron gates which support ornate lampposts.

Take the second path on the left past the monument to Guy de Maupassant ③ (1897). This is only one of a series of six Belle Epoque monuments of prominent French writers and musicians which are picturesquely scattered throughout the park. Most of them feature a solemn bust of a great man who is accompanied by a swooning muse.

Straight ahead is the most important remaining folly, a moss-covered Corinthian colonnade ④ running around the edge of a charming tiny lake with the requisite island in the center. Walk around the colonnade and under a 16th-century arch ⑤ transplanted from the old Paris Hôtel de Ville (*see p102*), which burned down in 1871.

Turn left on the Allée de la Comtesse de Ségur and go into Avenue Velasquez, a

wide tree-lined street with 19th-century Neoclassical mansions. At No. 7 is the splendid Cernuschi museum ⑥, which houses a collection of Far Eastern art.

Colonnade in Parc Monceau ④

Avenue Velasquez to Avenue Van Dyck

Re-enter the park and turn left onto the second small winding path, which is bordered by an 18th-century mossy pyramid ⑦, antique tombs, a stone arcade, an obelisk and a small Chinese stone pagoda. The romantically melancholy tone of these false ruins suits the spirit of the late 18th century.

Turn right on the first path past the pyramid and walk back to the central avenue. Straight ahead a Renaissance bridge fords the little stream running from the lake. Turn left and walk past the

monument (1902) to the musician Ambroise Thomas ⑧. Immediately behind there is a lovely artificial mountain with cascade. Turn left on the next avenue and walk to the monument (1897) to the composer Charles Gounod ⑨ on the left. From here follow the first winding path to the right toward the Avenue Van Dyck. Ahead to the right, in the corner of the park, is the Chopin monument ⑩ (1906), and looking along the Allée de la Comtesse de Ségur, the monument to the 19th-century French poet Alfred de Musset.

Ambroise Thomas statue ⑧

Avenue Van Dyck to Rue de Monceau

Leave the park and pass onto Avenue Van Dyck. No. 5 on the right is an impressive Parc Monceau mansion ⑪, a Neo-Baroque structure built by chocolate manufacturer Emile Menier; No. 6 is in the French Renaissance style that came back into favor in the 1860s. Straight ahead, beyond the ornate grille, there is a fine view of Avenue Hoche and in the distance the Arc de Triomphe. Walk past the gate

The mountain cascade ⑧

and turn left into Rue de Courcelles and left again into Rue Murillo, bordered by more elaborate town houses in 18th-century and French Renaissance styles ⑫. At the crossing of Rue Rembrandt, on the left, is another gate into the park and on the right a massive apartment building from 1900 (No. 7) and an elegant French Renaissance house with an elaborately carved wooden front door (No. 1). At the corner of the Rue Rembrandt and the Rue de Courcelles is the oddest of all the neighborhood buildings, a striking five-story red Chinese pagoda ⑬. It is an exclusive emporium of Chinese art.

Turn left onto the Rue de Monceau, walk past Avenue Ruysdaël and continue to the Musée Nissim de Camondo at No. 63 Rue de Monceau ⑭. Some nearby buildings worth having a look at are Nos. 52, 60 and 61 ⑮.

Boulevard Malesherbes

At the junction of Rue de Monceau and Boulevard Malesherbes turn right. This long boulevard with dignified six-story apartment buildings is typical of the great avenues cut through Paris by Baron Haussmann, prefect of the Seine during the Second Empire (*see pp34–5*). They

greatly pleased the Industrial Age bourgeoisie, but horrified sensitive souls and writers who compared them with the buildings of New York.

No. 75 is the stylish marble front of Benneton, the most fashionable Paris card and stationery engraver ⑯. On the left, approaching the Boulevard Haussmann, looms the greatest 19th-century Paris church, St-Augustin ⑰, built by Victor-Louis Baltard. Enter the church through the back door on Rue de la Bien-faisance. Walk through the church and leave by the main door. On the left is the huge stone building of the French Officers' club, the Cercle Militaire ⑱. Straight ahead is a bronze statue of Joan of Arc ⑲. Continue on to Place St-Augustin to St-Augustin metro station.

Joan of Arc statue ⑲

KEY

••• Walk route

☀ Good viewing point

Ⓜ Metro station

0 meters   250

0 yards   250

Chinese pagoda emporium ⑬

TIPS FOR WALKERS

Starting point: Blvd de Courcelles.
Length: 2 miles (3 km).
Getting there: The nearest metro is Monceau, reached by bus No. 30; No. 84 goes to metro Courcelles and No. 94 stops between Monceau & Villiers metros.
St Augustin church: Open 8:30am–7pm daily (closed 12:30–3:30pm public hols).
Stopping-off points: Near the Renaissance bridge in the Parc Monceau there is a kiosk serving coffee and sandwiches. There are two cafés at Place de Rio de Janeiro and several brasseries around Place St-Augustin. The Square M Pagnol is a pleasant place to relax and take in the beauty of the park at the end of the walk.

A 90-Minute Walk along the Canal St-Martin

The walk along the quays on each side of the Canal St-Martin is an experience of Paris very different from that of tonier districts. Here, the older surviving landmarks of the neighborhood – the factories, warehouses, dwellings, taverns and cafés – hint at life in a thriving 19th-century industrial, working-class world. But there are also the softer charms of the old iron footbridges, the tree-lined quays, the inevitable fishermen, the river barges, and the still waters of the broad canal basins. A walk along the canal, which connects the Bassin de la Villette with the Seine, will evoke images of the Pernod-drinking, working-class Paris of Jean Gabin and Edith Piaf.

The 18th-century Barrière de la Villette ②

Bassin de la Villette looking north ③

Place de Stalingrad to Avenue Jean-Jaurès

From the Stalingrad metro station ①, follow Boulevard de la Villette to the new square in front of the Barrière de la Villette ②. This is one of the few remaining 18th-century tollhouses in Paris, designed by the celebrated Neoclassical architect Nicolas

Ledoux in the 1780s. The fountains, square and terraces were designed in the 1980s to provide an attractive setting and fine views of the Bassin de la Villette ③ to the north.

Walk toward Avenue Jean-Jaurès. On the left is the first lock ④ leading down to the canal.

Quai de Valmy to Rue Bichat

Cross over to the Quai de Jemmapes, which runs the whole length of the east side

TIPS FOR WALKERS

Starting point: Place de Stalingrad.
Length: 2 miles (3.5 km).
Getting there: The nearest metro is Stalingrad: bus No.54 stops there, and No.26 at metro Jaurès.
Hôpital St-Louis: Chapel open 2–5pm Fri–Sun; the courtyard is open daily.
Stopping-off points: Ethnic food shops and restaurants abound in the lively Rue du Faubourg du Temple and nearby streets. The Quai de Valmy also has plenty of modish restaurants and bars (Antoine et Lili, La 25e Image, l'Atmosphère), and is lined with benches to rest on; and there is a shady public garden on Boulevard Jules Ferry.

View from Rue E Varlin bridge ⑦

KEY

- ••• Walk route
- ☆ Good viewing point
- Ⓜ Metro station

| 0 meters | 500 |
| 0 yards | 500 |

Courtyard garden of Hôpital St-Louis ⑭

Iron footbridges over the canal ⑤

of the canal and down to the first bridge on Rue Louis Blanc. Cross the bridge to the Quai de Valmy. From the corner there is a glimpse of the oblique granite and glass front of the new Paris Industrial Tribunal ⑥ on the Rue Louis Blanc.

Continue along Quai de Valmy. At Rue E Varlin cross the bridge ⑦, from where there is an attractive view of the second canal lock, lock-keeper's house, public gardens and old lampposts. At the other side of the bridge and slightly to the left, go along the pedestrianized Rue Haendel, which provides a good view of the towering, terraced buildings of a public housing complex ⑧. Nearby is the French Communist

Party headquarters ⑨ on Place du Colonel Fabien. The building can be recognized by its curving glazed tower.

Return to the Quai de Jemmapes, where at No. 134 ⑩ stands one of the few surviving brick-and-iron industrial buildings that used to line the canal in the 19th century. At No. 126 ⑪ is another notable modern building, a residence for the elderly, with monumental concrete arches and glazed bay windows. Further along, at No. 112 ⑫, is an Art Deco apartment building with bay windows, decorative iron balconies and tiles. On the ground floor there is a typical 1930s proletarian café. Here the canal curves gracefully into the third lock, spanned by a charming transparent iron footbridge ⑬.

Hôpital St-Louis to Rue Léon Jouhaux

Turn left onto Rue Bichat, which leads to the remarkable 17th-century Hôpital St-Louis ⑭. Enter through the hospital's old main gate with its high-pitched roof and massive stone arch. Pass into the courtyard. The hospital was founded in 1607 by Henri IV, the first Bourbon king, to care for the victims of the plague. Leave the courtyard from the central gate on the wing on your left. Here you pass by the 17th-century hospital chapel ⑮ and out into the Rue de la Grange aux Belles.

Turn left and walk back to the canal. At the junction of

Rue de la Grange Batelière and the Quai de Jemmapes stood, until 1627, the notorious Montfaucon gallows ⑯, one of the chief public execution spots of medieval Paris. Turn into the Quai de Jemmapes. At No. 101 ⑰ is the original front of the Hôtel du Nord, which was made famous in the eponymous 1930s movie. In front is another iron footbridge and a drawbridge ⑱ for traffic, providing a charming setting with views of the canal on each side. Cross over and continue down the Quai de Valmy until the last footbridge ⑲ at the corner of the Rue Léon Jouhaux. From here the canal can be seen disappearing under the surface of Paris, to continue its journey, through a great stone arch.

Entrance to Hôpital St-Louis ⑭

Square Frédéric Lemaître to Place de la République
Walk along Square Frédéric Lemaître ⑳ to the start of Boulevard Jules Ferry, which has a public garden stretching down its center. The garden was built over the canal in the 1860s. At its head stands a charmingly nostalgic statue of a flower girl of the 1830s, *La Grisette* ㉑. On the left is a busy working-class street, Rue du Faubourg du Temple ㉒, with flourishing ethnic shops and restaurants. Follow the street to the right and on to the metro station in the Place de la République.

A shop front in Rue du Temple ㉒

A 90-Minute Walk around the Ile St-Louis

The walk around this charming, tiny island passes along the enchanting, picturesque tree-lined quays from Pont Louis-Philippe to Quai d'Anjou, taking in the sumptuous 17th-century *hôtels* that infuse the area with such a powerful sense of time. It then penetrates into the heart of the island along the main street, Rue St-Louis-en-l'Ile, enlivened by chic restaurants, cafés, art galleries and boutiques, before returning to the north side of the island and back to Pont Marie. For more information on the main sights, see pages 77 and 87.

Left Bank view of the Ile St-Louis

Fishing on a St-Louis quayside

Metro Pont Marie to Rue Jean du Bellay

From the Pont Marie metro station ① walk down Quai des Celestins and Quai de l'Hôtel de Ville, lined with traditional bookstands, from where there is a good view of Ile St-Louis. Turn left at Pont Louis-Philippe ② and, having crossed it, take the steps down to the lower quay immediately to the right. Walk around the tree-shaded west point of the island ③, then up the other side to the Pont St-Louis ④. Across from the bridge, on the corner of Rue Jean du Bellay, is Le Flore en l'Ile ⑤, the toniest café-cum-tea salon on the island.

Quai d'Orléans

From the corner of the Quai d'Orléans and the Rue Jean du Bellay there are fine views of the Panthéon's dome and Notre-Dame. Along the quay, Nos. 18–20, the Hôtel Rolland has unusual Hispano-Moorish windows. No. 12 ⑥ is one of several stately 17th-century houses with handsome wrought-iron balconies. At No. 6 the former Polish library,

KEY

• • • Walk route

☼ Good viewing point

Ⓜ Metro station

0 meters	250
0 yards	250

Seine barge passing a St-Louis quay

founded in 1838, now houses the Société Historique et Littéraire Polonaise, focusing on the life of Polish poet Adam Mickiewicz ⑦; it also contains some Chopin scores and autographs by George Sand and Victor Hugo. On the right, the Pont de la Tournelle ⑧ links the island to the Left Bank.

Quai de Béthune to Pont Marie

Continue beyond the bridge and onto Quai de Béthune, where the Nobel-laureate Marie Curie lived at No. 36 ⑨, and where beautiful wrought-iron balconies gracefully decorate Nos. 34 and 30. The Hôtel Richelieu ⑩ at No. 18 is one of the island's most beautiful houses.

St-Louis church door ⑰

It features a fine garden where it has retained its original Classical blind arcades.

If you turn left down Rue Bretonvilliers there is an imposing 17th-century house ⑪, with a high-pitched roof resting on a great Classical arch spanning the street. Back on the Quai de Béthune, proceed to the Pont de Sully ⑫, a late 19th-century bridge joining the riverbanks. Ahead is the charming 19th-century Square Barye ⑬, a shady public garden at the east point of the island, from where there are fine river views. From here travel toward the Quai d'Anjou as far as the corner of Rue St-Louis-en-l'Ile to see the most famous house on

small, chic, bistro-style restaurants with pleasantly old-fashioned decors. No. 31 is the original Berthillon shop ⑱, No. 60 an art gallery ⑲ with an original 19th-century window front,

Gargoyle at No. 51 Rue St-Louis-en-l'Ile ⑳

and at No. 51 is one of the few 18th-century *hôtels* on the island, Hôtel Chernizot ⑳, with a superb Rococo balcony which rests on leering gargoyles.

Turn right into Rue Jean du Bellay and along to Pont Louis-Philippe. Turn right again into the Quai de Bourbon, which is lined by one of the island's finest rows of *hôtels*, the most notable being Hôtel Jassaud at No. 19 ㉑. Continue to the 17th-century Pont Marie ㉒ and cross it to the Pont Marie metro on the other side.

The 17th-century Pont Marie ㉒

the island, the Hôtel Lambert ⑭ (*see pp26–7*). Continue into the Quai d'Anjou where Hôtel de Lauzun ⑮ at No. 17 has a severe Classical front and a beautiful gilded balcony and drain-pipes. Now turn left into Rue Poulletier and note the convent of the Daughters of Charity ⑯ at No. 5 bis. Further on, at the corner of Rue Poulletier and Rue St-Louis-en-l'Ile, is the island church, St-Louis ⑰, with its unusual tower, projecting clock and carved main door.

Proceed along Rue St-Louis-en-l'Ile, which abounds in

Windows of the Hôtel Rolland

TIPS FOR WALKERS

Starting point: Pont Marie metro.
Length: 1.6 miles (2.6 km).
Getting there: The walk starts from the Pont Marie metro. However, bus route 67 takes you to Rue du Pont Louis-Philippe and also crosses the island along Rue des Deux Ponts and Blvd Pont de Sully; routes 86 and 87 also cross the island along Blvd Pont de Sully.
Stopping-off points: There are cafés, such as Flore en l'Ile, and the Berthillon shops for ice cream (see p317). Restaurants on the Rue St-Louis-en-l'Ile include Auberge de la Reine Blanche (No. 30) and Au Gourmet de l'Isle (No. 42), as well as a pâtisserie and a cheese shop. Good resting-points are the tree-shaded quays and Square Barye to the eastern end of the island.

A 90-Minute Walk in Auteuil

Part of the fascination of the walk around this bastion of bourgeois life in westernmost Paris lies in the contrasting nature of the area's streets. The old village provincialism of Rue d'Auteuil, where the walk begins, leads on to the masterpieces of luxurious modern architecture along Rue La Fontaine and Rue du Docteur Blanche. The walk ends at the Jasmin metro station. For more on the sights of Auteuil, see page 254.

Obelisk, Place d'Auteuil ①

Rue d'Auteuil

The walk begins at Place d'Auteuil ①, a leafy village square with a striking Guimard-designed metro station entrance, an 18th-century funerary obelisk, and the 19th-century Neo-Romanesque Notre Dame d'Auteuil. Walk down Rue d'Auteuil, the main street of the old village, and take in the sense of an old provincial world. The Auberge du Mouton Blanc brasserie ② now occupies the premises of the area's oldest tavern, favored by Molière and his actors in the 17th century. The house at Nos. 45–47 ③ was the residence of American presidents John Adams and his son John Quincy Adams. Move on to the pleasantly shaded Place Jean Lorrain ④, the site of the local market. Here there is a Wallace drinking fountain,

Wallace fountain ④

donated by the English millionaire Richard Wallace in the 19th century. On the right, down Rue Donizetti, is the Villa Montmorency ⑤, a private enclave of luxury villas built on the former country estate of the Comtesse de Boufflers.

Rue La Fontaine

Continue the walk along Rue La Fontaine, renowned for its many Hector Guimard buildings. Marcel Proust was born at No.96. Henri Sauvage's ensemble of artists' studios at No. 65 ⑥ is one of the most original Art Deco buildings in Paris. No. 60 is a Guimard Art Nouveau house ⑦ with elegant cast-iron balconies. Further along there is a small Neo-Gothic chapel at No. 40 ⑧ and Art Nouveau apartment buildings at Nos. 19 and 21 ⑨. No. 14 is Guimard's most spectacular building, the Castel Béranger ⑩, with a superb iron gate.

TIPS FOR WALKERS

Starting point: *Place d'Auteuil.*
Length: *2 miles (3 km).*
Getting there: *The nearest metro station to the starting point is Eglise d'Auteuil, and buses that take you there are Nos. 22, 52 and 62.*
Stopping-off points: *Along Rue d'Auteuil is the inexpensive, trendy brasserie L'Auberge du Mouton Blanc, with 1930s decor. No. 17 Rue La Fontaine is a tiny 1900 Art Nouveau café with old tiled floors and original zinc-covered bar. Place Jean Lorrain is a pleasantly shaded square where walkers can rest, and on Rue La Fontaine there is a small park in front of the Neo-Gothic chapel at No. 40. Further on at Place Rodin there is a pleasant public garden.*

Doorway of No. 28 Rue d'Auteuil.

KEY

••• Walk route

🔆 Good viewing point

Ⓜ Metro station

0 meters	250
0 yards	250

Rue de l'Assomption to Rue Mallet Stevens

At the corner of Rue de l'Assomption there is a view of the massive Maison de Radio-France ⑪ built in 1963 to house French radio and television (see p200). It was one of the first modern postwar buildings in the city. Turn left onto Rue de l'Assomption and walk to the fine 1920s apartment building at No. 18 ⑫. Turn left into Rue du Général Dubail and follow the street to Place Rodin, where the great sculptor's bronze

Shuttered bay window at No. 3 Square Jasmin ⑲

nude, *The Age of Bronze* (1877) ⑬, occupies the center of the rotary.

Take the Avenue Théodore Rousseau back to Rue de l'Assomption and turn left

were altered dramatically by the addition of an extra three storys in the 1960s.

Continue on Rue du Docteur Blanche until coming to Villa du Docteur Blanche on the left. At the end of this small cul de sac is the most celebrated modern house in Auteuil, Le Corbusier's Villa Roche ⑰. Together with the adjoining Villa Jeanneret, it is now part of the Corbusier Foundation (see pp38–9). Built for an art collector in 1924 using the new technique of reinforced concrete, the house, with its geometric forms and lack of ornamentation, is a model of early Modernism.

No. 18 Rue de l'Assomption, detail ⑫

Rue du Docteur Blanche to Rue Jasmin

Walk back to Rue du Docteur Blanche and turn right into Rue Henri Heine. No. 18 bis ⑱ is a very elegant Neo-classical 1920s apartment building offering a good contrast to one of Guimard's last creations from 1926 next door – an Art Nouveau facade much tamer than that at Castel Béranger but still employing brick, and with projecting bay windows and a terraced roof. Turn left on Rue Jasmin. In the second cul de sac on the left there is another Guimard house at No. 3 Square Jasmin ⑲. Toward the end of Rue Jasmin is the metro station.

toward Avenue Mozart. Cut through in the 1880s, this is the principal artery of the 16th arrondissement, linking north and south and lined with typical bourgeois apartment buildings of the late 19th century. Cross the avenue and continue to the Avenue des Chalets where there is a typical collection of weekend villas ⑭ recalling the quieter suburban Auteuil of the mid-19th century. Further along Rue de l'Assomption, Notre-Dame de l'Assomption ⑮ is a Neo-Renaissance 19th-century church. Turn left into Rue du Docteur Blanche. At No. 9 and down the adjoining Rue Mallet Stevens ⑯ there is a row of celebrated modern houses in the International Modern style by the architect Robert Mallet Stevens. In this expensive, once avant-garde enclave lived architects, designers, artists and their modern-minded clients. The original proportions, however,

Courtyard of No. 14 Rue La Fontaine

The Age of Bronze ⑬

A 90-Minute Walk in Montmartre

The walk begins at the base of the sand-stone *butte* (hill), where old theaters and dance halls, once frequented and depicted by painters from Renoir to Picasso, have now been taken over by nightclubs. It continues steeply uphill to the original village, along streets which still retain the atmosphere caught by artists like Van Gogh, before winding downhill to end at Place Blanche. For more on the main sights of Montmartre and the Sacré-Coeur, see pages 218–27.

Montmartre seen from a distance

Place Pigalle to Rue Ravignan

The walk starts at the lively Place Pigalle ① and follows Rue Frochot to the Rue Victor Massé. At the corner is the ornate entrance to an exclusive private street bordered by turn-of-the-century chalets ②. Across, at No. 27 Rue Victor Massé, is an ornate mid-19th century apartment building, and No. 25 is where Vincent Van Gogh and his

brother Theo lived in 1886 ③. The famous Chat Noir ④, Montmartre's most renowned artistic cabaret in the 1890s, flourished at No. 12. At the end of the street begins the wide tree-lined Avenue Trudaine. Take Rue Lallier on the left to Boulevard de Rochechouart. Continue east. No. 84 is the first address of the Chat Noir and No. 82 was the Grand Trianon ⑤, Paris's oldest movie theater, from the

Entrance gate to Avenue Frochot

TIPS FOR WALKERS

Starting point: *Place Pigalle.*
Length: *1.4 miles (2.3 km). The walk goes up some very steep streets to the top; if you do not feel like the climb, consider taking the Montmartrobus, which covers most of the walk and starts at Place Pigalle.*
Getting there: *The nearest metro is Pigalle; buses that take you there are Nos. 30, 54 and 67.*
Stopping-off points: *There are many cafés and shops in Rue Lepic and the Rue des Abbesses. Rayons de la Santé, to the right of the theater in Place Charles Dullin, is one of the city's best vegetarian restaurants. For shade and a rest, Place Jean-Baptiste Clément and Square S Buisson at Avenue Junot are charming public squares.*

early 1890s. Further along, No. 74 is the original front of Montmartre's first great cancan dance hall, the Elysée-Montmartre ⑥.

Turn left on to Rue Steinkerque, which leads to Sacré-Coeur gardens, and then left into Rue d'Orsel, which leads to the leafy square Place Charles Dullin, where the small early 19th-century Théâtre de l'Atelier ⑦ stands. Continue up the hill on Rue des Trois Frères and turn left on Rue Yvonne le Tac, which leads to Place des Abbesses ⑧. This is one of the most pleasant and liveliest squares in the area. It has conserved its entire canopied Art Nouveau metro entrance by Hector Guimard. Nearby is St-Jean l'Evangéliste ⑨, an unusual brick and mosaic Art

Rue André Antoine ⑩

Nouveau church. To the right of the church a flight of steep steps leads to the tiny Rue André Antoine where the Pointillist painter Georges Seurat lived at No. 39 . Continue along Rue des Abbesses and turn right at Rue Ravignan.

Rue Ravignan
From here there is a sweeping view of Paris. Climb the steps straight ahead to the deeply shaded Place Emile Goudeau ⑪. To the left, at No. 13, is the original entrance to the Bateau-Lavoir, the most important cluster of artists' studios in

St-Jean l'Evangéliste, detail ⑨

Montmartre. Here Picasso lived and worked in the early 1900s. Further up, at the corner of Rue Orchampt and Rue Ravignan, there is a row of picturesque 19th-century artists' studios ⑫.

Rue Ravignan to Rue Lepic
Continue up the hill along the small public garden Place Jean-Baptiste Clément ⑬. At the top, cross Rue Norvins. Nearby is an old Monmar-tois restaurant, Auberge de la Bonne Franquette ⑭, which, as Aux Billards en Bois, used to be a favorite gathering place for 19th-century artists. Continue along the narrow Rue St-Rustique, from where Sacré-Coeur can be seen. At the end and to the right is Place du Tertre ⑮, the main village square. From here go north on Rue du Mont Cenis and turn left to Rue Cortot. Erik Satie, the eccentric composer, lived in No. 6 ⑯, and at No. 12 is the Musée de Montmartre ⑰. Turn right on Rue des Saules and walk past the very pretty Montmartre vineyard ⑱ to the Au Lapin Agile ⑲ at the corner

of Rue St-Vincent. Go back down Rue des Saules and right on Rue de l'Abreuvoir, an attractive street of turn-of-the-20th-century villas and gardens. Continue into l'Allée des Brouillards, a leafy pedestrian alley. No. 6 ⑳ was Renoir's last house in Montmartre. Take the steps down into the Rue Simon Dereure and immediately turn left into a small park, which can be crossed to reach Avenue Junot. Here, No. 15 ㉑ was the house of Dadaist Tristan Tzara in the early 1920s. Continue up Avenue Junot, turn right on Rue Girardon and right again on Rue Lepic.

Au Lapin Agile nightclub ⑲

Rue Lepic to Place Blanche
At the corner is one of Montmartre's few surviving windmills, the Moulin du Radet ㉒. Continue along Rue Lepic: to the right at the top of a slope is another windmill survivor, the Moulin de la Galette ㉓. Turn left on Rue de l'Armée d'Orient, with its picturesque artists' studios ㉔, and left again into Rue Lepic. Van Gogh lived at No. 54 ㉕ in June 1886. Continue to Place Blanche, and on Boulevard de Clichy to the right is one of the area's great landmarks, the Moulin Rouge ㉖.

Artist selling his work at Place du Tertre ⑮

KEY

••• Walk route

☆ Good viewing point

Ⓜ Metro station

0 meters   250

0 yards   250

Moulin Rouge nightclub near the Place Blanche ㉖

A 90-Minute Walk in Buttes-Chaumont

This area in the east of the city is little known to many visitors, yet it contains one of Paris' biggest and most beautiful parks and some fascinating architecture. The walk is quite strenuous with many steps, and takes in a charming micro-village, the Butte Bergeyre, which is perched high above the city and has rare houses in contrasting styles. After descending from the village, the walk continues in Buttes-Chaumont park, a vast hill complete with a lake with a huge island and folly, rocky outcrops and a wonderful variety of trees and plants.

a small garden ⑩. This is owned by the city but tended by local residents who can often be found working here.

Head back down the Rue Georges Lardennois to the Rue Michel Tagrine and take the ivy-draped steps back down to the main road ⑪. Continue straight and then turn right onto the Avenue Mathurin-Moreau, noting the fine Art Deco building ⑫ at 42 with its glittering gold-colored tile detail. At the end of the road, cross the Rue Manin to the entrance to the park.

View across city toward Sacré-Coeur ⑧

The Butte Bergeyre

From the metro Buttes-Chaumont ① take the Rue Botzaris, turning right onto the Avenue Simon Bolivar until you reach the stairs at 54 ②, which lead up into the Butte Bergeyre. At the top of the stairs pause to absorb the enchanting atmosphere of this micro-village of five little streets. Construction started in the 1920s but there are also some modern buildings. Carry on into the Rue Barrelet de Ricou ③ to admire the ivy-covered house at 13 ④, then continue to the end of the road to take a left into the Rue Philippe Hecht ⑤ where the chalet-style house at 7 ⑥ is an interesting contrast to the creeper-covered Art Deco gem at 13 ⑦. At the end of the street take a left up to the corner of the Rue Georges Lardennois and the Rue Rémy-de-Gourmont for a wonderful view across the city ⑧ of Montmartre with its wedding-cake Sacré-Coeur on top. Be sure to admire the tiny patch of grapevines ⑨ in the residents' garden below. Close to this mini-vineyard is

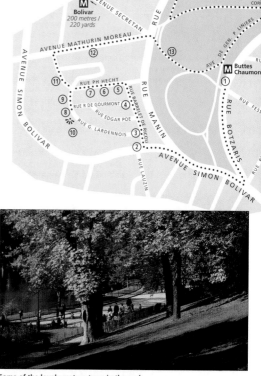

Some of the lovely mature trees in the park

The suspension bridge, for the best view of the park ⑯

TIPS FOR WALKERS

Starting point: Metro Buttes-Chaumont.

Length: 1.5 miles (2.5 km). Note: Very steep walk in parts, with many steps.

Getting there: Go to Buttes-Chaumont metro station, on line 7bis. Or take buses Nos. 26, 60 and 75 to the stop for Buttes Chaumont park.

Stopping off points: The park is full of lovely spots to rest, and the benches near the lake are good if bringing your own refreshments. Le Kaskade café across from the park (at 2 Place Armand-Carrel) is a fashionable spot for snacks and drinks with a terrace that is ideal on a sunny day.

PARC DES BUTTES CHAUMONT

㉓ Ⓜ Botzaris

Clifftop folly, the park's summit ㉒

The Buttes-Chaumont Park

Commissioned by Napoleon III and Baron Haussman in 1864, the park covers 61 acres (25 ha) and took four years to complete. It was built by the engineer Adolphe Alphand and the architect Gabriel Davioud. Today, the hilly park is popular with joggers as it provides a fierce workout. It is packed with mature trees including planes, poplars, ash, maples, chestnuts, sequoias and beautiful magnolias. At the entrance to the park

there is a man-made rock structure ⑬ with steps carved out of the façade; climb them to the top. Go on along a tree-lined path to join the Avenue de General Puebla Liniers and follow this until reaching the Carrefour de la Colonne ⑭ where there is a red brick mansion house. With your back to this go ahead to a little bridge lined with terracotta tiles. Take the bridge ⑮ then branch left down the steps within man-made rock to an impressive 206-ft (63-m) long bridge ⑯. Towering over the lake, this provides wonderful views of the park. Cross the bridge and follow the path down to the lake. The lake ⑰ is encircled by weeping willows and benches for breaks to admire the 164-ft (50-m) high man-made island ⑱. Follow the lake around until you hear rushing water. One of the park's most impressive features is the 105-ft (32-m) high waterfall ⑲ hidden inside a grotto. Walk right up to the waterfall looking up to see a patch of sky and some glorious man-made stalactites. Take a stepping-stone to the other

side of the cave and then exit and rejoin the path around the lake, heading left. Ascend the few steps, then veer to the left and up the hill ⑳. Bear left over the terracotta-tiled bridge. Take the right branch of steps and head up to the top of the cliff. Cross a tiny bridge ㉑ and turn left up some steps to the folly ㉒, a copy of the Temple of Sibylle near Rome. This is the highest point in the park providing views across the city all the way to the Sacré-Coeur. Now take the path on the right back to the Carrefour de la Colonne. Turn left and continue along the Avenue de la Cascade all the way to the exit ㉓. From here you can take the metro from station Botzaris.

KEY

••• Walk route

☼ Good viewing point

Ⓜ Metro station

0 meters   200

0 yards   200

Man-made waterfall, inside the grotto ⑲

A 90-Minute Walk in Faubourg St-Antoine

In the east of the city a few steps away from the bustle of the Bastille lies the Faubourg St-Antoine district, traditionally a working-class neighborhood full of furniture designers, carpenters and artisans, and this legacy can still be seen today. From the Place de la Bastille, the walk takes in Paris' pleasure-boat port, the artisan area around the Viaduc des Arts – a former bridge with arts and crafts studios nestling in the arches – and onto the Promenade Plantée for a fascinating tree-filled stroll.

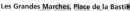

Les Grandes Marches, Place de la Bastille

The Port de Plaisance, with many pleasure boats ④

Port de Plaisance

Tucked away near the traffic of Place de La Bastille ① lies an area of tranquillity that's of interest to boat-lovers and landlubbers alike. The Port de Plaisance and Paris-Arsenal garden ② was inaugurated in 1983 to provide a harbor for pleasure craft. Linking the Seine to the Canal St-Martin, the harbor was previously where commercial barges loaded and unloaded cargo. Today, it's a pretty spot full of with yachts, dingies and Parisians out for a stroll. The cobbled stones on the quayside and old-fashioned lampposts add to the port's atmosphere. The lawns are perfect for a picnic and the children's play areas, while small, are well stocked with rocking chairs, slides and climbing apparatus ③. Continue to the end of the marina to the lock ④. Cross over the lock bridge, observing the pedestrian crossing sign, and head down on the other quayside turning back toward the Place de La Bastille. Just before the gray

steel bridge ⑤, take the stairs up and then the bridge over to the Boulevard de la Bastille ⑥. Cross the Boulevard and take a right and then left onto the Rue Jules César ⑦ all the way to the end of the street, turn left and then cross the Rue de Lyon turning right onto the Avenue Daumesnil and the start of the Viaduc des Arts ⑧.

Viaduc des Arts

In 1859 the Paris Viaduct was built to take a railroad line that linked the Faubourg St-Antoine district with the suburbs. In 1994 the restored and revamped Viaduc des Arts opened with 50 shops and studios nestling in the bridge's rose stone archways.

In keeping with the tradition of the area, the ateliers are all linked to the arts, and some of the city's master crafters call the arches home. The superb window

Place de la Bastille with the impressive Opéra de Paris Bastille ①

displays at the first studio "Fleur d'Art Guillet" ⑨ give a hint of the quality of craftsmanship to come. Guillet specializes in providing silk flowers for Paris' top theater and fashion houses. The "Ateliers du Temps Passé" ⑩ at 5 is a restorer of paintings, while Lorenove at 11 restores period glass. Number 13 is the base for hot interior designer Cherif, and the whimsical "Au Bonheur des Dames" ⑪ at 17 provides all kinds of materials for embroidery fans. For refreshment, stop at the Viaduc Café at 43 ⑫, which dishes up simple meals and hearty salads to the area's hip creatives. The SEMAEST

One of the arts and crafts shop fronts under the Viaduc des Arts ⑧

gallery space at 55/57 ⑬ hosts temporary exhibitions. Moving on past the metal furniture-maker Baguès at 73, the antique lace restorers Marie Lavande at 83, the Atelier Le Tallec 93/95, which specializes in hand-painted porcelain, it is clear that the spirit of the old artisans' area is alive and well. For those of a musical bent, Allain Cadinot repairs and sells Boehm flutes at 99, while Roger Lanne is a violin- and cello-maker at 103. With the coppersmith at 111, the terracotta tile specialist at 113 and the frame-maker at 117, you are close to the end of the viaduct, where the last atelier Jean-Charles Brosseau-Licences ⑮ perhaps sums up the street's diversity specializing in making hats, scent and cutlery.

Promenade Plantée

Turn left, follow the signs and take the steps up to the Promenade Plantée ⑯, a walkway on top of the viaduct. It is 2-3/4 miles (4.5 km) long and goes all the way to the Vincennes woods. For a longer walk, turn right here and go through tunnels to the city's edge and the woods. Or turn left and head back toward the Bastille. This narrow walkway offers wonderful views of the rooftops, and you can also see into some apartments. With bamboo, roses, lavender and maples, the walkway is a delight. At the end ⑰, take the steps down to the Rue de Lyon ⑱ leading to the Bastille metro, pausing only to admire the splendid Opéra de Paris Bastille ⑲ *(see p98)*.

Promenade Plantée, a lovely rooftop walkway ⑯

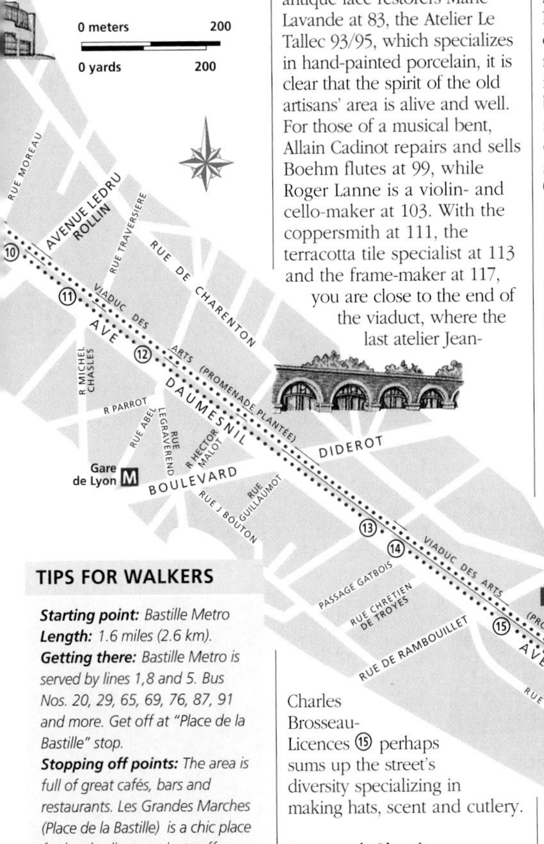
0 meters 200
0 yards 200
RUE MOREAU
AVENUE LEDRU ROLLIN
RUE TRAVERSIERE
RUE DE CHARENTON
VIADUC DES ARTS (PROMENADE PLANTÉE)
AVE DAUMESNIL
R MICHEL CHASLES
R PARROT
RUE ABEL
RUE LEGRAVEREND
R HECTOR MALOT
Gare de Lyon
BOULEVARD DIDEROT
RUE GUILLAUMOT
RUE J BOUTON
PASSAGE GATBOIS
RUE CHRETIEN DE TROYES
RUE DE RAMBOUILLET
AVENUE DAUMESNIL
RUE DU CHAROLAIS
Montgallet 300 metres / 330 yards
Bois de Vincennes 3 km / 2 miles
Dugommier 450 metres / 500 yards

TIPS FOR WALKERS

Starting point: *Bastille Metro*
Length: *1.6 miles (2.6 km).*
Getting there: *Bastille Metro is served by lines 1,8 and 5. Bus Nos. 20, 29, 65, 69, 76, 87, 91 and more. Get off at "Place de la Bastille" stop.*
Stopping off points: *The area is full of great cafés, bars and restaurants. Les Grandes Marches (Place de la Bastille) is a chic place for lunch, dinner or just coffee before you start or afterward. Nearby Rue de Lappe is lined with some fun bars. During the walk, take a break at the Viaduc Café (43 Viaduc des Arts).*

KEY

- Walk route
- Detour route
- Good viewing point
- Metro station

A 90-Minute Walk in Butte-aux-Cailles

This walk takes place in and around the Butte-aux-Cailles, a lovely "village" set on a hill that is all quiet streets, leafy squares and buzzy local bistrots. The area made history in 1783 when the first manned balloon flight touched down here. In the 1800s it was home to many workers from the small factories in the area and was one of the first areas to fight during the Paris Commune. However, it only really developed after 1910 and the architecture reflects the social ideals of the day – that individual houses and green spaces aid health.

de la Butte-aux-Cailles ⑪. Head up the street to the Place de la Commune de Paris ⑫, which today looks unremarkable yet was the site of a major battle in May 1871. Continue up the Rue de la Butte-aux-Cailles. Les Abeilles at 21 ⑬ is a curious store dedicated to bee-keeping and a delight for honey lovers. Pancakes in the old-fashioned crêperie Des Crêpes et des Cailles at 13 may satisfy if you are just peckish, but further down at 20 is the area's best-known restaurant Les Temps de Cerises ⑭. Fittingly, as it's only a few minutes' walk from the Place de la

Quiet, cobbled streets typify the Butte-aux-Cailles ⑪

Buttes-aux-Cailles

Take the "Auguste Blanqui" exit out of the Place d'Italie metro station ①, noting the Guimard decoration. Follow the bustling Rue Bobillot until you reach the Rue Paulin-Méry ② and take your first steps into the peace of the Butte-aux-Cailles. The contrast is surprising as you walk the quiet, narrow, cobbled streets with their old-fashioned street lamps. Note the lovely lilac painted shutters on 5 ③ and the trees in the small garden in front of the facing house. Continue straight ahead, cross over the Rue du Moulin-des-Près and turn left into the Rue Gérard past the red brick terraces and plant-decked villas ④. Keep on into the Rue Samson and then turn right onto the Rue Jonas and left onto the Rue des Cinq Diamants ⑤. The charming theater at 10 performs well-reviewed shows, while at 43 ⑥ Hansel et Gretel is a quaint old candy shop with a few tables and chairs. Those

interested in history may appreciate the Association des Amis de la Commune de Paris at 46 ⑦, which sells T-shirts, books and pamphlets on that bloody episode in Parisian history. Turn right into the Passage Barrault, a cobbled alleyway with ivy-covered walls and a countryside feel ⑧. At the end of the passage, turn left onto the Rue Barrault and continue up the street until the right turn onto the Rue Daviel. At 10 Rue Daviel the row of cottages known as "Little Alsace" ⑨ because of their chalet style are, in fact, one of the first public housing programs in Paris. Walk down the nearby Villa Daviel ⑩, a tiny street of terraces with small front gardens overflowing with greenery. Retrace your steps back up to the Rue Barrault, turn left and then right onto the artery of the area, the Rue

Road sign in the Butte aux Cailles area

13ᵉ Arrᵗ

RUE DE LA BUTTE AUX CAILLES

Theater, Rue des Cinq-Diamants ⑤

RUE DE TOLBIAC

BOULEVARD   AUGUST

Corvisart Ⓜ

CINQ DIAMANTS

RUE

PASSAGE BARRAULT

RUE BARRAULT

RUE ALPHAND

RUE DES

RUE SAMSON

RUE DE LA BUTTE AUX CAI

RUE DAVIEL

VILLA DAVIEL

RUE DE CHÉREAU

RUE DE POUY

RUE BOBILLOT

RUE DE L'ESPÉRANCE

MICHAL

RUE BUOT

PASSAGE BOITON

RUE MARTIN BERNARD

Le Temps des Cerises, full of bohemian atmosphere ⑭

TIPS FOR WALKERS

Starting point: Place de l'Italie metro.
Length: 1.6 miles (2.6 km).
Getting there: Start from the Place D'Italie metro via lines 5, 6 and 7. Or take buses Nos 27, 47, 57, 67 or 83 and get off at the stop "Place d'Italie".
Stopping-off Points: The Rue de la Butte-aux-Cailles is full of great cafés, bars and restaurants. Les Cailloux (No 58) is a chic place for lunch, Les Temps des Cerises (No 20) is very atmospheric, while L'Oisive Thé (No 10) is a lovely little tearoom. Chez Gladines (30 Rue des Cinq Diamants) is a great bet for a good lunch.

Crêpes from Des Crêpes et des Cailles

Commune. It's run as a co-operative and is also the unofficial neighborhood HQ. At the end of the road is the Place Paul Verlain ⑮. On the other side of the square is the red brick Art Nouveau swimming pool ⑯. Built in 1924, it houses one indoor pool and two lovely outdoor swimming areas. Take the steps in front of the building to find the modern fountain on the place ⑰. This is supplied by a local well 1,902 ft (580 m) deep, dating from 1863, and was refurbished in 2000. You may see locals lined up to fill plastic bottles here. Exit the square, take a right and then another right past the chic restaurant Chez Nathalie with its flowery terrace, which is always packed in summer, into the Rue Vandrezanne. Continue down this pedestrianized street into the passage Vandrezanne, a steep cobbled alleyway with antiquated lampposts ⑱. Cross over the Rue Moulinet and take the Rue Moulin des Pres until you come to the Rue Tolbiac. Cross this busy road then take a right stepping back into another time at the Square des Peupliers ⑲. Built in 1926, each house is different, reflecting the ideals of the time. All have pretty little gardens, most have lovely Art Nouveau porches and the ornate gilded lampposts are very special. Leave the Square des Peupliers and take a right back onto the Rue du Moulin-des-Pres. Head down the street, noting the interesting rough stone houses ⑳, straight past an unusual purple Art Nouveau-style house at 104 ㉑. Take a right onto the Rue Damesme, turn right into the Rue du Docteur Leray and then right again onto Rue Dieulafoy ㉒. Here are several unique, colorful cottages. At the end of the row, take a right onto the Rue Henri Pape, a left onto the Rue Damesme, walk up to the Rue Tolbiac and back out into modern, busy, Paris. Turn right and walk up to the metro Tolbiac ㉓.

Square des Peupliers, with its unique houses ⑲

KEY

••• Walk route

Ⓜ Metro station

0 meters   200

0 yards   200

TRAVELERS' NEEDS

WHERE TO STAY

Paris has more guest rooms than any other city in Europe. Its hotels vary from magnificent luxurious places like the Ritz (the French call them *palaces*) and exclusive establishments like L'Hôtel, where Oscar Wilde died beyond his means, to much simpler hotels in charming older parts of Paris. It is worth noting that *hôtel* does not always mean "hotel". It can also mean a town hall (*hôtel de ville*), hospital (*Hôtel-Dieu*) or a mansion.

We have inspected hotels in all price brackets and have selected a broad range, all of which are good value for your money. The listings on pp284–91 are organized by area, as in the sightseeing section of the guide, and according to hotel price. Other types of accommodation such as bed and breakfast rooms, efficiency apartments and hostels (*see pp278–9*) are also well worth considering, especially for visitors who are on a tight budget.

WHERE TO LOOK

Hotels in Paris tend to cluster by type in particular areas, with the river separating the business and leisure districts. Luxury hotels tend to be on the north side and *hôtels de charme* on the south side.

In the fashionable districts near the Champs-Elysées lie many of the grandest hotels in Paris, including the Royal Monceau, the Bristol, the Four Seasons George V, the Meurice and the Plaza Athénée. Several less well known but elegant hotels can be found in the residential and ambassadorial quarter near the Palais de Chaillot.

To the east, still on the Right Bank, in the regenerated Marais, a number of the old mansions and palaces have been converted into exceptionally attractive small hotels at reasonable prices. The nearby areas around Les Halles and the Rue St-Denis,

however, attract prostitutes and drug addicts. Just south of the Marais across the Seine, the Ile St-Louis and Ile de la Cité have several charming hotels.

The Left Bank covers some of the most popular tourist areas and has an excellent range of small hotels of great character. The atmosphere subtly changes from the much upgraded Latin Quarter and the chic and arty areas north and south of Boulevard St-Germain, to the rather shabby Boulevard itself and the staid institutional area toward Les Invalides and the Eiffel Tower. The hotels tend to reflect this.

Further from the center, Montparnasse has several large business hotels in high-rise blocks, and the Porte de Versailles area to the south is usually packed with trade fair participants. The station areas around Gare du Nord and Gare de Lyon offer a number of basic hotels (choose

Hôtel de Crillon (*see pp282, 285*)

carefully). Montmartre has one or two pleasant hotels if you don't mind the hilly location, but beware of hotels allegedly in Montmartre but actually in the red-light, sex-show district of Pigalle. If you are looking for a hotel in person, the best times for inspecting are late morning or mid-afternoon. If the hotels are full, try again after 6pm, when unclaimed provisional reservations become free. Don't rely on the impression of a hotel given by reception: ask to see the room offered, and if it isn't acceptable, ask to be shown another, if available. (For airport hotels *see p379.*)

HOTEL PRICES

Hotel prices aren't always cheaper in low season (mid-November to March or July and August) because fashion shows and other major events

The Hôtel du Louvre (*see p285*), between the Louvre and the Palais Royal

throughout the year can pack rooms, raising prices. However, in the older hotels differences in the size and position of rooms can have a marked effect on cost. Small rooms tend to be cheapest.

Twin rooms are slightly more expensive than doubles; single occupancy rates as high or nearly as high as for two people sharing (rates are nearly always quoted per room, not per person). Single rooms are rare and many are extremely poky or poorly equipped. Rooms without a bath tend to be about 20% cheaper than those with. You might find a half-board arrangement unnecessary with such a wide choice of good restaurants around.

It's always worth asking for a discount: you may get a corporate rate, for instance. In some hotels special deals are offered for students, families or senior citizens.

HIDDEN EXTRAS

By law, tax and service must be included in the price quoted or displayed at the reception desk or in the rooms. Tips are unnecessary other than for exceptional service – if the concierge reserves show tickets, for instance, or if the maid does some washing for you. However, before you make a reservation you should always establish whether breakfast is included in the price or not. Beware of extras such as drinks or snacks from

The Hôtel Meurice *(see p285)* in the Tuileries Quarter

a mini-bar, which will probably be pricey, as will laundry services, garage parking or telephone calls from your room – especially telephone calls made through the switchboard.

Exchange rates in hotels invariably tend to be lower than in a bank, so make sure you have enough cash to pay your bill unless you are paying by credit card or using traveler's checks.

HOTEL RATINGS

French hotels are classified by the tourist authorities into five broad categories: one to four stars, plus a four-star deluxe rating. Some very simple places are unclassified. Star ratings indicate something about the level of facilities you can expect (for example, any hotel with more than three stars should have an elevator). But the French rating system is no reliable guide to friendliness, cleanliness or tastefulness of the decor.

FACILITIES

Few Parisian hotels below a four-star rating have a restaurant, although there is nearly always a breakfast room. Quite a few hotel restaurants close in August. Many of the older hotels also lack a public lounge area. More modern or expensive hotels have correspondingly better facilities and generally some kind of bar. Inexpensive hotels may not have an elevator – significant when you are dragging suitcases upstairs.

Usually only the more expensive hotels have parking facilities. For exceptions to this rule, see the listings on pages 284–91. If you are driving you may prefer to stay in one of the peripheral motel-style chain hotels *(see pp279–80)*.

All but the very simplest of city hotels will have a telephone in the bedroom; many also have television. Business facilities (fax and internet) are now available in the grander hotels. Double beds *(grands lits)* are common, but you must specify whether or not you want one.

Four Seasons George V *(see p290)*

Statue in the Hôtel Relais Christine *(see pp283, 287)*

The Plaza Athénée *(see p291)* in Champs-Elysées

WHAT TO EXPECT

Many hotel beds still stick to the time-honored French bolster, a sausage-shaped headrest that can be uncomfortable if you are unused to it. If you prefer pillows, ask for *oreillers*. If you want to make sure you get a toilet, specify a *WC*, and if you want a bath, ask for a *bain*. Otherwise, a *cabinet de toilette* is just a basin and bidet, and *eau courante* means simply a basin with hot and cold running water. A duplex room is a suite on two floors.

The traditional French hotel breakfast of fresh coffee, croissants, jam and orange juice in Paris gradually changing into an elaborate buffet breakfast with cold meats and cheeses. Whatever the type, insist on an *orange pressée* (freshly squeezed orange juice) and not a *jus d'orange*, which will usually be from a can. Some of the luxury hotels are now such popular venues for breakfast that it is worth reserving a place in the breakfast area if you don't want to eat in your room. A pleasant alternative is to head for the nearest café where French workers are enjoying breakfast over a newspaper.

Checkout time is usually noon and if you stay longer you will pay for an extra day.

SPECIAL BREAKS

As Paris is such a popular destination with leisure as well as business travelers, weekend packages are rare. Providing there are no major events taking place, you can reduce costs by visiting in low season and negotiating a discount, or by seeking out an all-inclusive package.

TRAVELING WITH CHILDREN

Families with young children will often find they can share a room at no or very little extra cost, and some operators offer packages with this in mind. Few hotels refuse to accept children, though facilities specifically for children are not universal.

DISABLED TRAVELERS

Our information about wheelchair access to hotels was gathered by question-naire and therefore relies on the hotels' own assessment of their suitability. Not many are well geared for use by disabled visitors. The **Association des Paralysés de France** and the **Groupement pour l'Insertion des Personnes Handicapées Physiques (GIHP)** have pertinent information. *(For addresses see p367.)*

EFFICIENCY UNITS

A program called **Résidence Internationale de Paris** provides units in specially run apartment blocks. Some hotel-type facilities are available, but you pay extra for them. Prices vary from around 90€ a night for a small studio to over 300€ a night for an apartment for several people. Either contact

The quiet Hôtel des Grands Hommes *(see p287)*

Paris-Séjour-Réservation or get in touch with each *rési-dence* directly. The **Office du Tourisme et des Congrès de Paris** also provides a full list of *résidences*.

Efficiency accommodation is an increasingly popular alternative for staying in Paris. The better known agencies include **Allo Logement Temporaire, At Home In Paris, ASLOM, Paris Appartements Services** and **France Appartements. Good Morning Paris** and **France-Lodge** also arrange efficiency apartments, as well as being B&B agencies *(see*

Directory p280). All provide furnished apartments for stays from one week to six months, sometimes in the apartment of a Parisian who is abroad. Prices are comparable to the Résidence Internationale de Paris, sometimes slightly cheaper for the larger apartments.

STAYING IN PRIVATE HOMES

Bed and breakfast, that US and British phenomenon, is known as *chambre d'hôte* or *café-couette* ("coffee and a quilt"). B&B accommodation is available at moderate prices, between 35€ and 75€ for a double room per night. **Alcôve & Agapes** offers rooms in some enviable districts of Paris, all within walking distance of a metro station. It is worth asking about suites and rooms with a private lounge, kitchen or terrace. All homes are routinely inspected.

France-Lodge is a good-value agency specializing in long-stay room rentals and apartments. A registration fee of 15€ a year is payable but rentals are generally cheaper than with other agencies. **Good Morning Paris** provides guest rooms and tourist information. A two-night minimum stay is required when reserving *(for details see Directory p280)*.

CHAIN HOTELS

A mushroom crop of motel-style establishments on the outskirts of Paris now host large numbers of both business and leisure visitors.

The garden of the Relais Christine *(see p287)*

The very cheapest chains such as Formule 1, Première Class and Fast Hotel, really have nothing except price to recommend them. Further up the ladder are **Campanile, Ibis** and **Primevère**. These places are practical, relatively inexpensive and useful if you have a car, but lack any real

The Hôtel Prince de Galles Sheraton *(see p291)*

Parisian atmosphere or character. Many are in charmless locations on busy roads and may suffer from traffic noise. The newer motels of these chains are better equipped and much better decorated than the older ones. Several chains (**Sofitel**, **Novotel** and **Mercure**) are especially geared to business travelers, providing better facilities at higher prices; indeed some of the more central ones are positively luxurious. Reductions can make these hotels good value on the

weekends. Many of the hotels have restaurants attached. Most of the chains produce their own brochures, often with useful maps detailing the motel's precise location *(see Directory p280)*.

HOSTELS AND DORMITORY ACCOMMODATION

There are several hostel networks in Paris. **Maisons Internationales de la Jeunesse et des Etudiants (MIJE)** provides dormitory accommodation for the 18–30s in three splendid mansions in the Marais. There are no advance reservations (except for groups) – call at the central offices on the day.

The **Bureau Voyage Jeunesse (BVJ)** has two 'hotels' with double rooms and dormitory accommodation (23–28€ and 25€ respectively), with breakfast and nearly private bathrooms. Reservations cannot be made more than a two weeks in advance.

La Maison de l'UCRIF (Union des Centres de Rencontres Internationales de France) has nine centers around Paris with individual, shared and dormitory rooms. No age limit is imposed. Cultural and sports activities are available at some centers.

Fédération Unie des Auberges de Jeunesse (FUAJ) is a member of the International Youth Hostels Federation. There is no age limit at their two Paris hostels. *(For addresses see Directory p280.)*

The Hôtel Atala terrace *(see p290)*

DIRECTORY

OFFICE DU TOURISME

25 Rue des Pyramides 750001.
Tel 08 92 68 30 30.
See p367 for other branches.
www.parisinfo.com

AGENCIES

Paris-Séjour-Réservation
90 Ave des Champs-Elysées 75008.
Tel 01 53 89 10 50.
Fax 01 53 89 10 59.

Ely 12 12
5 Rue d'Artois 75008.
Tel 01 43 59 12 12.
www.ely1212.com

EFFICIENCY UNITS

Allo Logement Temporaire
64 Rue du Temple 75003.
Tel 01 42 72 00 06.
Fax 01 42 72 03 11.

At Home in Paris
16 Rue Médéric 75017.
Tel 01 42 12 40 40.
Fax 01 42 67 71 43.

ASLOM
6 Passge Duris 95020.
Tel 01 43 49 67 79.
www.aslom.com

France Appartements
97 Ave des Champs-Elysées 75008.
Tel 01 56 89 31 00.
www.rentapart.com

Paris Appartements Services
20 Rue Bachaumont 75002.
Tel 01 40 28 01 28.
Fax 01 40 28 92 01.
www.paris-apts.com

RESIDENCES DE TOURISME

Résidence Inter-nationale de Paris
44 Rue Louis Lumière 75020.
Tel 01 40 31 45 45.
www.residence-inter-paris.com

Les Citadines
27 Rue Esquirol 75013.
Tel 08 25 01 03 29.
www.citadines.com

Pierre et Vacances
10 Pl Charles-Dullin 75018.
Tel 01 42 57 14 55.
Fax 01 42 54 48 87.
www.pierre-vacances.fr

Résidence du Roy
8 Rue François-1er 75008.
Tel 01 42 89 59 59.
www.hroy.com

BED & BREAKFAST

Alcôve & Agapes
8bis Rue Coysevox 75018.
Tel 01 44 85 06 05.
Fax 01 44 85 06 14

France-Lodge
41, Rue La Fayette 75009.
Tel 01 53 20 09 09.
www.apartments-in-paris.com

Good Morning Paris
43 Rue Lacépède, 75005.
Tel 01 47 07 28 29.
Fax 01 47 07 44 45.

CHAIN HOTELS

Campanile
Tel 01 64 62 46 46
(central reservations).
www.campanile.fr

Ibis
Tel 08 03 88 22 22
(central reservations).
www.accorhotels.com

Primevère
Tel 08 00 12 12 12
(central reservations).
www.choicehotels.com

Royal Garden St-Honoré
218 Rue du Faubourg St-Honoré 75008.
Tel 01 49 53 03 03.
www.gtshparis.com

Hilton
18 Ave de Suffren 75015.
Tel 01 44 38 56 00.
www.hilton.com

Holiday Inn St-Germain-des-Prés
92 Rue de Vaugirard 75006.
Tel 01 49 54 87 00.
www.holiday-inn.com

Holiday Inn République
10 Pl de la République 75011.
Tel 01 43 14 43 50.
www.holiday-inn.com

Mercure Paris Bercy
77 Rue de Bercy 75012.
Tel 01 53 46 50 50.
www.mercure.com

Mercure Pont Bercy
6 Blvd Vincent Auriol 75013.
Tel 01 45 82 48 00.
www.mercure.com

Mercure Paris Montparnasse
20 Rue de la Gaîté 75014.
Tel 01 43 35 28 28.
www.mercure.com

Mercure Paris Tour-Eiffel
64 Blvd de Grenelle 75015.
Tel 01 45 78 90 00.
www.mercure.com

Mercure Paris Porte de Versailles
69 Blvd Victor 75015.
Tel 01 44 19 03 03.
www.mercure.com

Méridien Montparnasse
19 Rue du Commandant René Mouchotte 75014.
Tel 01 44 36 44 36.
www.lemeridien-montparnasse.com

Novotel Paris Bercy
85 Rue de Bercy 75012.
Tel 01 43 42 30 00.
www.novotel.com

Novotel Paris Les Halles
8 Pl Marguerite de Navarre 75001.
Tel 01 42 21 31 31.
www.novotel.com

Novotel Tour Eiffel
61 Quai de Grenelle 75015.
Tel 01 40 58 20 00.
www.novotel.com

Hotel Sofitel Scribe
1 Rue Scribe 75009.
Tel 01 44 71 24 24.
www.sofitel.com

Sofitel Paris Forum Rive Gauche
17 Blvd St-Jacques 75014.
Tel 01 40 78 79 80.
www.sofitel.com

Sofitel Paris La Défense Centre
34 Cours Michelet, 92060.
Tel 01 47 76 44 43.
www.sofitel.com

Sofitel Le Faubourg
15 Rue Boissy d'Anglas 75008.
Tel 01 44 94 14 14.
www.sofitel.com

Warwick Champs-Elysées
5 Rue de Berri 75008.
Tel 01 45 63 14 11.

HOSTELS

FUAJ – Centre National
27 Rue Pajol 75018.
Tel 01 44 89 87 27.
Fax 01 44 89 87 49.
www.fuaj.org

MIJE
Head Office: 11 Rue du Fauconnier 75004.
Tel 01 42 74 23 45.
Fax 01 40 27 81 64.

BVJ
20 Rue Jean-Jacques Rousseau 75001.
Tel 01 53 00 90 90.
Fax 01 53 00 90 91 or
44 Rue des Bernardins 75005.
Tel 01 43 29 34 80.

La Maison de l'UCRIF
27 Rue de Turbigo 75002.
Tel 01 40 26 57 64.
Fax 01 40 26 58 20.

CAMPING

Camping du Bois de Boulogne/Ile de France
Allée du Bord de l'Eau 75016.
Tel 01 45 24 30 00.
Fax 01 42 24 42 95.

Camping International de Jablines
Jablines-Annet 77450.
Tel 01 60 26 09 37.
Fax 01 60 26 43 33.

FFCC
78 Rue de Rivoli 75004.
Tel 01 42 72 84 08.

CAMPING

The only campsite in Paris itself is the **Camping du Bois de Boulogne/Ile de France** (around 9€–25€ per night). This well-equipped site next to the Seine is open all year but is usually full during the summer. Sites for tents, campers as well as rental of mobile homes are available. There are many other campsites in the surrounding region, some close to an RER line. The **Camping International de Jablines** (around 18€–23€ per night) is conveniently located just 5.5 miles (9km) from Disneyland Paris and a 25-minute RER train ride from central Paris. Details of other sites can be obtained from the Paris tourist office or from a booklet produced by the **Fédération Française de Camping-Caravanning (FFCC)** (see Directory p280).

RESERVATIONS

The busiest Paris tourist seasons are May, June, September and October, but special events such as fashion shows, trade fairs or major exhibitions can fill most rooms in Paris throughout the year. Disneyland Resort Paris has further increased the pressure to find accommodation, as many visitors choose to stay in the capital and commute to the park on the RER. July and August are quieter, as many Parisians are on their annual vacation. But the August shutdown of old is no longer the case – around half the hotels, restaurants and shops remain open.

If you have decided on a hotel, it is vital to reserve at least a month ahead as Paris is a popular destination. The hotels in the listings are among the best in their category and will fill particularly fast. Make a reservation six weeks in advance between May and October. The best way is to reserve directly with the hotel. If you make your initial inquiry by telephone, call during the day if possible – you are more likely to find staff authorized to take

Tourist information desk, Charles de Gaulle airport

reservations. During busy periods you must send confirmation of your reservation (websites or email addresses are provided where available).

If you prefer to use an agency, **Ely 12 12** and **Paris-Séjour-Réservation** can reserve hotels and other kinds of accommodation, sometimes even a barge along the Seine.

If you aren't too picky about where you stay, or if all the hotels are reportedly full, you can reserve via the **Office du Tourisme et des Congrès de Paris**, which offers an on-the-spot reservation service for a reasonable fee.

DEPOSITS

If you make a reservation by telephone you will be asked for either your credit card number (from which any cancellation fee may be deducted) or a deposit (arrhes). These arrhes can be as much as the price of a night's stay, but usually cost only about 15% of this. Pay your deposit by credit card or by sending an international money order. You can sometimes send an ordinary check for an amount equivalent to the deposit as evidence of your intention to keep the reservation. Usually the hotel will simply keep your foreign check as security until you arrive, then return it to you and give you one total bill when you leave. But do check with the hotel before sending an ordinary check. It's also perfectly acceptable in France to specify your choice of room

when you reserve.

Try to arrive at your hotel by 6pm on the day you have reserved, or at least telephone to say you will be late, otherwise you may well lose the room. A hotel that breaks a confirmed, prepaid booking is breaking a contract and the client is entitled to compensation of at least twice any deposit paid. If you have any problems, consult the Office du Tourisme.

TOURIST INFORMATION DESKS

You can reserve hotel rooms at all airport information desks but only in person and for the same day. The Gare de Lyon and the Tour Eiffel (seasonal) information desks provide a similar reservation arrangement for all forms of accommodation. Many Paris information desks also keep a complete list of city hotels and some reserve entertainment, excursions etc (see Practical Information p367).

USING THE LISTINGS

The hotels on pages 284–91 are organized according to area and price. All are centrally situated. The symbols after the hotel's address summarize the facilities it offers.

📋 air-conditioning in all rooms
🏋 gym/fitness facilities
🏊 swimming pool in hotel
🧒 children's facilities: baby/toddler cribs and babysitting service
🛗 elevator
🅿 hotel parking available
🍴 restaurant
🚫 no credit cards accepted

Price categories for a double room for one night including breakfast, tax and service:

€ under 90 euros
€€ 90–140 euros
€€€ 141–180 euros
€€€€ 181–260 euros
€€€€€ over 260 euros

Paris's Best: Hotels

Paris is famous for its hotels. It excels in all categories from the glittering opulent *palaces* (the top luxury hotels) to the *hôtels de charme*, full of character and romantic appeal, to the simpler good-value family hotels in quiet back streets. As a center of culture and fashion, the city has long been a mecca for the rich and famous, great and good from all walks of life. Not surprisingly, therefore, it can boast some of the most magnificent hotels in the world and has more than a thousand hotels in the inner city alone. Whatever the price level, however, the hotels in our listings *(see pp284–91)* all show that inimitable style and taste that Parisians bring to everything they do. These are a selection of the very best.

Bristol
In the chic heart of Paris, this epitomizes luxury. (See p290.)

Champs-Elysées

Chaillot Quarter

R I V E R   S E

Invalides and Eiffel Tower Quarter

Balzac
Small but stylish, this hotel exudes period charm. The restaurant, Pierre Gagnaire, is highly rated. (See p290.)

Hôtel de Crillon
One of the great palace *hotels, this was built for Louis XV.* (See p285.)

Plaza Athénée
In the heart of haute couture *Paris, this is the favorite haunt of the fashion world. Magnificent decor and a superb restaurant are the main attractions.* (See p291.)

Duc de St-Simon
Bedrooms overlook a leafy garden in this comfortable and peaceful hôtel de charme *situated in an 18th-century mansion south of the Seine.* (See p289.)

Le Grand Hôtel Intercontinental
Built for Napoleon III in 1862, this historic hotel has been patronized by the rich and famous from Mata Hari to Winston Churchill. (See p291.)

L'Hôtel
Best known as the last home of Oscar Wilde, this stylish hotel boasts rooms both impressive and slightly bizarre. One room was furnished and occupied by the music hall star Mistinguett. (See p287.)

Relais Christine
An oasis of calm in the hub of the city, this charming hotel offers traditional comforts such as a welcoming open fire in the drawing room. (See p287.)

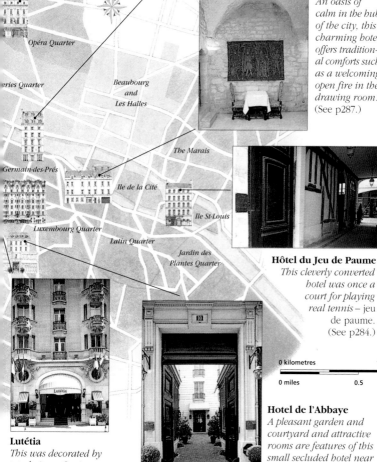

Opéra Quarter

eries Quarter

Beaubourg and Les Halles

Germain-des-Prés

The Marais

Ile de la Cité

Ile St-Louis

Luxembourg Quarter

Latin Quarter

Jardin des Plantes Quarter

Hôtel du Jeu de Paume
This cleverly converted hotel was once a court for playing real tennis – jeu de paume. (See p284.)

| 0 kilometres | 1 |
| 0 miles | 0.5 |

Hotel de l'Abbaye
A pleasant garden and courtyard and attractive rooms are features of this small secluded hotel near the Jardins du Luxembourg. (See p286.)

Lutétia
This was decorated by top designer Sonia Rykiel. (See p287.)

Choosing a Hotel

The choice of hotels listed in the following pages have all been individually inspected and assessed specially for this guide. The list covers all the areas and price categories with additional information to help you choose a hotel that best meets your needs. Hotels within the same category are listed alphabetically.

PRICE CATEGORIES
For a standard double room per night including breakfast and necessary charges:

€ under 90 euros
€€ 190–140 euros
€€€ 141–180 euros
€€€€ 181–260 euros
€€€€€ over 260 euros

THE MARAIS

Hôtel Acacias Hôtel de Ville   €€

20 Rue du Temple, 75004 **Tel** 01 48 87 07 70 **Fax** 01 48 87 17 20 **Rooms** 33   **Map** 13 C1

From the hotel it's a short walk to Notre Dame, the Louvre and the banks of Seine. Solid wooden furniture and fine prints make for a charming atmosphere in the rooms, all of which are individually decorated. Services also include Wi-Fi facilities. **www.acacias-hotel.com**

Hôtel de la Bretonnerie   €€

22 Rue Ste-Croix de la Bretonnerie, 75004 **Tel** 01 48 87 77 63 **Fax** 01 42 77 26 78 **Rooms** 29   **Map** 13 C3

Carved stone walls and an arched dining room in the basement are some of the charming features of Hôtel de la Bretonnerie, housed in a 17th-century mansion. One of the most comfortable hotels in the area, it has spacious bedrooms with wooden beams and antique furniture. Service is warm and friendly. **www.bretonnerie.com**

Hôtel du Bourg Tibourg   €€€

19 Rue du Bourg Tibourg, 75004 **Tel** 01 42 78 47 39 **Fax** 01 40 29 07 00 **Rooms** 30   **Map** 13C

This stylish spot was decorated by top interior designer Jacques Garcia and is extremely popular with fashionable visitors to Paris. Rooms are opulent and all bathrooms are fully clad in black marble. The beautiful interior courtyard is a pleasant surprise. **www.hotelbourgtibourg.com**

Hôtel du Septieme Art   €€€

20 Rue St-Paul, 75004 **Tel** 01 44 54 85 00 **Fax** 01 42 77 69 10 **Rooms** 23   **Map** 14 D4

A film buff's dream, this charming little spot is stuffed full of mementoes of the movies. The rooms are clean and all have a cinematic touch, from advertising posters to mini-statuettes of Marilyn Monroe. Staff are very friendly too. An ideal place to retire after a long day of sightseeing. **www.hotel7art.com**

St-Merry   €€€

78 Rue de la Verrerie, 75004 **Tel** 01 42 78 14 15 **Fax** 01 40 29 06 82 **Rooms** 12   **Map** 13 B3

A historic hotel which was the presbytery of the adjoining church in the 17th century and later became a bordello. It is today a simply lovely place to stay. Furnished in Gothic style, note the flying buttresses crossing room 9. **www.hotelmarais.com**

St-Paul-le-Marais   €€€

8 Rue de Sévigné, 75004 **Tel** 01 48 04 97 27 **Fax** 01 48 87 37 04 **Rooms** 28   **Map** 14 D3

Close to the historic Place des Vosges, this hotel has wooden beams and old stone, although the furnishings are simple and modern. Ask for bedrooms facing the courtyard to avoid the noise of traffic coming from the Rue de Sévigné. **www.hotelsaintpaullemarais.com**

Hôtel des Deux-Iles   €€€€

59 Rue St-Louis-en-l'Ile, 75004 **Tel** 01 43 26 13 35 **Fax** 01 43 29 60 25 **Rooms** 17   **Map** 13 C4

It's a privilege to be able to stay on the Ile St-Louis, and this converted 17th-century mansion offers an affordable way to do so. Here the atmosphere is peaceful, the small bedrooms are attractive and the lounge has a real fire. **www.deuxiles-paris-hotel.com**

Hôtel du Jeu de Paume   €€€€

54 Rue St-Louis-en-l'Ile, 75004 **Tel** 01 43 26 14 18 **Fax** 01 40 46 02 76 **Rooms** 30   **Map** 13 C4

Standing on the site of a former real tennis court, the hotel has been skillfully converted into a warm, elegant place to stay. Features include a glass-walled elevator, wooden beams, old terracotta paving, a sauna and several charming duplex rooms. **www.hoteljeudepaume.com**

Pavillon de la Reine   €€€€€

28 Pl des Vosges, 75003 **Tel** 01 40 29 19 19 **Fax** 01 40 29 19 20 **Rooms** 56   **Map** 14 D3

Set back from the marvelous Place des Vosges, the Pavillon de la Reine is the best hotel in the Marais. Incredibly romantic, the courtyard is a haven of peace and the bedrooms are sumptuous and furnished with excellent reproduction antiques. **www.pavillon-de-la-reine.com**

Key to Symbols *see back cover flap*

BEAUBOURG AND LES HALLES

Hôtel Roubaix €

6 Rue Grenetta, 75003 **Tel** *01 42 72 89 91* **Fax** *01 42 72 58 79* **Rooms** *53* **Map** *13B*

Hôtel Roubaix is pleasantly old-fashioned and inexpensive in an area with few good places to stay. The owners are exceptionally friendly and the rooms are clean, if a little shabby. The hotel is popular with return guests, so be sure to reserve a room in advance. **www.hotel-de-roubaix.com**

TUILERIES QUARTER

Hôtel St-Honoré €

85 Rue St-Honoré, 75001 **Tel** *01 42 36 20 38* **Fax** *01 42 21 44 08* **Rooms** *29* **Map** *12 F2*

Close to Concorde, Tuileries, Louvre and Palais-Royal, the St-Honoré has an attractive green façade. The rooms, recently renovated and equipped with all modern amenities, are extremely well kept. Very good value considering the excellent location. A few rooms have been designed for families. **www.parishotel.com**

Brighton €€€

218 Rue de Rivoli, 75001 **Tel** *01 47 03 61 61* **Fax** *01 42 60 41 78* **Rooms** *65* **Map** *12 D1*

A real insiders' location, the Brighton provides a much-sought after Rivoli address without the sky-high prices. The bedrooms have beautiful, high ceilings and large windows that look out either on to the Jardin des Tuileries or on to the courtyard. **www.esprit-de-france.com**

Clarion St-James et Albany €€€€€

202 Rue de Rivoli, 75001 **Tel** *01 44 58 43 21* **Fax** *01 44 58 43 11* **Rooms** *200* **Map** *12 E1*

This quiet and clean hotel is currently undergoing a much–needed renovation to do away with its aura of faded grandeur. It is perfectly situated in the heart of Paris, across from the Tuileries gardens, and boasts a charming spa and swimming pool area. **www.clarionstjames.com**

Hôtel Costes €€€€€

239 Rue St Honoré, 75001 **Tel** *01 42 44 50 00* **Fax** *01 42 44 50 01* **Rooms** *82* **Map** *12 D1*

One of the most fashionable places to stay in Paris, the Costes is a favorite with models and movie stars. A sumptuous affair, it is designed to resemble a Second Empire palace. The balcony rooms are the most in demand. In summer, eat in the Italianate courtyard. **www.hotelcostes.com**

Hôtel de Crillon €€€€€

10 Pl de la Concorde, 75008 **Tel** *01 44 71 15 00* **Fax** *01 44 71 15 02* **Rooms** *147* **Map** *11 C1*

With its magnificent location on the glittering Place de la Concorde, the Crillon offers unsurpassed elegance. The hotel has a fine Royal Suite and terrace, a sublime dining room and a fashionable bar designed by Sonia Rykiel. **www.crillon.com**

Hôtel du Louvre €€€€€

Pl André Malraux, 75001 **Tel** *01 44 58 38 38* **Fax** *01 44 58 38 01* **Rooms** *177* **Map** *12 E1*

The first luxury hotel in France was built in 1855 by order of Napoleon III. The lavish rooms have spectacular views: the Pissarro Suite is where the artist painted his view of Place du Théâtre Français, while if you reserve room 551 you can admire the opera house from your bath! **www.hoteldulouvre.com**

Intercontinental €€€€€

3 Rue de Castiglione, 75001 **Tel** *01 44 77 11 11* **Fax** *01 44 77 14 60* **Rooms** *445* **Map** *12 D1*

This elegant late 19th-century hotel is situated between the Jardin des Tuileries and the Place Vendôme. It was designed by Charles Garnier, architect of the Paris Opéra. Bedrooms are quiet – the best overlook one of the courtyards. **www.paris-ic-intercontinental.com**

Meurice €€€€€

228 Rue de Rivoli, 75001 **Tel** *01 44 58 10 10* **Fax** *01 44 58 10 15* **Rooms** *160* **Map** *12 D1*

The Meurice is a perfect example of successful restoration, with excellent replicas of the original plasterwork and furnishings. The staff here are unstintingly helpful and the hotel offers personalized shopping and art buying tours. There is also a top spa. **www.meuricehotel.com**

Regina €€€€€

2 Pl des Pyramides, 75001 **Tel** *01 42 60 31 10* **Fax** *01 40 15 95 16* **Rooms** *120* **Map** *12 E1*

Surprisingly, the Regina is not known to many tourists, even though it is popular with the media. The wood detail in the lounge is stunning Art Nouveau and many movies have been shot here. Some of the rooms have superb views. **www.regina-hotel.com**

Ritz

€€€€€

15 Pl Vendôme, 75001 **Tel** *01 43 16 30 30* **Fax** *01 43 16 31 78* **Rooms** *162* **Map** *6 D5*

A legendary address, the Ritz still lives up to its reputation, combining elegance and decadence. The Louis XVI furniture and chandeliers are all originals, and the floral arrangements are works of art. The Hemingway Bar is home to the glitterati. **www.ritzparis.com**

ST-GERMAIN-DES-PRÈS

Hôtel du Globe

€

15 Rue des Quatre-Vents, 75006 **Tel** *01 46 33 62 69* **Fax** *01 46 33 62 69* **Rooms** *15* **Map** *12 F4*

A 17th-century building right by the Jardin du Luxembourg, with excellent accommodation. Antique furniture and colorful fabrics liven up the guestrooms. Breakfast is brought to your room. Extremely popular, so reserve in advance. **www.globe-paris-hotel.com**

Grand Hôtel des Balcons

€€

3 Rue Casimir Delavigne, 75006 **Tel** *01 46 34 78 50* **Fax** *01 46 34 06 27* **Rooms** *50* **Map** *12 F5*

Embellished with Art Nouveau features, this hotel has a beautiful hall with stained-glass windows and striking 19th-century-style lamps and wood paneling. Most guestrooms, quiet and well-decorated, enjoy a balcony. High-speed Internet access with Wi-Fi available. **www.balcons.com**

Hôtel de Lille

€€

40 Rue de Lille, 75007 **Tel** *01 42 61 29 09* **Fax** *01 42 61 53 97* **Rooms** *20* **Map** *12 D2*

The jewel-like Hôtel de Lille is situated near the Orsay and Louvre museums in the heart of Faubourg St-Germain. The modern, standard bedrooms are small and the bar is minute. There is a charming lounge in the arched basement. **www.hotel-paris-ville.com**

Hôtel du Quai Voltaire

€€

19 Quai Voltaire, 75007 **Tel** *01 42 61 50 91* **Fax** *01 42 61 62 26* **Rooms** *33* **Map** *12 D2*

Overlooking the river, this hotel was once the favorite of Blondin, Baudelaire and Pissarro, and has featured in several movies. Bedrooms on the quay are better avoided, as they suffer from traffic noise. Higher floors are quieter, though, and the views are superb. **www.quaivoltaire.fr**

Hôtel d'Angleterre

€€€

44 Rue Jacob, 75006 **Tel** *01 42 60 34 72* **Fax** *01 42 60 16 93* **Rooms** *27* **Map** *12 E3*

Once the British Embassy, the Hôtel d'Angleterre has retained many of the original features, including the fine old staircase, the exquisite garden and the salon mantelpiece. Bedrooms are individually decorated, many have exposed beams and wonderful four-poster beds. **www.hotel-dangleterre.com**

Hôtel des Marronniers

€€€

21 Rue Jacob, 75006 **Tel** *01 43 25 30 60* **Fax** *01 40 46 83 56* **Rooms** *37* **Map** *12 E3*

Situated between a courtyard and a garden, this hotel provides perfect peace. The decor is unremarkable, but bedrooms on the fourth floor, garden side provide very special views over the Parisian rooftops and the St-Germain-des-Prés church steeple. **www.paris-hotel-marronniers.com**

Hôtel des Sts-Pères

€€€

65 Rue des Sts-Pères, 75006 **Tel** *01 45 44 50 00* **Fax** *01 45 44 90 83* **Rooms** *39* **Map** *12 E3*

The hotel occupies one of the old aristocratic mansions of St-Germain-des-Prés. The lounge bar is very popular with authors from the publishing houses nearby. The bedrooms are quiet and roomy – the best has an outstanding ceiling fresco. **www.espritfrance.com**

Hôtel de Fleurie

€€€€

32/34 Rue Grégoire de Tours, 75006 **Tel** *01 53 73 70 00* **Fax** *01 53 73 70 20* **Rooms** *29* **Map** *12 F4*

The statue-filled façade is enough to make one want to stay in this welcoming, family-run hotel. Inside, the woodwork and white stone create the same light feel, as do the bedrooms, all of which are beautifully decorated, with well-equipped bathrooms. **www.hotel-de-fleurie.tm.fr**

Hôtel de l'Abbaye St-Germain

€€€€

10 Rue Cassette, 75006 **Tel** *01 45 44 38 11* **Fax** *01 45 48 07 86* **Rooms** *44* **Map** *12 D5*

A 17th-century abbey, just steps from the Jardin du Luxembourg, this charming hotel has been a preferred hideout for artists and writers. Its finely furnished guestrooms and apartments have been tastefully done up and provided with modern facilities. **www.hotel-abbaye.com**

Lenox

€€€€

9 Rue de l'Université, 75007 **Tel** *01 42 96 10 95* **Fax** *01 42 61 52 83* **Rooms** *34* **Map** *12 D3*

The charm of the Lenox lies in its simplicity and literary history – T. S. Elliot, Ezra Pound and James Joyce all lived here. The staff are extremely friendly and the cocktail bar is lovely. The rooms are impeccably decorated. The hotel enjoys a great location in the heart of St-Germain-des-Prés. **www.lenoxsaintgermain.com**

Key to Price Guide *see p284* **Key to Symbols** *see back cover flap*

L'Hôtel

  €€€€€

13 Rue des Beaux-Arts, 75006 **Tel** *01 44 41 99 00* **Fax** *01 43 25 64 81* **Rooms** *20*

Map *12 E3*

A riot of exuberance and opulence, this Jacques Garcia designed hotel is gloriously decadent. Each room is different, the hotel's most famous one is the Oscar Wilde suite, where the author died and which boasts period furnishings. There's also a beautiful spa. **www.l-hotel.com**

Lutétia

 €€€€€

45 Blvd Raspail, 75006 **Tel** *01 49 54 46 46* **Fax** *01 49 54 46 00* **Rooms** *230*

Map *12 D4*

The Lutétia is a mainstay of glamour on the south side of the river. The building is partly Art Nouveau and partly Art Deco, and has been restored throughout. Publishers and chic shoppers are regular customers in the restaurant. Convenient location. **www.lutetia-paris.com**

Montalembert

 €€€€€

3 Rue de Montalembert, 75007 **Tel** *01 45 49 68 68* **Fax** *01 45 49 69 49* **Rooms** *56*

Map *12 D3*

Situated in the heart of the publishing district, this fashionable hotel combines modernity and timeless elegance. The bedrooms boast fine wood and designer fabrics with excellent quality linen sheets, towels and bathrobes. The eighth-floor suites have good views. Wi-Fi facilities are provided. **www.montalembert.com**

Relais Christine

€€€€€

3 Rue Christine, 75006 **Tel** *01 40 51 60 80* **Fax** *01 40 51 60 81* **Rooms** *51*

Map *12 F4*

Always full, the Relais Christine is the epitome of the *hôtel de charme*. It is part of the cloister of a 16th-century abbey and is a romantic haven of peace. The bedrooms are bright and spacious, especially the duplex rooms. Wi-Fi facilities are available. **www.relais-christine.com**

LATIN QUARTER

Esmeralda

€

4 Rue St-Julien-le-Pauvre, 75005 **Tel** *01 43 54 19 20* **Fax** *01 40 51 00 68* **Rooms** *19*

Map *13 A4*

The much-loved bohemian Esmeralda lies in the heart of the Latin Quarter. With old stone walls and beamed ceilings, its charm has seduced the likes of Terence Stamp and Serge Gainsbourg. The best rooms overlook Notre-Dame. No breakfast provided.

Hôtel des Grandes Ecoles

 €€

75 Rue Cardinal Lemoine, 75005 **Tel** *01 43 26 79 23* **Fax** *01 43 25 28 15* **Rooms** *51*

Map *13 B5*

This hotel is a cluster of three small houses around a beautiful garden, where you can breakfast in good weather. The rooms are all comfortable and furnished with traditional 18th-century-style floral wallpaper, some open onto the courtyard. Internet access available. **www.hotel-grandes-ecoles.com**

Hôtel des Grands Degrès de Notre Dame

€€

10 Rue des Grands Degrès, 75005 **Tel** *01 55 42 88 88* **Fax** *01 40 46 95 34* **Rooms** *10*

Map *13 B4*

An exceptionally friendly place to stay. The staff are genuinely welcoming and the wood paneling and oak beams around the building make it even more special. Lovely, very clean bedrooms with Internet access available. The Bar Restaurant and Tea Room serves great food at a low price. **www.lesdegreshotel.com**

Hôtel de Notre-Dame

€€€

19 Rue Maître Albert, 75006 **Tel** *01 43 26 79 00* **Fax** *01 46 33 50 11* **Rooms** *34*

Map *13 B5*

The picturesque Hôtel de Notre-Dame overlooks Notre-Dame cathedral and the Seine on one side and the Panthéon on the other. The furnishings are functional, but some rooms have beams or an old stone wall. The main appeal here is the location. The hotel has its own sauna and Wi-Fi access. **www.hotel-paris-notredame.com**

Hôtel des Grands Hommes

 €€€€

17 Pl du Panthéon, 75005 **Tel** *01 46 34 19 60* **Fax** *01 43 26 67 32* **Rooms** *31*

Map *17 A1*

Teachers at the Sorbonne frequent this quiet family hotel close to the Jardin du Luxembourg. It boasts a great view of the Panthéon from the attic rooms on the upper floor. The bedrooms are comfortable. Wi-Fi services available. **www.hoteldesgrandshommes.com**

Hôtel du Panthéon

€€€€

19 Pl du Panthéon, 75005 **Tel** *01 43 54 32 95* **Fax** *01 43 26 64 65* **Rooms** *36*

Map *17 A1*

This hotel is managed by the same family as the Hôtel des Grands Hommes: the welcome is equally warm and the decor similarly classical. Extra romance and luxury can be found in room 33 with its divine four-poster bed. Wi-Fi available in the reception room only. **www.hoteldupantheon.com**

Hôtel Residence Hotel IV

 €€€€

50 Rue des Bernardins, 75005 **Tel** *01 44 41 31 81* **Fax** *01 46 33 93 22* **Rooms** *13*

Map *13 B5*

Overlooking a pretty park square and with window boxes full of geraniums in season, this hotel is a real jewel. Bedrooms are bright and airy, some of the larger rooms have attached kitchens and there is also an apartment for four people available. Wi-Fi services provided. Very quiet for the area. **www.residencehenri4.com**

LUXEMBOURG QUARTER

Hôtel Récamier
3 bis Pl St-Sulpice, 75006 **Tel** *01 43 26 04 89* **Fax** *01 46 33 27 73* **Rooms** *30*   €€

Map *12 E4*

Hotel Récamier, which is situated on the quiet Place St-Sulpice, is a family hotel with an air of old-fashioned Parisian charm. The hotel was constructed in 1905 and remains a favorite both with writers and Left Bank tourists. Bedrooms overlooking the square have lovely views.

Aviatic
105 Rue de Vaugirard, 75006 **Tel** *01 53 63 25 50* **Fax** *01 53 63 25 55* **Rooms** *43*   €€€€

Map *12 E5*

True to its Parisian past and longstanding family hotel tradition, the much-loved Aviatic combines bohemian style with modern comforts. The rooms are individually decorated with charming pieces found at local flea markets and warm, bright textiles. Parking is available for 23 euros per day. **www.aviatic.fr**

MONTPARNASSE

Hôtel Apollon Montparnasse
91 Rue Ouest, 75014 **Tel** *01 43 95 62 00* **Fax** *01 43 95 62 10* **Rooms** *33*   €€

Map *15 C3*

Close to the Parc des Expositions of the Porte de Versailles, the Apollon Montparnasse is decorated with Grecian statues, fine furnishings and lots of peach. You can get simple, well-equipped guestrooms. Parking is available for 12 euros per day. The hotel also provides Wi-Fi facilities. **www.apollon-montparnasse.com**

Hôtel Delambre
35 Rue Delambre, 75014 **Tel** *01 43 20 66 31* **Fax** *01 45 38 91 76* **Rooms** *30*   €€

Map *16 D2*

Located a few steps away from Montparnasse cemetery, and close to the Jardin de Luxembourg and Latin Quarter, this hotel stylishly mixes modern and classical styles. Guestrooms are simply furnished with all modern amenities. **www.hoteldelambre.com**

Ferrandi
92 Rue du Cherche-Midi, 75006 **Tel** *01 42 22 97 40* **Fax** *01 45 44 89 97* **Rooms** *42*   €€€

Map *15 C1*

The Rue du Cherche-Midi is well-known to lovers of antiques. The Hôtel Ferrandi is a quiet hotel with a fireplace in the lounge and comfortable bedrooms filled with dark wood and decorated in warm tones. Four-poster beds in some rooms. **www.123france.com**

Ste-Beuve
9 Rue Ste Beuve, 75006 **Tel** *01 45 48 20 07* **Fax** *01 45 48 67 52* **Rooms** *22*   €€€

Map *16 D1*

The Ste-Beuve is a small, carefully restored hotel for aesthetes and habitués of the Rive Gauche galleries. There is a fireplace in the hall, the rooms are pleasantly decorated in pastel shades and there are several classic, contemporary paintings. **www.paris-hotel-charme.com**

Villa des Artistes
9 Rue de la Grande Chaumière, 75006 **Tel** *01 43 26 60 86* **Fax** *01 43 54 73 70* **Rooms** *59*   €€€

Map *16 D2*

The Villa des Artistes aims to recreate Montparnasse's artistic heyday when Modigliani, Beckett and Fitzgerald were all visitors here. The bedrooms are clean, but the main draw is the large patio garden and fountain, where you can breakfast in peace. **www.villa-artistes.com**

Le Saint-Grégoire
43 Rue de l'Abbé Grégoire, 75006 **Tel** *01 45 48 23 23* **Fax** *01 45 48 33 95* **Rooms** *20*   €€€€

Map *11 C5*

Le Saint-Grégoire is a fashionable townhouse hotel with immaculately decorated bedrooms and 19th-century furnishings. At the center of the drawing room is a charming fireplace with a real fire. Reserve a room with a delightful private terrace. Parking costs 13 euros a day. **www.lesaintgregoire.com**

INVALIDES AND EIFFEL TOWER QUARTER

Grand Hôtel Levêque
29 Rue Cler, 75007 **Tel** *01 47 05 49 15* **Fax** *01 45 50 49 36* **Rooms** *50*   €€

Map *10 F3*

On a street with a quaint fruit-and-vegetable market, the Levêque lies between the Eiffel Tower and the Invalides. The great location isn't the only attraction – guestrooms are well-kept and the hotel also provides Internet facilities. **www.hotel-leveque.com**

Key to Price Guide *see p284* **Key to Symbols** *see back cover flap*

Hôtel de Varenne

44 Rue de Bourgogne, 75007 **Tel** *01 45 51 45 55* **Fax** *01 45 51 86 63* **Rooms** *24*

€€

Map *11 B2*

Beyond its severe façade, this hotel conceals a narrow courtyard garden where guests breakfast in the summer. The bedrooms, recently refurbished in elegant Louis XVI or Empire style, are impeccable. The hotel is popular with French government officials. **www.hoteldevarenne.com**

Hôtel Bourgogne et Montana

3 Rue de Bourgogne, 75007 **Tel** *01 45 51 20 22* **Fax** *01 45 56 11 98* **Rooms** *32*

€€€

Map *11 B2*

Situated in front of the Assemblée Nationale, the hotel has an air of sobriety. Features include a mahogany bar, an old elevator and a circular hall with pink marble columns. The bedrooms were recently refurbished in an aristocratic style. Extremely stylish. **www.bourgogne-montana.com**

Hôtel de Suède St-Germain

31 Rue Vaneau, 75007 **Tel** *01 47 05 00 08* **Fax** *01 47 05 69 27* **Rooms** *40*

€€€

Map *11 B4*

Located near the Orsay and Rodin museums, the Hôtel de Suède St-Germain offers elegant rooms, decorated in late 18th-century styles in pale colors and the owners' welcome is exceptionally warm. Deluxe rooms offer a view over the park. A lovely little garden to breakfast in completes the picture. **www.hoteldesuede.com**

Eiffel Park Hôtel

17 bis Rue Amélie, 75007 **Tel** *01 45 55 10 01* **Fax** *01 47 05 28 68* **Rooms** *36*

€€€€

Map *10 F3*

In the heart of the Champs de Mars, the charming Eiffel Park Hôtel has been entirely renovated. It offers individually designed guestrooms with intricate wallpaper in some and exotic furniture in others. On the top floor is a breakfast terrace. Wi-Fi facilities provided. **www.eiffelpark.com**

Duc de St-Simon

14 Rue de St-Simon, 75007 **Tel** *01 44 39 20 20* **Fax** *01 45 48 68 25* **Rooms** *34*

€€€€€

Map *11 C3*

The Hôtel Duc de St-Simon is justifiably one of the most sought-after hotels on the south side of the Seine. A charming 18th-century mansion furnished with antiques, it lives up to its aristocratic pretensions. **www.hotelducdesaintsimon.com**

CHAILLOT QUARTER

Costes K

81 Ave Kléber, 75016 **Tel** *01 44 05 75 75* **Fax** *01 44 05 74 74* **Rooms** *83*

€

Map *4 D5*

This hotel, not to be confused with the more expensive Hôtel Costes, is situated steps from the Eiffel Tower. A piece of modern art by Spanish architect Ricardo Bofill, who used sycamore, stucco, marble and stainless steel in the construction. Cool Asian interiors for the guestrooms. **www.hotelcostesk.com**

Hameau de Passy

48 Rue de Passy, 75016 **Tel** *01 42 88 47 55* **Fax** *01 42 30 83 72* **Rooms** *32*

€€

Map *9 B3*

In the heart of the residential quarter of Passy, a stone's throw from the Eiffel Tower and the Trocadero, Hameau de Passy lies in a private lane, which is an oasis of greenery. Rooms overlook the garden. Breakfast can be served in your room upon request. **www.hameaudepassy.com**

Hôtel du Bois

11 Rue du Dôme, 75016 **Tel** *01 45 00 31 96* **Fax** *01 45 00 90 05* **Rooms** *41*

€€€

Map *4 D5*

Two minutes from the Arc de Triomphe and the Champs Elysées, Hôtel du Bois is ideal for haute-couture boutique lovers. Behind a typically Parisian façade, is an interior exuding charm – Georgian furniture in the lounge, thick patterned carpeting and fine prints in the bedrooms. **www.hoteldubois.com**

Hôtel de Banville

166 Blvd Berthier, 75017 **Tel** *01 42 67 70 16* **Fax** *01 44 40 42 77* **Rooms** *38*

€€€€

Map *4 D1*

This charming 1930s hotel was a family house, and it has retained something of a family atmosphere. There is a grand piano in the lobby and live music on Tuesday evenings. The bedrooms are very comfortable and the superior rooms are stunning. **www.hotelbanville.com**

Concorde La Fayette

3 Pl du Général Koenig, 75017 **Tel** *01 40 68 50 68* **Fax** *01 40 68 50 43* **Rooms** *950*

€€€€€

Map *3 C2*

The formulaic Concorde La Fayette with its fascinating egg-shaped tower is thoroughly high-tech. It has numerous facilities, including a fitness club, a bar on the 33rd floor, restaurants, a shopping gallery, and identical bedrooms with some absolutely splendid views. **www.concorde-lafayette.com**

Raphaël

17 Ave Kléber, 75016 **Tel** *01 53 64 32 00* **Fax** *01 53 64 32 01* **Rooms** *85*

€€€€€

Map *4 D4*

The epitome of discreet elegance, movie stars come here to be sheltered from the paparazzi. The decor is opulent and the roof terrace bar is the loveliest in Paris and extremely popular with the jet set. There are amazing views of the city and its principal monuments illuminated at night. **www.raphael-hotel.com**

Square

3 Rue de Boulainvilliers, 75016 **Tel** 01 44 14 91 90 **Fax** 01 44 14 91 99 **Rooms** 22   **Map** 9 A4

An exceptional hotel, the curvy granite façade hides 22 rooms and suites furnished with exotic fabrics and woods. The hotel boasts a fashionable restaurant and nightclub and, most unusually, a small but well-stocked modern art gallery. **www.hotelsquare.com**

St-James

43 Ave Bugeaud, 75016 **Tel** 01 44 05 81 81 **Fax** 01 44 05 81 82 **Rooms** 48   **Map** 3 B5

The St-James occupies a mansion with a small park near the Avenue Foch and the Bois de Boulogne. Reminiscent of a gentleman's club, guests here become "temporary members" and a token fee is included in the room price. Aristocratic atmosphere. **www.saint-james-paris.com**

Villa Maillot

143 Ave de Malakoff, 75016 **Tel** 01 53 64 52 52 **Fax** 01 45 00 60 61 **Rooms** 42   **Map** 3 C4

Conveniently situated for Porte Maillot and La Défense, the hotel was once an embassy and remains suitably refined with delightful Art-Deco style furnishings. The rooms have large beds, concealed kitchenettes and marble bathrooms. A new spa area offers massages. **www.lavillamaillot.fr**

CHAMPS-ELYSÉES

Atala

10 Rue Chateaubriand, 75008 **Tel** 01 45 62 01 62 **Fax** 01 42 25 66 38 **Rooms** 48   **Map** 4 E4

Situated in a quiet street near the Champs-Elysées, the Atala's rooms overlook a tranquil garden with tall trees. The bedrooms are functional rather than charming, so reserve a room on the eighth floor with spectacular views of the Eiffel Tower. **www.hotelatala.com**

Résidence Lord Byron

5 Rue Chateaubriand, 75008 **Tel** 01 43 59 89 98 **Fax** 01 42 89 46 04 **Rooms** 31   **Map** 4 E4

Close to the Etoile, the Résidence Lord Byron is a discreet, small hotel with a courtyard garden for breakfast. Its bright bedrooms are quiet but small; if you want more space, ask for a salon bedroom or a ground-floor room. **www.escapade-paris.com**

Balzac

6 Rue Balzac, 75008 **Tel** 01 44 35 18 00 **Fax** 01 44 35 18 05 **Rooms** 70   **Map** 4 F4

The Balzac is known mainly for its restaurant, run by Pierre Gagnaire. But this is more than just a restaurant with rooms and deserves to be visited for its own sake. Philip Starck's "Bar à Cigares" is exceptional. **www.hotelbalzac.com**

Bristol

112 Rue du Faubourg-St-Honoré, 75008 **Tel** 01 53 43 43 00 **Fax** 01 53 43 43 01 **Rooms** 180   **Map** 5 A4

One of Paris's finest hotels, the Bristol's large rooms are sumptuously decorated with antiques and magnificent marble bathrooms. The period dining room, with its Flemish tapestries and glittering crystal chandeliers, has been winning rave reviews. Wonderful swimming pool. **www.lebristolparis.com**

Claridge-Bellman

37 Rue François 1er, 75008 **Tel** 01 47 23 54 42 **Fax** 01 47 23 08 84 **Rooms** 42   **Map** 4 F5

The Claridge-Bellman is a miniature version of the old Claridge Hotel and is managed by its former directors. The hotel has a truly traditional feel. It is quiet, sober and efficiently run, and is furnished throughout with tapestries and antiques. **www.hotel-claridge-bellman.com**

Four Seasons George V

31 Ave George V, 75008 **Tel** 01 49 52 70 00 **Fax** 01 49 52 71 10 **Rooms** 246   **Map** 4 E5

This legendary hotel, dotted with salons, old furniture and art, lost a little of its charm when it was renovated. But it gained a stunning restaurant, Le Cinq, which boasts the world's top sommelier and an award-winning chef. Great spa. **www.fourseasons.com/paris**

Hôtel de la Trémoille

14 Rue de la Trémoille, 75008 **Tel** 01 56 52 14 00 **Fax** 01 40 70 01 08 **Rooms** 93   **Map** 10 F1

The Hôtel de la Trémoille is an impressive, yet relaxed, establishment. Rooms are decorated with comfortable antiques and the bathrooms are extremely luxurious. A fashionable restaurant, Senso, by Terence Conran is now a hit with Paris's beautiful people. **www.hotel-tremoille.com**

Hôtel Franklin Roosevelt

18 Rue Clément Marot, 75008 **Tel** 01 53 57 49 50 **Fax** 01 53 57 49 59 **Rooms** 48   **Map** 4 F5

Chic interior throughout, complete with period furniture, old paintings and a fireplace in the lounge. The bedrooms are generally very large. Cozy atmosphere at the Lord's bar, though the cafés of the Champs-Elysées are also nearby. **www.hrroosevelt.com**

Key to Price Guide see p284 **Key to Symbols** see back cover flap

Hôtel Vernet

26 Rue Vernet, 75008 **Tel** *01 44 31 98 00* **Fax** *01 44 31 85 69* **Rooms** *51*   **Map** *4 E4*

Gustave Eiffel, architect of the Eiffel Tower, created the dazzling glass roof of the dining room here. The hotel lobby is impressive with Persian rugs, precious woods, antiques and parquet flooring. The large, quiet bedrooms are pleasantly furnished and guests have free use of the Royal Monceau's fitness club. **www.hotelvernet.com**

Plaza Athénée

25 Ave Montaigne, 75008 **Tel** *01 53 67 66 65* **Fax** *01 53 67 66 66* **Rooms** *188*   **Map** *10 F1*

The legendary Plaza Athénée is popular with honeymooners, aristocracy and haute couture shoppers. The restaurant by Alain Ducasse is wonderfully romantic, while Le Bar du Plaza is now the hottest address in Paris for cocktails. The last word in luxury. **www.plaza-athenee-paris.com**

Prince de Galles

33 Ave George V, 75008 **Tel** *01 53 23 77 77* **Fax** *01 53 23 78 78* **Rooms** *168*   **Map** *4 E5*

Less prestigious than its neighbor the Four Seasons George V, the Prince de Galles most definitely has its own identity and charm. The marble and chandelier-filled lobby gives way to subdued elegance in the bedrooms. Wi-Fi facilities available. **www.luxurycollection.com/princelegalles**

Royal Monceau

37 Ave Hoche, 75008 **Tel** *01 42 99 88 00* **Fax** *01 42 99 89 90* **Rooms** *180*   **Map** *4 F3*

The Royal Monceau champions subtle luxury. The breakfast room is unusual – a striking glass gazebo with curved walls. Its health club is one of the most fashionable in Paris. The bedrooms are elegant – reserve a room overlooking the courtyard. **www.royalmonceau.com**

San Régis

12 Rue Jean Goujon, 75008 **Tel** *01 44 95 16 16* **Fax** *01 45 61 05 48* **Rooms** *44*   **Map** *11 A1*

Since it opened in 1923 the San Régis has been popular with the jet set, who enjoy its quiet but central location. This particularly welcoming, intimate luxury hotel is full of excellent antiques, overstuffed sofas and a distinctly opulent air. **www.hotel-sanregis.fr**

OPÉRA QUARTER

Ambassador

16 Blvd Haussmann, 75009 **Tel** *01 44 83 40 40* **Fax** *01 42 46 19 84* **Rooms** *300*   **Map** *6 E4*

One of the best of Paris's Art Deco hotels, it has been restored to its former glory and has deep carpeting and antique furniture. The ground floor has pink marble columns, Baccarat crystal chandeliers and Aubusson tapestries. The restaurant, 16 Haussmann, is extremely popular with Parisian gourmets. **www.hotelambassador-paris.com**

Edouard VII Hotel

39 Ave de l'Opéra, 75002 **Tel** *01 42 61 56 90* **Fax** *01 42 61 47 73* **Rooms** *69*   **Map** *6 E5*

The only hotel on the impressive Avenue de l'Opéra, the Edourd VII is centrally located between the Louvre and the Opéra Garnier, which makes it perfect for sightseeing. Ask for a room at the front for a breathtaking view over the Opéra House. **www. edouard7hotel.com**

Le Grand Hôtel Intercontinental

2 Rue Scribe, 75009 **Tel** *01 40 07 32 32* **Fax** *01 40 07 32 02* **Rooms** *478*   **Map** *6 D5*

Directly next to the Opéra Garnier, the hotel is a sumptuous example of good taste. The bedrooms all have pictures with a musical theme reflecting the hotel's location. The renowned restaurant, the Café de La Paix, is an opulent affair in Opéra Quarter. **www.paris.intercontinental.com**

MONTMARTRE

Regyn's Montmartre

18 Pl des Abbesses, 75018 **Tel** *01 42 54 45 21* **Fax** *01 42 23 76 69* **Rooms** *22*   **Map** *6 E1*

Near Sacré-Coeur, this is an impeccably kept hotel. Top-floor guestrooms have views of the Eiffel Tower. Around the corner from here is Tabac des Deux Moulins on 15 Rue le Pic where Amelie worked in the film *Amelie*. **www.regynsmontmartre.com**

Terrass Hôtel

12-14 Rue Joseph-de-Maistre, 75018 **Tel** *01 46 06 72 85* **Fax** *01 42 52 29 11* **Rooms** *100*   **Map** *6 E1*

Montmartre's most luxurious hotel, the rooms here are comfortably, if unremarkably, furnished. A few bedrooms retain the original Art-Deco woodwork. The big draw is the rooftop restaurant, where in the summer fashionable Parisians take in a world-class view. **www.terrass-hotel.com**

RESTAURANTS, CAFES AND BARS

The French national passion for good cuisine makes eating out one of the greatest pleasures of a visit to Paris. Everywhere in the city you see people eating – in restaurants, bistros, tea salons, cafés and wine bars.

Most restaurants serve French food but there is a range of Chinese, Vietnamese and North African eateries in many areas as well as Italian, Greek, Lebanese and Indian places. The restaurants in the list-ings *(see pp300–315)* have been selected from the best that Paris can offer across all price ranges. The list-ings are organized by area, as in the sightseeing section of the guide, and by price. Most places will serve lunch from noon until around 2pm, and the menu often includes fixed-price meals. Parisians usually start to fill restaurants for dinner around 8:30pm and most places serve from around 7:30pm until 11pm. *(See also Light Meals and Snacks pp316–19.)*

WHAT TO EAT

A tremendous range of food is available in Paris, from the rich meat dishes and perfect pâtisserie for which France is most famous to simpler French regional cuisines *(see pp296–7)*. The latter are available in brasseries and bistros – the type usually depends on the birthplace of the chef. At any time of day simple, tasty meals can be had in cafés, wine and beer bars, and brasseries, bistros and cake shops – or pâtisseries – abound. Some cafés, like the Bar du Marché *(see p318)* in St-Germain-des-Prés, are known for their excellent cold food and don't offer hot meals at lunchtime.

The best ethnic food comes from France's former colonies: Vietnam and North Africa. North African places are known as *couscous* restaurants and serve filling, somewhat spicy, inexpensive food that varies in quality. Vietnamese restaurants are also good value and provide a light alternative to rich French food. Paris also has some good Japanese restaurants, notably around Rue Monsieur le Prince (6th arrondissement); Rue de la Roquette (11th) and Rue de Belleville (19th) have others.

WHERE TO FIND GOOD RESTAURANTS AND CAFES

You can eat well in almost any part of Paris. Wherever you are, as a rule of thumb you will find that the most out-standing restaurants and cafés are those that cater predomin-antly to a French clientele.

The Left Bank probably has the greatest concentration of restaurants, especially in tourist areas like St-Germain-des-Prés and the Latin Quarter. The quality of food varies, but there are some commendable bistros, outdoor cafés and

Beauvilliers restaurant *(see p312)*

wine bars – see pages 316–19 for a selection of the best places to go in Paris for light meals and snacks. The Latin Quarter also has a high concentration of Greek restaurants centered chiefly around Rue de la Huchette.

In the Marais and Bastille areas, small bistros, tea salons and cafés are plentiful, some new and fashionable. There are also many good, traditional long-established bistros and brasseries.

In the Champs-Elysées and Madeleine area it is difficult to find inexpensive good food. Sadly, this area tends to be overrun with fast food joints and pricy but not very good cafés. There are, however, some very good expensive restaurants here.

Montparnasse still has some great cafés from the 1920s, including Le Sélect and La Rotonde, on the Boulevard du Montparnasse *(see p319)*. Sensitive renovation has

The prim Mariage Frères shop and tea room *(see p318)*

recaptured much of their old splendor. There are excellent bistros in this area as well.

There are many noteworthy restaurants, bistros and cafés in the Louvre-Rivoli area, competing with tourist-oriented, overpriced cafés. Just to the east, Les Halles is filled with fast food joints and mediocre restaurants but there are few places of note.

Good Japanese food can be found near the Opéra together with some fine brasseries, but otherwise the area around the Opéra and Grands Boulevards is not the best for restaurants. Near the Bourse are a number of reputable restaurants and bistros frequented by stockbrokers.

Montmartre has a predictable number of tourist restaurants, but it also has a few very pleasant small bistros. One expensive and luxurious exception is Beauvilliers *(see p312)*, a Montmartre landmark tucked on the far side of the Butte.

Quiet neighborhoods in the evening, the Invalides, Eiffel Tower and Palais de Chaillot tend to have less noisy, more serious restaurants than areas with lively nightlife. Prices can be high.

Two Chinatowns, one in the area south of the Place d'Italie, the other in the traditionally working-class, hilltop area of Belleville, have concentrations of ethnic food but few French restaurants of note. There are a number of Vietnamese venues as well as large, inexpensive Chinese ones, and Belleville is packed with small North African restaurants.

Le Grand Véfour in the Tuileries *(see p304)*

TYPES OF RESTAURANTS AND CAFES

One of the most enjoyable aspects of eating in Paris is the diversity of places to eat. Bistros are small, often moderately priced restaurants with a limited selection of dishes. Those from the Belle Epoque era are particularly beautiful, with zinc bars, mirrors and attractive tiles. The food is generally, but not always, regional and traditional. Many chefs from the toniest restaurants have now also opened bistros and these can be very good value.

Brasseries are generally large bustling eateries, many with an Alsatian character serving carafes of Alsatian wine and platters of sauerkraut and sausage. They have immense menus, and most serve food throughout the day and are open late. Outside you may well see impressive sidewalk displays of shellfish, with apron-clad oyster shuckers working late into the night.

A typical bistro menu

Cafés open early in the morning, and apart from the large tourist cafés, the majority close by around 10pm. They serve drinks and food all day long from a short menu of salads, sandwiches and eggs. At lunch most also offer a small choice of hot daily specials. Café prices vary from area to area, in direct proportion to the number of tourists. Upscale cafés, like Café de Flore and Les Deux Magots serve food until late at night. Those cafés specializing in beer almost always include onion tarts, French fries and hearty bowls of steamed mussels on the menu. Brunch is now served in many places on weekends, from around 15€.

Wine bars are informal. They usually have a moderately priced, simple lunch menu and serve wine by the glass. They serve snacks at any time of day – such as marvelous open sandwiches *(tartines)* made with sourdough Poilâne bread topped with cheese, sausage or pâté – until around 10pm, but a few are open for dinner.

Tea salons open for breakfast or mid-morning until the early evening. Many offer lunch, as well as a selection of sweet pastries for afternoon tea. They are at their best in the middle of the afternoon and offer coffee and hot chocolate as well as fine teas. Some, like Le Loir dans la Théière, are casual with sofas and big tables, while Mariage Frères is more formal. Angélina on the Rue de Rivoli is famous for its hot chocolate, and Ladurée has excellent chocolate macaroons. *(For addresses see pp318–19.)*

Tour d'Argent decoration *(see p306)*

VEGETARIAN FOOD

Vegetarian restaurants in Paris are few, and non-vegetarian restaurant menus are usually firmly oriented toward meat and fish. However, you can get a good salad almost anywhere and you can often fare well by ordering two courses from the list of *entrées* (first courses). The North African restaurants will serve you *couscous nature* – which doesn't have meat.

Never be timid about asking for a change in a dish. If you see a salad with ham, bacon or *foie gras*, ask the waiter for it without the meat. If you are going to an upscale restaurant, telephone ahead and ask the manager if it is possible to prepare a special meal for you. Most restaurants will be happy to oblige.

Organic produce is starting to be used in French cuisine.

HOW MUCH TO PAY

Prices for meals in Paris range from extremely economic to astronomical. You can still enjoy a hearty restaurant or café lunch for 12€, but a typical good bistro, brasserie or restaurant meal in central Paris will average 30€–38€ with wine. (Remember that the better French wines will increase the size of your bill significantly.) More expensive restaurants begin at about 45€ with wine and go up to 150€ for the top places. Many places offer a *formule* or *prix-fixe* (fixed price) menu, especially at

Le Carré des Feuillants *(see p304)*

lunch, and this will almost always offer the best value. Some restaurants feature menus for under 15€ – a few at this price include wine. Coffee usually carries an extra charge.

All French restaurants are obliged by law to display their menu outside. The posted rates include service but a tip for particularly good service will always be appreciated (any amount from one euro to 5 percent of the total).

The most widely accepted credit card is Visa. Few restaurants accept American Express, and some bistros do not accept credit cards at all, so it is wise to ask when you call. Traveler's checks are not widely accepted either, and cafés require cash.

MAKING RESERVATIONS

It is best to reserve a table in all restaurants, brasseries and bistros. Although you can usually get into a brasserie without a reservation, you may have to wait for a table.

Le Pavillon Montsouris near the Parc Montsouris *(see p315)*

DRESS CODE

Except for some three-star restaurants which can be rather formal, you can dress up or down in Parisian restaurants – within reason. The restaurant listings *(see pp300–319)* indicate which places require formal dress.

READING THE MENU AND ORDERING

Menus in small restaurants and bistros, and even in big brasseries, are often handwritten and can be difficult to decipher, so ask for help if necessary.

The waiter usually takes your choice of *entrée* (first course), then the *plat* (main course). Dessert is ordered after you have finished your main course, unless there are some hot desserts which have to be ordered at the start of

The Angélina restaurant, also known for its tea room *(see p318)*

the meal. The waiter will tell you this, or the dessert section of the menu will be marked *à commander avant le repas*.

The first course generally includes a choice of seasonal salads or vegetables, pâté and small hot or cold vegetable dishes or tarts. Small fish dishes like smoked salmon, grilled sardines, herring, fish salads and tartares are also offered. Brasseries have shellfish such as oysters, which can also be eaten as a main course. (The French tend to eat shellfish only when the month ends in 're'!)

Main dishes usually include a selection of meat, poultry and fish and upmarket restaurants offer game in the

Le Train Bleu station restaurant in the Gare de Lyon *(see p314)*

fall. Most restaurants also offer daily specials *(plats du jour)*. These dishes will incorporate fresh, seasonal produce and are usually good value.

Cheese is eaten either as a dessert or as a pre-dessert course. Some people have a green salad with their cheese. Coffee is served after, not with, dessert. You will need to ask specifically if you want it *au lait* (with milk). Decaffeinated coffee *(décaféiné)* and herbal teas *(tisanes)* are also popular after-dinner beverages.

In most restaurants you will be asked if you would like a drink before ordering food. A typical apéritif is *kir* (white wine with a drop of crème de cassis, a blackcurrant liqueur) or *kir royal* (champagne with crème de cassis). Spirits, however, are rarely drunk before a

meal in France *(see* What to Drink in Paris *pp298–9).*

Bistros and brasseries usually include the wine list with the menu. The more expensive restaurants have separate wine lists, which are generally brought to the table by the wine waiter after you have seen the meal menu.

SERVICE

As eating is a leisurely pastime in France, although the general standard of service in Paris restaurants is high, it is not always fast. In small restaurants in particular don't expect rapid attention: there may be only one waiter, and dishes are cooked to order.

CHILDREN

Children are usually very welcome, but there may be little room in a busy restaurant for strollers or baby carriages. Nor are special facilities like highchairs or baby seats commonly provided in eating places.

SMOKING

France has passed strict legislation forcing restaurants to provide nonsmoking tables. These are often not the best tables in the house, and while most restaurants abide

by the regulation, cheaper eating places, specially cafés, still tend to be very smoky.

WHEELCHAIR ACCESS

Wheelchair access may be restricted, and tables can be tightly packed in. Parisian restaurants are generally accommodating, however, and a word when you are reserving should ensure that you are given a more conveniently situated table and help when you arrive.

USING THE LISTINGS

Key to symbols used in the restaurant listings on pp300–315.

- 🚶 children's portions
- ♿ wheelchair access
- 🍴 formal dress required
- 🪑 outside tables
- 💳 no credit cards accepted
- 🅿 parking

Price categories for a three-course meal including a half-bottle of house wine, tax and service:

- € under 25 euros
- €€ 26–35 euros
- €€€ 36–50 euros
- €€€€ 51–75 euros
- €€€€€ over 75 euros

Lucas Carton restaurant *(see p312)*

The Flavors of Paris

From the glittering temples of haute cuisine to the humblest neighborhood bistro, Paris is a paradise for food lovers, whether you dine on foie gras and truffles or steak-frites, a seafood platter or a perfumed Moroccan couscous. France is immensely proud of its cuisine, from its classic origins to the most rustic of regional dishes. All are available in the capital and, though the French them-selves will debate endlessly about the ideal sauce to complement meat or fish, or the right wine to accompany them, they will always be in total agreement that theirs is the best food in the world.

Girolles (chanterelles) on a stall in rue Mouffetard market

the season. Even if you are not shopping for food to cook, the markets are worth browsing and, after an hour or so in the crowded, narrow streets of the rue de de Buci or rue Moufettard you will be more than ready for lunch.

The food of the French provinces, once despised for its rusticity, is now celebrated and almost every region is represented in the capital,

from the rich, bourgeois cuisines of Burgundy and Lyon to the celebrated healthy Mediterranean diet of Provence. Paris itself is surrounded by top quality market gardens which supply young peas, carrots and pot-atoes. Salmon, asparagus, and wild mushrooms come from the Loire; Normandy brings salt-marsh lamb, apples and Camembert.

What all French chefs agree on is the importance of using the finest quality ingredients, and there is no better place to appreciate the quality of French produce than in the markets of Paris. Here, top chefs may be seen early in the morning, alongside local shoppers, seeking inspiration and the prize ingredients of

Comté

Brie de Meaux

Tomme de chevre

Ami du Chambertin

Roquefort

Selection of fine French cheeses in perfect condition

CLASSIC FRENCH CUISINE

What is usually thought of as classic French cuisine developed in kings' palaces and noble châteaux, with the emphasis on luxury and display, not frugality or health. Dishes are often bathed in rich sauces of butter or cream, enhanced with luxurious ingredients like truffles, foie gras, rare mushrooms and alcohol. Meat is treated with reverence, and you will usually be asked how you want your beef, lamb or duck cooked; the French tend to like their beef rare (*bleu* or *saignant*) and their lamb and duck pink (*rose*). For well-cooked meat, ask for *"bien cuit"* but still expect at least a tinge of pinkness. The most famous country classics include slowly cooked casseroles like *coq au vin* and *boeuf à la bourguignonne*, as well as the bean, sausage and duck baked dish *cassoulet*, from the southwest.

Escargots à la Bourguignonne
are plump Burgundy snails served in their shells with garlic, butter and parsley.

Salers beef and lentils come from the Auvergne; beef and Bresse chickens from Burgundy; not forgetting Basque ham, Collioure anchovies, lamb from the Pyrenees, or fragrant Provençal melons.

THE NEW STYLE

In recent years, innovative chefs have developed new styles of cooking, reacting against the richness of traditional cookery, and using fresh ingredients, lightly cooked to retain their flavor.

Mouthwatering display in a Parisian patisserie

Sealed jars of whole duck-liver foie gras, a luxury item

Sauces are made of light reductions to enhance, not obscure, the main ingredient of a dish. A wave of invention and originality has resulted in a plethora of unusual ingredients, fresh twists on the classics, and sometimes wonderful new combinations and flavors, such as sea bass with bean purée and red wine sauce, or with fermented grape juice; sole with quince juice and tarragon; tempura of langoustines with cinnamon beurre blanc; rabbit with Indian spices and tomato polenta; and rosemary ice cream or lavender sorbet.

FOREIGN FOOD

Paris can also offer diners an amazing selection of world flavors, especially those of France's former colonies – for example, Moroccan tajines and Cambodian fish with coconut milk. Most fascinating of all is to observe how these cuisines are developing, as young chefs adapt and combine traditional ingredients and culinary styles with those of France.

ON THE MENU

Andouillettes Sausages made of pork intestines

Blanquette de veau Veal stew with eggs and cream

Crottin chaud en salade Goat's cheese on toast with salad

Cuisses de grenouille Frogs' legs in garlic butter

Iles flottantes Meringues floating in creamy sauce

Plateau de fruits de mer Platter of raw and cooked seafood

Ris de veau Veal sweetbreads

Rognons à la moutarde Kidneys in mustard sauce

Salade frisée aux lardons Endive salad with fried bacon

Sole meunière Fried sole with melted butter

Moules marinière *are mussels steamed in a fragrant sauce of white wine, garlic, parsley and sometimes cream.*

Coq au vin *is a male chicken braised with red wine, herbs, garlic, baby onions and button mushrooms.*

Tarte tatin *is a caramelized upside-down buttery apple tart, created at the hotel Tatin in the Loire Valley.*

What to Drink in Paris

Paris is the best place in France to sample a wide range of the country's many different wines. It's cheapest to order wine by the carafe, normally referred to by size: 25cl (*quart*), 33cl (*fillette*), 50cl (*demi*) or 75cl (*pichet*, equivalent to a bottle*). Cafés and wine bars always offer wine by the glass – *un petit blanc* is a small glass of white, a larger glass of red, *un ballon rouge*. House wine is nearly always reliable.

Paris's last vineyard, near Sacré-Coeur *(see p220)*

RED WINE

Some of the world's finest and most expensive red wines come from the Bordeaux and Burgundy regions, but for everyday drinking choose from the enormous range of basic Bordeaux or Côtes du Rhône wines. Alternatively try Beaujolais, which comes from the southern end of Burgundy and is light enough to serve chilled.

Distinctive bottle shapes for Bordeaux and Burgundy

Bordeaux châteaux include Margaux, which makes some of the world's most elegant red wines.

Burgundy includes some big, strong red wines from the village of Gevrey-Chambertin in the Côte de Nuits.

Beaujolais Nouveau, the fruity first taste of the year's new wine, is released on the third Thursday of November.

The Loire has very good red wines from the area around Chinon. They are usually quite light and very dry.

Southern Rhône is famous for its dark, rich red wines from Châteauneuf-du-Pape, north of Avignon.

Northern Rhône has some dark, fragrant red wines, best aged for at least 10 years, from Côte-Rôtie near Vienne.

FINE WINE VINTAGE CHART

	2002	2001	2000	1999	1998	1997	1996	1995	1994
BORDEAUX									
Margaux, St-Julien, Pauillac, St-Estèphe	7	7	8	7	7	7	8	8	6
Graves, Pessac-Léognan (red)	8	7	8	7	8	7	8	8	6
Graves, Pessac-Léognan (white)	7	7	8	8	7	8	7	7	7
St-Emilion, Pomerol	7	8	8	7	7	7	8	8	6
BURGUNDY									
Chablis	7	8	8	8	8	9	8	9	6
Côte de Nuits (red)	7	7	7	7	7	8	7	8	5
Côte de Beaune (white)	6	8	7	7	8	9	8	9	6
LOIRE									
Bourgueil, Chinon	8	7	8	8	7	9	9	8	6
Sancerre (white)	7	8	8	8	7	9	8	8	7
RHONE									
Hermitage (red)	8	7	7	8	8	7	9	8	7
Hermitage (white)	8	8	9	7	8	8	8	7	7
Côte-Rôtie	7	7	8	8	8	7	9	8	7
Châteauneuf-du-Pape	7	7	8	7	8	7	8	8	7

The quality scale from 1 to 10 represents an overall rating for the year and is only a guideline.

WHITE WINE

The finest white Bordeaux and Burgundy are best with food, but for everyday drinking try a light dry wine such as Entre-Deux-Mers from Bordeaux, or Anjou Blanc or Sauvignon de Touraine from the Loire. Alsace makes some reliable white wines. Sweet wines such as Sauternes, Barsac or Coteaux du Layon are delicious with *foie gras*.

Alsace Riesling and Burgundy

Alsace wines are usually labeled by grape variety. Gewürztraminer is one of the most distinctive.

Loire wines include Pouilly-Fumé, from the east of the region. It is very dry, often with a slightly smoky perfume.

SPARKLING WINE

In France champagne is the first choice for a celebration drink, and styles range from nonvintage to deluxe. Many other wine regions make sparkling wines by the champagne method which tend to be a lot cheaper. Look out for Crémant de Loire, Crémant de Bourgogne, Vouvray Mousseux, Saumur Mousseux and Blanquette de Limoux.

Champagne

Burgundy wines include Chablis, a fresh, full-flavored dry wine from the northernmost vineyards.

The Loire has the perfect partner to seafood dishes in Muscadet, a dry white wine from the Atlantic Coast.

Champagne vineyards east of Paris produce the famous sparkling wine. Billecart-Salmon is a light, pink Champagne.

Sweet Bordeaux are luscious, golden-colored dessert wines, the most famous being Barsac and Sauternes.

APERITIFS AND DIGESTIFS

Kir, white wine mixed with a small amount of blackcurrant liqueur or *crème de cassis*, is the ubiquitous apéritif. Also common is aniseed-flavored *pastis* which is served with ice and a pitcher of water and can be very refreshing. Vermouths, especially Noilly-Prat, are also common apéritifs. *Digestifs*, or after-dinner drinks, are often ordered with coffee and include *eaux-de-vie*, the strong colorless spirits infused with fruit, and brandies such as Cognac, Armagnac and Calvados.

Kir: white wine with cassis

BEERS

Beer in France is sold either by the bottle or, more cheaply, on tap by the glass – *un demi*. The cheapest is lager-style *bière française*, and the best brands are Meteor and Mutzig, followed by "33", "1664" and Kronenbourg. A maltier beer is Leffe, which comes as *blonde* (lager) or *brune* (darker, more fully flavored). Pelforth makes very good dark beer and lager. Some bars and cafés specialize in foreign beers, especially from Belgium, and these are very malty and strong; others brew their own beer. (For beer bars see p317.)

OTHER DRINKS

The brightly colored drinks consumed in cafés all over Paris are mixtures of flavored syrups and mineral waters, called *sirops à l'eau*. The emerald-green drinks use mint syrup, the red ones grenadine. Fruit juices and tomato juice are sold in bottles unless you specify *citron pressé* or *orange pressée* (freshly squeezed lemon or orange), which is served with a pitcher of water and with sugar or sugar syrup for you to dilute and sweeten to taste. If you ask for water, you will be served mineral water, sparkling (*gazeuse*) or still (*naturelle*); if you don't want to be charged, ask for tap water (*eau de robinet*).

Fresh lemon juice is served with water and sugar

Choosing a Restaurant

The restaurants listed on the following pages have been selected for their good value or exceptional food. The chart below lists restaurants in Paris by area, and the entries are alphabetical within each price category. Details on snack and sandwich bars are in Light Meals and Snacks on pages 316–319.

PRICE CATEGORIES
For a three-course meal per person, with a half-bottle of house wine, including tax and service.
€ under 25 euros
€€ 26–35 euros
€€€ 36–50 euros
€€€€ 51–75 euros
€€€€€ over 75 euros

ILE DE LA CITÉ AND ÎLE SAINT-LOUIS

Au Rendez-Vous des Camionneurs   €

72 Quai des Orfèvres, 75001 **Tel** *01 43 54 88 74*   **Map** *12 F3*

There aren't many *camionneurs* (truck drivers) on picturesque Ile de la Cité, but this restaurant can satisfy the biggest appetite. Veal stew in white sauce is the house specialty, along with *foie gras* terrine and puff pastry filled with tomato, basil and mozzarella. Extra charges for evenings.

L'Ane et la Mule   €€

74 Quai des Orfèvres, 75001 **Tel** *01 43 54 16 71*   **Map** *12 F3*

Formerly called Ristorante il Delfino, this is a comfortable and stylish Italian restaurant, complete with fireplace and 17th-century cellar, and well suited to a romantic dinner. Pasta, tiramisu and the Delfino escalope (breaded veal cutlet) deserves its place as house specialty.

Nos Ancêtres les Gaulois   €€

39 Rue St-Louis en l'Ile, 75004 **Tel** *01 46 33 66 07*   **Map** *13 C4*

This restaurant has a jolly atmosphere and caters to big appetites. Only one set menu, which includes assorted salads, a buffet of cooked meats, one grilled meat, cheeseboard, fruit, dessert and plenty of wine. Satisfying and entertaining. Children's menu available for 10 euros.

La Rose de France   €€€

24 Pl Dauphine, 75001 **Tel** *01 43 54 10 12*   **Map** *12 F3*

Majestic setting, looking onto a 17th-century square. The cooking updates French classics, with specialties like the John Dory with rhubarb, ginger and Basmati rice. More traditional is the duck fillet in ratatouille. A *cuisine du marché* restaurant, La Rose uses the freshest produce from the day's market.

Le Vieux Bistro   €€€€

14 Rue du Cloître-Notre-Dame, 75004 **Tel** *01 43 54 18 95*   **Map** *13 B4*

This authentic bistro is popular with many Paris restaurateurs and entertainers. The slightly rundown decor suits the place and the rendition of favorites like *boeuf bourguignon, gratin dauphinois* (sliced potatoes baked in cream), *tarte tatin* (upside-down apple tart) and profiteroles are good.

THE MARAIS

Aux Vins de Pyrénées   €

25 Rue Beautrellis, 75004 **Tel** *01 42 72 64 94*   **Map** *13 C3*

A very old bistro with a friendly and typically Parisian atmosphere. The day's menu, written up on a blackboard, typically offers a selection of grilled meats. There is an excellent selection of wines by the glass (particularly good value Bordeaux and lesser-known wines from Southwest France). Extra charges for a menu *à la carte*.

Galerie 88   €

88 Quai de l'Hotel de Ville, 75004 **Tel** *01 42 72 17 58*   **Map** *13 B4*

The bare-walled decor in this tiny restaurant on the banks of the Seine appeals to students and people on a budget. Prices are low, service is friendly if slow, and you really know you are in Paris. The food is old-fashioned, and includes terrines and a selection of delicious homemade tarts. A few vegetarian dishes too.

Il Piccolo Teatro   €

6 Rue des Ecouffes, 75004 **Tel** *01 42 72 17 79*   **Map** *13 C3*

Established in the 1970s, Il Piccolo Teatro is one of Paris's first vegetarian restaurants. Delicious cuisine, with a Mediterranean accent, is served here. Specialties include moussaka, lasagne and stuffed aubergines (eggplant). Lots of organic produce is used.

Key to Symbols *see back cover flap*

Le Baracane €

38 Rue des Tournelles, 75004 **Tel** *01 42 71 43 33* **Map** 14 E3

A tiny restaurant with good quality food at reasonable prices. The fixed-price menu is particularly good value. The Southwestern cuisine includes a delicious rabbit *confit*, braised oxtail, pears poached in Madeira and Cassis (blackcurrant liqueur), and superb homemade chestnut bread.

Le Passage des Carmagnoles 🏃 €

18 Passage de la Bonne Graine, 75011 **Tel** *01 47 00 73 30* **Map** 14 F4

A short walk from the Place de la Bastille, the proprietor Soizik may personally greet you. Although it calls itself a wine bar (and the selection of wines by the glass and bottle is excellent), it offers a full menu including five styles of *andouillette* (tripe sausage) and a variety of daily specials. Excellent cheeses; desserts include a vast chocolate éclair.

Brasserie Bofinger 🏃 €€

3 Rue de la Bastille, 75004 **Tel** *01 42 72 87 82* **Map** 14 E4

Established in 1864, Bofinger claims to be the oldest brasserie in Paris. It is certainly one of the prettiest, with stained glass, leather banquettes, brass decorations and murals by the Alsatian artist Hansi. It serves good shellfish, as well as respectable *choucroute*, and grilled meats.

Chez Jenny 🏃♿� €€

39 Blvd du Temple, 75003 **Tel** *01 44 54 39 00* **Map** 14 D1

This huge brasserie on the Place de la République has been a bastion of Alsatian cooking since it was founded over 60 years ago. Service by women in Alsatian dress adds to the atmosphere. The *choucroute* (sauerkraut) *spéciale Jenny* makes a hearty meal with a fruit tart or sorbet, served with a fruit liqueur for dessert.

Le Colimaçon 🏃 €€

44 Rue Vieille du Temple, 75004 **Tel** *01 48 87 12 01* **Map** 13 C3

Le Colimaçon (snail) refers to the restaurant's centerpiece: a corkscrew staircase. A building dating to 1732, it has period wooden beams in the ceiling. Snails are also on the menu along with frogs' legs in parsley and tomato sauce and *gigot de sept heures*.

Le Repaire de Cartouche 🏃♿ €€

8 Blvd des Filles du Calvaire, 75011 **Tel** *01 47 00 25 86* **Map** 14 D2

Like its "sister" establishment, Le Villaret, this restaurant is run by former employees of Astier, to the same excellent standards. It too has a changing seasonal menu, which includes roast pigeon with leeks in a vinegar sauce and rabbit terrine with chocolate. Its decor is reassuringly traditional.

Trésor 🏃♿🚥 €€

5–7 Rue du Trésor, 75004 **Tel** *01 42 71 35 17* **Map** 13 C3

The decor of the tiny and trendy Trésor is defined by a contemporary elegance, with a touch of kitsch. Lasagne, grilled steak in wine sauce and tiramisu show the blending of French and Italian cooking. A wide selection of wines, whiskeys and cocktails are available here. The dining room opens onto a very pleasant terrace.

Auberge Nicolas Flamel 🏃 €€€

51 Rue de Montmorency, 75003 **Tel** *01 42 71 77 78* **Map** 13 B1

Housed in Paris's oldest building (1407) and named after the famous alchemist. The restaurant's specialties include *Tatin de foie gras poellé* and *Gala au pain d'épices*, while the *tour de force* here is *gigot de sept heures* following a medieval recipe. Comprehensive wine list.

La Guirlande de Julie 🚥 €€€

25 Pl des Vosges, 75003 **Tel** *01 48 87 94 07* **Map** 14 D3

Consummate restaurant professional Claude Terrail of the Tour d'Argent *(see p306)* has employed a good chef here, and the decor is fresh and appealing. For the best views, ask for a table near the window in the first dining room. In good weather meals are served under the cool vaulted stone arcades.

Le Bar à Huitres 🅿🏃♿🚥 €€€

33 Blvd Beaumarchais,75003 **Tel** *01 48 87 98 92* **Map** 14 E3

Oysters predominate in Paris's three Bars à Huîtres (the others are in Montparnasse and St-Germain-des-Prés). You can compose your own seafood platter to start, followed by a choice of hot fish dishes, with meat on offer for carnivores. Convenient for the Place de la Bastille and the Marais.

Hiramatsu 🅿🏃♿ €€€€€

52 Rue de Longchamps, 75016 **Tel** *01 56 81 08 80* **Map** 9 C1

Where Zen culture and French *haute cuisine* meet. Its menu reflects extreme refinement in cuisine and presentation: frog consommé with morel sauce and ginger vegetables. Reservations essential. The seasonal cuisine might include *Foie gras de canard de choux frisé au jus de truffe et madaire*.

L'Ambroisie 🅿🏃♿🚥🍸 €€€€€

9 Pl des Vosges, 75004 **Tel** *01 42 78 51 45* **Map** 14 D3

Housed in a former jewelry shop restored by Chef Mousieur Pacaud, this is one of only seven Michelin three-star restaurants in Paris. The cuisine includes a mousse of sweet red peppers, *truffle feuilleté* (layered pastry) and langoustines. Reservations are accepted one month in advance.

BASTILLE

Boca Chica
58 Rue de Charonne, 75011 **Tel** *01 43 57 93 13*   **€€**

Map *14 F4*

The upbeat Boca Chica boasts a funky decor, trendy tunes and Spanish fare. Tapas, paella, grilled sardines, pork ribs and *gâteau Basque* are all on the menu. On Mondays, there's a clairvoyance night here, while salsa is featured every Wednesday night.

Barrio Latino
46 Rue du Faubourg St-Antoine, 75012 **Tel** *01 55 78 84 75*   **€€€**

Map *14 F4*

Three floors of exuberant and luxurious South American decor. Exotic food includes *guacamole, quesadillas* (grilled cheese-filled tortillas), Brazilian grilled pork and Uruguayan-style scallops on a skewer with salsa. Cheaper lunch. Children are not allowed into the restaurant from 10pm onward. Discotheque and salsa.

China Club
50 Rue de Charenton, 75012 **Tel** *01 43 43 82 02*   **€€€**

Map *14 F5*

Chinese restaurants can be kitsch, but this one is revolutionary in an extremely glamorous way. China Club has a colonial chic decor as well as superior Asian cuisine. Specialties include five-spice crispy pigeon and sautéed sole with ginger-plum sauce.

Blue Elephant
43 Rue de la Roquette, 75011 **Tel** *01 47 00 42 00*   **€€€€**

Map *14 F3*

An island of refinement in the trendy Bastille area, with a tropical decor of lush plants, gurgling fountains and Thai woodwork. Superbly presented Thai cuisine: *som tam* (green papaya, dried shrimp and lime salad) and cashew nut chicken served in a fresh pineapple. Sunday brunch.

BEAUBOURG AND LES HALLES

Au Crocodile
28 Rue Léopold Bellan, 75002 **Tel** *01 42 36 92 44*   **€**

Map *13 A1*

The limited menu of this welcoming neighborhood restaurant is seasonal, with dishes such as marinated sardines, salmon profiteroles and sea trout with basil. Natural products used. The varnished ivory-colored ash wood decor with abundant flowers is refreshing.

Aux Tonneau des Halles
28 Rue Montorgueil, 75001 **Tel** *01 42 33 36 19*   **€**

Map *13 A1*

A genuine Parisian bistro, Aux Tonneau des Halles is one of the last of its kind, with its real zinc bar, smoky interior and one of the tiniest kitchens in Paris. Service is not quick, but when the food is this good, who cares! The wines are original and good value.

La Victoire Suprême du Coeur
41 Rue des Bourdonnais, 75001 **Tel** *01 40 41 93 95*   **€**

Map *13 A2*

Comforting vegetarian fare served in a bright blue and white dining room. Mushrooms are a specialty here, as in mushroom pâté or roast mushrooms with blackberry sauce. Desserts include a famous berry crumble. No alcohol served except cider; try the biodynamic carrot juice.

Le Bistrot Beaubourg
25 Rue Quincampoix, 75004 **Tel** *01 42 77 48 02*   **€**

Map *13 B2*

This arty but chic establishment serves classic French food. Skate with "black" butter sauce and rib-eye steak with green pepper sauce are typical of their excellent menus, changed daily. Lingering over one's meal is no sin here. Equally pleasurable inside, or outside on the sunny terrace.

Le Grizzli
7 Rue St-Martin, 75004 **Tel** *01 48 87 77 56*   **€**

Map *13 B3*

A change of ownership has breathed new life into the Grizzli, founded in 1903 when it was one of the last Parisian places to have dancing bears! The owner orders much produce from his native Southwest including local ham, lamb chops, cooked on a sizzling slate, cheeses and wines made by his family.

Au Pied de Cochon
6 Rue Coquillière, 75004 **Tel** *01 40 13 77 00*   **€€**

Map *12 F1*

This colorfully restored brasserie was once popular with high society, who came to observe the workers in the old market and to relish the onion soup. Although touristy, this gigantic place is fun, and has a menu with something for everyone (including excellent shellfish). Still one of the best places after a night out.

Key to Price Guide *see p300* **Key to Symbols** *see back cover flap*

Café Beaubourg

43 Rue Saint-Merri, 75004 **Tel** *01 48 87 63 96* **Map** *13 B2*

With views of the animated piazza of the Beaubourg museum, Café Beaubourg has an elegant and contemporary decor. Simple and reliable, if slightly overpriced, fare is guaranteed – a variety of tartares, grilled meats and fish. The menu even offers a Thai salad.

Le Loubechem

31 Rue Berger, 75001 **Tel** *01 42 33 12 99* **Map** *12 F2*

A former butcher's shop, meat is what this no-nonsense eatery is all about, with portions designed more for rugby players than ballet dancers. *L'assiette du rôtisseur* is a classic (3-meat roast platter, each with its own sauce), and the *aiguillette à la ficelle* are still prepared in the traditional manner.

Le Tire-bouchon

22 Rue Tiquetonne, 75002 **Tel** *01 42 21 95 51* **Map** *13 A1*

The chef elaborates on various regional classics adding a gourmet touch. *Confit de canard*, prawns in puff pastry with saffron sauce and roast pigeon with morels. One of the popular dishes served at the restaurant is the honey-roasted *Magret de canard au miel*.

Le 404

69 Rue Gravilliers, 75003 **Tel** *01 42 74 57 81* **Map** *13 B1*

Magnificently located in the *hôtel particulier* built for Gabrielle d'Estrées (Henri IV's mistress) in 1737, Le 404 is impeccably run by debonair actor Smaïn, who also owns London's Momo restaurant. The food is deeply rooted in his native Morocco: genuine-tasting *couscous*, tajine and vegetarian delicacies. Cheaper lunches.

Pharamond

24 Rue de la Grand-Truanderie, 75001 **Tel** *01 40 28 45 18* **Map** *13 A1*

Founded in 1870, this bistro is a charming remnant of its age, with tiles and mosaics, handsome woodwork and mirrors. Specialties include *tripes à la mode de Caen* (tripe cooked with onions, leeks, cider and Calvados) and *boeuf en daube* (beef stew). The Normandy cider is strongly recommended.

Saudade

34 Rue des Bourdonnais, 75001 **Tel** *01 42 36 30 71* **Map** *13 A2*

This is probably Paris's finest Portuguese restaurant, with all the tiles you expect to see along the Tajo not the Siene. The staple salt cod is prepared in fritters, with tomato and onion or with potatoes and eggs. Roast suckling pig and *cozido* (Portuguese stew) are other dishes. A good selection of wines and ports.

Georges

19 Rue Beaubourg, 75004 **Tel** *01 44 78 47 99* **Map** *13 B2*

On the top floor of the Pompidou Centre, the Georges offers stunning views. Light and inspired cuisine, such as cherry tomato and goat's cheese cake, *sole meunière*, lamb with chutney and macaroons. Roasted scallops with lemon butter is a hit. Terrace seating too. Decor is minimalist, with lots of steel and aluminum.

Joe Allen

30 Rue Pierre Lescot, 75001 **Tel** *01 42 36 70 13* **Map** *13 A2*

Known to offer some of the best burgers in Paris, Joe Allen's boasts an American menu, with chicken wings, grilled tuna with pesto and cheesecake. Chilled but chic atmosphere, candlelit in the evening. The restaurant serves an excellent brunch on Sunday.

Benoît

20 Rue St-Martin, 75004 **Tel** *01 42 72 25 76* **Map** *13 B2*

A gem of a Parisian bistro. The owner has retained the faux-marble, polished-brass and lace-curtain decor created by his grandfather in 1912. The menu includes *saladiers* (assorted cold salads), house *foie gras*, *boeuf à la mode* and *cassoulet* (white bean and meat stew). The wine list is outstanding.

TUILERIES QUARTER

Toraya

10 Rue St-Florentin, 75001 **Tel** *01 42 60 13 00* **Map** *11 C1*

One of the oldest Japanese pâtisseries in Paris, Toraya offers a slice of Japan to Parisians. Dark wood contrasts with the vivid colors of the leather armchairs. Beautifully crafted Japanese pastries are on the menu: red-bean or green-tea-flavored macaroons and many authentic, delicate rice dishes.

Gaya

17 Rue Duphot, 75001 **Tel** *01 42 60 43 03* **Map** *5 C5*

Monsieur Goumard's *bistrot de la mer* (seafood bistro) was once his upmarket fish restaurant before he restored the 19th-century Goumard Prunier. The menu consists of simply prepared fish dishes; the dining area on the ground floor is particularly eye-catching, with its colorful Portuguese tiles.

Il Palazzo at Hôtel Normandy
€€

7 Rue de l'Echelle, 75001 **Tel** *01 42 60 91 20*
Map *12 E1*

High-class venue with French and Italian cuisine. Roast pigeon flambéed with grappa with a mushroom fricassée and potato pancakes and scallops with green asparagus and truffle. Currently being refurbished, the restaurant is open only for lunch.

La Muscade
€€

36 Rue Montpensier, 75001 **Tel** *01 42 97 51 36*
Map *12 E1*

The epitome of French classicism: a Regency-style dining room nestled at the heart of the Palais Royal gardens. Mediterranean-inspired food such as the orange, glazed tomatoes and veal tagine. Tearoom in the afternoon, with pastries such as fig pastilla (in filo).

Le Carré des Feuillants
€€

213 Blvd St-Germain, 75007 **Tel** *01 42 22 06 57*
Map *11 C3*

Situated at the far end of the Boulevard St-Germain near the Assemblée Nationale, this friendly neighborhood place offers hearty, unpretentious cuisine. This features specialties from the Southwest, including a good *cassoulet* (white bean and meat stew). Pastries come from the excellent pâtisserie Peltier.

Le Grand Louvre
€€

Le Louvre, 75001 **Tel** *01 40 20 53 41*
Map *12 F2*

It's rare to find such a good restaurant situated under the Louvre's glass pyramid entrance. The menu draws inspiration from Southwest France – stuffed goose neck, *foie gras*, *boeuf en daube* (beef stew), prune ice cream with Armagnac – and was originally developed by André Daguin, one of the region's gastronomic stars.

Barlotti
€€€€

35 Pl du Marché St-Honoré, 75001 **Tel** *01 44 86 97 97*
Map *12 D1*

From the creators of super-trendy Buddha Bar and Barrio Latino is this showy Italy-themed restaurant with its impressive atrium. Aubergine (eggplant) pasta, prawn risotto and cod satisfy the most delicate palates. Great Sunday brunch. Lunch at Barlotti is a little cheaper than dinner.

Café Marly
€€€€

93 Rue de Rivoli, 75001 **Tel** *01 49 26 06 60*
Map *12 E2*

Wonderful views of the Louvre and inventive French cuisine: *carpaccio*, caramel and coconut duck, salmon with spinach cream and raspberry macaroons. Beef with Roquefort cream sauce is one of the main draws, while for the raw-fish lovers, there's spiced avocado and tuna *tartare*.

Goumard
€€€€€

9 Rue Duphot, 75001 **Tel** *01 42 60 36 07*
Map *5 C5*

Opened in 1872 and still possessing many original features such as glass chandeliers and inlaid wood paneling. Quality seafood on the menu including *bouillabaisse* and sea bass with oyster sauce as well as plenty of champagne (over 150 vintages).

Le Grand Véfour
€€€€€

17 Rue de Beaujolais, 75001 **Tel** *01 42 96 56 27*
Map *12 F1*

This 18th-century restaurant is considered by many to be Paris's most attractive. The chef Guy Martin effortlessly maintains his third Michelin star with dishes such as scallops with Beaufort cheese, cabbage ravioli with a truffle cream and endive *galette* (pancake).

SAINT-GERMAIN-DES-PRÈS

Aux Charpentiers

€

10 Rue Mabillon, 75006 **Tel** *01 43 26 30 05*
Map *12 E4*

There are no surprises at this old-established bistro, popular with students and St-Germain-des-Prés locals. The menu changes daily but you can count on bistro standards such as Marengo veal, *boeuf à la mode* and homey pastries, served at reasonable prices. Extra charges for dinner.

Chez les Filles
€

64 Rue du Cherche Midi, 75006 **Tel** *01 45 48 61 54*
Map *11 C5*

Moroccan sisters run this charming little tea room, where afternoons offer an exotic tea break. Tagines, salads and *couscous* are on the lunch menu, and a Berber brunch is served on Sundays. Featuring wrought-iron work and kilims bearing Moroccan accents.

Le Petit Saint-Benoît

€

4 Rue St-Benoît, 75006 **Tel** *01 42 60 27 92*
Map *12 E3*

This is the place for anyone who wants to mix with the locals; the waitresses speak their mind and you might be seated at a table with others. Not much has been done to the decor, but the good-value food is simple and homey. Its *cuisine du marché* offers six *plats du jour*, different every day.

Key to Price Guide *see p300* **Key to Symbols** *see back cover flap*

Polidor

🍽🚻♿ €

41 Rue Monsieur le Prince, 75006 **Tel** *01 43 26 95 34* **Map** *12 F5*

Once frequented by Verlaine and Rimbaud, this is bohemian Paris incarnate. The place has kept its reputation by sticking to traditional cuisine at rock-bottom prices. Grilled steak, *daube de boeuf* and Marengo veal (slow cooked with tomatoes). Various tarts such as chocolate, lemon or apple.

Coffee Parisien

🚻♿ €€

4 Rue Princesse, 75006 **Tel** *01 43 54 18 18* **Map** *12 E1*

With wooden paneling, punctuated with pictures of American presidents, this is one of the best places for brunch. American classics on the menu including one of the best burgers in Paris (bacon and cheese), eggs Benedict and all kinds of pancakes and sundaes.

L'Arbuci

🚻♿🍴 €€

25 Rue de Buci, 75006 **Tel** *01 44 32 16 00* **Map** *12 E4*

The Blanc brothers, owners of venerable institutions such as Procope, experiment at this unwaveringly contemporary venue. The menu boasts a great deal of seafood, including shellfish platters; other dishes accommodate foreign spices and vegetables, as exemplified in the lemon grass tuna and pineapple kebobs.

Alcazar

🚻♿ €€€

62 Rue Mazarine, 75006 **Tel** *01 53 10 19 99* **Map** *12 F4*

A fashionable club in the 1970s, Alcazar was bought by Sir Terence Conran in 1999. He converted it into a new brasserie-bar, and the result is this huge, elegant and thoroughly modern establishment which serves simple but well-made cuisine. Cheaper lunches.

Barocco

🚻 €€€

23 Rue Mazarine, 75006 **Tel** *01 43 26 40 24* **Map** *12 F3*

Serving Brazilian cuisine: *seijoada* (black bean casserole), *churrasco* (grilled meat) and Portuguese-style cod. A chic and cosy interior, complete with a library. Brazilian musical groups perform at the Barocco every Tuesday, Wednesday, Thursday and Sunday.

Bouillon Racine

🚻♿ €€€

3 Rue Racine, 75006 **Tel** *01 44 32 15 60* **Map** *12 F5*

Stuffed roast suckling pig, licorice-flavored lamb and seafood risotto are all served at Bouillon Racine. This was where the *bouillons*, the popular meat-flavored soups, first made an appearance. Its building, dating to 1906, is an Art Nouveau masterpiece.

Brasserie Lipp

🅿🚻♿🍴 €€€

151 Blvd St Germain, 75006 **Tel** *01 45 48 53 91* **Map** *12 E4*

This is the brasserie that everyone loves to hate. Yet, its clientele, which includes entertainers and politicians, keeps returning for the good food. The dishes include herring in cream and a huge *millefeuille* pastry. Ask to be seated downstairs with the "in" crowd: the first floor is referred to as Siberia.

Rôtisserie d'en Face

🅿🚻 €€€

2 Rue Christine, 75006 **Tel** *01 43 26 40 98* **Map** *12 F4*

Jacques Cagna's rôtisserie is located across from his eponymous gastronomic restaurant. Perfectly mastered traditional recipes on the menu: veal chop with morel sauce and mashed potato and pan-fried red mullet with capers, lemon and caramelized chicory (endive).

Tan Dinh

🍽🚻♿ €€€

60 Rue de Verneuil, 75007 **Tel** *01 45 44 04 84* **Map** *12 D3*

The relatively high prices in this Franco-Vietnamese restaurant run by the discreet Vifian family are due to a combination of the good quality cuisine and an outstanding wine list with one of the biggest collections of Pomerols in the city. There are no Oriental lanterns here – the interior decor is sober.

Yugaraj

🚻 €€€

14 Rue Dauphine, 75006 **Tel** *01 43 26 44 91* **Map** *12 F3*

Yugaraj is still considered by many to be the best Indian restaurant in Paris. The chef, proud of his high-quality products, emphasizes dishes from his native northern India, and key spices are brought in directly from the subcontinent. The wine list is perhaps surprisingly good too.

Procope

€€€€

13 Rue de l'Ancienne Comédie, 75006 **Tel** *01 40 46 79 00* **Map** *12 F4*

Opened in 1686, Paris's oldest café welcomed literary and political figures such as Voltaire and Diderot. Nowadays, it's still a hub for the intelligentsia, who sit alongside those curious about this historical monument. *Coq au vin* is the specialty. Shellfish platters, too.

Jacques Cagna

🅿🚻♿🍷 €€€€€

14 Rue des Grands Augustins, 75006 **Tel** *01 43 26 49 39* **Map** *12 F4*

This elegant 17th-century townhouse showcases chef-owner Jacques Cagna's trinkets and excellent classic-cum-modern cuisine. Try the red mullet salad with *foie gras*, pigeon *confit* with turnips, and a classic Paris-Brest (choux pastry filled with praline-flavored cream). The wine list is admirable.

Lapérouse
P & T   €€€€€

51 Quai des Grands Augustins, 75006 **Tel** *01 43 26 68 04*

Map 12 F4

This famous establishment from the 19th century was once one of the glories of Paris. Under the impeccable management of owner-chef Alain Hacquard, this is still the case. The series of salons have kept their 1850s decor. The best tables are by the window. Valet parking available.

LATIN QUARTER

Le Grenier de Notre Dame
P & &   €

18 Rue de la Bûcherie, 75005 **Tel** *01 43 29 98 29*

Map 13 A4

Le Grenier de Notre Dame opened in the 1970s and still exudes its original hippie atmosphere. Mostly organic ingredients are used to make the filling meals such as fish gratin, vegetarian casserole or vegetarian escalope in breadcrumbs. The wine list offers a good choice of reasonably priced labels, including Château Chaurignac Bordeaux.

Loubnane
&   €€

29 Rue Galande, 75005 **Tel** *01 43 26 70 60*

Map 9 A4

A Lebanese restaurant where specialties include delicious and generous *mezzes*, served under the watchful eye of a patron whose main aim in life actually seems to be the happiness of his customers. Live Lebanese music is often performed in the basement.

Fogon Saint-Julien
&   €€€

10 Rue St-Julien le Pauvre, 75005 **Tel** *01 43 54 31 33*

Map 13 A4

Authentically Spanish and truly stylish. The elegant straw-colored interior, with wrought iron accents, does credit to the fine cuisine. Savory tapas and all kinds of paella using gourmet produce such as lobster and black rice. Chef Alberto Henaiz makes delicious tapas.

Le Balzar
& &   €€€

49 Rue des Ecoles, 75005 **Tel** *01 43 54 13 67*

Map 13 A5

There's a fair choice of brasserie food here but the main attraction is the ambience. It's typically Left Bank: traditionally dressed waiters weave their way among the hustle and bustle providing express service, with archetypal brasserie decor to match: there are large mirrors and comfortable leather seats.

Le Petit Pontoise
& &   €€€

9 Rue Pontoise, 75005 **Tel** *01 43 29 25 20*

Map 13 B5

Popular neighborhood venue. Inventive use of herbs and spices: pan-fried quail with honey, dried fruits and nuts and prawns Provençal. A perfect menu will probably be composed of a *Risoto à la Truffe*, followed by a duck *parmentier* and stir-fried *foie gras* and, finally, a hot vanilla *soufflé*. Reservations recommended.

Les Bouchons de François Clerc
€€€

12 Rue de l'Hôtel Colbert, 75005 **Tel** *01 43 54 15 34*

Map 13 A4

A comprehensive wine list with vintages offered at wine growers' prices complements dishes such as marrow-flavored roast beef with potato gratin and Morello cherry soufflé. The chef recommends pan-fried scallops, lentils with *foie gras* sauce or a pan-roasted beef of *bavière* with bone marrow and ground pepper.

Moissonnier
& & &   €€€

28 Rue des Fossés St-Bernard, 75005 **Tel** *01 43 29 87 65*

Map 13 B5

This family-run bistro serves favorites which have Lyonnais overtones, such as *saladiers* (assorted salads), *tahlier de sapeur* (ox tripe), *quenelles de brochet* (pike dumplings) and chocolate cake. Beaujolais wines are traditionally served in a small bottle known as a pot. Ask to be seated downstairs.

Rôtisserie du Beaujolais
&   €€€

19 Quai de la Tournelle, 75005 **Tel** *01 43 54 17 47*

Map 13 B5

Facing the Seine and owned by Claude Terrail of the Tour d'Argent next door, the restaurant has a large rôtisserie for roasting poultry and meats. Many of the meats and cheeses are ordered specially from the best suppliers in Lyon. A Beaujolais is, of course, the wine you should order here.

L'Atelier Maître Albert
P & &   €€€€

1 Rue Maître Albert, 75005 **Tel** *01 56 81 30 01*

Map 13 B5

The antique fireplace is purely decorative, yet dishes from the rôtisserie are this restaurant's specialty. Traditional fare such as veal kidneys and mouthwatering chocolate cake are the chief attractions. Other specialties include veal, mixed salad *du moment* and chicken livers.

La Tour d'Argent
P & & T   €€€€€

15–17 Quai de la Tournelle, 75005 **Tel** *01 43 54 23 31*

Map 13 B5

Established in 1582, the Tour appears to be eternal. Patrician owner Claude Terrail has hired young chefs who have rejuvenated the classic menu. The ground-floor bar is also a gastronomic museum; from here take an elevator to the luxurious panoramic restaurant. One of the finest wine cellars. Lunch menu is for 60 euros.

Key to Price Guide *see p300* **Key to Symbols** *see back cover flap*

JARDIN DES PLANTES QUARTER

Les 5 Saveurs d'Anada €

72 Rue du Cardinal Lemoine, 75005 **Tel** *01 43 29 58 54*   **Map** *17 A1*

Les 5 Saveurs d'Anada offers a small menu, featuring high-class macrobiotic, organic and (mostly) vegetarian food. Inventive soups are flavored with butternut squash or cinnamon; mains include fish *bento* or *seitan* (gluten) curry. Good choice of organic wines, plus fruit cocktails.

Marty Restaurant €€€

20 Ave des Gobelins, 75005 **Tel** *01 43 31 39 51*   **Map** *17 B3*

Authentic Art Deco interior but the cuisine steals the show. Serves a hearty fare, such as roast duck or rabbit casserole. Insist on seasonal dishes such as gazpacho. Excellent *crème brûlée*. The Marty was established by E Marty in 1913 and is still family-run.

Mavromatis €€€€

42 Rue Daubenton, 75005 **Tel** *01 43 31 17 17*   **Map** *17 B2*

With an elegant decor, this restaurant is manned by the Mavrommatis brothers, one in the kitchen, the other welcomes guests. Its Greek specialties include roast lamb and *moussaka*. The Hellenic excursion continues with Greek yogurt and *baklava* for dessert.

MONTPARNASSE

Aux Petits Chandeliers €

62 Rue Daguerre, 75014 **Tel** *01 43 20 25 87*   **Map** *16 D3*

Unpretentious bistro, established in 1962 and still featuring the small chandeliers after which it was named. This was the first restaurant in Paris to serve cuisine from the island of Réunion. On the menu are Creole-style pudding, exotic fruit sorbets and coconut-and-vanilla punch.

La Bretonne €

56 Rue du Montparnasse, 75014 **Tel** *01 43 20 89 58*   **Map** *16 D2*

La Bretonne is a little piece of Brittany, complete with antique furniture and decorative plates. Tasty pancakes such as Provençal (mushrooms and snail butter), *Guéménée* (with chitterling sausages), and a large choice of flambéed varieties for dessert.

La Coupole €€

102 Blvd du Montparnasse, 75014 **Tel** *01 43 20 14 20*   **Map** *16 D2*

This famous brasserie has been popular with the fashionistas, artists and thinkers since its creation in 1927. Under the same ownership as Brasserie Flo, it has a similar menu: shellfish, smoked salmon and good desserts. Lamb curry is a specialty. Open from breakfast to 2am.

La Régalade €€

49 Ave Jean Moulin, 75014 **Tel** *01 45 45 68 58*   **Map** *15 C5*

Gourmet fare for a bargain at this traditional bistro. Duck *foie gras* casserole and pan-fried cod with leek vinaigrette are main courses. Grand Marnier soufflé is the chef's specialty dessert. The seasonal menu, based on a *cuisine du marché*, is often renewed, depending on market. Reservations essential.

L'Echanson €€

89 Rue Daguerre, 75014 **Tel** *01 43 22 20 00*   **Map** *15 C3*

Quintessential Parisian bistro serving cuisine that couldn't be more French yet the chef shows creativity by reinventing classics, such as *magret de canard* with peaches, or poached fish with orange cream and spinach-filled pasta. The courses on the seasonal menu keep changing: in winter, duck is served with a blackcurrant sauce.

Natacha €€

17 bis Rue Campagne Première, 75014 **Tel** *01 43 20 79 27*   **Map** *16 E2*

Long drapes by the entrance and theater seats bring drama to an otherwise simple interior of the Natacha restaurant. You can get a hint of the exotic on the menu, which includes chicken terrine with pistachios and glazed kumquats and steamed fish with herb dressing. Brunch on Sundays.

Café des Délices €€€

87 Rue d'Assas, 75006 **Tel** *01 43 54 70 00*   **Map** *16 E2*

Nothing seems too audacious for young chef Gilles Choukroun. Scallops with chocolate is one of his inventions. Dishes don't stay on the menu for too long except for the citrus dessert, the house specialty. Casual-chic defines the café's atmosphere.

La Cagouille

10–12 Pl Constantin Brancusi, 75014 **Tel** *01 43 22 09 01*

€€€

Map *15 C3*

This large venue, on the stark new Place Brancusi in the rebuilt Montparnasse district, is one of Paris's best fish restaurants. Big fish are served simply with few fancy sauces or adornments. You might also find unusual seasonal delicacies like black bay scallops and *vendangeurs* (tiny red mullet).

Contre-Allée

83 Ave Denfert-Rochereau, 75014 **Tel** *01 43 54 99 86*

€€€€

Map *16 E3*

Michel Inizian (former chef of Le Procope) conjures up *Escalope de foie gras de canard d'Auvergne poêlée* with apple chutney and exotic fruits, truffle-flavored baby spinach, half-cooked red tuna mince with spices and rizotto au Parmesan. The decor is minimalist and the service is young and energetic.

INVALIDES AND EIFFEL TOWER QUARTER

Sip Babylone

46 Bd Raspail, 75007 **Tel** *01 45 48 87 17*

€

Map *12 D4*

Close to Le Bon Marché and great for a tasty shopping break, this is more a snack bar than a restaurant. Tea and pastries are served all day long in the elaborate dining room. For lunch, try the cheese platters, bacon and Parmesan salad or a plate of smoked salmon, *taramasalata* and aubergine (eggplant).

Au Sauvignon

80 Rue des Sts-Pères, 75007 **Tel** *01 45 48 49 02*

€€

Map *12 D4*

This restaurant revolves around wine. Walls are plastered with posters of the beverage, and the wine list boasts fine vintages accompanied by savory snacks such as fine cheese or smoked salmon toast. Desserts include puff pastry with apple, plum or other seasonal fruit. Sunny terrace.

L'Oeillade

10 Rue de St-Simon, 75007 **Tel** *01 42 22 01 60*

€€

Map *11 C3*

A welcoming restaurant with a good-value and varied set menu featuring deep-fried smelt, *pipérade* (stewed sweet peppers, tomatoes and garlic) with poached egg, *sole meunière*, cod *brandade* (salt cod and garlic purée), roast lamb with cumin and *ile flottante* (meringue in vanilla custard). Extra charges depending on wine.

La Serre

29 Rue de l'Exposition, 75007 **Tel** *01 45 55 20 96*

€€

Map *10 F3*

Owners Mary-Alice and Philippe Beraud offer good home cooking, using the freshest ingredients at reasonable prices. Specialties from the Southwest include *cuisse de canard confite* (preserved leg of duck) with sautéed potatoes and a perfect pot-roasted calves' liver served with a *confiture d'onions*.

Thoumieux

79 Rue St-Dominique, 75007 **Tel** *01 47 05 49 75*

€€

Map *11 A2*

This bustling traditional French bistro offers good value. Ingredients are fresh and almost everything is made on the premises, including *foie gras*, duck *rillettes* (similar to *pâté*), *cassoulet* (white bean and meat stew) and chocolate mousse. Prompt service.

La Villa Corse

164 Bd de Grenelle, 75015 **Tel** *01 53 86 70 81*

€€€

Map *10 E5*

In a pleasant neighborhood, La Villa Corse is regarded as one of the city's best, serving fresh and strongly flavored Corsican-Mediterranean cuisine. The menu features wild boar stew, olive veal, Brocciu cheese and chestnut bread, a specialty from the city of Bonifacio. Good choice of Corsican wines.

'R'

6 Rue de la Cavalerie, 75015 **Tel** *01 45 67 06 85*

€€€

Map *10 E5*

Following a recent revamp, the modern R sports a new look, with new interiors and menu. Pristine white dominates its neo-pop decor by designer Christophe Pillet. The Eiffel Tower is on view from this eighth-floor resto-bar serving an eclectic spread. DJ music on every Thursday, Friday and Saturday.

Le Récamier

4 Rue Récamier, 75007 **Tel** *01 45 48 86 58*

€€€€

Map *12 D4*

A Paris institution, attracting writers, publishers, journalists and political figures, the Récamier is reputed for its classic French character. The menu features Burgundian specialties, such as *boeuf bourguignon*, pike mousse and Grand-Marnier soufflé. Tucked away in a pedestrian street, its terrace is one of the best in Paris.

L'Arpège

84 Rue de Varenne, 75007 **Tel** *01 45 51 47 33*

€€€€€

Map *11 B3*

Alain Passard's three-star restaurant near the Musée Rodin is one of the most highly regarded in Paris. It has striking pale-wood decor and sprightly young service as well as good food. Passard's lobster and turnip vinaigrette and duck Louise Passard are classics. Don't miss the apple tart.

Key to Price Guide *see p300* **Key to Symbols** *see back cover flap*

Le Jules Verne

2nd platform, Eiffel Tower, 75007 **Tel** *01 45 55 61 44*

Map *10 D3*

This is no tourist trap: the Jules Verne on the second platform of the Eiffel Tower is now one of the hardest dinner reservations to obtain in Paris. The sleek, all-black decor suits the monument perfectly and the pretty, flavorful cuisine is very good indeed.

Vin sur Vin

20 Rue de Monttessuy, 75007 **Tel** *01 47 05 14 20*

Map *10 E2*

Owner Patrice Vidal is justly proud of his eight-table restaurant. The menu is seasonal and original, the wine list fabulous with interesting wines at reasonable prices. Dishes might include *pot-au-feu de foie gras*, *salade folle* and *cote de veau de Cantal*.

CHAILLOT AND PORTE MAILLOT

Chez Géraud

31 Rue Vital, 75016 **Tel** *01 45 20 33 00*

Map *9 B3*

Géraud Rongier, the jovial owner, is a scrupulous observer of *cuisine du marché*, using what's best at the market that day to create dishes like shoulder of lamb cooked on a spit, *sabodet* sausage in red wine sauce, skate with mustard, roast pigeon with port sauce and bitter chocolate cake. The mural was specially created.

Oum El Banine

16 bis Rue Dufrenoy, 75016 **Tel** *01 45 04 91 22*

Map *9 A1*

The owner of this small, authentic restaurant in the chic residential quarter learned her art from her mother in Morocco. There is good *harira* soup (a thick, spicy soup), flavorful tagines, *pastilla* (a savory puff-pastry tart) and *brik* (stuffed pastry triangle). Couscous is served with five choices of ragoût.

6 New York

6 Ave de New York, 75016 **Tel** *01 40 70 03 30*

Map *10 E1*

A trendy restaurant, with an impressive minimalist interior, 6 New York marries pale wood and soft tones of gray. Though known to be a fashionable venue, it serves a surprisingly traditional cuisine, featuring pig's trotters (feet), Niçoise sole and vegetable risotto.

L'Astrance

4 Rue de Beethoven, 75016 **Tel** *01 40 50 84 40*

Map *9 C3*

The inventive cuisine of L'Astrance's two chefs have made it so popular that you must reserve at least a month ahead. Dishes include sautéed pigeon with a caramelized hazelnut sauce and apple and celery minestrone with roasted spice ice cream. The Menu Surprise is as lovely as the mountain flower this restaurant is named after.

L'Huitrier

16 Rue Saussier Leroy, 75017 **Tel** *01 40 54 83 44*

Map *4 E2*

This freshly decorated restaurant specializes in shellfish, especially oysters which you order by the half-dozen or dozen. It also serves several hot fish dishes and makes a good restorative stop before or after visiting the animated market in the nearby Rue Poncelet.

La Butte Chaillot

110 Bis Ave Kléber, 75016 **Tel** *01 47 27 88 88*

Map *4 D5*

This is the boutique restaurant of the renowned, not to say deified, chef Guy Savoy. The country bistro cuisine includes snail salad, oysters with a cream mousse, roast breast of veal with rosemary and apple tart. The clientele are chic, so make sure you dress up.

La Plage

Port Javel 75015 **Tel** *01 40 59 41 00*

Map *9 B5*

A spectacular site facing the Statue of Liberty on the Ile aux Cignes. Thankfully, the cuisine's as good as the view. The huge terrace is the place to be seen at lunchtime, as well as an idyllic spot for a candlelit dinner on a balmy summer's eve. The decor is an attractive mix of wood and pastel tones.

Zebra Square

3 Pl Clément Ader, 75016 **Tel** *01 44 14 91 91*

Map *9 B4*

Part of the Hotel Square complex, a modern building with minimalist decor spiced up by splashes of zebra prints. Equally modern fare: crab cakes, aubergine (eggplant) *carpaccio* and salmon tartare. Brunch on Sundays. Stylish rooms done up in rich, soothing colors. A hit with the fashion and media crowd.

59 Poincaré

59 Ave Raymond Poincaré, 75016 **Tel** *01 47 27 59 59*

Map *9 C1*

In this historic townhouse, Alain Ducasse creates France's great "classic" dishes. Each culinary region is featured, particularly his native Southwest. Dishes include *turbot de Bretagne*, *chevreuil* (venison) *d'Alsace* and *fois gras de canard des Landes*. The enviable wine list highlights the Bordeaux region.

Le Timgad
21 Rue Brunel, 75017 **Tel** *01 45 74 23 70*

€€€€

Map *3 C3*

This has been Paris's best-known, most elegant Maghrebian restaurant for years, hence the need to reserve in good time. The menu has many different *briks*, tagines and *couscous* dishes as well as specialties like grilled pigeon, *pastilla* and *méchoui* (whole roast lamb), which needs to be ordered in advance.

Prunier
16 Ave Victor Hugo, 75116 **Tel** *01 44 17 35 85*

€€€€

Map *4 D4*

One of the prettiest seafood restaurants, Prunier was founded in 1925. Its dazzling Art-Deco interior features wooden panels in the upstairs dining room. Wonderful seafood including smoked salmon and a variety of caviars. The menu changes with the season. Valet parking available.

CHAMPS-ELYSÉES

Ladurée
16 Rue Royale, 75008 **Tel** *01 42 60 21 79*

€

Map *4 F5*

Celebrated as one of the best tearooms in town since 1862, Ladurée hasn't lost any of its class. This elegant tearoom, famous for its Renaissance-style interior, still serves its renowned macaroons, which come in all kinds of inventive flavors: aniseed, caramel, chestnut, lime and basil.

Le Stübli
11 Rue Poncelet, 75017 **Tel** *01 42 27 81 86*

€

Map *4 E3*

A little corner of Germany with a patisserie, deli and tea room. For lunch, try the great classics, such as sauerkraut. Their apple *strudel*, *linzertorte* and authentic Viennese hot chocolate make for a fine afternoon tea. Lunch is served on the terrace. German beer and wine is available.

La Fermette Marbeuf 1900
5 Rue Marbeuf, 75008 **Tel** *01 53 23 08 00*

€€

Map *4 F5*

Fabulous Belle Époque mosaics, tiles and ironwork were discovered beneath the formica walls of this Champs-Elysées bistro. La Fermette Marbeuf also serves good brasserie-style food including a commendable set menu with many *appellations contrôlées* wines – a measure of their quality.

Le Boeuf sur le Toit
34 Rue du Colisée, 75008 **Tel** *01 53 93 65 55*

€€

Map *5 A4*

Highly inspired by the 1930s – *Les Années Folles* – the building (The Ox on the Roof) was formerly a venue hosting cabarets. Exemplifying the classic Paris Art-Deco brasserie, its changing menu can include *sole meunière*, snails, *foie gras* and *crème brûlée*.

Sébillon
66 Rue Pierre Charron, 75008 **Tel** *01 43 59 28 15*

€€€

Map *4 F5*

The current restaurant is an offshoot of the original Sébillon based in the bourgeois suburb of Neuilly since 1913. The menu is the same with shellfish, lobster salad, scallops *à la Provençale*, ribroast of beef and gigantic éclairs. The great specialty here is leg of lamb – as much as you want, sliced at your table.

Verre Bouteille
85 Ave des Ternes, 75017 **Tel** *01 45 74 01 02*

€€€

Map *3 C2*

Verre Bouteille proves that simple can be tasty. The house specialty is steak tartare, but goat's cheese ravioli, *foie gras* and chocolate cake are also superb. Lunch is much cheaper than dinner. If you liked what you ate here, and feel audacious enough to try the recipe, you can find it on their website: www.leverrebouteille.com

Flora Danica
142 Ave des Champs-Elysées, 75008 **Tel** *01 44 13 86 26*

€€€€

Map *4 E4*

On the ground floor of the House of Denmark, this venue is more relaxed and less pricey than Copenhague upstairs. Original Scandinavian cuisine, with just a touch of France. Specialties include grilled salmon and strawberries with mulled wine. Interiors are prettily done in Danish style. Valet parking available.

L'Avenue
41 Ave Montaigne, 75008 **Tel** *01 40 70 14 91*

€€€€

Map *10 F1*

Located at the hub of *couture* fashion, L'Avenue attracts an elegant crowd. The unusual Neo-1950s decor is fresh and colourful. Service can get a bit hectic at peak lunch and dinner times, but then this is a brasserie. The cuisine is varied and supper is served until late.

Man Ray
34 Rue Marbeuf, 75008 **Tel** *01 56 88 36 36*

€€€€

Map *4 F5*

A high resto-bar filled with golden Buddhas, Chinese lanterns and Oriental artifacts. French-Asian fusion cuisine features citrus and ginger tuna and wok-fried scampi with oyster mushrooms. Great selection of sushi. A live orchestra plays Mozart on occasional Monday evenings.

Key to Price Guide *see p p300* **Key to Symbols** *see back cover flap*

Tanjia

P X €€€€

23 Rue de Pontieux, 75008 **Tel** *01 42 25 95 00*

Map *5 A5*

A celebrity hotspot, run by Cathy and David Guetta, the glossy Tanjia has a warm Moroccan feel. Serves authentic food: the Tanjia tagine is cooked with 25 spices for no less than 10 hours. After dinner, there is water-pipe smoking in the lounge.

Guy Savoy

T €€€€€

18 Rue Troyon, 75017 **Tel**

Map *4 D3*

A handsome dining room and professional service further complement the remarkable cuisine of Guy Savoy himself. The three-starred Michelin menu includes oysters in aspic, Bresse chicken with a sherry vinegar glaze, poached or grilled pigeon with lentils, and then an extraordinary dessert.

La Maison Blanche

P X & 🔲 T €€€€€

15 Ave Montaigne, 75008 **Tel** *01 47 23 55 99*

Map *10 F1*

The popular Maison Blanche restaurant affixed 15 Avenue Montaigne to its name when it moved here. Although the decor is modern, the restaurant is almost opulently vast. The cuisine, with its Provençale and Southwestern influences, is flavorsome and is the main attraction for its worldly clientele.

Le Cercle Ledoyen

P X T €€€€€

1 Ave Dutuit, 75008 **Tel** *01 53 05 10 02*

Map *11 B1*

The refined cuisine at Le Cercle Ledoyen mainly features turbot breast and mashed potatoes with truffle butte (a sea fish recipe) and *mille-feuilles de Krampouz croustillante avec crème de citron*. Ask for a table in the dining room – a re-creation of an 1950s grill room – or on the terrace.

OPÉRA QUARTER

Chartier

X & €

7 Rue du Faubourg Montmartre, 75009 **Tel** *01 47 70 86 29*

Map *6 F4*

Despite its impressive 1900s decor, Chartier still caters to people on a budget, mostly students and tourists, though some of the old habitués still come for the basic cuisine (hard-boiled eggs with mayonnaise, house pâté, roast chicken and pepper steak). Expect to wait, as the waiters are very busy.

Chez Clément

X €

17 Blvd des Capucines, 75002 **Tel** *01 53 43 82 00*

Map *6 E5*

Just two minutes walk from the Opéra, this comfortable bistro (part of a chain) serves its signature dishes of roast meats until well after midnight every day of the year. The dish of the day is always good value and, unusually, is available for both lunch and dinner.

La Vaudeville

X 🔲 €€

29 Rue Vivienne, 75002 **Tel** *01 40 20 04 62*

Map *6 F5*

This is one of seven brasseries owned by Paris's reigning brasserie king, Jean-Paul Bucher. Good shellfish, Bucher's famous smoked salmon, many different fish dishes as well as classic brasserie standards like pig's trotters and *andouillette*. A quick, friendly service and noisy ambience make it lots of fun.

Le Noces de Jeanette

X & €€

14 Rue Favart, 75002 **Tel** *01 42 96 36 89*

Map *6 F5*

A typical Parisian bistro, named for the one-act curtain-raising opera performed at the Opera Comique across the street. An ornate interior belies the cozy atmosphere. The fixed-price menu offers a wide choice of classic dishes. Try the vichyssoise or *terrine de crustacés à la crème d'Oseille*. Menu changes regularly.

Angl'Opéra

X 🔲 €€€

39 Ave de l'Opéra, 75002 **Tel** *01 42 61 86 25*

Map *6 E5*

In this chic, informal restaurant, top chef Gilles Choukroun flexes his culinary muscles with his trademark cooking of blending and marrying flavors in ways quite unlike anywhere else in Paris's food circuit. Expect iconoclastic dishes such as *crème brulée* of foie gras.

Café Runtz

& €€€

16 Rue Favart, 75002 **Tel** *01 42 96 69 86*

Map *6 F5*

One of the few genuine Alsatian *weinstub* (wine bars) in Paris, Café Runtz has been doing business since the turn-of-the-19th century. Photos of entertainment stars remind you that the Salle Favart (the former Opéra Comique) is next door. Regional specialties include Gruyère salad, onion tart, *choucroute*, *jambonneau* and fruit tarts.

Le Grand Colbert

€€€

2–4 Rue Vivienne, 75002 **Tel** *01 42 86 87 88*

Map *6 F5*

Situated in the restored Galérie Colbert owned by the Bibliothèque Nationale, this must be one of the prettiest brasseries in Paris. The menu offers classic brasserie fare – herring fillets with potatoes or cream, snails, onion soup, classic whiting Colbert (in breadcrumbs) and grilled meats.

Willi's Wine Bar

13 Rue des Petits-Champs, 75001 **Tel** *01 42 61 05 09*

Map 12 F1

Original wine posters cover the walls and over 250 vintages are in the cellar at Willi's Wine Bar. The menu includes onion tart with a salad topped with pine nuts, beef *fricassée* with braised chicory (endive) and rosemary sauce and bitter chocolate terrine.

Café Drouant

18 Rue Gaillon, 75002 **Tel** *01 42 65 15 16*

Map 6 E5

Founded in the 19th century, this is one of Paris's most historic restaurants. The café, not to be confused with the more expensive restaurant, is a fashionable spot which serves excellent food until late and has an extremely good value menu at dinner. The interior has a famous shellfish-motif ceiling.

La Fontaine Gaillon

1 Rue de la Michodière, 75002 **Tel** *01 47 42 63 22*

Map 6 E5

In a 17th-century mansion, Fontaine Gaillon is partly owned by legendary film actor Gérard Depardieu. The menu showcases sautéed John Dory, Merlan Colbert with sorrel purée, *confit de canard* and lamb chops. Comfortable interiors and a good wine list.

Lucas Carton

9 Pl de la Madeleine, 75008 **Tel** *01 42 65 22 90*

Map 5 C5

The audacious three-Michelin-starred cuisine of super-chef Alain Senderens is something you will either love or hate. His legendary creations include *foie gras* with cabbage, spicy duck Apicius and a mango *mille-feuille vanille*. The Belle-Époque decor is stunning and the crowd is certainly glamorous.

MONTMARTRE

Au Grain de Folie

24 Rue la Vieuville, 75018 **Tel** *01 42 58 15 57*

Map 6 F1

Paris has only a handful of vegetarian restaurants, and Au Grain de Follie has a truly cozy feel. Main courses consist of salads with interesting combinations of vegetables and grains (most of which are organic). The apple crumble is highly recommended.

Musée de la Halle St-Pierre

2 Rue Ronsard, 75018 **Tel** *01 42 58 72 89*

Map 7 A1

Formerly a covered market, this venue now hosts a library, the Max Fourny primitive art museum and a restaurant. This is a popular spot for afternoon tea and pastries. At lunch, the menu is more substantial with savory bites such as quiche, pies and tarts. Children's activities provided.

Le Restaurant

32 Rue Véron, 75018 **Tel** *01 42 23 06 22*

Map 6 E1

Almost invisible from the main road, this place teems with locals every night of the week. Its original distressed-chic decor provides a unique setting, while the kitchen offers French food with a twist. The split-pea soup with giant *gambas* (prawns) is a must, as is the delicious chocolate tart.

Le Wepler

14 Pl de Clichy, 75018 **Tel** *01 45 22 53 24*

Map 6 D1

Retro-style brasserie open until late into the night. Good for afternoon tea, early evening cocktails and pre- or post-show suppers. Large shellfish platters as well as sauerkraut, *andouillette* and *confit de canard*. An institution, established in 1892.

Beauvilliers

52 Rue Lamarck, 75018 **Tel** *01 42 54 54 42*

Map 2 E5

Montmartre's best and one of the most festive in Paris, this is where effusive chef Edouard Carlier delves into old cookbooks for ideas. Favorites are *escabèche* of red mullet (the fish is cooked and marinated), veal *rognonnade* (part of à loin of veal with the kidney) and a very lemony lemon tart.

FARTHER AFIELD

Dao Vien

82 Rue Baudricourt, 75013 **Tel** *01 45 85 20 70*

Map 18 D5

In the heart of original Paris Chinatown, this friendly Vietnamese restaurant is especially pleasant. *Soupe Saïgonnaise* is a Dao Vien specialty, along with delicious egg-stuffed crêpes, chicken with ginger, and jasmine tea.

Key to Price Guide *see p300* **Key to Symbols** *see back cover flap*

Favela Chic
18 Rue Fbg du Temple, 75011 **Tel** *01 40 21 38 14*   €

Map *8 D5*

Not much of Brazil is missing from this lively haven, run by Jerome and Roseanne. The *caipirinha* (fresh lime, cane-sugar alcohol and lots of crushed ice) has lost none of its buzz, and the *feijoada* tastes just as it does back in Salvador Bahia. The place gets noisy as the evening progresses, so come early.

L'Occitanie
96 Rue Oberkampf, 75011 **Tel** *01 48 06 46 98*   €

Map *14 F1*

As the name indicates, the cuisine here is deeply rooted in the Southwest, as is the welcome from the Occitan-speaking *bon-viveur* owner. *Cassoulet*, *confit* or *potage à rouzole* (soup with sausage-meat and herb dumplings) are some of the typical dishes served here. Helpings are generous.

Le Baron Rouge
1 Rue Théophile Roussel, 75012 **Tel** *01 43 43 14 32*   €

Map *14 F5*

Right next to the lively Marché d'Aligre (see p338), Parisians rush here on weekends to sample the divine oysters, brought straight from Cap Ferret on the Atlantic coast. These can be eaten out on the sidewalk, standing around large wine barrels. Also a good wine bar during the week.

Le Volant
13 Rue Beatrix Dussane, 75015 **Tel** *01 45 75 27 67*   €

Map *10 D5*

The owner of Le Volant (The Steering Wheel) is fanatical about auto racing. There's nothing racy, however, about the cooking: it is simple, traditional French cuisine at its best; *boeuf bourguignon*, mouthwatering homemade fruit tarts and the never-to-be-forgotten chocolate mousse.

Restaurant 8
1 Rue Maillard, 75011 **Tel** *01 44 64 11 92*   €

Showbiz and good eating combine in this unique restaurant, where Italian cuisine is served in the basement of Kiron Espace's film studio. The menu changes regularly, but do try the cappelleti pasta with ribbons of parma ham and the layered ricotta cream dessert with figs and maraschino-soaked biscuit.

Astier
44 Jean-Pierre Timbaud, 75011 **Tel** *01 43 57 16 35*   €€

Map *14 E1*

Quality here is among the best for the price in Paris, and the dining rooms are always full in this hugely popular bistro. The food is very good, including mussel soup with saffron, rabbit in mustard sauce, duck breast with honey, and good cheeses and wines.

Brasserie Flo
7 Cour des Petites-Ecuries, 75010 **Tel** *01 47 70 13 59*   €€

Map *7 B4*

This authentic Alsatian brasserie is situated in a passageway in a slightly unsavory neighborhood. But it is worth the effort to find it: the rich wood and stained-glass decor is unique and very pretty and the straightforward brasserie menu includes good shellfish and *choucroute* (sauerkraut).

Chez Fernand
17-19 Rue de la Fontaine au Roi, 75011 **Tel** *01 43 57 46 25*   €€

Map *8 E5*

The banal decor and modest prices of this small restaurant near the Place de la République are no reflection of the good Normandy-based cuisine: mackerel *rillettes* (similar to pâté), skate with Camembert, *tarte Normande* (apple tart) flambéed with Calvados.

Chez Prune
36 Rue Beaurepaire, 75010 **Tel** *01 42 41 30 47*   €€

Map *8 D4*

With wonderful views of Canal Saint-Martin, this is a top spot for brunch on Sundays, with a choice of smoked salmon or ham with croissants. Upmarket cuisine for lunch: saffron and lime fish and three-cheese ravioli. Platters of cold meats and cheeses in the evening. Daily food based on *cuisine du marché*.

Julien
16 Rue du Faubourg St-Denis, 75010 **Tel** *01 47 70 12 06*   €€

Map *7 B5*

With its superb 1880s decor, Julien is upmarket but reasonable. Under the same ownership as Brasserie Flo, it has the same friendly service and wide dessert variety. The imaginative brasserie cuisine includes hot *foie gras* with lentils, breaded pig's trotter and Julien's version of *cassoulet*.

La Mère Lanchaise
78 Bd de Menilmontant, 75020 **Tel** *01 47 97 61 60*   €€

This is a friendly bistro with a split personality. A great terrace and two dining rooms – one traditional and the other plastered in aluminum. Uncomplicated food includes asparagus and citrus fruit salad, beef with potato gratin, *charcuterie* and crumble with seasonal fruit.

Le Bistro des Deux Théâtres
18 Rue Blanche, 75009 **Tel** *01 45 26 41 43*   €€

Map *6 D3*

If you are on a strict budget this formula restaurant in the theater district is a real find. The reasonable set menu includes an apéritif, a choice of first and main courses, cheese or dessert and a half bottle of wine. The food is reliably good, including duck *foie gras* and smoked salmon with *blinis* (small savory pancakes).

Le Clos Morillons

50 Rue des Morillons, 75015 **Tel** *01 48 28 04 37*

This discreet family-run restaurant's menu evolves constantly. The Far Eastern travels of chef Philippe Delacourcelle are evident in specialties such as cod roasted with cinnamon, pigeon with sesame and monkfish and lobster with ginger. Other dishes are more French. Respectable Loire wines complement the set menu which changes regularly.

Le Paprika

28 Ave Trudaine, 75009 **Tel** *01 44 63 02 91*

Map *6 F2*

Gourmet Hungarian cuisine and live gypsy music (October–April and June). A dish such as the *csáky bélszin* (beef with morels and *foie gras*) is familiar to the French palate, but desserts such as apple and cinnamon strudel offer a taste of Central Europe. Occasional live music.

Pause Café

41 Rue de Charonne, 75011 **Tel** *01 48 06 80 33*

Map *14 F4*

Since the shooting of *Chacun Cherche son Chat*, this has been a top spot to be seen. Luckily this has not ruined the friendly ambience nor the fine cuisine: light dishes such as steak tartare, tarts with salads and excellent homemade pastries. The stone and glass interior lends a rustic-elegant charm

Piston Pélican

15 Rue de Bagnolet, 75020 **Tel** *01 43 70 35 00*

A long bar, wooden benches and a collection of old advertisements adorn this quaint venue. Salads served in hollowed-out bread, salmon tartare with sesame oil and caramel-centered chocolate cake exemplify the menu's twist on classic dishes.

L'Auberge du Bonheur

Allée de Longchamps, Bois de Boulogne, 75016 **Tel** *01 42 24 10 17*

Map *3 A3*

This is probably the only affordable restaurant in the Bois. In summer you can sit on the gravel terrace under chestnut and plane trees, surrounded by wisteria and bamboo. It's also delightful in cool weather inside the cozy chalet. The simple service complements cuisine that emphasizes grilled meats.

La Marine

55 Quai Valmy, 75010 **Tel** *01 42 39 69 81*

Map *8 D5*

For several years now this establishment has been the headquarters of the Internet trade, and as such, is usually packed, so call ahead. The main courses are good and mainly fishy, such as red mullet in puff pastry, fish steak with a creamy nettle sauce, or fish stew. The desserts aren't so highly recommended.

Le Bistro d'à Côté Flaubert

10 Rue Gustave Flaubert, 75017 **Tel** *01 42 67 05 81*

Map *4 E2*

This was the first and remains the most appealing of star-chef Michel Rostang's boutique bistros. Many Lyonnais dishes are served including lentil salad, *cervelas* or *sabodet* sausage, *andouillette*, and macaroni gratin. Popular with executives at lunch and with the upper layers of the bourgeoisie at night.

Le Chardenoux

1 Rue Jules Vallès, 75011 **Tel** *01 43 71 49 52*

This classic bistro is one of the prettiest in Paris. Both fish and meat feature on the traditional French menu, with dishes such as roasted cod, preserved duck and fricasée of kidney. The wine list covers all of France's wine regions. The menu changes depending on the market.

Le Clou

132 Rue Cardinet, 75017 **Tel** *01 42 27 36 78*

Map *5 A1*

Traditional bistro, complete with a collection of old advertisements and blackboard menus. Scallops, grilled beef and desserts such as glazed nougat and chocolate cake never leave the menu. The well-priced wine list features a great range of French wines from various regions.

Le Train Bleu

Pl Louis Armand, 75012 **Tel** *01 43 43 09 06*

Map *18 E1*

Train station restaurants were once grand places for a meal. Today this is not usually so, but the Train Bleu (named after the fast train that once took the élite to the Riviera) in the Gare de Lyon is a pleasant exception. Upmarket brasserie cuisine such as hot Lyonnais sausage, with excellent pastries. The Belle Époque decor is a landmark.

Le Villaret

13 Rue Ternaux, 75011 **Tel** *01 43 57 89 76*

Map *14 E2*

Tucked away on the Oberkampf district's northern fringes, this restaurant is run by the former staff from nearby Astier. Well-known for its *cuisine du marché* (using the freshest ingredients from the day's market), carefully chosen and prepared meat and big cheese selection. Packed on weekends.

Les Allobroges

71 Rue des Grands-Champs, 75020 **Tel** *01 43 73 40 00*

It's worth the trip out to taste chef Olivier Pateyron's fresh and innovative cooking. Specialties include *Canettes aux épices* (duck with spices) and *Souris d'agneau ail en chemise et purée de poix* (lamb with garlic and bean mash). A complementary *amuse-gueule*, different every day of the year, is offered.

Key to Price Guide *see p300* **Key to Symbols** *see back cover flap*

Les Amognes

243 Rue du Faubourg St-Antoine, 75011 **Tel** *01 43 72 73 05*

Chef Thierry Coué has worked under Alain Senderens *(see p312)*, and his small restaurant is not pretty, but the food is original and good. The cod fritters with tomatoes and basil, tuna with artichokes and bell pepper, sea bream with a chilli-oil and pineapple soup with Pina Colada are worth the trip. Seasonal menu.

Au Pressoir

257 Ave Daumesnil, 75012 **Tel** *01 43 44 38 21*

Chef Séguin and his wife are passionate about quality, and it shows. Dishes are often unusual, such as monkfish with bacon and split peas, *foie gras* with Jerusalem artichokes, pigeon with aubergine *blinis* and chocolate soup with brioche. Excellent service and wine list. Comfortable surroundings.

L'Oulette

15 Pl Lachambeaudie, 75012 **Tel** *01 40 02 02 12*

L'Oulette's vast new premises may lack intimacy, but Chef Marcel Baudis's cuisine, reflecting his native Quercy, remains excellent. Dishes include duck *foie gras* cooked *en terrine* and jurancon sauce, lamb from the Pyrenées, and *pain d'épices* (a kind of spiced cake).

Le Chalet des Îles

14 Chemin Ceinture du Lac Inférieur du Bois de Boulogne, 75116 **Tel** *01 42 88 04 69*   **Map 3 A4**

Idyllic setting, nestled on an island in the middle of a lake. The country-style interior suits the bucolic environment, but the cuisine showcases a modern approach: pan-fried sole with a Creole-style sauce, coconut and lemon chicken with red rice and chocolate cake with a red berry *coulis*.

Le Pavillon Montsouris

20 Rue Gazan, 75014 **Tel** *01 43 13 29 00*

This restored building once counted Trotsky, Mata Hari and Lenin among its clientele. Today the attractive interior and terrace make fine surroundings for a good value set menu. Specialties include fish tartar, wild boar with bacon and wine sauce, and *crème brulée à la vanille Bourbon*.

Tante Jeanne

116 Blvd Pereire, 75017 **Tel** *01 43 80 88 68*   **Map 4 E1**

The late Bernard Loiseau opened this place where a stylish crowd now enjoys *croustillant de langoustine et pied de cochon jus iodé* (pig's feet in a fish-flavored sauce), *filet de bar grille au fenouil "confit-purée-jus"* (anis-flavored grilled fish), and *rafraichi de pamplemousse, gelée de Campari* (grapefruit, Campari sauce).

Apicius

122 Ave de Villiers, 75017 **Tel** *01 43 80 19 66*   **Map 4 D1**

Although chef-owner Jean-Pierre Vigato looks more like a model, his cuisine is hearty: he enjoys preparing offal and treating fish like meat. Dishes include roast sweetbreads, pig's trotters roasted *en crépinette* (with small sausages), all-caramel or all-chocolate desserts. Personal service by lovely Madame Vigato.

Auguste

98 Rue de Tocqueville, 75017 **Tel** *01 47 63 39 97*   **Map 5 A1**

This reliable restaurant serves excellent fish and a few meat dishes. The *salade augusta* is generously garnished with shellfish and the house specialty *bouillabaise* with potatoes must be one of the best in Paris. An unusual dish is langoustines flavored with tarragon and saffron.

Au Trou Gascon

40 Rue Taine, 75012 **Tel** *01 43 44 34 26*

This authentic 1900s bistro owned by star-chef Alain Dutournier (of Carré des Feuillants) is one of Paris's most popular places. The delicious Gascon food includes ham from the Chalosse region, great *foie gras*, lamb from the Pyrenees and local poultry. Dutournier's desserts are also worth finding room for.

Dessirier

9 Pl du Maréchal Juin, 75017 **Tel** *01 42 27 82 14*   **Map 4 E1**

Dedicated to seafood since 1883, this is one of Paris's best-known fish restaurants. Oyster risotto, whole grilled sea bass and langoustine salad feature. A combination of fish brasserie and wet-fish market, it offers a variety of fish-based dishes, depending on the season. Affordable wine list available. Valet parking.

Faucher

123 Ave de Wagram, 75017 **Tel** *01 42 27 61 50*   **Map 4 E2**

Monsieur and Mme Faucher take a great interest in their restaurant and guests. The big dining room with large windows is pretty and the terrace a delight in fine weather. The original food includes *mille-feuille* of spinach and sliced raw beef, truffle-stuffed egg, turbot with caviar cream and a good selection of desserts.

Le Pré Catelan

Route de Suresnes, Bois de Boulogne, 75016 **Tel** *01 44 14 41 14*

This elegant Belle Époque restaurant in the Bois is a delight, either in midsummer when you can dine on the terrace, or in midwinter when the lights inside are magical. The menu is luxurious, with huge langoustines, special Duclair duck with spices and sea urchin soufflé. Divine desserts. There is a cheaper menu at lunchtime.

Light Meals and Snacks

Good food and drink are so much a part of everyday life in Paris that you can eat and drink well without ever going to a restaurant. Whether you want to enjoy a meal or casual drink at a café, wine bar or tearoom, buy a crêpe from a street stand or a quiche or crusty *baguette* sandwich from a bakery, or put together a picnic from cheeses, breads, salads and *pâtés*, informal eating is one of the city's great gastronomic strengths.

Paris is also a wonderful city for drinking. Wine bars in every quarter offer various wines by the glass. Beer bars have astounding selections, and Irish pubs are much-loved spots which serve Guinness in a relaxed, sometimes rowdy atmosphere. Or choose from chic hotel bars or fun late-night bars. *(See also pp298–9.)*

CAFES

Paris is famous for its cafés, and rightly so. You can't walk far in this city without passing one. They range in size from tiny to huge, some with pin-ball machines, a tobacconist and betting stations, some with elegant Belle Epoque decorations and immaculately attired waiters. Every Parisian has their favorite local café and these establishments function as the heart of any neighborhood. The life of a café changes throughout the day and it's always fascinating to check out the locals at leisure, sipping their morning espresso, tucking into a hearty lunch or drinking an *apéritif* after work. Most cafés will serve you light food and drink at any time of day.

Breakfast definitely is one of the busiest times and fresh croissants and *pains au chocolat* (chocolate-filled pastries) sell fast. The French often eat these dipped in a bowl or large cup of milky coffee or hot chocolate. Eating breakfast out at a café, or at least grabbing a quick caffeine fix in the morning, is a fundamental part of the French lifestyle.

The café lunch usually includes *plats du jour* (daily specials) and, in the smaller cafés, is one of the great Parisian bargains, rarely costing more than 12€ for two courses with wine. The specials are often substantial meat dishes such as *sauté d'agneau* (sautéed lamb) or *blanquette de veau* (veal with

a white sauce), with fruit tarts for dessert. For a simpler lunch, salads, sandwiches and omelettes are usually available at any time of day. One of the best places for this kind of food is the **Bar du Marché** in St-Germain-des-Prés. **Le Rostand** by the Luxembourg Gardens is also an excellent place to eat as is **Le Café du Marché** in the Invalides district.

Most museums have reliable cafés, but those at the Pompidou Centre *(see pp110–11)* and the Musée d'Orsay *(see pp144–5)* are especially good. When visiting the Louvre, it is worth waiting till you re-emerge from the galleries and stopping at the upmarket **Café Marly** in front of the glass pyramid for an expensive, yet memorable drink or meal. Should you find yourself in the department store **La Samaritaine** *(see p321)*, it's worth going to the café for the fabulous views over Paris.

Cafés in the main tourist and nightlife areas (Boulevard St-Germain, Avenue des Champs-Elysées, Boulevard Montparnasse, the Opéra and Bastille) generally stay open late – some until 2am.

It is important to note that prices change depending on where in the café you choose to enjoy your drink. Standing at the bar with a glass of beer is usually a little cheaper than sitting at one of the tables, and heading outside to the terrace will normally cost you more again.

TEA SALONS

Tearooms have become increasingly popular in Paris over the last few years and the selection of teas is normally impressive. Some tea salons also offer light lunches, as well as breakfast and afternoon tea, including **Bernardaud**, the porcelain manufacturers, where you can choose which tea service to eat off. **Mariage Frères** in the Marais is well known for its exhaustive drink list and also sells loose tea and lovely teapots to take home. **Ladurée** on the Champs Elysées is a Parisian institution where well-heeled ladies sip tea and nibble the house specialty macaroons. For another type of tea, visit the mosaic-tiled **Café de la Mosquée**, at Paris's mosque in the Jardin des Plantes area, for sticky pastries and excellent mint tea.

WINE BARS

Most Parisian wine bars are small, convivial neighborhood places. They open early, many doubling as cafés for breakfast, and offer a small, good-quality lunch menu. It's best to get there early or after 1:30pm if you want to avoid the crowd. Most wine bars are usually closed by 9pm.

Wine bar owners tend to be passionate about wine, most of them buying directly from producers. Young Bordeaux wines and those from the Loire, Rhône and the Jura can be surprisingly good, and wine bar owners usually seek out interesting tipples. The **L'Ecluse** chain specializes in Bordeaux, but for the most part you will find delicious lesser-known wines at very reasonable prices. Serious oenophiles might like to visit wine bars which form part of wine shops so that any interesting vintages tasted can be ordered by the case-load and enjoyed at home. There are several examples of this type of place in Paris – **Juveniles**, **Lavinia** and

Legrand Filles et Fils in the Opéra district are among the finest. Juveniles is a small shop with a zinc bar run by a Scotsman. The selection is very good, especially for wines from the New World and great food is also served here. Lavinia is Europe's largest wine store. The choice is vast, there are regular tastings and the sleek bar serves many wines by the glass. The climate-controlled fine wines section is also worth a visit. Legrand is an old-fashioned vintner which is extremely popular with Parisian wine buffs. The bar has a lovely selection and knowlegable staff. The most fashionable wine bar of this type is **Wine and Bubbles** in the Beaubourg and Les Halles district. This is a great place to spend a whole evening.

BEER BARS AND PUBS

Paris has both pubs and beer bars. Whereas pubs are simply for drinking, beer bars also serve a particular style of food and are larger. *Moules-frites* (a generous bowl of steamed mussels served with French fries), *tarte aux poireaux* (leek tart) and *tarte aux oignons* (onion tart) are classic examples of the food they serve. The chief reason for going to a beer bar, however, is for the beer. The lists are often vast: some specialize in Belgian *gueuze* (heavy, malty, very alcoholic beer), others have beers from all around the world.

Some beer bars are open from noon, whereas pubs open later in the afternoon. Pubs are usually open every day, often until 1 or 2am. The pubs in Paris have a good mix of expatriate and French clients. Some pubs are also microbreweries serving beer brewed on the premises. The **Frog and Princess** and the **Frog and Rosbif** are good examples of this type of pub, serving several types of home-brewed beer. The bar staff are very friendly and will happily help you choose the pint that's right for you. Aside from traditionally English pubs such as **The Bombardier**

in the Latin Quarter, Paris has dozens of Irish pubs and a few Scottish pubs. The best Irish pubs include **Coolin** and **Corcoran's** in St-Germain-des-Prés, **Kitty O'Sheas** and **Carrs** in the Tuileries district and **O'Sullivans by the Mill** in Montmartre. A Highland fling and good whisky can be found in the **Highlander** in St-Germain-des-Prés and **The Auld Alliance** in the Marais.

BARS

In such an elegant city, it's no surprise that Paris has more than its share of cocktail and late-night bars too. Some pretty Paris brasseries, such as **La Coupole**, **La Rotonde** and **La Closerie des Lilas**, have long wooden or zinc bars, accomplished bartenders, a glamorous ambience and a sense of distinguished times past. Hotel bars are some of the loveliest places for cocktails in Paris. **The Hemingway Bar** at the Ritz *(see p286)* is the most famous hotel bar in Paris. It is full of nostalgia, small, intimate, lined with heavy wood and has the official Best Bartender in the World, Colin Peter Field. The cocktails here are wonderful and each drink for a lady comes complete with a fresh flower. Other hotel bars of note include the bar at the hotel Four Seasons George V *(see p290)* where the bartenders will shake your martini at your table and present it in an individual silver shaker, the rooftop terrace at the Hôtel Raphaël *(see p289)* and the fashion-able bar at the hotel Plaza Athénée *(see p291)*.

La Mezzanine de l'Alcazar is one of Paris' most fashionable bars, while **Le Rosebud** and the **China Club** are young and trendy. Other hip bars include **Le Fumoir** next to the Louvre with its long elegant bar and excellent cocktails, **Andy Wahloo** which is tiny with a Moroccan design, **De LaVille** café which is popular as a pre-club destination, **Rhubarb** which has a wonderful martini menu and **The Lizard Lounge**, which attracts a noisy, young crowd. The

Philippe Starck designed bar and restaurant **Kong**, on top of the Kenzo store near the Pont Neuf, is currently Paris's trendiest place for drinks.

Bars which are less trendy but great for a relaxing drink include the tiny, stone-clad **Stolly's** in the Marais and **Harry's Bar**, a legendary American bar which claims to have invented the Bloody Mary.

TAKE-OUT FOOD

Crêpes are the traditional Parisian street food. Although there are fewer good crêpe stands than there used to be, they still exist. Sandwich bars provide *baguettes* with a wide range of fillings, a Parisien – a type of *baguette* – is normally Emmental cheese with ham, Camembert-filled sandwichs tend to be delicious, but beware the misguidingly named *crudités* (salad) which normally includes tuna and mayonnaise along with the *crudités*. The best fast food in Paris is freshly-baked flat *focaccia* bread sprinkled with savory flavorings. It is sold fresh from a wood-burning oven and filled with one or more fillings of your choice. You can buy it at **Cosi** in Rue de Seine. Busy tourist areas also have their share of *kebab* shops, if this is what appeals.

Ice-cream stands open around noon, and stay open late in summer. It's worth waiting for the city's best ice-cream at **Maison Berthillon**. Seasoned gourmets come from across the city to line around the block for a scoop or two of their delicious concoctions. Chocoholics will be delighted with their intense cocoa ice-cream, while fruit fans can expect sorbets packed with flavor. There are several branches of Berthillon in the city but the Ile St Louis store is recom-mended: nothing beats stroll-ing along the Seine catching the drips from a divine ice-cream cone. Ice-cream obsessives might also like to head to **Amorino** which makes Italian-style *gelati*. Don't miss the *ameretto gelati* which comes sprinkled with crushed *ameritti* biscuits.

DIRECTORY

ILE DE LA CITÉ AND ILE ST-LOUIS

WINE BARS
Le Franc Pinot
1 Quai de Bourbon 75004.
Map 13 C4.

TEA SALONS
Le Flore en l'Isle
42 Quai d'Orléans 75004.
Map 13 B4.

ICE-CREAM PARLORS
Amorino
47 Rue St-Louis-en-l'Ile
75004.
Map 13 C4.

Maison Berthillon
31 Rue St-Louis-en-l'Ile
75004. **Map** 13 C4.

TUILERIES QUARTER

CAFÉS
Café Marly
93 Rue de Rivoli
Cour Napoleon du Louvre
75001.
Map 12 F1.

WINE BARS
La Cloche des Halles
28 Rue Coquillière 75001.
Map 12 E2.

Juveniles
47 Rue de Richelieu
75001. **Map** 12 E1.

TEA SALONS
Angélina
226 Rue de Rivoli 75001.
Map 12 D1.

Bernardaud
11 Rue Royale 75008.
Map 5 C5.

Ladurée
16 Rue Royale 75008.
Map 5 C5.

PUBS
Carrs
1 Rue Mont Thabor
75001. **Map** 12 D1.

Kitty O'Sheas
10 Rue des Capucines
75002.
Map 6 D5.

BARS
Bars du Ritz
15 Pl Vendôme 75001.
Map 6 D5.

Le Comptoir
37 Rue Berger 75001.
Map 12 F2.

Le Fumoir
6 Rue de l'Amiral-de-
Coligny 75001.
Map 12 F2.

Harry's Bar
5 Rue Danou 75002.
Map 6 E5.

THE MARAIS

CAFÉS
Au Petit Fer à Cheval
30 Rue Vieille du Temple
75004. **Map** 13 C3

Café du Trésor
5 Rue du Trésor 75004.
Map 13 C3.

Feria Café
4 Rue du Bourg Tibourg
75004. **Map** 13 C3

L'Etoile Manquante
34 Rue Vieille du Temple
75004. **Map** 13 C3.

Ma Bourgogne
19 Pl des Vosges 75004.
Map 14 D3.

TEA SALONS
Le Loir dans la Théière
3 Rue des Rosiers 75004.
Map 13 C3.

Mariage Frères
30–32 Rue du Bourg-
Tibourg 75004.
Map 13 C3.

BEER BARS
Café des Musées
49 Rue de Turenne 75003.
Map 14 D3.

WINE BARS
Le Coude Fou
12 Rue du Bourg-
Tibourg 75004.
Map 13 C3.

Le Passage des Carmagnoles
18 Passage de la Bonne-
Graine 75011.
Map 14 F4.

La Tartine
24 Rue de Rivoli 75004.
Map 13 C3.

PUBS
The Auld Alliance
80 Rue François Miron
75004.
Map 13 C3.

BARS
L'Apparement Café
18 Rue des Coutures St-
Gervais 75004.
Map 14 D2.

La Belle Hortense
31 Rue Vieille du
Temple 75004.
Map 13 C3.

Chez Richard
37 Rue Vieille du
Temple 75004.
Map 13 C3.

China Club
50 Rue de Charenton
75012. **Map** 14 F5.

Le Connetable
55 Rue des Archives
75004.
Map 13 C2.

Les Etages
35 Rue Vielle du
Temple 75004.
Map 13 C3.

The Lizard Lounge
18 Rue du Bourg-Tibourg
75004. **Map** 13 C3.

Stolly's
16 Rue Cloche Perce
75004. **Map** 13 C3.

BEAUBOURG AND LES HALLES

CAFÉS
Bistrot d'Eustache
(See p109).

Café Beaubourg
100 Rue St Martin 75004.
Map 13 B2.
(See p108).

WINE BARS
Wine and Bubbles
3 Rue Français 75001.
Map 13 A1.

PUBS
Flann O'Brien
6 Rue Bailleul 75001.
Map 12 F2.

Frog and Rosbif
116 Rue Saint-Denis
75001. **Map** 13 B1.

BARS
Andy Wahloo
69 Rue des Gravilliers
75003.
Map 13 B1.

Kong
1 Rue Pont Neuf 75001.
Map 13 A2.

ST-GERMAIN-DES-PRÉS

CAFÉS
Le Bar du Marché
75 Rue de Seine 75006.
Map 12 E4.

Café de Flore
(See p139).

Café de la Marie
8 Place St-Sulpice 75006.
Map 12 E4.

Les Deux Magots
(See p138).

La Palette
43 Rue de Seine 75006.
Map 12 E4.

SANDWICH BARS
Cosi
54 Rue de Seine 75006.
Map 12 E4.

WINE BARS
Au Sauvignon
80 Rue des Sts-Pères
75007.
Map 12 D4.

Bistro des Augustins
39 Quai des Grands-
Augustins 75006.
Map 12 F4.

PUBS
Coolin
15 Rue Clément 75006.
Map 12 E4.

Corcoran's
28 Rue Saint-André
des Arts 75006.
Map 12 F4.

Frog and Princess
9 Rue Princesse 75006.
Map 12 E4.

Highlander
8 Rue de Nevers 75006.
Map 12 F3.

The Moosehead
16 Rue des Quatre-Vents
75006.
Map 12 F4.

BARS
Le Bar Dix
10 Rue de l'Odéon
75006.
Map 12 F4.

Le Bar du Marché
75 Rue de Seine
75006.
Map 11 B2.

DIRECTORY

Birdland
8 Rue Guisarde 75006.
Map 12 E4.

Café Mabillion
164 Blvd St-Germain
75006.
Map 12 E4.

Don Carlos
66 Rue Mazarine 75006.
Map 12 F4.

Fu Bar
5 Rue St Sulpice 75006.
Map 12 F4.

**La Mezzanine de
l'Alcazar**
62 Rue Mazarine 75006.
Map 12 F4.

LATIN QUARTER

CAFÉS
Panis
21 Quai Montebello
75005.
Map 13 A4.

WINE BARS
Les Pipos
2 Rue de l'Ecole
Polytechnique 75005.
Map 13 A5.

BEER BARS
La Gueuze
19 Rue Soufflot 75005.
Map 12 F5.

PUBS
The Bombardier
2 Place du Panthéon
75005.
Map 17 A1.

BARS
Le Piano-Vache
8 Rue Laplace 75005.
Map 13 A5.

Rhubarb
8 Rue Laplace 75005.
Map 13 A5.

JARDIN DES
PLANTES

CAFÉS
Le Verre à Pied
118 bis Rue Mouffetard
75005.
Map 17 B2.

TEA SALONS
Café de la Mosquée
39 Rue Geoffroy St-Hilaire
75005.
Map 17 C2.

PUBS
Finnegan's
9 Rue des Boulangers
75005.
Map 17 B1.

ICE-CREAM
PARLORS
Häagen-Dazs
3 Pl de la Contrescarpe
75005.
Map 17 A1.

LUXEMBOURG
QUARTER

CAFÉS
Au Petit Suisse
16 Rue de Vaugirard
75006.
Map 21 F5.

Le Rostand
6 Place Edmond
Rostand 75006.
Map 12 F5.

BEER BARS
**L'Académie de
la Bière**
88 Blvd de Port-Royal
75005. **Map** 17 B3.

MONTPARNASSE

CAFÉS
Café de la Place
23 Rue d'Odessa 75014.
Map 15 C2.

La Rotonde
7 Pl 25 Août 1944 75014.
Map 16 D2.

**Le Sélect
Montparnasse**
99 Blvd du Montparnasse
75006.
Map 16 D2.

WINE BARS
Le Rallye
6 Rue Daguerre
75014.
Map 16 D4.

TEA SALONS
Max Poilâne
29 Rue de l'Ouest 75014.
Map 15 C3.

BARS
La Closerie des Lilas
171 Blvd du
Montparnasse 75014.
Map 16 D2.

**La Coupole
(Café Bar)**
102 Blvd du Montparnasse
75014.
Map 16 D2.
(See p178).

Cubana Café
45 Rue Vavin 75006.
Map 12 F5.

Le Rosebud
11 bis Rue Delambre
75014.
Map 16 D2.

INVALIDES AND
EIFFEL TOWER
QUARTER

CAFÉS
Le Café du Marché
38 Rue Cler 75007.
Map 10 F3.

PUBS
O'Brien's
77 Rue Saint-Dominique
75007.
Map 10 F3.

BARS
Café Thoumieux
4 Rue de la Comète
75007.
Map 11 A3.

CHAMPS-ELYSÉES

WINE BARS
L'Ecluse
64 Rue François Premier
75008.
Map 4 F5.

Ma Bourgogne
133 Blvd Haussmann
75008.
Map 5 B4.

TEA SALONS
Ladurée
75 Ave des Champs-
Elysées 75008.
Map 4 F5.

BARS
**Le Bar du Plaza
at the Plaza
Athénée**
(See p291).

Hôtel Raphaël
(See p289).

**Le V at
Four Seasons
George V**
(See p290).

OPÉRA QUARTER

CAFES
Café de la Paix
12 Blvd des Capucines
75009. **Map** 6 E5.
(See p213).

WINE BARS
Bistro du Sommelier
97 Blvd Haussmann
75008.
Map 5 C4.

Lavinia
3-5 Blvd de la Madeleine
75008.
Map 6 D5.

Legrand Filles et Fils
1 Rue de la Banque
75002.
Map 12 F1.
***Tel** 01 42 60 07 12.*

MONTMARTRE

CAFÉS
Le Chinon
49 Rue des Abbesses
75018.
Map 6 E1.

Le Sancerre
35 Rue des Abesses
75018.
Map 6 E1.

PUBS
**O'Sullivans by
the Mill**
92 Blvd de Clichy
75018.
Map 6 E21.

FURTHER AFIELD

WINE BARS
Le Verre Volé
67 Rue de Lancry 75010.
Map 8 D4.

BARS
L'Autre Café
62 Rue Jean-Pierre
Timbaud 75011.
Map 8 F5.

Café Charbon
109 Rue Oberkampf
75011. **Map** 14 E1.

Chez Prune
36 Rue Beaurepaire
75010. **Map** 8 D4.

Pause Café
41 Rue de Charonne
75011.
Map 14 F4.

SHOPS AND MARKETS

Paris seems to be the very definition of luxury and good living. Beautifully dressed people sip wine by the banks of the Seine against a backdrop of splendid architecture, or they hurry down gallery-lined streets carrying bags from various specialty shops. The least expensive way of joining the chic set is to create French style with accessories or with costume jewelry.

Alternatively, splurge on the fashion, or the wonderful food and related items from kitchen gadgets to tableware. Remember too that Parisian shops and markets are the ideal place to indulge in the French custom of strolling through the streets, seeing and being seen. For high fashion there's the exquisite *couture* house window displays on Avenue Montaigne or browse around the bookstalls along the Seine. A survey of some of the most famous places to shop follows.

OPENING HOURS

Shops are usually open from 10am to 7pm, Monday to Saturday, but hours can vary. Many department stores stay open late on Thursday, while boutiques may shut for an hour or two at midday. Markets and local neighborhood shops close on Mondays. Some places shut for the summer, usually in August, but they may leave a note on the door suggesting an open equivalent nearby.

HOW TO PAY

Cash is readily available from the ATMs in most banks, which accept both credit and bank debit cards. Visa and MasterCard are the most widely accepted credit cards.

VAT EXEMPTION

A sales tax (TVA) from 5.5–19.6 percent is imposed on most goods and services in EU countries. Non-EU residents shopping in France are entitled to a refund of this if they spend a minimum of 175€ in one shop in one day. You must have been resident in France for less than six months and either carry the goods with you out of the country within three months of purchase or get the shop to forward them to you. If shopping in a group, you can usually buy goods together in order to reach the minimum.

Larger shops will generally supply a form (*bordereau de détaxe* or *bordereau de vente*) and help you to fill it in. When you leave France or the EU you present the form to Customs, who either permit you to be reimbursed right away, or forward your claim to the place where you bought the merchandise; the shop eventually sends you a refund. If you know someone in Paris it may be quicker if they can pick up the refund for you at the

Shopping in Avenue Montaigne

shop. Alternatively at large airports such as Orly and Roissy some banks may have the facilities to refund you on the spot. Though the process involves a lot of paperwork, it can be worth it. There is no refund on food, drink, tobacco, cars and motorcycles. Bicycles, however, can be reimbursed.

SALES

The best sales (*soldes*) are held in January and July, although you can sometimes find sale items before Christmas. If you see goods labeled *Stock*, it means that they are stock items. *Dégriffé* means designer labels marked down, frequently from the previous year's collections. *Fripes* indicates that the clothes are second-hand. The sales tend to occupy prime floor space for the first month and are then relegated to the back of the store.

La Samaritaine department store in Beaubourg and Les Halles

DEPARTMENT STORES

Much of the pleasure of shopping in Paris is derived from going to the small specialty shops. But if time is short, try the *grands magasins* (department stores). Some still operate a ticket system for selling goods. The shop assistant writes up a ticket for goods from their own boutique which you take to one of the cashiers. You then return with your validated ticket to pick up your purchase. This can be time-consuming, so go early in the morning and don't shop on Saturdays. The French don't pay much attention to lines, so be assertive! One peculiarity of a visit is that the security guards may ask to inspect your bags as you leave. These are random checks and should not be taken as an implication of theft.

Though department stores have different emphases, all have places to eat. **Au Printemps** is noted for its exciting and innovative household goods section, and large menswear store. The clothes departments for women and children are well-stocked. Fashion shows are held at 10am on Tuesdays (and Friday from April to October: by invitation only,

Snails from the *charcuterie*

Kenzo designerwear in the Place des Victoires *(see pp324–25)*

distributed to certain overseas hotels, airlines and travel agencies). The lovely domed restaurant in the cupola often hosts chic after-hours parties; these are private, but do visit the restaurant during shopping hours.

BHV (Le Bazar de l'Hôtel de Ville) is a home improvement paradise. The Left Bank **Le Bon Marché** was Paris's first department store and today is its chicest. The designer clothing sections are well-sourced, the high-end accessories are excellent and the own-brand linen has a good quality to price ratio. The prepared food sections serve restaurant quality fare for take-out.

Galeries Lafayette is perhaps the best-known department store and has a wide range of clothes available at all price levels. Its first-floor trends section plays host to lots of innovative designers.

La Samaritaine is one of the city's oldest shops and is full of bargains. It often carries the same items as Galeries Lafayette at lower prices. As a plus, there is a panoramic view of the Seine from the restaurant, Le Toupary. **Virgin Megastore** is open until late and has an excellent record selection and an impressive book section. **FNAC** specializes in records, books (foreign editions can be found at Les Halles) and electronic equipment, while **FNAC Digitale** sells a wide range of the latest technological equipment.

Bookstall, Vanves market *(see p339)*

ADDRESSES

Au Printemps
64 Blvd Haussman 75009.
Map 6 D4. *Tel* 01 42 82 50 00.

BHV
52–64 Rue de Rivoli 75004.
Map 13 B3. *Tel* 01 42 74 90 00.

Le Bon Marché
24 Rue de Sèvres 75007.
Map 11 C5. *Tel* 01 44 39 80 00.

FNAC
Forum des Halles, 1 Rue Pierre Lescot 75001. **Map** 13 A2. *Tel* 0140 41 40 00.

FNAC Digitale
77–81 Blvd St-Germain 75006.
Map 13 A5. *Tel* 01 44 41 31 50.

Galeries Lafayette
40 Blvd Haussmann 75009.
Map 6 E4. *Tel* 01 42 82 34 56.

La Samaritaine
19 Rue de la Monnaie 75001.
Map 12 F2. *Tel* 01 40 41 20 20.

Virgin Megastore
52–60 Ave des Champs-Elysées 75008.
Map 4 F5. *Tel* 01 49 53 50 00.

Lionel Poilâne's bread bearing his trademark – a square *(see pp333–5)*

Paris's Best: Shops and Markets

Old-fashioned and conservative yet full of surprises, Paris is a treasure trove of quality shops and boutiques. Time-honored emporia mix with modern precincts in a city that buzzes with life in its inner quarters, not least in the markets. Here you can buy everything from exotic fruit and vegetables to fine china and antiques. Whether you're shopping for handmade shoes, perfectly cut clothes or traditionally made cheeses, or simply soaking in the atmosphere, you won't be disappointed.

Place de la Madeleine
Top-class groceries and delicacies are sold on the north side of this square.
(See p214.)

THE CENTER OF PARIS COUTURE

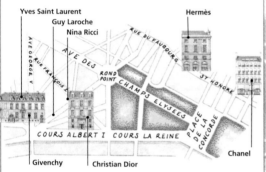

Yves Saint Laurent
Guy Laroche
Nina Ricci
Hermès

RUE DU FAUBOURG
AVE GEORGE V
RUE FRANÇOIS 1
AVE DES
ROND POINT
CHAMPS ELYSEES
ST HONORE
COURS ALBERT I   COURS LA REINE
PLACE DE LA CONCORDE
Chanel

Givenchy   Christian Dior

See inset map

Champs-Elysées

R I V E R

Invalides and Eiffel Tower Quarter

Chanel
Coco Chanel (1883–1971) reigned over the fashion world from No. 31 Rue Cambon. The main boutique is on Avenue Montaigne. (See p325.)

Rue de Rivoli
Inexpensive mementos like this Paris snow globe can be found in the shops on the Rue de Rivoli. (See p130.)

Marché de la Porte de Vanves
This charming and relaxed market sells old books, linen, postcards, china and musical instruments.
(weekends only – see p339.)

Kenzo
The Japanese designer has colorful apparel for men, women and children in his clothes shops. (See p327.)

Cartier
The early Cartier jewelry designs with their beautifully cut stones are still highly sought after. This shop on Rue de la Paix sells all the Cartier lines. (See p329.)

Rue de Paradis
You can buy porcelain and crystal at reduced prices at the company showrooms on this street. Look out for Porcelainor, Baccarat and Lumicristal. (See pp330–32.)

Passage des Panoramas
This once-prosperous arcade at Les Galeries has an old engraving house. (See p216.)

0 kilometers 1

0 miles 0.5

Opéra Quarter

Tuileries Quarter

Beaubourg and Les Halles

The Marais

St-Germain-des-Prés

Ile de la Cité

Ile St-Louis

Latin Quarter

Rue des Francs-Bourgeois
La Maison Rouge is a charming antiques shop stocking light fixtures and furniture. (See pp336–7.)

Luxembourg Quarter

Jardin des Plantes Quarter

Montparnasse

Rue Mouffetard
The market sells cheeses and other quality foods. (See p339.)

Forum des Halles
This modern glass arcade has many shops. (See p109.)

Clothes and Accessories

For many people Paris is synonymous with fashion and Parisian style is the ultimate in chic. More than anywhere else in the world, women in Paris seem to be in tune with current trends, and when a new season arrives they appear, as one, to don the look. Though less trend-conscious generally, Parisian men are aware of style and mix and match patterns and colors with élan. Finding the right clothes at the right price means knowing where to shop. For every luxury boutique on the Avenue Montaigne, there are ten young designers' shops waiting to become the next Jean-Paul Gaultier – and hundreds more selling imitations.

HAUTE COUTURE

Paris is the home of *haute couture*. The original *couture* garments, as opposed to the imitations and adaptations, are one-of-a-kind creations, designed by one of the nine *haute couture* houses listed with the Fédération Française de la Couture. The rules for being classified are fairly strict, and many of the top designers are not included. Astronomical prices put *haute couture* beyond the reach of all but a few immensely deep pockets, but it's still the lifeblood of the fashion industry providing inspiration for the mass market.

The fashion seasons are launched with the *couture* shows in January and July. Most shows are held in the Carrousel du Louvre *(see p123)*. If you want to see a show, you stand a much better chance of getting a seat at the private *couture* shows (the main shows are for buyers and the press). To do this call the press offices of the *haute couture* houses a month in advance. You can only be sure you have a place when you receive the ticket. For the private shows, telephone the fashion house or, if you're in Paris, try going to the boutique and asking if there's a show – and remember to dress the part.

Most *couture* houses make *prêt-à-porter* clothes as well – ready-to-wear clothes fitted on a standard model. They're still not cheap, but give you an idea of some of the designer elegance and creativity at a fraction of the cost.

WOMEN'S CLOTHES

The highest concentration of *couture* houses is on the Right Bank. Most are on or near the Rue du Faubourg-St-Honoré and the classier Avenue Montaigne: **Christian Dior**, **Pierre Cardin**, **Chanel**, **Christian Lacroix**, **Marcel Marongiu**, **Givenchy**, **Louis Féraud**, **Nina Ricci** and **Yves Saint Laurent**. This is where you will rub shoulders with the rich and famous.

Hermès has classic country chic. **MaxMara's** Italian elegance is quite popular in France and no one can resist a **Giorgio Armani** suit. **Karl Lagerfeld** has a shop where the latest creations from his own line, Lagerfeld Gallery, are exhibited.

The theatrical **Paco Rabanne** has a store on the Left Bank, which is surrounded by many other fine fashion houses. Try **Sonia Rykiel** for knitwear, **Junko Shimada** for sporty casuals and **Barbara Bui** for soft, feminine clothes.

Many designers have a Left Bank branch in addition to their Right Bank bastions, and they all have ready-to-wear shops here. For sheer quality there's **Georges Rech**, but don't forget Yves Saint Laurent or **Jil Sander** for their exquisite tailoring. Try Armani's St-Germain temple of fashion, or Prada's affordable boutique, **Miu Miu**, in the Rue de Grenelle. **Onward Kashiyama France** has its cult following for some imaginative clothes, and **Irié** is the place for reasonably priced clothes which are trendy but will stand the test

of time. Also in the Saint-Germain-des-Près district, the **Comptoir des Cotonniers** stocks excellent basics, **Diapositive** has glamorous evening wear and **Vanessa Bruno** is extremely popular for feminine flair. Quirky looks can be found at **Corinne Sarut**, who has a growing following among French fashionistas.

Ready-to-wear shops blanket Paris, and in the beautiful Place des Victoires they thrive off shoppers visiting the Rue du Faubourg-St-Honoré. The **Victoire** boutique offers one of the best collections of current designer labels with Michael Klein, Helmut Lang and Thierry Mugler among many others. **Kenzo** is here (although a new flagship store now exists near the Pont Neuf), along with fellow Japanese designers **Comme des Garçons**, with its avant-garde, quirky fashion for both sexes, and **Yohji Yamamoto** just down the street, near Ventilo. The nearby Rue Jean-Jacques-Rousseau has now become one of the city's prime shopping stops.

Moving east to the Rue du Jour, **Agnès B** and **Claudie Pierlot's** clothes have timeless elegance. There are also many shops selling inexpensive copies of new designs in the center. **Corinne Cobson** near the Tuileries has quintessentially chic womenswear and **Martin Margiela** carries excellent quality basics with a twist.

The Marais is a haven for up-and-coming designers and is always busy on Saturdays. One of the best streets is the Rue des Rosiers, which includes Issey Miyake's **Pleats Please**, **L'Eclaireur** and a branch of **Tehen** for clothes. **Nina Jacob** is on the neighboring Rue des Francs-Bourgeois, and daring designer **Azzedine Alaïa's** shop is just around the corner. **Plein Sud** stocks sexy creations, **A-Poc** is an offshoot of Issey Miyake and has daring designs.

The Bastille area has trendy boutiques, as well as some

DIRECTORY

WOMEN'S CLOTHES

Agnès B
2–3–6–10–19 Rue du Jour 75001. **Map** 13 A1.
Tel 01 45 08 56 56.
One of several branches.

A-Poc
47 Rue des Francs-Bourgeois 75006.
Map 14 D3.
Tel 01 44 54 07 05

Azzedine Alaïa
7 Rue de Moussy 75004.
Map 13 C3.
Tel 01 42 72 19 19.

Barbara Bui
23 Rue Etienne-Marcel 75001. **Map** 13 A1.
Tel 01 40 26 43 65.
www.barbarabui.com
One of two branches.

Chanel
42 Ave Montaigne 75008.
Map 5 A5.
Tel 01 47 23 47 12.
One of several branches.

Christian Dior
30 Ave Montaigne 75008.
Map 10 F1.
Tel 01 40 73 73 73.
www.doir.com

Christian Lacroix
73 Rue du Faubourg-St-Honoré 75008. **Map** 5 B5.
Tel 01 42 68 79 00.
www.christian-lacroix.com

Claudie Pierlot
1 Rue Montmartre 75001.
Map 13 A1.
Tel 01 42 21 38 38.
www.claudie-pierlot.com
One of two branches.

Colette
213 Rue St-Honoré 75001.
Map 12 D1.
Tel 01 55 35 33 90.
www.colette.fr

Comme des Garçons
54 Rue du Faubourg St-Honoré 75008. **Map** 4 E3.
Tel 01 53 30 27 27.

Comptoir des Cotonniers
59 Rue Bonaparte 75006.
Map 12 E3.
Tel 01 43 26 07 56.

Corrine Cobson
6 Rue du Marché Saint-Honoré 75001.
Map 12 D1.
Tel 01 42 60 48 64.

Corrine Sarut
6 Rue du Marché Saint-Honoré 75001.
Map 12 D1.
Tel 01 42 61 71 60.

Diapositive
42 Rue du Four 75006.
Map 12 E4.
Tel 01 45 48 85 57.

L'Eclaireur
3 ter Rue des Rosiers 75004. **Map** 13 C3.
Tel 01 48 87 10 22.

Eres
2 Rue Tronchet 75008.
Map 5 C5.
Tel 01 47 42 28 82.
One of two branches.

Gaëlle Barré
17 Rue Keller 75011.
Map 14 F4.
Tel 01 43 14 63 02.

Georges Rech
54 Rue Bonaparte 75006.
Map 12 E3.
Tel 01 43 26 84 11.
www.georges-rech.fr
One of several branches.

Giorgio Armani
6 Pl Vendôme 75001.
Map 6 D5.
Tel 01 42 61 55 09
www.giorgioarmani.com

Givenchy
28 Rue du Faubourg-St-Honoré 75008.
Map 5 C5.
Tel 08 25 82 55 90.
www.givenchy.com

Hennes
15 Rue Commerce 75015.
Map 10 E5.
Tel 01 40 57 24 60.
One of several branches.

Hermès
24 Rue du Faubourg-St-Honoré 75008. **Map** 5 C5.
Tel 01 40 17 47 17.
www.hermes.com
One of several branches.

Irié
8 Rue du Pré-aux-Clercs 75007. **Map** 12 D3.
Tel 01 42 61 18 28.

Isabel Marant
16 Rue de Charonne 75011. **Map** 14 F4.
Tel 01 49 29 71 55.

Jean-Paul Gaultier
6 Rue Vivienne 75002.
Map 12 F1.
Tel 01 42 86 05 05.
One of two branches.

Jil Sander
52 Ave Montaigne 75008.
Map 10 F1.
Tel 01 44 95 06 70.

Junko Shimada
13 Rue St-Florentin 75008.
Map 11 C1.
Tel 01 42 60 94 12.
One of two branches.

Kenzo
3 Pl des Victoires 75001.
Map 12 F1.
Tel 01 40 39 72 00.
One of several branches.

Kookaï
82 Rue Reaumur 75002.
Map 13 B1.
Tel 01 45 08 93 69.
One of several branches.

LA City
141 Rue de Rennes 75006.
Map 16 D1.
Tel 01 45 44 71 18.
One of several branches.

Lolita Lempicka
46 Ave Victor Hugo 75016. **Map** 3C5.
Tel 01 45 02 14 46.

Louis Féraud
22 Ave Victor Hugo 75016. **Map** 3 B5.
Tel 01 45 00 61 49.

Mac Douglas
9 Rue de Sèvres 75006.
Map 12 D4.
Tel 01 45 48 14 09.
One of several branches.

Marcel Marongiu
203 Rue St-Honoré 75001.
Map 13 A2.
Tel 01 49 27 96 38.

Martin Margiela
25 Rue de Montpensier 75001. **Map** 12 E1.
Tel 01 40 15 07 55.

MaxMara
37 Rue du Four 75006.
Map 12 D4.
Tel 01 43 29 91 10.
One of two branches.

Miu Miu
16 Rue de Grenelle 75007.
Map 12 D4.
Tel 01 53 63 20 30.
www.miumiu.com

Morgan
165 Rue de Rennes 75006.
Map 16 D1.
Tel 01 45 48 96 77.
One of several branches.

Nina Jacob
23 Rue des Francs-Bourgeois 75004.
Map 14 D3.
Tel 01 42 77 41 20.

Nina Ricci
39 Ave Montaigne 75008.
Map 10 F1.
Tel 01 40 88 64 51.
www.ninaricci.fr

Onward Kashiyama France
147 Blvd St-Germain 75006. **Map** 12 E4.
Tel 01 55 42 77 55.

Paco Rabanne
83 Rue des Sts-Pères 75006. **Map** 12 D4.
Tel 01 45 48 82 26.

Pierre Cardin
27 Ave de Marigny 75008.
Map 5 B5.
Tel 01 42 66 68 98.
www.pierrecardin.com
One of two branches.

Pleats Please
3 bis Rue des Rosiers 75004. **Map** 13C3.
Tel 01 40 29 99 66.
One of two branches.

Plein Sud
21 Rue des Francs-Bourgeois 75004.
Map 14 D3.
Tel 01 42 72 10 60.

Promod
60 Rue Caumartin 75009.
Map 6 D4.
Tel 01 45 26 01 11.
One of several branches.

Ragtime
23 Rue de l'Echaudé 75006. **Map** 12 E4.
Tel 01 56 24 00 36.

Sinequanone
16 Rue Four 75006.
Map 12 E4.
Tel 01 56 24 27 74.
One of several branches.

more established names. Designer **Jean-Paul Gaultier** has a boutique in the Rue du Faubourg St-Antoine. His "senior" and "junior" collections reflect price and attitude. **Isabel Marant's** boutique is renowned for its originality, and **Gaëlle Barré** is a stylist with a fast-growing reputation. The swimsuit store is **Eres**, while for leather, it's **Mac Douglas**.

Young designers' clothes are found at **Colette**, **Stella Cadente** and **Zadig & Voltaire**, while **Zucca** now has several boutiques. For fabulous, if somewhat pricey, clothes from the 1920s to the 1950s, try **Ragtime**.

Not all Parisians have pocketbooks that allow them to shop on the Avenue Montaigne, but those on smaller budgets still manage to look chic in clothes from some chain stores. There are many large chains here which have branches in other European cities. Chain stores tend to stock each store differently, depending on the desires and buying patterns of the local clientele. Because of this it is possible to find quintessentially French fashion in large chains such as **Zara**, particularly at the branches in Passy and near the Opera.

Mighty Swedish retailer **Hennes** has an exciting concept store for young fashion in Paris's 15th arrondissement and stocks designs by Karl Lagerfeld in some of its larger shops. French chain stores are also numerous. Well-known names such as **Kookaï** and **Morgan** stock fresh and funky items. **Sinéquanone** and **LA City**, on the other hand, are rather classic in their designs, while **Promod** is a very cheap store for fun merchandise.

CHILDREN'S CLOTHES

Lots of options for children exist in various styles and many price ranges. Many top designers of adult clothes also have boutiques for children. These include **Kenzo**, **Baby Dior**, **Agnès B**, **Sonia Rykiel** and **Teddy's**.

Ready-to-wear shops such as **Jacadi** and **Du Pareil au Même** are serviceable and wide-ranging; and **Tartine et Chocolat's** best-selling garments are overalls. **Bonpoint** stocks adorably chic clothing for mini-Parisians. **Petit Bateau** is coveted as much by grown-ups as it is by children. The inevitable has finally happened – children now have their own concept store in **Bonton**.

For little feet, **Froment-Leroyer** probably offers the best all-round classics. **Six Pieds Trois Pouces** has a huge choice of styles.

MEN'S CLOTHES

Men don't have the luxury of *haute couture* dressing and their choice is limited to ready-to-wear. Still, some men's clothes, mostly by womens-wear designers, can be very expensive.

On the Right Bank, there's **Giorgio Armani**, **Pierre Cardin**, **Kenzo**, **Lanvin** (also good for accessories) and **Yves Saint Laurent**. On the Left Bank, **Michel Axael** and **Jean-Charles de Castelbajac** are known for their ties and **Francesco Smalto's** elegant creations are worn by some of the world's leading movie stars. **Yohji Yamamoto's** clothes are for those who are intent on making a serious fashion statement, while **Gianni Versace** is classic, suave and Italian in style. **APC**, **Paul Smith** and **Ron Orb** garments are rather more contemporary, and **Olivier Strelli**, **Polo by Ralph Lauren** and **Loft Design By** are chic without being overtly trendy, and thus are likely to have a longer shelf life.

The ultimate in Parisian elegance for men is a suit, custom-made shirt or silk tie from **Charvet**. A trip to the **Place Vendôme** store is a pleasure in itself. Be sure to ask the charming and friendly staff for a tour around their atelier for an insight into how such exquisite creations are crafted. **Madelios** is a great shopping mall for men which mixes designer and chain store brands.

LIFESTYLE STORES

Since **Colette** first burst on to the Parisian shopping scene six years ago, the fad for lifestyle shops has shown no sign of slowing down. Concept stores tend to be high-end affairs crammed with designer labels, some obscure, some household names, all grouped together to equip you with everything you could possibly need. From fashionable books to shoes, beauty products, household goods, music and furniture via designer mineral water, purses, sneakers and evening gowns, the one-stop shopping experience provides the ultimate in retail therapy.

Spree in Montmartre mixes fashion, art and design so that you can buy a great outfit and some interesting art at the same time, while **View on Fashion** in the Bastille focuses on designer street wear. The **Castelbajac Concept Store** has designers' clothes alongside furniture and interesting knick-knacks.

VINTAGE AND SECOND-HAND STORES

The vintage craze hit Paris some time back and there are some wonderful shops to plunder for a retro look. The best of the bunch is **Didier Ludot**, where an Alladin's Cave of chic *haute couture* is elegantly displayed. From vintage Courrèges dresses to excellent condition Chanel suits, this is the place for top-of-the-line retro. The **Depôt-Vente de Buci-Bourbon** is another good place to bargain hunt. A cheaper option and a way to access more recent looks is to head for one of the many second-hand or consignment stores in the city. Chic Parisians discard their outfits with the seasons so it is very easy to pick up some quality items which are normally in top condition from places such as **Réciproque** in Passy or **Alternatives** in the Marais. Sample pieces, sale stock and last season's collection pieces can be found at **Le Mouton à Cinq Pattes**.

DIRECTORY

Sonia Rykiel
175 Blvd St-Germain
75006. **Map** 12 D4.
Tel 01 49 54 60 60.
One of several branches.

Stella Cadente
4 Quai des Célestins
75004. **Map** 13 C4.
Tel 01 44 78 05 95.
www.stella-cadente.com

Vanessa Bruno
25 Rue St-Sulpice 75006.
Map 12 E5.
Tel 01 43 54 41 04.

Ventilo
27 bis Rue du Louvre
75002. **Map** 12 F2.
Tel 01 44 76 83 00.
One of six branches.

Victoire
2 Rue du Mail 75002.
Map 12 F1.
Tel 01 42 96 46 76.
One of several branches.

Yohji Yamamoto
25 Rue du Louvre 75001.
Map 12 F1.
Tel 01 42 21 42 93.

Yves Saint Laurent
38 Rue du Faubourg-St-
Honoré 75008. **Map** 5 C5.
Tel 01 42 65 74 59.
One of several branches.

Zadig & Voltaire
9 Rue du 29 Juillet 75001.
Map 12 D1.
Tel 01 42 92 00 80.

Zara
53 Rue Passy 75016.
Map 9 B3.
Tel 01 45 25 07 00.
One of several branches.

Zucca
8 Rue St-Roch 75001.
Map 12 E1.
Tel 01 44 58 98 88.

CHILDREN'S CLOTHES

Agnès B
(See p325).

Baby Dior
(See p325 Christian Dior).

Bonpoint
15 Rue Royale 75008.
Map 5 C5.
Tel 01 47 42 52 63.
www.bonpoint.com
One of several branches.

Bonton
82 rue de Grenelle 75007.
Map 10 F3.
Tel 01 44 39 09 20.

Du Pareil au Même
15-17 Rue des
Mathurins 75008.
Map 6 D4.
Tel 01 42 66 93 80.
One of several branches.

Froment-Leroyer
7 Rue Vavin 75006.
Map 16 E1.
Tel 01 43 54 33 15.
www.froment-leroyer.fr
One of several branches.

Jacadi
17 Rue Tronchet 75008.
Map 5 C5.
Tel 01 42 65 84 98.
www.jacadi.fr

Kenzo
(See p325).

Petit Bateau
116 Ave des Champs
Elysées 75008.
Map 4 E4.
Tel 01 40 74 02 03.

Six Pieds Trois Pouces
78 Ave de Wagram
75017. **Map** 4 E2.
Tel 01 46 22 81 64.
One of several branches.

Tartine et Chocolat
105 Rue du Faubourg-St-
Honoré 75008.
Map 5 B5.
Tel 01 45 62 44 04.

Teddy's
38 Rue François-1er
75008.
Map 10 F1.
Tel 01 47 20 79 79.

MEN'S CLOTHES

APC
45 Rue Madame 75006.
Map 12 E5.
Tel 01 45 48 43 71.

Charvet
28 Place Vendôme 75001.
Map 6 D5.
Tel 01 42 60 30 70.

Francesco Smalto
44 Rue François-1er
75008. **Map** 4 F5.
Tel 01 47 20 96 04.
www.smalto.com

Jean-Charles de Castelbajac
10 Rue de Vauvilliers
75001.
Tel 01 45 48 40 55.
www.jedecastelbajac.com

Gianni Versace
62 Rue du Faubourg St-
Honoré 75008.
Map 5 C5.
Tel 01 47 42 88 02.
www.versace.com

Giorgio Armani
(See p325).

Kenzo
(See p325).

Lanvin
15 Rue du Faubourg St-
Honoré 75008.
Map 14 F4.
Tel 01 44 71 31 33.
www.lanvin.com
One of several branches.

Loft Design By
56 Rue de Rennes 75006.
Map 16 D1.
Tel 01 45 44 88 99.
One of several branches.

Michel Axael
121 Blvd St-Germain
75006.
Map 12 E4.
Tel 01 43 26 01 96.

Olivier Strelli
7 Blvd Raspail 75007.
Map 12 D4.
Tel 01 45 44 62 21.
www.strelli.be
One of two branches.

Paul Smith
22 Blvd Raspail 75007.
Map 12 D4.
Tel 01 42 84 15 30.

Pierre Cardin
(See p325).

Ron Orb
39 Rue Etienne Marcel
75001.
Map 13 A1.
Tel 01 40 28 09 33.

Yohji Yamamoto
47 Rue Etienne
Marcel 75001.
Tel 01 45 08 82 45.

Yves Saint Laurent
12 Pl St-Sulpice 75006.
Map 12 D4.
Tel 01 43 26 84 40.

LIFESTYLE STORES

Castelbajac Concept Store
31 Pl du Marché-St-
Honoré 75001.
Map 12 E1.
Tel 01 42 60 41 55.

Colette
(See p325).

Spree
16 Rue de La Vieuville
75018. **Map** 6 F1.
Tel 01 42 23 41 40.

View on Fashion
27 Rue des Taillandiers
75011. **Map** 6 F1.
Tel 01 43 55 05 03.

VINTAGE AND SECOND-HAND STORES

Alternatives
18 Rue du Roi-de-Sicile
75004. **Map** 13 C3.
Tel 01 42 78 31 50

Depôt-Vente de Buci-Bourbon
6 Rue de Bourbon-le-
Château 75006.
Map 12 E4.
Tel 01 46 34 45 05.

Didier Ludot
19-24 Galerie Montpensier
75001. **Map** 12 E1.
Tel 01 42 96 06 56.

Le Mouton à Cinq Pattes
19 Rue Grégoire-de-Tours
75006. **Map** 12 F4.
Tel 01 43 29 73 56.
One of several branches.

Réciproque
95 Rue de la Pompe
75016. **Map** 9 A1.
Tel 01 47 04 30 28.

JEWELRY

Agatha
97 Rue de Rennes 75006.
Map 12 D5.
Tel 01 45 48 81 30.
www.agatha.fr
One of several branches.

JEWELRY

The *couture* houses probably stock some of the best jewelry and scarves. **Chanel's** jewels are classics and **Christian Lacroix's** are fun. **Boutique YSL** is a great place for accessories.

Among the main expensive Paris jewelry outlets are **Boucheron**, **Mauboussin** and **Poiray**. They are for the serious jewelry buyer. Other top retailers include **Harry Winston** and **Cartier**. **Dinh Van** has some quirky pieces, while **Mikimoto** is a must for pearls and **H Stern** has some innovative designs using semi-precious and precious stones. For a range of more unusual jewelry and accessories, try the **Daniel Swarovski Boutique**, which is owned by the Swarovksi crystal family.

Trends and imitations can be found around the Marais, the Bastille and Les Halles, in that order for quality. Those of note include **Scooter**, where chic young Parisians shop, and **Agatha** for copies of Chanel designs and basics.

Imitations in precious metals are available at **Verlor**, a cheap jeweller where one can find copies of pieces by top jewelers using genuine stones. Another reasonably priced Parisian jeweller is **Chaput**, where decent jewelry, especially the pieces made with semi-precious stones, can be found at good prices.

SHOES, BAGS AND BELTS

For sheer luxury **Harel** has a wide range of exotic leather footwear. Go to **Charles Jourdan** for a big selection of colors or to **Sidonie Larizzi** who will make up shoes from one of numerous leather swatches. Current favorites with the fashion set include **Michel Perry**, **Bruno Frisoni** and **Robert Clergerie**. **Rodolphe Ménudier** and **Christian Louboutin** are mainstays for sexy stilettos. **Carel** stocks stylish basics, **Mosquitos** make comfortable but trendy shoes and **Jonak** is a must for good imitations of designer footwear. **Bowen** has a selection of traditional men's shoes and **Fenestrier** creates chic versions of classics. **J M Weston** or **Berluti** are the last words in elegance for many Parisian men.

Christian Lacroix makes wonderful purses and belts. Beautifully made leather goods can also be found at **Longchamp**, **Gucci** and **Hermès**. For ladies purses, nothing can beat **Chanel** or **Dior** at the top end of the scale, although **Goyard** comes close. Mid-range bags from **Furla** are a great compromise as are colorful leather bags from up-and-coming Danish designer **Christiansen at AB33**. Fabric bags from **Jamin Puech**, **Vanessa Bruno** or **Hervé Chapelier** are a feature in every chic Parisian closet. For a great range of shoes, boots and bags at reasonable prices, try **Jet-Set**. Cheap, cheerful and very stylish bags can be found at **Lollipops**.

HATS

One of Paris's favorite milliners is **Marie Mercié**. **Anthony Peto** now creates men's hats at the old shop in Rue Tiquetonne. **Manon Martin** is offbeat and imaginative and **Philippe Model** is one of the most creative and stylish hatmakers in Paris. **Tête en L'Air** in Montmarte has a wonderful selection of fun and stylish headgear.

LINGERIE

For modern lingerie go to **Fifi Chachnil**, whose shop is filled with colorful underwear. **La Boite à Bas** sells fine French stockings, whereas **Princesse Tam Tam** offers quality items at reasonable prices, while divine designer underwear can be found at cult store **Sabbia Rosa**. The ultimate in Parisian lingerie can be bought off the shelf or made to order at **Cadolle**, the store which invented the bra.

SIZE CHART

For Australian sizes follow the British and American conversions.

Children's clothing

French	2-3	4-5	6-7	8-9	10-11	12	14	14+ (years)
British	2-3	4-5	6-7	8-9	10-11	12	14	14+ (years)
American	2-3	4-5	6-6x	7-8	10		12	14	16 (size)

Children's shoes

French	24	25½	27	28	29	30	32	33	34
British	7	8	9	10	11	12	13	1	2
American	7½	8½	9½	10½	11½	12½	13½	1½	2½

Women's dresses coats and skirts

French	34	36	38	40	42	44	46
British	6	8	10	12	14	16	18
American	2	4	6	8	10	12	14

Women's blouses and sweaters

French	81	84	87	90	93	96	99 (cms)
British	31	32	34	36	38	40	42 (inches)
American	6	8	10	12	14	16	18 (size)

Women's shoes

French	36	37	38	39	40	41
British	3	4	5	6	7	8
American	5	6	7	8	9	10

Men's suits

French	44	46	48	50	52	54	56	58
British	34	36	38	40	42	44	46	48
American	34	36	38	40	42	44	46	48

Men's shirts

French	36	38	39	41	42	43	44	45
British	14	15	15½	16	16½	17	17½	18
American	14	15	15½	16	16½	17	17½	18

Men's shoes

French	39	40	41	42	43	44	45	46
British	6	7	7½	8	9	10	11	12
American	7	7½	8	8½	9½	10½	11	11½

DIRECTORY

Boucheron
26 Pl Vendôme 75001.
Map 6 D5.
Tel 01 42 61 58 16.
www.boucheron.com

Boutique YSL
38 Rue du Faubourg-St-Honoré 75008.
Map 5 C5.
Tel 01 42 65 74 59.

Cartier
13 Rue de la Paix 75002.
Map 6 D5.
Tel 01 42 18 53 70.
One of several branches.

Chanel
(See p325).

Chaput
53 Rue Passy 75016.
Map 9 B3.
Tel 01 42 24 50 40.
One of several branches.

Christian Lacroix
(See p325).

Daniel Swarovski Boutique
7 Rue Royale 75008.
Map 5 C5.
Tel 01 40 17 07 40.
www.daniel-swarovski.com

Dinh Van
15 Rue de la Paix
75002. **Map** 6 D5.
Tel 01 42 86 02 66.
One of several branches.

H Stern
3 Rue Castiglione 75001.
Map 12 D1.
Tel 01 42 60 22 27.
One of several branches.

Harry Winston
29 Ave Montaigne 75008.
Map 10 F1.
Tel 01 47 20 03 09.
www.harrywinston.com

Mauboussin
20 Pl Vendôme 75001.
Map 6 D5.
Tel 01 44 55 10 00.
www.mauboussin.com

Mikimoto
8 Pl Vendôme 75001.
Map 6 D5.
Tel 01 42 60 33 55.

Poiray
1 Rue de la Paix 75002.
Map 6 D5.
Tel 01 42 61 70 58.

Scooter
10 Rue de Turbigo 75001.
Map 13 A1.
Tel 01 45 08 50 54.
One of several branches.

Verlor
19 Rue de la Paix 75002.
Map 6 D5.
Tel 01 40 07 08 86.
One of several branches.

SHOES, BAGS AND BELTS

Bowen
5 Pl des Ternes 75017.
Map 4 E3.
Tel 01 42 27 09 23.
One of several branches.

Berluti
26 Rue Marbeuf 75008.
Map 4 F5.
Tel 01 53 93 97 97.

Bruno Frisoni
13 Rue de Monsigny
75002. **Map** 6 E5.
Tel 01 42 65 20 40.

Carel
4 Rue Tronchet 75008.
Map 6 D4.
Tel 01 43 12 37 00.
One of several branches.

Charles Jourdan
23 Rue François-1er
75008.
Tel 01 47 20 81 28.
One of several branches.
www.charles-jourdan.com

Christian Louboutin
38-40 Rue de Grenelle
75007. **Map** 10 F3.
Tel 01 42 22 33 07.

Christiansen at AB33
33 Rue de Charlot 75003.
Map 14 D1.
Tel 01 42 71 02 82.

Fenestrier
23 Rue du Cherche-Midi
75006.
Map 12 D5.
Tel 01 42 22 66 02.

Furla
8 Rue de Sevres 75006.
Map 11 C5.
Tel 01 40 49 06 44.
One of several branches.

Goyard
233 Rue St Honoré 75001.
Map 5 C5.
Tel 01 42 60 57 04.

Gucci
350 Rue St-Honoré 75001.
Map 5 C5.
Tel 01 42 96 83 27.
www.gucci.com
One of two branches.

Harel
7 Rue Tournon 75006.
Map 12 E5.
Tel 01 43 54 16 16.

Hermès
(See p325).

Hervé Chapelier
1 Rue du Vieux-Colombier
75006. **Map** 12 D4.
Tel 01 44 07 06 50.

Jamin Puech
61 Rue de Hauteville
75010. **Map** 7 B4.
Tel 01 43 54 16 16.

Jet-Set
85 Rue de Passy 75016.
Map 9 B3.
Tel 01 42 88 21 59.
One of two branches.

Jonak
70 Rue de Rennes 75006.
Map 16 D1.
Tel 01 45 48 27 11.

Lollipops
60 Rue Tiquetonne 75002.
Map 13 A1.
Tel 01 42 33 15 72.
www.lollipops.fr

Longchamp
404 Rue St-Honoré 75001.
Map 5 C5.
Tel 01 43 16 00 18.
www.longchamp.com

Michel Perry
4 Rue des Petits-Pères
75002. **Map** 12 F1.
Tel 01 42 44 10 07.

Mosquitos
25 Rue du Four 75006.
Map 12 E4.
Tel 01 43 25 25 16.

Robert Clergerie
5 Rue du Cherche-Midi
75006. **Map** 12 D1.
Tel 01 42 71 02 82.

Rodolphe Ménudier
14 Rue de Castiglione
75001. **Map** 12 D1.
Tel 01 42 60 86 27.

Sidonie Larizzi
8 Rue de Marignan 75008.
Map 4 F5.
Tel 01 43 59 38 87.

Vanessa Bruno
(See p327).

HATS

Anthony Peto
56 Rue Tiquetonne 75002.
Map 13 A1.
Tel 01 40 26 60 68.

Manon Martin
19 Rue de Turenne 75004.
Map 14 D3.
Tel 01 48 04 00 84.

Marie Mercié
23 Rue St-Sulpice 75006.
Map 12 E4.
Tel 01 43 26 45 83.

Philippe Model
33 Pl du Marché St-Honoré 75001.
Map 12 D1.
Tel 01 42 96 89 02.

Tête en L'Air
65 Rue des Abbesses
75018.
Map 6 E1.
Tel 01 46 06 71 19.

LINGERIE

La Boîte à Bas
27 Rue Boissy-d'Anglas
75008. **Map** 5 C5.
Tel 01 42 66 26 85.

Cadolle
14 Rue Cambon 75001.
Map 6 D5.
Tel 01 42 60 94 94.

Fifi Chachnil
26 Rue Cambon 75001.
Map 6 D5.
Tel 01 42 60 38 86.
One of several branches.

Princesse Tam Tam
9 Rue Bréa 75006.
Map 16 D1.
Tel 01 42 34 99 31.
One of several branches.

Sabbia Rosa
73 Rue des Sts-Pères
75006.
Map 12 D4.
Tel 01 45 48 88 37.

Gifts and Souvenirs

Paris has a wealth of stylish gifts and typical souvenirs, from designer accessories and perfume to French delicacies and Eiffel Tower paperweights. Shops on the Rue de Rivoli and around major tourist attractions such as Nôtre Dame or Sacré Coeur offer a range of cheap holiday paraphernalia, or go to some of the souvenir shops such as **Les Drapeaux de France**. Mementos can often be found in museum shops, including reproductions and creations by young designers. Try **Le Musée du Louvre**, **Musée d'Orsay** or **Musée Carnavalet**.

GIFTS

Au Printemps has excellent own-label accessories, especially ladies purses. The luxury floor is ideal for window-shopping or high-end purchases such as Tiffany jewelry or Cartier watches. It also stocks small, reasonably priced items.

For those looking to take home gastronomic tasters, the famed food hall at **Le Bon Marché**, La Grande Epicerie, offers anything and everything you might need for a gourmet feast or quick snack.

Galeries Lafayette now boasts the world's biggest lingerie department.

PERFUME AND COSMETICS

Many shops advertise discounted perfume and cosmetics. Some even offer duty-free perfume to shoppers outside the EU, with discounts on the marked prices when you show your passport. They include **Eiffel Shopping** near the Eiffel Tower. The **Sephora** chain has a big selection, or try the department stores for a range of designers' perfumes. In particular, the beauty department at **Au Printemps** is one of Europe's biggest with one of the world's largest perfume selections. It stocks many beauty brands which are hard to find elsewhere.

Parfums Caron has many scents created at the turn-of-the-19th century, which are unavailable elsewhere; so this is the place to find exclusive presents that you will almost certainly decide to keep for yourself. Beautifully packaged perfumes made from natural essences are available from **Annick Goutal**. **Guerlain** has the ultimate in beauty care, while the elegant shops of **L'Artisan Parfumeur** specialize in exquisitely packaged scents which evoke specific memories. They have also reissued favorites from the past, including perfume made to exactly the same formula as one that was worn at the court of Versailles. **Frédéric Malle** is another big name in top-of-the-line scent. Exclusive perfumes can also be found in the beautiful surroundings of the **Salons du Palais Royal**, an upscale Shiseido store. Serge Lutens, the company's creative director and a renowned parfumier creates exquisite and exotic scents which can only be bought in this store. **Lunx** is another designer perfumery where you can choose between one of their ten exclusive fragrances.

If you want to purchase yourself a little *je-ne-sais-quoi* then lipstick, powder and paint from **Stephane Marais** is an absolute must. A sought-after makeup artist who worked with catwalk models and *haute couture* designers, Marais created his own cosmetics line a few years back. His store on the Rue Saint Honoré gets an interior makeover every few months. Another *haute* cosmetics designer is Terry de Gunzberg, whose store **By Terry** stocks fantastic products. Personalize your gift by having a message inscribed on the sleek, silver packaging. Further custom beauty products can be found at the **Galerie Noemi**, where lipstick can be mixed up just for you.

HOUSEHOLD GOODS

Though certain items are obviously rather delicate to carry home, it is difficult to ignore some of the world's most elegant tableware, found in Paris's chic shops. If you are wary of loading up your cases with breakable pieces, many shops will arrange to ship crockery overseas. Luxury household goods can be found on the Rue Royale, where many of the best shops are located. They sell items such as rustic china and reproduction and modern silverware. **Lalique's** Art Nouveau and Art Deco glass sculptures are collected all over the world. Impeccable silverware including fine photograph frames and even chopsticks comes from **Christofle**.

For significant savings on porcelain and crystal, try **Lumicristal**, which stocks Baccarat, Daum and Limoges crystal, or go to **Baccarat** itself. Baccarat also has a boutique on the Place de la Madeleine. The interior designer **Pierre Frey** has an upstairs showroom displaying fabrics which have been made into a fabulous array of cushions, bedspreads and tablecloths. Excellent quality bed linen can also be found at **Yves Delorme**.

La Chaise Longue has a selection of well-designed *objets*, along with fun gift ideas. **Home Autour du Monde** is contemporary, while **La Tuile à Loup** carries more traditional French handicrafts. **DOM** and **Why** stock an excellent range of cheap, kitsch accessories for funky homes. A newly opened interior design store at **Galeries Lafayette** has everything from fancy mops to cutting-edge, three-piece suites. The **Sentou Gallery** is a clutch of stores full of chic pieces for Parisian living. One shop carries interesting tableware, while another focuses on practical purchases, with the final store dedicated to high-end furniture.

Kitchen equipment which can't be beaten comes from

E. Dehillerin. A must-have item in many Parisian homes is a scented candle from **Diptyque**. Figuier is their most popular fragrance.

The basement at **BHV** (see p321) is filled with tools and equipment for decorating your house and garden.

BOOKS, MAGAZINES AND NEWSPAPERS

Many English and American publications can be found at large magazine stands or at some of the bookshops listed. If French is no obstacle the weeklies *Pariscope*, *L'Officiel des Spectacles* and *Zurban* have the most comprehensive listings of what's going on around town.

The *International Herald Tribune*, an English-language daily newspaper, is published in Paris and contains good American news coverage. Two periodicals, *Paris Free Voice* and the biweekly *France–US Contacts*, are also published in English.

Some of the large department stores have a book section (see Department Stores p321). There is a large branch of **W H Smith** and a useful **Galignani**, or try **Brentano's**. A small, somewhat disorganized, but cozy and convivial bookshop is **Shakespeare & Co**. The American-influenced **Village Voice** has a good literary and intellectual selection of new books, while **The**

Abbey Bookshop does the same for second-hand books. **Tea and Tattered Pages** is a British second-hand bookshop.

French-language bookshops include **La Hune**, specializing in art, design, architecture, photography, fashion and movies; **Gibert Joseph**, selling general and educational books; and **Le Divan** which has social science, psychology, literature and poetry sections. French food lovers and cooks will adore browsing at **Food**, a cornucopia of cookbooks in several languages, edible goodies and tableware.

FLOWERS

Some Parisian florists such as **Christian Tortu** are very well known, so be sure to buy one of Tortu's signature vases. **Aquarelle** and **Monceau Fleurs** offer a good selection at reasonable prices; and **Mille Feuilles** is the place to go to in the Marais. (See also Specialty Shops p332.) Stunning silk flowers can be found at **Hervé Gambs**, whose chic store is brimming over with beautiful artifical blooms.

SPECIALTY SHOPS

For cigars, **A La Civette** is perhaps Paris's most beautiful tobacconist. It is also probably the most devoted to its wares and has humidified shop windows to preserve its merchandise.

Go to **A L'Olivier** in the Rue de Rivoli for a wonderful selection of exotic oils and vinegar. Or, if honey is your favorite condiment, try **La Maison du Miel** where you can buy all kinds of fine honeys, including those made from the flowers of lavender and acacia. You can also buy refreshing beeswax soap and candles here. **Mariage Frères** has become a cult favorite for its 350 varieties of tea; it also sells teapots.

Couture fabrics can be purchased from a range at **Wolff et Descourtis**. For an unusual gift of traditional French card games or tarot cards, go to **Jeux Descartes**. One of the world's most famous and delightful toyshops is **Au Nain Bleu**, while the name **Cassegrain** is synonymous with high-quality stationery and paper products. **Calligrane** sells a tempting range of high-quality desk accessories and paper products.

The **La Maison de la Fausse Fourrure** offers just about everything made in fake fur. From floor-length coats to shopping carts, via hot-water bottle covers and tactile lampshades, an unusual gift is sure to result from a trip here. However, the ultimate in eccentric shopping can be found at **Deyrolle**, Paris's most famous taxidermist, which profides gifts for the person who truly has everything.

DIRECTORY

SOUVENIR AND MUSEUM SHOPS

Les Drapeaux de France
14 Galerie Montpensier
75001. **Map** 12 E1.
Tel 01 42 97 55 40.

Le Musée
Niveau 2, Forum des Halles, Porte Berger 75001.
Map 13 A2.
Tel 01 40 39 97 91.

Musée Carnavalet
(See p97).

Le Musée du Louvre
(See p123).

Musée d'Orsay
(See p145).

GIFTS

Au Printemps
64 Blvd Haussman 75009.
Map 6 D4.
Tel 01 42 82 50 00.

Le Bon Marché
24 Rue de Sèvres 75007.
Map 11 C5.
Tel 01 44 39 80 00.

Galeries Lafayette
40 Blvd Haussmann
75009.
Map 6 E4.
Tel 01 42 82 34 56.
One of two branches.

PERFUME AND COSMETICS

Annick Goutal
16 Rue de Bellechasse
75007.
Map 11 C3.
Tel 01 45 51 36 13.
One of several branches.

L'Artisan Parfumeur
24 Blvd Raspail 75007.
Map 16 D1.
Tel 01 42 22 23 32.
One of several branches.

By Terry
21 Galerie Véro-dodat
75001.
Map 12 F2.
Tel 01 44 76 00 76.

Eiffel Shopping
9 Ave de Suffren 75007.
Map 10 D3.
Tel 01 45 66 55 30.

DIRECTORY

Frédéric Malle
37 Rue de Grenelle 75007.
Map 11 C3.
Tel 01 42 22 77 22.

Galerie Noemi
92 Ave des Champs
Elysées 75008.
Map 4 F5.
Tel 01 45 62 78 27.

Guerlain
68 Ave des Champs-
Elysées 75008.
Map 4 F5.
Tel 01 45 62 52 57.
One of several branches.
www.guerlain.com

Lunx
48-50 Rue de l'Université
75007. **Map** 12 D3.
Tel 01 45 44 50 14.

Parfums Caron
34 Ave Montaigne 75008.
Map 10 F1.
Tel 01 47 23 40 82.

Sephora
70 Ave des Champs-
Elysées 75008.
Map 11 B1.
Tel 01 53 93 22 50.
www.sephora.fr
One of several branches.

**Salons du Palais
Royal**
25 Rue de Valois 75001.
Map 12 F1.
Tel 01 49 27 09 09.

Stephane Marais
217 Rue St-honoré 75001.
Map 12 D1.

HOUSEHOLD
GOODS

Baccarat
11 Pl de la Madeleine
75008. **Map** 5 C5.
Tel 01 42 65 36 26.
(See also p201).

La Chaise Longue
30 Rue Croix-des-Petits-
Champs 75001.
Map 12 F1.
Tel 01 42 96 32 14.
One of several branches.

Christofle
24 Rue de la Paix 75002.
Map 6 D5.
Tel 01 42 65 62 43.
One of several branches.

Diptyque
34 Bld St Germain 75006.
Map 13 B5.
Tel 01 43 26 45 27.

DOM
21 Rue Ste-Croix de la
Bretonnerie 75004.
Map 13 B3.
Tel 01 42 71 08 00.

E. Dehillerin
18 Rue Coquillière 75001.
Map 12 F1.
Tel 01 42 36 53 13.

**Home Autour
du Monde**
8 Rue des Francs-Bourgeois
75003. **Map** 14 D3.
Tel 01 42 77 06 08.

Lalique
11 Rue Royale 75008.
Map 5 C5.
Tel 01 53 05 12 12.

Lumicristal
22 bis Rue de Paradis
75010. **Map** 7 B4.
Tel 01 42 46 96 25.

Pierre Frey
7 Rue Jacob 75006.
Map 12 E3.
Tel 01 46 33 73 00.

Point à la Ligne
67 Ave Victor Hugo
75116. **Map** 3 B5.
Tel 01 45 00 87 01.

La Tuile à Loup
35 Rue Daubenton 75005.
Map 17 B2.
Tel 01 47 07 28 90.

Why
41 Rue des Francs-
Bourgeois 75004.
Map 13 C2.
Tel 01 44 61 72 75.

Sentou Gallery
18 & 24 Rue Pont Louis-
Philippe 75004.
Map 13 C3.
Tel 01 42 71 00 01.

Yves Delorme
8 Rue Vavin 75006.
Map 16 D1.
Tel 01 44 07 23 14.

BOOKS, MAGAZINES
AND NEWSPAPERS

Abbey Bookshop
29 Rue de la Parcheminerie
75005. **Map** 13 A4.
Tel 01 46 33 16 24.

Brentano's
37 Ave de l'Opéra 75002.
Map 6 E5.
Tel 01 42 61 52 50.
www.brentanos.fr

Le Divan
203 Rue de la Convention
75015. **Map** 12 E3.
Tel 01 53 68 90 68.

Food
58 Rue Charlot 75003.
Map 14 D2.
Tel 01 42 72 68 97.

Galignani
224 Rue de Rivoli 75001.
Map 13 A2.
Tel 01 42 60 76 07.

Gibert Joseph
26 Blvd St-Michel 75006.
Map 12 F5.
Tel 01 44 41 88 88.

La Hune
170 Blvd St-Germain
75006. **Map** 12 D4.
Tel 01 45 48 35 85.

Shakespeare & Co
37 Rue de la Bûcherie
75005. **Map** 13 A4.
Tel 01 43 26 96 50.

**Tea and Tattered
Pages**
24 Rue Mayet 75006.
Map 15 B1.
Tel 01 40 65 94 35.

Village Voice
6 Rue Princesse 75006.
Map 12 E4.
Tel 01 46 33 36 47.
www.villagevoicebookshop.
com

W H Smith
248 Rue de Rivoli 75001.
Map 11 C1.
Tel 01 44 77 88 99.

FLOWERS

Aquarelle
1 Rue Abbé de l'Epée
75005. **Map** 16 F1.
Tel 01 44 07 15 00.
One of several branches.

Christian Tortu
6 Carrefour de l'Odéon
75006. **Map** 12 F4.
Tel 01 43 26 02 56.

Hervé Gambs
9 Bis Rue des Blancs
Manteaux 75004.
Map 13 C3.
Tel 01 44 59 88 88.

Monceau Fleurs
84 Blvd de Raspail 75006.
Map 12 D4.
Tel 01 45 48 70 10.

SPECIALTY SHOPS

A La Civette
157 Rue St-Honoré 75001.
Map 12 F2.
Tel 01 42 96 04 99.

A L'Olivier
23 Rue de Rivoli 75004.
Map 13 C3.
Tel 01 48 04 86 59.

Au Nain Bleu
408 Rue St-Honoré 75008.
Map 5 C5.
Tel 01 42 60 39 01.
www.aunainbleu.com
One of several branches.

Calligrane
4 Rue du Pont-Louis-
Philippe 75004.
Map 13 B4.
Tel 01 48 04 31 89.

Cassegrain
422 Rue St-Honoré 75008.
Map 5 C5.
Tel 01 42 60 20 08.
www.cassegrain.fr

Deyrolle
46 Rue du Bac 75007.
Map 12 D3.
Tel 01 42 22 30 07.

Jeux Descartes
52 Rue des Écoles 75005.
Map 13 A5.
Tel 01 43 26 79 83.
One of three branches.

**La Maison de la
Fausse Fourrure**
34 Boulevard Beaumarchais
75011. **Map** 14 E3.
Tel 01 43 55 24 21.

La Maison du Miel
24 Rue Vignon 75009.
Map 6 D5.
Tel 01 47 42 26 70.

Mariage Frères
30 Rue du Bourg-Tibourg
75004. **Map** 13 C3.
Tel 01 42 72 28 11.
www.mariagefreres.com
One of several branches.
(See p286).

Wolff et Descourtis
18 Galerie Vivienne
75002. **Map** 12 F1.
Tel 01 42 61 80 84.

Food and Drink

Paris is as famous for food as it is for fashion. Gastronomic treats include *foie gras*, cold meats from the *charcuterie*, cheese and wine. Certain streets are so overflowing with food shops that you can put together a picnic for 20 in no time: try the Rue Montorgueil *(see p339)*. The Rue Rambuteau, running on each side of the Pompidou Centre, has a marvelous row of fish stores, cheese delicatessens and shops selling prepared foods. *(See also* What to Eat and Drink in Paris *pp296–99* and Light Meals and Snacks *pp316–19*.)

BREAD AND CAKES

There is a huge range of breads and pastries in France's capital. The *baguette* is often translated as "French bread"; a *bâtard* is similar but thicker, while a *ficelle* is thinner. A *fougasse* is a crusty, flat loaf made from *baguette* dough, often filled with onions, cheese, herbs or spices. Since most French bread contains no fat it goes stale quickly: the sooner you eat it, the better. The French would never eat day-old bread so be sure to be up in time to make it to the bakery for breakfast!

Croissants can be bought *ordinaire* or *au beurre* – the latter is flakier and more buttery. *Pain au chocolat* is a chocolate-filled pastry eaten for breakfast and *chausson aux pommes* is filled with apples. There are also pear, plum and rhubarb variations. A *pain aux raisins* is a bread-like wheel filled with custard and raisins.

Poilâne sells perhaps the only bread in Paris known by the name of its baker (the late Lionel, brother of Max) and his hearty wholewheat loaves are tremendously popular, with freshly baked loaves being jetted around the world to satisfy the cravings of certain movie stars. There are always big lines on the weekend and around 4pm when a fresh batch comes out of the oven.

Many think **Ganachaud** bakes the best bread in Paris. Thirty different kinds, including ingredients such as walnuts and fruit are made in the old-fashioned ovens. Although **Les Panetons** is

part of a larger chain, it is one of the best of its kind with a broad range of breads. Favorites here include five-grain bread, sesame rolls and *mouchoir aux pommes*, a variation on the traditional *chausson*.

It is very important to remember that every Parisian has a favorite neighborhood bakery, so when you are buying bread locally simply go for the shop with the longest lines.

Many of the Jewish delicatessens have the best ryes and the only pumpernickels in town. The best known is **Jo Goldenberg's**.

Le Moulin de la Vierge uses a wood fire to bake organic breads and rich pound cakes. **Maison Meli** is second only to **Max Poilâne** in the Montparnasse area with *baguettes*, *fougasses*, cakes and pastries. **J L Poujauran** is known for his black-olive bread and nut-and-raisin wholegrain breads. **Pierre Hermé** is to cakes what Chanel is to fashion, while **Ladurée** macaroons are legendary.

CHOCOLATE

Like all food in France, chocolate is to be savored. **Christian Constant's** low-sugar creations are made with pure cocoa and are known to connoisseurs. **Dalloyau** makes all types of chocolate and is not too expensive (it's also known for its *pâtisserie* and cold meats). **Fauchon** is world famous for its luxury food products. Its chocolates are excellent, as is the *pâtisserie*. **Lenôtre** makes classic truffles and pralines. Robert Linxe at **La Maison du Chocolat** is

constantly inventing fresh, rich chocolates with mouthwatering exotic ingredients. **Richart** boasts beautifully presented and hugely expensive chocolates, which are usually coated with dark chocolate or liqueur-filled. **Debauve & Gallais** are best known for their wonderful and delicious glacé chestnut treats *(marron glacés)*.

CHARCUTERIE AND FOIE GRAS

Charcuteries often sell cheese, snails, truffles, smoked salmon, caviar and wine as well as cold meats. **Fauchon** has a good grocery, as does the department store **Le Bon Marché**. **Hédiard** is a luxury shop similar to Fauchon, and **Maison de la Truffe** sells *foie gras* and sausages as well as truffles. For Beluga caviar, Georgian tea and Russian vodka go to **Petrossian**.

The Lyon and Auvergne regions of France are the best known for their *charcuterie*. Examples can be bought from **Chretienne Jean-Jacques**. **Aux Vrais Produits d'Auvergne** has a number of outlets where you can stock up on dried and fresh sausages and delicious Cantal cheese (rather like cheddar). **Pou** is a sparklingly clean and popular shop selling *pâté en croute* (pâté baked in pastry), *boudins* (black and white puddings), Lyonnais sausages, ham and *foie gras*. Just off the Champs-Elysées, **Vignon** has superb *foie gras* and Lyonnais sausages as well as popular prepared foods.

Together with truffles and caviar, *foie gras* is the ultimate in gourmet food. The quality (and price) depends upon the percentage of liver used. Though most specialty food shops sell *foie gras*, you can be sure of quality at **Comtesse du Barry**, which has six outlets in Paris. **Divay** is relatively inexpensive and will ship overseas. **Labeyrie** has a range of beautifully packaged *foie gras* suitable for giving as presents.

CHEESE

Although Camembert is undoubtedly a favorite, there is an overwhelming range of cheeses available.

A friendly *fromager* will help you choose. **Marie-Anne Cantin** is one of the leading figures in the fight to protect traditional production methods, and her fine cheeses are available from the shop that she inherited from her father. Some say that **Alléosse** is the best cheese delicatessen in Paris – the façade may be in need of renovation, but all the cheeses are made according to traditional methods. **Fromagerie Quatrehomme** sells farm-made cheeses, many of which are in danger of becoming extinct; these include a rare and delicious truffle Brie (when in season). **Boursault** is one of the best shops in Paris for all types of cheese – the *chèvre* (goat's cheese) is particularly good, and outside on the sidewalk the daily specials are offered at remarkably reasonable prices. **Barthelemy** in the Rue de Grenelle has a truly exceptional Roquefort. **Androuet** is a Parisian institution with several branches across the city. Try a pungent Munster or a really ripe Brie. A charming cheese shop on the bustling Rue Montorgueil market street, **La Fermette**, offers a dazzling array of dairy products, which the helpful and friendly staff will happily encase in plastic for the journey home. This is imperative when bringing cheese through customs, so don't forget to ask your *fromager* to wrap it for you. Well-heeled locals line in the street to buy oozing *livarot* and sharp *chèvre* from **La Fromagerie d'Auteuil**.

WINE

The chain store which has practically cornered the everyday drinking market is **Nicolas** – there's a branch in every neighborhood with a range of wines to suit all pockets. As a rule, the salespeople are knowledgeable

and helpful. Try the charming **Legrand Filles et Fils** (see p319) for a carefully chosen selection. **Caves Taillevent** on the Rue du Faubourg-St-Honoré is worth a sightseeing tour. It is an enormous, overwhelming cellar with some of the most expensive wine. **Cave Péret** on the Rue Daguerre has a vast selection of wines and can offer personal advice to help you with your purchase. The beautiful **Ryst-Dupeyron**, in the St-Germain quarter, displays whiskies, wines, ports, and Monsieur Ryst's own Armagnac. He will even personalize a bottle for that special occasion.

Other great wine stores include **Lavinia** (see p319) which is the largest in Europe, and **Di'Vin** in the 16th arrondissement where Emmanuel, the owner, will guide you through his complex and interesting selection. The staff in **Les Caves Augé** are also very knowledgable and friendly.

CHAMPAGNE

Fabulous fizz can be found at most wine stores, but some know their bubbles better than others. The **Nicolas** chain, mentioned above, frequently has great offers on well-known brands, so this is a good place to come and stock up on your favorite famous bubbly. **Tchin Tchin** on the Rue Martyrs is a friendly and well-stocked wine shop with charming staff to help you with your selection. The **Repaire du Bacchus** on the Rue d'Auteuil is a good place to go for hard-to-find vintages. The *sommelier* here is very knowledgable and able to provide excellent alternative advice if your preferred brand is out of stock. **Legrand Filles et Fils** on the Rue de la Banque, is one of the few shops in Paris to stock Salon, a rare high-end champagne. They also sell champagne by Jacques Selosse which is little-known but well-loved by champagne connoisseurs. **Les Caves du Panthéon** on the Rue Saint Jacques is a small, but lovely wine shop which has a

particularly interesting selection of champagnes. Close by is **Nectar**, a corner wine shop which is distinguished both by its charming and helpful staff and also by its frequent deals on champagne. The climate-controlled section of **Hédiard** at the Place de la Madelaine is a good place to find rare, fine sparkling wines. **Caprices de l'Instant** is a fashionable wine store which stocks good quality champagne including bottles by some lesser-known producers. A stroll along the Boulevard St-Germain can be enhanced with a visit to **La Maison du Millesimes**, a wonderful store carrying excellent vintages of household name champagnes.

OYSTERS

The ultimate aphrodisac for some, a slippery sea creature for others, there is no doubt that the once humble oyster can cause heated debate. In Paris, the argument tends to be over the best place to purchase these creatures, with every seafood fan worth his platter claiming a favorite spot; and it is, of course, important to get it right. A deciding factor for some is the grace with which your fish seller will agree to open them for you. In general, a polite request will be honored, although sometimes you may have to wait a while before being presented with a platter perfect for a picnic. The fish seller on the Rue Cler market street, **La Sablaisse Poissonerie**, has an excellent reputation as does the **Poissonerie du Dôme** in the city's 14th arrondissement. Over in the traditionally rough area around the Rue Oberkampf, you can find excellent oysters at the **Poissonerie Lacroix**. If you prefer to eat your oysters on the spot then head to an *huitrerie* (oyster shop) such as the **Huiterie Garnier** on the Avenue Mozart in the chic 16th arrondissement, where you can enjoy your shellfish right away at the few tables tucked into the corner of the store.

DIRECTORY

BREAD AND CAKES

Ganachaud
226 Rue des Pyrénées
75020. *Tel 01 43 58 42 62.*

J L Poujauran
20 Rue Jean-Nicot 75007.
Map 10 F2.
Tel 01 43 17 35 20.

Jo Goldenberg
15 Rue des Rosiers 75004.
Map 13 C3.
Tel 01 48 87 70 39.

Maison Meli
4 Pl Constantin Brancusi
75014. **Map** 15 C3.
Tel 01 43 21 76 18.

Max Poilâne
29 Rue de l'Ouest 75014.
Map 15 B3.
Tel 01 43 27 24 91.

**Le Moulin de
la Vierge**
105.Rue Vercingétorix
75014. **Map** 15 A4.
Tel 01 45 43 09 84.
One of several branches.

Les Panetons
113 Rue Mouffetard
75005. **Map** 17 B2.
Tel 01 47 07 12 08.

Pierre Hermé
72 Rue Bonaparte 75006.
Map 12 E4.
Tel 01 43 54 47 77.

Poilâne
8 Rue de Cherche-Midi
75006. **Map** 12 D4.
Tel 01 45 48 42 59.

CHOCOLATE

Christian Constant
37 Rue d'Assas 75006.
Map 16 E1.
Tel 01 53 63 15 15.

Dalloyau
101 Rue du Faubourg-St-
Honoré 75008. **Map** 5 B5.
Tel 01 42 99 90 00.

Debauve & Gallais
30 Rue des Saints-Pères
75007. **Map** 12 D4.
Tel 01 45 48 54 67.
One of two branches.

Fauchon
26 Pl de la Madeleine
75008. **Map** 5 C5.
Tel 01 47 42 91 10.
www.faucho.fr

Lenôtre
15 Blvd de Courcelles
75008. **Map** 5 B2.
Tel 01 45 63 87 63.

**La Maison du
Chocolat**
225 Rue du Faubourg-St-
Honoré 75008.
Map 4 E3.
Tel 01 42 27 39 44.

Richart
258 Blvd St-Germain
75007. **Map** 11 C2.
Tel 01 45 55 66 00.

CHARCUTERIE
AND FOIE GRAS

**Chretienne Jean-
Jacques**
58 Rue des Martyrs 75009.
Map 6 F2.
Tel 01 48 78 96 45.

Comtesse du Barry
1 Rue de Sèvres 75006.
Map 12 D4.
Tel 01 45 48 32 04.
One of several branches.

Divay
4 Rue Bayen 75017.
Map 4 D2.
Tel 01 43 80 16 97.

Fauchon
26 Pl de la Madeleine
75008. **Map** 5 C5.
Tel 01 47 42 60 11.

Hédiard
21 Pl de la Madeleine
75008. **Map** 5 C5.
Tel 01 43 12 88 88.

Labeyrie
11 Rue d'Auteuil 75016.
Tel 01 42 24 17 62.

Maison de la Truffe
19 Pl de la Madeleine
75008. **Map** 5 C5.
Tel 01 42 66 10 01.

Petrossian
18 Blvd Latour-Maubourg
75007. **Map** 11 A2.
Tel 01 44 11 32 22.

Pou
16 Ave des Ternes 75017.
Map 4 D3.
Tel 01 43 80 19 24.

Vignon
14 Rue Marbeuf 75008.
Map 4 F5.
Tel 01 47 20 24 26.

CHEESE

Alléosse
13 Rue Poncelet 75017.
Map 4 E3.
Tel 01 46 22 50 45.

Androuët
23 Rue des Acacias 75017.
Map 4 D3.
Tel 01 40 68 00 12.

Barthelemy
51 Rue de Grenelle 75007.
Map 12 D4.
Tel 01 45 48 56 75.

Boursault
71 Ave du Général-Leclerc
75014. **Map** 16 D5.
Tel 01 43 27 93 30.

La Fermette
86 Rue Montorgueil
75002. **Map** 13 A1.
Tel 01 42 36 70 96.

**La Fromagerie
d'Auteuil**
58 Rue d'Auteuil 75016.
Tel 01 45 25 07 10.

**Fromagerie
Quatrehomme**
62 Rue de Sèvres 75007.
Map 11 C5.
Tel 01 47 34 33 45.

Marie-Anne Cantin
12 Rue du Champ-
de-Mars 75007.
Map 10 F3.
Tel 01 45 50 43 94.

WINE

Les Caves Augé
116 Blvd Haussman
75008. **Map** 5 C4.
Tel 01 45 22 16 97.

Cave Péret
6 Rue Daguerre 75014.
Map 16 D4.
Tel 01 43 22 08 64.

Caves Taillevent
199 Rue du Faubourg-St-
Honoré 75008.
Map 4 F3.
Tel 01 45 61 14 09.

Di'vin
123 Ave Mozart 75016.
Map 9 A3.
Tel 01 53 92 04 60.

Nicolas
35 Blvd Malesherbes
75008. **Map** 5 C5.
Tel 01 42 65 00 85.

Ryst-Dupeyron
79 Rue du Bac 75007.
Map 12 D3.
Tel 01 45 48 80 93.

CHAMPAGNE

Caprices de l'Instant
12 Rue Jacques Couer
75004. **Map** 14 E4.
Tel 01 40 27 89 00.

**Les Caves du
Panthéon**
174 Rue St Jacques
75005. **Map** 13 A5.
Tel 01 46 33 90 35.

Hédiard
2 Place de la Madeleine
75008. **Map** 5 C5.
Tel 01 43 12 88 88.

**La Maison de
Millesimes**
137 Boulevard Saint
Germain 75006.
Map 12 F4.
Tel 01 40 46 80 01.

Nectar
25 Rue des Ecoles 75005.
Map 13 A5.
Tel 01 43 26 99 43.

Repaire du Bacchus
58 Rue d'Auteuil 75016.
Tel 01 45 25 09 75.

Tchin Tchin
39 Rue Martyrs 75009.
Map 6 F3.
Tel 01 40 16 80 27.

OYSTERS

Huiterie Garnier
114 Avenue Mozart
75016. **Map** 9 A3.
Tel 01 40 50 17 27.

**Poissonerie du
Dôme**
4 Rue Delambre 75014.
Map 16 D2.
Tel 01 43 35 23 95.

Poissonerie Lacroix
44 Rue Oberkampf 75011.
Map 14 E1.
Tel 01 47 00 93 13.

**La Sablaise
Poissonerie**
28 Rue Cler 75007.
Map 10 F3.
Tel 01 45 51 61 78.

Art and Antiques

In Paris you can either buy art and antiques from shops and galleries with established reputations, or from flea markets and avant-garde galleries. Many of the prestigious antiques shops and galleries are located around the Rue du Faubourg-St-Honoré and are worth a visit even if you can't afford to buy. On the Left Bank is Le Carré Rive Gauche, an organization of 30 antiques dealers. *Objets d'art* over 50 years old, worth more than a given amount (values vary for all categories of art object), will require a *Certificat pour un bien culturel* to be exported anywhere in the world (provided by the vendor), plus a *licence d'exportation* for non-EU countries. Seek professional advice from the large antique shops.

EXPORTING

The Ministry of Culture designates *objets d'art*. Export licenses are available from the **Centre Français du Commerce Extérieur**. The **Centre des Renseignements des Douanes** has a booklet, *Bulletin Officiel des Douanes*, with all the details.

MODERN CRAFTS AND FURNITURE

One of the best places for furniture and *objets d'art* by up-and-coming designers is **Sentou**, where you can find objects and textiles, as well as furniture by contemporary designers. Another essential venue is the showroom of the Italian designer, **Giulio Cappellini**. **Le Viaduc des Arts** is a railroad viaduct, each arch of which has been transformed into a storefront and workshop space. Stroll along this street for a great show of contemporary metalwork, tapestry, sculpture, ceramics and much more.

ANTIQUES AND OBJETS D'ART

If you wish to buy antiques, you might like to stroll around the areas that boast many galleries – in Le Carré Rive Gauche around Quai Malaquais, try **L'Arc en Seine** and **Anne-Sophie Duval** for Art Nouveau and Art Deco. Rue Jacob is still one of the best places to seek beautiful objects, antique or modern. Close to the Louvre, the **Louvre des Antiquaires** (see

p120) sells expensive, quality furniture. On the Rue du Faubourg-St-Honoré you will find **Didier Aaron**, expert on furniture from the 17th and 18th centuries. **Village St-Paul** between the Quai des Célestins, the Rue Saint Paul and the Rue Charlemange, is the most charming group of antiques shops and is also open on Sundays.

La Calinière has a superb range of *objets d'art* and old lighting fixtures. Glassware from the 19th century to the 1960s is sold at **Verreglass**. **La Village Suisse** in the south of the city also groups many art and antiques dealers.

REPRODUCTIONS, POSTERS AND PRINTS

A beautiful, contemporary art gallery called **Artcurial** on the Place des Champs-Elysées has one of the best selections of international art periodicals, books and prints. On the Boulevard Saint Germain, **La Hune** is a popular bookshop, particularly for art publications. The museum bookshops, especially those in the Musée d'Art Moderne *(see p201)*, Louvre *(see p123)*, Musée d'Orsay *(see p145)* and Pompidou Centre *(see p111)* are good for recent art books and posters.

Galerie Documents on the Rue de Seine sells original antique posters. Or leaf through the second-hand bookstalls along the banks of the Seine.

ART GALLERIES

Established art galleries are located on or around the Avenue Montaigne. The **Louise Leiris** gallery was founded by D H Kahnweiler, the dealer who "discovered" both Georges Braque and Pablo Picasso. The gallery still shows Cubist masterpieces.

Artcurial holds many exhibitions and has an impressive permanent collection of 20th-century art, including works by Joan Miró, Picasso, Alberto Giacometti and Max Ernst. **Galerie Lelong** is devoted to contemporary artists.

On the Left Bank **Adrian Maeght** has a tremendous stock of paintings at prices to suit most budgets; he also publishes fine art books. **Galerie 1900–2000** specializes in works by Surrealist and Dada artists, and **Galerie Jeanne Bucher** represents postwar Abstraction with artists like Nicolas de Staël and Vieira da Silva. **Dina Vierny** is a bastion of Modernism, founded by sculptor Aristide Maillol's famous model of the same name. Rue Louise-Weiss has become the area for cutting-edge creativity and innovation. **Galerie Emmanuel Perrotin** has two sites in this area, which is known as "Scène Est". The **Air de Paris** gallery is also popular. In the Marais try **Yvon Lambert, Galerie Templon** – specializing in American art, and **Galerie du Jour Agnès B**, and in the Bastille, **Levignes-Bastille** and **L et M Durand-Dessert**, also a fashionable place to buy catalogs on new artists, if not their actual works.

AUCTIONS AND AUCTION HOUSES

The great Paris auction center, in operation since 1858, is **Drouot-Richelieu** *(see p216)*. Bidding can be intimidating since most of it is done by dealers. Beware of the auctioneer's high-speed patter. *La Gazette de L'Hôtel Drouot* tells you what auctions are coming up when. Drouot-Richelieu has its own auction catalog as well. The house only accepts cash and French checks, but there is an exchange desk in house. A 10–15 perent commission to the house is charged, so add it on to any price you hear. You may view from 11am to 6pm on the day before the sale, and from 11am to noon on the morning of the sale. Items considered

not good enough for the main house are sold at **Drouot-Nord**. Here auctions take place from 9am to noon and viewing is just 5 minutes before the sales begin. The most prestigious auctions are held at **Drouot-Montaigne**.

The **Crédit Municipal** holds around 12 auctions a month, and almost all the items on sale are small objects and furs off-loaded by rich

Parisians. The rules follow those at Drouot. Information can also be found in *La Gazette de L'Hôtel Drouot*.

Service des Domaines sells all kinds of odds and ends, and here you can still find bargains. Many of the wares come from bailiffs and from Customs and Excise *(see p374)* confis-cations. Viewing is from 10am to 11:30am on the day of the sale.

DIRECTORY

EXPORTING

Centre Français du Commerce Extérieur
10 Ave d'Iéna 75116.
Map 10 D1.
Tel 01 40 73 30 00.
www.cfce.fr

Centre des Renseignements des Douanes
84 Rue d'Hauteville 75010.
Tel 08 25 30 82 63.
www.douane.gouv.fr

MODERN CRAFTS AND FURNITURE

Cappellini
4 Rue des Rosiers 75004.
Map 13 C3.
Tel 01 42 78 39 39.
www.cappellini.it

Sentou
18 Rue du Pont-Louis-Philippe 75004.
Map 13 C3.
Tel 01 42 77 44 79.

Le Viaduc des Arts
Ave Daumesnil 750012.
Map 14 F5.
Tel 01 43 40 75 75.
This comprises a series of shops on the Avenue.

ANTIQUES AND OBJETS D'ART

Anne-Sophie Duval
5 Quai Malaquais 75006.
Map 12 E3.
Tel 01 43 54 51 16.

L'Arc en Seine
31 Rue de Seine 75006.
Map 12 E3.
Tel 01 43 29 11 02.

La Calinière
68 Rue Vieille-du-Temple 75003. **Map** 13 C3.
Tel 01 42 77 40 46.

Didier Aaron
118 Rue du Faubourg-St-Honoré 75008.
Map 5 C5.
Tel 01 47 42 47 34.

Louvre des Antiquaires
2 Pl du Palais Royal 75001.
Map 12 E2.
Tel 01 42 97 27 27.

Verreglass
32 Rue de Charonne 75011. **Map** 14 F4
Tel 01 48 05 78 43.

Village St-Paul
Between the Quai des Célestins, the Rue St-Paul and the Rue Charlemagne 75004. **Map** 13 C4.

La Village Suisse
78 Ave de Suffren 75015.
Map 10 E4.
www.levillagesuisseparis.com

REPRODUCTIONS, POSTERS, PRINTS

Artcurial
7 Pl des Champs-Elysées M. Dassaulf 75008.
Map 5 A5.
Tel 01 42 99 16 16.

Galerie Documents
53 Rue de Seine 75006.
Map 12 E4.
Tel 01 43 54 50 68.

La Hune
170 Blvd St-Germain 75006.
Map 12 D4.
Tel 01 45 48 35 85.

ART GALLERIES

Adrian Maeght
42 Rue du Bac 75007.
Map 12 D3.
Tel 01 45 48 45 15.

Air de Paris
32 Rue Louise-Weiss 75013.
Map 18 E4.
Tel 01 44 23 02 77.

Dina Vierny
36 Rue Jacob 75006.
Map 12 E3.
Tel 01 42 86 00 87.

Galerie 1900–2000
8 Rue Bonaparte 75006.
Map 12 E3.
Tel 01 43 25 84 20.

Galerie Emmanuel Perrotin
5 & 30 Rue Louise-Weiss 75013.
Map 18 E4.
Tel 01 42 16 79 79.

Galerie Jeanne Bucher
53 Rue de Seine 75006.
Map 12 E4.
Tel 01 44 41 69 55.

Galerie du Jour Agnès B
44 Rue Quincampoix 75004.
Map 13 B2.
Tel 01 44 54 55 90.

Galerie Lelong
13 Rue de Téhéran 75008.
Map 5 A3.
Tel 01 45 63 13 19.

Galerie Templon
30 Rue Beaubourg 75003.
Map 13 B1.
Tel 01 42 72 14 10.
Open by appt only.

L et M Durand-Dessert
28 Rue de Lappe 75011.
Map 14 F4.
Tel 01 48 06 92 23.

Levignes-Bastille
27 Rue de Charonne 75011.
Map 14 F4.
Tel 01 47 00 88 18.

Louise Leiris
47 Rue de Monceau 75008. **Map** 5 A3.
Tel 01 45 63 28 85.

Yvon Lambert
108 Rue Vieille-du-Temple 75003.
Map 14 D2.
Tel 01 42 71 09 33.

AUCTION HOUSES

Crédit Municipal
55 Rue des Francs-Bourgeois 75004.
Map 13 C3.
Tel 01 44 61 64 00.
www.creditmunicipal.fr

Drouot-Montaigne
15 Ave Montaigne 75008.
Map 10 F1.
Tel 01 48 00 20 80.
www.drouot.fr

Drouot-Nord
64 Rue Doudeauville 75018.
Tel 01 48 00 20 99.

Drouot-Richelieu
9 Rue Drouot 75009.
Map 6 F4.
Tel 01 48 00 20 20.

Service des Domaines
15–17 Rue Scribe 75009.
Map 6 D4.
Tel 01 45 11 62 62.

Markets

For eye-catching displays of wonderful food or a lively shopping atmosphere, there is no better place than a Paris market. There are large covered food markets, markets where stalls change regularly, and permanent street markets with a mixture of shops and stalls which are open on a daily basis. Each has its own personality reflecting the area in which it is located. A list of some of the more famous markets, with approximate opening times, follows. For a complete list of markets contact the Paris Office du Tourisme (see p280). And while you're enjoying browsing around the stalls remember to keep an eye on your money – and be prepared to bargain.

FRUIT AND VEGETABLE MARKETS

The French treat food with the kind of reverence usually reserved for religion. Most still shop on a daily basis to be sure of buying the freshest produce possible, so food markets tend to be busy. The majority of fruit and vegetable markets are open from around 8am to 1pm and from 4pm to 7pm Tuesday to Saturday, and from 9am to 1pm Sunday.

Watch what you buy in the food markets or you may find you have purchased a kilo of fruit or vegetables from a marvelous display only to discover later that all the produce hidden underneath is rotten. To avoid this, try to buy produce loose rather than in boxes. Most outdoor stalls prefer to serve you rather than allow you to help yourself, but you can point to the individual fruit and vegetables of your choice. A little language is useful for specifying *pas trop mûr* (not too ripe), or *pour manger ce soir* (to be eaten tonight). If you go to the same market every day you'll become familiar to the stall holders and are far less likely to be cheated. You will also get to know the stalls worth buying from and the produce worth buying. Seasonal fruit and vegetables are, of course, usually a good buy, tending to be fresher and cheaper than at other times of the year. Finally, go early in the day when the food is freshest and the lines are shortest.

FLEA MARKETS

It's often said that you can no longer find bargains at the Paris flea markets. Though this may be true, it's still worth going to one for the sheer fun of browsing. And bear in mind that the price quoted is not the one that you are expected to pay – it's generally assumed that you will bargain. Most flea markets are located on the city's boundaries. Whether you pick up any real bargains has as much to do with luck as with judgment. Often the sellers themselves have little or no idea of the true value of their goods – which can work either for or against you. The biggest and most famous market, incorporating several smaller ones, is the Marché aux Puces de St-Ouen. Keep your eye on your wallet, as pickpockets frequent these markets.

SPECIALTY MARKETS

Try the Marché aux Fleurs Madeleine in the Opéra, the Marché aux Fleurs on the Ile de la Cité (see p81) or the Marché aux Fleurs Ternes in the Champs-Elysées district for fresh flowers. On the Ile de la Cité on Sundays the Marché aux Oiseaux bird market replaces the flower market. Stamp collectors will enjoy the permanent Marché aux Timbres where you can also buy old postcards. In Montmartre the Marché St-Pierre, famous for cheap fabrics, is patronized by professional designers.

Marché d'Aligre

(See p233.)

Reminiscent of a Moroccan bazaar, this must be the cheapest and liveliest market in the city. Here traders hawk ingredients such as North African olives, groundnuts and hot peppers and there are even a few halal butchers. The noise reaches a crescendo on weekends when the cries of the market boys mingle with those of militants of all political persuasions as the latter petition and protest in the Place d'Aligre. The stalls on the square sell mostly second-hand clothes and bric-à-brac. This is a less affluent area of town with few tourists and many Parisians.

Rue Cler

(See p190.)

This high-class, pedestrianized food market is patronized mainly by the politicians and captains of industry who live and work in the vicinity, so it's good for people-spotting! The produce is excellent – there's a Breton delicatessen and some good cheese delicatessens.

Marché Enfant Rouges

39 Rue de Bretagne 75003. **Map** 14 D2. **M** Temple, Filles-du-Calvaire. ⏰ 8am–noon, 3pm–8pm Tue–Fri, 8am–8pm Sat, 8am–1pm Sun.

This long-established, charming fruit and vegetable market on the Rue de Bretagne is part covered, part outdoors and dates from 1620. The items on sale are famous for their freshness, and on Sunday mornings street singers, performers and accordionists sometimes enliven the proceedings.

Marché aux Fleurs Madeleine

Pl de la Madeleine 75008. **Map** 5 C5. **M** Madeleine. ⏰ 7am–8pm Tue–Sun.

Marché aux Fleurs Ternes

Pl des Ternes 75008. **Map** 4 E3. **M** Ternes. ⏰ 8am–8pm Tue–Sun.

Marché St-Pierre

Pl St-Pierre 75018. **Map** 6 F1. **M** Anvers. ⏰ 2–7pm Mon, 9am–7pm Tue–Sat.

Marché aux Timbres

Cour Marigny 75008. **Map** 5 B5. **M** Champs-Elysées. ⏰ 8am–7pm Thu, Sun & public hols.

Marché St-Germain

Rue Mabillon and Rue Lobineau
75005. **Map** 12 E4. Ⓜ *Mabillon*.
◗ 8am–1pm, 4pm–8pm Tue–Sat,
8:30am–1pm Sun.

St-Germain is one of the few
covered markets left in Paris and
has been enhanced by renovation.
Here you can buy Italian, Mexican,
Greek, Asian and organic produce
and other goods.

Rue Lepic

75018. **Map** 6 F1. Ⓜ *Blanche*,
Lamarck-Caulaincourt.
◗ 8am–2pm Tue–Sun.

The Rue Lepic fruit and vegetable
market is situated conveniently
close to the sights of Montmartre
in this refreshingly unspoiled
winding old quarry road. The
market is at its liveliest on the
weekend.

Rue de Lévis

Blvd des Batignolles 75017. **Map** 5 B2.
Ⓜ *Villiers*. ◗ 8am–1pm, 4pm–7pm
Tue–Sat, 9am–2pm Sun.

Rue de Lévis is a bustling, popular
food market near the Parc
Monceau with a number of good
pâtisseries, an excellent cheese
delicatessen and a *charcuterie*
which is known for its savory
pies. The part of the street that
leads to the Rue Legendre sells
haberdashery and fabrics.

Rue Montorgueil

75001 & 75002. **Map** 13 A1.
Ⓜ *Les Halles*. ◗ 8am–1pm,
4pm–7pm Tue–Sat, 9am–1pm Sun.

The Rue Montorgueil is what
remains of the old Les Halles
market. The street has now been
repaved and restored to its former
glory. Here you can buy exotic
fruit and vegetables like green
bananas and yams from the
market gardeners' stalls, or sample
offerings from the delicatessens or
from the Stohrer pastry shop.
Alternatively pick up some of the
pretty Moroccan pottery for sale.

Rue Mouffetard

(See p166.)

Rue Mouffetard is one of the oldest
market streets in Paris. Although it
has become touristy and somewhat
overpriced, it's still a charming
winding street full of quality food
products. It's worth waiting for
the freshly made bread at Les
Panetons bakery at No. 113 *(see
pp333–5)*. There is also a lively
African market down the nearby
side street of Rue Daubenton.

Rue Poncelet

75017. **Map** 4 E3. Ⓜ *Ternes*.
◗ 8am–noon, 4pm–7:30pm
Tue–Sat, 8am–12:30pm Sun.

The Rue Poncelet food market is
situated away from the main
tourist areas of Paris but is worth
visiting for its authentic French
atmosphere. Choose from the
many bakeries, pâtisseries and
charcuteries or enjoy authentic
Auvergne specialties from Aux
Fermes d'Auvergnes.

Marché de la Porte de Vanves

Ave Georges-Lafenestre & Ave Marc-
Sangnier 75014. Ⓜ *Porte-de-Vanves*.
◗ 8am– 7pm Sat & Sun.

Porte de Vanves is a small market
selling good-quality bric-à-brac
and junk as well as some second-
hand furniture. It's best to get to
the market early on Saturday
morning for the best choice of
wares. Artists exhibit nearby in the
Place des Artistes.

Marché Président-Wilson

Situated in Ave du Président-Wilson,
between Pl d'Iéna & Rue Debrousse
75016. **Map** 10 D1. Ⓜ *Alma-Marceau*.
◗ 7am–1pm Wed & Sat.

This very chic food market on
Avenue Président-Wilson is close
to the Musée d'Art Moderne and
the Palais Galliera fashion museum.
It has become important because
there are no other food shops
nearby. It is best for meat.

Marché aux Puces de Montreuil

Porte de Montreuil, 93 Montreuil
75020. Ⓜ *Porte-de-Montreuil*.
◗ 8am–6pm Sat, Sun & Mon.

Go early to the Porte de Montreuil
flea market, where you'll have a
better chance of picking up a
bargain. The substantial second-
hand clothes section attracts many
young people. There's also a wide
variety of items including used
bicycles, bric-à-brac and an exotic
spices stand.

Marché aux Puces de St-Ouen

(See p231.)

This is the most well known, the
most crowded and the most
expensive of all the flea markets,
situated on the northern outskirts
of the city. Here you'll find a range
of markets, locals dealing from
their car trunks and a number of
extremely large buildings packed
with stalls. Some of them are very

upmarket, others sell junk. The
flea market is a 10–15 minute walk
from Clignancourt metro – don't
be put off by the somewhat sleazy
Marché Malik which you have to
pass through on your way from
the metro. A *Guide des Puces*
(guide to the flea markets) can be
obtained from the information
kiosk in the Marché Biron on the
Rue des Rosiers. The more
exclusive markets will take credit
cards and arrange for goods to be
shipped home. New stock arrives
on Friday, the day when pro-
fessionals come from all over the
world to sweep up the best buys.

Among the markets here the
Marché Jules Vallès is good for
turn-of-the-19th century *objets
d'art*. Marché Paul-Bert is
more expensive, but charming.
Items on sale include furniture,
books and prints. Both markets
deal in second-hand goods rather
than antiques.

In a different league, Marché
Biron sells elegant, expensive
antique furniture of very high
quality. Marché Vernaison is the
oldest and biggest market, good for
collectables such as jewelry as
well as lamps and clothes. No
information about the Marché aux
Puces is complete without
mentioning Chez Louisette in the
Vernaison market. This café is
always full of locals enjoying the
home cooking and the well-
intentioned renditions of Edith Piaf
songs. Marché Cambo is a fairly
small market with beautifully
displayed antique furniture.
Marché Serpette is popular with
the dealers: everything sold here
is in mint condition.

Marché Raspail

Situated on Blvd Raspail between Rue
du Cherche-Midi & Rue de Rennes
75006. **Map** 12 D5. Ⓜ *Rennes*
(closed Suns, use Sevres Babylone).
◗ 7am–2pm Tue, Fri & Sun.

The Raspail market sells typical
French groceries as well as
Portuguese produce on Tuesdays
and Fridays. But Sunday is the day
for which it's famous, when health-
conscious Parisians turn up in
droves for the organically grown
produce. Marché Raspail is not a
cheap market, but it is very good.

Rue de Seine and Rue de Buci

75006. **Map** 12 E4. Ⓜ *Odéon*.
◗ 8am– 1pm, 4pm–7pm Tue–Sat,
9am–1pm Sun.

The stalls here are expensive
and crowded but sell quality
fruit and vegetables. There is
also a large florist's and two
excellent pâtisseries.

ENTERTAINMENT IN PARIS

Whether you prefer classical drama or cabaret, leggy showgirls or ballet, opera or jazz, movies or dancing the night away, Paris has it all. Free entertainment is aplenty as well, from the street performers outside the Pompidou Centre to musicians busking in the metros. Parisians themselves enjoy strolling along the boulevards or sitting at a sidewalk café, and nursing a drink. Of course, for the ultimate "oh-la-la!" experience, showgirls await you at celebrated cabarets while supermodels pose in nightclubs. For fans of spectator sports there is tennis, the Tour de France, horse racing, soccer or rugby. Recreation centers and gyms cater to the more active, while the municipal swimming pools delight waterbabies. And for those disposed either way, there's always the popular type of lawn bowling played in Paris, *pétanque*.

PRACTICAL INFORMATION

For the visitor in Paris there is no shortage of information about what's on offer.

The **Office du Tourisme** near the Tuileries and Opera is the city's main tourism distribution point for leaflets and schedules of events. It has a recorded information telephone service giving details of free concerts and exhibitions along with information on transportation to the venues. Its website is also extremely useful. Your hotel reception desk or concierge should also be able to help you with any such information. They usually keep a wide range of brochures and leaflets for guests, and will generally be more than happy to make reservations for you.

BUYING TICKETS

Depending on the event, tickets can be bought at the door, but for blockbuster concerts it is necessary to do so well in advance. For most major events, including some classical music concerts and museum shows, tickets can be purchased at the **FNAC** chain or **Virgin Megastore**. For popular events be sure to do so well in advance, Parisians can be very quick on the draw for hot tickets. However, for theater, opera and dance performances, you can often buy inexpensive tickets at the last minute. If the tickets are marked *sans visibilité* you will be able to see the stage only partially, or perhaps not at all. Often, obliging ushers

Ballerina of the Ballet de l'Opéra

Nightclubbing in Paris

will put you in a better seat, depending on availability, but don't forget to tip.

Theater box offices are open daily from approximately 11am–7pm. Most box offices accept credit card reservations made by phone or in person. But you may have to arrive early to pick up your tickets if you reserved by telephone, as they may be sold to someone else at the last minute. If you

Concert at Opéra National de Paris Garnier (see p348)

LISTINGS MAGAZINES

Paris has several good listings magazines. Among them are *Pariscope,* the simplest to use, *L'Officiel des Spectacles* and *Zurban.* They are published every Wednesday and are widely available. *Le Figaro* also has a good listings section on Wednesdays. Two English publications, *Paris Free Voice* and the quarterly *The City,* are both available at newsstands or **W H Smith** *(see p332).*

Buying tickets at the box office of a comedy club

are really eager and can't get a hold of tickets, you can always turn up at the box office just before the perform-mance in case there are unclaimed or returned tickets.

TICKET TOUTS

If you must have a ticket to a sold-out performance, do as the French do: stand at the entrance with a sign that says *cherche une place* (or *deux*, etc). Many people have an extra ticket to sell. Often the people selling the extra tickets are simply doing so because a person in their party has stood them up and they will simply sell the ticket at face value. It is fine to buy these tickets, but watch out for touts and be sure you don't buy a coun-terfeit or overpriced ticket.

Pétanque players

DISCOUNT TICKETS

Half-price tickets to current plays are sold on the day of performance at **Kiosque Théâtre**. Credit cards are not accepted and a small commis-sion is charged per ticket. There is a booth on the Place de la Madeleine *(see p214)*, open 12:30–8pm, Tuesday–Saturday, 12:30–4pm Sunday, and in the Parvis de la Gare Montparnasse 12:30–6pm Tuesday–Saturday. This is a great way to buy tickets without doing so weeks or even months in advance and, of course, has the added benefit of costing less. The *kiosque* is a Parisian institu-tion and often has passes for the season's top shows.

DISABLED VISITORS' FACILITIES

Where facilities do exist, they are either very good or dreadful. Many venues have wheelchair space, but always phone in advance to make sure it's properly equipped. As far as public transportation is concerned, the metro, with its long stairways, is completely inaccessible to wheelchairs. Some bus lines are equipped with ramps for wheelchair accessibility; check with the city's transportation authority, the RATP, to find out which lines have facilities.

USEFUL ADDRESSES

FNAC
Forum des Halles, 1 Rue Pierre-Lescot 75001. **Map** 13 A2. *Tel* 01 40 41 4000.

The Grand Rex theater *(see p354)*

FNAC
26 Ave des Ternes 75017.
Map 4 D3. *Tel* 01 44 09 18 00.

G7 Taxis
Tel 01 47 39 47 39.
Tel 01 41 27 66 99 *(in English).*

Office du Tourisme
25 Rue des Pyramides 75001.
Map 12 E1. *Tel* 08 92 68 30 00.
www.parisinfo.com

Taxis Bleus
Tel 01 49 36 10 10.

Virgin Megastore
52–60 Ave des Champs-Elysées 75008.
Map 4 F5. *Tel* 01 49 53 50 00.

Theater

From the grandeur of the Comédie Française to slap-stick farce and avant-garde drama, theater is flourishing in Paris and the suburbs – the training ground for the best young actors and directors. The city also has a long tradition of playing host to visiting companies, and it attracts many foreign productions, often in the original languages.

There are theaters scattered throughout the city and the theater season runs from September to July; national theaters close during August but many commercial ones stay open. For complete listings of what's on read *Pariscope*, *Zurban* or *L'Officiel des Spectacles (see p340)*.

NATIONAL THEATERS

Founded in 1680 by royal decree, the **Comédie Française** *(see p120)*, with its strict conventions regarding the style of acting and interpretation, is the bastion of French theater. Its aim is to keep classical drama in the public eye and also to perform works by the best modern playwrights.

The Comédie Française (inextricably linked in the national consciousness to Molière) is the oldest national theater in the world and one of the few institutions of *ancien-régime* France to have survived the Revolution. It settled into its current home after players occupied the Palais-Royal during the Revolution. The traditionally styled red velvet auditorium has a huge stage equipped with the latest technology.

The majority of the reper-toire is classical, dominated by Corneille, Racine and Molière, followed by second strings Marivaux, Alfred de Musset and Victor Hugo. The company also performs modern plays by French and foreign playwrights.

The **Odéon Théâtre de l'Europe**, also known as the Théâtre National de l'Odéon *(see p140)*, was at one time the second theater of the Comédie Française. It now specializes in performing plays from other countries in their original languages.

Next door the **Petit Odéon** features new plays and those in foreign languages.

The **Théâtre National de Chaillot** is a huge under-ground auditorium in the Art Deco Palais de Chaillot *(see p198)*. It stages lively productions of mainstream European classics and, occasionally, musical revues. The theater also contains a studio, the **Salle Gémier**, for more experimental work.

The **Théâtre National de la Colline** has two performance spaces and specializes in contemporary dramas.

FARTHER AFIELD

A thriving multi-theater complex in the Bois de Vincennes, the **Cartoucherie** houses five separate avant-garde theaters, including the internationally famous **Théâtre du Soleil**.

INDEPENDENT THEATERS

Among the most important of the serious independents are the **Comédie des Champs-Elysées**, the **Hébertot** and the **Atelier**, which aims to be experimental. Other notable venues include the **Théâtre Marigny**, for excellent modern French drama, the **Montparnasse** and the **Théâtre Antoine** which pioneered the use of realism on stage. The **Madeleine** maintains consistently high standards and the **Huchette** specializes in Ionesco plays. The avant-garde producer/ director Peter Brook has a loyal following at the **Bouffes-du-Nord**.

For over a hundred years the **Palais Royal** has been the temple of risqué farce. With fewer French Feydeau-style farce writers these days, translations of English and American sex comedies are filling the gap. Other notable venues include the **Bouffes-Parisiens**, **La Bruyère**, the **Michel** and the **St-Georges**. The **Théâtre Marie Bell** presents popular one-man comedy shows.

CAFE-THEATERS AND CHANSONNIERS

There is a long tradition of entertainment in cafés, but the café-theaters of today have nothing in common with the "café-concerts" of the turn-of-the-19th century. These modern entertainments have originated because young actors and new playwrights could not find work, while drama students were unable to pay to rent established theaters. Don't be surprised if there is an element of audience participation, or alternatively, in small venues, if the actors can sometimes seem a little too close for comfort. This form of theatre is now so popular in Paris that one can often see posters advertising classes for café-theater or notices inviting people to join small troupes. Café-theaters rose to prominence during the 1960s and 70s, when unknowns such as Coluche, Gérard Depardieu and Miou-Miou made their debut at the **Café de la Gare** before going on to success on the screen, so who knows who you might see at your local café.

Good venues for seeing new talent include the **Théâtre d'Edgar** and **Au Bec Fin**, while **Chez Michou** is an old-fashioned spot which is very popular and tends to specialize in broad caricature. Traditional *chansonniers* – cabarets where ballads, folk songs and humor abound – include **Au Lapin Agile** *(see p223)*, in the heart of Mont-martre. Political satire is on offer at the **Caveau de la République** and the **Deux Anes**, also in Montmartre. Another form of café entertainment that often veers toward the theatrical is café-philosophique. These are philosophical discussions or debates, held on topics such as justice, war or love, in which skilled orators take to the floor to declaim their positions. Audience participation is encouraged. Such evenings are held in many locations, but the best known are held at **Le 7 Lézards**. The debates take place in French, but English language events also exist: the monthly play-reading at the **Café de Flore** is a fine example of the genre.

CHILDREN'S THEATER

Some Paris theaters, such as the **Gymnase-Marie Bell**, the **Porte St-Martin** and the **Café d'Edgar**, have children's matinees on Wednesdays and weekends. In the city parks there are several tiny puppet theaters (marionnettes), which are sure to delight children and adults alike. *(See Independent Theaters p344.)* The **Lido** also has a new show for children.

OPEN-AIR THEATER

During the summer, weather permitting, open-air performances of Shakespeare in French and classic French plays are held in the Shakespeare Garden in the Bois de Boulogne. There are also occasional performances in the Tuileries and in Montmartre as part of Paris's summer festival. Check listings magazines for these events.

ENGLISH-LANGUAGE THEATER IN PARIS

The On Stage Theater Company and The Dear Conjunction Theater are both Paris-based companies who perform in English (details in listings magazines). There are also several English language poetry societies which host poetry and play readings; the best is the Live Poets Society. **Kilometre Zero** is an interesting English language arts collective that performs plays, publishes a magazine and hosts open-mike recital evenings. The **Hôtel du Nord** puts on excellent stand-up comedy acts in English each week. An historic venue, it is much-loved by expatriates and plays host to some of the finest comic talent on the circuit at the moment.

STREET THEATER

Street theater thrives during the summer. Jugglers, mime artists, fire-eaters and musicians can be seen mainly in tourist areas such as the Pompidou Centre *(see pp110–11)*, St-Germain-des-Prés and Les Halles.

CABARET

The music hall revue is the entertainment form most associated with turn-of-the-19th-century Paris. It evokes images of bohemian artists and champagne-induced debauchery. Today, most of the girls are likely to be American and the audience is made up mainly of foreign businessmen and tour groups.

When it comes to picking a cabaret the rule of thumb is simple: the better-known places are the best. Lesser-known shows resemble nothing so much as Grade-B strip shows. All the cabarets listed here guarantee topless women sporting outrageous feather- and sequin-encrusted headpieces, an assortment of vaudeville acts and, depending on your point of view, a spectacularly entertaining evening or an exercise in high kitsch.

The **Lido** is the most Las Vegas-like of the cabarets and stars the legendary Bluebell Girls. The **Folies-Bergères** is renowned for lively entertainment. It is the oldest music hall in Paris and probably the most famous in the world.

The **Crazy Horse** features some of the more risqué costumes and performances, and dancers with names such as Betty Buttocks, Fila Volcana and Nouka Bazooka. It has been transformed from its Wild West barroom into a jewel-box theater with a champagne bucket fastened to each seat. Here, the lowly striptease of burlesque shows has been refined into a vehicle for comedy sketches and international beauties.

Paradis Latin is the most "French" of all the city's cabaret shows. It has variety acts with remarkable special effects and scenery in a beautiful, old Left Bank theater, partially designed by Gustave Eiffel.

The **Don Camillo Rive Gauche** has more elegant, less touristy shows, with excellent *chanson* singers, comedians and all kinds of other variety acts. The **Moulin Rouge** *(see p226)*, once the haunt of Toulouse-Lautrec, is the birthplace of the cancan. Today, the Moulin Rouge is less extravagant than the screen version portrayed in the famous movie, but cabaret fans can still be certain of an evening of glamour, glitz and good times. Outrageously camp, transvestite parodies of these showgirl reviews can be seen at **Chez Madame Arthur**.

BUYING TICKETS

Tickets can be bought at the box office, by telephone or through theater agencies. Box offices are open daily from about 11am–7pm; some accept credit card purchases by telephone or in person.

TICKET PRICES

Ticket prices range from 7€–30€ for the national theaters and 8€–38€ for the independent. Reduced-price tickets and student stand-bys are available in some theaters 15 minutes before curtain-up. For cabaret, expect to pay from 23€–60€; 68€–105€ including dinner.

The **Kiosque Théâtre** offers half-price tickets on the day-of-performance: credit cards are not accepted and a small commission is charged for each ticket sold. There is a ticket booth in the Place de la Madeleine and one in front of Gare Montparnasse.

DRESS

These days, evening clothes are only worn to gala events at the Opéra National de Paris Garnier, the Comédie Française or the premiere of an upmarket play.

DIRECTORY

NATIONAL THEATERS

Comédie Française
Salle Richelieu, 1 Pl Colette 75001.
Map 12 E1.
Tel 08 25 10 16 80.
www.comedie-francaise.fr

Odéon Théâtre de l'Europe
8 Blvd Berthier 75017.
Map 12 F5.
Tel 01 44 85 40 40.
www.theatre-odeon.fr

Théâtre National de Chaillot
Pl du Trocadéro 75016.
Map 9 C2.
Tel 01 53 65 31 00.

Théâtre National de la Colline
15 Rue Malte-Brun 75020.
Tel 01 44 62 52 52.

FURTHER AFIELD

Cartoucherie
Route du Champ-de-Manoeuvre 75012.

Théâtre de l'Aquarium
Tel 01 43 74 99 61.

Théâtre de l'Epée de Bois
Tel 01 48 08 39 74.

Théâtre de la Tempête
Tel 01 43 28 36 36.

Théâtre du Chaudron
Tel 01 43 28 97 04.

Théâtre du Soleil
Tel 01 43 74 24 08.

INDEPENDENT THEATERS

Atelier
Pl Charles Dullin 75018.
Map 6 F2.
Tel 01 46 06 49 24.

Bouffes-du-Nord
37 bis Blvd de la Chapelle 75010.
Map 7 C1.
Tel 01 46 07 34 50.

Bouffes-Parisiens
4 Rue Monsigny 75002.
Map 6 E5.
Tel 01 42 96 92 42.

La Bruy`ere
5 Rue La Bruy`ere 75009.
Map 6 E3.
Tel 01 48 74 76 99.

Cinq Diamants
10 Rue des Cinq Diamants 75013.
Map 17 B5.
Tel 01 45 80 51 31.

Comédie des Champs-Elysées
15 Ave Montaigne 75008.
Map 10 F1.
Tel 01 53 23 99 10.

Hébertot
78 bis Blvd des Batignolles 75017.
Map 5 B2.
Tel 01 43 87 23 23.

Huchette
23 Rue de la Huchette 75005.
Map 13 A4.
Tel 01 43 26 38 99.

Madeleine
19 Rue de Surène 75008.
Map 5 C5.
Tel 01 42 65 07 09.

Maison du Metallos
94 Rue Jean-Pierre Timbaud 75011.
Map 14 F1.
Tel 01 47 00 68 45.

Marigny
7 Ave de Marigny 75008.
Map 5 A5.
Tel 01 53 96 70 30.

Michel
38 Rue des Mathurins 75008.
Map 5 C4.
Tel 01 42 65 35 02.

Montparnasse
31 Rue de la Gaîté 75014. **Map** 15 C2.
Tel 01 43 22 77 30.

Palais Royal
38 Rue Montpensier 75001.
Map 12 E1.
Tel 01 42 97 59 81.

Porte St-Martin
16 Blvd St-Martin 75010.
Map 7 C5.
Tel 01 42 08 00 32.

Scene du « 8 »
8 Rue Hippolyte Lebas 75009.
Map 6 F3.
Tel 01 42 82 13 70.

St-Georges
51 Rue St-Georges 75009.
Map 6 E3.
Tel 01 48 78 63 47.

Théâtre Antoine
14 Blvd de Strasbourg 75010.
Map 7 B5.
Tel 01 42 08 77 71 & 01 42 08 76 58.

Théâtre Marie Bell
38 Blvd Bonne-Nouvelle 75010.
Map 7 A5.
Tel 01 42 46 79 79.

Théâtre Sudden
14 bis Rue Sainte-Isaure 75018.
Map 2 F4.
Tel 01 42 62 35 00.

CAFE-THEATERS AND CHANSONNIERS

Au Bec Fin
6 bis Rue Thérèse 75001.
Map 12 E1.
Tel 01 42 96 29 35.

Au Lapin Agile
22 Rue des Saules 75018.
Map 2 F5.
Tel 01 46 06 85 87.

Café de Flore
See 139.

Café de la Gare
41 Rue du Temple 75004.
Map 13 B2.
Tel 01 42 78 52 51.

Caveau de la République
23 Place République 75003.
Map 8 D5.
Tel 01 42 78 44 45.

Chez Michou
80 Rue des Martyrs 75018.
Map 6 F3.
Tel 01 46 06 16 04.

Deux Anes
100 Blvd de Clichy 75018.
Map 6 D1.
Tel 01 46 06 10 26.

Hôtel du Nord
102 Quai de Jemmapes 75010.
Map 8 D3.
Tel 01 40 40 78 78.

Le Point Virgule
7 Rue St-Croix-de-la-Bretonnerie. 75004.
Map 13 C3.

Le 7 Lézards
10 Rue des Rosiers 75004.
Map 13 C3.
Tel 01 48 87 08 97.

Théâtre d'Edgar
58 Blvd Edgar-Quinet 75014.
Map 16 D2.
Tel 01 42 79 97 97.

CABARET

Chez Madame Arthur
75 bis Rue des Martyrs 75018.
Map 6 F2.
Tel 01 42 54 40 21.

Crazy Horse
12 Ave George V 75008.
Map 10 E1.
Tel 01 47 23 32 32.

Don Camillo Rive Gauche
10 Rue des Sts-Pères 75007. **Map** 12 E3.
Tel 01 42 60 82 84.

Folies-Bergères
32 Rue Richer 75009.
Map 7 A4.
Tel 01 44 79 98 98.

Lido
116 bis Ave des Champs-Elysées 75008.
Map 4 E4.
Tel 01 40 76 56 10

Moulin Rouge
82 Blvd de Clichy 75018.
Map 6 E1.
Tel 01 53 09 82 82.
www.moulinrouge.fr

Classical Music

The music scene in Paris has never been so busy and exciting. Government spending has ensured that there are many first-class venues with an excellent range of opera, and classical and contemporary music productions. There are also numerous concerts in churches and many music festivals.

Information about what's on is listed in *Pariscope*, *Zurban* and *L'Officiel des Spectacles*. A free monthly listing of musical events is given out at most concert halls. Also, try the Office du Tourisme in the Rue des Pyramides *(see pp340–41)* for details of many free and open-air classical music performances.

OPERA

Opera lovers will find themselves well catered for, with many productions mounted at the Bastille and the beautifully renovated **Opéra National de Paris Garnier**. Opera is also an important part of the programming at the Théâtre du Châtelet, as well as being produced intermittently by a variety of small organizations, and there are occasional large-scale lavish productions at the **Palais Omnisports de Bercy** or POB *(see p359)*.

The Opéra de Paris's ultra-modern home is the **Opéra National de Paris Bastille** *(see p98)*, where performances have finally begun to make full use of the house's mind-boggling array of high-tech stage mechanisms. There are 2,700 seats, all with a good view of the stage, and the accoustics are excellent.

Productions feature classic and modern operas, and its interpretations are often avant-garde: Philippe Mamoury's *K...*; Bob Wilson's production of *The Magic Flute*, done in the style of Japanese Noh, with some of the cast delivering their lines while balancing on one leg; Messiaen's *St Francis of Assisi*, with video screens and neon added to bring the story up to date.

There are also occasional dance performances, when the Bastille plays host to the ballet company from the Opéra National de Paris Garnier *(see p215)*. The house includes two smaller spaces, the **Auditorium** (500 seats) and the **Studio** (200 seats) for smaller-scale events

connected to the current productions on the main stages here and at the Opera Garnier.

The **Opéra Comique** (also known as the Salle Favart), now run by Jérôme Savary, no longer has opera, but stages a wide range of eccentric, light-weight productions, including some popular music-hall-style work and operetta. Savary is also behind several large-scale musicals at the Palais des Congrès exhibtion space and some municipal events (such as a public ball held to celebrate the 50th anniversary of the liberation of Paris).

CONCERTS

Paris is the home of three major symphony orchestras, and a good half-dozen other orchestras; it is also a major venue for touring European and American orchestras. Chamber music is also flourishing, either as part of the programming of the major venues, or in smaller halls and churches.

The **Salle Pleyel** is Paris's principal concert hall, with 2,300 seats, and was, until recently, the home of the Orchestre de Paris (now at the Théâtre Mogador). Its season runs from October to June, with an average of two concerts a week. The Salle Pleyel is also the main base for the Ensemble Orchestral de Paris and such reputable orchestral associations as the Lamoureux, the Pasdeloup and the Colonne, which organize concert seasons from October to Easter. The building also includes two smaller halls for chamber

music – the Salle Chopin (470 seats) and the Salle Debussy (120 seats).

Over the last few years the **Théâtre du Châtelet** has become one of the city's principal venues for all kinds of concerts, opera and dance. The high-quality program includes opera classics from Mozart's *Così fan tutte* to Verdi's *La Traviata*, and more modern works, such as Boessman's *Contes d'Hiver*, and occasional concerts by international opera stars. Great attention is also devoted to 20th-century music here, and throughout the season there are lunchtime concerts and recitals in the foyer.

The beautiful Art Deco **Théâtre des Champs-Elysées** is a celebrated classical music venue which also produces some opera and dance. Radio-France is part-owner of the theater, and its Orchestre National de France gives concerts here, as do many touring orchestras and soloists. The Orchestre des Champs-Elysées, directed by Philippe Herreweghe, is in residence here, and gives period-instrument performances. Other concerts range from Baroque to 20th-century music, and the Concerts du Dimanche Matin organization stages excellent concerts, mostly chamber music, on Sundays at 11am.

Radio-France is the biggest single concert organizer in Paris, with a musical force that includes two major symphony orchestras: the Orchestre National de France and the Orchestre Philharmonique. Many of its concerts are given in Paris's other concert halls, but the **Maison de Radio-France** has a large hall and several smaller studios that are used for concerts and broadcasts open to the public *(see p200, Musée de Radio France)*.

The **Salle Gaveau** is a medium-sized concert hall with a busy schedule of chamber music and recitals. Since its recent renovation, the Salle Gaveau has had the capacity to hold ambitious orchestral concerts.

The **Auditorium du Louvre** was built as part of the ongoing expansion of the Louvre *(see pp122–9)* and it is used mostly for chamber music recitals. The Musée d'Orsay's *(see pp144–7)* **Auditorium du Musée d'Orsay** is a medium-sized auditorium, with an active concert program. Lunchtime concerts are free with museum tickets, while evening concerts have varying prices.

Other museums often hold concerts as part of an exhibition theme – such as troubadours at the Musée National du Moyen Age *(see p154–7)* – so check the listings magazines.

The Musique à la Sorbonne holds a concert series in the **Grand Amphithéâtre de la Sorbonne** and the **Amphithéâtre Richelieu de la Sorbonne**. Productions have included the Slavonic Music festival, featuring the works of East European composers.

Occasionally concerts are given in the **Conservatoire d'Art Dramatique**, where Beethoven was introduced to Paris audiences in 1828 and where Hector Berlioz's major work, *La Symphonie Fantastique*, was first performed. Otherwise, it's not usually open to public.

CONTEMPORARY MUSIC

Contemporary music in Paris has a high profile and is definitely alive and kicking. Although no longer at the head of any orchestra, Pierre Boulez is still a major figure in the capital's contemporary music scene. Jonathan Nott now directs the experimental Ensemble InterContemporain, which is lavishly supported by the French state in its home at the Cité de la Musique *(see pp234–5)*. **IRCAM**, the vast laboratory of "digital signal processing" underneath the Pompidou Centre, is still the envy of the world, architecturally at least. Musically, it is beginning to live up to its promise.

Other bright stars among the many talented composers include Pascal Dusapin, Philippe Fénelon, George

Benjamin and Philippe Manoury, as well as Georges Aperghis, who specializes in musical theater.

The fabulously designed **Cité de la Musique** complex at Parc de la Villette includes both a spectacularly domed *salle de concerts* surrounded by a glass-roofed arcade, and the **Conservatoire National de Musique** with its opera theater and two small concert halls. The Chamber Orchestra of Europe is in residence here. Both venues are used for regular performances, including jazz, ethnic and contemporary music, as well as *chansons* and early music.

For details either phone the venue concerned or consult the listings magazines. For those interested in contemporary music, the quarterly magazine *Résonance* is published by IRCAM at the Pompidou Centre.

FESTIVALS

Some of the most important music festivals are the result of the work of the **Festival d'Automne à Paris**, which acts as a behind-the-scenes stimulator, commissioning new works, subsidizing others and in general enlivening the Parisian musical, dance and theatrical scene from September to December.

The **Festival St-Denis**, running throughout June and July, holds concerts with an emphasis on choral works. Most performances are given in the Basilique St-Denis.

The **Musique Baroque au Château de Versailles**, from around the middle of September to the middle of October, is an offshoot of the Baroque Music Center, founded in Versailles in 1988. Operas, concerts, recitals, chamber music, dance and theater are on offer in the fabulous surroundings of Versailles *(see pp248–53)*.

Other interesting festivals include the Chopin festival, held in the Orangerie in the Bois de Boulogne from mid-June to mid-July, and the Quartier d'Eté festival, which host a series of outdoor classical music concerts.

For tickets, it is usually necessary to go to the theater box office or venue concerned, though some festivals may run an advance postal reservation service.

CHURCHES

Music is everywhere in Paris' churches, in the form of classical concerts, organ recitals or religious services. The most outstanding churches which hold regular concerts include **La Madeleine** *(see p214)*, **St-Germain-des-Prés** *(see p138)*, **St-Julien-le-Pauvre** *(see p152)* and **St-Roch** *(see p121)*. Music is also performed in the **Eglise des Billettes**, **St-Sulpice** *(see p172)*, **St-Gervais–St-Protais** *(see p99)*, **Notre-Dame** *(see pp82–5)*, **St-Louis-en-l'Ile** *(see p87)* and **Sainte-Chapelle** *(see pp88–9)*.

A great proportion, but not all, of these concerts are free. If you have any difficulty contacting the church in question, try the Office du Tourisme for information *(see pp340–41)*.

EARLY MUSIC

A number of early-music ensembles have taken up residence in Paris. The Chapelle Royale gives a concert series at the **Théâtre des Champs-Elysées** with programs ranging from Renaissance vocal music to Mozart. Their enchanting sacred music concerts (look out for Bach cantatas) take place in the **Notre-Dame-des-Blancs-Manteaux** *(see p102)*.

Baroque opera is more the domain of Les Arts Florissants, founded and directed by American-born William Christie, who perform French and Italian operas from Rossi to Rameau, and Les Musiciens du Louvre, directed by Marc Minkowski. Both companies perform regularly at the Théâtre du Châtelet and the Opera National Garnier. The **Théâtre de la Ville** and the charming Rococo 1900s **Théâtre du Grévin** *(see p216)*, are both excellent venues in which to hear Baroque chamber music.

BUYING TICKETS

For tickets, it's always best to deal directly with the relevant box office. Reserving tickets at the main venues is possible by mail up to two months before the performance and by telephone two weeks to a month in advance. If you want a good seat, it's best to order in advance as tickets tend to sell quickly. Last-minute tickets may also be available at the box office, and certain venues, such as the Opéra National de Paris Bastille, keep some tickets for the cheaper seats aside for the purpose. Ticket agents, notably in the **FNAC** stores *(see p341)*, and a good hotel concierge can also help. These agencies accept credit card orders – a useful service as not all venues are guaranteed to accept them.

Half-price tickets on the day of performance can be bought at the **Kiosque Théâtre** *(see p341)* which is found in the Place de la Madeleine and also at the RER station at Parvis de la Gare Montparnasse. However, these agencies usually only deal for performances taking place at private theaters.

Note, however, that many theaters and concert halls may be closed during the holiday season in August, so inquire first to avoid disappointment.

TICKET PRICES

Ticket prices can range from 8€–85€ for the Opéra de Paris Bastille and the principal classical music venues, and from 5€–25€ for the smaller halls and concerts in churches around the city, such as Sainte-Chapelle.

DIRECTORY

CLASSICAL MUSIC VENUES

Amphithéâtre Richelieu de la Sorbonne
17 Rue de la Sorbonne 75005.
Map 12 F5.
Tel 01 42 62 71 71.

Auditorium
See Opéra National de Paris Bastille.

Auditorium du Louvre
Musée du Louvre, Rue de Rivoli 75001.
Map 12 E2.
Tel 01 40 20 84 00.

Auditorium du Musée d'Orsay
102 Rue de Lille 75007.
Map 12 D2.
Tel 01 40 49 49 66.

Cité de la Musique
Parc de La Villette, 221 Ave Jean-Jaurès 75019.
Tel 01 44 84 44 84.
www.cite-musique.fr

Conservatoire d'Art Dramatique
2 bis Rue du Conservatoire 75009. **Map** 7 A4.
Tel 01 42 46 12 91.

Eglise des Billettes
24 Rue des Archives 75004. **Map** 13 C2.
Tel 01 42 72 37 08.

Festival d'Automne
156 Rue de Rivoli 75001.
Map 12 F2 5
Tel 01 53 45 17 00.

Festival Chopin
Orangerie de Bagatelle Bois de Boulogne 75016.
Map 3 A4.
Tel 01 45 00 22 19.

Grand Amphi-théâtre de la Sorbonne
45 Rue des Ecoles 75005.
Map 13 A5.
Tel 01 42 62 71 71.

IRCAM
1 Pl Igor Stravinsky 75004.
Map 13 B2.
Tel 01 44 78 48 43.

La Madeleine
Pl de la Madeleine 75008.
Map 5 C5.
Tel 01 42 50 96 18.

Maison de Radio-France
116 Ave du Président-Kennedy 75016.
Map 9 B4.
Tel 01 42 20 42 20.

Musique Baroque au Château de Versailles
Château de Versailles, Chapelle Royal 78000. Versailles.
Tel 01 30 83 78 00.

Notre-Dame
Pl du Parvis-Notre-Dame.
Map 13 A4.
Tel 01 42 34 56 10.

Notre-Dame-des-Blancs-Manteaux
1 Rue Abbé Migne 75004.
Map 13 A4.
Tel 01 42 72 09 37.

Opéra Comique
(Salle Favart) 5 Rue Favart 75002. **Map** 6 F5.
Tel 08 25 00 00 58.

Opéra National de Paris Bastille
120 Rue de Lyon 75012.
Map 14 E4.
Tel 08 92 89 90 90.
www.operadeparis.fr

Opéra National de Paris Garnier
Place de l'Opéra 75009.
Map 6 E4.
Tel 08 92 89 90 90.

Pompidou Centre
19 Rue Beaubourg 75004.
Map 13 B2.
Tel 01 44 78 12 33.

Quartier d'Eté Festival
Various venues.
Tel 01 44 94 98 00.

Sainte-Chapelle
4 Blvd du Palais.
Map 13 A3.
Tel 01 53 73 78 50.

St-Germain-des-Prés
Pl St-Germain-des Prés 75006. **Map** 12 E4.
Tel 01 55 42 81 33.

St-Gervais–St-Protais
Pl St-Gervais 75004.
Map 13 B3.
Tel 01 48 87 32 02.

St-Julien-le-Pauvre
1 Rue St-Julien-le-Pauvre 75005. **Map** 13 A4.
Tel 01 42 26 00 00.

St-Louis-en-l'Ile
19 bis Rue St-Louis-en-l'Ile 75004. **Map** 13 C5.
Tel 01 46 34 11 60.

St-Roch
296 Rue St-Honoré 75001.
Map 12 D1.
Tel 01 42 44 13 20.

St-Sulpice
Pl St-Sulpice 75006.
Map 12 E4.
Tel 01 46 33 21 78.

Salle Gaveau
45 Rue La Boétie 75008.
Map 5 B4.
Tel 01 49 53 05 07.

Salle Pleyel
252 Rue du Faubourg St-Honoré 75008.
Map 4 E3.
Tel 01 45 61 53 00.

Studio
See Opéra National de Paris Bastille.

Théâtre de la Ville
2 Pl du Châtelet 75004.
Map 13 A3.
Tel 01 42 74 22 77.

Théâtre des Champs-Élysées
15 Ave Montaigne 75008.
Map 10 F1.
Tel 01 49 52 50 50.

Théâtre du Châtelet
1 Pl du Châtelet 75001.
Map 13 A3.
Tel 01 40 28 28 40.

Théâtre du Grévin
10 Blvd Montmartre 75009. **Map** 6 F4.
Tel 01 47 70 85 05.

Dance

When it comes to dance, Paris is more a cultural crossroads than a cultural center. Due to a deliberate government policy of decentralization, many of the top French dance companies are based in the provinces, although they frequently visit the capital. In addition, the greatest dance companies from all over the world perform here. Paris has a well-deserved reputation as a center of excellence for modern and experimental dance, and has numerous workshops and places in which to learn its many forms.

CLASSICAL BALLET

The opulent **Opéra National de Paris Garnier** *(see p215)* is the home of the Ballet de l'Opéra de Paris, which is earning a reputation as one of the world's best classical dance companies.

Since the Opéra National de Paris Bastille opened in 1989, the Opéra National de Paris Garnier has been used almost exclusively for dance. It is one of the largest theaters in Europe, with performance space for 450 artists and a seating capacity of 2,200.

Modern dance companies such as the Martha Graham Company, Paul Taylor, Merce Cunningham, Alvin Ailey, Jerome Robbins and Roland Petit's Ballet de Marseille also regularly perform here.

The Opéra National de Paris Garnier, extensively restored both inside and out, now shares operatic productions with the **Opéra National de Paris Bastille**.

MODERN DANCE

Government support has helped the **Théâtre de la Ville** (once run by Sarah Bernhardt) to become Paris's most important venue for modern dance, with subsidies keeping ticket costs relatively low. Through performances at the Théâtre de la Ville, modern choreographers such as Jean-Claude Gallotta, Regine Chopinot, Maguy Marin and Anne Teresa de Keersmaeker have gained international recognition. Here you may also see troupes such as Pina Bausch's Wuppertal Dance Theater, whose tormented, existential choreography may not be to everyone's taste, but is always popular with Parisian audiences.

Music performances also run throughout the season and include chamber music, recitals, world music and jazz.

The **Maison des Arts de Créteil** presents some of the most interesting dance works in Paris. It is located in the Paris suburb of Créteil, where local government gives strong support to dance. Créteil's company choreographer, Maguy Marin, has won consistent praise for her darkly expressive work.

The Maison des Arts also brings in such innovative companies as the Sydney Ballet, and the Kirov from St Petersburg, which is more inclined toward the classical.

Set amid the opulent *couture* shops and embassies, the elegant Art Deco **Théâtre des Champs-Élysées** has 1,900 seats. It is frequented by an upmarket audience who watch major international companies perform here. It was here that Nijinsky first danced Stravinsky's iconoclastic *The Rite of Spring*, which led to rioting among the audience.

The theater is more famous as a classical music venue, but recent visitors have included the Harlem Dance Company and London's Royal Ballet, and it is here that Mikhail Baryshnikov and American choreographer Mark Morris perform when they are in Paris. It also sponsors the popular *Géants de la Danse* series, an evening-length sampling of international ballet.

The lovely old **Théâtre du Châtelet** is a renowned opera and classical music venue, but it is also host to international contemporary dance companies such as the Tokyo Ballet and the Birmingham Royal Ballet.

Experimental dance companies perform in the **Théâtre de la Bastille**, where innovative theater is also staged. Many directors and companies start here, then go on to international fame.

New companies to look out for include La P'tit Cie and L'Esquisse, but they have no fixed venue.

EVENTS LISTINGS

To find out what's on, read the inexpensive weekly entertainment guides *Pariscope* and *L'Officiel des Spectacles*. Posters advertising dance performances are widely displayed in the metros and on the streets, especially on the green advertisement columns, the *colonnes Morris*.

TICKET PRICES

Expect to pay 10€–100€ for tickets to the Opéra de Paris Garnier (5€–60€ for a ballet), 6€–75€ for the Théâtre des Champs-Élysées, and anything from 9€–27€ for other venues.

DANCE VENUES

Maison des Arts et de la Culture de Créteil
Pl Salvador Allende 94000 Créteil.
Tel 01 45 13 19 19.

Opéra National de Paris Garnier
See p214-5.

Opéra National de Paris Bastille See p98.

Théâtre de la Bastille
76 Rue de la Roquette 75011.
Map 14 F3.
Tel 01 43 57 42 14.

Théâtre de la Ville
See p334.

Théâtre des Champs-Elysées
See p334.

Théâtre du Châtelet
See p334.

Rock, Jazz and World Music

Music lovers will find every imaginable form of music in Paris and its enviorns, from international pop stars in major venues to buskers of varying degrees of talent in the metro. There's a huge variety of styles on offer, with reggae, hip-hop, world music, blues, folk, rock and jazz – Paris is said to be second only to New York in the number of jazz clubs and jazz recordings, and there is always an excellent selection of bands and solo performers.

On the summer solstice (June 21) each year, the Fête de la Musique takes place, when anyone can play any form of music, anywhere, without a license, and when the whole city parties all night. Ears may be assailed by a heavy metal rock band or lulled by an accordionist playing traditional French songs.

For complete listings of what's happening, buy *Zurban* or *Pariscope* (published every Wednesday) at any kiosk. For jazz fans there's the monthly *Jazz* magazine for schedules and in-depth reviews.

MAJOR VENUES

The top international acts are often at the enormous arenas: **Palais Omnisports** at Bercy, **Stade de France** at St-Denis or the **Zénith**. Other venues such as the legendary *chanson* center of the universe, the **Olympia**, or the **Grand Rex** (also a movie theater), have assigned seating and a more intimate atmosphere. They host everyone from bewigged and cosmetically enhanced iconic first ladies of country to acid jazz stars. *(See Directories p350 & p359).*

ROCK AND POP

Until recently, Paris's indigenous rock groups (Les Négresses Vertes are probably the best-known, and are still going strong) drew foreign attention precisely because they were French. For too long, Paris pop meant Johnny Hallyday and insipid covers of US and UK hits, or Serge Gainsbourg and his brand of faintly naughty decadence. Paris rock traditionally (and deservedly) attracted either patronizing praise or outright mockery.

That is no longer the case. The international success of the groups Daft Punk and Air and the contribution to the music scene of producer, songwriter and musician Bertrand Burgalat have led to a growth in confidence in the local music scene. The phrase French Touch often describes hip producers, writers or singers, now in demand all over the world. Banlieue- (suburb-) based rap, rai and reggae no longer sound like versions of imported forms, instead they now have their own identity.

There is no shortage of gigs. The latest bands usually play at **La Cigale** and its downstairs den of din, **La Boule Noire**, the **Divan du Monde** and the **Elysée-Montmartre**, while the **Bataclan** and the **Rex** club are the best places for R&B. The **Olympia** is the city's most famous rock venue, attracting top acts. Many nightclubs also double up as live music venues *(see pp351–3).*

JAZZ

Paris is still jazz-crazy. Many American musicians have made the French capital their home because of its receptive atmosphere. All styles, from free-form to Dixieland and swing, and even hip-hop-jazz crossover, are on offer. Clubs range from quasi-concert halls to piano bars and publike venues. One of the most popular places, though not the most comfortable, is the **New Morning**. It's hot and smoky, and the table service can be a little erratic, but all the great jazz musicians continue to perform here, as they have in the past. Arrive early to ensure a good seat. **Le Duc des Lombards** is a lively jazz club in Les Halles, which also features salsa.

Many jazz clubs are also cafés, bars or restaurants. The latter includes the intimate **Bilboquet**, with its Belle Epoque interior. This stylish place is favored by movie stars. Dining might not be a requirement, but it's always wise to check first.

Other hotspots are **Le Petit Journal Montparnasse** for modern jazz, **Le Petit Journal St-Michel** for Dixieland and the **Sunset**. A trendy crowd is drawn to the **7 Lézards**, in the Marais. **Caveau de la Huchette** looks like the archetypal jazz joint, but today it favors swing and big-band music, and is popular with students. The **Caveau des Oubliettes** has a growing reputation for cutting-edge jazz.

For a change, try the local talent at small, friendly bars such as the less expensive **Bistrot d'Eustache**, or the trendy **China Club**, with its 1940s *film noir* decor. The **Jazz-Club Lionel Hampton** in the Méridien hotel is a well-respected venue which features Sunday jazz brunch. On the other side of town, the renovated **Trabendo** has an intriguing mix of up-and-comers and down-and-outers.

The **Slow Club**, with its neon sign, has swinging jazz and a dance-happy crowd. Paris does not neglect blues fans either. The **Quai du Blues** is the best-known haunt, hosting concerts by established performers.

Paris has two international jazz festivals in summer: the Paris Jazz Festival *(see p63)* which is the mainstay of the summer calendar, and the JVC Halle That Jazz at the **Grande Halle de la Villette** in July, with movies on jazz, debates and discussions and *boeufs* (jam sessions).

WORLD MUSIC

With its large populations from West Africa and the countries of the Maghreb, the Antilles and Latin America, Paris is a natural center for world music. The **Chapelle des Lombards** has played host to top acts; it also has jazz, salsa and Brazilian music. **Aux Trois Maillets** is a medieval cellar with everything from blues to tango and rock and roll covers, while **Kibélé** is a great place for North African sounds. Many jazz clubs intersperse their programs with ethnic music. These include **New Morning**, which also has shows with South American artists, and **Baiser Salé**, for popular acts including Makossa, Kassav, Malavoi and Manu Dibango.

World music in a stunning setting can be found at the Institut du Monde Arabe, a wonderful architectural feat *(see p164)* which draws stars from the Arab music world to its concert hall.

TICKET PRICES

Prices at jazz clubs can be steep, and there may be a cover charge of over 15€ at the door, which usually includes the first drink. If there is no cover charge, the drinks will be expensive and at least one must be bought.

Tickets can be bought from FNAC outlets and Virgin Megastore *(see p341)*, or directly from venue box offices and at the door of the clubs themselves.

DIRECTORY

MAJOR VENUES

Grand Rex
1 Blvd Poissonnière 75002.
Map 7 A5.
Tel 01 45 08 93 89.

Olympia
28 Blvd des
Capucines 75009.
Map 6 D5.
Tel 08 92 68 33 68.
www.olympiahall.com

**Palais Omnisports
de Paris-Bercy**
8 Blvd de Bercy
75012.
Map 18 F2.
Tel 08 92 69 23 00.

Zénith
211 Ave de Jean-
Jaurès 75019.
Tel 01 42 08 60 00.

ROCK AND POP

Bataclan
50 Blvd Voltaire
75011.
Map 14 E1.
Tel 01 43 14 35 35.

**La Cigale/
La Boule Noire**
120 Blvd Rochechouart
75018.
Map 6 F2.
Tel 01 49 25 81 73.

Divan du Monde
75 Rue des Martyrs 75018.
Map 6 F2.
Tel 01 42 52 02 46.

Elysée-Montmartre
72 Blvd Rochechouart
75018.
Map 6 F2.
Tel 01 42 23 46 50.

Rex Club
5 Blvd Poissonnière 75002.
Map 7 A5.
Tel 01 42 36 83 98.

JAZZ

Baiser Salé
58 Rue des Lombards
75001.
Map 13 A2.
Tel 01 42 33 37 71.

Bilboquet
13 Rue St-Benoît 75006.
Map 12 E3.
Tel 01 45 48 81 84.

Bistrot d'Eustache
37 Rue Berger, Carré des
Halles 75001.
Map 13 A2.
Tel 01 40 26 23 20.

**Caveau de la
Huchette**
5 Rue de la Huchette
75005.
Map 13 A4.
Tel 01 43 26 65 05.

**Caveau des
Oubliettes**
52 Rue Galande 75005.
Map 13 A4.
Tel 01 46 34 23 09.

China Club
50 Rue de Charenton
75012. Map 14 F5.
Tel 01 43 43 82 02.

**Le Duc des
Lombards**
42 Rue des Lombards
75001.
Map 13 A2.
Tel 01 42 33 22 88.

**La Grande Halle
de la Villette**
211 Ave Jean-Jaurès
75019.
Map 8 F1
Tel 01 40 03 75 75.

**Jazz-Club Lionel
Hampton**
Hôtel Méridien, 81 Blvd
Gouvion-St-Cyr 75017.
Map 3 C3.
www.jazzclub-paris.com

New Morning
7–9 Rue des
Petites-Écuries 75010.
Map 7 B4.
Tel 01 45 23 51 41.

Paris Jazz Festival
Parc Floral Bois de
Vincennes 75012.
Tel 01 55 94 29 29.

**Le Petit Journal
Montparnasse**
13 Rue du Commandant-
Mouchotte 75014.
Map 15 C2.
Tel 01 43 21 56 70.

**Le Petit Journal
St-Michel**
71 Blvd St-Michel 75005.
Map 16 F1.
Tel 01 43 26 28 59.

7 Lézards
10 Rue des Rosiers
75004.
Map 13 C3.
Tel 01 48 87 08 97.

Slow Club
130 Rue de Rivoli 75001.
Map 13 A2.
Tel 01 42 33 84 30.

Sunset
60 Rue des Lombards
75001.
Map 13 A2.
Tel 01 40 26 46 60.

Trabendo
211 Ave Jean-Jaurès
75019.
Map 8 F1.
Tel 01 42 01 12 12.

WORLD MUSIC

Aux Trois Maillets
56 Rue Galande
75005.
Map 13 A4.
Tel 01 43 54 42 94.

Baiser Salé
See Jazz.

**Chapelle des
Lombards**
19 Rue de Lappe
75011. Map 14 F4.
Tel 01 43 57 24 24.

**Institut du
Monde Arabe**
See p164.

Kibélé
12 Rue de l'Echiquier
75010.
Map 7 B5.
Tel 01 48 24 57 74.

New Morning
7 Rue des Petites-Ecuries
75010.
Map 7 B4
Tel 01 45 23 51 41

Quai du Blues
17 Blvd Vital-Bouhot
92200.
Neuilly sur Seine.
Tel 01 46 24 22 00.

Nightclubs

The club scene in Paris is now somewhat under siege as government legislation on noise levels slightly hampers establishments' *modus operandi*. The city council is waging war on noise pollution and while this suits those with neighbors who possess large stereos, it's bad news for people who like to dance till dawn. They carry on regardless, albeit with fewer decibels, and you will still find every type of sound (and a great deal of creativity) on the club scene. There are clubs to suit every taste and it's worth noting that bouncers often treat foreign would-be entrants preferentially, so be sure to stand proud, ditch the attempts at French and speak English when you get near the door. The magazine *Zurban* lists up-to-the-minute information, with opening times and brief descriptions of club nights. Alternatively, read the posters at the Bastille metro station or listen to Radio NOVA 101.5 FM, which gives details of the night's best raves. Flyers advertising what's on at which clubs can be found on café, bar and shop counters. Popular nighttime options for the more mature set include ballroom dancing and visits to suave piano bars. If you're wondering about what to wear, the dressy side of the dressy-casual approach is usually the safest bet. Attire for nightclubs varies, for upscale venues be sure to put your designer-labeled best foot forward, while more relaxed ones will accept an urban look, but generally, sweats, jeans and trainers are definite no-nos.

MAINSTREAM

A huge yet convivial venue, **Le Bataclan** is a showcase for current bands. After the show on Saturday nights, it becomes one of the best nightclubs in Paris, legendary for its mouth-watering choice of funk, soul and new jack swing.

Club 79 is a lively, "retro"-oriented disco; the inexpensive **La Scala** attracts a large, young crowd, and has recently played host to ultra-fashionable party producers la Johnson. Linked to the **Alcazar**, which is a fashionable Terence Conran bar and restaurant very popular with a pre-club crowd, **WAGG** just next door is a wonderful spot for some uninhibited dancing. WAGG is unpretentious although the door staff are discriminating, and the disco and soul played in the stone cellars make for a great night out.

Les Bains, one-time Turkish bath, is the glitzy nightspot for fashion and show business people; its upstairs restaurant, now serving Thai food, is a popular place for private dinner parties. This is the place to be, so reserve a table for dinner if you're concerned about gaining entry and getting a much-coveted seat. The dance floor is tiny and music is mainly house, with 1970s and 80s disco on Mondays, and R&B on Wednesdays. Gay night is *Café con Leche* on Sundays. Legendary promoters and Parisian nightowls David and Cathy Guetta left Les Bains a while ago and took some of their regulars with them, but the club is still a flashy place to be and there is always the possibility of spotting a movie star. Advertising executives and filmmakers frequent the **Rex Club**. Despite the essentially conservative nature of the clientele, the music on different nights ranges from glam rock and house to "exotique" – funk, reggae and world music. Sounds are mainly rock and roll at the smart and non-ageist **Zed Club**. The vast **La Locomotive** caters to mainstream tastes most nights, with rock, house, groove and dance music each occupying a different floor.

The **Bus Palladium** is another mainstream venue where you can let loose and dance to classic pop music. It is very popular with stylish Parisians and is renowned as a good place to mingle. Utterly unpretentious, **Club Med World** is the place to go for 1980s classics and unselfconscious dancing.

EXCLUSIVE

Being rich, beautiful and famous may not be enough to get you into **Castel's**, but it could help. It is a strictly private club and the happy few who make it, dine in one of two very good restaurants before heading down to the dance floor.

Regine's is mostly full of be-suited executives and wealthy foreigners who dine and dance to the easy-listening music. However, it is now enjoying something of a renaissance, especially on ladies nights, when a trained physiognomist picks out only the best looking women to come in for a girls-own session for a few hours, complete with male strip show. Predictably, when the doors open to men later in the evening, it becomes one of Paris's top nightspots for seeing and being seen.

The wood-paneled, cozy **Ritz Club** in the legendary Ritz hotel is open only to members and hotel guests, though the chic and elegant are welcome. The ambience is upmarket and the music makes for easy listening. A younger, glamorous set have recently begun to make the Ritz Club their home, attracted, no doubt, by its old-fashioned star quality.

La Suite is currently one of the hardest places to get into in Paris. Run by the Guettas formerly of Les Bains, the smooth decor sets off the expensive tans sported by the jetsetters, supermodels and movie stars who come here.

Reserving a table at the expensive, but decent, restaurant is a good way to ensure access. Equally chic, **Le VIP** is populated by wannabes attracted by the name. Private parties are often held here, so it's a good idea to call ahead.

Nirvana Lounge is an opulent affair with a designer music soundtrack compiled by Claude Challe. The bar is open all day and stays busy with party-goers on the dance floor until four in the morning. Another extremely upscale spot is **L'Etoile** situated near the Arc de Triomphe. Be prepared to make the effort to look your best (and most-solvent) to get in here.

The most popular of the chic clubs, and the most laid-back and friendly once you're inside, is **Le Cab** (formerly known as Cabaret). The interior has recently been redesigned by Ora Ito, and today, anybody who's anybody comes here to dance like crazy or lay back and take it all in on one of the sumptuous mattresses in the chillout area.

TRENDY

Once a working-class music hall frequented by famous Parisians Edith Piaf and Jean Gabin, **Balajo** has now gone upmarket although it still emits a friendly vibe and remains one of the best clubs in Paris for dancing; they even hold ballroom dancing nights. It's also one of the few clubs open on Mondays.

An ultrahip young crowd flock to the small and cozy **Folie's Pigalle**, one-time strip joint and present-day venue for live music. Its original theme nights make for some of the best fun clubbing around. For a top dancing night out, try the biweekly "Bal" with live big band at the **Elysée Montmartre**. Here too, look out for "Return to the Source", Goa-trance nights that come all the way from London's Fridge.

Paris's trendy clubs seem to have a longer shelf life than those in some other cities and another hip venue that's still going strong is **Le Gibus**

which offers different dance styles throughout the week. Check the flyers to pick your own style of party.

The **Batofar**, the scarlet lighthouse ship moored on the Seine in the 13th arrondissement, is now a mainstay of the Paris club scene. The music here varies from underground techno to reggae depending on the night of the week, but the crowd are always friendly and relaxed. In the summer, try not to miss their wonderfully chilled-out afternoon sessions on the quayside.

The **Nouveau Casino** behind the ever trendy Café Charbon (see p319) in Oberkampf pulls in an eclectic crowd for events varying from dub to air-guitar competitions. Newcomer **Le Triptyque** has made an impressive mark on the Paris club scene with its mixed programming and excellent live music agenda. House music fans will love the hardcore sounds at the **Red Light**, which attracts big name DJs on a regular basis.

If bigger is always better, then head to superclub at **Studio 287** for a huge clubbing experience. While if it's just a large dance floor that's needed then Johnny Hallyday's club **L'Amnesia** should suffice.

WORLD MUSIC

A stylish and expensive African-Antillean club, **Keur Samba** is popular with the jetset. Things get going after 2am and last long into the night. **Le Casbah** is exclusive, jazzy and one of the best established venues on the Paris club scene. Its African-Middle Eastern decor has always been a magnet for models and trendies who, in between dances, do a little nocturnal shopping in the club's downstairs boutique. Le Casbah is currently enjoying something of a renaissance of its 'chicest of the chic' reputation.

If your nervous system responds favorably to the heaving rhythms and throbbing beat of authentic Latin music, you should head for **La Java**, which combines

glorious sounds with the quaint appeal of a Belleville dance hall. **Les Etoiles** is the place to go for salsa with soul. The **Latina Café**, on the other hand, is a more upmarket venue for Latin music. Other lively world music nights are held at **Trottoirs de Buenos-Aires**, **Chapelle des Lombards** and the cellar bar at **Aux Trois Maillets** (see Rock, Jazz and World Music pp349–50).

GAY AND LESBIAN

The gay scene in Paris is thriving. **Le Queen** boasts a great line-up of DJs. Monday is disco night, Friday and Saturday are garage and soul and the rest of the week is drum and bass and house. Some of the raunchier events are men-only. Girls should go with pretty boys. Sunday nights at **La Locomotive** are the Gay Tea Dance. Wednesday is Respect, formally of Le Queen. **Le Champmeslé**, one of the most venerable fixtures of Paris's ever more upfront and confident lesbian scene, continues to evolve and attract a new clientele. **Pulp** is the city's biggest and best lesbian club. Men are admitted in the week, but the weekend is strictly for ladies. For a pre-club venue, lesbian bars **Boobs Bourg** and **Les Scandaleuses** are the hippest and busiest. Scream is the gay night at the **Elysée Montmartre**. **Le Depôt** is rumored to be one of the most fun gay clubs in Paris, with a much-talked about backroom. Their Gay Tea Dance, held every Sunday, is legendary.

ADMISSION CHARGES

Some clubs are strictly private, others have a more generous admission policy. Prices can range from 12€ to 15€ or 30€, or more, and may be higher after midnight and on weekends. But quite often there are concessions for women.

In general, one drink (une consommation) is included in the entry price; thereafter it can become an extremely expensive evening.

DIRECTORY

DISCO AND CLUB VENUES

Alcazar
62 Rue Mazarine 75006.
Map 12 F4.
Tel 01 53 10 19 99.

L'Amnesia
33 Ave Maine 75015.
Map 15 C3.
Tel 01 56 80 37 37.

Les Bains
7 Rue du Bourg-
L'Abbé 75003.
Map 13 B1.
Tel 01 48 87 01 80.

Balajo
9 Rue de Lappe 75011.
Map 14 E4.
Tel 01 47 00 07 87.

Le Bataclan
50 blvd Voltaire 75011.
Map 13 E1.
Tel 01 43 14 35 35.

Batofar
Moored opposite 11
Quai Francois Mauriac
75013.
Tel 01 56 29 10 00.

Bus Palladium
6 Rue Fontaine 75009.
Map 6 E2.
Tel 01 53 21 07 33.

Le Cab
2 Pl de Palais Royale
75001.
Map 12 E1.
Tel 01 58 62 56 25.

**Le Cabaret
Milliardaire**
68 rue Pierre Charon
75008.
Map 4 F5.
*Tel 01 42 89 44 14 &
01 53 5 49 49.*

Castel's
15 Rue Princesse
75006.
Map 12 E4.
Tel 01 40 51 52 80.

Club 79
22 Rue Quentin
Bauchard 75008.
Map 4 F5.
Tel 01 47 23 68 75.

Club Med World
39 Cour St-Emilion
75012.
Tel 08 10 81 04 10.

**Dancing de la
Coupole**
104 Boulevard
Montmartre 75014.
Map 15 C1
Tel 01 43 27 56 00.

Le Duplex
2 Bis Avenue Foch
75002.
Map 4 D4.
Tel 01 45 00 45 00.

Elysée Montmartre
72 Blvd Rochechouart
75018.
Map 6 F2.
Tel 01 44 92 45 38.

L'Etoile
12 Rue de Presbourg
75016.
Map 4 D4.
Tel 01 45 00 78 70.

Folie's Pigalle
11 Pl Pigalle 75009.
Map 6 E2.
Tel 01 48 78 55 25.

Le Gibus
18 Rue du Faubourg-du-
Temple 75011.
Map 8 E15.
Tel 01 47 00 78 88.

Hammam Club
54 Rue d'Amsterdam
75009.
Map 6 D2.
Tel 01 55 07 80 00.

La Locomotive
90 Blvd de Clichy
75018.
Map 4 E4.
Tel 01 53 41 88 88.

Nouveau Casino
109 Rue Oberkampf
75011.
Map 14 E1.
Tel 01 43 57 57 40.

Nirvana Lounge
3 Ave Matignon 75008.
Map 5 A5.
Tel 01 53 89 18 91.

Les Plances
40 Rue de Colisee 75008.
Map 5 A4.
Tel 01 42 25 11 68.

Pulp
25 Blvd Poissoniere 75002.
Map 7 A5.
Tel 01 40 26 01 93.

Red Light
34 Rue du Depart 75014.
Map 15 C2.

Regine's
49–51 Rue Ponthieu
75008.
Map 5 A5.
Tel 01 43 59 21 13.

Rex Club
5 Blvd Poissonière
75002.
Map 7 A5.
Tel 01 42 36 10 96.

Ritz Club
Hôtel Ritz, 15 Pl
Vendôme 75001.
Map 6 D5.
Tel 01 43 16 30 30.
www.ritzparis.com

La Scala
188 bis Rue de Rivoli
75001.
Map 12 E2.
Tel 01 42 61 64 00.

La Suite
40 Ave George V
75008.
Map 4 E5.
Tel 01 53 5 49 49.

Studio 287
33 Ave de la Porte
d'Aubervilliers
75018.
Map 8 D1.
Tel 01 48 34 00 00.

Triptyque
142 rue Montmartre
75002.
Map 13 A1.
Tel 01 40 28 05 55.

VIP
78 Ave des Champs-
Elysées 75008.
Map 4 E4.
Tel 01 56 69 16 66.

WAGG
62 Rue Mazarine 75006.
Map 12 F4.
Tel 01 55 42 22 00.

Zed Club
2 Rue des Anglais
75005.
Map 13 A5.
Tel 01 43 54 93 78.

WORLD MUSIC

Le Casbah
18-20 Rue de la Forge-
Royale 75011.
Tel 01 43 71 04 39.

Les Etoiles
61 Rue Château d'Eau
75010.
Map 7 C5.
Tel 01 45 00 78 70.

La Java
105 Rue du Faubourg-du-
Temple 75010.
Map 8 E5.
Tel 01 42 02 20 52.

Latina Café
114 Ave des Champs-
Elysées 75008.
Map 4 E4.
Tel 01 42 89 98 89.

Keur Samba
79 Rue de la Boétie
75008.
Map 5 A4.
Tel 01 43 59 03 10.

GAY AND LESBIAN VENUES

Boobs Bourg
26 Rue de Montmorency
75003.
Map 13 C2.
Tel 01 42 74 04 82.

La Champmeslé
4 Rue Chabanais 75001.
Map 12 E1.
Tel 01 42 96 85 20.

Le Depôt
10 Rue aux Ours 75003.
Map 13 B2.
Tel 01 44 54 96 96.

Le Queen
102 Ave des Champs-
Elysées 75008.
Map 4 E4.
Tel 01 53 89 08 90.

Les Scandaleuses
8 Rue des Ecouffes 75004.
Map 13 C3.
Tel 01 48 87 39 26.

Movies

Paris is the world's capital of film appreciation. With more than 300 screens within the city limits, distributed among 100 theaters and multiplexes, a fabulous cornucopia of films are screened, both brand-new and classic. Although American movies dominate the market more than ever, virtually every filmmaking industry in the world has found a niche in the city's art houses. Theaters change their programs on Wednesdays. The cheapest practical guides to what's on are *Pariscope* and *L'Officiel des Spectacles (see p340)* with complete theater listings and timetables for some 300 films. *Zurban* also has features on current releases. Films shown in subtitled original language versions are coded "VO" *(version originale)*; dubbed films are coded"VF" *(version française)*. The Fête du Cinéma is held one day in June. The system is that you pay full price for one film and then every film seen subsequently in any theater on that day costs 1€. Film buffs think nothing of taking in six or seven screenings on the day.

MOVEMENTS IN CINEMA

Paris was the cradle of the cinematograph over 100 years ago, when Auguste and Louis Lumière invented the early film projector. Their screening of *L'Arrivée d'un Train en Gare de la Ciotat* ('Arrival of a Train at la Ciotat Station) in Paris in 1895, is considered by many to mark the birth of the medium. The French reverence for film as a true art form is based on a theory of one of the world's first film critics, Ricciotto Canudo, an Italian intellectual living in France, who dubbed cinematography "the Seventh Art" in 1922. The title holds true even today. The city was of course also the incubator of that very Parisian vanguard movement, the New Wave, when film directors such as Claude Chabrol, François Truffaut, Jean-Luc Godard and Eric Rohmer in the late 1950s and early 60s revolutionized the way films were made and perceived. The exploration of existential themes, the use of long tracking shots and the rejection of studios for outside locations are some of the characteristics of New Wave film. In 2001, the success of *Amélie Poulain* revitalized the Parisian filmmaking scene; many of its locations are easy to spot as you walk around town. When the movie version

of the *Da Vinci Code*, also featuring *Amelie* star Audrey Tautou, hits movie screens in 2006, similar location spotting will be possible.

MOVIE ZONES

Most Paris theaters are concentrated in several cinema belts, which enjoy the added appeal of nearby restaurants and shops.

The Champs-Elysées remains the densest theater strip in town, where you can see the latest Hollywood smash hit or French *auteur* triumph, as well as some classic re-issues, in subtitled original language versions. Theaters in the Grands Boulevards, in the vicinity of the Opéra de Paris Garnier, show films in both subtitled and dubbed versions. The Place de Clichy is the last Parisian stronghold of Pathé, which operates no less than 13 screens there, all showing dubbed versions. A major hub of Right Bank movie activity is in the Forum des Halles shopping mall.

The Left Bank, historically associated with the city's intellectual life, remains the center of the art and repertory cinemas. Yet, it has equally as many of the latest blockbusters. Since the 1980s, many theaters in the Latin Quarter have closed down and the main area for Left Bank

theaters is now the Odéon-St-Germain-des-Prés area. The Rue Champollion is an exception. It has enjoyed a revival as a mini-district for art and repertory films.

Further to the south, Montparnasse remains a lively district of new films in both dubbed and subtitled prints.

BIG SCREENS AND PICTURE PALACES

Among surviving landmark theaters are two Grands Boulevards venues, the 2,800-seat **Le Grand Rex** with its Baroque decor, and the **Max Linder Panorama**, which was refurbished by a group of independent film buffs in the 1980s for both popular and art film programming.

Boasting the largest screen in the entire country is the **Gaumont Grand Ecran Italie** in the Place d'Italie district. The huge new 14-screen **MK2 Bibliothèque** theater (plus bar, shops and exhibition space), recently opened up in the revitalised 13th arrondissement. Just across the river, the **Bercy** theater complex is well worth a visit too.

In the Cité des Sciences et de l'Industrie at La Villette, scientific films are shown at **La Géode** *(see p235)*. This has a hemispheric screen (once the world's largest) and an "omnimax" projector which uses 70-mm film shot horizontally to project an image which is nine times larger than the standard 35-mm print.

REVIVAL AND REPERTORY HOUSES

Each week, more than 150 titles representing the best of world cinema can be seen. For old Hollywood films, the independent **Grand Action** mini-chain can't be beaten. Other active and thoughtful repertory and re-issue venues include the excellent **Reflets Médicis** screens in the Rue Champollion and the **Pagode**. The latter is particularly striking, the Oriental pagoda was constructed in 1895 and has been recently renovated.

The **Studio 28** in Montmartre is a lovely old movie house with lights in the theater designed by Jean Cocteau and a charming garden bar full of starry lights and kitsch cutouts of old movie stars. Opened in the 1920s, Studio 28 claims to be the first ever avant-garde cinema and once played host to film greats such as Luis Buñuel and Abel Gance. They screen everything from the latest releases through to Fellini festivals and documentary shows. There are at least ten films screened here each week, including art-house classics and pre-releases. The theater also holds regular debates with well-known directors and actors. Another Parisian institution, the **Studio Galande** has shown the *Rocky Horror Picture Show* to costumed movie-goers every Friday night for over 20 years.

CINÉMATHÈQUE FRANÇAISE

The private "school" of the New Wave generation, this famous film archive and repertory cinema was created by Henri Langlois in 1936 *(see p198)*. It has lost its monopoly on classic film screenings, but it is still a must for cinephiles in search of that rare film no longer in theatrical circulation or, perhaps, recently restored or rescued. The **Cinémathèque Française Grands Boulevards** encompasses two theaters, one in the Palais de Chaillot *(see p198)*, and the other in the 10th arrondissement. By autumn 2005, the planned Maison du Cinéma in the Gehry-designed building on the Rue de Bercy should eventually house these and other theaters. Tickets are priced at about 4€, and there are subscriptions and special rates for students and children.

NON-THEATRICAL VENUES

In addition to the Cinémathèque Française, film programs and festivals are integral parts of two highly popular Paris cultural institutions, the Musée d'Orsay *(see pp144–5)* and

the Pompidou Centre *(see pp110–11)* with its **Salle Garance**. The Musée d'Orsay regularly schedules film programs to complement current art exhibitions and is usually restricted to silent films. The Pompidou Centre organizes vast month-long retrospectives, devoted to national film industries and on occasion to some of the major companies.

Finally, the **Forum des Images** *(see p109)* in the heart of Les Halles is a high-tech film and video library with a huge selection of films and documentaries featuring the city of Paris from the late 19th century to the present day. The archives here are amazing and include news-reels and advertisements featuring Paris alongside the feature films and documentaries. The Forum has three theaters, all of which run daily screenings of feature films, beginning at 2.30pm. One ticket allows the visitor access to both the video library and to the cinema screenings. In the video library it is possible to search the database of over 6,000 films and then watch your choice on your own personal screen. The movie screenings are frequently grouped according to theme or director, making it possible to spend several hours enjoying a mini-retrospective.

TICKET PRICES

Expect to pay around 7€ at first-run venues or even more for movies of unusual length or special media attention. However, exhibitors practice a wide array of collective discount incentives, including discount admissions for students, the unemployed, the elderly, veterans and large families. Wednesday is discount day for everybody at all the city's theaters – prices are slashed to as low as 4€.

France's three exhibition giants, Gaumont, UGC and MK2, also sell special discount cards and accept credit card reservations for their flagship houses, while repertory houses issue "fidelity" cards.

MOVIES WITH STRONG IMAGES OF PARIS

Historical Paris (studio-made)
An Italian Straw Hat
(René Clair, 1927)

Sous les toits de Paris
(René Clair, 1930)

Les Misérables
(Raymond Bernard, 1934)

Hôtel du Nord
(Marcel Carné, 1937)

Les Enfants du Paradis
(Marcel Carné, 1945)

Casque d'Or
(Jacques Becker, 1952)

La Traversée de Paris
(Claude Autant-Lara, 1956)

Playtime
(Jacques Tati, 1967)

New Wave Paris (location-made)
Breathless
(Jean-Luc Godard, 1959)

Les 400 coups
(François Truffaut, 1959)

Documentary Paris
Paris 1900
(Nicole Vedrès, 1948)

La Seine a rencontré Paris
(Joris Ivans, 1957)

Paris as seen by Hollywood
Seventh Heaven
(Frank Borzage, 1927)

Camille
(George Cukor, 1936)

An American in Paris
(Vincente Minnelli, 1951)

Gigi
(Vincente Minnelli, 1958)

Irma La Douce
(Billy Wilder, 1963)

Le Divorce
(James Ivory, 2003)

The Bourne Identity
(Doug Liman, 2002)

Frantic
(Roman Polanski, 1988)

French Kiss
(Lawrence Kasdan, 1995)

Moulin Rouge
(Baz Luhrmann, 2001)

Before Sunset
(Richard Linklater, 2004)

The Ninth Gate
(Roman Polanski, 1999)

Paris when it Sizzles
(Richard Quine, 1964)

Film Festivals

Film festivals are a way of life for Parisian movie buffs, there are several major events each year and lots of small themed festivals happening at any given time around the city. The annual Paris Film Festival, held at the end of March, may be dwarfed by its glitzier sister in Cannes, but the capital's version is a far friendlier event for the public to attend – and there are still more than enough opportunities to spot celebrities.

OPEN-AIR FESTIVALS

There are several outdoor cinema festivals throughout the summer, including the Festival Silhouette which shows short films in the lovely Buttes Chaumont (see p232), the Cinema au Clair du Lune festival which has projections of films at Parisian sites which are relevant to the movie and Le Cinema en Plein Air which draws crowds to a lawn in La Villette (see pp234-35), where a giant inflatable screen shows old and contemporary classics. This is one of the summer's most popular events so be sure to get there early and don't forget to take a hamper full of goodies to nibble on throughout the movie.

INDOOR FESTIVALS

During the annual Paris Film Festival, over 100 films are shown at the Gaumont Marignon on the Champs-Elysées. The city's gay and lesbian film festival at the Forum des Images enjoyed its tenth year in 2004 and will return in November. Paris Tout Court is an impressive short film festival held at the Arlequin in St-Germain which also stages lectures and meetings with renowned directors and artists. Other film festivals include the Les Etranges festival which shows weird and wonderful offbeat films from around the world to enthusiastic audiences.

DIRECTORY

THEATERS

Action Christine Odeon
4 Rue Christine 75006.
Map 12 F4.
Tel 01 43 29 11 30.

Action Ecoles
23 Rue des Ecoles 75005.
Map 13 A5.
Tel 01 43 29 79 89.

Arelquin
76 Rue de Rennes 75006.
Map 12 E4.
Tel 01 45 44 28 80.

Le Balzac
1 Rue Balzac 75008.
Map 4 E4.
Tel 08 92 68 31 23.

Le Champo
51 Rue des Ecoles 75005.
Map 13 A5.
Tel 01 43 29 79 89.

Cinémathèque Française
4 Rue de Longchamp 75116.
Tel 01 56 26 01 01.

Cinema Studio Galande
42 Rue Galande 75005.
Map 13 A4.
Tel 08 92 68 06 24.

Forum des Images
Porte St-Eustache, Forum des Halles 75001.
Map 13 A2.
Tel 01 44 76 62 00.

Gaumont Grand Ecran Italie
30 Place d'Italie 75013. **Map** 17 C4.
Tel 01 40 30 20 10.

Gaumont Marignan
27 Ave Champs-Elysées 75008.
Map 5 A5.
Tel 01 42 89 12 74.

La Géode
26 Ave Corentin-Cariou 75019.
Tel 08 92 68 45 40.
www.cite-sciences.fr

Goethe Institut
17 Ave d'Iena 75016.
Map 10 D1.
Tel 01 44 43 92 30.

Grand Action
Action Rive Gauche, 5 Rue des Ecoles 75005.
Map 13 B5.
Tel 01 43 54 47 62.

Le Grand Rex
1 Blvd Poissonnière 75002.
Map 7 A5.
Tel 08 92 68 70 23.

Images d'Ailleurs
21 Rue de la Clef 75005.
Map 13 B2.
Tel 01 45 87 18 09.

Latina
20 Rue du Temple 75004.
Map 7 C2.
Tel 08 92 68 07 51.

Lucenaire
53 Rue Notre-Dame-des-Champs 75006.
Map 16 E2.
Tel 01 45 44 57 34.

Max Linder Panorama
24 Blvd Poissonnière 75009.
Map 7 A5.
Tel 08 92 68 00 31.

Majestic Bastille
4 Blvd Richard Lenoir 75011.
Map 14 E4.
Tel 01 47 00 02 48.

MK2 Beaubourg
50 Rue Rambuteau 75003.
Map 7 B2.
Tel 08 92 69 84 84.

MK2 Bibliothèque
128-162 Ave de France 75015. **Map** 18 F4.
Tel 08 92 69 84 84.

Pagode
57 bis Rue de Babylone 75007. **Map** 11 C4.
Tel 01 45 55 48 48.

Quartier Latin
9 Rue Champollion 75005.
Map 13 A5.
Tel 01 43 26 84 65.

Racine Odeon
6 Rue de l'Ecole de Medecine 75006.
Map 12 F4.

Reflets Médicis
3-7 Rue Champollion 75005.
Map 12 F5.
Tel 01 46 33 25 97.

Salle Garance
Centre Georges Pompidou, 19 Rue Beaubourg 75004.
Map 13 B2.

St-Andre des Arts
30 Rue St Andre des Arts 75006.
Map 12 F4.
Tel 01 43 26 48 18.

Studio 28
10 Rue Tholozé 75018.
Map 6 E1.
Tel 01 46 06 36 07.

UGC Ciné Cité Bercy
2 Cour St-Emilion 75012.
Tel 08 36 68 68 58.

UGC Cine-Cite les Halles
7 Place de la Rotonde 75001.
Map 7 A2.
Tel 08 92 70 00 00

Sports and Fitness

There is no end to sports activities in Paris. Certain events such as the Roland Garros tennis tournament and the Tour de France bicycle race are national institutions. The only drawback is that many of the facilities are on the outskirts of the city.

For details regarding all sports events in and around Paris contact **Paris Infos Mairie** – a free information service run by the Town Hall. The weekly entertainment guides *L'Officiel des Spectacles*, *Pariscope* and the Wednesday edition of *Le Figaro* also have good listings of the week's sports events *(see p340)*. For in-depth sports coverage there is the daily paper *L'Equipe*. See also *Children's Paris* on page 362.

OUTDOOR SPORTS

The annual Tour de France bicycle race finishes in July in Paris to city-wide frenzy, when the French president awards the coveted *maillot jaune* (yellow jersey) to the winner. For over 20 years now the final stage of the tour has taken place on the Champs-Elysées with the riders racing up the famous avenue. Traffic across the city grinds to a halt and sports fans and couch potatoes alike flock to cheer on the cyclists. Finding a spot to watch can be extremely tough; it's best to hunt down your speck several hours before the riders are expected.

For those brave enough to tackle cycling through the city traffic, bikes may be rented throughout Paris, including at **Paris Vélo** in the Rue du Fer-à-Moulin and **Maison Roue Libre** in Passage Mondétour, headquarters of the RATP's bicycle rental service, Roue Libre *(see p359)*. In summer (weekends and public holidays only) old RATP buses rent bicycles from five locations (Place de la Concorde, Stalingrad, Place du Châtelet, Porte d'Auteil and Parc Floral de Vincennes). The **Fédération Française de Cyclotourisme** in the Rue Louis Bertrand will give you information on over 300 cycling clubs around Paris. Things are gradually improving for those who favor pedal power. All year long, the city council shuts down some of the quaysides on Sundays and national holidays to allow cyclists freewheeling next to the Seine. The city has also undertaken a program of expansion for its cycle lanes. Be aware though that Paris traffic is heavy and Parisian drivers not especially two-wheel friendly. Those who can't wait for the quais along the Seine to be closed on Sundays should head over to the Bois de Vincennes or the Bois de Boulogne for a leisurely bike ride through the woods. The more ambitious can pick up a copy of the free Paris à Vélo map from a tourist office to find details of all the city's cycle lanes. If you'd prefer to take an organized cycle tour through the city, there are several organizations who run fun trips. **Fat Tire Bike Tours** in the Rue Edgar Faure have daily trips in spring and summer in which knowledgeable guides shepherd cyclists around the streets while imparting interesting information on the city's landmarks. **Paris à Vélo c'est Sympa** runs multi-lingual tours to offbeat parts of the city.

Inline skates can enjoy parades through the city on Friday nights. The police close off boulevards around the city allowing thousands of skate fans to join the trip every week. The parade starts outside the Gare de Montparnasse at 10pm but you can join the route at any point if the whole circuit seems like too much. Contact www.pari-roller.com for details of the route. Beginners can enjoy a free lesson prior to the departure of the parade if they arrive at the start point at 8pm. There are many good outlets in the city for skate rental. The parade's website provides useful links to recommended outlets. As a safety precaution the trip is canceled if the weather is inclement and the roads wet.

Parisians enjoy Sunday afternoon boating in the Bois de Vincennes *(see p233)*, the Bois de Boulogne *(see p254)* and the Parc des Buttes-Chaumont *(see p232)*. Just line up to rent a boat.

All the golf courses are outside Paris. Many are private clubs, but some will admit non-members – for further information contact the **Fédération Française du Golf** in the Rue Anatole-France. Otherwise try the **Golf de Chevry**, **Golf de St-Pierre du Perray**, **Golf de St-Quentin en Yvelines** or the **Golf de Villennes**. Expect to pay at least 25€ each time you want to play.

You can go horseback riding in both the Bois de Boulogne and the Bois de Vincennes. For details, contact the **Ligue Equestre de Paris** in the Rue Laugier.

Tennis can be played at municipal courts such as the **Tennis Luxembourg** in the Jardin du Luxembourg. Courts are available every day on a first-come first-served basis. **Tennis de la Faluère** in the Bois de Vincennes has some of the better courts, but these must be reserved at least 24 hours in advance.

INDOOR SPORTS

There are plenty of gyms in Paris which you can use with a day pass. Expect to pay 20€ or more, depending on the facilities.

Club Med Gym is a well-equipped, popular chain of gyms with more than 20 sites in Paris and the suburbs. Good choices include the branches in Rue de Berri and Rue de Rennes. **Club Jean de Beauvais** in the Rue Jean de Beauvais is a state-of-the-art gym with personalized fitness programs. The **Ken Club** on Avenue President Kennedy is an upmarket gym complete with pool and sauna in the chic 16th arronssissement. Its proximity next to a major radio studio means French media personalities are often to be found there working out on their lunch break. In theory the **Ritz Gym**, which has the finest indoor swimming pool in Paris, is for guests or members only, but if the hotel is not too full you can buy a day pass.

Skating is a cheap pastime and can be enjoyed year-round at the **Patinoire d'Asnières-sur-Seine** located on Boulevard Pierre de Coubertin.

Squash can be played at **Squash Club Quartier Latin** in the Rue de Pontoise, where options also include billiards, gym and a sauna. Other good clubs include the **Squash Montmartre**, **Squash Rennes-Raspail** and the **Squash Front de Seine**.

SPECTATOR SPORTS

A day out at the races is a chance to see the rich in all their finery. The world-famous Prix de l'Arc de Triomphe is held at the **Hippodrome de Longchamp** in the Bois de Boulogne on the first Sunday in October. More racing takes place at the **Hippodrome de St-Cloud** and **Maisons Lafitte**, which are a short drive west of Paris. For steeple-chasing go to the **Hippodrome d'Auteuil** in the Bois de Boulogne. The **Hippodrome de Vincennes** on Route de la Ferne hosts the trotting races. For detailed information on all of these, consult **France Galop** on phone or check their Internet service.

The 24-hour car race at Le Mans, 115 miles (185 km) southwest of Paris, is one of the best-known road races in the world. It takes place every year in mid-June. Contact the **Automobile Club de l'Ouest** for details. The **Palais Omnisports de Paris-Bercy** sports stadium in Boulevard Bercy is the venue for a huge range of events, including the

Paris tennis open, the six-day cycling race, showjumping, world-class martial arts demonstrations, tournaments in everything from figure skating to handball and major rock concerts.

Parc des Princes can hold 50,000 people. It is home to the main Paris soccer team, Paris St-Germain, and hosts the rugby internationals.

Despite its glorious baptism in 1998 with France's World Cup victory, the **Stade de France** has failed to win a home team; meanwhile, it makes do with the Six Nations Trophy, Tina Turner and Johnnie Halliday.

The **Stade Roland Garros** in Avenue Gordon-Bennett is famous for its international tennis tournament. From late May to mid-June everyone lives and breathes tennis. Business meetings are transferred from the conference room to the stadium. Apply for tickets several months ahead. Don't miss a trip to the stadium's excellent museum of tennis featuring everything from prototype rackets to a Bjorn Bjorg headband. Also, be sure to reserve a table at one of the swanky restaurants here, which are transformed into a place to see and be seen during the tournament. Tennis fans should also be sure to catch the mens' masters series at the Palais Omnisports de Paris Bercy in November and the womens' tournament 'Open Gaz de France', which takes place at the **Stade Pierre de Coubertin** on Avenue Georges Lafont, in March.

SWIMMING

There is a huge aquatic fun park, known as **Aquaboulevard**, in south Paris (see p362). Besides an exotic artificial beach, swimming pools, water toboggans and rapids, there are tennis and squash courts, golf, bowling, table tennis, billiards, a gym, bars and shops.

Of the many municipal swimming pools, one of the best is the **Piscine des Halles** in Place de la Rotonde, with an Olympic-sized swimming pool in the

underground shopping complex. For a lovely 1930s mosaic decor with two levels of private changing rooms, a whirlpool, sauna and water jets, go to the **Piscine Pontoise-Quartier Latin**. This complex also has a small gym overlooking the pool, where fitness fans can pump a little iron before taking a dip. The **Piscine Henry de Montherlant** is part of a municipal sports complex that includes tennis courts and a gym. The beautiful Art Nouveau pool in the Butte aux Cailles (see pp272-3) is a treat for serious swimmers and sunbathers. A decent-sized indoor pool is perfect for laps while the two outdoor swimming areas are great for lounging. The villagey atmosphere of the surrounding area only serves to reinforce the feeling of relaxing on vacation miles away from the city. A fantastic view of the Eiffel Tower can be spied mid-crawl at the **Piscine Emile-Anthoine**. Some of the upscale hotels and gyms also have their own pools. It is possible to buy a day pass to the chic **Sofitel Paris Club Med Gym** in the Rue Louis Armand and have access to their 15-meter pool. Similarly at the **Novotel Tour Eiffel**, non-guests are welcomed to their health club and pool which has a retractable roof for swimming under the sun in spring and summer. It is important to note that all municipal pools and some private ones insist that bathers wear swimming caps and that male swimmers wear close-fitting swimsuits rather than baggy trunks or shorts.

MISCELLANEOUS

Baseball, fencing, jogging in the parks, volleyball, windsurfing at La Villette (see pp234–9) and bowling are just some of the other sports activities that can be enjoyed during your stay.

Fishing on the Seine is fast becoming a popular pastime with Parisiens. Due to a clean-up operation the Seine is now home to a variety of freshwater fish.

DIRECTORY

OUTDOOR SPORTS

Fat Tire Bike Tours
24 Rue Edgar Faure 75015.
Map 10 E4.
Tel 01 56 58 10 54

Fédération Française de Cyclotourisme
12 Rue Louis Bertrand
94200, Ivry-sur-Seine.
Tel 01 56 20 88 88.

Fédération Française du Golf
68 Rue Anatole France,
92300 Levallois Perret.
Tel 01 41 49 77 00.

France Galop
Tel 01 49 10 20 30.
www.france-galop.com

Golf de Chevry
91190 Gif-sur-Yvette.
Tel 01 60 12 40 33.

Golf de St-Pierre du Perray
91380 St-Pierre du Perray.
Tel 01 60 75 17 47.
www.bluegreen.com

Golf de St-Quentin en Yvelines
78190 Trappes.
Tel 01 30 50 86 40.

Golf de Villennes
Route d'Orgeval,
78670 Villennes-sur-Seine.
Tel 01 39 08 18 18.

Ligue Equestre de Paris
69 Rue Laugier 75017.
Tel 01 42 12 03 43.

Maison Roue Libre
1 Passage Mondétour
75001.
Map 13 B2.
Tel 08 10 44 15 34.

Paris à Vélo c'est Sympa
37 Blvd Bourdon 75004.
Map 14 E4.
Tel 01 48 87 60 01.

Paris Infos Mairie
(Mon–Fri: 8am–7pm;
Sat: 8:30am–1pm).
Tel 08 20 00 75 75.

Paris Vélo
2 Rue du Fer-à-Moulin
75005. **Map** 17 C2.
Tel 01 43 37 59 22.

Tennis de la Faluère Route de la Pyramide
Bois de Vincennes 75012.
Tel 01 43 74 40 93.

Tennis Luxembourg Jardins du Luxembourg
Blvd St-Michel 75006.
Map 12 E5.
Tel 01 43 25 79 18.

INDOOR SPORTS

Club Jean de Beauvais
5 Rue Jean de Beauvais
75005. **Map** 13 A5.
Tel 01 46 33 16 80.

Club Med Gym
26 Rue de Berri 75008.
Map 4 F4.
Tel 01 43 59 04 58.
149 Rue de Rennes
75006. **Map** 15 C1.
Tel 01 45 44 24 35.
www.clubmedgym.com

Ken Club
100 Ave President
Kennedy 75016.
Tel 01 46 47 41 41.

Patinoire d'Asnières-sur-Seine
Blvd Pierre de Coubertin,
92600 Asnières.
Tel 01 47 99 86 37.

Ritz Gym
Ritz Hotel, Pl Vendôme
75001. **Map** 6 D5.
Tel 01 43 16 30 30.

Squash Club Quartier Latin
19 Rue de Pontoise
75005.
Map 13 B5.
Tel 01 55 42 77 88.

Squash Front de Seine
21 Rue Gaston-de-
Caillavet 75015.
Map 9 B5.
Tel 01 45 75 35 37.

Squash Montmartre
14 Rue Achille-Martinet
75018.
Map 2 E4.
Tel 01 42 55 38 30.

Squash Rennes-Raspail
149 Rue de Rennes
75006. **Map** 16 D1.
Tel 01 35 44 24 35.

SPECTATOR SPORTS

Automobile Club de l'Ouest
Tel 02 43 40 24 24.

Hippodrome d'Auteuil
Bois de Boulogne 75016.
Tel 01 40 71 47 47.

Hippodrome de Longchamp
Bois de Boulogne 75016.
Tel 01 44 30 75 00.

Hippodrome Maisons Lafitte
1 Ave de la Pelouze,
78600 Maisons Lafitte.
Tel 01 39 62 06 77.

Hippodrome de St-Cloud
1 Rue de Camp
Canadien, 92210 St-
Cloud.
Tel 01 47 71 69 26.

Hippodrome de Vincennes
2 Route de la Ferme,
75012 Vincennes.
Tel 01 49 77 17 17.

Palais Omnisports de Paris-Bercy
8 Blvd Bercy 75012.
Map 18 F2.
Tel 08 25 0 3 00 31.

Parc des Princes
24 Rue du Commandant-
Guilbaud 75016.
Tel 08 25 07 50 77.

Stade de France
93210 La Plaine St-Denis.
Tel 01 55 93 00 00.

Stade Pierre de Coubertin
82 Ave Georges Lafont
75016.
Tel 01 45 27 79 12.

Stade Roland Garros
2 Ave Gordon-Bennett
75016.
Tel 01 47 43 48 00.
www.fft.fr

SWIMMING

Aquaboulevard
4 Rue Louis-Armand
75015.
Tel 01 40 60 10 00.

Piscine Butte-aux-Cailles
5 Pl Paul-Verlaine 75013.
Map 17 A5.
Tel 01 45 89 60 05.

Piscine des Amiraux
6 Rue Hermann-Lachapelle
75018.
Tel 01 46 06 46 47.

Piscine des Halles
10 Pl de la Rotonde,
Niveau 3, Entrance Porte
St Eustache, Les Halles
75001. **Map** 13 A2.
Tel 01 42 36 98 44.

Piscine Emile-Anthoine
9 Rue Jean Rey 75015.
Map 10 D3.
Tel 01 53 69 61 59.

Piscine Henry de Montherlant
32 Blvd de Lannes 75016.
Tel 01 40 72 28 30.

Piscine Pontoise-Quartier Latin
19 Rue de Pontoise
75005.
Map 13 B5.
Tel 01 55 42 77 88.

Piscine St Germain
12 Rue Lobineau 75006.
Map 12 E4.
Tel 01 43 29 08 15.

Piscine Saint-Merri
16 Rue de Renard 75004.
Map 13 B3.
Tel 01 42 72 29 45.

Sofitel Paris Club Med Gym
8 Rue Louis Armand
75015.
Tel 01 45 54 79 00.

Novotel Tour Eiffel
61 Quai de Grenelle
75015. **Map** 9 B5.
Tel 01 40 58 20 00.

CHILDREN'S PARIS

It's never too early to instill a lifelong taste for this magical city in your children. A trip to Disneyland Resort Paris *(see pp242–5)* or down the Seine *(see pp72–3)*, the dizzy heights of the Eiffel Tower *(see pp192–3)* or a visit to Notre-Dame *(see pp82–5)* are fun at any age, and with children in tow you will see old haunts through new eyes. The historic parks are probably best appreciated by older children and adults, but everyone will love the technological wizardry of the Disneyland Paris theme park. During the summer, carnivals, circuses and all kinds of impromptu events are staged in gardens and parks, notably in the Bois de Boulogne *(see pp254–5)*. Or, take children to an entertainment center, museum or adventure playground, or to a show at one of the café-theaters.

La Cité des Enfants at La Villette

PRACTICAL ADVICE

Paris welcomes young families in hotels *(see p278)* and most restaurants *(see p295)*. Many sights and attractions offer child discounts, while infants under three or four enter free. The upper age limit for discounts is usually about 12 but can vary considerably. Many museums are free on Sundays; others allow children under 18 in free at any time. Ask at the Office du Tourisme *(see p280)* for full details of child discounts, or check in the weekly entertainment guides such as *Pariscope, L'Officiel des Spectacles, Paris Mômes* and *Zurban*.

A lot of the children's activities are geared to end-of-school times, including Wednesday afternoons when French children have time off. For information on museum workshops, contact the **Ministère de la Culture** or visit **www.paris-frimousse.com**, which has information on events for 2–12-year olds.

Cribs and strollers can be rented from major baby-sitting agencies like **Home Service**. **Mamynoo** and **Kid Services** are other specialized baby-sitting organizations.

MUSEUMS

Top of the museum list for children is undoubtedly the Cité des Sciences et de l'Industrie *(see pp234–9)* at Parc de la Villette. Hands-on activities and changing exhibitions illuminate many aspects of science and modern technology in this immense complex. There are sections for children called La Cité des Enfants and Techno Cité. In central Paris, the Palais de la Découverte, within the Grand Palais *(see p206)*, is an old-fashioned but lively science museum where staff adopt the role of mad scientists.

The Louvre *(see pp122–9)* organizes special sessions designed to introduce children to various aspects of art, while the Galerie des Enfants at the Pompidou Centre *(see pp110–13)* does the same with modern art.

Other enjoyable museums for children include the Musée de la Marine *(see p199)* and the Musée de la Poupée *(see p114)*. The former covers the history of the French maritime tradition and includes scale models. The latter displays handmade dolls dating from the mid-19th century, and also offers doll-making classes for both adults and children.

USEFUL CONTACTS

Home Service
2 Rue Pierre Semard 75009.
Map 7 A5.
Tel *01 42 82 05 04.*
www.homeserviceidf.com

Kid Services
Tel *08 20 00 02 30.*

Mamynoo
Tel *08 20 00 07 82.*
www.mamynoo.com

Ministère de la Culture
3 Rue de Valois 75001.
Map 12 F1.
Tel *01 40 15 80 00.*

The Café d'Edgar theater

The Guignol marionnettes

PARKS, ZOOS AND ADVENTURE PLAYGROUNDS

The best children's park within Paris is the Jardin d'Acclimatation in the Bois de Boulogne *(see pp254–5)*, with a children's theater and circus, a pony club, a mini railroad and boats. The Musée en Herbe *(see p254)* is a museum created especially for children offering entertaining educational activities.

Pony rides, Jardin d'Acclimatation

France Miniature recreates France on a small scale, complete with all its monuments.

The Bois de Vincennes *(see p233)* has simple amusements for children in the inexpensive

Parc Floral. It also has Paris's largest zoo and the largest carnival in France, open from Palm Sunday through to the end of May. Perhaps the most appealing zoo is the small Ménagerie in the Jardin des Plantes *(see p164)*.

ENTERTAINMENT CENTERS

There are many supervised children's activity centers in Paris. The Atelier des Enfants in the Pompidou Centre *(see pp110–11)* has a workshop on Wednesday and Saturday afternoons from 2.30 to 4pm. The medium of instruction is French but the circuses, mimeshows, marionnettes and craft or museum workshops focus on actions rather than words.

Several café-theaters, including Café d'Edgar *(see p343)* and Au Bec Fin *(see p342)*, offer children's shows where mime, dance or music form part of the content. The most spectacular cinematic experience is in La Géode at the Cité des Sciences et de l'Industrie (see p237). The theater **Le Saint Lambert** specializes in children's films and comic strips in French, though most films for children

Lion in the Bois de Vincennes zoo

will not have English subtitles. Movie tickets are cheaper on Wednesdays, with no child discounts on weekends.

The **Cirque de Paris** offers children a day's entertainment when they can meet the animals, put on clown makeup or practice tightrope walking. Shows are in the afternoon, after lunch with the *artistes*.

The Guignol marionnette puppet shows are a summer tradition in Paris. The themes are similar to the traditional English Punch and Judy shows. Most of the main parks hold Guignol shows in summer on Wednesday afternoons and on weekends. One or two shows are free. Consult the entertainment guides such as *Pariscope, L'Officiel des Spectacles* and *Paris Mômes*.

ADDRESSES

Cirque de Paris
115 Blvd Charles de Gaulle, 92390 Villeneuve-la-Garenne. *Tel* 01 47 99 40 40.

France Miniature
25 Route du Mesnil, 78990 Elancourt.
Tel 01 30 16 16 30.
www.franceminiature.com

Le Saint Lambert
6 Rue Peclet 75015. *Tel* 01 45 32 91 68.

Circus acrobats training at the Cirque de Paris

Fireworks over Sleeping Beauty Castle, Disneyland Resort Paris

THEME PARKS

The two parks of Disneyland Resort Paris *(see pp242–5)* are the biggest and most spectacular of the Paris theme parks. Six hotels, each with a different, imaginative theme, and a campsite provide on-site accommodation. The complex also includes a golf course, shops and restaurants.

Parc Asterix is a French theme park centering around the legendary world of Asterix the Gaul. Here six themed "worlds" feature gladiators, slave auctions and rides among the many attractions. The park is situated 24 miles (38 km) northeast of Paris. Take the RER line B to Charles de Gaulle Airport then the shuttle bus to Parc Asterix.

Donald Duck

SPORTS AND RECREATION

The giant waterpark **Aqua-boulevard** is one of the best places to take energetic youngsters. Also good is the indoor pool at **Forum des Halles**. The weekly entertainment guide *Pariscope* lists the swimming pools in and around Paris. Accomplished roller-skaters and skate-boarders practice outside the Palais de Chaillot *(see p198)*. There is an official roller-skating rink in Parc Monceau *(see pp258–9)*, and the Parc des Buttes-Chaumont *(see p232 and pp268–9)* and Disneyland Resort Paris *(see pp242–5)* have ice-skating rinks. Disneyland also has a range of other sports facilities. Old-fashioned fairground

carousels are situated near Sacré-Coeur *(see pp224–5)* and Forum des Halles *(see p109)*. A great way of inspiring interest in the city's history, and great fun too, is a boat trip. Several companies compete *(see pp72– 3)* from different departure points, and pass a host of waterfront sites including Notre-Dame, the Louvre and the Musée d'Orsay. Boats departing from La Villette travel along the Paris canal system. Radio-controlled model boats are popular on the ponds of the Jardin du Luxembourg *(see p172)*. Or, take the family boating on the lakes of the Bois de Boulogne *(see pp254–5)* or the Bois de Vincennes *(see p233)*. Riding is also popular in these parks *(see p357 Directory)*.

ADDRESSES

Aquaboulevard
4 Rue Louis Armand 75015.
Tel *01 40 60 10 00.* ⏰ *9am–11pm Mon–Thu, 9am– midnight Fri, 8am–midnight Sat, 8am–11pm Sun.*

La Piscine des Halles
Forum des Halles, 10 Pl de la Rotonde, Les Halles 75001. **Map** 12 F2. **Tel** *01 42 36 98 44.* ⏰ *11:30am–10pm Mon–Fri, 9am–7pm Sat–Sun.*

Parc Asterix
BP8 Plailly 60128. 🏠 *08 26 3010 40, 08 26 68 30 10.* ⏰ *Apr–mid-Oct: 10am–6pm Mon–Fri, 9am–7pm w/e & hols.* **www**.parcasterix.fr

Apache
46 Rue Saint-Placide 75006.
Map 12 D5. **Tel** *01 53 63 27 10. One of several branches.*

CHILDREN'S SHOPS

There is no shortage of chic children's fashion in Paris. A good place to start is the Rue du Jour in Beaubourg and Les Halles which has a number of children's boutiques. The city has many appealing toy shops such as Au Nain Bleu *(see p331)* or the branches of Apache *(see Addresses)*, but, like the clothes shops, they can be prohibitively expensive. *(See also p326.)*

Characters from the book Tintin, in Au Nain Bleu toy shop

Roller-skaters near the Eiffel Tower

Carousel near Sacré-Coeur

STREET LIFE AND MARKETS

Outside the Pompidou Centre (see pp110–11) street enter-tainers draw the crowds on sunny afternoons. Musicians, conjurors, fire-eaters and artists of all kinds perform here. In Montmartre there is a tradition of street-painting, predominantly in the Place du Tertre (see p222) where

Model boats for rent in the Jardin du Luxembourg

someone will always be willing to draw your child's portrait. It's also fun to take the funicular up the hill to Sacré-Coeur (see pp224–5), then walk down through the pretty streets.

Parisian markets are color-ful and animated. Try taking children to the Marché aux Fleurs on the Ile de la Cité (see p81) or to the food mar-kets on the Rue Mouffetard, in the Jardin des Plantes Quarter (see p166 and p339), or the Rue de Buci in St-Germain-des-Prés. The biggest flea market, Marché aux Puces de St-Ouen is on weekends in Place Clignan-court (see p231 and p339). Alternatively take children to the quiet Ile de la Cité or Ile St-Louis on the Seine.

VIEWPOINTS AND SIGHTSEEING

Top of the sightseeing list for children is a trip up the Eiffel Tower (see pp192–3). On a clear day spectacular views over Paris will enable you to point out a number of sights, and at night the city is magically lit up. Elevators run until 11pm and lines are much shorter in the evenings. If you are pushing a baby stroller, bear in mind that the ascent is in three stages, using two separate elevators.

Other interesting sights for children include Sacré-Coeur (see pp224–5) with its ovoid dome – the second highest point in Paris after the Eiffel Tower – and Notre-Dame cathedral (see pp82–3) on the Ile de la Cité. Children will enjoy feeding the pigeons in the cathedral square, counting the 28 kings of Judah on the West Front and listening to you recount the story of the hunchback of Notre-Dame. There are incomparable views from the towers. Children and adults alike will appreciate the enchanting Sainte-Chapelle (see pp88–9), also on the Ile de la Cité. There are discounts for children under the age of 17.

Contrast ancient and modern Paris with a visit to the Pom-pidou Centre (see pp110–13) and enjoy a ride on the caterpillar-like escalators outside, or go to the café on the roof terrace for the views. There is also the 56-story Montparnasse Tower (see p178) with some spectacular telescopic views from the top terrace; and there is the huge arch at La Défense (see p255) which has elevators to exhibition platforms where visitors can overlook the whole complex.

OTHER INTERESTS

Children are quick to see the funny side of unusual spectacles. Les Egouts, Paris's sewers, now welcome apprehensive visitors for a

Escalators at the Pompidou Centre

short tour of the city's sewer-age system (see p190). Display boards in several languages explain the processes.

The Catacombs (see p179) are a long series of quarry tunnels built in Roman times, now lined with ancient skulls.

On the Ile de la Cité is the Conciergerie (see p81), a turreted prison where many hapless aristocrats spent their final days. The Grévin wax-works are in Boulevard Mont-martre (see p216). The museum's Revolution rooms will especially appeal to older children, with gruesome scenes and grisly sound effects, demon-strating the reality of social upheaval.

EMERGENCIES

Enfance et Partage is a free 24-hour child helpline (also for adults). One of Paris's largest children's hospitals is **Hôpital Necker**.

Enfance et Partage
Tel 08 00 05 12 34.

Hôpital Necker 149 Rue de Sèvres 75015. **Map** 15 B1. **Tel** 01 44 49 40 00.

A young visitor to Paris

SURVIVAL
GUIDE

PRACTICAL INFORMATION

As with most large cities, it's easy to waste your limited sightseeing time in Paris either in transit or in lines. A little forward planning can minimize this. Call in advance to confirm the sight is open, and isn't closed for refurbishment or holidays – a phonecard, or *télécarte*, is a wise investment *(see p372)*. Purchase a *carnet* or travel pass to economize and simplify transportation on the buses and metro *(see pp384–7)*. Buying a *Paris Carte-Musées-Monuments* will give unlimited access to museums and monuments, and cuts down on lines. Beware the Paris lunch break (around 1–3pm), as many essential services shut down, as well as some museums. Guided tours are often the best way to see the essential sights before you get your bearings. If you're on a tight budget, admission prices are sometimes lower at certain times of day, or on Sundays; card-carrying students can obtain discounts on some tickets and admissions *(see p374)*.

MUSEUMS AND MONUMENTS

There are 172 museums and monuments open to the public in Paris. Most are open Monday (or Tuesday) to Sunday, and from 10am to 5:40pm. Some offer evening visits. The national museums are closed on Tuesdays, except Versailles and the Musée d'Orsay, which are closed on Mondays. The municipal museums, such as those run by the city of Paris (Ville de Paris) are usually closed on Mondays.

An admission fee is usually charged, or a donation is expected. The entrance fee to national museums is totally waived on the first Sunday of each month. Those under 18 are admitted free and those 18–25 and over 60 pay a reduced rate. The municipal museums, and some other museums, do not charge a fee to see their permanent collections on Sundays. Those under 7 and over 60 are admitted free at all times. To obtain the discounts you will have to provide absolute proof of who you are and how old you are.

Train station sign for information services

The *Paris Carte-Musées-Monuments* gives the bearer unlimited access to 70 museums and monuments for 1, 3 or 5 days, without standing in line – a significant advantage in the Paris high season. The pass can be purchased at any of the city's museums as well as main metro stations, Batobus stops, FNAC ticket counters and at the headquarters of the **Office du Tourisme** or **Paris Convention and Visitors' Bureau**.

OPENING HOURS

This guide lists opening times for each sight individually. Most Paris shops and businesses are open from 9am to 7pm. While many stay open all day, others close for an hour or two from noon or 12:30. Some smaller food shops open earlier, around 7am, and take a longer midday break. Almost all business is closed on Sunday, and many shops close Monday too. Some restaurants close at least one day a week. Many shops close for a month or more during summer. Banks are open from around 9am to 4:30–5:15pm Mon–Fri, 9am–noon Sat. Some close noon–2pm. The day before a public holiday they close at noon.

TOURIST INFORMATION

There is one main tourist office in Paris, near the Tuileries garden, the **Office du Tourisme et des Congrès de Paris**, which provides the latest maps, information and brochures. Its state of the art equipment gives a comprehensive picture of events in the city, and it is well worth a visit, despite summer lines. There are also tourist offices at the Eiffel Tower, the Carrousel du Louvre, at Place du Tertre in Montmartre, at the Gare du Nord and Gare de Lyon, and in the Opéra quarter.

PARIS Convention and Visitors Bureau
Tourist Office logo

ENTERTAINMENT

The main listings magazines in Paris, available at all newsstands, are *Pariscope* and *L'Officiel des Spectacles (see p340)*. Each Wednesday they present full information on the week's current theater, movies and exhibits, as well as on cabarets, dinner clubs and some restaurants.

Paris museum pass, for saving time and money

Paris sightseeing tour bus

FNAC ticket agencies sell for all the entertainment venues, including temporary museum shows. There are FNAC branches throughout Paris. For more information call one of their branches (see p341).

For theater events only, the Kiosque Théâtre sells same-day tickets at 50 per cent discount. The two locations are Place de la Madeleine and the Parvis de la Gare Montparnasse (see p341).

Visitors should be aware that smoking is generally not allowed in theaters or movies.

Kiosque Théâtre ticket kiosk

GUIDED TOURS

Double-decker bus tours with commentaries in English, Italian, Japanese and German are organized by **France Tourisme**, **Cityrama** and **Paris Vision**. The tours begin from the city center and take about two hours. They pass the main sights but do not stop at all of them. Departure times vary. **Les Cars Rouges** runs British double-decker bus tours, stopping at many of the sights in Paris, which allow you to leave the bus at any of the stops and to continue later (ticket valid for 2 days). Monum (Centre des Monuments Nationaux) (see p95) offers guided walking tours.

DISABLED ACCESS

Services for disabled people in Paris are still comparatively limited. Although most sidewalks are contoured to allow wheelchairs an easier passage, many restaurants, hotels, and even museums are poorly equipped. (They may claim otherwise.) However, better facilities are being incorporated into all renovated and new buildings, and the French are usually more than ready to help disabled people who are having difficulty. For up-to-date information on public facilities for the disabled, contact the **Groupement pour l'Insertion des Personnes Handicapées Physiques (GIHP)**.

DISABILITY INFORMATION

Les Compagnons du Voyage
17 Rue Pablo Néruda 92532, Levallois-Perret Cedex.
Tel 01 45 19 15 00.
6:30am–8pm Mon–Fri; 7:30am–6pm Sat; 9:30am–10pm Sun. 7-day escort services on all transportation. Costs vary. **www**.compagnons.com

Association des Paralysés de France
17 Blvd August Blanqui 75013.
Map 17 B5. *Tel* 01 40 78 69 00.
Fax 01 45 89 40 57.
www.apf-asso.com

GIHP
10 Rue Georges de Porto-Riche 75014. *Tel* 01 43 95 66 36.
Fax 01 45 40 40 26.
www.gihpnational.org

DIRECTORY

CITY CENTER TOURIST OFFICES

Office du Tourisme et des Congrès de Paris / Paris Convention and Visitors' Bureau
25 Rue des Pyramides 75001. **Map** 12 E1.
Tel 08 92 68 30 00.
10am–7pm Mon–Sat.
www.parisinfo.com

Carrousel du Louvre
99 Rue de Rivoli 75001.
Map 13 A2.
10am–7pm daily.

Eiffel Tower
Champ de Mars 75007.
Map 10 F3.
11am–6:40pm daily.
Oct–Apr & May.1

Gare de Lyon
20 Blvd Diderot 75012.
Map 18 F1. 8am–6pm Mon–Sat. May.1

Gare du Nord
18 Rue de Dunkerque 75010. **Map** 7 B2.
8am–6pm daily. May.1

Montmartre
21 Place du Tertre 75018.
Map 6 F1.
10am–7pm daily.

Opéra
11 Rue Scribe 75009.
Map 6 D4.
9am–6.30pm Mon–Sat.

FOREIGN FRENCH TOURIST OFFICES

Australia
Level 22, 25 Bligh St, Sydney NSW 2000.
Tel (2) 9255 1788.

Canada
1981 Ave McGill College, Suite 490, Montréal QUE H3A 2W9.
Tel 514 876 9881.

United Kingdom
178 Piccadilly, London WIV OAL. *Tel* (0906) 8244 123 (within UK only).
info@mdlf.co.uk

United States
444 Madison Ave, New York, NY 10022.
Tel (212) 838 7800.

BUS TOUR OPERATORS

Cityrama
4 Place des Pyramides 75001.
Map 12 E1.
Tel 01 44 55 61 00.
www.graylineparis.com

France Tourisme
5 Ave de la Grande Armée 75116.
Map 9 C4.
Tel 01 45 02 88 50.
www.francetourisme.com

Les Cars Rouges
17 Quai de Grenelle 75015.
Map 9 C4.
Tel 01 53 95 39 53.
www.carsrouges.com

Paris Vision
214 Rue de Rivoli 75001.
Map 12 D1.
Tel 01 42 60 30 01.
www.parisvision.com

Personal Security and Health

Paris is as safe or as dangerous as you make it – common sense is usually sufficient to stay out of trouble. If, on the other hand, you are sick during your visit, pharmacists are an excellent source of advice. In France pharmacists can diagnose many health problems and suggest appropriate treatment. For more serious medical help, someone at the emergency numbers below will be able to deal with most inquiries. There are many specialized services available, including a general advice line for English-speakers in crisis, an English-speaking Alcoholics Anonymous group, and a phoneline for psychiatric help.

French pharmacy sign

Emergency button at metro stations

EMERGENCY NUMBERS

SAMU (ambulance)
Tel 15 (toll free).

Police
Tel 17 (toll free).

**Pompiers
(fire department)**
Tel 18 (toll free).

European Emergency Call
Tel 112 (toll free).

**SOS Medecin
(doctor, house calls)**
Tel 01 47 07 77 77.

SOS Dentaire (dentist)
Tel 01 43 37 51 00.

Burn Specialists
Tel 01 58 41 41 41.

**SOS Help (English
language crisis line)**
Tel 01 46 21 46 46.

**SOS Dépression
(for psychiatric help)**
Tel 01 40 47 95 95.

Sexual Disease Center
Tel 01 40 78 26 00.

Family Planning Center
Tel 01 48 88 07 28.

Anti-Poison Center
Tel 01 40 05 48 44.

PERSONAL SECURITY

For a city of over 2 million people, Paris is surprisingly safe. The center of the city in particular has little violent crime. Muggings and brawls do occur, but they are rare compared to many other world capitals. However, try to avoid poorly lit or isolated places. Beware of pickpockets, especially on the metro during the rush hour. Keep all valuables securely concealed, and if you carry a purse or case, never let it out of your sight.

When traveling late at night, it is a good idea, for women especially, to avoid long transfers in metro stations such as Montparnasse and Châtelet-Les Halles. Generally, areas around RER train stations tend to attract groups of youths from outlying areas who come to Paris for entertainment, and

may become unruly. The last runs each night of RER trains to and from outlying areas should also be avoided. In an emergency in the metro, call the station agent by using the yellow telephone marked *Chef de Station* on all metro and RER platforms, or go to the ticket booth at the entrance. Most metro stations also have emergency buttons. Coaches also have alarm pulls. If there is a problem outside stations, or at bus stops, telephone the police by dialing 17.

PERSONAL PROPERTY

Take great care with your personal property at all times. Make sure you insure your possessions before arrival. On sightseeing or enter-tainment trips do not carry valuables with you. Also, only take as much cash as you think you will need. Traveler's checks are the

Paris fireman   Policewoman   Policeman

Typical Paris police car

Paris fire engine

Paris ambulance

safest method of carrying large sums of money. You should never leave your luggage unattended in metro or train stations – it may be stolen. For missing persons, or in the case of robbery or assault, call the police or go to the nearest police station *(Commissariat de Police)*. For lost or stolen passports call your consulate *(see p375)*.

MEDICAL TREATMENT

All European Union nationals are entitled to French Social Security coverage. However, treatment must be paid for, and hospital rates vary widely. Reimbursements may be obtained if you are carrying Form E111 (available free to EU citizens), but the process is long and involved. All travelers should consider purchasing travel insurance, and obtain a Form E111 in case of emergencies. Non-EU

nationals must carry their own medical insurance.

In the case of a medical emergency, call **SAMU** *(see box on facing page)* or the **Pompiers** (fire department). Fire department ambulances are often the quickest to arrive at an emergency. In addition, first-aid and emergency treatment is provided at all fire stations.

Hospitals with emergency departments are shown on the Street Finder *(see p390)*. For English-language visitors, there are two hospitals with English-speaking staff and doctors: the **American Hospital** and the **British Hospital**.

There are many pharmacies throughout the city, and a short list is provided here. Pharmacies are recognized by the green crosses on the shop front. At night and on Sundays, pharmacies hang in their doorway the address of the nearest one open.

Banking and Local Currency

Visitors to Paris will find that the banks usually offer them the best rates of exchange. Privately owned bureaux de change, on the other hand, have variable rates, and care should be taken to check small print details relating to commission and minimum charges before any transaction is completed.

BANKING

There is no restriction on the amount of money or currency you may bring into France. It is wise to carry large sums in the form of travelers' checks. To exchange travelers' checks or cash, bureaux de change are located at airports, large railroad stations, and in some hotels and shops.

Many bank branches in central Paris have their own bureaux de change. They generally offer the best exchange rates but also charge a commission for doing the exchange.

Many independent, non-bank exchange offices do not charge commission, but they offer poorer rates of exchange. Central Paris non-bank exchanges are usually open 9am–6pm Mon–Sat, and are found along the Champs-Elysées, around the Opéra and Madeleine, and near some tourist attractions and monuments. They can also be found at all main railroad stations, open 8am–9pm daily. Note that the bureaux located at Gare St-Lazare and Gare d'Austerlitz are closed on Sunday. Airport offices are open 7am–11pm daily.

Sign at bureau de change

CARDS AND CHECKS

Travelers' checks can be obtained from **American Express, Travelex** or from your bank. If you know that you will spend most of them, it is best to have them issued in euros. American Express

checks are widely accepted in France and, if the checks are exchanged at an Amex office, no commission will be charged. In the case of theft, your checks will be replaced at once.

Because of the high commissions charged, many French businesses do not accept the American Express credit card. The most commonly used credit card is Carte Bleue/Visa. Eurocard/Mastercard is also widely accepted.

French ATM

French credit cards are now "smart cards", with a *puce* (a microchip capable of storing data) instead of a magnetic strip on the back. Many retailers have machines designed to read both smart cards and magnetic strips. Conventional non-French cards cannot be read in the smart card slot. Ask the cashier to swipe the card through the magnetic reader *(bande magnétique)*. You may also be asked to type in your PIN code *(code confidentiel)* and press the green key *(validez)* on a small keypad by the cash desk.

CONVERSION CHART

The following is a rough guide to equivalent currency values, rounded up or down for ease of use.

Euros	Francs
1	6.5
5	33
20	130
50	330
100	650

DIRECTORY

AFTER-HOURS BUREAUX DE CHANGE

Ancienne Comédie
5 Rue Ancienne-Comédie 75006.
Map 12 F4.
Tel 01 43 26 33 30.
9am–10pm daily.

CCF
103 Ave des Champs-Elysées 75008.
Map 4 E4.
Tel 01 40 70 27 22.
8:45am–7pm Mon–Fri, 10am–6:30pm Sat (Nov–end Apr);
8:45am–8pm Mon–Fri, 9:30am–6:30pm Sat (May–end Oct).

Global Change
134 Blvd St-Germain 75006.
Map 12 F4.
Tel 01 40 46 87 75.
9am–10:30pm daily.

Europullman
10 Rue Alger 75001.
Map 12 D1.
Tel 01 42 60 55 58.
9am–7pm Mon–Sat.

FOREIGN BANKS

American Express
11 Rue Scribe 75009.
Map 6 D5.
Tel 01 47 14 50 00.

Barclays
45 Blvd Haussman 75009.
Map 6 F4.
Tel 01 55 27 55 27.
One of several branches.

HSBC
20 Place Vendôme 75001.
Map 6 D5.
Tel 01 44 86 18 61.

Travelex
8 Place de l'Opéra 75009.
Tel 01 47 42 46 52.

LOST CARDS AND TRAVELERS' CHECKS

American Express
Tel 01 47 77 70 00 Cards.
Tel 08 00 90 86 00 Checks.

Mastercard
Tel 01 45 67 53 53 Cards.

Visa/Carte Bleue
Tel 08 92 70 57 05 Cards.

THE EURO

The euro (€), the single European currency, is now operational in 12 of the 25 member states of the EU. Austria, Belgium, Finland, France, Germany, Greece, Ireland, Italy, Luxembourg, Netherlands, Portugal and Spain all chose to join the new currency; Denmark, the UK and Sweden chose to stay out, with an option to review their decision. France's Overseas Departments (Réunion etc) also all now use the euro.

Euro bills are identical throughout all 12 countries, bearing architectural drawings of fictitious monuments. The coins, however, have one side identical (the value side), and one side unique to each country. Both bills and coins are valid and interchangeable within each of the 12 countries.

Bills

Euro bills have seven denominations. The 5€ bill (gray in color) is the smallest, followed by the 10€ bill (pink), 20€ bill (blue), 50€ bill (orange), 100€ bill (green), 200€ bill (yellow) and 500€ bill (purple). All bills show the stars of the European Union.

5 euros

10 euros

20 euros

50 euros

100 euros

200 euros

500 euros

2 euros

1 euro

50 cents

20 cents

10 cents

Coins

The euro has eight coin denominations: 1€ and 2€; 50 cents, 20 cents, 10 cents, 5 cents, 2 cents and 1 cent. The 1€ and 2€ coins are both silver and gold in color. The 50-, 20- and 10-cent coins are gold. The 5-, 2- and 1-cent coins are bronze.

5 cents

2 cents

1 cent

Telephone and Postal Service

The French telecommunications agency is called France Télécom, the postal service is La Poste. Both work efficiently, though customer service at post offices may not be great. So, be prepared to wait in lines. There are many *bureaux des postes* scattered throughout the city. These are identified by the blue-on-yellow La Poste sign *(see p373)*. Public telephones are located in most public places, including on the streets and in railroad and metro stations. If you are dialing abroad from Paris, the best way is to purchase a telephone card *(télécarte)*, then find a quiet location to call from.

Telephone Booths
Coin-operated telephone booths are now rare. Card-operated telephones are cheap and easy to use, but you must buy a télécarte first.

Modern, card-operated phonebox

Older-style phonebox

USING A PHONECARD (TELECARTE) TELEPHONE

1 Lift the receiver and wait for a dial tone.

2 Holding the *télécarte* with the arrow side up, insert it into the slot in the direction that the arrow is pointing.

3 Wait for the display screen to indicate how many units are stored on the card. The screen will then tell you to dial.

4 Dial the number and wait to be connected.

5 If you want to make another call do not replace the receiver, simply press the green follow-on call button.

6 When you have finished the call, replace the receiver. The card will emerge from the slot. Remove it.

FRANCE TELECOM
600 AGENCES
PARTOUT
EN FRANCE
TELECARTE 50

Télécarte phonecard

USING THE TELEPHONE

Most French telephones have push-buttons, but some older dial telephones are still found in cafés and restaurants. Telephone directories *(annuaires)* are found in post offices, cafés and restaurants, but not usually in telephone booths *(cabines)*.

To use a Paris payphone, you generally need a phone card *(télécarte)*. Sold in *tabacs*, post offices and some news-stands, these are available in 50 or 120 telephone units, and are simple to use. Remember to buy a new card before the old one runs out! Coin telephones have virtually disappeared from the streets of Paris. They can still be found in cafés but they are reserved for the use of customers. Collect calls are known as *PCV* in France. Most telephone booths can be called from anywhere. The phone booth number is displayed above the telephone unit.

All French telephone numbers have ten digits. The first two digits indicate the region: 01 indicates Paris and the Ile de France; 02, the northwest; 03, the northeast; 04, the southeast; and 05, the southwest. Do not dial the initial zero when phoning from abroad.

Most new cell phones brought from another European or Mediterranean country can be used in France. Alert your network ahead of time that you plan to use the phone abroad so that they can enable it. However, US-based mobiles need to be "triple band" to be used in France. Remember that the making and receiving of international cell phone calls can be very expensive.

REACHING THE RIGHT NUMBER

- **In the case of emergencies,** dial 17.

- **Directory assistance** dial 12.

- **International directory assistance**, for all countries, dial 32 12.

- **International telegrams** dial 0800 33 44 11.

- **Home Direct** (collect calls), dial 0800 99, then the country code (preceded by 00).

- To make direct international calls, dial 00, wait for the tone, then dial the country code, area code (omit the intital 0) and the number.

- The country codes for the following are: **Australia**: 61; **Canada and USA**: 1; **Ireland (Eire)**: 353; **New Zealand**: 64; **UK**: 44.

- **Low-rate period** (for most places): 7pm–8am Mon–Fri, all day Sun and public holidays.

- The middle pages of the telephone directory give the cost of calls per minute for each country and list their country codes, Home Direct codes, etc.

- To telephone **France** from your home country, dial: from the UK 00 33; from the US 011 33; from Australia: 00 11 33. Omit the first 0 of the French area code.

Mail and Postal Services – Using La Poste

Post office sign

In addition to all normal services – telegrams, postage stamps, registered letters, special delivery, delivery of packages and books – the post office also sells collectors' stamps, and will cash or send international money orders. Fax and telex services, as well as public telephones and Minitel, are available in all main offices.

SENDING A LETTER

Common postage stamps *(timbres)* are sold singly or in *carnets* of ten. These are valid for letters and postcards up to 20 g (approximately an ounce) to most EU countries. Stamps can often be bought in *tabacs*. Paris post office hours are 8am–7pm (or 8pm) Mon–Fri, 8am–noon Sat. At post offices you can consult the phonebook *(annuaire)*, buy phonecards *(télécartes)*, send or receive money orders *(mandats)* and call anywhere in the world.

Letters are dropped into yellow mailboxes.

For poste restante (mail holding), the sender should write the recipient's name in block letters, then "Poste Restante", then the address of the Paris-Louvre post office.

Paris Arrondissements

The districts or arrondissements of Paris are numbered from 1 to 20 (see p390). The first three numbers of the postal code – 750 (or 751) – indicate Paris; the last two give the arrondissement number. The first arrondissement's postal code is 75001.

When sending a letter poste restante, it is wise to underline the last name, as French officials otherwise sometimes assume the first name listed is the family name.

MAIN POST OFFICES

Paris-Louvre
52 Rue de Louvre 75001. **Map** 12 F1. *Tel* 01 40 28 76 00. *Fax* 01 45 08 12 82. ◯ 24 hrs daily.

Paris-Forum des Halles
Forum des Halles 75001. **Map** 13 A2. *Tel* 01 44 76 84 60. ◯ 8am–6pm Mon–Fri, 8am–noon Sat.

Paris-Champs Elysées
71 Ave des Champs Elysées 75008. **Map** 4 F5. *Tel* 01 53 89 05 80. *Fax* 01 42 56 13 71. ◯ 9am–7:30pm Mon–Fri, 10am–7pm Sat.

Destinations

Paris mailbox

CUSTOMS AND IMMIGRATION

For travelers coming from within the EU's "Schengen" zone (ie. those that agreed to the Schengen Treaty), no documentation at all is needed to enter France. For "non-Schengen" nationals, including the UK, a passport (or similar) is required. Visitors from the US, Canada, Australia and New Zealand do not currently need a visa if staying under 3 months. However, for a trip over 3 months, a visa must be applied for from the French consulate in the visitor's own country before leaving. It is always advisable to double-check visa requirements as these can be subject to change at any time.

TAX-FREE GOODS

The purchase of goods "duty free" for export to another EU country is no longer possible. Visitors resident outside the European Union can reclaim the sales tax (TVA, or VAT; *see p320*) they pay on French goods if they spend more than 175 in the same shop in one day and take the goods

out of France. *Détaxe* receipts can be issued on purchase to reclaim the tax paid, and reimbursements are collected when exiting the EU, which must be within 3 months of purchase. There are some goods you cannot claim a rebate on, namely food and drink, medicines, tobacco, cars and motorcycles.

DUTY-PAID AND DUTY-FREE GOODS

There are no longer any restrictions on the quantities of duty-paid and VAT-paid goods you can take from one EU country to another, as long as they are for your own use and not for resale.

Bottle of scent

You may be asked to prove the goods are for your own use if they exceed the EU suggested quantities. If you cannot do so, the entire amount of the goods (not just the deemed excess) may be confiscated and destroyed. The suggested limits are: 10 liters of spirits (i.e. drinks over 22° proof), 90 liters of wine, 110 liters of beer and 800 cigarettes. Some dangerous goods are illegal. Visitors under the age of 17 are not allowed to import duty-paid tobacco or alcohol.

IMPORTING OTHER GOODS

In general, all personal goods (eg. car or bicycle) may be imported to France if they are obviously for personal use and not for sale. The brochure *Voyagez en toute liberté* clarifies this. It is available from customs (below), which also gives advice on import regulations (usually in French).

CUSTOMS INFORMATION

Centre des Renseignements des Douanes
84 rue d'Hauteville 75010.
Tel 08 25 30 82 63. *Fax* 01 53 24 68 30. ⬛ 9am–5:30pm Mon–Fri.
www.douane.gouv.fr

ELECTRICAL ADAPTORS

The voltage in France is 220 volts. Plugs have two small round pins; heavier-duty installations have two large round pins. Better hotels offer built-in adaptors for razors only. Adaptors can be bought at department stores, such as BHV *(see p321).*

French two-pin electrical plug

STUDENT INFORMATION

Students with valid ID cards benefit from discounts of 25–50 percent at theaters, museums, movies and many public monuments. An ISIC card (the International Student ID card) may be purchased from main travel agencies, Office de Tourisme de l'Université offices (**OTU**) and the Centre d'Information et de Documentation Jeunesse (**CIDJ**). CIDJ provides information on student life in Paris and can furnish a list of inexpensive accommodation, including the Bureau Voyage Jeunesse (**BVJ**), which has 2 hostels in central Paris with double rooms and dormitory accommodation at reasonable prices *(see pp279-80 and 375).*

PUBLIC TOILETS IN PARIS

Most old-fashioned urinals and toilets have been replaced by modern pay toilets. They are found on sidewalks all over the city. In some units, classical music is played. It is crucial that children under 10 are not allowed into these toilets on their own. They have an automatic cleaning function which can be a danger to small children.

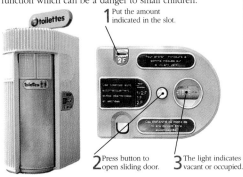

1 Put the amount indicated in the slot.

2 Press button to open sliding door.

3 The light indicates vacant or occupied.

INTERNATIONAL BOOKSHOPS

Brentano's
37 Ave de l'Opéra 75002.
Map 6 E5. **Tel** *01 42 61 52 50.*
🕐 *10am–7:30pm Mon–Sat.*

Gibert Jeune
5 Place St-Michel 75005.
Map 13 A4. **Tel** *01 56 81 22 22.*
🕐 *9:30am–7:30pm Mon–Sat.*

W H Smith
248 Rue de Rivoli 75001. **Map** 11 C1.
Tel *01 44 77 88 99.* 🕐 *9am–7:30pm
Mon–Sat; 1–7pm Sun.*

TV, RADIO, PRESS

Some American and British
papers can be bought on the
day of publication at *maisons*

Foreign newspapers from kiosks

de la presse or *kiosques*
(newsstands) throughout the
city. Some of these are
European or international
editions, such as *USA Today,
The Sun, Financial Times
Europe* and the *Guardian
International, The Weekly
Telegraph, The Economist,* and
*The International Herald
Tribune.*

The main French national
dailies are – from right to left
on the political spectrum – *Le
Figaro, France Soir, Le Monde,
Libération* and *L'Humanité.*
The weeklies include satirical
Le Canard Enchaîné, news
magazines *Marianne, Le
Nouvel Observateur* and
L'Express, and numerous titles
devoted to fashion, gossip and
gastronomy.

The French TV channels are
TF1 and *France 2,* both with a
lightweight mix, *France 3,*
with documentaries, debate
and classic movies, *5e* ("La
Cinquième") and the Franco-
German high-culture *ARTE,*
which share a channel specializing in arts, classical music
and films, and *M6* which
devotes a lot of time to pop
and rock. Cable and satellite
channels include CNN, Sky
and a variety of BBC channels.

BBC Radio 4 can be picked
up during the day, while at

night *BBC World Service* uses
the same channel (648AM or
198 Long Wave). *Radio France
International* (738AM) gives
excellent daily news in English
on their web site www.rfi.fr.

PARIS TIME

Paris is one hour ahead of
Greenwich Mean Time
(GMT) all year long. The
French use the 24-hour
clock, therefore, 9am is
09.00, 9pm is 21.00. New
York is some 6 hours behind
Paris, Los Angeles 9 hours
behind and Auckland 11
hours ahead.

CONVERSION CHART

Imperial to metric
1 inch = 2.54 centimeters
1 foot = 30 centimeters
1 mile = 1.6 kilometers
1 ounce = 28 grams
1 pound = 454 grams
1 pint = 0.48 liter
1 gallon = 4.6 liters

Metric to imperial
1 millimeter = 0.04 inch
1 centimeter = 0.4 inch
1 meter = 3 feet 3 inches
1 kilometer = 0.6 mile
1 gram = 0.04 ounce
1 kilogram = 2.2 pounds
1 liter = 2.1 pints

DIRECTORY

STUDENT INFO

OTU Voyages
119 Rue St-Martin 75004.
Map 13 B2.

1 Pl du M.al de Lattre de
Tassigny 75016.
Map 3 A4.

39 Ave Georges Bernanos
75005. **Map** 16 F2.
Tel *0820 817 817 (all 3).*

CIDJ
101 Quai Branly 75015.
Map 10 E2. **Tel** *01 44 49
13 40.* 🕐 *9:30am–6pm
Mon–Fri (7pm Tue & Thu),
9:30am–1pm Sat.*

BVJ
20 Rue Jean-Jacques
Rousseau 75001. **Map** 12
F2. **Tel** *01 53 00 90 90.*

44 Rue des Bernardins
75005. **Map** 13 B5.
Tel *01 43 29 34 80.*

EMBASSIES

Australia
4 Rue Jean Rey 75015.
Map 10 D3.
Tel *01 40 59 33 00.*

Canada
35 Ave Montaigne 75008.
Map 10 F1.
Tel *01 44 43 29 00.*

Great Britain
35 Rue du Faubourg St-
Honoré 75008.
Map 5 C5.

Consulate (visas) 18bis
Rue d'Anjou 75008.
Tel *01 44 51 31 00.*

Ireland (Eire)
12 Ave Foch 75016. **Map**
3 B4. **Tel** *01 44 17 67 00.*

New Zealand
7 ter, Rue Léonard de Vinci
75116. **Map** 3 C5.
Tel *01 45 01 43 43.*

USA
2 Ave Gabriel 75008.
Map 5 B5.
Tel *01 43 12 22 22.*

RELIGIOUS SERVICES

PROTESTANT

American Church
65 Quai d'Orsay 75007.
Map 10 F2.
Tel *01 40 62 05 00.*

Church of Scotland
17 Rue Bayard 75008.
Map 10 F1.
Tel/Fax *01 48 78 47 94.*

St George's Anglican Church
7 Rue Auguste Vacquerie
75116. **Map** 4 E5.
Tel *01 47 20 22 51.*

CATHOLIC

Basilique du Sacré-Coeur
35 Rue du Chevalier de la
Barre 75018.
Map 6 F1.
Tel *01 53 41 89 00.*

Cathédrale de Notre-Dame
Pl du Parvis Notre-Dame
75004. **Map** 13 A4.
Tel *01 42 34 56 10.*

JEWISH

Synagogue Nazareth
15 Rue Notre Dame de
Nazareth 75003. **Map**
7 C5. **Tel** *01 42 78 00 30.*

MUSLIM

Grande Mosquée de Paris
Place du Puits de l'Ermite
75005. **Map** 17 B2.
Tel *01 45 35 97 33.*

GETTING TO PARIS

Paris is a major hub of European air, road and rail travel. Direct flights from around the world serve the French capital's two main international airports. Paris is also at the center of Europe's growing high-speed rail network, with arrivals throughout the day of Eurostar from London, Thalys from Brussels, Amsterdam and Cologne, and TGVs from Marseille and Geneva. Approaching by road, *autoroutes* (highways) converge on Paris from all directions, including – via Eurotunnel's Channel rail shuttle – the UK.

Boeing 737 passenger jet

ARRIVING BY AIR

The main British airlines with regular flights to Paris are **British Airways** and **British Midland**. The main French airline is **Air France**. From the United States there are regular flights direct to Paris mainly on **American, United, Northwest, Continental, Delta, Virgin** and **British Airlines**. From Canada, **Air France** and **Air Canada** fly direct to Paris. **Qantas** is one of the few providing connecting flights from Australia and New Zealand.

High airport charges have generally deterred Europe's no-frills low-cost airlines from flying to Paris, though **Easyjet** does offer a very inexpensive London-Paris CDG service.

Ryanair flies from Dublin and Glasgow (Prestwick) to Beauvais, an hour or more's bus journey west of Paris. For airline offices in Paris, see page 379.

The peak summer season in Paris is from July to September. Airline fares are at their highest during this time. Different airlines, however, may have slightly different high summer season periods, so check with the airlines or an agent as to which months are covered by these fares.

If you are prepared to look around for the best deals, there are very good ones on offer from reputable discount agents. If you book a cheap deal with a discount agent, check whether you will get a refund if the agent or operator goes out of business, and do not part with the full fare until you actually see the ticket.

Addresses of reputable discount agencies in Paris are listed on page 379. These offer charters and regular scheduled flights at competitive prices. Many of them have representatives in other countries. Note that children can travel more cheaply than adults.

Flight Times
Here are some flight times to Paris from cities in different parts of the world: London 1 hour; Dublin 90 minutes; Montreal 7.5 hours; New York 8 hours; Los Angeles 12 hours; Sydney 23 hours.

CHARLES DE GAULLE AIRPORT

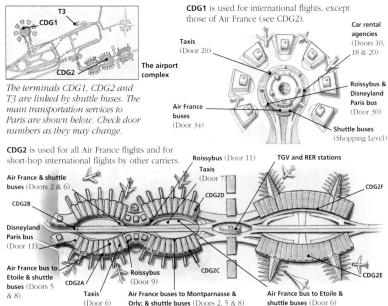

T3
CDG1
CDG2

The terminals CDG1, CDG2 and T3 are linked by shuttle buses. The main transportation services to Paris are shown below. Check door numbers as they may change.

CDG1 is used for international flights, except those of Air France (see CDG2).

Taxis (Door 20)

Car rental agencies (Doors 10, 18 & 20)

The airport complex

Roissybus & Disneyland Paris bus (Door 30)

Air France buses (Door 34)

Shuttle buses (Shopping Level)

CDG2 is used for all Air France flights and for short-hop international flights by other carriers.

Air France & shuttle buses (Doors 2 & 6)

CDG2B

Disneyland Paris bus (Door 11)

Air France bus to Etoile & shuttle buses (Doors 5 & 8)

CDG2A

Taxis (Door 6)

Roissybus (Door 9)

Air France buses to Montparnasse & Orly; & shuttle buses (Doors 2, 5 & 8)

CDG2C

Roissybus (Door 11)

Taxis (Door 7)

CDG2D

TGV and RER stations

CDG2F

CDG2E

Air France bus to Etoile & shuttle buses (Door 6)

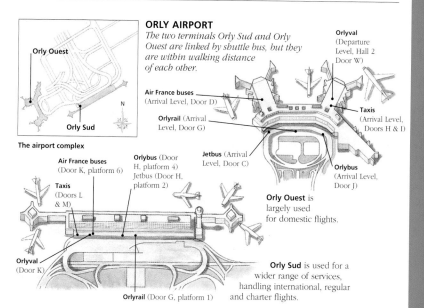

ORLY AIRPORT

The two terminals Orly Sud and Orly Ouest are linked by shuttle bus, but they are within walking distance of each other.

Orly Ouest

Orlyval (Departure Level, Hall 2 Door W)

Air France buses (Arrival Level, Door D)

Orlyrail (Arrival Level, Door G)

Taxis (Arrival Level, Doors H & I)

The airport complex

Orly Sud

N

Air France buses (Door K, platform 6)

Orlybus (Door H, platform 4) Jetbus (Door H, platform 2)

Jetbus (Arrival Level, Door C)

Orlybus (Arrival Level, Door J)

Taxis (Doors L & M)

Orly Ouest is largely used for domestic flights.

Orlyval (Door K)

Orly Sud is used for a wider range of services, handling international, regular and charter flights.

Orlyrail (Door G, platform 1)

CHARLES DE GAULLE (CDG) AIRPORT

This is Paris's main airport, lying 19 miles (30 km) north of the city. It has two main terminals, CDG1 and CDG2, and a charter flight terminal, T3. CDG2 straddles the TGV-RER station and comprises six linked halls, referred to as CDG2A, CDG2B, CDG2C, CDG2D, CDG2E and CDG2F.

Getting into Town

Buses, trains and taxis all run to central Paris. Air France operates two services: one to Porte Maillot and Charles de Gaulle-Etoile, which leaves about every 12 minutes and takes about 40 minutes; the other goes to the Gare de Lyon and Montparnasse TGV train station, leaving every 30 minutes and taking about 50 minutes. The Roissybus service, run by the RATP, takes travelers to Opéra. This journey takes about 50 minutes and the buses leave every 15 minutes, between 5:45am and 11pm. All three services connect up in central Paris with the metro, the RER and the RATP bus network.
Disneyland Resort Paris runs a bus service (8:30am–7:45pm) every 30-45 minutes from both of the Charles de Gaulle terminals.

The TGV station is in CDG2, and there are RER train stations (Line B) at CDG1 and CDG2. Trains leave every 5–15 minutes and take about 35 minutes to reach the city center, at the Gare du Nord, where there is a link to the metro and to other RER lines.
Airport Shuttle provides door to door service in a small mini-bus for both airports, for 22€ for one person, or 14€ each for two or more (must reserve at least 48 hours ahead). Normal taxis to the center run between 36€ (daytime) and 45€, often with long waits.

ORLY AIRPORT (ORY)

This is Paris's second airport, which is located 9 miles (15 km) south of the capital. It has two terminals, Orly Sud and Orly Ouest.

Getting into Town

Transportation services take travellers to the southern part of the city and a special bus links the airport with Disney-land Resort Paris, leaving every 45 minutes.
Travelers arriving at Orly can take a taxi, bus or train to central Paris. The bus services are run by Air France and RATP (Orlybus). Air France buses take about 30 minutes to reach the city center,

stopping at Les Invalides and Gare de Montparnasse. The Orlybus, also leaving every 12–20 minutes, takes about 25 minutes to reach the city center at Denfert-Rochereau. The Jet Bus service takes travelers from the airport to Villejuif-Louis Aragon metro station every 15–20 minutes.
A bus (confusingly called Orlyrail) links the airport with RER Line C at Pont de Rungis, from where trains leave every 15 minutes (half hour after 9pm), taking 25 minutes to reach the Gare d'Austerlitz. An automatic train, Orlyval, links the airport with RER Line B at Antony station, from where trains leave every 4–8 minutes for Châtelet in central Paris (35-minute total journey).
Taxis to the city center take 25–45 minutes, depending on the traffic, and cost 20€–30€.

Orlyval train leaving Orly Airport

CROSSING THE CHANNEL

Travelers coming to Paris from Britain by road will need to cross the English Channel. The simplest and most popular way is on the vehicle-carrying train shuttles through the Channel Tunnel. Operated by **Eurotunnel**, these run between the terminals at Folkestone and Calais. You are directed onto the trains and remain with your vehicle, though you may get out of your car and walk around inside the train. The journey through the tunnel takes about 30 minutes, is unaffected by sea conditions or weather, and trains depart every 15-30 minutes, depending on demand. On both the English and the French side, the tunnel terminal has direct motorway access.

There are also several ship or catamaran car ferries across the Channel. On the short Dover-Calais route, there are up to 100 crosssings per day, operated by several operators running frequent, fast services. **Stena Line** ships make this crossing in 75 minutes, **SeaFrance** takes 90 minutes, while **Hoverspeed**'s Seacat catamarans cross in just 45 minutes. Hoverspeed's Super Seacat does the crossing between Newhaven and Dieppe in 2 hours. **Transmanche Ferries**, part of Corsica Ferries, also run this route, but take nearly 4 hours. **Norfolkline** has a 2-hour Dover to Dunkerque crossing.

Two companies ply the longer western routes across the Channel. **Brittany Ferries** crossings from Plymouth to Roscoff take 6 hours, and from Poole to Cherbourg they take $4^{1/4}$ hours on conventional ferry, or $2^{1/4}$ hours on the Condor Vitesse (fast ferry). From Portsmouth, Brittany take 6 hours to Caen, and $8^{3/4}$ hours overnight to St-Malo, while **P&O Portsmouth** takes $5^{1/2}$ hours to Le Havre, and 5 hours to Cherbourg, or $2^{1/2}$ hours on the Portsmouth Express. Driving to Paris from Cherbourg takes 4–5 hours; from Dieppe or Le Havre, about $2^{1/2}$–3 hours; from Calais, 2 hours.

ARRIVING BY BUS

The main bus operator to Paris is **Eurolines**, based at the Gare Routière Internationale in eastern Paris. Its buses travel to Belgium, Holland, Ireland, Germany, Scandinavia, United Kingdom, Italy and Portugal.

Their terminus in London is Victoria Coach Station, from where there are between three and five daily departures for Paris, depending on the season. The journey from London to Paris takes between 8 and 9 hours.

A long-haul bus

USEFUL CONTACTS

Eurostar
London Waterloo International.
Tel 08705-186 186.
www.eurostar.com

Eurotunnel
www.eurotunnel.com

Brittany Ferries
www.britannyferries.com

Hoverspeed/Seacat
www.hoverspeed.co.uk

Norfolkline
www.norfolkline.co.uk

P&O Portsmouth
www.poferries.com

Stena Line
www.stenaline.co.uk

SeaFrance
www.seafrance.com

Transmanche Ferries
www.transmancheferries.com

Eurolines
Ave de Général de Gaulle, Bagnolet.
Tel 08 92 89 90 91.
Victoria Coach station, London SW1.
Tel 08705-143 219.
www.eurolines.com

ARRIVING BY RAIL

Eurostar trains travel directly from central London (Waterloo) to central Paris (Gare du Nord) in 2 hours and 35 minutes. There are up to 24 departures daily. Other high-speed services into Paris

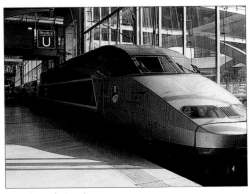

The high-speed TGV train

THE TGV

Trains à Grande Vitesse, or TGV high-speed trains, travel at speeds up to 186mph (300 km/h). TGVs for northern France leave from the Gare du Nord for the Atlantic Coast and Brittany from Gare Montparnasse, and for Provence and the southeast from Gare de Lyon. The network serves a large number of stations on routes to these destinations, and the number of stations served is growing all the time, making this an ever-more convenient form of transportation (see pp380–81).

include **Thalys**, from Brussels, Amsterdam and Cologne, and **TGVs** from throughout France. These services must be pre-purchased, though reservations can be made up to the last moment. Prices are much cheaper reserved ahead.

As the railroad hub of France and the continent, Paris has five major international railroad stations operated by the French state railroads, known as SNCF (*see p388*). The Gare de Lyon in eastern Paris is the city's main station, serving the south of France, the Alps, Italy, Switzerland and Greece. The Gare de l'Est serves eastern France, Austria, Switzerland and Germany.

Arriving at the Gare du Nord are trains from Holland, Belgium and Scandinavia. Trains from some Channel ports arrive at the Gare St-Lazare. The terminus for trains from Spain, as well as from the Brittany ports, is the Gare Montparnasse. The other main stations are: Massy-Palaiseau (SW of city); Marne-la-Vallée for Disneyland Resort Paris (E); Aeroport Charles-de-Gaulle (NE).

There is a tourist office at the Gare de Lyon where you can reserve accommodation (*see p367*). All the railroad stations are served by buses, the metro and RER trains. Directional signs show where to make connections to the city transportation system.

ARRIVING BY CAR

Paris is an oval-shaped city. It is surrounded by an outer beltway called the Boulevard Périphérique. All highways leading to the capital link in to the Périphérique, which separates the city from the suburbs. Each former city gate, called a *porte,* now corresponds to an exit from (or entrance to) the Périphérique. Arriving drivers should check their destination address and consult a map of central Paris to find the closest corresponding *porte.* For example, a driver who wants to get to the Arc de Triomphe should exit at Porte Maillot.

DIRECTORY

MAIN AIRLINES SERVING PARIS

Aer Lingus
52 Rue Belle Feuille 92100 Boulogne-Billancourt.
Tel 01 70 20 00 72.
www.aerlingus.com

Air Canada
106 Blvd Haussmann 75008. **Map** 6 D4.
Tel 0825 880 881.
www.aircanada.ca

Air France
30 Ave Léon Gaumont 75985.
Tel 0820 820 820.
www.airfrance.com

American Airlines
Charles de Gaulle airport
Tel 0810 872 872.
www.aa.com

British Airways
13–15 Blvd de la Madeleine 75001.
Map 6 D5.
Tel 0825 825 400.
www.ba.com

British Midland
18 Blvd Malesherbes, 75008. **Map** 5 B3.
Tel 01 41 91 87 04.
www.flybmi.com

Delta Airlines
119 Ave de Champs-Elysées 75008. **Map** 4 E4.
Tel 0800 354 080.
www.delta.com

Easyjet
Tel 08 25 08 25 08.
www.easyjet.com

Qantas Airways
13–15 Blvd de la Madeleine 75001. **Map** 6 D5. *Tel* 0820 820 500.
www.qantas.com

Ryanair
Tel 0892 555 666 (France).
www.ryanair.com

DISCOUNT TRAVEL AGENCIES

Directours
90 Ave des Champs-Elysées 75008. **Map** 4 E4.
Tel 01 45 62 62 62.
www.directours.com

Forum Voyages
1 Rue Cassette 75006.
Map 12 D5.
Tel 01 45 44 38 61.
www.forumvoyages.com

Jet Tours
29 Ave de la Motte Picquet 75007. **Map** 10 F4.
Tel 01 47 05 01 95.
www.jettours.com

Nouvelles Frontières
109 Rue du Fbg St Honoré 75008. **Map** 4 E3.
Tel 08 25 00 07 47.
www.nouvelles-frontieres.fr

USIT Voyages
85 Blvd St-Michel 75005.
Tel 08 25 08 25 25.

52 Grosvenor Gardens London SW1W 0AG.
Tel 020 7730 7285.
www.usitconnections.fr

AIRPORT INFORMATION

www.adp.fr

Information/paging
Tel 01 48 62 22 80 (CDG).
Tel 01 49 75 15 15 (Orly).
Tel 0892 681 515 (CDG & Orly: same day flight info).

Disabled Assistance
To order free guide *Guide Passager à mobilité réduite:*
Tel 01 49 75 06 92.
@ dccmp3@adp.fr

Air France Buses
Tel 0892 350 820.

RATP (Roissybus/ Orlybus)
Tel 08 92 68 77 14 (French) or 08 92 68 41 14 (English).
www.ratp.fr

RER Trains
Tel 01 53 90 20 20.

TGV
Tel 08 92 35 35 35.

SNCF
Tel 01 53 90 20 20.
www.sncf.com

Airport Shuttle
Tel 01 30 11 11 90 or 1 888 426 2705 (from US).
www.airportshuttle.fr

CDG Airport Hotels

Ibis
Tel 01 49 19 19 20.
@ H1404@accor-hotels.com
www.accorhotels.com

Holiday Inn
Tel 01 34 29 30 00.
@ hiroissy@alliance-hospitality.com

Novotel
Tel 01 49 19 27 27.
@ H1014@accor-hotels.com
www.accorhotels.com

Sofitel
Tel 01 49 19 29 29.
@ H0577@accor-hotels.com

ORLY SUD AIRPORT HOTELS

Ibis
Tel 01 56 70 50 50.
@ H1413@accor-hotels.com

Hilton Hotel
Tel 01 45 12 45 12.
@ oryhitwRM @hilton.com. www.hilton.com

Mercure
Tel 01 49 75 15 50.
@ H1246@accor-hotels.com
www.accorhotels.com

Arriving in Paris

This map depicts the bus and rail services between the two main airports and the city. It shows the ferry-rail links from the UK, the main railroad links from other parts of France and Europe, and the long-haul bus services from other European countries. It also shows the main city railroad and coach terminals, the airport shuttle connections and the airport bus and rail stops. The frequency of services and journey times from the airport are provided, as are the approximate times of rail journeys from other cities. Metro and RER line connections to other parts of Paris are indicated at the terminals and route stops.

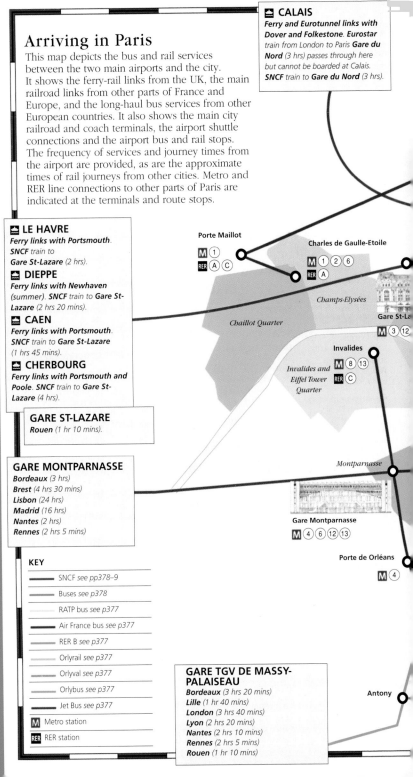

CALAIS
Ferry and Eurotunnel links with Dover and Folkestone. Eurostar train from London to Paris **Gare du Nord** *(3 hrs) passes through here but cannot be boarded at Calais.* **SNCF** *train to* **Gare du Nord** *(3 hrs).*

Porte Maillot
M (1)
RER (A) (C)

Charles de Gaulle-Etoile
M (1) (2) (6)
RER (A)

Champs-Elysées

Chaillot Quarter

Gare St-La
M (3) (12)

Invalides
M (8) (13)
RER (C)

Invalides and Eiffel Tower Quarter

LE HAVRE
Ferry links with Portsmouth. **SNCF** *train to* **Gare St-Lazare** *(2 hrs).*
DIEPPE
Ferry links with Newhaven (summer). **SNCF** *train to* **Gare St-Lazare** *(2 hrs 20 mins).*
CAEN
Ferry links with Portsmouth. **SNCF** *train to* **Gare St-Lazare** *(1 hrs 45 mins).*
CHERBOURG
Ferry links with Portsmouth and Poole. **SNCF** *train to* **Gare St-Lazare** *(4 hrs).*

GARE ST-LAZARE
Rouen (1 hr 10 mins).

GARE MONTPARNASSE
Bordeaux (3 hrs)
Brest (4 hrs 30 mins)
Lisbon (24 hrs)
Madrid (16 hrs)
Nantes (2 hrs)
Rennes (2 hrs 5 mins)

Montparnasse

Gare Montparnasse
M (4) (6) (12) (13)

Porte de Orléans
M (4)

KEY

————	SNCF *see pp378–9*
————	Buses *see p378*
————	RATP bus *see p377*
————	Air France bus *see p377*
————	RER B *see p377*
————	Orlyrail *see p377*
————	Orlyval *see p377*
————	Orlybus *see p377*
————	Jet Bus *see p377*
M	Metro station
RER	RER station

GARE TGV DE MASSY-PALAISEAU
Bordeaux (3 hrs 20 mins)
Lille (1 hr 40 mins)
London (3 hrs 40 mins)
Lyon (2 hrs 20 mins)
Nantes (2 hrs 10 mins)
Rennes (2 hrs 5 mins)
Rouen (1 hr 10 mins)

Antony

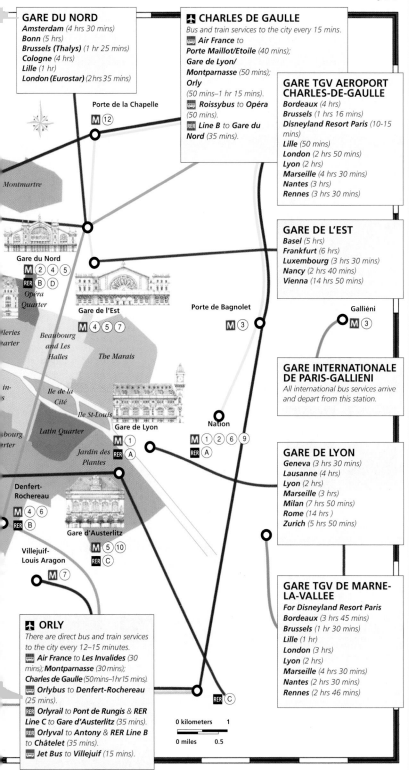

GARE DU NORD
Amsterdam *(4 hrs 30 mins)*
Bonn *(5 hrs)*
Brussels (Thalys) *(1 hr 25 mins)*
Cologne *(4 hrs)*
Lille *(1 hr)*
London (Eurostar) *(2 hrs 35 mins)*

✈ CHARLES DE GAULLE
Bus and train services to the city every 15 mins.
🚌 **Air France** to
Porte Maillot/Etoile *(40 mins)*;
Gare de Lyon/
Montparnasse *(50 mins)*;
Orly
(50 mins–1 hr 15 mins).
🚌 **Roissybus** to **Opéra**
(50 mins).
RER **Line B** to **Gare du**
Nord *(35 mins)*.

GARE TGV AEROPORT CHARLES-DE-GAULLE
Bordeaux *(4 hrs)*
Brussels *(1 hr 16 mins)*
Disneyland Resort Paris *(10-15 mins)*
Lille *(50 mins)*
London *(2 hrs 50 mins)*
Lyon *(2 hrs)*
Marseille *(4 hrs 30 mins)*
Nantes *(3 hrs)*
Rennes *(3 hrs 30 mins)*

Porte de la Chapelle
M ⑫

Montmartre

Gare du Nord
M ② ④ ⑤
RER Ⓑ Ⓓ

Opéra
Quarter

Gare de l'Est
M ④ ⑤ ⑦

Porte de Bagnolet
M ③

Galliéni
M ③

GARE DE L'EST
Basel *(5 hrs)*
Frankfurt *(6 hrs)*
Luxembourg *(3 hrs 30 mins)*
Nancy *(2 hrs 40 mins)*
Vienna *(14 hrs 50 mins)*

GARE INTERNATIONALE DE PARIS-GALLIENI
All international bus services arrive and depart from this station.

leries
arter

Beaubourg
and Les
Halles

The Marais

Ile de la
Cité

Ile St-Louis

Latin Quarter

bourg
rter

Gare de Lyon
M ①
RER Ⓐ

Nation
M ① ② ⑥ ⑨
RER Ⓐ

GARE DE LYON
Geneva *(3 hrs 30 mins)*
Lausanne *(4 hrs)*
Lyon *(2 hrs)*
Marseille *(3 hrs)*
Milan *(7 hrs 50 mins)*
Rome *(14 hrs)*
Zurich *(5 hrs 50 mins)*

Jardin des
Plantes

Denfert-
Rochereau
M ④ ⑥
RER Ⓑ

Gare d'Austerlitz
M ⑤ ⑩
RER Ⓒ

Villejuif-
Louis Aragon
M ⑦

GARE TGV DE MARNE-LA-VALLEE
For Disneyland Resort Paris
Bordeaux *(3 hrs 45 mins)*
Brussels *(1 hr 30 mins)*
Lille *(1 hr)*
London *(3 hrs)*
Lyon *(2 hrs)*
Marseille *(4 hrs 30 mins)*
Nantes *(2 hrs 30 mins)*
Rennes *(2 hrs 46 mins)*

✈ ORLY
There are direct bus and train services to the city every 12–15 minutes.
🚌 **Air France** to **Les Invalides** *(30 mins)*; **Montparnasse** *(30 mins)*;
Charles de Gaulle *(50 mins–1hr 15 mins)*.
🚌 **Orlybus** to **Denfert-Rochereau** *(25 mins)*.
RER **Orlyrail** to **Pont de Rungis** & **RER Line C** to **Gare d'Austerlitz** *(35 mins)*.
RER **Orlyval** to **Antony** & **RER Line B** to **Châtelet** *(35 mins)*.
🚌 **Jet Bus** to **Villejuif** *(15 mins)*.

RER Ⓒ

0 kilometers   1

0 miles   0.5

GETTING AROUND PARIS

Central Paris is compact. The best way to get around is to walk. Cycling and inline skating are increasingly popular with Parisians and tourists alike but they are not without risk. Visitors unfamiliar with the rules of the road and undisciplined French driving need to take care.

Driving a car in the city center is not fun. Traffic is often heavy, there are many one-way streets, and parking is notoriously difficult and expensive. The bus, metro and RER train system operated by the RATP makes getting around cheap and easy. The city is divided into five travel zones: zones 1 and 2 corresponding to the center and zones 3, 4 and 5 to the suburbs and the airport. The city is also divided into 20 arrondissements, which will help visitors in their search for addresses (*see p373*).

Parisian drivers do not always respect pedestrian crossings.

Stop sign

Walk sign

WALKING IN PARIS

Australian, British, Irish and New Zealand visitors need to remember that cars drive on the right-hand side of the road. There are many two-stage road crossings where pedestrians wait on an island in the center of the road before proceeding. These are marked *piétons traversez en deux temps*.

Walking tours are cited in the weekly listings magazines (*see p340*).

CYCLING IN PARIS

Paris is an excellent city for cyclists. It's reasonably flat, manageably small, has many backstreets where car traffic is restricted, and about 103 miles (150 km) of cycle lanes (*pistes cyclables*). Parisian drivers are increasingly respectful of cyclists as more

and more of their fellow citizens turn to two wheels.

The RATP's own cycling center, the **Maison Roue Libre**, in the heart of Paris, is very helpful for rental and organized tours, as well as for repairs and storage. The free map *Paris à Vélo* (Paris by Bike), available here and in most RATP metro, RER and bus stations, is a useful starting point. Bicycles may be taken on SNCF trains, and

A Parisian cyclist

TICKETS AND TRAVEL PASSES

Travel by public transportation is easy in Paris, and the options for payment and budgeting are varied. The tickets and passes on offer will suit most tourists. Tickets can be purchased at all main metro and RER stations, at the airports and several tourist offices. Individual tickets are relatively cheap and you can buy a block of ten (*carnet*) at a discount. The *Paris Visite* pass for one, two, three or five days includes discounted entry to some sights but is comparatively expensive unless you intend to travel fairly extensively. The daily, weekly and monthly travel card system is in the process of development. Currently, visitors can still buy a one-day *Mobilis* card or a Monday–Sunday weekly (*hebdomadaire*) or monthly *Carte Orange* for selected zones.

Paris Visite pass and one-day ticket

Mobilis card

Carte Orange

Tickets for use on metro, RER or bus

Carte Orange one-month travel ticket for zones 1 and 2

* G E T T I N G   A R O U N D   P A R I S **383*

some suburban train stations rent bicycles.

There are now bicycle shops throughout Paris, most of them renting bikes from about 14€ a day, and many also organize guided tours. **Mike's Bike Tours** offer tours in English, departing from near the Eiffel Tower, as do **Paris Vélo** and others (*see Directory*).

No entry sign

INTERDIT
SUR TOUTE LA LONGUEUR
DE LA VOIE

Parking Interdit (no parking)

DRIVING IN PARIS

Though driving and parking can be difficult in central Paris, a rental car can be useful for visiting outlying areas. To rent a car, a valid driving license and passport are required (most companies also require one major credit card). For payment by check or cash, additional ID may be required (including airline tickets and credit cards). International driving licenses are not needed for drivers from the EU, North America, Australia and New Zealand.

Cars drive on the right-hand side of the road and must yield to traffic merging from the right, even on main roads, unless marked by a *priorité* sign, which indicates right of way. Cars on a rotary usually have right of way, though one exception is the Arc de Triomphe where cars yield to traffic from the right – one of Paris's most hair-raising experiences!

AXE ROUGE

ARRÊT GÊNANT

Tow-away zone

30

Speed limit sign in km/h

PARKING

Parking in Paris is difficult and expensive. Never park where there are *Parking (Stationnement) Interdit* signs. Park only in areas with a large "P" or a *Parking Payant* sign on the sidewalk or road, and pay at the *horodateur* machine. For towed or clamped cars, phone or go to the nearest police station (*Commissariat de Police*). For towing away there is a fine, plus a fee for each day the car is held. There are 7 car pounds (*perfourrières*) in Paris, where cars are kept for 48 hours, then sent to outlying long-term garages (*fourrières*).

USING AN HORODATEUR MACHINE

Horodateurs (parking meters) operate from 9am–7pm Mon–Fri. Unless otherwise indicated, parking is free Sat–Sun, public holidays and in August.

Card-only machine

1 If using coins, insert according to the rate shown. If using a card, see step 2.

MARIE DE PARIS
PARIS CARTE
1

Parking card

2 If using a card, insert and press blue button for each 15 minutes required.

3 Press green button for ticket.

4 Remove ticket and place inside car windshield.

BICYCLE RENTAL, REPAIR & TOURS

Maison Roue Libre
1 Passage Mondétour 75001.
Map 13 B2.
Tel 0810 44 15 34.
Bicycle rental, storage, repair.

Mike's Bike Tours
Ave Gustave Eiffel 75007 & 22 Rue Edgar Foure 75015.
Map 10 D3.
Tel 01 56 58 10 54.
www.mikesbiketoursparis.com
English language bicycle tours.

Paris à vélo c'est sympa!
28 Rue Baudin, 75011.
Tel 01 48 87 60 01.
www.parisvelosympa.com
Bicycle rental, repairs, tours.

Paris Vélo
2 Rue du Fer-à-Moulin 75005.
Map 17 C2. **Tel** 01 43 37 59 22.
www.paris-velo-rent-a-bike.fr
Bicycle rental, tours.

RATP Information
Tel 08 92 68 77 14.
www.ratp.fr

SNCF Information
Tel 08 92 35 35 35.
www.sncf.fr

CAR RENTAL

Car rental agencies abound in Paris. Here is a list of major companies with agencies at Charles de Gaulle and Orly airports, main railroad stations and city-center locations. Telephone for reservations and pick-up and drop-off information.

ADA
Tel 08 92 68 40 02.

Avis
Tel 0820 05 05 05

Budget
Tel 0825 003 564.

Europcar
Tel 01 45 00 08 06.

Hertz
Tel 0825 861 861.

National Citer
Tel 01 44 38 61 61.

Sixt-Eurorent
Tel 01 48 62 57 66.

Traveling by Metro

The RATP (Paris transit authority) operates 14 metro lines, referred to by their number and terminus names, criss-crossing Paris and its suburbs. This is often the fastest and cheapest way to get across the capital, as there are dozens of stations scattered around the city. Metro stations are easily identified by their logo, a large circled "M", and sometimes their elegant Art Nouveau entrances. Neighborhood maps are found in all stations, near the exits. The metro and RER (Paris rail network) systems operate in much the same way, though RER coaches are slightly larger. The first trains leave their terminals at 5:30am and the last return at 1:15am.

RATP logo

Art Nouveau metro sign

Modern metro sign

Reading the Metro Map

Metro and RER lines are shown in various colors on the metro map. Metro lines are identified by a number, which is located on the map at each end of a line. Some metro stations serve only one line, others serve more than one. There are stations sharing both metro and RER lines and some are linked to one another by interconnecting passages.

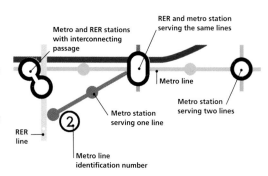

Metro and RER stations with interconnecting passage

RER and metro station serving the same lines

Metro line

Metro station serving two lines

Metro station serving one line

RER line

Metro line identification number

USING THE RER

The RER is a system of commuter trains, traveling underground in central Paris and above ground in outlying areas. Both metro tickets and passes are valid on it. There are five lines, known by their letters: A, B, C, D and E. Each line forks. For example, Line C has six forks, labeled C1, C2 etc. All RER trains bear names (for example, ALEX or VERA) to make it easier to read RER timetables in the station halls and on platforms. Digital panels on all RER platforms indicate train name, direction of travel (terminus) and upcoming stations.

RER stations are identified by a large circled logo. The main city stations are: Charles de Gaulle-Etoile, Châtelet-Les-Halles, Gare de Lyon, Nation, St-Michel-Notre-Dame, Auber-Haussmann St-Lazare and the Gare du Nord-Magenta.

The RER and metro systems overlap in central Paris. It is often quicker to take an RER train to a station served by both, as in the case of La Défense and Nation. However, getting into the RER stations, which are often linked to the metro by a maze of corridors, can be very time-consuming.

The RER is particularly useful for getting to Paris airports and to many of the outlying towns and tourist attractions. Line B3 serves Charles de Gaulle airport; Lines B4 and C2 serve Orly airport; Line A4 goes to Disneyland Resort Paris; and Line C5 runs to Versailles.

RER logo

BUYING A TICKET

Ordinary metro and RER tickets can be bought either singly or as a *carnet* of 10, from ticket booths or ticket machines in the station halls (carry some 1 and 2 euro coins). The useful **Paris Visite** bus, metro and RER pass (*see p382*) is widely available, and you can also buy it in advance at certain travel agencies and rail ticket agents abroad (eg. Rail Europe in London). One metro ticket "section urbaine" entitles you to travel anywhere on the metro, and on RER trains in central Paris. RER trips outside the center (such as to airports) require special tickets. Fares to suburbs and nearby towns vary. Consult the fare charts posted in all RER stations. Passengers on all city transportation must retain their tickets during the trip, as regular inspections are made and fines can be imposed for not having a ticket.

MAKING A JOURNEY BY METRO

1 To determine which metro line to take, travelers should first find their destination on a metro map. (Maps can be found inside stations and also on the inside back cover of this book.) Trace the metro line by following the color coding and the number of the line. At the end of the line you will see the number of the terminus – remember this, as it will help you to find the correct train.

Insert the train ticket in the first barrier.

Remove the ticket from the second barrier.

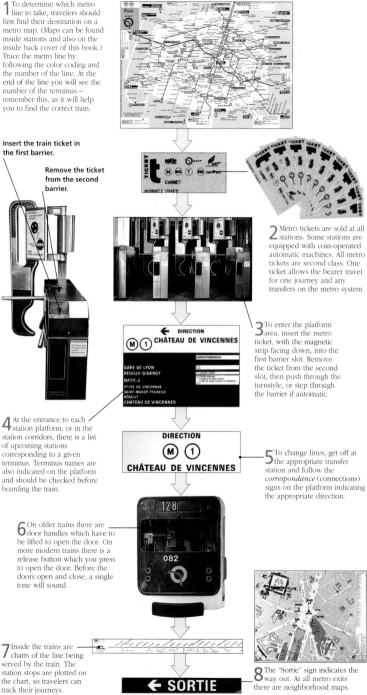

2 Metro tickets are sold at all stations. Some stations are equipped with coin-operated automatic machines. All metro tickets are second class. One ticket allows the bearer travel for one journey and any transfers on the metro system.

3 To enter the platform area, insert the metro ticket, with the magnetic strip facing down, into the first barrier slot. Remove the ticket from the second slot, then push through the turnstyle, or step through the barrier if automatic.

4 At the entrance to each station platform, or in the station corridors, there is a list of upcoming stations corresponding to a given terminus. Terminus names are also indicated on the platform and should be checked before boarding the train.

5 To change lines, get off at the appropriate transfer station and follow the *correspondance* (connections) signs on the platform indicating the appropriate direction.

6 On older trains there are door handles which have to be lifted to open the door. On more modern trains there is a release button which you press to open the door. Before the doors open and close, a single tone will sound.

7 Inside the trains are charts of the line being served by the train. The station stops are plotted on the chart, so travelers can track their journeys.

8 The "Sortie" sign indicates the way out. At all metro exits there are neighborhood maps.

Traveling by Bus

The bus is an excellent way to see the great sights of Paris. The bus system is run by the RATP, as is the metro, so you can use the same tickets for both. There are over 200 bus lines in greater Paris and over 3,500 buses in daily circulation at rush hour. This is often the fastest way to travel short distances. However, buses can get caught up in heavy traffic and are often crowded during peak hours. Visitors should check the times for the first and last buses as they vary widely, depending on the line. Most buses run from Monday to Saturday, from early morning to mid-evening (6am–8:30pm).

Ticket-canceling machine

Bus Stop Signs

Signs at bus stops display route numbers. A white background indicates a service every day all year; a black one means no service on Sundays or public holidays.

Bus terminus sign

Bus stop　　**Night bus sign**

TICKETS AND PASSES

A single bus ticket entitles the bearer to a single journey on a single line. If you want to make a change, you'll need another ticket. Exceptions to this rule are the buses Balabus, Noctambus, Orlybus and Roissybus, and lines 221, 297, 299, 350 and 351.) Children under four are allowed to travel for free, and those aged between four and ten may travel at half price.

You can purchase a *carnet* of 10 tickets, each of them valid for a single bus or metro journey. However, a *carnet* can be obtained only at the metro stations, not on the buses. Metro tickets may be used for bus travel. Bus-only tickets are purchased on board the bus, from the driver, and these must be canceled to be valid. To do this insert the ticket into the canceling machine inside the main doors of the bus. Be sure

Red exit button

Canceling a Bus Ticket

Insert the ticket into the machine in the direction of the arrow, then withdraw it.

to hold onto your ticket until the end of the journey. Inspectors do make random checks and are empowered to levy on-the-spot fines if you cannot produce a valid canceled ticket for the duration of your journey.

Travel passes are an economical idea if you are planning a number of journeys during your stay. For a set fee, you can enjoy the freedom of unlimited travel on Paris buses (*see p382*). Never cancel these as it will render them invalid. They should be shown to the bus driver when ever you board a bus, and to a ticket inspector on request.

Paris's Buses
Passengers can identify the route and destination of a bus from the information on the panels at the front. Some buses have open rear platforms, although these are becoming more rare.

Passengers enter the bus at the front door

Bus route number

Bus destination

Bus route number on rear of bus

Bus front displaying information

Open rear platform

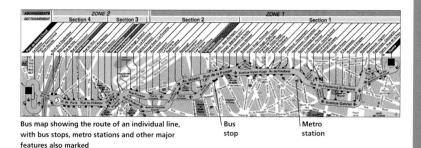

Bus map showing the route of an individual line, with bus stops, metro stations and other major features also marked | **Bus stop** | **Metro station**

USING THE BUSES

Bus stops and shelters are identified by the number shields of the buses that stop at them, and by the distinctive RATP logo. Route maps at bus stops indicate transfers and nearby metro and RER stops. Bus stops also display timetables, and show first and last buses. Neighborhood maps are also displayed at most bus shelters.

Most buses must be flagged down. Some models have multiple doors which must be opened by pressing a red button inside the bus to exit, or outside the bus to enter. All buses have buttons and bells to signal for a stop. Some buses do not go all the way to their terminus; in that case, there will be a slash through the name of the destination on the front panel.

Buses are gradually being equipped with access for wheelchairs, and all buses already have some seats reserved for disabled and elderly persons, veterans and pregnant women. These seats are identified by a sign and must be given up on request.

NIGHT AND SUMMER BUSES

There are 18 night bus lines, called Noctambus, for Paris and its suburbs (running 1:00–5:30am daily). The terminus for most of the lines is Châtelet, at Avenue Victoria or Rue St-Martin. Noctambus stops are clearly identified by a shield bearing an owl and a yellow moon. Noctambus must be flagged down. Travel passes are valid, but the normal metro tickets are not. Fares vary according to destination. Travelers may buy tickets on board the bus.

The RATP also operates buses in the Bois de Vincennes and Bois de Boulogne during the summer. The **RATP Information** is extremely helpful on these services and on the best and cheapest ways to get around the city.

RATP Information

54 Quai de la Rapée 75012.
Tel 08 92 68 77 14
www.ratp.fr

USEFUL BUS ROUTES

Here is a selection of the best sightseeing bus routes around the center of Paris, taking in some of the great sights of the city. The routes show the major bus stops, the nearest metro stations and locations of some of the notable sights.

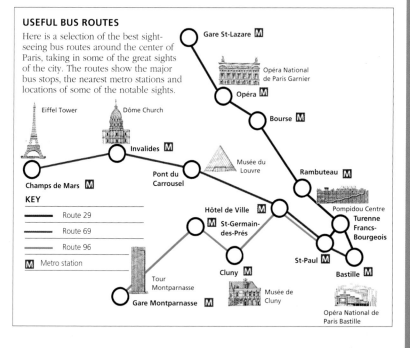

Using the SNCF Trains

The French state railroad, Société Nationale des Chemins de Fer (**SNCF**), has two kinds of service in Paris: the Banlieue suburban service and the Grandes Lignes, or long-distance service. The suburban services all operate within the five-zone network (*see p382*). The long-distance services operate throughout France. These services allow travelers to visit parts of France close to Paris in a daytrip. The TGV high-speed service is particularly useful for such journeys, as it is capable of traveling about twice as fast as the normal trains (*see pp378–9*).

Gare de l'Est railroad
station in 1920

RAILROAD STATIONS

As the railroad hub of France and the Continent, Paris boasts six major international railroad stations operated by the SNCF. The railroad stations are the Gare du Nord, Gare de l'Est, Gare de Lyon, Gare d'Austerlitz, Gare St-Lazare and Gare Montparnasse.

All the main train stations have long-distance and suburban destinations. Some of the main suburban locations, such as Versailles and Chantilly, are served by both long-distance and suburban trains.

The stations have departures and arrivals boards showing the train number, departure and arrival time, delay, platform number or letter, provenance, and main stops along the route. For those with heavy luggage,

Rail traveler with
luggage cart

there are carts, requiring a 1 euro coin (refunded when the cart is returned).

TICKETS

Tickets to suburban destinations can often be purchased at coin-operated automatic machines located inside station halls, so it is useful to carry coins (the machines give change).

Otherwise you can buy tickets at the ticket counters.

Before boarding a train, travellers must time-punch (*composter*) their tickets and reservations in a *composteur* machine. Inspectors do check travelers' tickets and anyone who fails to time-punch their ticket can be fined.

Ticket booths are marked with panels indicating the kind of tickets (*billets*) sold: *Banlieue* for suburban tickets, *Grandes Lignes* for mainline tickets, and *Internationale* for international tickets.

Substantial fare discounts of 25-50 percent are offered to over 60s (*Découverte Senior*), under 26s (*Découverte 12-25*),

Composteur Machine

The composteur machines are located in station halls and at the head of each platform. Tickets and reservations must be inserted face up.

A time-punched ticket

up to four adults traveling with a child under 12 (*Découverte Enfant Plus*), or anyone buying more than 30 days or more than 8 days in advance (*Découverte J30 or J8*).

STUDENT AND YOUTH DISCOUNT TICKETS

Nouvelles Frontières
87 Blvd de Grenelle 75015. **Map** 10D4.
Tel 08 25 00 08 25 / 01 53 95 65 65.
www.nouvelles-frontieres.fr

Wasteels
12 Rue La Fayette 75009. **Map** 6 E4.
Tel 0825 88 70 05.
www.wasteels.fr

SUBURBAN TRAINS

Suburban lines are found at all main Paris train stations and are clearly marked Banlieue. Tickets for city

A double-decker Banlieue train

transit cannot be used on Banlieue trains, with the exception of some RER tickets to stations with both SNCF and RER lines. Several tourist destinations are served by Banlieue trains, including Chantilly, Chartres, Fontainebleau, Giverny and Versailles (*see pp248–53*). Telephone the SNCF for details on 08 92 35 35 35 or try their website: **www**.sncf.fr

Traveling by Taxi

Taxis are more expensive than trains or buses, but they are an advantage after 1am, when the metro has stopped running. There are taxi stands (*station de taxis*) throughout the city; a short list is provided below.

A Paris taxi stand sign

CATCHING A TAXI

There are over 10,000 taxis operating in central Paris. Yet there never seem to be enough of them to meet demand, particularly during rush hours and on Friday and Saturday nights.

Taxis can be hailed in the street, but not within 165 ft (50 m) of a taxi stand. Since stands always take priority over street stops, the easiest way to get a cab is to find a stand and join the line. Stands are found at many busy cross-roads, at main metro and RER stations, and at all hospitals, train stations and airports. An illuminated white light on the roof shows that the taxi is available. A small light lit below means that the taxi is occupied. If the white light is covered the taxi is off duty. Taxis on their last run can refuse to take passengers.

The meter should have a specified initial amount showing at the taxi stand, or when it is hailed. Initial charges on radio taxis vary widely, depending on the distance the taxi covers to arrive at the pickup point. Payment by check is not accepted but some cars take credit cards.

Rates vary with the part of the city and the time of day. Rate A, in the city center, is charged per kilometer. The higher rate B applies in the city center on Sundays, holidays and at night (7pm–7am), or daytime in the suburbs or airports. Even higher rate C applies to the suburbs and airports at night. Taxis charge for each piece of luggage. There's no need to give a tip.

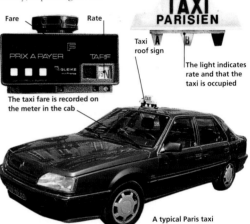

Fare   Rate

The taxi fare is recorded on the meter in the cab

Taxi roof sign

The light indicates rate and that the taxi is occupied

A typical Paris taxi

DIRECTORY

STREET FINDER

T he map references given with all sights, hotels, restaurants, shops and entertainment venues described in this book refer to the maps in this section (*see* How the Map References Work *opposite*). A complete index of street names and all the places of interest marked on the maps can be found on the following pages. The key map shows the area of Paris covered by the *Street Finder*, with the arrondissement numbers for each district. The maps include not only the sightseeing areas (which are color-coded), but the whole of central Paris with all the districts important for hotels, restaurants, shopping and entertainment venues. The symbols used to represent sights and features on the *Street Finder* maps are listed opposite.

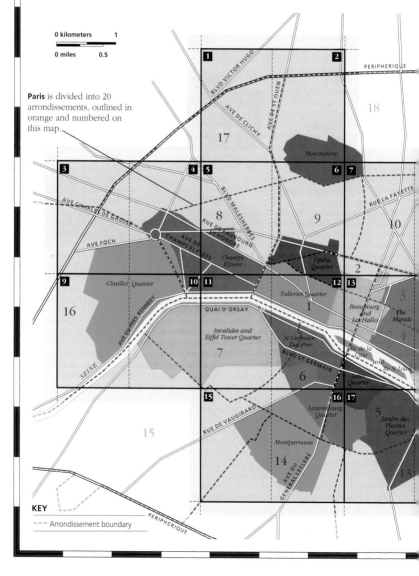

Paris is divided into 20 arrondissements, outlined in orange and numbered on this map.

0 kilometers 1

0 miles 0.5

BLVD VICTOR HUGO
AVE DE ST OUEN
PERIPHERIQUE
AVE DE CLICHY
18
17
Montmartre
RUE LA FAYETTE
AVE CHARLES DE GAULLE
BLVD MALESHERBES
RUE DU FAUBOURG ST HONORE
AVE DE FRIEDLAND
CHAMPS ELYSEES
AVE FOCH
8
9
10
Champs Elysées
Opéra Quarter
2
AVE DES CHAMPS ELYSEES
Chaillot Quarter
QUAI D'ORSAY
Tuileries Quarter
1
Beaubourg and Les Halles
The Marais
16
AVE DU PRES KENNEDY
Invalides and Eiffel Tower Quarter
7
St Germain Des-Prés
Ile de la Cité
Ile St Louis
BLVD ST GERMAIN
6
Latin Quarter
4
SEINE
RUE DE VAUGIRARD
Luxembourg Quarter
Jardin des Plantes Quarter
5
15
Montparnasse
14
AVE DU GENERAL LECLERC
13
PERIPHERIQUE

KEY
- - - Arrondissement boundary

HOW THE MAP
REFERENCES WORK

The first figure tells you
which *Street Finder* map
to turn to.

Hôtel de Ville **⓳**

4 Pl de l'Hôtel-de-Ville 75004.
Map 13 B3. *Tel* 01 42 76 50 49.
M *Hôtel de Ville.* ◯ *groups: by
arrangement.* ● *public hols, official
functions*   ♿ 🅿

The letter and number give
the grid reference. Letters go
across the map's top and
bottom; figures on its sides.

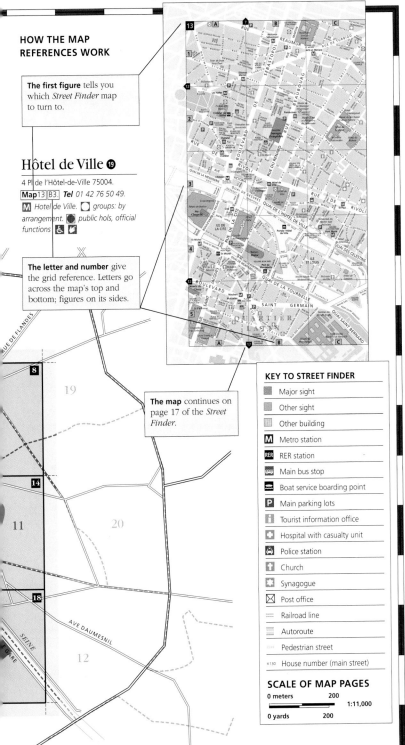

The map continues on
page 17 of the *Street
Finder.*

KEY TO STREET FINDER

▧	Major sight
▨	Other sight
▥	Other building
M	Metro station
RER	RER station
🚏	Main bus stop
⛴	Boat service boarding point
P	Main parking lots
ℹ	Tourist information office
✚	Hospital with casualty unit
🛡	Police station
✝	Church
✡	Synagogue
⊠	Post office
=	Railroad line
▬	Autoroute
⋯	Pedestrian street
⫶130	House number (main street)

SCALE OF MAP PAGES

0 meters	200	
		1:11,000
0 yards	200	

Street Finder Index

Each place name is followed by its arrondissement number, and then by its Street Finder reference.

Each place name is followed by its arrondissement number, and then by its Street Finder reference.

Each place name is followed by its arrondissement number, and then by its Street Finder reference.

Each place name is followed by its arrondissement number, and then by its Street Finder reference.

Each place name is followed by its arrondissement number, and then by its Street Finder reference.

Each place name is followed by its arrondissement number, and then by its Street Finder reference.

Each place name is followed by its arrondissement number, and then by its Street Finder reference.

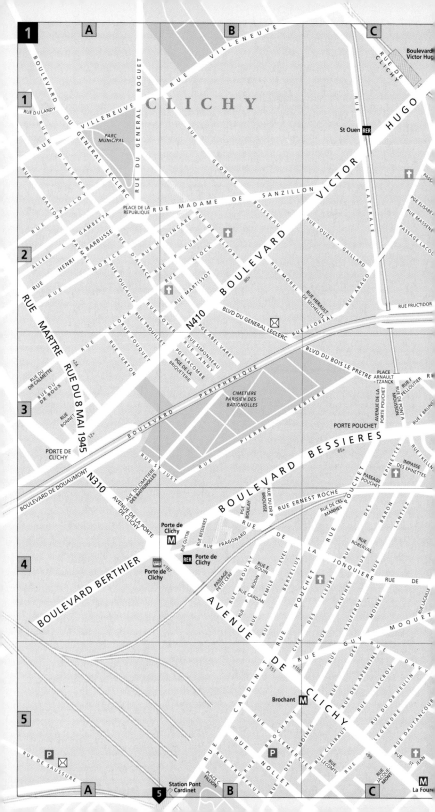

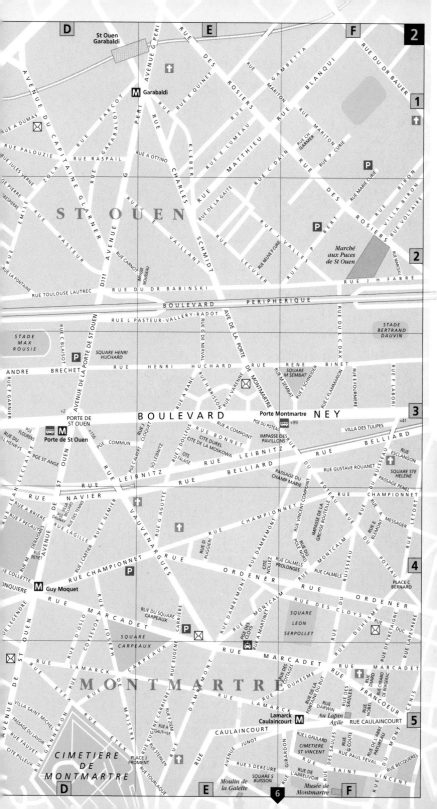

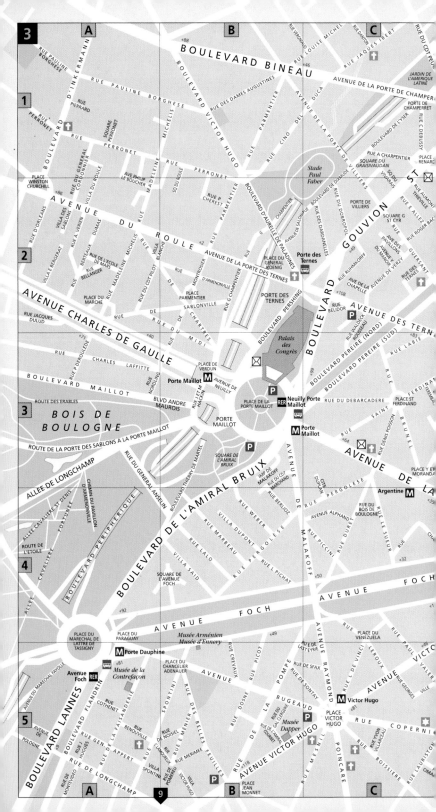

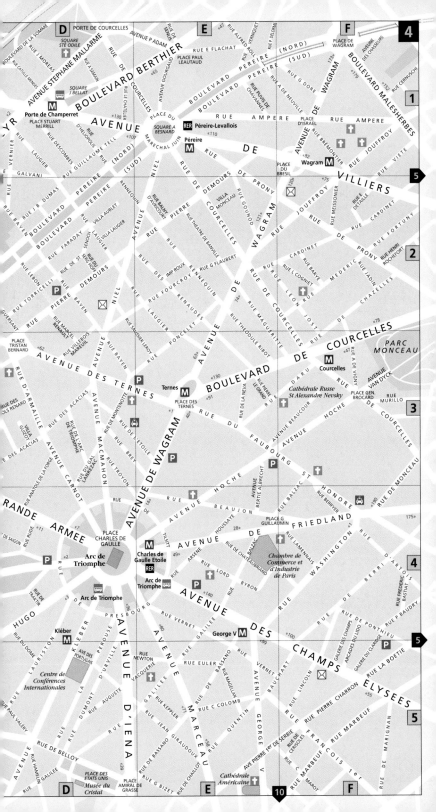

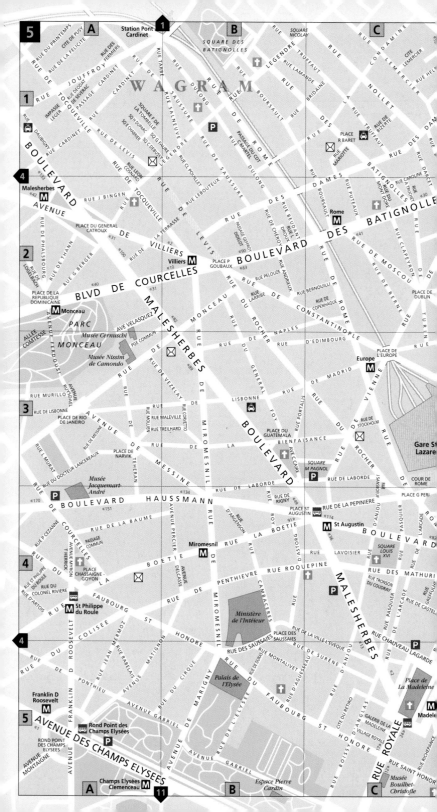

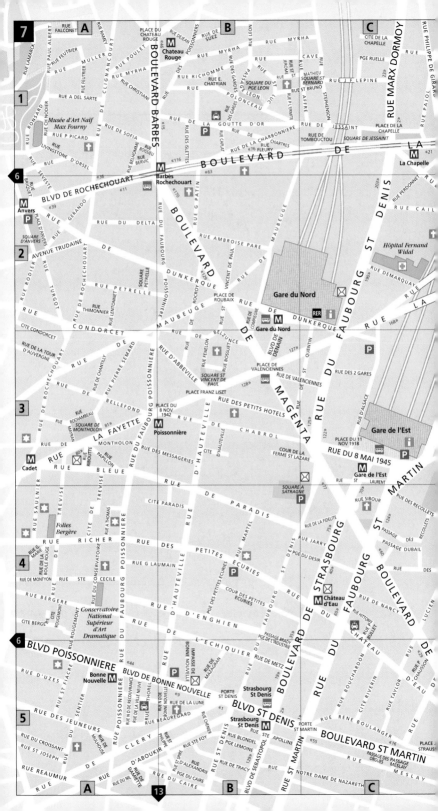

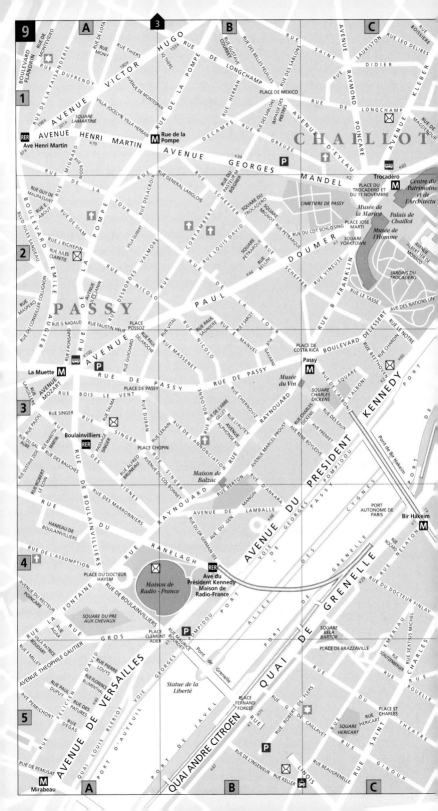

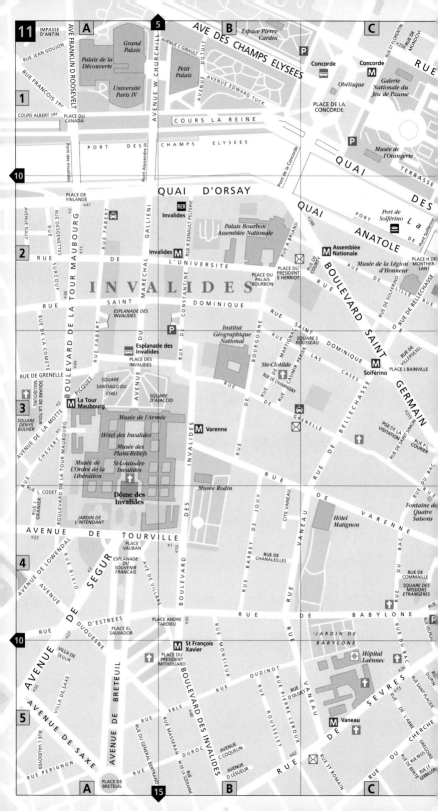

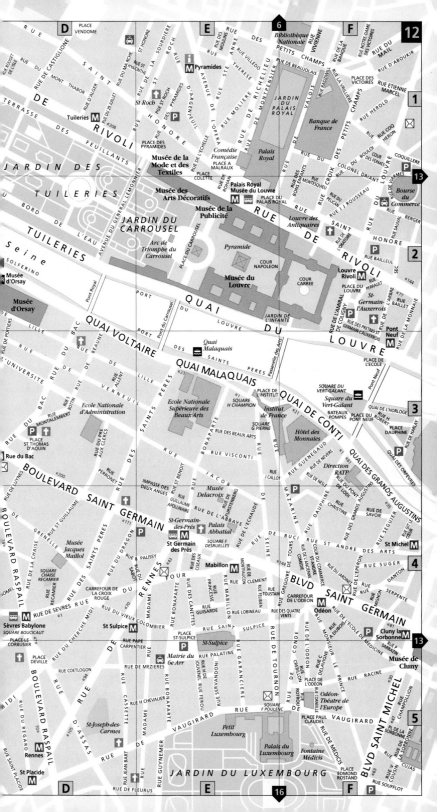

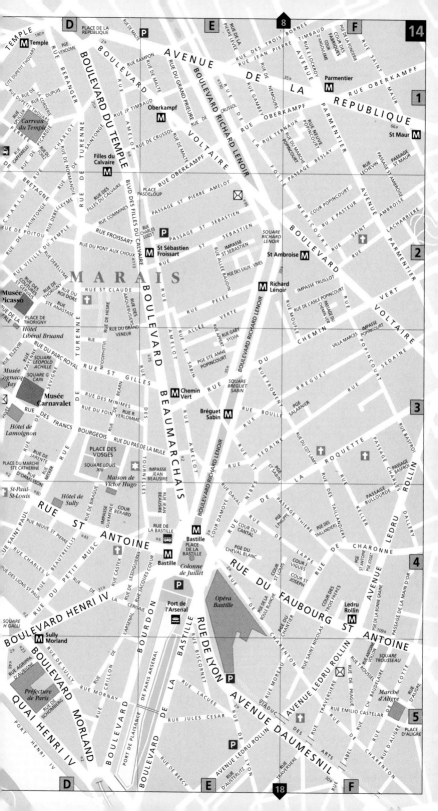

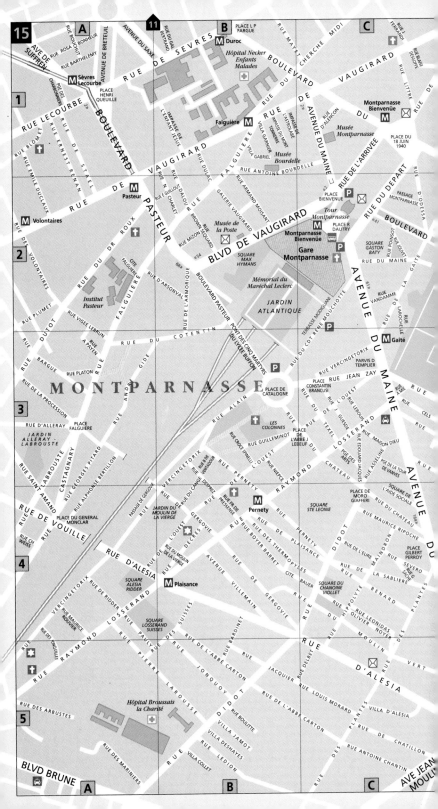

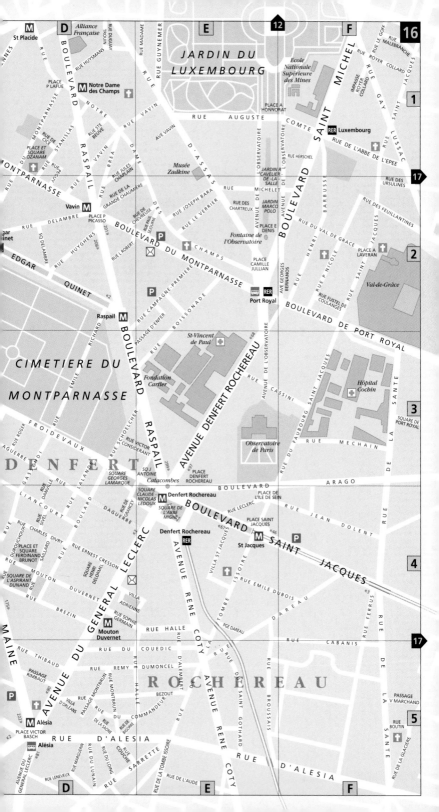

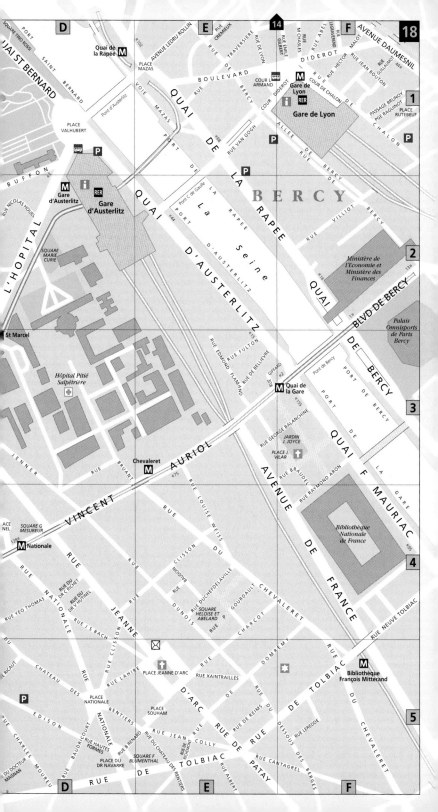

General Index

Acknowledgments

Dorling Kindersley would like to thank the many people whose help and assistance contributed to the preparation of this book.

Main Contributor
Alan Tillier has lived in all the main areas of Paris for 25 years, during which time he has been Paris correspondent for several journals including *Newsweek, The Times* and the *International Herald Tribune*. He is the author of several *Herald Tribune* guides for business travelers to Europe.

Contributors
Lenny Borger, Karen Burshtein, Thomas Quinn Curtiss, David Downie, Fiona Dunlop, Heidi Ellison, Alexandre Lazareff, Robert Noah, Andrew Sanger, Martha Rose Shulman, David Stevens, Ian Williams, Jude Welton.

Dorling Kindersley wishes to thank the following editors and researchers at Websters International Publishers: Sandy Carr, Siobhan Bremner, Valeria Fabbri, Gemma Hancock, Sara Harper, Annie Hubert, Celia Woolfrey.

Additional Photography
Andy Crawford, Michael Crockett, Lucy Davies, Mike Dunning, Philip Gatward, Steve Gorton, Alison Harris, Andrew Holligan, Chas Howson, Britta Jaschinski, Dave King, Ranald MacKechnie, Oliver Knight, Eric Meacher, Neil Mersh, Ian O'Leary, Alok Pathak, Stephen Oliver, Poppy, Susannah Price, Tim Ridley, Philippe Sebert, Steve Shott, Peter Wilson, Steven Wooster.

Additional Illustrations
John Fox, Nick Gibbard, David Harris, Kevin Jones Associates, John Woodcock.

Cartography
Andrew Heritage, James Mills-Hicks, Suresh Kumar, John Plumer, Chez Picthall (DK Cartography). Advanced Illustration (Cheshire), Contour Publishing (Derby), Euromap Limited (Berkshire). Street Finder maps: ERA-Maptec Ltd (Dublin) adapted with permission from original survey and mapping by Shobunsha (Japan).

Cartographic Research
Roger Bullen, Tony Chambers, Paul Dempsey, Ruth Duxbury, Ailsa Heritage, Margeret Hynes, Jayne Parsons, Donna Rispoli, Andrew Thompson.

Design and Editorial
MANAGING EDITOR Douglas Amrine
MANAGING ART EDITOR Geoff Manders
SENIOR EDITOR Georgina Matthews
SERIES DESIGN CONSULTANT Peter Luff
EDITORIAL DIRECTOR David Lamb
ART DIRECTOR Anne-Marie Bulat
PRODUCTION CONTROLLER Hilary Stephens
PICTURE RESEARCH Naomi Peck
DTP DESIGNER Andy Wilkinson
Janet Abbott, Emma Ainsworth, Vandana Bhagra, Hilary Bird, Vanessa Courtier, Maggie Crowley, Lisa Davidson, Guy Dimond, Elizabeth Eyre, Simon Farbrother, Fay Franklin, Eric Gibory, Paul Hines, Fiona Holman, Gail Jones, Nancy Jones, Stephen Knowlden, Chris Lascelles, Rebecca Milner, Fiona Morgan, Lyn Parry, Shirin Patel, Pamposh Raina, Philippa Richmond, Philippe Rouin, Andrew Szudek, Alka Thakur.

Special Assistance
Miranda Dewer at Bridgeman Art Library, Editions Gallimard, Lindsay Hunt, Emma Hutton at Cooling Brown, Janet Todd at DACS.

Photographic Reference
Musée Carnavalet, Thomas d'Hoste.

Photography Permissions
DORLING KINDERSLEY would like to thank the following for their kind permission to photograph at their establishments: Aéroports de Paris, Basilique du Sacré-Coeur de Montmartre, Beauvilliers, Benoit, Bibliothèque Historique de la Ville de Paris, Bibliothèque Polonaise, Bofinger, Brasserie Lipp, Café de Flore, Caisse Nationale des Monuments Historiques et des Sites, Les Catacombes, Centre National d'Art et de Culture Georges Pompidou, Chartier, Chiberta, La Cité des Sciences et de l'Industrie and L'EPPV, La Coupole, Les Deux Magots, Fondation Cousteau, Le Grand Colbert, Hôtel Atala, Hôtel Liberal Bruand, Hôtel Meurice, Hôtel Relais Christine, Kenzo, Lucas-Carton, La Madeleine, Mariage Frères, Memorial du Martyr Juif Inconnu, Thierry Mugler, Musée Armenien de France, Musée de l'Art Juif, Musée Bourdelle, Musée du Cabinet des Medailles, Musée Carnavalet, Musée Cernuschi: Ville de Paris, Musée du Cinema Henri Langlois, Musée Cognacq-Jay, Musée de Cristal de Baccarat, Musée d'Ennery, Musée Grévin, Musée Jacquemart-André, Musée de la Musique Méchanique, Musée National des Châteaux de Malmaison et Bois-Préau, Collections du Musée National de la Légion d'Honneur, Musée National du Moyen Age-Thermes de Cluny, Musée de Notre-Dame de Paris, Musée de l'Opéra, Musée de l'Ordre de la Libération, Musée

d'Orsay, Musée de la Préfecture de la Police, Musée de Radio France, Musée Rodin, Musée des Transports Urbains, Musée du Vin, Musée Zadkine, Notre-Dame du Travail, A l'Olivier, Palais de la Découverte, Palais de Luxembourg, Pharamond, Pied de Cochon, Lionel Poilâne, St Germain-des-Prés, St Louis en l'Ile, St Médard, St Merry, St-Paul– St-Louis, St-Roch, St-Sulpice, La Société Nouvelle d'Exploitation de La Tour Eiffel, La Tour Montparnasse, UNESCO, and all the other museums, churches, hotels, restaurants, shops, galleries and sights too numerous to thank individually.

Picture Credits

t=top; tc=top center; tr=top right; cla=center left above; ca=center above; cra=center right above; cl=center left; c=center; cr=center right; clb=center left below; cb=center below; crb=center right below; bl=bottom left; bc=bottom center; br=bottom right.

Works of art have been reproduced with the permission of the following copyright holders:
© SUCCESSION H MATISSE/DACS 1993: 111ca; © ADAGP/SPADEM, Paris and DACS, London 1993: 44cl; © ADAGP, Paris and DACS, London 1993: 61br, 61tr, 105tc, 107cb, 109b, 111tc, 111cb, 112bl, 112t, 112br, 113bl, 113br, 119c, 120b, 179tl, 180bc, 181cr, 211tc; © DACS 1993: 38tl, 45cr, 50br, 55cr, 57tl, 100t, 100br, 100clb, 100cl, 100ca, 101t, 101ca, 101cr, 101bl, 104, 107cra, 113c, 137tl, 178cl, 178ca, 208br.

CHRISTO–THE PONT NEUF WRAPPED, Paris, 1975-85: 40cla; © CHRISTO 1985, by kind permission of the artist. Photos achieved with the assistance of the EPPV and the CSI pp 234-9; Courtesy of ERBEN OTTO DIX: 110bl; Photos of DISNEYLAND ® PARIS: 242tr, 243bl, 243cr. The characters, architectural works and trademarks are the property of THE WALT DISNEY COMPANY. All rights reserved; FONDATION LE CORBUSIER: 59t, 254b; Courtesy of THE ESTATE OF JOAN MITCHELL: 113t; © HENRY MOORE FOUNDATION 1993: 191b. Reproduced by kind permission of the Henry Moore Foundation; BETH LIPKIN: 241t; Courtesy of the MAISON VICTOR HUGO, VILLE DE PARIS: 95cl; Courtesy of the MUSÉE D'ART NAIF MAX FOURNY PARIS: 221b, 223b; MUSÉE CARNAVALET: 212b; MUSÉE DE L'HISTOIRE CONTEMPORAINE (BDIC), PARIS: 208br; MUSÉE DE L'ORANGERIE: 130tr; MUSÉE DU LOUVRE: 125br, 128c; MUSÉE NATIONAL DES CHÂTEAUX DE MALMAISON ET BOIS-PRÉAU: 255cr; MUSÉE MARMOTTAN: 58c, 58cb, 59c, 60tl, 131tr; MUSÉE DE LA MODE ET DU COSTUME PALAIS GALLIERA: 57br; MUSÉE DE MONTMARTRE, PARIS: 221t; MUSÉE DES MONUMENTS FRANÇAIS: 197tc, 198cr; MUSÉE NATIONAL DE LA LÉGION D'HONNEUR: 32bc, 143bl; MUSÉE DE LA VILLE DE PARIS: MUSÉE DU PETIT PALAIS: 54cl,

205cb; © SUNDANCER: 362bl.

The Publishers are grateful to the following individuals, companies and picture libraries for permission to reproduce their photographs:

ADP: 377b; ALAMY: Bertrand Collet 269cl; Glenn Harper 212tl; Image State 270br; ALLSPORT UK: Sean Botterill 41br; ALLVEY & TOWERS: 378bl; THE ANCIENT ART AND ARCHITECTURE COLLECTION: 22clb; JAMES AUSTIN: 88t.

BANQUE DE FRANCE: 133t; NELLY BARIAND: 165c; GÉRARD BOULLAY: 84tl, 84tr, 84bl, 84br, 85t, 85cra, 85crb, 85br, 85bl; BRIDGEMAN ART LIBRARY, LONDON: (detail) 21br, 22cr, 23cl, 30cr–31cl, (detail) 35br; British Library, London (detail) 18br, (detail) 23bl, (detail) 24tl, (detail) 31tl; B N, Paris 19bl, (detail) 23tc, (detail) 23cr; Château de Versailles, France 19tr, 19bc, (detail) 19br, (detail) 30br, (detail) 155b; Christie's, London 8–9, (detail) 24cb, 34cla, 36tl, 44c; Delomosne, London 32clb; Giraudon 16, (detail) 26bl, (detail) 26clb, (detail) 27br, (detail) 30bl, (detail) 30cla, (detail) 31bl, 33cb, 58br, (detail) 60bl, 60ca, 60c; Lauros– Giraudon 23tr; Louvre, Paris 56t, 60br, 61bl, 61tl; Roy Miles Gallery 27tr; Musée de L'Armée, Paris (detail) 83br; Musée Condé, Chantilly (detail) 4tr, 18bl, 19tcl, (detail) 19tcr, (detail) 19c, (detail) 22tl, (detail) 26bc; Musée Crozatier, Le Puy en Velay, France (detail) 25bl; Musée Gustave Moreau, Paris 56b, 231tr; National Gallery (detail) 29tl, (detail) 44b; Musée de la Ville de Paris, Musée Carnavalet (detail) 30bc, (detail) 31tr, 31crb, 97t. Collection Painton Cowen 40cla; Palais du Tokyo, Paris 59b; Temples Newsham House, Leeds 25cr; Uffizi Gallery, Florence (detail) 24br; © THE BRITISH MUSEUM: 31tc.

CITÉ DE LA MUSIQUE: Eric Mahondieu 235br; CITÉ DES SCIENCES ET DE L'INDUSTRIE: Bernard Baudin Lar Le Floréal 239tl; Christophe Foubert Alcaline 239bl; Michel Lamoureux 236cb, 236b, 236tl, 237tl, 237tr, 238clb, 238t, 239cra, 239crb; Pascal Prieur 238cla; Michel Virad 236clb, 237tl; CORBIS: Burnstein Collection 227b; Ray Juno 10cl; Richard List 11cl; Sylvain Saustier 268b; TOM CRAIG: 273t, 273br.

R Doisneau: RAPHO 143t.

ESPACE MONTMARTRE: 220bl; EUROPEAN COMMISSION 371; MARY EVANS PICTURE LIBRARY: 38bl, 81br, 89tl, 94b, 130b, 141cl, 191c, 192cr, 193crb, 209b, 224bl, 247br, 251t, 253b, 388t.

GIRAUDON: (detail) 22bl, (detail) 23crb; Lauros–Giraudon (detail) 33bl; Musée de la Ville de Paris: Musée Carnavalet (detail) 211t; LE GRAND VÉFOUR: 293t.

ROBERT HARDING PICTURE LIBRARY: 22br, 26tl, 29ca, 29br, 36cla, 38tl, 41tl, 45cr, 65br, 240cb, 381cr; B M 27ca; B N 191tr, 208bc; Biblioteco

Reale, Turin 127t; Bulloz 208cb; P Craven 380b; R Francis 82clb; I Griffiths 376t; H Josse 208br; Musée National des Châteaux de Malmaison et Bois-Préau 33tc; Musée de Versailles 26cl; R Poinot 361b; P Tetret 251crb; Explorer 12bl; F. Chazot 341b; Girard 65c; P Gleizes 62bl; F Jalain 378b; J Moatti 340bl, 340cl; Walter Rawlings 43bc; A Wolf 123br, 123tl; ALISON HARRIS: Musée de Montparnasse 179cl; Pavillon des Arts 108br; Le Village Royale 132tl; JOHN HESELTINE PHOTOGRAPHY: 174; HULTON GETTY: 45cl, 101br, 181tc, 231bl, 232c; Charles Hewitt 40clb; Lancaster 181tc.

© IGN PARIS 1990 Authorisation Nº 90–2067: 13b; INSTITUT DU MONDE ARABE: Georges Fessey 165tr.

THE KOBAL COLLECTION: 44t, 140b; Columbia Pictures 181br; Société Générale de Films 38tc; Les Films du Carrosse 109t; Montsouris 197cra; Georges Méliès 198bl; KONG: Patricia Bailer 10b.

THE LEBRECHT COLLECTION: 227br; FRANÇOIS LEQUEUX 194cl.

MAGNUM: Bruno Barbey 64b; Philippe Halsmann 45b; MINISTÈRE DE L'ECONOMIE ET DES FINANCES: 371c; MINISTÈRE DE L'INTÉRIEUR SGAP DE PARIS: 368bc, 368br, 369t; COLLECTIONS DU MOBILIER NATIONAL-CLICHÉ DU MOBILIER NATIONAL: 167cr; © photo MUSÉE DE L'ARMÉE, PARIS: 189cr; MUSÉE DES ARTS DÉCORATIFS, PARIS: L Sully Jaulmes 54t; MUSÉE DES ARTS DE LA MODE– Collection UCAD– UFAC: 121b; MUSÉE BOUILHET-CHRISTOFLE: 57tr, 132t; MUSÉE CANTONAL DES BEAUX-ARTS, LAUSANNE: 115b; MUSÉE CARNAVALET: Dac Karin Maucotel 97b; MUSÉE D'ART ET D'HISTOIRE DU JUDAÏSME/ Christophe Fouin 103br; MUSÉE NATIONALE DE L'HISTOIRE NATURELLE: D Serrette 167cl; MUSÉE DE L'HOLOGRAPHIE: 109cl; © MUSÉE DE L'HOMME, PARIS: D Ponsard 199c, 199cl; © PHOTO MUSÉE DE LA MARINE, PARIS: 32bl, 196cl; MUSÉE NATIONAL D'ART MODERN– CENTRE GEORGES POMPIDOU, PARIS: 61tr, 110br, 110bl, 111t, 111ca, 111cb, 112t, 112bl, 112br, 113t, 113c, 113bl, 113br; MUSÉE DES PLANS-RELIEFS, PARIS: 186crb; MUSÉE DE LA POSTE, PARIS: 179tl; MUSÉE DE LA SEITA, PARIS: D Dado 190t.

© PARIS TOURIST OFFICE: Catherine Balet 270cl; David Lefranc 268c, 269t, 269br, 270tr, 271t, 271br, 272cl, 272bl, 272br; PHILIPPE PERDEREAU:

132b, 133b; CLICHÉ PHOTOTHÈQUE DES MUSÉES DE LA VILLE DE PARIS– © DACS 1993: 21ca, 21crb, 28cr–29cl, 96tr; POPPERFOTO: 227t.

PAUL RAFERTY 246b; RATP.SG/G.I.E. TOTHEME 54; 386; REDFERNS: W Gottlieb 38clb; © PHOTO RÉUNION DES MUSÉES NATIONAUX: Grand Trianon 26crb; Musée Guimet 54cb, 200tr; Musée du Louvre: 27cb, (detail) 32cr–33cl, 55tl, 123bl, 124t, 124c, 124b, 125t, 125c, 126c, 126bl, 126br, 127b, 128t, 128b, 129t, 129c; Musée Nationaux d'Art Moderne © DACS/ADAGP 111crb; Musée Picasso 55cr, 100t, 100c, 100cl, 100clb, 100br, 101bl, 101cr, 101ca, 101t; ROGER- VIOLLET: (detail) 24clb, (detail) 39bl, (detail) 192bc, (detail) 209t; ANN RONAN PICTURE LIBRARY: 173cr; PHILIPPE RUAULT: Fondation Cartier 179bl.

LA SAMARITAINE, PARIS: 115c; SEALINK PLC: 378cl; SIPAPRESS: 222c; SNCF – SERVICE PRESSE VOYAGES FRANCE EUROPE: 388bl; FRANK SPOONER PICTURES: F Reglain 64ca; P Renault 64c; SYGMA: 35crb, 240cl; F Poincet 40tl; Keystone 40bc, 241cra; J Langevin 41br; Keler 41crb; J Van Hasselt 41tr; P Habans 62c; A Gyori 63cr; P Vauthey 65bl; Y Forestier 188t; Sunset Boulevard 241br; Water Carone 340t.

TALLANDIER: 25cb, 25tl, 28cl, 28clb, 28bl, 29bl, 30tl, 31cr, 31ca, 32tl, 32cb, 32br, 38cla, 39ca, 39br, 40cb, 52cla; B N 28br, 32crb, 38bc; Brigaud 39crb; Brimeur 34bl; Charmet 36cb; Dubout 17b, 20br, 24ca, 25br, 26br, 30c, 33cr, 33tr, 34br, 35bl, 36clb, 36bl, 36br, 37bl, 37br, 37clb, 37tl, 38crb; Josse 20cla, 20tc, 20c, 20clb, 21tl, 36bc; Josse-B N 20bl; Joubert 38c; Tildier 37ca; Vigne 34clb; LE TRAIN BLEU: 295t.

VIDÉOTHÈQUE DE PARIS: Hoi Pham Dinh 106lb

AGENCE VU: Didier Lefèvre 340cr.

Front Endpaper: JOHN HESELTINE PHOTOGRAPHY br. © DACS 1993: cra. Back endpaper: RATP CML AGENCE CARTOGRAPHIQUE.

COVER:
FRONT COVER: DK IMAGES: Eric Meacher bl; TIPS IMAGES: Chad Ehlers main image. BACK COVER: DK IMAGES: all. SPINE: DK IMAGES: b; TIPS IMAGES: Chad Ehlers t.

DORLING KINDERSLEY SPECIAL EDITIONS

Dorling Kindersley books can be purchased in bulk quantities at discounted prices for use in promotions or as premiums. We are also able to offer special editions and personalized jackets, corporate imprints, and excerpts from all of our books, tailored specifically to meet your own needs.

To find out more, please contact: (in the United Kingdom) – Sarah.Burgess@dk.com or Special Sales, Dorling Kindersley Limited, 80 Strand, London WC2R 0RL

(in the United States) – Special Markets Department, DK Publishing, Inc., 375 Hudson Street, New York, NY 10014.

Phrase Book

In Emergency

Help!	**Au secours!**	*oh sekoor*
Stop!	**Arrêtez!**	*aret-ay*
Call a doctor!	**Appelez un médecin!**	*apuh-lay uñ medsañ*
Call an ambulance!	**Appelez une ambulance!**	*apuh-lay oon oñboo-loñs*
Call the police!	**Appelez la police!**	*apuh-lay lah pob-lees*
Call the fire department!	**Appelez les pompiers!**	*apuh-lay leh poñ-peeyay*
Where is the nearest telephone?	**Où est le téléphone le plus proche?**	*oo ay luh teblehfon luh ploo prosh*
Where is the nearest hospital?	**Où est l'hôpital le plus proche?**	*oo ay l'opeetal luh ploo prosh*

Communication Essentials

Yes	**Oui**	*wee*
No	**Non**	*noñ*
Please	**S'il vous plaît**	*seel voo play*
Thank you	**Merci**	*mer-see*
Excuse me	**Excusez-moi**	*exkoo-zay mwah*
Hello	**Bonjour**	*boñzhoor*
Goodbye	**Au revoir**	*oh rub-vwar*
Good night	**Bonsoir**	*boñ-swar*
Morning	**Le matin**	*matañ*
Afternoon	**L'après-midi**	*l'apreb-meedee*
Evening	**Le soir**	*swar*
Yesterday	**Hier**	*eeyebr*
Today	**Aujourd'hui**	*ob-zboor-dwee*
Tomorrow	**Demain**	*dubmañ*
Here	**Ici**	*ee-see*
There	**Là**	*lah*
What?	**Quoi, Quel, quelle?**	*kwah, kel, kel*
When?	**Quand?**	*koñ*
Why?	**Pourquoi?**	*poor-kwah*
Where?	**Où?**	*oo*

Useful Phrases

How are you?	**Comment allez-vous?**	*kom-moñ talay voo*
Very well, thank you.	**Très bien, merci.**	*treb byañ, mer-see*
Pleased to meet you.	**Enchanté de faire votre connaissance.**	*oñsboñ-tay dub febr votr kon-ay-sans*
See you soon.	**A bientôt.**	*byañ-toh*
That's fine	**Voilà qui est parfait**	*vwalah kee ay par-fay*
Where is/are...?	**Où est/sont...?**	*oo ay/soñ*
How far is it to...?	**Combien de kilometres d'ici à...?**	*kom-byañ dub keelo-metr d'ee-see ah*
Which way to...?	**Quelle est la direction pour...?**	*kel ay lah deer-ek-syoñ poor*
Do you speak English?	**Parlez-vous anglais?**	*par-lay voo oñg-lay*
I don't understand.	**Je ne comprends pas.**	*zhuh nub kom-proñ pah*
Could you speak slowly please?	**Pouvez-vous parler moins vite s'il vous plaît?**	*poo-vay voo par-lay mwañ veet seel voo play*
I'm sorry.	**Excusez-moi.**	*exkoo-zay mwah*

Useful Words

big	**grand**	*groñ*
small	**petit**	*pub-tee*
hot	**chaud**	*show*
cold	**froid**	*frwah*
good	**bon/bien**	*boñ/byañ*
bad	**mauvais**	*moh-veb*
enough	**assez**	*assay*
well	**bien**	*byañ*
open	**ouvert**	*oo-ver*
closed	**fermé**	*fer-meb*
left	**gauche**	*gobsh*
right	**droit**	*drwah*
straight on	**tout droit**	*too drwah*
near	**près**	*preb*
far	**loin**	*lwañ*
up	**en haut**	*oñ ob*
down	**en bas**	*oñ bah*
early	**de bonne heure**	*dub bon urr*
late	**en retard**	*oñ rub-tar*
entrance	**l'entrée**	*l'on-tray*
exit	**la sortie**	*sor-tee*
toilet	**les toilettes, le WC**	*twab-let, vay-see*
free, unoccupied	**libre**	*leebr*
free, no charge	**gratuit**	*grah-twee*

Making a Telephone Call

I'd like to place a long-distance call.	**Je voudrais faire un appel á l'étranger.**	*zhuh voo-dreb febr uñ apel a laytroñ-zhay*
I would like to make a collect call.	**Je voudrais faire une communication en PCV.**	*zhuh voo-dreb febr oon komoonikab-syoñ oñ peb-seb-veb*
I'll try again later.	**Je rappelerai plus tard.**	*zhuh rapel-eray ploo tar*
Can I leave a message?	**Est-ce que je peux laisser un message?**	*es-keb zhuh puh leb-say uñ mebsazb*
Hold on.	**Ne quittez pas, s'il vous plaît.**	*nuh kee-tay pah seel voo play*
Could you speak up a little please?	**Pouvez-vous parler un peu plus fort?**	*poo-vay voo par-lay uñ pub ploo for*
local call	**la communication locale**	*komoonikab-syoñ low-kal*

Shopping

How much does this cost?	**C'est combien s'il vous plaît?**	*say kom-byañ seel voo play*
I would like ...	**je voudrais...**	*zhuh voo-dray*
Do you have?	**Est-ce que vous avez?**	*es-kuh voo zavay*
I'm just looking.	**Je regarde seulement.**	*zhuh rubgar sublmoñ*
Do you take credit cards?	**Est-ce que vous acceptez les cartes de crédit?**	*es-kuh voo zaksept-ay leb kart duh kreb-dee*
Do you take traveler's cheques?	**Est-ce que vous acceptez les cheques de voyages?**	*es-kuh voo zaksept-ay leb shek dub vuayazb*
What time do you open?	**A quelle heure vous êtes ouvert?**	*ab kel urr voo zet oo-ver*
What time do you close?	**A quelle heure vous êtes fermé?**	*ab kel urr voo zet fer-may*
This one.	**Celui-ci.**	*subl-wee-see*
That one.	**Celui-là.**	*subl-wee-lah*
expensive	**cher**	*shebr*
cheap	**pas cher, bon marché**	*pab shebr, boñ mar-shay*
size, clothes	**la taille**	*tye*
size, shoes	**la pointure**	*pwañ-tur*
white	**blanc**	*bloñ*
black	**noir**	*nwabr*
red	**rouge**	*roozb*
yellow	**jaune**	*zbobwn*
green	**vert**	*vebr*
blue	**bleu**	*bluh*

Types of Shop

antique shop	**le magasin d'antiquités**	*maga-zañ d'oñteekee-tay*
bakery	**la boulangerie**	*booloñ-zburee*
bank	**la banque**	*boñk*
bookstore	**la librairie**	*lee-brebree*
butcher	**la boucherie**	*boo-shebree*
cake shop	**la pâtisserie**	*patee-sree*
cheese shop	**la fromagerie**	*fromazb-ree*
dairy	**la crémerie**	*krem-ree*
department store	**le grand magasin**	*groñ maga-zañ*
delicatessen	**la charcuterie**	*sbarkoot-ree*
drugstore	**la pharmacie**	*farmab-see*
fish seller	**la poissonnerie**	*pwasson-ree*
gift shop	**le magasin de cadeaux**	*maga-zañ dub kadob*
greengrocer	**le marchand de légumes**	*mar-sboñ dub lay-goom*
grocery	**l'alimentation**	*alee-moñta-syoñ*
hairdresser	**le coiffeur**	*kwafubr*
market	**le marché**	*marsb-ay*
newsstand	**le magasin de journaux**	*maga-zañ dub zboor-no*
post office	**la poste, le bureau de poste, le PTT**	*pobst, booroh dub pobst, peb-teb-teb*
shoe shop	**le magasin de chaussures**	*maga-zañ dub show-soor*
supermarket	**le supermarché**	*soo pebr-marsbay*
tobacconist	**le tabac**	*tabab*
travel agent	**l'agence de voyages**	*l'azboñs dub vwayazb*

Sightseeing

abbey	**l'abbaye**	*l'abay-ee*
art gallery	**la galerie d'art**	*galer-ree dart*
bus station	**la gare routière**	*gabr roo-tee-yebr*

cathedral	la cathédrale	katay-dral
church	l'église	l'aygleez
garden	le jardin	zhar-dañ
library	la bibliothèque	beebleeo-tek
museum	le musée	moo-zay
railroad station	la gare (SNCF)	gabr (es-en-say-ef)
tourist information office	les renseignements touristiques, le syndicat d'initiative	roñsayn-moñ toorees-teek, sandee-ka d'eenee-syateev
town hall	l'hôtel de ville	l'obtel dub veel
closed for public holiday	fermeture jour férié	fèrbmeh-tur zhoor fehree-ay

Staying in a Hotel

Do you have a vacant room?	Est-ce que vous avez une chambre?	es-kub voo-zavay oon shambr
double room, with double bed	la chambre à deux personnes, avec un grand lit	shambr ab dub pebr-son avek un gronñ lee
twin room	la chambre à deux lits	shambr ab dub lee
single room	la chambre à une personne	shambr ab oon pebr-son
room with a bath, shower	la chambre avec salle de bains, une douche	shambr avek sal dub bañ, oon doosh
porter	le garçon	gar-soñ
key	la clef	klay
I have a reservation.	J'ai fait une réservation.	zhay fay oon rayzebrva-syoñ

Eating Out

Do you have a table?	Avez-vous une table de libre?	avay-voo oon tabbl dub leebr
I want to reserve a table.	Je voudrais réserver une table.	zhub voo-dray rayzebr-vay oon tabbl
The bill please.	L'addition s'il vous plaît.	l'adee-syoñ seel voo play
I am a vegetarian.	Je suis végétarien.	zhub swee vezbay-tebryañ
Waitress/ waiter	Madame, Mademoiselle/ Monsieur	mab-dam, mab-demwabzel/ mub-syub
menu	le menu, la carte	men-oo, kart
fixed-price menu	le menu à prix fixe	men-oo ab pree feeks
cover charge	le couvert	koo-vebr
wine list	la carte des vins	kart-deb vañ
glass	le verre	vebr
bottle	la bouteille	boo-tay
knife	le couteau	koo-tob
fork	la fourchette	for-sbet
spoon	la cuillère	kwee-yebr
breakfast	le petit déjeuner	pub-tee deb-zhub-nay
lunch	le déjeuner	deb-zhub-nay
dinner	le dîner	dee-nay
main course	le plat principal	plab prañsee-pal
starter, first course	l'entrée, les hors d'oeuvre	l'oñ-tray, or-dubvr
dish of the day	le plat du jour	plab doo zhoor
wine bar	le bar à vin	bar ab vañ
café	le café	ka-fay
rare	saignant	say-noñ
medium	à point	ab pwañ
well done	bien cuit	byañ kwee

Menu Decoder

apple	la pomme	pom
baked	cuit au four	kweet ob foor
banana	la banane	banan
beef	le boeuf	bubf
beer, draught	la bière, bière	bee-yebr, bee-yebr
beer	à la pression	ab lab pres-syoñ
boiled	bouilli	boo-yee
bread	le pain	pan
butter	le beurre	burr
cake	le gâteau	gab-tob
cheese	le fromage	from-azh
chicken	le poulet	poo-lay
chocolate	le chocolat	shoko-lah
cocktail	le cocktail	cocktail
coffee	le café	kab-fay
dessert	le dessert	deb-ser
dry	sec	sek
duck	le canard	kanar
egg	l'oeuf	l'uf

fish	le poisson	pwab-ssoñ
fresh fruit	le fruit frais	frwee freb
garlic	l'ail	l'eye
grilled	grillé	gree-yay
ham	le jambon	zhoñ-boñ
ice, ice cream	la glace	glas
lamb	l'agneau	l'anyob
lemon	le citron	see-troñ
lobster	le homard	omabr
meat	la viande	vee-yand
milk	le lait	leb
mineral water	l'eau minérale	l'ob meeney-ral
mustard	la moutarde	moo-tard
oil	l'huile	l'weel
olives	les olives	leb zoleev
onions	les oignons	leb zonyoñ
orange	l'orange	l'oroñzb
French fries	les frites	freet
fresh orange juice	l'orange pressée	l'oroñzb press-eb
fresh lemon juice	le citron pressé	see-troñ press-eb
pepper	le poivre	pwavr
poached	poché	posb-ay
pork	le porc	por
potatoes	les pommes de terre	pom-dub tebr
prawns	les crevettes	krub-vet
rice	le riz	ree
roast	rôti	rou-tee
roll	le petit pain	pub-tee pañ
salt	le sel	sel
sauce	la sauce	sobs
sausage, fresh	la saucisse	sobsees
seafood	les fruits de mer	frwee dub mer
shellfish	les crustaces	kroos-tas
snails	les escargots	leb zes-kar-goh
soup	la soupe, le potage	soop, poh-tazb
steak	le bifteck, le steack	beef-tek, stek
sugar	le sucre	sookr
tea	le thé	tay
toast	pain grillé	pan greeyay
vegetables	les légumes	lay-goom
vinegar	le vinaigre	veenaygr
water	l'eau	l'ob
red wine	le vin rouge	vañ roozb
white wine	le vin blanc	vañ bloñ

Numbers

0	zéro	zeb-rob
1	un, une	uñ, oon
2	deux	dub
3	trois	trwab
4	quatre	katr
5	cinq	sañk
6	six	sees
7	sept	set
8	huit	weet
9	neuf	nerf
10	dix	dees
11	onze	oñz
12	douze	dooz
13	treize	trebz
14	quatorze	katorz
15	quinze	kañz
16	seize	sebz
17	dix-sept	dees-set
18	dix-huit	dees-sweet
19	dix-neuf	dees-nerf
20	vingt	vañ
30	trente	tront
40	quarante	karoñt
50	cinquante	sañkoñt
60	soixante	swasoñt
70	soixante-dix	swasoñt-dees
80	quatre-vingts	katr-vañ
90	quatre-vingt-dix	katr-vañ-dees
100	cent	soñ
1,000	mille	meel

Time

one minute	une minute	oon mee-noot
one hour	une heure	oon urr
half an hour	une demi-heure	oon dub-mee urr
Monday	lundi	luñ-dee
Tuesday	mardi	mar-dee
Wednesday	mercredi	mebrkrub-dee
Thursday	jeudi	zhub-dee
Friday	vendredi	voñdrub-dee
Saturday	samedi	sam-dee
Sunday	dimanche	dee-moñsb

ATHENS REGIONAL LIBRARY SYSTEM

3 3207 00436 3091

6/10

Madison County Library
P O Box 38 1315 Hwy 98 West
Danielsville, GA 30633
(706)795-5597
Member Athens Regional Library System

Paris Metro and Regional Express Railway (RER)

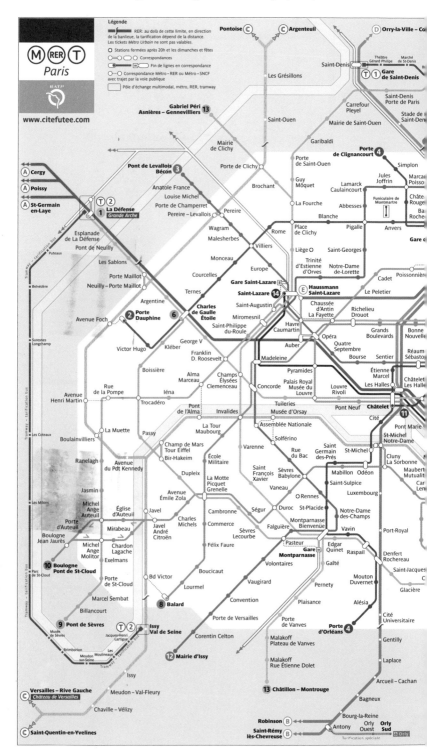